VICTORIAN TRAVELLERS GUIDE TO 19TH CENTURY ENGLAND AND WALES

MENAI TUBULAR & SUSPENSION BRIDGES.

Published by A. & C. Black. Edinburgh. July 1852.

VICTORIAN TRAVELLERS GUIDE TO 19TH CENTURY

ENGLAND & WALES

CONTAINING CHARTS OF ROADS, RAILWAYS, INTERESTING LOCALITIES, VIEWS OF SCENERY AND A COMPREHENSIVE LIST OF HOTELS

BRACKEN BOOKS
LONDON

FIRST PUBLISHED 1864 BY ADAM AND CHARLES BLACK
AS BLACK'S GUIDE TO ENGLAND AND WALES

THIS EDITION PUBLISHED BY BRACKEN BOOKS,
A DIVISION OF BESTSELLER PUBLICATIONS LTD,
BRENT HOUSE, 24 FRIERN PARK, NORTH FINCHLEY, LONDON, ENGLAND

ISBN 0 946495 69 6

PRINTED AND BOUND IN FINLAND BY WERNER SÖDERSTRÖM OY.

PREFACE.

ACCURACY, conciseness, and a just discrimination of the importance of the several objects described, being the qualifications most valued in a Guide-Book, it has been the aim of the Editor to devote his most anxious attention to the attainment of these requisites; and it is believed that the present work will be found to contain a larger amount of well-digested information than has ever been presented in any volume of such convenient size.

To have given all the roads of England within the limits of such a volume as the present was obviously impossible. Only the main roads have therefore been described, although the distances between places on the various tours by the cross-roads are very generally given. By reference to the maps and charts, the routes by the cross-roads will readily be ascertained, and by turning to the index, the reader will be directed to the pages where all the places of any importance are described.

The names, position, and distances of the various places have been copied from the maps of the Ordnance Survey; and the same valuable authority has been the basis of the several charts and district-maps with which the volume is illustrated.

The names of the proprietors of the various mansions described have been carefully compared with Burke's Peerage, Baronetage, and History of the Landed Commoners. In consequence of the frequent changes in the possession of the smaller mansions and villas, it has been deemed better to omit the names of the occupants of these, than to give information which a short period of time might render inaccurate.

The memorable incidents mentioned in connection with the various localities have been carefully selected from the best county histories and other topographical works of authority.

The population is according to the last census of 1861.

The expense of travelling, and the gratuities paid to servants at hotels, are subjects so materially influenced by the habits of the traveller, and the style of the establishment at which he sojourns, that it is difficult to afford precise information in regard to them. At the same time, the Publishers have reason to believe that a few particulars on those heads will be generally acceptable to tourists, and they have accordingly embodied in the following note the result of the inquiries which they have made upon the subject.

HOTEL CHARGES.

THE following scale shows the average charge for the several items which enter into the traveller's bill. The prices in the *first* division of the scale are rarely exceeded in any of the ordinary Hotels, while, in some, charges even more moderate may sometimes be met with. The prices in the *second* division show the charges in Hotels of the highest class in the principal cities.

Bed, 1s. 6d. to 2s. 6d.	3s. to 5s.
Breakfast, 1s. 6d. to 2s.	2s. to 3s.
Dinner, 2s. to 3s.	3s. 6d. to 5s.
Tea, 1s. to 1s. 6d.	1s. 6d. to 2s.
Supper, 1s. 6d. to 2s.	According to what is ordered.
Port or Sherry, per bottle, 3s. 6d. to 5s.	5s. to 6s.
Porter or Ale, per bottle, 1s.	
Brandy or other spirits, per measure, 6d.	9d. to 1s.
Attendance, 1s. to 1s. 6d.	2s. to 5s.
Private Room, 2s. to 5s.	5s. to 10s.

*** If the Traveller requires his table to be furnished beyond the ordinary scale of comfort, he must be prepared for a proportionate increase of charge.

The payment of the gratuities to servants at Inns is a source of great annoyance to travellers. It largely contributes to the tourist's comfort when the charges under this head are included in the bill. This practice has now been adopted by many Hotel-keepers. When this is not done, the following rules will enable the tourist to calculate the charges for himself.

GRATUITIES TO SERVANTS.

1.

A single gentleman, taking the general accommodation of the Hotel for one or two meals as a passing traveller, Waiter, Boots, and Chambermaid, 6d. This includes the removal of any reasonable weight of luggage; but extra messages and parcels are charged separately.

2.

A single gentleman, staying a day and night, and taking his meals in the hotel, 1s. 6d. or 2s. for servants, and if he stays several days, 1s. or 1s. 6d. per day.

3.

A gentleman and his wife, occupying a sitting room and bed-room, 2s. 6d. to 3s. 6d. per night for servants. If accompanied by sons or daughters, or other relatives, half this rate from each; but no charge for children under nine years of age.

4.

A party of four or six for one night about 1s. 6d. each.

In country and village inns, even the lowest of the payments above quoted may be unnecessarily liberal, while in some of the fashionable hotels in London, the highest may be considerably under par.

DESCRIPTION OF DISTRICTS TRAVERSED BY ROADS AND RAILWAYS.

WALES.

END OF WALES.

THE LAKE DISTRICT.

MAPS AND CHARTS

VIEWS.

THE

PICTURESQUE TOURIST OF ENGLAND.

LONDON.

GOOD HOTELS, WITH MODERATE CHARGES.

Abbreviations used.—Bd. Bed; Bt. Breakfast; Dr. Dinner: T. Tea; At. Attendance; P. R. Private Room.

At Railway Stations.—Euston Square Hotel, Euston Grove, Great Northern, King's Cross—Bd. 2s. to 3s.; bt. 1s. 6d. to 2s. 6d.; dr. as per bill of fare; at. 1s. 6d., after 1s.; p. r. 3s. to 4s., lights extra. Great Western, Paddington.—Grosvenor Hotel, Victoria Station, Pimlico, per bill of fare and printed rates; each of these hotels can accommodate 200 persons at least.

In or near the city and East End.—Albion, 153 Aldersgate Street. Anderton's, 162 Fleet Street—Bd. 2s.; bt. 1s. 6d.; dr. 2s. to 3s.; t. 1s. 6d.; at. optional. Bridge House, Wellington Street, London Bridge—Bd. 2s.; bt. 2s.; dr. 2s. 6d.; t. 1s. 6d. to 2s.; at. 1s. 6d. Castle and Falcon, 5 Aldersgate Street—Bd. 2s. to 3s.; bt. 3s. to 2s. 6d.; dr. 3s. 6d.; t. 1s. 6d. to 2s. 6d.; at. 1s. 6d. to 2s. Cathedral, 48 St. Paul's Churchyard—Bd. 1s. 6d.; bt. 1s. 6d.; dr. 2s.; t. 1s.; at. 1s. 6d. Guildhall, 33 Gresham Street, Cheapside. Portugal, 154 Fleet Street. Queen's, St. Martin's-le-Grand. Radley's, 10 New Bridge Street.

Central, between City and West End.—Ashley's, 13 Henrietta Street, Covent Garden—Bd. 1s. 6d.; bt. 1s. 3d. to 1s. 9d.; dr. 2s. to 3s.; t. 1s. 3d.; at. charged on bill; p. r. 3s. Bedford, 14 Piazza, Covent Garden—Bd. 3s.; bt. 2s.; dr. 3s. 6d.; t. 1s. 6d.; at. 1s. 6d.; p. r. lights and fire. Craven, 45 Craven Street—Bd. 2s. 6d.; bt. 2s. 6d.; dr. 3s.; t. 1s. 6d.; p. r. lights. Exeter Hall, 375 Strand—Bd. 2s.; bt. 1s. 6d.; dr. 2s.; t. 1s. 6d.; at. 1s.; p. r. 3s. 6d. to 5s. Golden Cross, 452 Strand—Bd. 3s.; bt. 2s. 6d.; dr. 3s. 6d.; t. 2s. 6d.; at. charged in bill, 1s. 9d.; p. r. 5s. to 10s., wax lights and fire extra. Morley's, Trafalgar Square—Bd. 3s.; bt. 2s. 6d.; dr. 3s. 6d. to 5s.; t. 2s.; at. optional; p. r. 5s. to 10s. New Hummums, Tavistock Row, Covent Garden—Bd. 2s. 6d.; bt. 2s.; dr. 3s. 6d.; t. 2s.; at. optional; p. r. 5s. Old Hummums, Tavistock Row, Covent Garden. Richardson's, Piazza, Covent Garden—Bd. 3s.; bt. 2s. 6d,; at. 2s.; p. r. lights. Tavistock, Piazza—Bd. 3s.; bt. 2s.; dr. 3s. 6d.; t. 1s. 6d.; at. 1s. 6d.; p. r. lights and fire.

West End.—Westminster Palace Hotel, Victoria Street. Palace Hotel, Buckingham Gate. The Grosvenor, Victoria Station, Pimlico. Ford's, 13 Manchester Street, Manchester Square—Bd. 2s. 6d.; bt. 2s.; dr. 3s. 6d.; t. 2s.; at. optional; p. r. 6s. Ginger's, 1 Bridge Street, Westminster.

For Foreigners.—Hotel de Provence, 17 Leicester Square. Hotel de Versailles, 2 Leicester Place. Hotel de l'Europe, 15 Leicester Place. Hotel de l'Univers, 2 Earl Street. Panton, 28 Panton Street. Royal, 26 New Bridge Street, Blackfriars – Introduction required. Sabloniere, 30 Leicester Square—Bd. 2s. to 3s.; bt. 2s.; dr. 3s.; t. 1s. 6d.; at. optional.

First Class Family Hotels, for the Aristocracy and Foreigners of Distinction—Clarendon, 169 New Bond Street. Farrance's, 11 Upper Belgrave Street. Claridge's, 42 to 45 Brook Street. Burlington, 19 and 20 Cork Street. Christie's, 57 St. James Street. Fenton's, 63 St. James Street. Grillon's, 7 Albemarle Street. Hatchett's, 67 Piccadilly. London, 43 Albemarle Street—Bd. 3s. to 5s.; bt. 2s. 6d. to 3s. 6d.; dr. 5s. to 8s.; t. 2s.; at. optional; p. r. 7s. to 12s. Long's, 16 New Bond Street—Bd. 3s. 6d.; bt. 2s. 6d.; dr. 4s. 6d. to 8s.; t. 2s.; at. optional; p. r. 6s. to 12s.

DINING HOUSES.

Some of these are famed for particular dishes; these are placed within brackets.
Hours 1 to 5 P.M.

City.—Lake's, 49 Cheapside. Joe's, Finch Lane, Cornhill (beef-steaks). The Cock, 201 Fleet Street (steaks, chops, and snipe kidneys). Williams, Old Bailey (boiled beef). Dolly's, Queen's Head Passage, Paternoster Row (quiet chop-house). Simpson's, Billingsgate Market (fish). Lord Mayor's Larder, Cheapside, opposite Bow Church. Thorn's, Bucklersbury.

Central (hours 1 to 7).—The London, 191 Fleet Street, corner of Chancery Lane. Simpson's Divan Tavern, 103 Strand. Upton's, 91 Strand. The Bedford, 2 Bedford Street, Strand.

West End (hours 3 to 7).—Pye's, 3 Church Place, Piccadilly. The Albany, 190 Piccadilly. The Wellington, formerly Crockford's, 160 Piccadilly (charge 2s. and upwards). Donald's, St. James' Hall, 28 Piccadilly, and 69 and 71 Regent Street. The Scotch Stores, corner of New Burlington Street, Regent Street.

RESTAURANTS.

Groom's, 16 Fleet Street, Close to Temple Bar. Verrey's, 229 Regent Street. Kammerers, 37 Cranbourne Street, Leicester Square.

SUBURBAN.

Those marked thus * are famous for white-bait.

RICHMOND—Star and Garter, and Castle. SYDENHAM—Crystal Palace Refreshment Department. BLACKWALL—*Lovegrove's Dock Tavern. GREENWICH—*Crown and Sceptre; *Trafalgar: The Ship. GRAVESEND—*The Ship. CREMORNE GARDENS, CHELSEA—Simpson's.

For further particulars see Black's Guide to London.

Best Cab fare Guide—"Mogg's." Price 1s. Book of fares published by Chas. Knight. Price 2s. 6d.

Best Omnibus Guide—"Bolton's."

ALPHABETICAL LIST
OF
PLACES, EXHIBITIONS, ETC., IN LONDON,

LIKELY TO PROVE MOST ATTRACTIVE TO THE STRANGER OR TOURIST.

*Those with an * no one should leave London without seeing.*

PLACES.	MODE OF OBTAINING ADMISSION.
Abbey, Westminster.	Admission free, during Divine service, to the Nave and Transept. Charge of 6d. for admission to Henry VII.'s and smaller Chapels.
Apsley House, Piccadilly. Long the residence of the late Duke of Wellington.	Admission by ticket of the proprietor.
Arcades—Burlington. Lowther. Exeter Hall.	Open to the public.
Army and Navy Club, Pall Mall.	Introduction by a member.
Arsenal, Woolwich. *See* Woolwich.	Order of Secretary for War.
Bank of England.	Admission free.
Battersea Park.	Open to the public.
Bazaars—Soho Square.	Admission free.
Pantheon.	Do.
Pantechnicon.	Do.
Prince of Wales, Regent St.	Do.
Baker St.	Do.
Bethlehem Hospital.	Order of a Governor, except on Sunday, Monday, or Saturday
Breweries—Barclay and Perkins.	Order of the Firm.
Meux's.	Do.
Whitbread's.	Do.
Bridges—London.	
Westminster.	
Waterloo.	
Charing Cross.	
Southwark.	
Hungerford Suspension.	For pedestrians only, charge one halfpenny.
Chelsea Suspension.	
* British Museum.	Admission free, on Monday, Wednesday, and Friday, from 10 to 5. Catalogues, 4d.
Buckingham Palace.	Admission (during the absence of the Court) by ticket signed by the Lord Chamberlain.
Cathedrals.	See St. Paul's and Westminster.
Chapels—Whitehall. The old Banqueting Hall.	Admission during divine service.
St. James's.	Do. do. (At 8 a.m. and 12 noon.)
Inner Temple.	Order of a Bencher.
Savoy.	Admission during Divine service.
Chelsea Hospital.	Open to the public.
Christ's Hospital.	Order of a Governor.
Clubs—Army and Navy, Pall Mall.	Introduction by a member.
Carlton, Pall Mall.	Do. do.

Places.	Mode of Obtaining Admission.
Clubs—*continued.*	
Conservative, St. James' St.	Introduction by a member.
Reform, Pall Mall.	Do. do.
Sen. United Service Club, Pall Mall.	Do. do.
Jun. United Service Club, Regent St.	Do. do.
Coal Exchange.	Open to the public.
Commons, House of.	Order of an M.P. for the ordinary Gallery, or of the Speaker for the Speaker's Gallery.
Cosmorama, Regent Street.	Admission, 1s.
Cremorne Gardens.	Admission, 1s.
Crosby Hall, Bishopsgate Street.	[Once the residence of Richard III., a fine specimen of the mansion of the fifteenth century.]
Courts of Law—Westminster Hall.	Open to the public.
Lincoln's Inn.	Do.
* Crystal Palace, Sydenham.	See Sydenham.
Custom House.	Long Room open to the public.
Docks.	Open to the public. The vaults by order of a Wine-Merchant to taste wines.
Dulwich Gallery.	Admission free, every day, from 10 till 4.
East India Office Museum.	Fridays, 10 till 4, free; Mondays and Thursdays, by order of a member of Council.
Egyptian Hall, Piccadilly.	Exhibitions various.
Entomological Society's Museum, 17 Old Bond Street.	Admission free on Tuesdays from 3 to 8.
Exchange, The. Open daily.	Admission free.
Exeter Hall. The May Meetings and Oratorios.	Do. Tickets, 3s. to 10s. 6d. for the Oratorios.
Foundling Hospital, Great Guildford St.	During Divine Service on Sundays.
Galleries, Picture.	
Bridgewater.	Tickets issued gratuitously by Mr. Smith, 137 New Bond Street.
Buckingham Palace.	Do. of the Lord Chamberlain.
Dulwich.	Open to the public.
Grosvenor.	Do. of the Proprietor.
Mr. Hope's, Piccadilly.	Do. do.
Mr. Holford's, Park Lane.	Do. do.
National, Trafalgar Square. Vernon, etc., in Kensington Museum.	Open to the public on Mondays, Tuesdays, Wednesdays, and Thursdays, from 10 to 5. Official Catalogue, 4d.
Sutherland.	Order of Proprietor.
Gardens, Public.	
Botanical, Regent's Park.	Ticket of a Subscriber or Member.
Kensington.	Open to the public.
Kew.	Week days from 1 to 6; Sundays from 2 to 6—free.
Zoological, Regent's Park.	Admission, 1s., and 6d.
Gates—Temple Bar.	
St. John's.	
Goldsmith's Hall, Foster Lane, Cheapside.	Order of the Secretary to the Company. [The Hall is fine. Here all articles of gold and silver manufacture are assayed and stamped.]
Greenwich Hospital.	Open to the public.
Guildhall.	Open to the public. [The Hall is famous for Lord Mayor's feasts and City elections, not forgetting the figures of Gog and Magog. In the library may be seen the signature of Shakespeare attached to a deed of conveyance.]
Hampton Court Palace.	Every day except Friday, from 10 till 4; Sundays, 2 to 6—free.
Holland House, Kensington.	Order of the Proprietor.

PLACES.	MODE OF OBTAINING ADMISSION.
Horse Guards.	Open to the public.
Hospitals—Bartholomew. Bethlehem or Bedlam.	Order of a Governor.
Chelsea.	Open to the public.
Christ's. Guy's. St. George's. Westminster. London.	Order of a Governor.
* Houses of Parliament.	See Lords and Commons.
Inns of Court— Gray's Inn, Holborn. Lincoln's Inn. Temple, Inner and Middle, Fleet Street.	Order of a Bencher. *See* the Temple Gardens and the Church, which is remarkably fine.
Kensington Gardens.	Open to the public.
* Kensington Museum.	Free, Monday, Tuesday, and Saturday, 10 to 5.
Kew Gardens.	Open to the public, on week days, from 1 to 6; Sundays, 2 to 6.
Lambeth Palace.	Order of the Archbishop.
Lincoln's Inn Hall.	Bencher's order.
Lords, House of.	Free on Wednesday and Saturday, by order from Lord Great Chamberlain's Office. On other days, order of a Peer, or of the Usher of the Black Rod.
Mansion House.	Open to the public on Tuesdays and Fridays.
Markets—Covent-Garden.	Open to the public.
Leadenhall.	Do.
Smithfield.	Do.
Mews, Royal.	Order of the Master of the Horse.
Mint, Tower-Hill.	Ticket signed by the Master. [When coining is going on the Mint is well worth a visit.]
Monuments—The Monument.	Admission to the top, 3d.
Duke of York.	Do. 6d.
Nelson's.	
In Westminster Abbey, St. Paul's, and Houses of Parliament.	Open to the public.
Museums—British.	Open to the public on Monday, Wednesday, and Friday.
Asiatic Society.	Order of a Director.
East India.	Order of a Member of Council.
Of Geology.	Open to the public on Monday, Tuesday, and Wednesday, from 10 to 4.
Sir J. Soanes'.	Open on Thursdays and Fridays, in April, May, and June.
United Service.	Member's ticket or introduction.
Kensington.	Free, Monday, Tuesday, and Saturday, 10 to 5.
* National Gallery, Trafalgar Square. See also Vernon Gallery.	Open to the public on Mondays, Tuesdays, Wednesdays, and Thursdays.
Opera Houses—Italian, Haymarket. Covent-Garden.	Single Tickets, from 8s. 6d. to 21s.
Parliament, Houses of.	Admission free to House of Lords on Wednesday and Saturday, by order from Lord Great Chamberlain's Office. The House of Lords is open during the hearing of Appeal Cases. To hear debates in House of Lords, order of a Peer, or in House of Commons, of a Member of Parliament.
Palaces—St. James'. Buckingham. Kensington.	Order of the Lord Chamberlain.
Panopticon of Science, Leicester Square.	Admission, 1s.
Pantechnicon, Halkin Street, West.	Open to the public. *See* Bazaar.

PLACES.	MODE OF OBTAINING ADMISSION.
Parks—Hyde. Green. Regent's. St. James'. Battersea. Victoria.	Open to the public.
Polytechnic, Regent Street.	Admission, 1s. [The Lectures on Scientific subjects and Experiments are very attractive and instructive.]
Police Courts.	Open to the public.
Post-Office, St. Martin's-le-Grand.	Order of the Postmaster-General or Secretary.
Prisons—Milbank. Pentonville, &c.	Order of the Home Secretary.
Queen's Mews.	Ticket of Secretary to the Master of the Horse.
Regent's Park.	Open to the public.
Royal Exchange.	Do.
Royal College of Surgeon's Museum.	Member's order or introduction.
Savoy Chapel.	Open during Divine Service.
Schools—Christ's Hospital. Charter House. St. Paul's. Westminster.	Order of a Governor.
Science and Art Department.	Open to the public. *See* Kensington Museum.
Soanes' Museum.	Admission by Ticket. [The Curiosities and Pictures are attractive.]
Society of Arts.	Every day except Wednesday, by Member's order
Somerset House.	Open to the public.
St. James' Palace.	Order of Lord Chamberlain.
* St. Paul's.	Admission to body of Cathedral free; to Whispering Gallery, 6d.; to the Ball, 1s. 6d.; to Model Room, Great Bell, Library, &c., 1s.; to the Clock, 2d.; to the Vaults, 1s. In all, 4s. 2d.
St. Stephen's, Walbrook.	Admission during Divine Service.
Statues—in Streets, Squares, etc. Queen Elizabeth, Fleet Street. Charles I., Charing Cross. Charles II., Soho Square. James II., Whitehall Gardens. William III., St. James' Square. Queen Anne, St. Paul's Churchyard. George I., Grosvenor Square. William, Duke of Cumberland, Cavendish Square. George III., Cockspur Street. George IV., Trafalgar Square. Wm. Pitt, Hanover Square. Fox, Bloomsbury Square. William IV., King William Street, City. Queen Victoria, Royal Exchange. Duke of Wellington, Piccadilly. Hyde Park. Royal Exchange. Sir R. Peel, Cheapside. Dr. Jenner, Trafalgar Square. Gen. Sir Chas. Napier, Trafalgar Square. Gen. Sir H. Havelock, Trafalgar Square. Guards' Memorial, Waterloo Pl. Lord Raglan, &c., Broad Sanctuary.	

CRYSTAL PALACE, SYDENHAM.

PLACES.	MODE OF OBTAINING ADMISSION.
Sydenham Palace.	Saturday, 2s. 6d. Other days 1s. Shut on Sunday. Hours of opening, Monday, 9 a.m., Tuesday, Wednesday, Thursday, and Friday, 10 a.m., Saturday, 12 noon. Closed at 6 p.m. Fares by Railway, from London Bridge or Pimlico Station, on one shilling days, including admission, 1st class, 2s. 6d.; 2d class, 2s.; 3d class, 1s. 6d.
Temple Church.	Order of a Bencher. Outer portion open to the public during divine service.
Bar. Gardens.	Open to the public.
Thames Tunnel.	Admission, 1d.
Theatres—Opera Houses, Italian, Covent Garden, and Haymarket.	
Adelphi, Strand (Webster's).	Boxes, 4s.; Pit, 2s. Opens 6.30 p.m.
Astley's, Westminster Bridge Road. (Horsemanship).	Opens 6.30 p.m.
Drury Lane, Drury Lane.	
St. James', King St.	
Haymarket (Buckstone's).	Boxes, 5s.; Pit, 3s. 6d. Opens 6.30 p.m.
Lyceum, Strand.	
Olympic, Wych Street (Wigans').	Boxes, 4s.; Pit, 2s. Opens 7 p.m.
Princess', Oxford Street.	Boxes, 5s.; Pit, 3s. 6d. Opens 6.30 p.m.
Sadler's Wells, Clerkenwell (Phelps).	
Strand, Strand.	
Surrey, Blackfriar's Road.	Boxes, 2s.; Pit, 1s.
Victoria, Waterloo Road.	
Marylebone, Church Street, Edgeware Road.	Boxes, 3s.; Pit, 1s.
New Great National Standard, Shoreditch, opposite to Eastern Counties Rail.	Boxes, 1s. 6d.; Pit, 6d.
Times Office.	Order of the Editor.
* Tower of London.	Admission, 6d. to the Armoury, and 6d. to view Regalia.
Tussaud's Exhibition, Baker Street.	Admission, 1s.
United Service Museum.	Daily from 11 till 4, by Member's order. [The collection of arms and armour is good.]
Vernon Gallery. Kensington Museum.	Open to the public. Days and hours same as National Gallery. Catalogue 2d.
* Westminster Abbey.	Admission free, during Divine Service, to Body of Church and Poets' Corner. To Chapels and Monuments, 6d.
Westminster, Palace of.	Open to the public (see Houses of Lords and Commons).
Whitehall Chapel.	Open during Divine Service.
* Windsor Castle.	Admission by ticket, to be obtained gratis from Ackermann, 96 Strand, on Monday, Tuesday, Thursday, and Friday, from 11 to 4.
Woolwich Arsenal, including the manufactory of Armstrong Guns.	Order of the Secretary for War.
* Zoological Gardens, Royal.	Admission, 1s., except on Monday, when the charge is 6d.

HOW TO SEE THE PRINCIPAL SIGHTS OF LONDON.

GROUP I. *West End.*—Starting from Charing Cross, and passing the Horse Guards and Whitehall Chapel, visit the Houses of Parliament, Westminster Abbey, Buckingham Palace, and the Park. All this may be accomplished in one forenoon, if the Tourist cannot spare more time.

GROUP II. *Central.*—Visit the National Gallery and British Museum.

GROUP III. *East End.*—Visit St. Paul's, and passing the Post Office and Goldsmith's Hall, proceed to Guildhall, the Bank of England, the Mansion House, and Exchange, and thence to the Tower, finishing the long day's work at the Thames Tunnel.

GROUP IV. Visit Regent's Park and the Zoological Gardens.

GROUP V. Starting per railway from the Victoria Station, Pimlico, the forenoon may be most satisfactorily spent at the Crystal Palace; and if time presses, the evening may be most agreeably passed at the Kensington Museum.

The visit to Windsor Castle will consume one day; and an excursion to Greenwich Park, including a visit to the Hospital, and the inspection of the Arsenal and Dockyard at Woolwich, will fill up another.

Note.—If there be abundance of time at command, most of these series can be subdivided as may suit the convenience of Tourists.

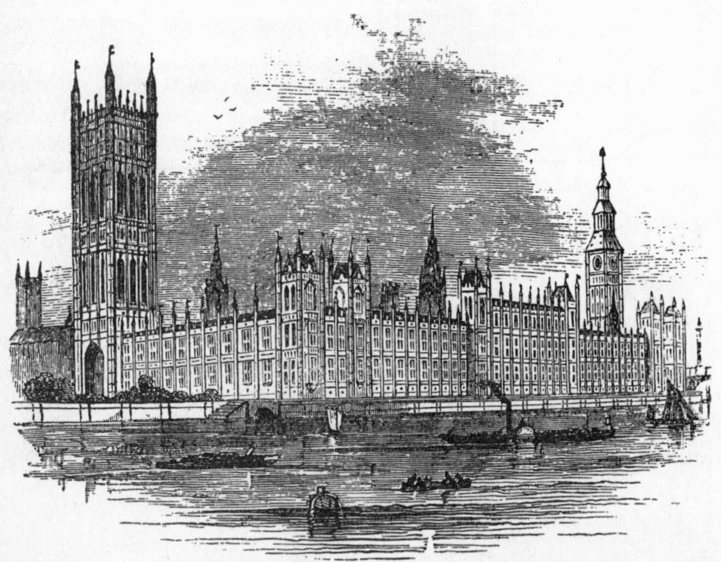

NEW HOUSES OF PARLIAMENT.

ROUTES THROUGH ENGLAND.

I. LONDON.—ROCHESTER.—CANTERBURY. [MARGATE.—RAMSGATE.—SANDWICH.—DEAL.] DOVER.

ON RIGHT FROM LOND.	From Dover.		From London.	ON LEFT FROM LOND.
	67	Deptford. cr. river Ravensbourn, to Greenwich, 1 mile, thence to Woolwich, 3¼.	4	Greenwich Hospital.
Morden College, consisting of almshouses for decayed merchants.	65½	Blackheath.	5½	Greenwich Park, a royal demesne, the favourite resort of Londoners. Woodlands. Charlton House, a fine specimen of the old manor house, the work of Inigo Jones, Sir T. M. Wilson, Bart.
Sevendroog Castle, erected to commemorate the reduction of Sevendroog in 1756, a strong fort on an island near Bombay.	62¾	Shooter's Hill.	8¼	Belvidere, the seat of Sir Culling E. Eardley, Bart.
Danson Park.	60¾	Welling.	10¼	Wickham.
Crayford derives its name from an ancient ford over the Cray. In this and the adjoining parish are a number of deep artificial caverns. A battle was fought here in 457 between the Saxons and the Britons.	57¾	Crayford. cr. river Cray.	13¼	
	56	Dartford. cr. river Darent.	15	At Dartford may be seen the remains of a nunnery founded by Edward III. A branch of the old Roman Watling St. passes through the town. Here Wat Tyler's rebellion commenced.
	54	Horn's Cross.	17	Ingress Park.
Wombwell Hall. Gravesend is considered the limit of the port of London, being the place where ships are obliged to lie till visited by custom-officers. Steam-	50¾	Northfleet.	20¼	Northfleet commands a very extensive view. The church contains several handsome monuments.
	49	Gravesend.	22	Milton Church.

ON RIGHT FROM LOND.	From Dover.		From London.	ON LEFT FROM LOND.
vessels ply regularly between this place and London. Opposite the Block House, on the Essex shore. is Tilbury Fort, having a strong battery.	47¾	Chalk St.	23¼	
Cobham Hall, (Earl of Darnley), surrounded by Cobham Woods.	44¾	Gads Hill.	26¼	Gads Hill is the scene of Falstaff's famous exploit.
	42½	Strood.	28½	
		cr. river Medway.		
Rochester is a city of great antiquity. The objects most deserving of notice in it are the Cathedral and the remains of the Castle, which occupy a commanding position, overlooking the Medway. Popul. (1861) 16,862. It returns two members to Parliament.	42	ROCHESTER.	29	Chatham is situated to the left of Rochester about ⅔ of a mile from the high road to Dover. It is celebrated for its extensive dockyards and naval arsenal. It has also an hospital for seamen and shipwrights, and a victualling-office for the navy. It is also a depot for troops destined for India Population (1861) 36,177. One Member. At the distance of 1 mile is Milton Royal, famous for its oysters.
	41	Chatham.	30	
Hartlip.	37	Rainham.	34	
	34	Newingham.	37	
	32¾	Key St.	38¼	
	31	Sittingbourne.	40	
Morris Court. Rodmersham, W. Lushington, Esq.	29¾	Basschild.	41¼	Linstead.
	28	Radfield.	43	
Linstead Lodge, Lord Teynham. Norton Court, Rt. Hon. S R. Lushington.		Green St.		At a short distance, Teynham.
Syndale House, W. Hyde, Esq.	25	Ospring.	46	Faversham, 1 mile distant. Popul. 5858.
Belmont, Lord Harris. At some distance to the right, Chilham Castle, J. B. Wildman, Esq., and Godmersham Park, R. Knight, Esq.	21¾	Boughton.	49¼	Nash Court. Hoath wood.
	17	Harbledown.	54	Hall Place.
	15½	CANTERBURY.	55½	Hales Place.

Canterbury is pleasantly situated on the Stour. It is the metropolitan see of all England. The chief object of attraction is the magnificent cathedral, with a fine choir, an altar-piece, designed by Sir James Burrough, a remarkable painted window, and the shrine of Thomas à Becket. It was begun in 1174, and not finished till the reign of Henry V. Under the Cathedral is a church for French Protestants, a colony of whom settled here after the revocation of the edict of Nantes, and established the silk manufacture, which still continues, though in a declining state. Besides the Cathedral, Canterbury contains fourteen parish churches—one of which, St. Martin's, is built of Roman bricks, and is supposed by antiquarians to have been erected so early as the second century of the Christian era. In the Church of the Holy Cross, St. Dunstan's, is buried the head of Sir Thomas More. In the eastern suburbs, a short distance from the Cathedral, are the remains of St. Augustine's Monastery, formerly a magnificent building, which, with its precincts, occupied 16 acres of ground; the ancient gateway, still remaining, is a fine specimen of architecture. This building for a long period lay almost entirely in ruins, and part of it was used as a common tavern and brewhouse. However, in 1844 it was purchased by

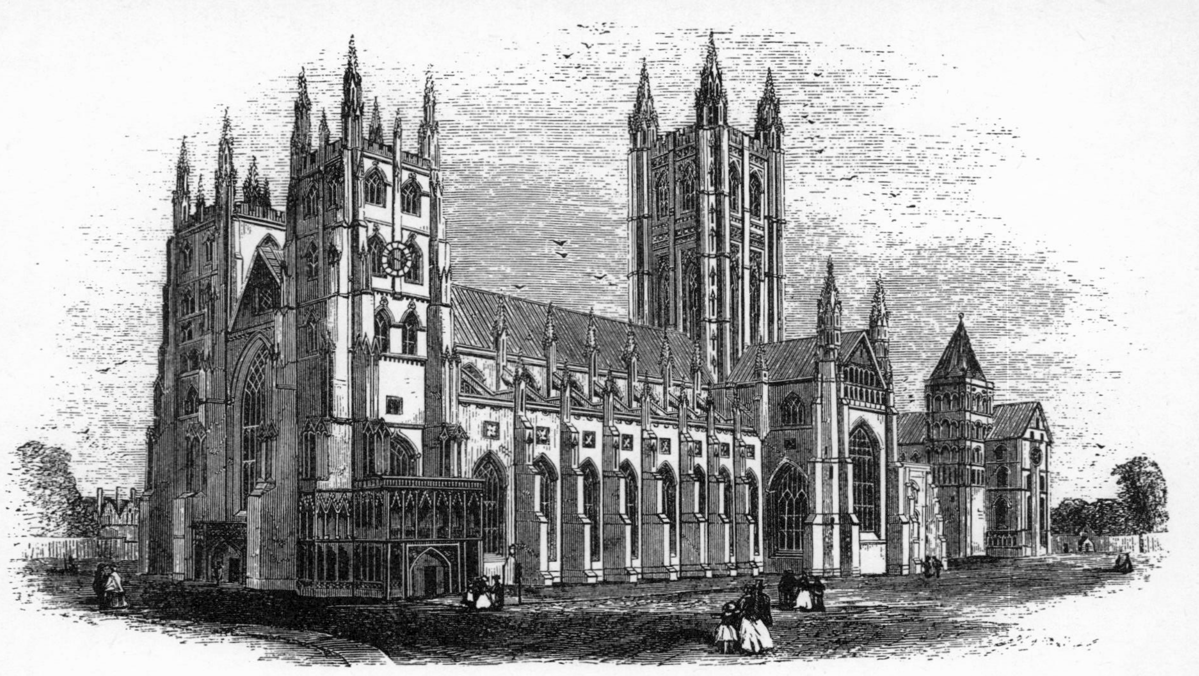

CANTERBURY CATHEDRAL.

A. J. B. Hope, Esq., M.P., a son of the author of "Anastasius," who not only saved it from further desecration, but has restored the gateway and built within the Abbey walls a Protestant missionary college.

Mercery Lane, one of the ancient avenues leading from the High Street to the Cathedral, is interesting to the visitor from its having been, according to tradition, the usual resort of the numerous pilgrims who in former times flocked to Canterbury to pay their devotions at the shrine of Thomas à Becket, where, as Chaucer expresses it—

> "And specially from every shire's ende
> Of Engle lond to Canterbury they wende." *

A pilgrimage to Canterbury will well repay the tourist, especially if he chance to be an ecclesiologist.

Of the walls by which Canterbury was anciently surrounded, some remains still exist; but all the gates have been taken down excepting one, Westgate, which forms the entrance by the London road. At the south-west extremity of the city are the remains of an ancient castle, a little to the east of which, and adjacent to the city wall, is a high artificial mound, called the Dane John (from Donjon), the sides of which are cut into serpentine walks, and tastefully adorned with trees and shrubs. The summit commands a fine prospect of the surrounding country, and the whole forms a favourite place of public resort.

Canterbury has no manufacture of any importance, and, since the formation of the railway to Dover, has lost much of the traffic which it formerly possessed. Many of the lower class of inhabitants are engaged in the hop grounds by which it is surrounded. Canterbury has some trade in corn, and good markets for provisions of all kinds. It returns two members to Parliament. Population 21,324.

Six miles distant from Canterbury is Whitstable, a fishing village on the north coast of Kent, and near the mouth of the Swale, the estuary which separates the island of Sheppey from the mainland. It is connected with Canterbury by a railway. Population, 1861, 3086. Four and a half miles further to the eastward is Herne Bay, which has of late years been partially frequented by the people of the metropolis as a summer bathing-place, for which its situation is well suited. But the extensive scale upon which it was laid out gives it an unfinished appearance, and the greater gaiety of Margate and Ramsgate attracts by far the larger number of visitors. The pier, or rather jetty, which is built on wooden piles, extends three-quarters of a mile into the sea, and forms a fine promenade. Herne Bay contains several charitable institutions, for which the inhabitants are chiefly indebted to the munificence of Mrs. Thwaits.

Nearly three miles to the east of Herne Bay is the ancient village of Reculver, the site of the Roman station Regulbium, and afterwards the seat of royalty

* Canterbury Tales, vol. ii. p. 1. Pickering's Edition of Chaucer.

under the Saxons. The encroachments of the sea on this part of the coast have swept away many of the houses and part of the churchyard, which is situated on the edge of a cliff; but this has been preserved by artificial means from further devastation, and the two lofty towers of the ruined church, which form a well-known landmark to sailors, are kept in repair under the direction of the Trinity House. Immediately beyond the Reculvers is the Isle of Thanet, on which are situated Margate and Ramsgate.

Margate (11 miles to the eastward of Herne Bay, and 16 miles, by the turnpike road, from Canterbury), originally an inconsiderable fishing village, has become of late years one of the most favourite and frequented watering-places in the kingdom. It contains numerous hotels, bazaars, assembly-rooms, a theatre, and other means of amusement for visitors during the bathing season. A stone pier, 903 feet long, and 60 feet wide in the broadest part, with a lighthouse at the extremity, forms a much-frequented promenade. During the summer and autumn, steamboats pass every day between Margate and London, performing the voyage in from six to seven hours. Population, 1861, 8874. Three miles west of Margate is Birchington Park, in which are two handsome towers, one of which has a peal of 12 bells. Two and a half miles east of Margate is Kingsgate, situated in a bay formed by an indentation in the chalk cliffs which line all this part of the Kentish coast. Kingsgate was formerly called Bartholomew's Gate, but received its present appellation in consequence of Charles II. landing here on his way to Dover in 1683. A mansion was erected here by Henry, third Lord Holland, on a plan resembling Tully's villa on the coast of Baiæ: it is now partly in ruins, which have a fantastic and not unpicturesque appearance. Adjacent to Kingsgate is the North Foreland, a bold promontory with a lighthouse on its summit.

About 1½ mile to the south of the North Foreland is the pleasant village and watering-place of Broadstairs, distant 3 miles from Margate and 2 from Ramsgate. Broadstairs is much resorted to during the bathing season, and is preferred by many on account of its quiet and retirement, as compared with the larger watering-places in its vicinity. It has a small pier for the protection of fishing-boats, but passengers from London are landed by boats from the Ramsgate steamers, which call here daily during the summer season. Population, 1549.

Near Broadstairs is Piermont, a villa which was the frequent residence of Her Majesty when a child.

Ramsgate, 16 miles (by road) from Canterbury, and 4 miles from Margate, is situated at the south-east extremity of the Isle of Thanet. Besides being greatly resorted to as a bathing-place by visitors from London and elsewhere, Ramsgate has also considerable coasting trade, and both ship-building and rope-making are carried on. The harbour, which embraces an area of 48 acres, is formed by two stone piers, of which the eastern extends 2000 feet in length, and is one of the finest works of the kind in the kingdom. The western pier is 1500 feet long, and has a lighthouse at its extremity. The harbour admits vessels of 500 tons burden, and is divided into two parts by a wall, fitted with sluices, and forming an inner and an outer harbour. The voyage between Ramsgate and London by steamboat occupies from seven to eight hours. Population 11,865.

On the east side of Ramsgate is East Cliff Lodge, the seat of Sir Moses Montefiore, Bart.; and a short distance to the southwest of the town is Pegwell Bay, famous for its shrimps. Pegwell Bay possesses also an interest of another kind, since it was here that, according to tradition, Hengist and Horsa landed, about the year 446 A. D.

A road also leads from Canterbury to Sandwich and Deal. At the distance of 3½ miles it passes Littlebourne, near which, on the right, is Lee Priory, Sir F. S. H. Brydges, Bart. Three miles farther on is Wingham, and near it, on the right, is Dane Court, E. R. Rice, Esq. A little farther in the same direction is Goodneston, Sir B. W. Bridges, Bart. Three miles and a quarter from Wingham is Ash; and three miles farther, the town of Sandwich. This was formerly a place of some importance, but its harbour has long been choked up with sand. It is a Cinque Port, and contains 2944 inhabitants.

About 5½ miles from Sandwich is Deal, also one of the Cinque Ports, and situated near the Downs, which extend about 8 miles in length and 6 in breadth, between this place and the Goodwin Sands. Deal was, before the general rise of steam tugs, the general rendezvous of the East India and other fleets. Here was also an establishment of pilots, for the more safe conveyance of shipping into and out of the Downs, and up the rivers Thames and Medway. Deal is defended by a castle, and along the coast are several martello towers. Between this place and Sandwich is Sandown Castle, built by Henry VIII; and about a mile from the town, on the other side, is Walmer Castle, held till his decease by the Duke of Wellington, as Warden of the Cinque Ports. Deal has of late years become frequented as a watering-place, and its appearance been in consequence greatly improved. The inhabitants are chiefly engaged in boat-building, sail-making, and other pursuits of a nautical character; and the Deal boatmen have a deservedly high repute for their skill and intrepidity in affording assistance to vessels in distress. For Parliamentary purposes Deal is included in the borough of Sandwich, which, conjointly with it, returns two members to Parliament. Population, 7531.

Six miles distant from Deal is the S. Foreland Lighthouse; and three miles beyond, Dover.

Margate, Ramsgate, and Deal are all connected with the metropolis by railways, for which see pages 10 and 11.

ON RIGHT FROM LOND.	From Dover.	Resuming the Route to Dover.	From London.	ON LEFT FROM LOND.
Nackington, Lord Sondes. Renwell. Pett House.		cr. the river Stour.		Bifrons, H. E. Taylor, Esq. Beaksbourne House, R. Peckham, Esq.
Bridge Place. Bourne Place.	12½	Bridge.	58½	Higham. Ileden, J. P. Plumptre, Esq.
Charlton Place.	10	Barham Dcwn.	61	Denhill.
Barham. Broome Park, Sir H. Oxenden, Bart. Wootton Court, Sir F. S. H. Brydges, Bart.	7½	Halfway House.	63½	Woolwich Wood.
	5	Lydden.	66	At a little distance, Waldershare, Earl of Guilford.
	3	Ewell.	68	
	1½	Buckland.	69½	
Just entering Dover, on the right, are the new barracks and fortifications.		cr. river.	71	
		DOVER.		

Dover is situated in a deep valley, formed by an opening in the chalk hills, which surround it in the form of an amphitheatre. On one of these, situated to the eastward of the town, and rising abruptly to a height of 320 feet above the sea, is situated the ancient Castle. The walls of Dover Castle embrace an area of nearly 35 acres of ground, within which space are contained towers and other buildings of various ages, from Roman to recent times. The appearance of the whole, from the commanding elevation which it occupies, is very imposing. Other portions of the heights adjacent to the town are also fortified. The harbour, which is formed artificially by piers and jetties, has recently been deepened and much improved, at vast expense. The town has been greatly extended of late years, and is now a fashionable and much-frequented watering-place, with every accommodation for the convenience of visitors. It is situated at the point of our island which makes the nearest approach to the coast of France, which is distant only 21 miles, and which is distinctly visible in clear weather. By means of the submarine electric telegraph, Dover now keeps up a constant communication with France, and through her, with a great portion of the continent. It was formerly the principal place of embarkation for the continent, but has been partially superseded in that respect by Folkstone. Dover is one of the Cinque Ports, and returns two members to Parliament. Population in 1861, 25,325. The hotels and inns are numerous.

About half a mile to the south-west of Dover is Shakespere's Cliff, a bold prominence of chalk, now tunnelled through by the railway, and the name of which is derived from the well-known description in the fourth act of "King Lear," which it is supposed to have suggested. But portions of the summit have fallen at various times, so that it now retires inland, and no longer "looks fearfully *in* the confined deep,"—though still affording a magnificent and

II. LONDON TO WOOLWICH, GRAVESEND ROCHESTER, AND CHATHAM, BY RAILWAY, 31 Miles.

ON RIGHT FROM LOND.	From Rochest.		From London.	ON LEFT FROM LOND.
Railway to Brighton and Dover branches off.		From London Bridge, by Greenwich railway, for 2½ miles. **Enter Kent.** The Greenwich railway was the first constructed line which had its commencement in the metropolis. It is constructed throughout upon arches, which form a viaduct 22 feet in height above the ground. This line forms the point of departure for both the Brighton and Dover lines.		Rotherhithe. Deptford, almost a suburb of London, has a royal dockyard, which embraces an area of 31 acres. The workhouse occupies the site of Sayes Court, the residence of the celebrated John Evelyn. Here Peter the Great studied shipbuilding. Pop. of Parish 40,242. To Greenwich, 1¼ mile.
The Railway passes through the centre of Woolwich, which is distant 8 m. from London by road, and about 9½ m. by water. Here is a Government dockyard, established in the reign of Henry VIII., consisting of a narrow strip of land, which extends for more than half a m. along the banks of the river. But the chief object of interest is the R. Arsenal, which covers more than 100 acres, and forms the grand depot of artillery for the use of the army and navy. It seldom contains fewer than 24,000 pieces of ordnance, besides smaller arms innumerable. Here are foundries for cannon, and every other description of warlike stores. On the adjacent common are extensive barracks, a Royal Military Academy for the education of young gentlemen designed for the military profession, and a Military Repository, containing weapons of destruction of almost every age and nation. There is a large convict establishment here employed in the Government Dockyard and the Arsenal. On the opposite side of the Thames a new town is springing up, called North-Woolwich. Pop. of Parish 41,695.		**cr. river Ravensbourne.**		Greenwich, the birthplace of Queen Bess and her father, distant 5 m. from London Bridge by road, is chiefly remarkable for its magnificent hospital, originally designed for a royal palace, but appropriated since 1694 to the purposes of an hospital for decayed seamen. Additions were made subsequent to this date by Sir Christopher Wren, &c. There is also a Royal Park, enclosing 200 acres, on an eminence of which stands the Observatory. The Park is greatly resorted to by the people of London for the purpose of recreation. The Ranger's house is occupied by the Earl of Aberdeen, who holds that office at present. Greenwich, Deptford, and Woolwich, form together the borough of Greenwich, which returns two members to Parliament. Pop. 139,436.
	27	**Lewisham Station.**	4	
	26	Blackheath St.	5	
	24	Charlton St. Close to the Station is the fine old manor house of Charlton, Sir T. M. Wilson, Bart.	7	
	23	Woolwich Dockyd. St.	8	
	22½	Woolwich Arsenal St.	8½	
Plumstead.	20	Abbey Wood St.	11	Plumstead and Erith Marshes; beyond, the Thames.
Belvidere Park, Sir C. E. Eardley, Bart.	18	Erith St. Erith can boast of a pretty ivy-covered church, containing a few monuments and brasses, but much defaced.	13	
Lesness Park. May place. Crayford.		cr. river Cray.		
	15	DARTFORD.	16	Dartford, a small town situated on the river Darent, is noted for its gunpowder and paper mills. The first paper mill in England was erected here. Pop. 5314.
		cr. river Darent.		
	12	**Greenhithe St.**	19	Greenhithe.
Swanscombe.		**Northfleet.**		**Ingress Abbey—The Hive.** At Northfleet some ship-building is carried on. Lime

ON RIGHT FROM LOND.	From Rochest.		From London.	ON LEFT FROM LOND.
Gravesend has greatly increased in size of late years, and become a favourite place of resort for the pleasure seekers of the metropolis. There are 3 excellent landing piers for the steamers and a variety of attractions for visitors. Pop. 18,782. Milton Church. Chalk.	8	**GRAVESEND.** Between Gravesend and Rochester the Railway passes through a tunnel, nearly along the line formerly occupied by the Thames and Medway Canal.	23	is extensively burnt in the neighbourhood. The church is ancient, and contains some interesting monuments. Rosherville gardens and pleasure grounds are well laid out, and with their adjuncts, form a great attraction to Cockney holiday-makers.
Cobham Hall, the noble seat of the Earl of Darnley, 3 miles. It contains a fine collection of pictures. Cobham Woods possess peculiar charms for those who delight in sylvan scenery.	3	**Higham St.**	28	3½ miles distant is Cowling Castle, built in the reign of Richard II., once a place of great strength: it is now chiefly in ruins, parts of which are very picturesque.
Strood, at which the railway terminates, forms a suburb of Rochester, with which it is connected by a handsome stone bridge. Together with the adjacent parish of Frinsbury, it forms a part of the borough of Rochester, which returns 2 members to Parliament.		**STROOD.**	31	2 miles from Stroud is Upnor Castle, on the west bank of the Medway, built in the reign of Elizabeth for the defence of the river. It forms a large ordnance depot for gunpowder.
		cr. river Medway to town of ROCHESTER (p. 2). CHATHAM (p. 2).		

III. LONDON TO FOLKSTONE AND DOVER, BY RAILWAY, 88 Miles.

ON RIGHT FROM LOND.	From Dover.		From London.	ON LEFT FROM LOND.
	67	From London Bridge, by Greenwich and Brighton railways, to Reigate Junc. St. (p. 24).	21	
Horne, 4 miles.		Through Bletchingley Tunnel, 1080 yards.		
Crowhurst.	61	Godstone St. Enter Kent.	27	**Godstone, 2 miles.** Tandridge Court, Earl of Cottenham.
Hever 3½ miles. Hever Castle, formerly the residence of Anne Boleyn, is	57	Edinbridge St.	32	Westerham, 5 miles. Population, 2162.
one of the most interesting relics in the kingdom. Many of the rooms are in the same state as when visited by Henry VIII. Adjacent to Hever is Chiddingstone, a village rich in specimens of old English architecture. It belonged till lately to the Waldo family.	52	Penshurst St. Penshurst, (Lord de Lisle and Dudley), the ancient seat of the Sydney family, who became possessed of the manor in the reign of Edward VI. Here Sir Philip Sydney was born in 1554. It is a fine old mansion, of quadrangular	37	Seven Oaks, 6 miles; and near it, Knowle Park, Countess Amherst (p. 16).

SOUTH EASTERN RAILWAY.

(REIGATE TO DOVER, CANTERBURY, DEAL, RAMSGATE & MARGATE.)

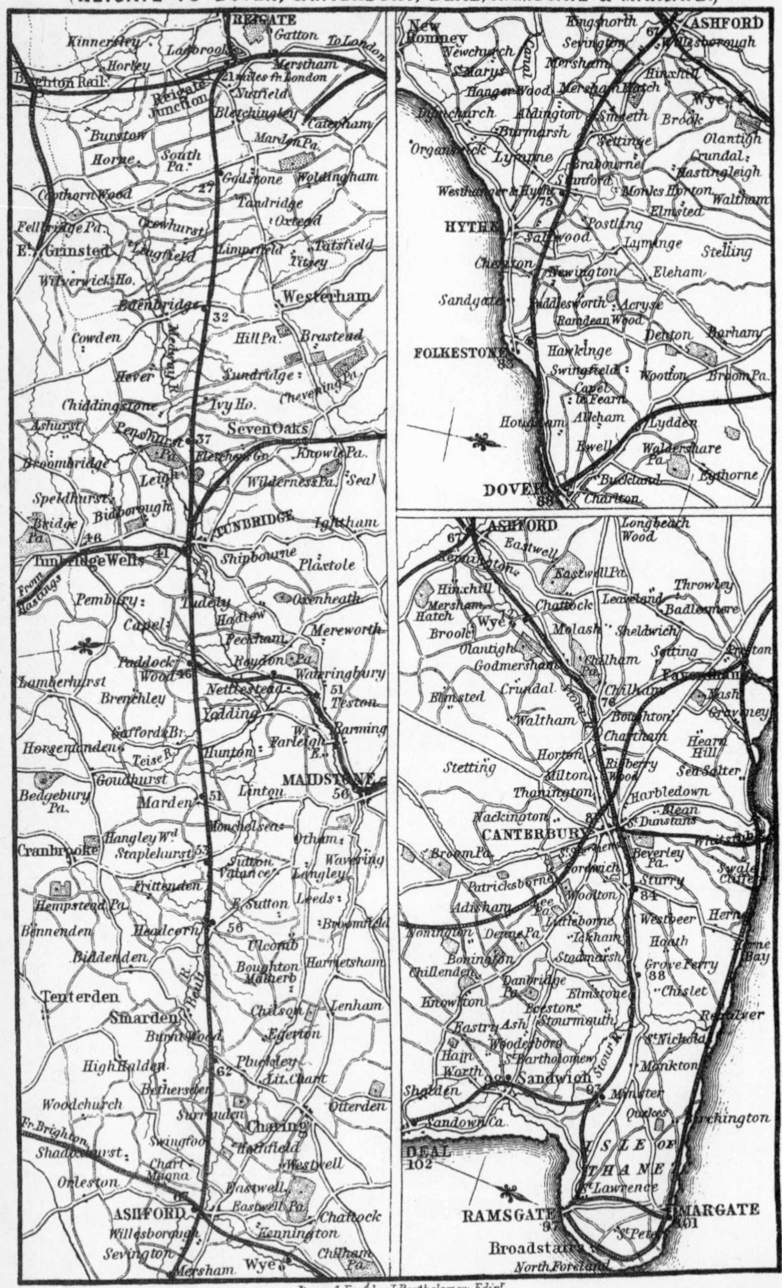

Drawn & Engd by J. Bartholomew, Edinr.

Published by A. & C. Black, Edinburgh.

ON RIGHT FROM LOND.	From Dover.		From London.	ON LEFT FROM LOND.
		form, enclosing a spacious court. The state apartments are adorned with rare portraits and paintings by eminent masters. Penshurt was also the birthplace of the famous Algernon Sydney.		
Branch to Tunbridge Wells, 5 miles.	47	Tunbridge Junction St. Here the central station of the railway is placed, covering 12 acres of ground, and consisting of offices, workhouses, and warehouses for the reception of goods.	41	Ightham, 7 miles.
Tudeley. Capel.	42	Paddock Wood Junction St.	46	Branch to Maidstone, 10 miles (p. 14).
Cranbrooke, $5\frac{1}{4}$ miles.		cr. river Teise.		
Frittenden, $3\frac{1}{2}$ miles.	38	Marden St.	50	
Sissinghurst Castle, 6 miles from the Staplehurst Station, is an ancient mansion now in ruins. It was used during one of the wars of the last century as a prison for French captives.	35	Staplehurst St.	53	
		cr. river Beult.		Sutton Valence, 4 m. Chart Sutton, 5 m. East Sutton, Sir E. Filmer, Bart.
	32	Headcorn St.	56	Boughton Malherb.
Biddenden, 4 miles. Tenterden, 9 miles. Smarden. Bethersden. Great Chart.	27	Pluckley St.	61	Charing, $5\frac{1}{2}$ miles. Population, 1241. Surrenden House, Sir E. C. Dering, Bart. Hothfield, Sir Richard Tufton, Bart. Goddinton House, Rev. N. Toke.
Branch to Rye and Hastings. Kingsworth. Aldington.	21	ASHFORD JUNCTION ST. (p. 13).	67	Branch to Canterbury, Ramsgate, &c. (see p.10). Willesborough. Sevington. Mersham Hatch, Sir N. J. Knatchbull, Bart.
Westenhanger House, an ancient manorial residence of the time of Richard I., Visct. Strangford.	13	cr. river Stour. Westenhanger and Hythe St. 2 miles west of Hythe is Lympne, the Portus Lemanis of the Romans: it has some remains of an ancient castle.	75	Smeeth: Sellinge. Standford. Monks Horton, $1\frac{3}{4}$ m. Postling. Beachborough, Rev. W. E. Brockman. Newington.
To Hythe, 3 m. (p. 14). Sandling Park, W. Deedes, Esq. Saltwood. Cheriton. Folkestone, $\frac{1}{2}$ mile.		Saltwood Tunnel, 952 yards.		
2 miles west of Folkestone is Sandgate (p. 14).	6	Folkestone St.	82	Hawkinge.
The engineering features of the line between Folkestone and Dover are well		Martello Tunnel, 636 yards. Abbot's Cliff Tunnel, 1937 yards.		Capel le Ferne. Hougham. $1\frac{1}{2}$ m. from Hougham,

ON RIGHT FROM LOND.	From Dover.		From London.	ON LEFT FROM LOND.
worthy of attention. The railway is alternately carried through tunnels, and upon artificial embankments formed on the face of the chalk cliffs, and washed at their base by the sea. In blasting the Round-down cliff for the occasion (in 1843), upwards of 19,000 pounds of gunpowder were used, and within a few seconds 400,000 cubic yards of chalk thrown down by the explosion to a depth of nearly 400 feet.		Shakespere's Cliff Tunnel, 1393 yards.		and 2½ from Dover, are the ruins of St Radigund's Monastery, founded at the close of the 12th century.
		DOVER (p. 6).	88	

IV. LONDON TO CANTERBURY, RAMSGATE, AND MARGATE, BY RAILWAY, 101 Miles.

ON RIGHT FROM LOND.	From Marg.		From London.	ON LEFT FROM LOND.
Leave main line to Dover.	34	From London Bridge to Ashford, as in preceding route.	67	**Kennington.**
Hinxhill, and beyond **Mersham Hatch, Sir N. J. Knatchbull, Bart.** Brook.		**Along the valley of the river Stour, which the line crosses 5 times between Ashford and Canterbury.**		Eastwell Park, Earl of Winchilsea and Nottingham, 2½ miles.
Crundell.	29	Wye St.	72	Godmersham Park, R. Knight, Esq.
Denge Wood. **Mystole House.**	25	Chilham St.	76	Chilham Park and Castle, J. B. Wildman, Esq. **To Feversham, 7 miles.**
Chartham. **Horton.** **Milton.** **Thanington.**		**CANTERBURY** (p. 2).	81	**Fishpond Wood.** **Harbledown: — Hall Place.** Hales Pl., **Railway to Whitstable, 6 miles.** **Beverley Park.**
Fordwich.	17	**Sturry St.**	84	**Herne Bay, 6 miles through the village of Herne.** **Westbere.**
Stodmarsh. **Grove Hill House.**	13	Grove Ferry St. cr. riv. Wantsum, and enter I. of Thanet.	88	**Hoath.** **Chislet Court.** **Sarre Bridge.** **Reculver, 3½ miles.** **Monkton.**
Branch to Sandwich and Deal, 9 miles. **Pegwell Bay.** **St Lawrence.**	8	Minster St.	93	**Birchington, 3 miles.**
Broadstairs, 2 miles from Ramsgate, and 3 from Margate, through St Peter's (p. 4).	4	**RAMSGATE** (p. 4).	97	**Dandelion.**
N. Foreland Lighthouse. **Kingsgate.**		**MARGATE** (p. 4).	101	**To Reculver, 8 miles.** **Herne Bay, 11 miles.**

ON RIGHT FROM LOND.	From Deal.		From London.	ON LEFT FROM LOND.
	9	From London Br. to Minster St. (p. 19).	93	
		cr. riv. Stour, and leave I. of Thanet.		About 1 mile before reaching Sandwich is Richborough Castle, the ancient Rutupiæ, a Roman station, and probably one of the earliest Roman works in the island. It is now a ruin, standing on a mound, the base of which is washed by the Stour.
Worth.	4	SANDWICH (p. 5).	98	
Sholden Lodge.		To Ramsgate, by coach, 6 miles.		Sandown Castle, where Col. Hutchinson died a prisoner.
From Deal to Dover, by coach, 8 miles, passing through Walmer and Ringswould.		DEAL (p. 5).	102	Deal Castle. Walmer Castle.

VI. LONDON TO TUNBRIDGE WELLS, BY RAILWAY, 46 Miles.

ON RIGHT FROM LOND.	From T. W.		From London	ON LEFT FROM LOND.
Mabledon Park, J. Deacon, Esq. Bidborough. Southborough Bounds. Nonsuch Green.	5	From London Br. to Tunbridge (p. 9).	41	Summerhill. Great Lodge. Pembury.
		TUNBRIDGE WELLS.	46	

Tunbridge Wells is a celebrated watering-place upon the borders of Kent and Sussex. The chalybeate spring, to which the town owes its origin, was first noticed in the reign of James I., by Dudley, Lord North. The town has much increased of late years, and contains all the usual requisites of a watering-place. It is celebrated for the salubrity of its air, and the neighbourhood is extremely picturesque and beautiful. Pop. 1861, 13,807. Excursions may be made to Penshurst, (Lord De Lisle and Dudley), 5 m. distant; Bridge Castle, 2 m. distant; Hever Castle, 7 m. distant; Bayham Abbey (Marquis Camden), 6 m. distant, the ruins of which are extremely picturesque. There is a modern mansion in the Gothic style. Two miles beyond Tunbridge Wells is Eridge Castle, the seat of the Earl of Abergavenny.

ON RIGHT FROM LOND.	From Folkest.		From London.	ON LEFT FROM LOND.
	68¼	Green-Man turnpike.	1½	
		cr. Surrey Canal.		
	67¼	Turk's Head or Half-way House.	2½	
		Hatcham.		
	66½	Newcross Square.	3¼	
		cr. Croydon Canal.		
	66	Newcross.	3¾	
		Enter Kent.		
Lewisham, a very populous village, extending near a mile on road to Bromley, 5 miles distant.	64¾	Lewisham.	5	Lee Lodge. Lee Manor House, F. Perkins, Esq.
		cr. river Ravensbourn.		
	64	Lee.	5¾	Lee Grove, T. Brandram, Esq.
Eltham Lodge.	61¾	Eltham. The church contains several interesting monuments. Here are the ruins of an old palace, in the time of Henry VII. one of the most magnificent royal edifices in England. The great hall is now used as a barn—the splendid roof of finely carved wood is in a good state of preservation. This is still Crown property.	8	Well-Hall, R. Sutton, Esq. Park Farm Place. To Dartford, 8½ miles.
	60¾	Southend.	9	
Kemnel.	58¼	Sidcup.	11½	
Frognal, Visct. Sydney.	57½	Foot's Cray.	12¼	North Cray. Foot's Cray Place.
		cr. river Cray.		
At a little distance, Chiselhurst.	55¾	Birchwood Corner.	14	
	53½	Pedham Place.	16¼	
Two miles distant. Lullingstone Castle, Sir P. Hart Dyke, Bart.	52¼	Farningham.	17½	
		cr. river Darent.		
	49	The Cock.	20¾	
To Seven-Oaks, 8 m. To Tunbridge, 8½. St. Clere, W. J. Evelyn, Esq., and 3 miles from Wrotham at Ightham, Oldbury Place, W. Elers, Esq.	45¾	Wrotham.	24	
		Wrotham Heath.		Addington.
Offham.	43½	Royal Oak.	26¼	Leybourne - Grange, Sir J. H. Hawley, Bt.
Bradbourne House, Sir W. Twysden, Bart.		A short distance to right, West Malling and East Malling.		
	39¾	Larkfield.	30	
	39	Ditton.	30¾	Aylesford and Friar's Place, Earl of Aylesford. Preston Hall.
		cr. river Medway.		
To Tunbridge, 13¼ m.	35¼	MAIDSTONE.	34½	

Maidstone, the county town of Kent, is situated on a pleasant declivity, chiefly on the right bank of the Medway. In the vicinity are very extensive hop plantations, and the town is surrounded by gardens and orchards. Maidstone has an extensive and flourishing trade in hops, grain, fruit, stone, &c. The paper-mills employ upwards of 300 hands. The Archbishop's Palace is a Gothic structure, rebuilt about the middle of the fourteenth century. It has undergone considerable alterations since that period, but is still a pleasant and convenient residence. Among the other buildings worthy of notice are, the County Hall, County Gaol, Chapel of Newark Hospital, All Saints Church, and a very ancient stone bridge. The town contains a grammar school, a proprietary school, 4 charity schools, 19 alms-houses, and 9 Dissenting meeting-houses. The county gaol was erected in 1818, on the improved radiating plan, at an expense of £200,000. Maidstone has returned two members of Parliament since the reign of Edward VI. It formerly contained a college, founded by Archbishop Courtenay in the reign of Richard II.; but it was suppressed by Edward VI. Population in 1861, 23,058. About 1½ miles north-east of the town is Pennenden Heath, where the county meetings have been held from a period prior to the Conquest. Roads lead from Maidstone to Hythe, Folkestone, and Dover, Canterbury, Rochester, Tenterden, and Romney, Tunbridge and Tunbridge Wells, and to Westerham. It is now connected with the metropolis by two railways.

ON RIGHT FROM LOND.	From Folkest.	Route to Folkestone continued.	From London.	ON LEFT FROM LOND.
Leeds Castle (C. W. Martin, Esq.) a fine old mansion, surrounded by a moat, situated in a wild park. Leeds village has an air of remote antiquity; and farther to the right East Sutton Place, Sir E. Filmer, Bart., and Ulcombe Ho.	30¼	Park Gate Inn.	39½	At a little distance Hollingbourn.
	28¼	Harrietsham.	41½	
Opposite Lenham, Chilstone House, G. Douglas, Esq.; Calehill Pk., H. Darell, Esq.; and further to the right, Surrenden-Dering, Sir E. C. Dering, Bart.	25¾	Lenham. The church is a large and handsome structure, and contains curious stalls and monuments.	44	Otterden.
	22¼	Charing on the left.	47½	To Faversham 10¾ m. To Canterbury 13½ m. Pett Place.
Hothfield Place, Sir R. Tufton, Bart. Goddinton, Rev. N. Toke.	19½	Hothfield Common.	50¼	At a distance, Eastwell Park, Earl of Winchilsea and Nottingham.
Four miles distant, Great Ollantigh.	16½	Ashford, At the confluence of two branches of the Stour. The church contains several monuments well worthy of notice. Pop. 5522.	53¼	To Faversham 14½ m. To Canterbury 14½ m.
	15¼	Willesborough.	54½	
	13¾	Mersham Hatch.	56	Mersham Hatch, Sir N. J. Knatchbull, Bart. At a distance Evington, Sir Courtenay Honywood, Bart.
	9¾	Sellinge. New-Inn Green.	60	Monks-Holton.

ON RIGHT FROM LOND.	From Folkest.	Route to Folkestone continued.	From London.	ON LEFT FROM LOND.
To New Romney 9 miles. This borough is one of the Cinque Ports. It formerly sent two members to Parliament,—the right of election being vested in the mayor, jurats, and commonalty; but it is now disfranchised. Pop. of parish, 1062.		HYTHE, One of the Cinque Ports, formerly a maritime town of great importance. It is a thoroughfare for persons going to or coming from France; the channel here being only 27 miles across to Calais, and the voyage being often made in one tide if the wind is fair. Returns 1 M.P. Pop. of town, 3001, and Parl. borough, 21,367.		Three miles distant, Sibton, J. Uneack, Esq. Hythe, near the church is the villa of Professor Coleman, and beyond, Beachborough, Rev. W. D. Brockman.
Sandgate is a village of considerable repute as a watering-place. It has a castle, originally built by Henry VIII., now employed as a martello tower.	6	Seabrook Bridge.	63¾	Marine Villa, Earl of Darnley.
	1¾	Sandgate.	68	
		FOLKESTONE.	69¾	

Folkestone was at one time a flourishing place, and is again rising into importance. It has greatly increased since the opening of the South-Eastern Railway, the directors of which have made it a principal station for communication with France. Swift steam-packets pass daily, and often twice a day between Folkestone and Boulogne (a direct distance of 29 miles), accomplishing the voyage in two hours. The harbour has been greatly extended and improved, and numerous modern buildings erected for the accommodation of visitors, by whom it is resorted to during the summer months. The surrounding country is very beautiful. Dr. William Harvey, the discoverer of the circulation of the blood, was a native, and left a sum of money, with which a school has been endowed. Customs dues collected in 1857, £135,381. Pop. 8507.

VIII. LONDON TO MAIDSTONE, BY RAILWAY, 43 Miles.

ON RIGHT FROM LOND.	From Maidst.		From London.	ON LEFT FROM LOND.
	12	From London Br. to Stroud St. (p. 7 and 8).	31	Rochester.
Cobham Hall, Earl of Darnley.	10	Cuxton St.	33	
	6	Snodland St.	37	
	4	Aylesford St.	39	
Leybourne Grange, Sir J. H. Hawley, Bart.		MAIDSTONE (p. 12).	43	The Mote, Earl of Romney.

65 Miles.

ON RIGHT FROM LOND.	From Winch.		From London.	ON LEFT FROM LOND.
		From London to Lewisham Bridge, see page 12.		
Well. Brockley.	60	Lewisham Bridge.	5	Lee. Horn Park. To Greenwich, 2½ miles.
Catsford Bridge.	59	Rushy Green.	6	Burnt Ash Grove.
Sydenham. Beckenham Place, J. Cator, Esq, Warren Ho.	57½	South End.	7½	
Clay Hill, Eden Farm, Lord Auckland (Bishop of Bath and Wells.)	56	BROMLEY.	9	Plaistow Hall. Camden Pl. Marq. Camden. Bromley House. Chiselhurst. Leesons, Lord Wynford 5 miles.

Bromley derives its name from the quantity of broom with which it was formerly surrounded. It is pleasantly situated on the Ravensbourn, and possesses a spring whose waters afford great relief in a variety of infirmities, from the chalybeate with which they are impregnated. The church contains a monument to the memory of Dr Hawkesworth, (the author of the Adventurer,) and the tomb of the wife of Dr Johnson. Bishop Warner, in 1666, here founded a college for 20 clergymen's widows. Population, 5505.

ON RIGHT FROM LOND.	From Winch.	Route continued.	From London.	ON LEFT FROM LOND.
	54½	Mason's Hill. Leaves Green.	10½	
Langley Pa., E. Goodhart, Esq. Hayes and Hayes Pl. Oakely Farm.				Southborough. Magpie Hall.
		Bromley Common.		
Holwood Ho.,(J. Ward,	52	Lock's Bottom.	13	
Esq.) once the seat of Mr. Pitt.	51	Farnborough.	14	Farnborough Hall.
High Elms, Sir J. W. Lubbock, Bart. New House.	49¾	Green Street Green.	15¼	Chelsfield.
	48¼	Spratt's Bottom.	16¾	Halstead and Halstead Place.
	47½	Richmore Hill.	17½	
Knockholt, Ashgrove Cottage.				Otford.
Chevening and Chevening Pa. Earl Stanhope. The third Earl possessed a	45	Morant's Court Hill, the summit of which commands a fine prospect.	20	Dunton Green.

ON RIGHT FROM LOND.	From Winch.		From Londcn.	ON LEFT FROM LOND.
great mechanical genius, and greatly improved the printing-press. Combe Bank. Chipsted Pl.				Bradbourne House.
	43	River Head.	22	Wilderness Park, Marquis Camden.
Montreal Pl. Earl Amherst. This seat received its name from the 1st Lord Amherst, in memory of his success in the reduction of Montreal, in Canada. To Westerham, $4\frac{1}{2}$ m. Keppington, Col. T. Austen. Ash Grove. Belle Vue.	41	SEVENOAKS is a pleasant town, and derives its name from seven oak-trees which formerly occupied the height on which it is built. The church is an elegant building, and, from its commanding situation, is a conspicuous object. The town has a Grammar-School, and a large range of alms-houses, instituted by Sir William de Sevenoke, a foundling, brought up by some charitable persons in the town from which he received his name. Population of parish, 4695.	24	Knowle Park (Earl Amherst), formerly the seat of the Sackvilles, Dukes of Dorset, whose title is now extinct. This magnificent mansion covers upwards of five acres of ground, and furnishes specimens of the architecture of a variety of ages,—the most ancient being as old as the Mareschels and Bigods, the most modern being the erection of Thomas, first Earl of Dorset, in the reign of James I. It has an invaluable collection of pictures and antique busts. The park contains herds of fine deer, a variety of excellent timber, and covers an extent of five or six miles in circumference.
Panthurst.	$40\frac{1}{4}$	River Hill.	$24\frac{3}{4}$	Rumsted.
Foxbush.	$37\frac{3}{4}$	Watt's Cross.	$27\frac{1}{4}$	Horn's Lodge.
		Flying Horse.		
Meopham Bank. Leigh Pa. Hall Pl. F. T. Bailey, Esq. Penshurst Pa., Lord de Lisle and Dudley. At a short distance is the famous oak, planted at the birth of Sir P. Sidney, and now 22 feet in circumference. The park is adorned by a noble sheet of water, called Lancup Well. See p. 8.	35	TUNBRIDGE, on the Medway, Is celebrated for its manufactures of turnery ware. It has a free grammar-school, founded and endowed by Sir A. Judde, a native of the place. Pop. of town, 5919. cr. River Medway To Tunbridge Wells, $5\frac{3}{4}$ miles.	30	To Maidstone, $13\frac{3}{4}$ miles. Postern Pa. J. E. West, Esq. Summer Hill, the residence of Cromwell's General Lambert after the civil wars.
Wood's Castle.	$30\frac{3}{4}$	Wood's Gate.	$34\frac{1}{4}$	Two and a-quarter miles distant is Tunbridge Wells.
	$28\frac{1}{2}$	Kipping's Cross.	$36\frac{1}{2}$	
	27	Lindridge.	38	

ON RIGHT FROM LOND.	From Winch.		From London.	ON LEFT FROM LOND.
		Enter Sussex.		
Two miles distant, Bayham Abbey (Marquis Camden), founded about the year 1200, beyond which, at Frant, is Shernfold, and Eridge Castle, Earl of Abergavenny.	25	Lamberhurst.	40	**Court Lodge.**
		cr. River Teise.		
	22	Stone Crouch, (Kent).	43	**Scotney Castle, an ancient seat situated in a deep vale on the banks of the Beulth.**
To Battle, 12 miles.	20¼	Flimwell.	44¾	**Bedgebury Park.**
Elfords.	17½	Highgate.	47½	**Oakfield Lodge.**
Lillesden.				
To Battle, 11 miles.				**To Cranbrook, five m.**
		Hawkhurst.		
	14¾	Sandhurst.	50¼	**To Tenterden, five m.**
Here a road leads to Four Oaks, through Whitebread Lane, saving 1½ mile.		Newinden.	52¾	
		cr. River Rother, and enter Sussex.		**Two miles distant, Merrington Place.**
At a distance are the ruins of Bodyham Castle, a magnificent building, supposed to have been built by one of the Dalyngriges, a family of great consequence in Sussex in the fourteenth and fifteenth centuries.	10¼	Nirthiam.	54¾	
	9¼	Beckley.	55¾	
	7¾	Four Oaks.	57¼	
	6	Peasemarsh.	59	
	2	RYE (p. 29.)	63	**Mountsfield, at the entrance of Rye.**
		WINCHELSEA.	65	Winchelsea Castle.

X. LONDON TO HASTINGS, 63¾ Miles.

ON RIGHT FROM LOND.	From Hastings.		From London.	ON LEFT FROM LOND.
To Tunbridge Wells, 13 miles.	19	London Bridge to Flimwell (Kent.) as above	44¾	To Rye, 18½ miles.
To Lewes, 24 miles.	16	Hurst Green (Sussex.)	47¾	**Iridge Pl. Lady Micklethwayt, Bart.**
		cr. river Rother. Robert's Bridge.		
Court Lo.; and, farther to the right, Darvell Bank.	11	Vine Hall.	52¾	
At a distance, Ashburnham House, Earl of Ashburnham.	9½	Wartlington.	54¼	
Battle Abbey, Lord H. Vane.	7¾	Battle.	56	
Battle Powder Mills. **Crowhurst Pl.**	5¾	Crowhurst Park.	58	**Beauport, Sir Charles M. Lamb, Bart.**
Hollington Lodge.				**1½ mile distant, Westfield.**
Ore Place—Sir H. Elphingstone, Bart.	2¼	Ore.	61½	**Bohemy House.**
		HASTINGS (p. 28.)	63¾	**To Winchelsea, 7½ miles, thence to Rye, 2 miles.**

ON RIGHT FROM LOND.	From Hastings		From London.	ON LEFT FROM LOND.
	37	London to Tunbridge (p. 16.)	30	Penshurst, Lord de Lisle and Dudley.
		cr. river Medway.		South Pa. Great Bounds, Viscount Hardinge.
	34	Southborough.	33	
		Nonsuch-Green.		
To Lewes, 24¾ miles.	31¼	Tunbridge Wells.	35¾	
	29¼	Frant (Sussex.)	37¾	
	24¾	Wadhurst.	42¼	
To East Bourne, 30 m.		Shover's Green.		
	21¾	Ticehurst.	45¼	
		Junction of the road		
	19	from Flimwell,	48	
		Thence to Hastings as by the preceding route.		

XII. LONDON.—UCKFIELD.—EAST BOURNE, 62¾ Miles.

ON RIGHT FROM LOND.	From E. Bourne.		From London.	ON LEFT FROM LOND.
Langley Park, E. Goodhart, Esq.	52¾	London Br. to Bromley (Kent.) (See p. 15.)	10	
Westerham is a small market-town. The manor was given to Abbey of Westminster by Edward I.—It is now the property of J. Ward, Esq. Gen. Wolfe and Bishop Hoadley were natives of this place. In the parish church there is a monument to the memory of the former, who is buried there.	48¼	Keston.	14½	Holwood Ho., J. Ward, Esq. The old mansion-house of Holwood was for many years the favourite retirement of Mr Pitt. On west side of Holwood Hill are the remains of an extensive encampment, supposed to be of Roman origin.
	47¼	Leaves Green.	15½	
	44	South Street.	18¾	
	41¼	Westerham.	21½	
		To Reigate, 13¾ m.		
		To East Grinstead, 16¾ miles.		
		To Maidstone, 22 m.		Hill Park.
	37½	Lindhurst.	25¼	
Squerries	36	Eden Br.	26¾	
		cr. river Eden.		
Hammerwood Lodge, J. D. Magens, Esq.	31¾	Kent Water, enter Suss.	31	
To East Grinstead, 6¾ m.	28¾	Hartfield.	34	Stoneland Park.
Two miles distant, Ashdown House, A. E. Fuller, Esq.		Ashdown Forest.		
	24¾	Junction of the road.	38	
Maresfield Park, Sir J. V. Shelley, Bart.		Maresfield.		Buckstead.
	19½	UCKFIELD.	43¼	Framfield Park, A. Donovan, Esq.
		In the neighbourhood are two chalybeate springs. Population, 1851, 1590.		
1¼ mile from Uckfield, a road leads off to Lewes 8 miles distant.		There is another and a shorter route from London to Uckfield (see p. 20.)		

ON RIGHT FROM LOND.	From E. Bour.		From Lond.	ON LEFT FROM LOND.
	14½	East Hoathley.	48¼	
The Broad.	12½	Whitesmith Green.	50¼	
	8½	Horsebridge.	54¼	Four m. distant, Hurstmonceux Park, H. M. Curteis, Esq.
		cr. riv. Cuckmere.		
	7	Hailsham.	55¾	
	3½	Polegate Green.	59¼	Ratton Park, Freeman Thomas, Esq.
	2¾	Willingdon.	60¾	
		EAST BOURNE.	62¾	Compton Place, Lord Chesham.

East Bourne is a fashionable sea-bathing place, situated in a valley at the extremity of the South Downs. It has a handsome church, in which are some monuments and a singular font. The bathing here is remarkably good; and it has also the advantage of a chalybeate spring. To the west of East Bourne is Beachy-Head, the loftiest cliff on this coast. It is 573 feet in height, and contains several caverns. Six miles east of East Bourne is Pevensey Castle, a fine specimen of ancient architecture. The date of its erection is unknown, but, from the quantity of Roman brick employed in the work, it is supposed to have been constructed out of some Roman fortress. The town and castle of Pevensey were conferred by William the Conqueror on his half-brother, Robert Earl of Montainge and Cornwall. They were afterwards forfeited to the Crown, and Henry III. granted them to his son Prince Edward and his heirs, Kings of England, so that they should never more be separated from the Crown. Notwithstanding of this, however, they were settled on the celebrated John of Gaunt. For many years Pevensey Castle was held by the Pelhams. It then came to Spencer Compton, Earl of Wilmington, and ultimately descended by marriage to the Duke of Devonshire. Six miles from Pevensey and 12 from East Bourne are the ruins of Hurstmonceux Castle, formerly a fortress of great magnificence and strength. Till 1777 it was the most perfect and regular castellated mansion in the kingdom; but about that period the roof was taken down, and the interior completely stript by the proprietor, the Rev. Mr Hare, who employed the materials thus obtained in the erection of some additional rooms in the modern mansion-house. The church contains some curious monuments of the family of Fiennes. Hurstmonceux is now the property of H. M. Curteis, Esq., who manifests a praiseworthy zeal in the preservation of its ruins.

The nearest road to East Bourne, and that which is most travelled, is through East Grinstead and Uckfield (see page 20). Its distance from London by the route is 61 miles. The population of East Bourne parish in 1861 was 5795.

XIII. LONDON TO LEWES AND BRIGHTON THROUGH CROYDON AND EAST GRINSTEAD, $58\frac{1}{4}$ Miles.

ON RIGHT FROM LOND.	From Bright.		From Lond.	ON LEFT FROM LOND.
	$56\frac{3}{4}$	Westminster Bridge to Kennington T. P.	$1\frac{1}{2}$	
	$55\frac{1}{4}$	Brixton.	3	
Streatham Park, where, while it was occupied by the Thrales, Dr. Johnson was a frequent visitor.	53	Streatham.	$5\frac{1}{4}$	The vicinity of Croydon is particularly celebrated for field-sports. The church is a fine ancient building, containing the monuments of Sheldon, Wake, Gridall, Whitgift, and Potter, Archbishops of Canterbury.
Beddington Pa., C. H. Carew, Esq., beyond which is Carshalton Ho., and Carshalton Pa.	49	CROYDON. To Epsom $9\frac{1}{4}$ miles.	$9\frac{1}{4}$	To Bromley $6\frac{1}{2}$ miles.
	$46\frac{3}{4}$	Purley House.	$11\frac{1}{4}$	Purley Ho. Here Horne Tooke resided. Sanderstead Co.
Hayling House.				
	$44\frac{1}{2}$	Rose and Crown Inn.	$13\frac{3}{4}$	
Quarry House.	43	Marden Park Lodge.	$15\frac{1}{4}$	Marden Park, Sir W. R. Clayton, Bart. Rook's Nest, C. H. Turner, Esq.
		Godstone Green.	19	Flower House. Lee Place. Stratton House.
Gasson House.				
	$37\frac{3}{4}$	Stanstead Borough.	$20\frac{1}{2}$	
	$35\frac{1}{4}$	Blindley Heath.	23	
	$33\frac{1}{4}$	New Chapel Green.	25	Felcourt.
Felbridge P.	$31\frac{1}{4}$	Felbridge (enter Sussex).	27	To Brighton through Lindfield 27 miles.
Framepost, and Saint Hill. At the east end of the town is Sackville College, erected by Robert, Earl of Dorset, for the residence of 24 aged persons.	$29\frac{3}{4}$	EAST GRINSTEAD. The church is a spacious building, containing a curious monument, with an inscription stating that the church was founded by R. Lewkner, Esq. and his wife, who was one of the ladies to the Queens of Edward IV. and Henry VII.	$28\frac{1}{2}$	East Co. East Grinstead formerly returned 2 M.P.'s., but is now disfranchised. Pop. of parish, 4266.
		cr. river Medway.		
Kidbrooke, Lord Colchester.	$26\frac{3}{4}$	Forest Row.	$31\frac{1}{2}$	Ashdown Pa., A. E. Fuller, Esq. Pixton House.
	$24\frac{3}{4}$	Wych Cross.	34	
To Cuckfield, 13 miles.	$21\frac{1}{4}$	Nutley.	37	
At a distance Sheffield Pa. Earl of Sheffield, and Fletching church, in which Gibbon the historian is interred.	$18\frac{1}{2}$	Maresfield.	$39\frac{3}{4}$	Maresfield Pa. Sir J. V. Shelley, Bart. Buxted Place.
	$16\frac{3}{4}$	Uckfield.	$41\frac{1}{2}$	

ON RIGHT FROM LOND.	From Bright.		From Lond.	ON LEFT FROM LOND.
	14¾	Horsted.	43½	Framfield, A. Donovan, Esq.
Malling House. Malling Deanery,	8¾	Cliff.	49½	Here a road leads off to East Bourne, distant 19½ miles.
		cr. river Ouse.		Plashet Park, Viscount Gage.
Combe Place, Rev. Sir G. Shiffner, Bart.	8¼	LEWES.	50	Glynde, 3 m. Lord Dacre and Glyndbourne.
Stanmer Park, Earl of Chichester.	6½	(See p. 28.)	51¾	Firle Place, Visct. Gage.
	4¼	Ashcombe.	54	
		Falmer.		
		BRIGHTON.	58¼	

XIV. LONDON TO BRIGHTON THROUGH CROYDON AND CUCKFIELD, 51¼ Miles.

ON RIGHT FROM LOND.	From Bright.		From Lond.	ON LEFT FROM LOND.
	34½	London to Merstham. At the 19th milestone, to Brighton, through Reigate.	17¾	
Near on Red-Hill Common Leith Hill Tower, a conspicuous object in this neighbourhood.	27½	Horley.	24	To Brighton through Hickstead, 24 miles.
		Enter Sussex.		
		Richman's Green.		
		Worth-Bridge.		
	24	Northfolk Arms.	27¼	
	21¾	Balcombe.	29½	
	20¼	Whiteman's Green.	31	
	18½		32¾	
	15	CUCKFIELD, Pop. of parish, 1851, 3196.	36¼	
	14¼		37	
	8½	Friar's Oak Inn.	42¾	
Danny, W. J. Campion, Esq.	6¾	Clayton.	44½	
Woolsonbury Beacon.	5¾	Piecombe.	45½	
	3	Patcham.	48¼	
	2¼	Withdean.	49	
		BRIGHTON.	51¼	

XV. LONDON TO BRIGHTON THROUGH CROYDON, REIGATE, CRAWLEY, AND HICKSTEAD, 52¼ Miles

ON RIGHT FROM LOND.	From Bright.		From Lond.	ON LEFT FROM LOND.
	43	Westminster Bridge to CROYDON.	9¼	
Up. Gatton House, W Currie, Esq.	34½	Merstham.	17¾	
Gatton Park, Lord Monson. Gatton is remarkable as having possessed the privilege of sending 2 M. P's. while it had seven electors.	31	REIGATE. The church contains several costly monuments. A castle formerly stood here, but no part of the building now remains. The Priory (Earl Somers) stands on the site of a convent of Augustines. Reigate returns one M. P. Pop .9975.	21¼	
Charlwood House, J. Fraser, Esq.		At the County Oak, enter Sussex.		
To Horsham, 7 miles.		CRAWLEY.	29¾	Tilgate Lodge.
	22½	cr. a branch of river Adur.		
	11½	HICKSTEAD.	40¾	
Albourne Place.	9½	Albourne Green.	42¾	Hurstpierpoint.
	6¼	Piecombe.	46	
	3¼	Patcham.	49	Stanmer Park, Earl of Chichester.
		BRIGHTON.	52¼	

XVI. LONDON TO BRIGHTON THROUGH SUTTON, REIGATE, AND CUCKFIELD 52¾ Miles.

ON RIGHT FROM LOND.	From Bright.		From Lond.	ON LEFT FROM LOND.
	49½	Clapham Common.	3¼	
	46¾	Tooting.	6	
At a distance Mordon Park.	45	Mitcham. cr. river Wandle, Once celebrated for the excellence of its trout.	7¾	Beddington Park, C. H. Carew, Esq. Carshalton House. Carshalton Park.
	41½	SUTTON.	11¼	Carshalton church contains a handsome monument to the Gaynesford family.
Nork Ho. E. of Egmont. Tadworth Court.	39¾	Banstead Downs. Obelisk.	13	The Oaks (formerly a seat of the Earls of Derby), a noble mansion, commanding fine views.
	34¾	Walton Heath.	18	
	33¾	Gatton Inn.	19	Upper Gatton House, W. Currie, Esq.
Gatton, a famous nomination borough, now disfranchised.	31¾	REIGATE. Thence to Brighton by Crawley and Cuckfield	21	Gatton Pa. a noble mansion, the approach to which is thought to equal anything of the kind in the kingdom, the seat of Lord Monson.

LONDON & BRIGHTON & SOUTH-COAST RAILWAYS.

(LONDON TO BRIGHTON, PORTSMOUTH & HASTINGS.)

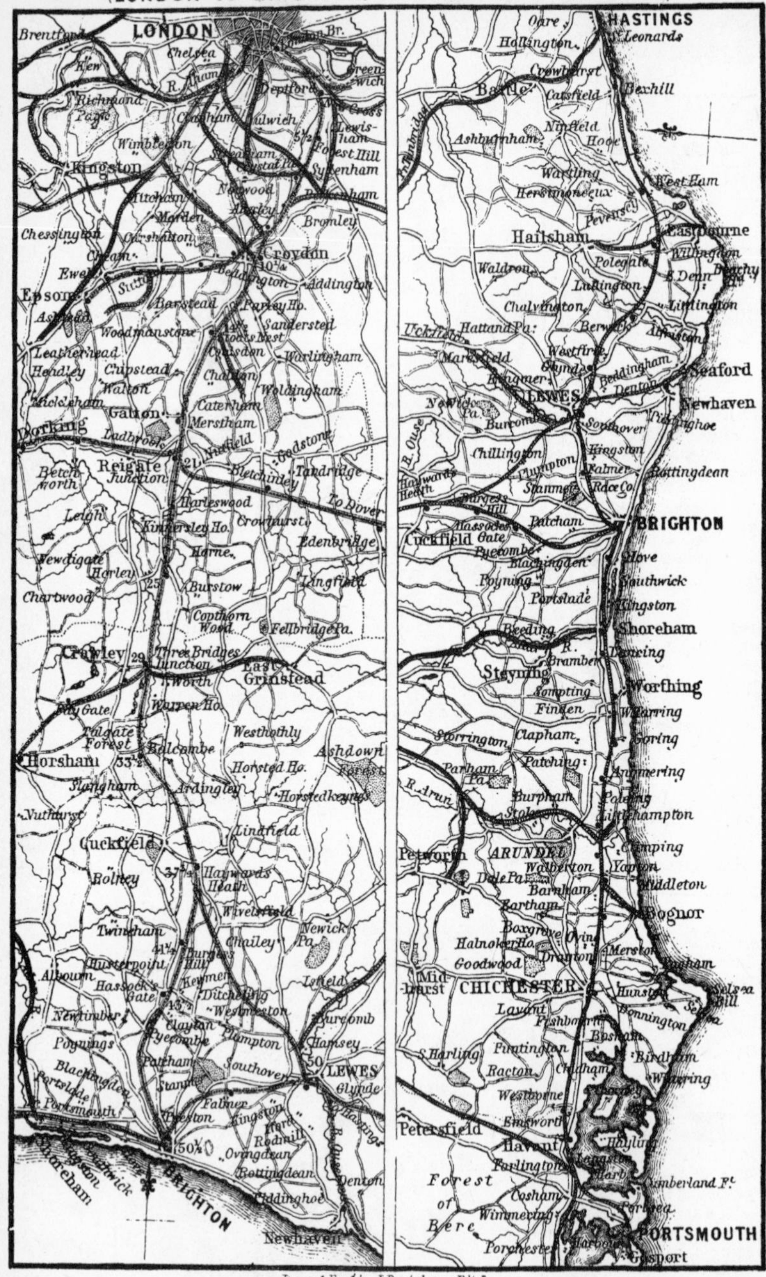

Drawn & Engd. by J. Bartholomew, Edinr.

Published by A. & C. Black, Edinburgh

ON RIGHT FROM LOND.	From Bright.		From London.	ON LEFT FROM LOND.
At New Cross is the Royal Naval School, founded in 1843.		From London Bridge by Greenwich Railway for 1¾ m. cr. Surrey Canal.		Deptford. **Greenwich (see p. 7).**
	48	New Cross St.	3	To Lee and Eltham.
One and a half m. distant is Dulwich, noted for its college and picture-gallery. The college was founded in 1639, by Edward Alleyn, a player, for the education and maintenance of poor scholars. The picture-gallery, bequeathed to the College by Sir Francis Bourgeois, R.A., and rich in specimens of the Dutch school, is open to the public.	45½	Forest Hill St. Sydenham. The resting-place of the Crystal Palace. Anerley. Norwood. From Upper Norwood, most extensive views of London and the surrounding country may be obtained.	5½	The scenery in the neighbourhood of this portion of the line presents many attractions; the country is richly cultivated, and the church spires rising in the distance form pleasing features in the landscape. Beckenham.
North Surrey Industrial Schools.		Sydenham, Anerley, and Norwood, are stations used only by the Croydon and Epsom trains.		Eden Farm, Lord Auckland (Bishop of Sodor and Man).
Beulah Spa, 1 mile, and beyond it Streatham, where Dr. Johnson was wont to spend much of his time with the Thrale family. Croydon and Epsom railway branches off. Hayling Park.	40¾	Croydon (East) St. The town of Croydon is to the right of the railway. (See p. 33).	10¼	Addiscombe College, for the education of cadets for the E. I. Co.'s service. Addington Park, 3½ m., Archbp. of Canterbury. Purley House, once the residence of John Horne Tooke, and whence the title of his work, "The Diversions of Purley," was derived.
Smitham Bottom, a broad open valley, through which the coach road passes; beyond are Banstead Downs.	37¾	Godstone Road St. To Godstone 8 miles, on left.	13¼	Sanderstead Court.
Two miles distant, The Oaks, formerly a seat of the Earls of Derby.	36¾	Stoat's Nest St.	14¼	Coulsdon. Chaldon.
Woodmansterne.		Merstham Tunnel, 1820 yards.		Marden Park, Sir W. R. Clayton, Bart.
Gatton Ho., Lord Monson, a magnificent structure, surrounded by an extensive park. The adjacent village of Gatton, long notorious as a rotten borough, was	32	Merstham St., used only by the South-Eastern trains.	19	Merstham House, Sir W. G. H. Jolliffe, Bart.

ON RIGHT FROM LOND.	From Bright.		From London.	ON LEFT FROM LOND.
disfranchised in 1832 by the Reform Act, a short time previous to which it had been purchased by the 5th Ld. Monson for L.100,000. Railway to Reading, through Dorking and Guildford, (p. 185). Reigate, situated on the Mole, and built upon a rock of white sand, much valued for the manufacture of fine articles of glass. An object of much curiosity here is the Baron's Cave. The town returns 1 member to parliament. Pop. 9975. 4927.	30	Redhill Junction St.	21	Leave South-Eastern line, to Dover, (p. 8).
		Earl's Wood embankment, over Earl's wood Common.		Nutfield. Many years ago a vast number of Roman coins were discovered here. Holmesdale Lodge.
		cr. 2 branches of the river Mole.		
	25	Horley St.	26	
Charlwood.		Cross county boundary and enter Sussex.		Burstow.
Crawley, 1½ mile.		cr. river Mole.		
Branch to Horsham, 8 m. (See p. 30).	21	Three Bridges St.	30	Worth, 1½ m. distant, has an ancient Saxon church.
		Pass through Tilgate Forest, part of The Weald.		
		cr. branch of R. Mole.		East Grinstead, 7 m, a market-town. Pop. of parish, 1861, 4266. It formerly returned two M.P.'s, but is now disfranchised. (See p. 20.)
		Balcombe Tunnel, 1120 yards.		
	17	Balcombe St. About 1½ mile from the station is the Ouse Viaduct, one of the most stupendous works of the kind in the kingdom. It consists of thirty-seven arches, of 30 feet span each. The height from the water to the surface of the road is 100 feet; height of the abutments, 40 feet; the length of the whole upwards of a quarter of a mile.	34	Balcombe House. 2½ m. distant, Wakehurst Pl., J. J. W. Peyton, Esq.
Slaugham Place.				Ardingley. Lindfield.
Cuckfield, 2 miles, is a small but pleasant market-town, with a fine and spacious church. Pop. of par. 3539.	13	Hayward's Heath St.	38	Branch to Lewes and Hastings, (p. 25). Wivelsfield.

ON RIGHT FROM LOND.	From Bright.		From London.	ON LEFT FROM LOND.
Cuckfield Place.				
Clayton Priory. Hurstpierpoint, 2 m.	9	Burgess Hill St.	42	
Albourne Place, 3 m.	7	Hassock's Gate St.	44	Keymer; Ditchling. To Lewes, by road, 9 m.
Danny Ho., W. J. Campion, Esq. Newtimber.		Clayton Tunnel, 2240 yards long, passes through the range of the S. Down hills.		Clayton. Pangdean.
Withdean.		Patcham Tunnel, 480 yards.		Patcham. Stanmer Park, 2 miles, Earl of Chichester.
				Preston.
Branch to Chichester and Portsmouth, (p. 79).		Descent to BRIGHTON.	51	Branch to Lewes and Hastings, 32½ miles.

XVIII. LONDON TO LEWES AND HASTINGS (ST LEONARD'S), BY RAILWAY, 74 Miles.

ON RIGHT FROM LOND.	From St Leon.		From London.	ON LEFT FROM LOND.
Leave line to Brighton.	36	From London Br. to Hayward's Heath (p. 24).	38	Wivelsfield.
Ditchling. — Ditchling Beacon, one of the highest points of the S. Downs, is 858 feet above the sea.	30	Cook's Bridge St.	44	Chailey, 2¾ m.
Westmeston. Plumpton. Combe Place, Rev. Sir G. Shiffner, Bart.—Hamsey Place.		The range of the South Down Hills lies to the right hand.		Chiltington. Wellingham, 2½ m.
	25½	LEWES.	48½	
Branch to Newhaven, 6¾ m. Newhaven is situated at the mouth of the Ouse, and forms the port of Lewes. Its harbour has recently been improved, and is the point of embarkation for Dieppe, the steamers which ply daily, making the passage in 4 or 5 hours. Pop. 1886.		Join line from Brighton (see p. 85). cr. river Ouse. The line here runs between the S. Down ranges.		Cliff: the highest point of Cliff Hill, round which the railway winds, is called Mount Caburn; it commands an extensive view.
	22½	Glynde St.	51½	Glynde Place, Lord Dacre. Glyndbourne.
Beddingham. Firle Place, Visct. Gage. Firle Hill, 820 feet high. Selmeston.		Line of S. Down Hills to the right.		
Berwick Court.	18	Berwick St.	56	

ON RIGHT FROM LOND.	From Hastings.		From London.	ON LEFT FROM LOND.
Willingdon. Branch to Eastbourne, 3 miles (p. 19).	14	cr. riv. Cuckmere. Polegate St. The railway now leaves the South Downs, which stretch southward to Beachy Head, and runs through a level tract, with the sea on the right hand.	60	Arlington. Branch to Hailsham, 3½ m. Hailsham is a small market-town, 59 m. from London by road. Pop., of Parish, 2098.
The coast is here lined by the martello towers, built at the period of the threatened French invasion, and which extend at intervals along great part of the Kentish and Sussex coasts.	10½	West Ham and Pevensey St. Pevensey is a very ancient place. It was probably the Anderida of the Romans, and the Andredesceaster of Saxon times.	63½	On the east of Pevensey are the ruins of Pevensey Castle (p. 19). Hurstmonceux Park, 3½ m., and ruins of Hurstmonceux Castle, H. M. Curteis, Esq. Beyond, Windmill Hill, H. M Curteis, Esq.
	4	Bexhill St.	70	Wartling. Hooe. Five m. from Bexhill St. is Ashburnham Ho. (Earl of Ashburnham), a fine modern edifice, standing in an extensive park. The parish church of Ashburnham contains some interesting relics of Charles I. such as the watch, shirt, &c. worn by him on the scaffold.
		Bulverhithe.		
St Leonard's consists wholly of modern structures, erected within the last few years for the accommodation of visitors, and is at present one of the most fashionable and frequented watering-places on the English coast. The esplanade is one of the finest in Europe.		Bopoop.		
	1	ST. LEONARD'S.	73	
		HASTINGS.	74	

Brighton is situated nearly in the centre of the bay stretching from Selsey Bill, in the west, to Beachy Head, the eastern extremity of the South Downs. It is protected on the north and north-east by this verdant chain of chalk hills, and on the west lies a level district of arable land. The sea has made considerable encroachments on this part of the coast. In the reign of Elizabeth the town of Brighton was situated on that tract where the chain-pier now extends into the sea, but the whole of the tenements under the cliff were destroyed by tremendous storms in 1703 and 1705, and no traces of this ancient town are now perceptible. The foundation of the prosperity of Brighton was laid by Dr Richard Russell, an eminent physician, whose work on the efficacy of sea water, combined with his successful practice, brought numerous visitors to the coast. But it

BRIGHTON.

was to George IV. when Prince of Wales, Brighton was indebted for its celebrity as a watering-place. His Royal Highness first visited Brighton in 1782. after which time he passed the summer and autumn months here for many years in succession. In 1784, he commenced the erection of the Pavilion, which was completed in its original design in 1787, and under the stimulus of royal patronage, what was formerly a fishing village, has now become the most attractive watering-place in Europe. The Pavilion having been purchased by the inhabitants in 1840, its gardens are used as a public promenade.

Brighton was made an incorporated town in 1854. It is divided into six wards, and the municipal affairs are managed by a mayor, recorder, twelve aldermen, and thirty-six councillors.

The fishery of Brighton was once very considerable, but has now declined to an almost incredible extent.

Of the public buildings of Brighton, the most distinguished is the Royal Pavilion, the architecture of which has been severely and justly censured. The Chain Pier is a light and elegant structure, erected in 1822, under the superintendence of Captain Brown, at an expense of L. 30,000. It has twice suffered from violent storms. The marine wall, which was completed in 1838, and was eleven years in building, is a splendid structure. It is nearly two miles in length, and cost about L.100,000. The celebrated spot called the Steyne, which was formerly a piece of waste land, is now a fashionable promenade, and is surrounded by beautiful buildings. In the northern enclosure stands the famous bronze statute of George IV. executed by Chantrey. The Town Hall is an immense pile of building, the cost of which is said to have been near L.30,000. Brighton contains numerous (13) places of worship in connection with the establishment, and many belonging to the various denominations of Christian Dissenters, and a Jews' synagogue. In the church-yard of the old church is a monument erected to the memory of Captain Tattersal, who assisted Charles II. in his escape to the continent after the battle of Worcester. There are a considerable number of schools in the town for the instruction of the children of the poor. Brighton contains barracks both for cavalry and infantry; the former affords accommodation for 625, and the latter for about 400 men. In the rear of the east part of the town is a pleasing rural retreat, called the Park, in which is the German spa establishment, where chemical imitations of the most celebrated mineral waters of Germany are prepared. At Wick, half a mile west of the town, there is a chalybeate spring, which has of late years been much frequented. Brighton is well supplied with baths, and every convenience for the accommodation of those who wish to avail themselves of the advantages of sea-bathing. The exteriors of many of the hotels are magnificent, and the interiors fitted up with much taste and convenience.

Brighton is not a manufacturing or commercial town, but it has an extensive retail trade.

To the north and north-east of the town, on the summit of the Downs, is the race-course, commanding an extensive view. A number of pleasant excursions may be made in the vicinity. The population of Brighton, which, at the commencement of the present century, was only 7339, was, by the census of 1841, 46,661, of 1851, 69,673, and by that of 1861, 77,693; while during the fashionable season, it is estimated at 90,000. Brighton returns two members to Parliament under the Reform Act.

At the distance of 8 miles from Brighton, stands the ancient market-town and borough of Lewes, pleasantly situated on a rising ground, and surrounded partly by hills, and watered by the river Ouse. Lewes is a place of great antiquity, and numerous remains of Roman art have been excavated in the town and neighbourhood. It was strongly fortified in the time of the Saxons. At the period of the Conquest, the rape of Lewes fell to the lot of William de Warren, son-in-law of William the Conqueror, who erected a castle in Lewes, and made it the place of his residence. It continued in the possession of his descendants until the beginning of the fourteenth century, when, in default of male issue, the barony passed into the family of Fitzalan, Earl of Arundel. On the death of Thomas, Earl of Arundel, in 1439, it was divided among the noble families of Norfolk, Dorset, and Abergavenny, in the possession of whose descendants it still remains. In the immediate vicinity of Lewes, a sanguinary battle was fought in May 1264, between the troops of Henry III., and those of the barons under Simon de Montfort, in which the former were defeated. A considerable portion of the castle still remains, and there are also some interesting ruins of the monastery of St. Pancras, founded by the first Earl de Warren in 1076. The annual revenue of the monastery at the time of the dissolution is valued at £1091 : 9 : 6. Lewes could also boast in former times of at least nine churches, but of these only two now remain. At present it contains six parish churches, and eight Dissenting chapels. The public buildings are, the County Hall, House of Correction, and Theatre. There is also an excellent race-course. A number of influential county families formerly had their principal residences at Lewes. The town has possessed the privilege of returning two members to Parliament since the time of Edward I. The population by the census of 1861 was 9716.

The distance from Lewes to London by Chailey is 49 miles ; by Uckfield, a mile more.

About forty miles east from Brighton is the borough of Hastings, a celebrated watering-place, and a place of great antiquity. The entrance to it from the London road is extremely beautiful. The town is well paved and lighted, and very neat and clean. It formerly possessed a good harbour ; but its chief dependence now lies on its fisheries, and on the influx of visitors. The citizens of the place are famous for their skill in boat-building. On a lofty rocky cliff westward of the town are the remains of a very ancient castle, the walls of which are still partly entire, and are in some places eight feet thick. The town contains a supply of hot and cold baths, libraries—a promenade, a theatre, an assembly room, &c. The notorious Titus Oates was born in this town, and officiated for some time as minister in All-Saints-Church. The vicinity of Hastings abounds in interesting and romantic scenery. The borough ranks as the first of the Cinque Ports in their official proceedings, and returns two members to Par-

HASTINGS.

liament. Population of the borough and Cinque Port, 22,837. Hastings is 64 miles distant from London, and is now completely joined to St. Leonards, there being no longer any space without houses between the two.

About seven miles north-west from Hastings is the market-town of Battle, which takes its name from that memorable contest, commonly called the Battle of Hastings, which put an end to the Saxon line of kings, and placed the crown of England on the head of a Norman. In the year following his victory, William, in fulfilment, it is said, of a vow made on the night previous to the battle, caused to be founded a splendid abbey, which, however, was not completed till seven years after his death. His conquering sword, and the robe which he had worn at his coronation, were offered at the altar. Here also was deposited the "Roll of Battel Abbey," consisting of a table of the Norman gentry who came into England with the Conqueror. This abbey was one of the mitred ones which conferred on the abbot the honour of a seat in Parliament. At the dissolution of the monasteries a grant of the house and site of the abbey was made to Sir Anthony Browne, the ancestor of the Montagu family, who continued to reside here in a part of the abbey which had been converted into a mansion, till the beginning of the eighteenth century, when it was sold to Sir Thomas Webster, Bart.; and it has lately passed by purchase to Lord Harry Vane. The abbey, when in its complete state, formed a square, three sides of which are now partly occupied with its ruins.

The town of Battle is celebrated for its manufacture of gunpowder. Pop. of Parish, 3293.

Ten miles east from Hastings stands the ancient town of Rye, situated on a rock near the mouth of the Rother. It was strongly fortified in the reign of Edward III., and part of the walls and some of the gates are still standing. Its harbour having been choked up by sand, a new one has been formed by cutting a large canal in a more direct line to the sea, sufficiently spacious to admit vessels of 200 tons up to the quay. The only objects worthy of notice are, the church, a very large stone building; Ypres Castle, originally built for the defence of the town, by William de Ypres, in the twelfth century, now occupied as a prison; the Town-Hall and the Market-place; and the remains of the town gates and walls. The fishermen of Rye send considerable supplies to the London market. Rye has for centuries been celebrated for a very extensive illicit trade, which is now, however, greatly diminished. Rye is one of the Cinque Ports; and, before the Reform Bill passed, returned two members to Parliament. It now, in conjunction with some of the neighbouring parishes, returns one. The population of Rye, Parl. Borough, 8202.

To the westward of Rye is the disfranchised borough of Winchelsea, formerly a place of considerable importance, but now greatly reduced, in consequence of the sea having deserted it. A part of one of its churches is all that remains out of three which it formerly possessed. It contains two monuments of Knights Templars, and there is a third in the vestry. The whole of Old Winchelsea was swallowed up by the sea in a tempest. The new town was built by Edward I. Between Winchelsea and Rye, and about two miles from the former, are the ruins of Winchelsea or Camber Castle, built by Henry VIII.

ON RIGHT FROM LOND.	From Worth.		From London.	ON LEFT FROM LOND.
Wimbledon Park, formerly the seat of the Earls Spencer, now subdivided into villas.	50	London to Tooting, (Page 22).	6	
	49	Merton Bridge. cr. river Wandle.	7	
Mordon Park.	46½	Mordon.	9½	
	43	Ewell. The church contains some curious monuments. Population (1851) 2186.	13	Nonsuch Park. Here was the royal palace of Nonsuch.
Durdans.	42	EPSOM. Famous for its mineral springs and its annual races. Parkhurst, the celebrated scholar, was buried in the church. Pop. 4890.	16	Nork House, Earl of Egmont. Woodcote Park.
Randall House.	38¼	Ashtead.	17¾	Ashtead Park.
To Guildford, 12 miles.	37	Leatherhead, on river Mole.	19	Thorncroft.
Norbury Park, T. Grissell, Esq. A beautiful seat, surrounded by fine plantations.	35½	Mickleham.	20½	
	34½	Burford Bridge. cr. river Mole.	21½	Box Hill, planted in the reign of Charles I., remarkable for the extent and beauty of its prospects.
Denbies, T. Cubitt, Esq. Bury Hill Park, C. Barclay, Esq. The Rookery, N. J. Fuller, Esq.	32½	DORKING. In the church are buried Tucker, author of "Light of Nature," and Hoole, translator of Ariosto. Pop. of township, 4061. The vicinity of Dorking is remarkable for its beautiful scenery, and abounds with mansions and villas. Two miles distant is Wotton, the birth and burial-place of John Evelyn, and now the property of his representative W. J. Evelyn, Esq.	21½	Betchworth Castle, in ruins. Deepdene, the beautiful seat of the late T. Hope, author of Anastasius, and now of his son, H. T. Hope, Esq.
Leith Hill Common and Tower, commanding a most extensive view. Anstie-bury. Here is a Roman encampment.	28½	Bear Green. To Arundel, 27¾ miles.	27½	
	27	Capel.	29	
Arnold House.	24½	Shiremark Mill, (Sussex).	31½	
Warnham. A little to the south is Chesworth, an ancient residence of the De Braose family.	19½	HORSHAM, Situated on the Adur. The church of St. Mary is a fine old building, and contains several ancient monuments, two of which are supposed to be those of Lord Braose and Lord Hoo, ancestors of the Duke of Norfolk. The town-hall is a handsome building, erected by the late Duke of Norfolk. Horsham returns one M.P. Population 6747.	36½	Horsham Park, R. H. Hurst, Esq. Denn Park. To Brighton by Henfield, 24½ miles.
Knepp Castle, Sir C. M. Burrell, Bart.	13¼	West Grinstead.	42¾	West Grinstead Park.
	9	Ashington.	47	Wiston Park.

EPSOM DOWNS

Continued.

ON RIGHT FROM LOND.	From Worth.		From London.	ON LEFT FROM LOND.
To Petworth, Col. Wyndham, 12 miles.	7½	Washington Common.	48½	To Steyning, 3½ miles.
Highden, Sir H. D. Goring, Bart.	4½	Findon.	51½	Cisbury Hill, surmounted by the ruins of a fort, said to have been constructed by Cisa, second King of the South Saxons.
Muntham. Offington House.	1¼	Broadwater.	54¾	
		WORTHING (p. 77).	56	

XX. LONDON TO ARUNDEL AND LITTLE HAMPTON, 59 Miles.

ON RIGHT FROM LOND.	From L. Ham.		From Lond.	ON LEFT FROM LOND.
Leith Hill, a beautiful eminence rising to an elevation of 993 feet, and surmounted by a tower, commanding a view of remarkable extent and beauty.	31½	London to Bear Green (page 30.)	27½	
	28¾	Stone Street.	30¼	Oakley Court.
	26	Denn Bridge (Sussex).	33	Eldersley Lodge.
				Field Place, Sir P. F. Shelley, Bart., son of the poet.
	21⅔	Park Street.	37¼	
	20	Buckman's Corner.	39	Somers.
	18	Billinghurst.	41	Clark's Land.
	13	Pulborough.	46	
	12	Hardham.	47	
Bignor Park, J. Hawkins, Esq. Here are Mosaic pavements and extensive Roman villa.	10¾	Coldwaltham.	48¼	
	8	Bury.	51	Houghton Hill. The views from the summit are particularly interesting.
To Chichester, 10 miles. To Salisbury, 64 miles. To Portsmouth, 40 miles.	3¾	ARUNDEL, (p. 77). cr. river Arun.	55¼	
		Leominster.		
	1¾	LITTLE HAMPTON,	57¼	
		A retired watering-place near the mouth of the Arun. It has a new Gothic church and Wesleyan chapel, a fort, and a ferry connecting Bognor and the Brighton Road. Bognor is 5 m. distant; Arundel Castle, Duke of Norfolk, 4 or 5; Worthing about 8 miles. Pop. 2350.	59	

ON RIGHT FROM LOND.	From Guildfrd.		From London.	ON LEFT FROM LOND.
	21	From London Bridge by Brighton Railway, to Reigate St. (p. 24).	21	Leave Line to Brighton.
Gatton Park, Lord Monson. Upper Gatton House, W. Currie, Esq. Headley Lodge. Buckland Green.	19	Town of REIGATE, (See p. 22).	23	The Priory, Earl Somers. Reigate Lodge, J. Phillips, Esq. Buckland. Buckland Court, Miss Carbonell. Wonham House, A. Way, Esq.
	16	Betchworth St.	26	Moor Place, J. W. Freshfield, Esq.
Box Hill, famed for its extensive prospect, and the beauty of the surrounding scenery. It received its name from the box-trees, planted in the reign of Charles I. Ashurst Lodge, J. M. Strachan, Esq. Headley Court, F. Ladbroke, Esq.	14	Box-Hill St.	28	Betchworth House. Betchworth Castle, a fine ruin. Broome Park, Sir B. Brodie, Bart. Shrub Hill, Lady Eliz. Wathen.
Burford Bridge, J. A. Gordon, Esq. Mickleham Hall, R. W. Crawford, Esq. Juniper Hill, Cuthbert Ellison, Esq. Juniper Hall, Miss Beardmore. Norbury Park, T. Grissell, Esq. The Denbies, T. Cubitt, Esq.	13	DORKING, Dorking is a market-town, noted for the excellence of its poultry. Limestone is found here in great abundance. Pop., 4061.	29	Deepdene, H. T. Hope, Esq. Bury Hill, C. Barclay, Esq. The Rookery, N. J. Fuller, Esq. Wotton Place, W. J. Evelyn, Esq. Abinger Hall, Lord Abinger.
Polsden, J. P. Bonsor, Esq. Great Bookham Court, Viscount Downe. Netley Place, in ruins.	8	Gomshall St.	34	Leith Hill, $4\frac{1}{2}$ m. distant, is the highest hill in the county of Surrey, and is 993 feet above the level of the sea.
Shere, E. Bray, Esq. Albury Park, Henry Drummond, Esq., and Lord Lovaine. Weston House.	7	Shere Heath St.	35	Hartswood Common, R. Clutton, Esq.
	4	Chilworth St.	38	Wonersh Park, Lord Grantley.
Shalford House. Sir Gosden House, John Sparkes, Esq.	2	Shalford St. cr. riv. Wey.	40	Loseley Place, Sir C. E. Scott. Bart., $1\frac{1}{4}$ mile. St. Catherine's Hill.
		GUILDFORD. Thence to Reading by railway, 25 m. (p. 185.)	42	Branch of South Western to Godalming, 4 m.

ON RIGHT FROM LOND.	From Epsom.		From London.	ON LEFT FROM LOND.
Mitcham, 3 m.	8	From London Br. to Croydon (as in p. 23).	10½	1½ m. before reaching Croydon, leave Brighton railway.
Beddington Park, C. H. Carew, Esq.		Croydon is a town of considerable antiquity, and much resorted to by the people of London since the opening of the railway. Sir William Walworth, famous for killing Wat Tyler, resided at Croydon Park. Here the Londoners were defeated by the army of Henry III. in 1264. Pop. 20,325.		Hayling Park.
In the village of Carshalton is the chief source of the river Wandle.	5½	Carshalton St.	13	Banstead Downs.
Carshalton House. Carshalton Park.				The Oaks. The drawing-room, on the first floor, is an octagon, and commands an extensive prospect, embracing Hampstead, Highgate, and part of London.
Mitcham, 3 miles.	3¾	Sutton St.	14¾	Sutton Lodge.
Mordon, 2¾ miles.		cross Reigate road.		Banstead, 2¾ miles. Nork Park, Earl of Egmont.
Nonsuch Park, W. F. G. Farmer, Esq.	2½	Cheam St.	15¾	
To Kingston, 5½ miles.	1¼	Ewell St.	17¼	Durdans.
		EPSOM. (See p. 30).	18¼	Woodcote Park.
This line of railway was for some time worked upon the atmospheric principle, which, however, was not found successful, and was finally abandoned in 1847. Since then it has been worked in the ordinary way, by locomotive engines.		From Epsom by road to Leatherhead 4 m. to Dorking 8 m.		

XXIII. LONDON TO CHICHESTER THROUGH GUILDFORD AND MIDHURST, 62 Miles, THENCE TO BOGNOR, $7\frac{1}{2}$ Miles.

ON RIGHT FROM LOND.	From Chiches.		From London.	ON LEFT FROM LOND.
	62 56	From the Surrey side of London Bridge to Wandsworth.	 6	Wimbledon Park, formerly Earl Spencer's, now subdivided for villas.
Richmond Park, the most charming of the Royal Parks in the neighbourhood of London, and a favourite resort of the citizens (See p. 88). Bushy Park (See p. 88). Hampton Court (See p. 50).	50	KINGSTON, on the Thames, over which is a handsome bridge of five arches. On the north side of the church is a stone, used, according to tradition, at the coronation of our Saxon Kings. Railway station. Pop. 9790.	12	Norbiton Place. Combe House. Combe Wood, H. R. H the Duke of Cambridge.
Ember Court, Sir C. Sullivan, Bart.	$48\frac{1}{4}$	Thames Ditton.	$13\frac{3}{4}$	Claremont (King of the Belgians), where the Princess Charlotte died, and more recently the residence of Louis Philippe and his family.
Esher Place.	46	ESHER. Esher Place was the seat of Cardinal Wolsey.	16	
Burhill, Burwood Ho., Sir R. Frederick, Bart. Byfleet.	$42\frac{1}{2}$	Cobham Street. cr. river Mole.	$19\frac{1}{2}$	Painshill Park. Pointers.
	$38\frac{1}{4}$	Ripley.	$23\frac{3}{4}$	Hatchfold. Ockham Park, Earl of Lovelace, a descendant of the sister of John Locke, and the husband of Lord Byron's only child, now dead.
Send Grove. Sutton Place, J. J. W. Weston, Esq. Stoke Place. Woodbridge, R. D. Mangles, Esq., M.P. Guildford gives the title of Earl to the North family. To Farnham, $11\frac{1}{2}$ m. To Odiham, $19\frac{1}{2}$ m. To Basingstoke, 26 m. Losely Place, Sir C. E. Scott, Bart. Northbrooke Place.	$32\frac{1}{2}$	GUILDFORD, the county town of Surrey, on the Wey. The principal buildings are the grammar school, erected in the reign of Edward VI.; three parish churches — one of which contains monuments in memory of Arch. Abbot and Mr. Speaker Onslow; Abbot's Hospital; several meeting-houses and charitable institutions; a new gaol, a theatre, the ruins of an ancient fortress, &c. The town carries on a considerable trade in corn and timber. In the neighbourhood are powder and paper mills. 2 M.P. Population 8020. er. river Wey.	$29\frac{1}{2}$	Clandon Park, Earl of Onslow. About 2 miles east of the town is the Merrows race-course. To Dorking, $11\frac{1}{4}$ m. To Horsham, 19 m. To Reigate, 18 m. Catherine Hill, on the summit of which are the ruins of a chapel of unknown origin, but rebuilt in the time of Edward I. Shalford House.
Westbrooke Place. At a distance, Pepper Harrow (Viscount Midleton), situated in a beautiful park, contains some good pictures.	$28\frac{1}{2}$	GODALMING, on the Wey, which is navigable from hence to the Thames. The chief trade is in timber, and in preparing silk and worsted for stockings and gloves. In the vicinity are several paper and corn mills. Pop. 2321.	$33\frac{1}{2}$	Gosden House, J. Sparkes, Esq., and at a distance Wonersh, Lord Grantley.

ON RIGHT FROM LOND.	From Chiches.		From London.	ON LEFT FROM LOND.
Eashing House. Lea House. Cosford House.	27	Milford.	35	Busbridge.
	20	HASLEMERE has a chapel containing some painted glass. It returned two M.P.'s till disfranchised by the Reform Act. Pop. of par. 1851, 955.	42	To Petworth, 9½ miles.
		Enter Sussex.		Cowdray Park, Earl of Egmont.
Iping House, Sir C. J. J. Hamilton, Bart.	17	Fernhurst.	45	Here a road leads to Chichester over Rook's Hill, and through East Lavant, 6 miles.
Woolbeding House.	15½	Henley Green.	46½	
	12¼	MIDHURST (See p. 76).	49¾	
Two miles distant, Chilgrove House.	6¾	Singleton.	55¼	
West Lavant House.	6	West Dean.	56	Cannon House, Rev. L. V. Harcourt.
Stoke House.	4	Binderton.	58	Molecombe.
Oakwood, J. Baring, Esq.	2	Mid-Lavant.	60	Goodwood, Duke of Richmond.
		CHICHESTER (p. 75).	62	

XXIV. LONDON TO CHICHESTER THROUGH GUILDFORD AND PETWORTH, 63½ Miles.

ON RIGHT FROM LOND.	From Chiches.		From London.	ON LEFT FROM LOND.
	63½	From London Bridge		
	28½	to Milford, Surrey.	35	
	26½	Witley.	37	
	23½	Chiddingfold.	40	
		Over Cripple Crouch Hill, and enter Sussex.		
To Haslemere, 3½ m.	20½	Fisher's Street.	43	Shillinglee Park, Earl of Winterton.
Pitshill, W. T. Mitford, Esq.	19½	North Chapel.	44	
Petworth House, Genl. Wyndham. To Midhurst, 6½ m.	14½	PETWORTH. Pop. 1851, 2427.	49	To Arundel, 11½ miles.
		cr. river Rother.		
Lavington House, Bishop of Oxford.	10¼	Duncton.	53¼	Burton Pa. (A. W. Biddulph, Esq.), a noble mansion, erected by Leoni, an Italian architect of great repute.
	7¾	Upper Waltham.	55¾	
Halnaker Pa. Duke of Richmond. Here are preserved two curfews, supposed to be as old as the time of William I. Goodwood, Duke of Richmond. (See p. 76).	3½	Halnaker. The church contains a rich monument of the De La Warr family.	60	Eartham (Mrs. E. Huskisson), built by Hayley the poet. Here Cowper the poet visited him. It was at one time the residence of the late Mr. Huskisson, M.P.
		CHICHESTER (p. 75).	63½	

XXV. LONDON TO PORTSMOUTH, THROUGH ESHER, GODALMING, AND PETERSFIELD, 72½ Miles.*

ON RIGHT FROM LOND.	From Portsm.		From London.	ON LEFT FROM LOND.
	72	From London Bridge to		
	37½	Milford, *Surrey*, (p. 35.)	35	To Petworth, 14 m.
	36¾	Mousehill.	35¾	Haslemere, 6½ m.
To the right of this place is a deep dell, called the Devil's Punch Bowl.	31¾	Hind Head Hill.	40¾	
	28¾	Seven Thorns, *Hants.*	43¾	
	26½	Liphook.	46	2 m. distant, Hollycombe.
	23	Rake, *Sussex.*	49½	
	19½	Sheet Bridge, *Hants.*	63	
To Alton, 13 miles. To Selborne, rendered famous by White's charming history, 10 miles.	18¼	PETERSFIELD, a small neat town, of considerable antiquity, is principally supported by its road trade. Near the chapel is an equestrian statue of William III. One M.P. Population, 5655.	54¼	To Haslemere, 12 m. Mickhurst, 9 miles. Rogate Lodge, Col. C. Wyndham. Heath House, Sir W. G. H Jolliffe, Bart.
	15½	Butser Hill, 917 feet high. The summit commands a most extensive view.	57	Ditcham, Earl of Limerick. Up Park. Idsworth Park, Sir J. C. C. Jervoise, Bart.
Catherington House.	10¾	Horndean. To Havant, 4¾ m. Thence to Hayling, 5 miles, a small island 5 or 6 miles east of Portsmouth. Its attractions as a watering-place are increasing. Over the Forest of Bere, comprehending about 16,000 acres, of which one-third is enclosed. The quantity of timber is trifling compared with what it once yielded. Some deer are kept.	61¾	Blendworth Lodge, Sir W. W. Knighton, Bt. Horndean Ho., and at a distance, Stanstead.
Southwick Pa. (T. Thistlethwayte, Esq.) an elegant mansion, erected on the site of an old manor-house, built here in the time of James I., and in which two monarchs were entertained, Charles I. and George I. The former was here at the time of Buckingham's assassination. Within the park stood the ancient priory of Black Canons, where Henry VI. and Margaret of Anjou were married.	6¾	Purbrook.	65¾	Purbrook House.
	5½	Portsdown Hill, 447 feet high, and runs east and west nearly seven miles. On the summit is a monument to the memory of Lord Nelson. It commands one of the most extensive and beautiful prospects in the south of England, including Chichester Cathedral, Portsmouth, Isle of Wight, Southampton Water, &c. A grand annual fair is held in July on the summit.	67	
Porchester Castle, on the Southwick estate, was used as a French prison during the war. It is now a fine ruin. In the interior is an old Saxon church, well preserved. The grounds are unfortunately, during the summer months, degraded into tea-gardens.	4¾	Cosham.	67¾	
	4¼	Portsea Bridge. Enter Portsea Island. Hillsea.	68¼	
		PORTSMOUTH, (p. 72).	72½	

* By the new road lately cut through hilly parts, the distance is reduced to 69 miles.

ON RIGHT FROM LOND.	From Gosport.		From London.	ON LEFT FROM LOND.
	78½ 22	From Hyde Pa. Corner to Filmer Hill, *Hants.* (p. 39.)	56½	
Brookwood Park.	19½	West Meon.	59	Hall Place. Westbury House, Viscount Gage.
	18	Warnford.	60½	Belmont. In the grounds are the remains of an ancient mansion, said to have
	16½	Exton.	62	been in a decayed state before 1610. About 2 m. from Exton is a Roman camp.
Corhampton House.	16	Corhampton.	62½	Midlington Place.
	14½	Droxford.	64	Hill Place.
Swanmore House.	12¼	Hill Pound Inn.	66¼	
		Forw. over Waltham Chase.		
Park Place.	9	Wickham, remarkable as the birthplace of William of Wykeham, the architect of Windsor Castle, and founder of the college at Winchester and New College, Oxford.	69½	Wickham church is an ancient building, containing several interesting tombs and monuments.
Uplands, J. Beardmore, Esq. Blackbrook, G. T. M. Purvis, Esq.	5½	FAREHAM. at the head of Portsmouth harbour, carries on a considerable trade in corn and coals. During summer it is much frequented for sea-bathing. Pop. 4011.	73	Roche Court, a mansion nearly 700 years old. Cams House, H. P. Delme, Esq., prettily situated at the head of Portsmouth Harbour.
	1	Forton.	77½	Fleetland House.
		GOSPORT, (p. 75.)	78½	Brockhurst.

XXVII. LONDON TO SOUTHAMPTON, THROUGH FARNHAM, ALTON, ALRESFORD, AND WINCHESTER, 77 Miles.

ON RIGHT FROM LOND.	From South.		From London.	ON LEFT FROM LOND.
	77	From Hyde Park Corner to		
	51	Bagshot, *Surrey*, p. 41.	26	
To Basingstoke, 17¾ m. Hawley House.	46¾	Frimley.	30¼	
Sandhurst Military College.		☞ cr. river Blackwater, and enter Hampshire.		
	45	Farnborough, (Railway station.)	32	
Clare House	38¾	FARNHAM, (*Surrey*,) on the Wey, is famous for its hops and its large wheat market. The church has a beautiful altar-piece, and handsome monuments. The castle, the residence of the	38¼	To Guildford, 10 m. 2½ m. distant is Moor Park, formerly the residence of Sir William Temple. Here is a cave in a rock through which flows a stream of pure water. The

ON RIGHT FROM LOND.	From South.		From London.	ON LEFT FROM LOND.
Willey Place, J. Ward, Esq. Northbrook House.		Bishops of Winchester, contains a good library, and a valuable collection of paintings. Wm. Cobbett was a native of this place. Population 3926.		spot is said to have been a favourite place of retirement with Swift when Secretary to Sir W. Temple. Fir Grove. Waverley Abbey, late Lord Sydenham. Pierrepont Lodge.
	$34\frac{3}{4}$	Bentley Green, *Hants.*	$42\frac{1}{4}$	Mareland House. Great Lodge. Arthur Young called the vale between Farnham and Alton the finest 10 miles in England.
Froyle Place, Rev. Sir T. C. Miller, Bart.		Froyle.		
	$30\frac{3}{4}$	Holybourne.	$46\frac{1}{4}$	
To Odiham 9 m., to Basingstoke, $10\frac{3}{4}$ m.	$29\frac{1}{2}$	ALTON on the Wey. The inhabitants are principally employed in the cultivation of hops, and in the manufacture of stuffs. Population 3286.	$47\frac{1}{2}$	To Selborne, 4 m.
	$28\frac{1}{4}$	Chawton.	$48\frac{3}{4}$	Chawton House, E. Knight, Esq.
	$22\frac{1}{4}$	Ropley Dean. Here the valley of the Itchin commences.	$54\frac{3}{4}$	
	21	Bishop's Sutton.	56	Tichborne House, Sir Edward Doughty, Bart.
To Winchester station, $7\frac{1}{2}$. New Place, J. Rawlinson, Esq. Upton House. Old Alresford House, Lord Rodney. Ovington. Avington (J. Shelley, Esq.) contains some valuable paintings. The park is 3 m. in circumference	$19\frac{3}{4}$	ALRESFORD, a neat little market-town on the Itchin, has a small manufacture of linseys. It formerly sent a representative to Parliament. In 1833, a large quantity of English silver coins of the reign of William I. were found in a field a short distance from this town. About 7000 of these coins are now in the British Museum. Pop. of parish of New Alresford 1546.	$57\frac{1}{4}$	
	$18\frac{3}{4}$	Seward's Bridge.	$58\frac{1}{4}$	To Bishop's Waltham, $10\frac{1}{4}$ m.
	12	WINCHESTER, (p. 52).	65	To Gosport, $22\frac{3}{4}$ m.
To Basingstoke, $17\frac{1}{4}$ m.—Whitchurch, 13—Andover, 13—Stockbridge, 9—Romsey, 11.	11	St. Cross.	66	Hursley Park (Sir W. Heathcote, Bart.), very picturesque, and containing remains of one of Cromwell's field fortifications.
	$9\frac{1}{2}$	Compton.	$67\frac{1}{2}$	
	$7\frac{1}{2}$	Otterbourne.	$69\frac{1}{2}$	
Cranbury Park, Thos. Chamberlayne, Esq.	$5\frac{1}{2}$	Chandler's Ford Bridge.	$71\frac{1}{2}$	
Chilworth House. Portswood House.	3	Junction of the Road.	74	North Stoneham Park, J. W. Fleming, Esq. South Stoneham Park.

ON RIGHT FROM LOND.	From South.		From London.	ON LEFT FROM LOND.
Bellevue.		**SOUTHAMPTON,** (p. 56.)	77	Midanbury House, M. Hoy, Esq. Bittern Lodge.
				Chessel House, Lord Ashtown.

XXVIII. LONDON TO SOUTHAMPTON, THROUGH BAGSHOT, BASINGSTOKE, AND WINCHESTER, 74½ Miles.

ON RIGHT FROM LOND.	From South.		From London.	ON LEFT FROM LOND.
	74½	From Hyde Park Corner to		
	29¼	BASINGSTOKE, *Hants*, (p. 52.)	45¼	
Hall Place.				
				Kempshot Park; and beyond, Farleigh House.
				Dummer House, once occupied by T. Terry, the actor and correspondent of Sir Walter Scott.
	22¼	Popham.	52¼	
	21½	East Stratton.	53½	Stratton Park, Rt. Hon. Sir F. T. Baring, Bart.
				Grange Park, Lord Ashburton.
	17½	Lunways Inn.	57½	
	14¼	Worthy.	60½	**Worthy.**
				Avington, J. Shelley, Esq.
	12	WINCHESTER, (p. 52.)	62½	
		Thence to Southampton, 12 miles, (See p. 38).	74½	

XXIX. LONDON TO SOUTHAMPTON THROUGH ALTON AND BISHOP'S WALTHAM, 75¼ Miles.

ON RIGHT FROM LOND.	From South.		From London.	ON LEFT FROM LOND.
		From Hyde Park Corner to		To Selborne, 2 miles, which has been rendered famous by "White's Natural History of Selborne."
	28	ALTON, *Hants*, (p. 38.)	47½	
	21½	Chawton.	48¾	Chawton House, E. Knight, Esq.
	24¾	Farringdon.	50½	To Selborne, 2 miles.
Pelham Place.				
Rotherfield **Park.**	23	East Tisted.	52¼	
				Basing Park.
Brookwood Park.	18¾	Filmer Hill.	56½	**To Gosport 22 miles.**

ON RIGHT FROM LOND.	From South.		From London	ON LEFT FROM LOND.
Northbrook House. Swanmore House. To Winchester, 10½ m.	10	BISHOP'S WALTHAM, a small town carrying on a considerable trade in leather. It has immemorially been the property of the See of Winchester. Here are the remains of the Bishop's castle, originally built by Bishop Henry de Blois, brother of King Stephen. It was demolished during the civil wars by the Parliamentary army under Waller. William of Wykeham, to whom it owed much of its grandeur, made it his favourite residence, and died here at the age of eighty. Pop. of Parish, 2267.	65¼	Eastward of the town is Waltham Chace, a waste of 2000 acres, belonging to the Bishop of Winchester. To Gosport 13 miles.
Botley Grange.	6½	Botley.	68¾	
	1	Northam Bridge. cross river Itchin.	74¼	
		SOUTHAMPTON, (p. 56.)	75¼	

XXX. LONDON.—BASINGSTOKE.—WHITCHURCH.—ANDOVER.—SALISBURY.—BLANDFORD.—DORCHESTER.—BRIDPORT, 134¾ Miles.

ON RIGHT FROM LOND.	From Bridport.		From Lond.	ON LEFT FROM LOND.
Kensington Palace, the favourite residence of Queen Anne, and in which Queen Victoria was born; and Holland House, Lord Holland. Here Addison spent his latter years, and died. During the Third Lord Holland's time this house was the famous resort of the Whig leaders.	131¼	From Hyde Park Corner to Kensington.	1½	
	130¾	Hammersmith.	4	
	129¾	Turnham Green.	5	Chiswick Ho., a beautiful seat of the Duke of Devonshire. Here both Fox and Canning died.
Gunnersbury House, the Baron Rothschild. Ealing Park. Brentford is the county town of Middlesex, being the place where the elections are held. Here stand the enormous gin distilleries of the late Sir Felix Booth, Bart. Two miles to the right is Osterley Park, Earl of Jersey. Sir Thomas Gresham's house stood on the site of the present one. Pop. 1861, 9521.	127¾	Brentford. cross Grand Junction Canal.	7	On the opposite side of the Thames is Kew, celebrated for the beautiful gardens and gigantic conservatory attached to the royal palace. Beyond Brentford is Sion Ho. the noble residence of the Duke of Northumberland.
Barracks. Powder Mills.	125¼	Hounslow. Twickenham, 2½ m. distant.	9½	Drilling ground. Hanworth Park.
West Bedfont, and farther to the right Stanwell Park, Sir J. Gibbons, Bart.	121¾	cr. the New river. Bedfont.	13	Feltham. Ashford.

ON RIGHT FROM LOND.	From Bridport		From Lond.	ON LEFT FROM LOND.
Two miles distant Ankerwycke House, G. S. Harcourt, Esq.	118¼	Staines.	16½	Laleham, Earl of Lucan. Hampton is 7 m., Kingston 9½ m., and Croydon 20¾ m. distant.
		cr. the Thames and enter Surrey.		
To the right is Runnymede, where the barons obtained from King John the grant of Magna Charta.	117	Egham. Windsor is 5 m. to the right.	17¾	Egham Park, Colonel H. Salwey; Kingswood Lodge and Beaumont Lodge, Viscount Ashbrook, are to the right of Egham.
Sunninghill, Silwood Park, and beyond Ascot race-ground.	113¾	Virginia Water. To Reading through Oakingham, 18 m.	21	Wentworth.
Bagshot Park.	108¾	Bagshot.	26	Hall Grove, and beyond Woodlands and Chobham Place.
Sandhurst Military College.	107¼	Golden Farmer.	27½	Obelisk which is visible for many miles around.
Yately House.	104¼	Blackwater, *Hants.*	30½	Hawley Ho.
Warren House. Bramshill Park, Rev. Sir W. H. Cope, Bart.; and beyond, Heckfield Place, Viscount Eversley.	99½	Hartford Bridge.	35½	Elvetham, Lord Calthorpe.
	98½	Hartley Row. To Odiham, 3 m.	36¼	Beyond, about 3 miles from the road (near Odiham), is Dogmersfield Park, Sir H. B. P. St. John Mildmay, Bart.
Tilney Hall.	96½	Murrell Green.	38¼	
Newnham.	95½	Hook.	39¼	Winchfield House.
Old Basing. Basing House, (p. 35.)	92	Maplederwell Hatch.	42¾	Hackwood Park, Lord Bolton, and farther to the left Herriard Park.
Basingstoke carries on a considerable trade in corn, malt, timber, and coals.	89½	BASINGSTOKE. To Alton, 6 m. To Winchester, 17½ m. To Stockbridge, 21 m.	45¼	
Worting House, and beyond, Tangier Manydown, Sir R. C. H. Rycroft, Bart.; and Malshanger.	87¼	Worting.	47½	
Ash House.	84¾	Clerken Green.	50	Hall Place. Ash Park.
Laverstoke Hall, M. Portal, Esq. Freefolk Priors, M. Portal Esq.	81¾	Overton.	53	
	78¼	WHITCHURCH. To Kingsclere, 7 m. thence to Reading, 16½ m. To Newbury, 13 m. To Winchester. 13 m.	56½	Whitchurch is a market-town, and disfranchised borough. Population in 1851 was 1911, half agricultural. Shalloons and serges are manufactured, also paper for the use of the Bank of England.
Hurstbourne Park, Earl of Portsmouth.	76¼	Hurstbourne.	58½	Long Parish House.
Andover is a well built town. The church is a spacious structure, and has existed as far back as the time of the Conqueror. The	71¼	ANDOVER, on the left bank of the Anton.	63½	Near Andover there are the remains of some Roman encampments. Andover is 11 m. west from

ON RIGHT FROM LOND.	From Bridport		From Lond.	ON LEFT FROM LOND.
borough returns two members to Parliament. The chief business is malting and the manufacture of silk. Pop., 5221. Amport Park, Marquis of Winchester.		To Newbury, 16 m. To Ludgershall, 7¼ m. thence to Devizes, 20 m. To Amesbury, 14 m. To Winchester, 14 m.		that part of the railway called the Andover Road Station, and 18 m. from the station at Basingstoke. Three m. beyond Andover, to the right, is Weyhill, celebrated for one of the greatest fairs in England for hops, cheese, cattle, &c.
Between Andover and the verge of the county are several remains of camps.	69¼	Little Anne.	65½	
	63¾	Middle Wallop. LobcombeCorner, en. Wilts.	71	
	59¾	Winterslow Hut. cr. the river Bourne.	75	
The College, J. H. Campbell Wyndham, Esq.	53¾	SALISBURY.	81	Laverstock House, a lunatic asylum.

Salisbury, the capital of Wilts, situated near the confluence of the rivers Willey, Avon, and Bourne, is distinguished for the pleasing arrangement of its buildings. It has ten principal streets, crossing at right angles, and through them at one time was conveyed a stream of water, taken from the Avon by sluices. That part of Salisbury denominated the Close is occupied by the Cathedral, the Bishop's palace, the houses of residentiary clergy, and many spacious private dwellings. The Cathedral, erected in the 13th century, is the most elegant and uniform structure of the kind in England. The spire, which was built a century later, is celebrated for its beauty and its height, which is upwards of 400 feet. The length of the Cathedral outside from west to east is 480 feet. The length of the grand transept is 232. The interior is particularly rich in sepulchral monuments. The great east window, the window at the west end over the central door, and the chapter-house, are also worthy of notice. Salisbury contains three parish churches, and several dissenting meeting-houses, a grammar school, where Addison received his education, Assembly Rooms, a Theatre, an Infirmary, and several charitable institutions. The Council-House, an elegant building, was erected at the sole expense of the 2d Earl of Radnor in 1795. Salisbury was formerly celebrated for its manufactories of cutlery, which, however, have of late years declined. The city returns two members to Parliament. Salisbury races generally take place in August, on the plain about three miles from the city. Population, 12,278.

About three miles from Salisbury, on the left, is Longford Castle, the seat of the Earl of Radnor. It contains a valuable collection of pictures. At the distance of 2½ miles stands Clarendon Castle, the ruins of which may still be traced, but not in such a state of preservation as to enable one to form any idea of the former grandeur of the building. It was here that, in the reign of Henry II., the laws regarding ecclesiastical authority, known by the name of the "Constitutions of Clarendon," were framed. Old Sarum, famous for the privilege it formerly possessed of returning two members to Parliament, was situated about one mile from Salisbury. The tree beneath which the election took place was cut down in 1831. There are visible traces of the walls of very extensive religious houses that once existed here.

At the distance of 8 miles from Salisbury, situated in the Plain near Amesbury, is the famous monument of antiquity called Stonehenge. It consists of a number of very large stones arranged in a circular form, and still partly connected with each other at the top by flat pieces placed in a transverse direction. Antiquarians are not agreed as to the object of this rude structure, or by whom it was made. By some it has been attributed to the Druids; by others, to the Danes; and by a third party, to the Romans.

About three miles from Salisbury is the ancient town of Wilton, at the conflux of the Willey and the Nadder, long noted for the manufacture of carpets; but this business has now declined. The town returns one member to Parliament. Pop. 1861, 8657. Adjoining the town is Wilton House, the celebrated seat of the Earls of Pembroke, now occupied by the Right Hon. Sidney Herbert, who has at a vast expense erected a fine church in the town. Here Sir Philip Sydney wrote his "Arcadia." Twelve miles from Wilton is Hindon, near which is the famous Fonthill Abbey, now the property of the Marquis of Westminster. A little to the south of Fonthill, and about ten or eleven miles from Wilton, is Wardour Castle, the seat of Lord Arundell of Wardour. In the grounds are the ruins of the ancient castle.

ON RIGHT FROM LOND.	From Bridport.	Resuming the route to Bridport.	From London.	ON LEFT FROM LOND.
Stratford, St. Anthony.	50½	Combe Basset.	84¼	
Handley. Rushmore Lodge, Lord Rivers.	43½	Woodgates Inn. (*Dorsetshire.*)	91¼	To Cranborne, 4 miles.
Chettle, Eastbury Park.	38½	Cashmore Inn.	96¼	St. Giles' Park, Earl of Shaftesbury. The garden is spacious and pleasant, and the park is about two miles in circumference. There is also a beautiful grotto, said to have cost L.10,000. At no great distance is Critchill House, H. C. Sturt, Esq.
Shaftesbury, about 11 miles distant, formerly possessed one of the richest nunneries in the kingdom. It returns one M.P. Population, 8983.	36¼	Tarrant Hinton.	98½	
	33½	Pimperne.	101¼	Blandford race ground.
Bryanston, the beautiful seat of Lord Portman. Down House, Sir J. J. Smith, Bart.	31¼	BLANDFORD. Population, 1851, 3913. To Shaftesbury, 11¼ miles. To Sturminster, 9 do. To Wimborne Minster, 10 do., thence to Poole, 6½ do. ☞ cross river Stour.	103½	Langton House.
Whatcombe House.	26	Winterborne Whitchurch.	108¾	

ON RIGHT FROM LOND.	From Bridport.		From Lond.	ON LEFT FROM LOND.
Milton Abbey.				
	23½	Milbourn.	111¼	
Dewlish House, J. Michel, Esq. Melcombe Bingham, R H. Bingham, Esq.				
		cross river Piddle.		
To Frampton 5 miles; Frampton House, R. B. Sheridan, Esq., grandson of R. Brinsley Sheridan.	20¼	Piddletown.	114½	Islington House. Kingston House. Stinsford House. To Wareham, 18 miles. To Weymouth, 8¼.
		cross river Frome.		
To Cerne Abbas, 7¼ m. Sherborne, 18 Yeovil, 19 Ilchester, 23¼ Somerton, 27¾ Glastonbury, 35¼ Crewkerne, 22 Beaminster, 17½	15¼	DORCHESTER. the capital of Dorset, a town of great antiquity on the Frome. Its ancient name was Durnovaria, signifying the passage of the river. It was strongly fortified. Several Roman antiquities have been discovered in it; and ¼ mile distant is Maumbury, the most perfect Roman amphitheatre in the kingdom. The church of St. Peter contains numerous monuments. Population 6823.	119½	Weymouth (and Melcombe Regis), is a place of considerable antiquity at the entrance of the Wey. It formerly carried on a good trade, but the harbour has been injured by sand, and it is now celebrated as a watering-place, this character having been derived from the frequent visits of Geo. III. and his family. It gives the title of Viscount to the Marquis of Bath. It returns two M.P.'s. Pop., 11,383. Weymouth Castle is about a mile south-west of the town, on a cliff facing Portland. It was one of the fortresses erected by Henry VIII. to guard against invasion.
	10¼	Winterborne Abbas.	124½	
Kingston Russell.				
	7	Longbredy Turnpike.	127¾	
Loders Court, Sir M. H. Nepean, Bart.	3¼	Traveller's Rest.	131½	
		BRIDPORT. Bridport is situated about a mile from the sea, and derives its name from its situation between two branches of the Brit. It appears to have been a considerable town before the Conquest, and is noted in Doomsday Book. It has a handsome town-hall and market-place, and a large and ancient church. It returns two members to Parliament. Population, 7719.	134¾	

About 6¼ miles from Bridport is the ancient town of Beaminster, which has suffered greatly by fire no less than three times during the last two centuries, but is now in a flourishing condition. Pop. of township 1861, 2614. Near it is Parnham house, Sir H. Oglander, Bart. From Bridport to Lyme Regis is about 9½ miles; to Axminster, 12 miles; to Honiton, 21¾ miles; to Exeter, 38¼ miles.

XXXI. LONDON TO EXETER, THROUGH BASINGSTOKE, SHAFTESBURY, AND HONITON, 168½ Miles.

ON RIGHT FROM LOND.	From Exeter.		From Lond.	ON LEFT FROM LOND.
	168½	From Hyde Park Corner to		
Longford Castle (Earl of Radnor), 2 m.	87½	**SALISBURY,** ***Wilts,*** **(p. 42.)**	81	Trafalgar House (Earl Nelson), 4 miles.
To Devizes, 22 m.				To Romsey, 15¾ miles, Southampton, through Romsey, 23¼ m., Lymington, 27 m., Fording Bridge, 12½ m.
	87	Fisherton.	81½	
To Warminster, 18¼ m.	84¾	Fugglestone.	83¾	
		cr. river Avon.		
	84¼	WILTON, (p. 43.)	84¼	
	83¼	Ugford.	85¼	Wilton House (Earl of Pembroke), occupied by Rt. Hon. Sidney Herbert.
	82¾	Burcombe.	85¾	
Hurdcott Ho., A. Powell, Esq.	81½	Barford.	87	
To Hindon, 9½ m.				
		cr. river Nadder.		
Compton Ho., J. H. Penruddock, Esq.	79¼	Compton Chamberlayne.	89¼	
Two m. distant, Dinton, W. Wyndham, Esq.	77¾	Fovant.	90¾	
Wardour Castle, Lord Arundell of Wardour. Within the grounds are the ruins of the old castle, famous for the defence made during the civil wars by a garrison of only 25 men under the command of Lady Blanch, against 1300 of the Parliament forces.	73¾	Wardour Park.	94¾	
	72½	Donhead.	96	**Fern Ho., T. Grove, Esq.**
Donhead Hall.	70½	Ludwell.	98	
To Hindon, 7 m.		Enter Dorsetshire.		
Pensbury House. Motcombe House, Marquis of Westminster.	67½	SHAFTESBURY, (p. 43.)	101	To Sturminster, 8 m.
	63¼	East Stour.	105¼	
		cr. river Stour.		
	62¼	West Stour.	106¼	Fifehead House.
	58	Henstridge Ash, *Somerset.*	110½	To Stalbridge, 1½ m. Stalbridge Pa., and, beyond, Thornhill.
	54	Milborne Port.	114½	Ven House, Sir W. C. Medlycott, Bart.
	52½	Oborne, *Dorset.*	116	
	51½	SHERBORNE, p.106.)	117	Sherborne Castle, Lord Digby. The centre was built by Sir W. Raleigh, whose family were deprived of the estate in a most disgraceful manner by James I. who bestowed it on his infamous favourite, Carr.
	49¼	Nether Compton.	119¼	
		cr. river Yeo.		

ON RIGHT FROM LOND.	From Exeter.		From London	ON LEFT FROM LOND.
Brympton House. To Castle Cary, 12¾ m. Ilchester, 4½. m., Ilminster, 14 m.	46¼	YEOVIL *(Somerset,)* an ancient town, with manufactories of linens, dowlas, ticking, and gloves. The vicinity is beautifully diversified with hill and dale. Pop., 7957.	122¼	Barwick House, J. Newman, Esq. To Dorchester, 19 m.
Three m. dist. Montacute House, W. Phelips, Esq.	41¼	East Chinnock.	127¼	
	39	Haselbury.	129¼	
To Ilchester, 10¼ m., Somerton, 14 m., Ilminster, 8 m.	36½	CREWKERNE, in a valley watered by the Axe and the Parret, has a fine Gothic church, richly adorned with carved work. Here are manufactories of sail-cloth, dowlas, and stockings. Pop. 3566.	132	To Dorchester, 22 m., Beaminster, 7¼ m., Lyme Regis, 16 m.
Hinton St George, Earl Poulett. To Ilminster, 4½ m.	33½	White Down.	135	To Axminster, 10½ m. Cricket Lodge, Lord Bridport, and 3 miles beyond it, Ford Abbey.
To Ilminster, 5¼ m., Taunton, 13 m.	28½	CHARD, a well-built manufacturing town, has a town hall—an ancient Gothic building, formerly a chapel—a handsome church, &c. Chard was the scene of the defeat of the Royalists under Col. Penruddock during the civil wars. Pop. 2276.	140	Four m. beyond Chard is a beautiful prospect on the left to the English Channel, and on the right to that of Bristol.
	22½	Stockland, Dorset.	146	To Axminster, 7 m. This town is distinguished for its manufactory of the best and most costly description of carpets. Pop., 2918.
	16½	HONITON, *Devon.*	152	
		EXETER, (p. 110.)	168½	

XXXII. LONDON TO EXETER THROUGH BASINGSTOKE, ANDOVER, AMESBURY, WINCANTON, ILMINSTER, AND HONITON, 164½ Miles.*

ON RIGHT FROM LOND.	From Exeter.		From London.	ON LEFT FROM LOND.
	164½	From Hyde Pa. Corner		
	101	to ANDOVER, *Hants,* (p. 41.)	63½	
To Ludgershall, 4 miles.	97¾	WEYHILL, celebrated for the greatest fair in England for hops, cheese, cattle, sheep, &c.		
	96¼	Mollens Pond.	68¼	Amport Park, Marquis of Winchester. Quarley House.

* It is proposed to carry on a line from the South Western Railway, at Basingstoke, by Andover to Salisbury, which will be connected by the Wilts, Somerset, and Weymouth line with the Great Western Railway, near Taunton, and also, by another branch, with Dorchester and Bridport.

ON RIGHT FROM LOND.	From Exeter.		From London.	ON LEFT FROM LOND.
Tedworth House, T. A. Smith, Esq.	92	Park House.	72½	Quarley Hill, the remains of an ancient encampment.
		Enter Wiltshire.		Wilbury Park, W. Cubitt, Esq.
Amesbury House was often the residence of Gay while under the patronage of the Duke and Duchess of Queensberry, and is now the property of Sir E. W. Antrobus, Bart.	87	AMESBURY, a small ancient town on the upper Avon. The church is supposed to have belonged to an abbey. Two miles distant on Salisbury Plain is that remarkable monument of antiquity, Stonehenge. Seventeen huge stones are now standing, which, with seven others lying on the ground, form the outer range. The inner circle is about 8 feet from the outer one, and has eleven stones standing, and eight fallen. Between these two circles is a walk of about 300 feet in circumference. Around are numerous barrows, many of which have been found to contain human skeletons, urns, and military weapons Dr Stukely fixes the date of the erection 460 B.C. Near Stonehenge is an inn called the Druid's Head. Pop. of parish, 1138.	77½	
To Warminster through Shrewton, 16¾ miles.		cross river Avon.		
Yarnbury Camp, a fine specimen of ancient fortification.	82½	Winterbourne Stoke.	82	
To Warminster, 10¼ m.	78	Deptford Inn.	86½	
	77¼	Willey.	87¼	
	72½	New Inn.	92	Fonthill Abbey (Marquis of Westminster), erected by the late Mr. Beckford, under the direction of Wyatt. The tower has now fallen down, and the edifice suffered greatly. Farther to the left is Pyt House, J. Benett, Esq., and Wardour Castle, Lord Arundell of Wardour.
Knoyle House, H. D. Seymour, Esq.	70½	HINDON. Pop. 604. To Shaftesbury 7 miles.	94	
To Bruton, 11½ miles.	67¾	Willoughby Hedge.	96¾	
To Frome, 11¼ miles.	63¾	MERE, formerly a place of considerable importance. It had a castle, of which very few traces now remain. The inhabitants are principally employed in the manufacture of dowlas and ticking.	100¾	
Stourhead House, the seat of Sir H. Hoare, Bart., a splendid mansion, situated in delightful grounds, and adorned with	61¾	Zeal's Green, Dorsetshire.	102¾	
	60¼	Bourton.	104½	

ON RIGHT FROM LOND	From Exeter.		From London.	ON LEFT FROM LOND.
a picture gallery, a library, &c. Within the grounds is a lofty tower, erected by H. Hoare, Esq., an ancestor of the present proprietor, to the memory of Alfred the Great, who here	57½	Bayford, *Somerset.*	107	To Shaftesbury, 10 m. Shanks House.
raised his standard against the Danes. To Bruton, 5 miles, Castle Cary, 5 miles. At a distance Redlynch, Earl of Ilchester.	56½	WINCANTON, an ancient town watered by the Cale. Here are the remains of an Augustine Priory. One mile distant is Horwood Spring Population of parish, 2450.	108	To Sherborne, 8 miles.
Holbrook House. Hadspen House.	54½	Holton.	110	
Yarlington Lodge, F. Rogers, Esq.	52¾	Blackford.	111¾	To Sherborne, 6 miles.
Cadbury Castle, or Camalet, was formerly one of the most stupendous fortifications in the kingdom. In it is a spot called King Arthur's Palace. Many Roman coins have been found here.	51	Cadbury, surrounded by beautiful scenery. The church contains a very curious epitaph in memory of Lady Magdalen Hastings.	113½	
To Bruton, 8 miles, Castle Cary, 4 miles.	49	Sparkford.	115½	To Sherborne, 8 miles. To Yeovil, 7¾ miles.
	43½	ILCHESTER, on the south bank of the Ivel, is a place of considerable antiquity, having been fortified in the time of the Romans. Pop. of par., 781.	121	To Yeovil, 4 miles.
	37½	Petherton Bridge.	127	
		cross river Parret.		
To South Petherton, 1 m.	34½	Seavington.	130	
Dillington House.	33	White Lackington.	131½	Hinton St George, Earl Poulett.
To Langport, 9¾ miles. Jordan's House, W. Speke, Esq.	31½	ILMINSTER was formerly famous for its manufacture of cloth. It has a handsome church, containing a monument in memory of Nicholas Wadham and his wife, the founders of Wadham College at Oxford. Pop. 3241.	133	To Chard, 5¼ miles. At Horton, 1½ mile distant, is a spring much celebrated for its efficacy in diseases of the eye.
	25½	Buckland St Mary.	139	
		cross river Haven, and enter Devonshire.		
	23½	Heathfield Arms.	141	
To Taunton, 11 miles. Four miles distant Wolford Lodge; near which is Hembury Fort, said to be the finest Roman camp in Devonshire. Tracey House.	16½	HONITON, a neatly built town, in a fine vale on the Otter, noted for the manufacture of lace. The church contains some ancient monuments. Two M.P. Pop., 3301.	148	To Axminster, 7 miles. Four miles distant Netherton House, Sir E. S. Prideaux, Bart. Bramble Hill.

ON RIGHT FROM LOND.	From Exeter.		From London.	ON LEFT FROM LOND.
Oakfield House. Deer Park.	15	Weston.	$149\frac{1}{2}$	Combe House.
Feniton Court, Right Hon. Sir J. Patteson. Corscombe House. Escot, Sir J. Kennaway, Bt. Larkbear House.	13	Fenny Bridges.	$151\frac{1}{2}$	To Ottery St. Mary, $2\frac{1}{2}$ miles. S. T. Coleridge was born here.
		cross river Otter.		
	$6\frac{1}{4}$	Rockbeare.	$158\frac{1}{4}$	Rockbeare House.
	$4\frac{1}{4}$	Honiton's Clist.	$160\frac{1}{4}$	Bishop's Court, Lord Graves, Winslade, and Farringdon House.
Poltimore, Lord Poltimore.		cross river Clist.		
Brockhill House.	$\frac{3}{4}$	Heavitree.	$163\frac{3}{4}$	Northbrook Lodge, H. D. Seymour, Esq. Higher Newcourt.
Pynes (Sir S. H. Northcote, Bart.), 2 miles.		EXETER (p. 110).	$164\frac{1}{2}$	Powderham Castle (Earl of Devon).

Nine miles from Honiton is SIDMOUTH, a fashionable watering-place, situated at the mouth of the river Sid, celebrated for the beauty of the surrounding scenery. It stands between two hills, nearly enclosing it on all sides but the south, which lies open to a beautiful bay of the English channel. The views between this place and Seaton are considered the finest on the south coast of Devon. The climate is extremely mild and salubrious. Sidmouth is much frequented by company in the bathing season, for whose accommodation there are warm baths, a public room, libraries, &c. It has also an ancient church and several meeting-houses. During the summer months tourists are admitted to Knowle Cottage (T. L. Fish, Esq.), gardens, conservatories, &c., on Mondays, between the hours of 2 and 4. The drawing-rooms are 100 feet long, and contain a fine collection of articles of *vertu*. Population, 2572.

Five miles from Sidmouth, and 12 miles from Exeter, is Bicton (Clinton Rolle, Esq.), the seat of the late Lord Rolle, and now occupied by Lady Rolle. The park, upwards of 1000 acres in extent, is stocked with deer and fine timber. The mansion is beautifully situated, and commands an extensive view of the sea.

About $8\frac{1}{2}$ miles from Sidmouth, and $10\frac{3}{4}$ miles from Exeter, is EXMOUTH, at the mouth of the Exe, the oldest and best frequented watering-place in Devon. It is celebrated for the mildness of its climate, the town being well sheltered from the north-east and south-east winds by some high hills which rise almost close behind it. The rides and walks in the neighbourhood are remarkably beautiful. Here are Assembly Rooms, baths, libraries, and other accommodations for visitors. The Beacon Hill, on which stands the handsome chapel of St Margaret, commands one of the finest views in the west of England. The road from Exmouth to Exeter through Topsham is remarkably beautiful. Population, 5228.

RAILWAY, 80 Miles.

ON RIGHT FROM LOND.	From South.		From London.	ON LEFT FROM LOND.
Battersea Fields. A public park is to be laid out here. Battersea Church contains a monument to Henry St. John, the celebrated Visc. Bolingbroke.	78	From Waterloo Road to Vauxhall Station.	2	Stockwell. Clapham, and Clapham Common.
Branches to Kew, Brentford, Richmond, and Windsor (p. 87).	75	Clapham Common St. cr. river Wandle. At the mouth of which, near the banks of the Thames, is Wandsworth: numerous people are here engaged in dyeing, printing calicoes, &c.	5	Balham Hill. Tooting. Garrat, a hamlet, the ancient practice of electing a mayor at which gave the title to Foote's farce, "The Mayor of Garrat."
Wimbledon Park, formerly Earl Spencer's, but now subdivided for villas. Prospect Place. Combe House, and beyond, Richmond Park. (See p. 88).	72	Wimbledon and Merton St.	8	To Merton, ¾ mile. Mitcham, 2 miles. Mordon, 2½ miles. Mordon Park. Cannon Hill.
	69½	Malden St. cr. riv. Hogsmill.	10½	Malden, 1½ mile.
One mile and three quarters beyond Kingston Station is a branch railway to Hampton Court, which the visitor reaches by a bridge across the Thames. Hampton Court palace and gardens form one of the most favourite places of holiday resort to the people of the metropolis, and are open to the public, free of charge, throughout the year, except upon Fridays. The palace originally belonged to Cardinal Wolsey, and was presented by him to Henry VIII. It was enlarged in 1694, under the direction of Sir Christopher Wren. Wolsey's apartments have lately been restored, and possess great attractions for the visitor. Both the house and gardens possess numerous objects of interest, not the least among which are the cartoons of Raphael, and many fine paintings.	68	Kingston St. The town of Kingston is 1¼ mile distant from the station. It contains the stone on which the Anglo-Saxon kings were crowned. Since the opening of the railway, a new town, distinguished as Kingston-on-rail, or New Kingston, has sprung into existence. Pop., 9790.	12	To Ewell, 4 miles. Long Ditton.
Thames Ditton (near which is Boyle Farm, Lord St. Leonard's). And further to the right. East and West Moulsey, all favourite places of resort to anglers. Ember Court, Sir C. Sullivan, Bart. Walton on Thames, 1¼ m.	65	Esher and Claremont Stations. cr. river Mole.	15	Esher, 1 mile, and Esher Place; beyond is Claremont, once the residence of the Princess Charlotte and Prince Leopold, now King of the Belgians, and latterly the asylum of the late Louis Philippe, ex-King of the French.
Ashley Park, Sir H. Fletcher, Bart. Mount Felix (Earl of Tankerville).	63	Walton and Hersham St.	17	Hersham Green. Burwood Park, Sir Richard Frederick, Bart.
Oatlands Park, lately subdivided to some extent, for villas. Weybridge, 1 mile. Ham Haw Park. Woburn Park.	61	Weybridge St. 1 mile beyond, on the right, is a branch railway to Addlestone and Chertsey, 3¼ miles long. Pop. of Weybridge, 1603.	19	Painshill Park, 2 m. From the summit of St. George's Hill (Earl of Ellesmere), about a mile distant, is a fine panoramic

ON RIGHT FROM LOND.	From South.		From London.	ON LEFT FROM LOND.
Basingstoke Canal. Ottershaw Park.		cr. river Wey, and Wey Navigation Canal. Ham Haw Common. Woking Heath.		view over the Thames and adjacent country, embracing Hampton Court, Chertsey, Windsor, &c. Byfleet. Wisley. Pyrford. Hoebridge Place.
Horsell. Chobham, 2½ miles. Knapp Hill, and The Hermitage. Bisley. Bisley Common. Chobham Hills.	55	Woking St. The line here continues alongside of the Basingstoke Canal, which afterwards crosses the railway. Cross Blackwater river, and enter Hants.	25	Branches to Guildford, Godalming, and Farnham (p. 82). Pirbright.
Frimley Green.		Cross line of Reading, Guildford, and Reigate Railway.		Continuation of Railway from Guildford to Portsmouth.
To Frimley 1½ mile; Bagshot, 5½ miles; Windlesham, 6½ miles. Sandhurst Military College, 3½ miles.	47	Farnborough St.	33	Farnborough Place. Farnham, 6½ miles (see p. 37). Aldershott Camp, on left of Farnborough Station.
Elvetham House, Lord Calthorpe, formerly a place of great extent and magnificence. Here a famous entertainment was given to Queen Elizabeth by the Earl of Hertford in 1591.	43	Fleetpond St.	37	
Beyond is Bramshill, the seat of Rev. Sir W. H. Cope, Bt., built for Henry Prince of Wales, eldest son of James I. Tilney Hall.	40	Winchfield St. Tunnel, 80 yards long.	40	Dogmersfield Park. Sir H. P. St. John Mildmay, Bart. Three miles south of Winchfield is Odiham, the birth-place of Lilly the Grammarian. Near it are the remains of an old castle, in which David, king of Scotland, was confined for eleven years after his capture at Neville's Cross. Population of Odiham parish, 2833.
Newnham. Chineham. Two miles from Old Basing is the Vine (W. L. W. Chute, Esq.), a mansion built by the first Lord Sandys. The ruins of Holy Ghost Chapel are visible from the line.		cr. Whitewater river. Embankment over valley of the Loddon. Line passes through the village of Old Basing, the scene of a severe battle fought in 871 between the Danes and the Saxons, when the latter, under the command of Alfred, were defeated.		Nateley Scures. Ruins of Basing House, famous for the gallant defence which it made under John, fifth Marquis of Winchester, against the Parliamentary troops. It held out during two years, and was ultimately stormed by Cromwell.

ON RIGHT FROM LOND.	From South.		From London.	ON LEFT FROM LOND.
Strathfieldsaye (Duke of Wellington), 6½ miles. Branch to Reading, 15 miles (see p. 187). Winklebury Hill, an ancient encampment. Worting House. Manydown House (Sir R. C. H. Rycroft, Bart). Malshanger House. Oakley Park. Hall Place.	32	Basingstoke St. Basingstoke is mentioned in Doomsday Book under the name of *Basingtoches*, and is described as having been always a royal manor. Malting and the corn trade form its principal business. Basingstoke had before the opening of the railway a very extensive coach traffic, from its position on one of the great western roads. Pop. 4654.	48	Hackwood Park, Lord Bolton, 1 mile. Herriard Park, 3 miles. Kempshot Park. North Waltham.
Ash Park. Overton, a large village, formerly a market town, 4½ miles. Whitchurch, 6 miles.		Lichfield Tunnel, 200 yards. Popham Hill Tunnel, 200 yards.		Popham Beacon, 460 feet high, affords a fine view from the summit.
Andover, 11½ miles.	22	Andover Road St.	58	Stratton Park, Rt. Hon. Sir F. T. Baring, Bart., contains a fine collection of paintings. Stratton belonged to Thomas Earl of Southampton, and by the marriage of his daughter to the illustrious patriot, Lord William Russell, it came into the possession of the Bedford family, who sold it to the grandfather of the present possessor.
Weston, Stoke Charity, Wonston, Hunton.		Over Micheldever embankment, raised more than 100 feet above the meadows.		Micheldever. 3 miles distant, the Grange, Lord Ashburton.
Winchester race course, on Worthy Down.		Lunways Inn Tunnel.		Kings Worthy, Headborn Worthy, Abbots Worthy, Easton; and beyond, Avington Park, J. Shelley, Esq.
	13	WINCHESTER.	67	

The origin of Winchester is involved in obscurity; but tradition, and the evidence of our oldest historical monuments, concur in representing it as one of the earliest settlements of the first inhabitants of the island. It was termed Caer Gwent by the Britons, Venta Belgarum by the Romans, and Wintanceaster by the Saxons. It became the capital of England under the Saxons when the country was united under the sway of Egbert, King of Wessex, in the beginning of the ninth century, and it retained this dignity till the reign of Edward the Confessor in the middle of the eleventh century. Here lie the bones of Alfred the Great and of the famous Canute. In this city, in 1002, commenced the horrid massacre of all the Danes who had settled in England. From this massacre sprung the old English custom of the Hocktide merriments. Here William the Conqueror built a castle and a palace, part of the foundations of which is yet to be seen. Here his son, William Rufus, was crowned, and here he was buried.

and here were the royal mint, treasury, and public record-office. Winchester suffered severely during the wars between Stephen and the Empress Matilda. Here Richard Cœur-de-Lion was crowned a second time with great pomp after his return from the crusades. Here John ratified his ignominious submission to the Pope's agent, Pandulph, and did homage to him for his crown. Henry III. was born here, and always bore the name of Henry of Winchester. Henry IV. here married Joan of Brittany. Parliaments were held in this city both in the fourteenth and fifteenth centuries. Prince Arthur, son of Henry VII., was born at the castle; and Henry VIII. entertained the Emperor Charles V. at the same place in 1522. At the Reformation, it suffered severely from the dissolution of its monasteries and other religious buildings, so that it had the appearance of a city sacked by a hostile army. Here Queen Mary was married to Philip of Spain. James I. made Winchester the scene of the disgraceful trials of Sir Walter Raleigh, Lords Cobham and Grey, and their assumed accomplices; and three of these royal victims, the Hon. George Brooke, brother of Lord Cobham, and the priests, Watson and Clarke, were executed here on the Castle-hill. The castle was garrisoned during the civil war, first by the adherents of the Parliament, from whom it was taken by the Royalists in 1643. After the battle of Naseby, it was retaken by Cromwell, who blew it up with gunpowder, battered to pieces the fortifications of the city, and demolished Wolvesey Castle, the bishop's palace. His troopers stabled their horses in the cathedral, and committed great excesses, demolishing the monuments, and mutilating and injuring parts of the edifice. The bishop's palace was rebuilt in 1684. Winchester was a favourite city of Charles II., who commenced the erection of a palace in 1682 on the site of the old castle, which, so far as finished, stands there now, and is occupied as barracks. Richard Cromwell, after resigning the Protectorate, passed the remainder of his life in retirement in the neighbourhood of this city, at the old manor of Merdon at Hursley.

Winchester is situated on the eastern slope of an eminence, at the foot of which flows the beautiful river Itchen. The city has a solemn and venerable appearance. It consists of several good streets, lighted with gas, and well paved. Of the five ancient gates only two are now remaining; and all traces of the ditches and old walls have been obliterated. The most interesting public building in Winchester is the cathedral. Kinegils, the first of the Saxon kings who embraced Christianity, laid the foundation of a cathedral here, which, after his death, was carried on by his son, Kenewalch, and completed in 648. It stood on the spot which is occupied by the existing building. Having fallen into decay, it was rebuilt by St Ethelwold in 980. Bishop Walkelyn, the prelate who was first appointed to the see after the conquest, rebuilt the central tower, and made various important repairs and additions. Bishop Godfrey de Lucy rebuilt a portion of the east end towards the close of the eleventh century. Various extensive improvements were made about the middle of the fourteenth century by Bishop William de Edington; and his illustrious successor, William de

Wykeham, who held the see of Winchester from 1366 to 1404, rebuilt nearly the whole of the cathedral to the westward of the central tower. A considerable part of the church to the east of this tower was restored by Bishop Richard Fox in the early part of the sixteenth century. The building is in the form of a cross, its length from east to west being 560 feet, and the breadth of the nave and aisles 86 feet. The nave, 250 feet in length, is considered one of the finest in England. The length of the transepts is 186 feet. The tower is 138 feet in height and 50 feet by 48 in breadth. By far the noblest part of the building is the west front, built by William of Wykeham, with its great central doorway, its noble window, rich with perpendicular tracery, its buttresses and pinnacled turrets, its crowning tabernacle, with its statue of the builder, and its pinnacled side aisles. The interior has a peculiarly solemn and magnificent appearance, and is richly ornamented. Around the walls are numerous monuments of bishops, deans, nobles, and gentlemen of neighbouring families. The chapels or chantries of Wykeham, Edington, Fox, Cardinal Beaufort, Waynflete, and Gardiner, are of the most beautiful and elaborate workmanship. "So delicately, so elaborately are they carved out, that they have more the appearance of being wrought in ivory than in stone. In these, on stately tombs, the sides of which are figured with the richest panelling, lie the effigies of these magnificent old prelates, and here were daily masses chanted for the repose of their souls." The workmanship of the choir is remarkably rich and beautiful. On the floor, a plain bevelled stone of dark marble marks the tomb of William Rufus; and arranged on each side of the sanctuary are six mortuary chests, containing the bones of many of the most eminent Saxon princes. Behind the altar is a magnificent stone screen of the most exquisite workmanship, erected by Bishop Fox; and a painting by West, of the raising of Lazarus, now occupies the place where the high altar formerly stood. In the floor of Prior Silkstede's chapel, in the old Norman south transept, is the tomb of Izaak Walton.

The most interesting building in Winchester next to the cathedral is St. Mary's College. William of Wykeham, by whom it was founded and endowed, was originally a poor boy of the neighbouring town of Wickham, who, having attracted the notice of Nicholas Uvedale, the lord of the manor, was sent by him to the old grammar-school of Winchester, which stood on the very spot where his college now stands. It has been justly said, that "his architectural works at Dover, Queenborough, Windsor, and other castles for the king—the building of his two colleges, this and New College, Oxford,—and his rebuilding the nave of his cathedral—mark him as the greatest architectural genius of the age." Winchester College was begun in the year 1387, and was completed six years afterwards. The society consisted of a warden and ten priests, who are perpetual fellows, three chaplains, three clerks, and sixteen choristers, a schoolmaster and under master, and seventy scholars. The establishment continues in the same condition; but besides the seventy scholars, there are now taught a considerable number of youths who are not on the foundation. The college is built round two courts with towers over each gateway. The buildings in the second court are in a far superior style to those in the first. The dining-hall is a splendid room in the ancient Gothic style, with a lofty groined roof. In a chamber adjoining the kitchen is a very singular emblematical figure in oil-painting, usually termed "the trusty servant." The chapel is lofty, finely roofed, and the large windows are filled with stained glass. On the south side of the chapel are the cloisters, enclosing a quadrangle of 132 feet square. In the midst of the quadrangle is a little Gothic chapel, where a monk used to perform a daily mass for the dead. It is now the library of the establishment, and contains a collection of valuable old books. To the westward of the cloisters and library is the school, a detached building, erected in 1687. Over the entrance is a fine bronze statue of Wykeham, cast and presented to the college by Caius Gabriel Cibber, father of Colley Cibber.

The Hospital of St Cross is situated about a mile from the city, in the centre of a delightful part of the valley of the Itchin. A pleasant path leads to it across the meadows. To the left is the hill of St Catherine's, near the summit of which there are traces of an ancient fortification. Behind St Catherine's, on the top of Twyford down, there are some vestiges of the great Roman road from *Portus Magnus* (Porchester) to Winchester. The Hospital of St Cross was erected in the time of King Stephen by Henry de Blois, and was originally intended for thirteen poor men, a master, a steward, four chaplains, thirteen clerks, and seven choristers. The hospital was built in a quadrangular form; and three sides of the square yet remain. On the outer front of the gateway tower is a statue of Cardinal Beaufort, who may be regarded as the second founder of the institution. The Church of St Cross, which is one of the most interesting monuments of architectural antiquity in the kingdom, consists of a nave and side aisles, with a chancel and transepts, and a massy Norman tower over the intersection. The view from the leads of the tower is very fine. The hospital was stripped of much of its income at the Reformation. It still, however, affords a handsome revenue to the master, and comfortable subsistence to thirteen poor brethren. The brethren wear black cloaks, with a silver cross on the breast. A small remnant of the ancient hospitality is still kept up; for any one who presents himself at the porter's lodge is entitled to receive a horn of ale and a slice of bread—the ale, however, being of the thinnest and the bread of the hardest.

The Winchester Museum, situated in Jewry Street, contains valuable specimens of archæology, ethnology, mammals, birds, &c. It is open on Mondays, Wednesdays, and Saturdays; admission free.

Winchester returns two members to Parliament. Population of city and liberty, 14,776.

A road leads from Winchester, a distance of 24 miles, to Gosport, passing through Twyford (where there was once a Roman Catholic seminary, at which Pope received part of his education), Botley and Titchfield, the church of which is an interesting structure, and contains the effigies of Wriothesley, first Earl of Southampton, and his wife and son. Near the town are the ruins of Titchfield House, in which Charles I. was twice concealed.

ON RIGHT FROM LOND.	From South.	(From Winchester.)	From London.	ON LEFT FROM LOND.
Compton.		The railway runs hence through the valley of the Itchen.		Hospital of St. Cross. (See p. 55.)
Otterbourne, and beyond, Cranbury Park, T. Chamberlayne, Esq.		Hursley, 5 miles from Winchester, was once the property of Richard Cromwell, in right of his wife, Dorothy Major. His daughters, after his death, sold the estate to Sir W. Heathcote, who caused the ancient mansion to be taken down. A seal was found on this occasion in one of the walls, which proved to be the seal of the Commonwealth; in the opinion of Virtue, the eminent artist, the very one taken away by Cromwell from the House of Parliament.		St. Catherine's Hill. Twyford House. Twyford Lodge. Shawford Lodge, and 4 miles distant, Rose Hill Park, Earl of Northesk.
Four miles distant, Hursley Park, Sir W. Heathcote, Bart. The park is very picturesque, and contains the very perfect remains of one of Cromwell's field fortifications.				Bambridge House, [illegible]-Gen. Sir John Hanbury, K.C.H. Marwell Hall.
Branch to Salisbury.	6	Bishopstoke St.	74	Branch to Gosport, 16 miles (p. 81).
North Stoneham Park, J. W. Fleming, Esq., well wooded, and commanding fine views. Beyond, Chilworth House.		Dr. Garnier, Dean of Winchester, holds the living of Bishopstoke. His gardens are most attractive, and admission is readily granted to any respectable person presenting a card, and signifying a wish to see them. The Himalayan collection is very fine.		Swathling. Townhill Park. South Stoneham Ho. Midanbury House. Bittern Grove. At Bittern was a Roman station, the Clausentum of the Itinerary. Roman remains are found here.
Portswood House.				
Bannister House.		Admiral Hawkes, one of the naval heroes of the reign of George II., is buried in North Stoneham church.		
Bevois Mount.		The line crosses the river Itchin by a viaduct.		
Bellevue.		SOUTHAMPTON.	80	Chessel House, Lord Ashtown.

Southampton is beautifully situated at the head of the bay called the Southampton Water, having the river Itchen on the one side, and the Test or Anton on the other. It was anciently fortified, and the remains of its walls and castle still exist. The town appears to have had its origin in the Saxon times, and is mentioned in the Saxon Chronicle under the year 873. During the ninth and tenth centuries it was frequently ravaged by the Danes; here Canute occasionally resided; and it was while he stayed at Southampton that the well-known incident occurred in which he rebuked the flattery of his courtiers. In the sixteenth century Southampton was visited by the Emperor Charles V., by Edward VI., Philip of Spain, and Queen Elizabeth; and it was for some time the residence of Charles I. Southampton possesses an excellent harbour for merchantmen, and its value and importance has been greatly increased by the recent formation of docks of a capacity sufficient to receive vessels of the largest class, and steam-vessels. This town has long been a place of great trade with Spain and Portugal, chiefly for the importation of wine and fruit. It has also a considerable trade with France, with the Baltic ports and Canada, and with the Channel Islands. It carries on a brisk coasting trade; and is the most convenient port for steam-boats plying to Guernsey, Jersey, St Malo, Granville, and Hâvre. There are also regular trading-smacks and schooners between London and Southampton. The total amount of the gross revenue collected at the custom-house in Southampton in 1861 amounted to £79,496. The formation of the South-Western Railway has proved of great benefit to the trade and local interests of Southampton, which is now the principal station for the West India, and also the Peninsular and Oriental packets, by the latter of which the overland communication with India, through Egypt and across the Isthmus of Suez, is maintained; this line of route has been further extended to Sydney and New Zealand.

Southampton was anciently defended by double ditches, battlements, and watch-towers. Of the gates, the only one remaining is an imposing structure called Bargate, on the north front of which are two figures, said by tradition to represent the famous Sir Bevois of Hampton and the giant Ascupart, whom he slew in single combat. Southampton contains a great number of large and well-built houses, and the principal streets are spacious and well paved.

Southampton contains five churches, of which St Michael's is remarkable for its high slender octagonal tower, which serves as a landmark to ships entering the harbour; it has also a Catholic chapel, and several places of meeting for dissenters of various denominations. There is a grammar-school, founded in the time of Edward VI. On the north side of the town is an asylum for female orphans, the children of soldiers; and there are various charitable institutions. About half a mile from the Bargate stand the barracks, which enclose an area of two acres, but this is not now a military station.

Since the fire which occurred at the Tower of London in 1841, the engraving department of the ordnance establishment has been removed to Southampton, at which town the execution of the national survey of Great Britain is at present carried on, and upon which numerous engravers are now employed. The Ordnance Survey of England and Wales, which was commenced in 1791, has been completed on a scale of one inch to a mile, with the exception of the six northern counties, at a total cost of L.662,000. The remaining portion, as well as a similar survey of Scotland, at present in progress, is being proceeded with upon the scales of six and three inches to a mile.

Southampton was incorporated into a borough by Charles I., and is also a county of itself: it is divided into five wards, and governed by a mayor, ten aldermen, and thirty councillors. It returns two members to Parliament. Population of Parliamentary borough, 46,960.

From Southampton to Salisbury is 21½ miles—Lymington, 20¼—Portsmouth, 17½—Gosport, 16½—Poole, 34—Winchester, 12.

The mildness of the air, the facility of making excursions by water as well as by land, the vicinity of the Isle of Wight and of the New Forest, contribute to render the town a desirable place for either a temporary or a permanent residence, which is further recommended by the excellent supplies of fish, fruit, meat, and other necessaries.

A number of pleasant excursions may be made in the neighbourhood of Southampton. About three miles from the town is the celebrated Netley Abbey,* one of the most picturesque ruins in England. The founder of this abbey was Peter Roche, Bishop of Winchester, who died towards the middle of the thirteenth century. Its inmates were of the Cistertian order. At the dissolution it was granted to Sir William Paulet, afterwards the celebrated Marquis of Winchester. The abbey is now a complete ruin, so that scarcely any part of it can be distinguished, except the remains of the chapel. The walk to it from the town of Southampton is one of enchanting beauty. The abbey itself is almost completely concealed by the luxuriant foliage of the trees among which it is embosomed, and, altogether, the spot is one of singular loveliness.

THE NEW FOREST.

In the neighbourhood of Southampton is that large tract of woodland termed the New Forest, than which there are probably few spots in England more interesting, or more worthy of being visited. The New Forest was originally formed by William the Conqueror in the year 1079, about thirteen years after the battle of Hastings. Its shape is a kind of irregular triangle, wide at the south, and drawing to a point towards the north, contained within a circumference of about fifty miles. Great odium has been heaped on the memory of William, particularly by the monkish historians, because of his alleged conduct in afforesting these woodlands, and it has been confidently asserted that he destroyed a large number of villages and churches, drove out the inhabitants, laid their lands waste, and formed the New Forest in their room. These statements, however, are greatly exaggerated, for it is obviously impossible that such an extensive depopulation could have taken place in a country which, from the nature of it, must have been from the first very thinly inhabited. At the same time, he cannot be absolved from all reproach in this matter, for it is evident that many persons must have been dispossessed of their lands ere such an extensive tract could have been wholly at his disposal. His son, William Rufus, was killed in this forest, according to popular tradition, by a random arrow, but the precise circumstances attending his death are involved in doubt. This event

* Leland states that the proper name of the place is Lettley, which is supposed to be a corruption of the Latin words *de Læto Loco.*

took place near Stoney Cross, at a short distance from Castle Malwood. An oak formerly stood on the spot, but this has now disappeared, and its site is marked by a triangular stone about five feet high, bearing the following inscription commemorative of the event:—

"Here stood the oak on which an arrow, shot by Sir Walter Tyrrell at a stag, glanced and struck King William II., named Rufus, in the breast, of which he instantly died, on the 2d of August A. D. 1100."

"King William II., surnamed Rufus, being slain as is before related, was laid in a cart belonging to one Purkess,* and drawn from hence to Winchester, and was buried in the cathedral church of that city."

"That where an event so memorable had happened might not hereafter be unknown, this stone was set up by John Lord Delaware, who has seen the tree growing in this place anno 1745."

Stoney Cross is visited in summer by great numbers of persons from Southampton, Winchester, and the neighbouring towns.

The New Forest has preserved its ancient boundaries more exactly, and retains more of the forest than any of our other forests. Part of it is now private property, but 65,845 acres belong to the Crown, subject to certain rights of common, of pasturage, pannage, and fuel, belonging to proprietors of estates within or adjacent to the forest. For local purposes, the forest is divided into nine bailiwicks, and these are again subdivided into fifteen walks. Formerly the chief officer of the forest was the Lord Warden, who was appointed by the crown during pleasure, by letters-patent under the Great Seal, and was generally some person of distinction; under him were a lieutenant, a bow-bearer, two rangers, a woodward, an under-woodward, four verderers, a high steward, an under-steward, twelve regarders, nine foresters, and fifteen under-foresters. Besides these ancient officers of the forest, there was one of later institution, called the purveyor, whose business it was to assign timber for the use of the navy. The forest is now managed by a deputy-surveyor under the Commissioners of Woods and Forests.

There is a numerous population within the limits of this forest. Their moral condition, though much improved of late years, is still low. "On the skirts of the forest," says William Howitt, "and round its vast heaths, are numbers of poor huts, whose inmates have very little visible means of existence, but profess themselves to be woodmen, charcoal-burners, and so on; but it is pretty well

* Purkess lived at Minstead, and maintained his family by burning charcoal. His male descendants have continued to occupy the same house, and to carry on the same trade till very recently. The last of the lineal occupiers of the hut died an old man a few years ago. It is said of this family that they always possessed a horse and cart, but never attained to the possession of a team. This tradition is thus referred to in Mr Stewart Rose's ballad of the Red King:—

"And still so runs our forest creed,—
Flourish the pious yeoman's seed,
Ev'n in the self-same spot;
One horse and cart their little store,
Like their forefathers, neither more
Nor less the children's lot."

understood that poaching and smuggling are their more probable vocations. Some of their cabins are the rudest erections of boughs, turf, and heather. Their poles for charcoal-burning are reared in huge pyramids, with the smallest end uppermost. * * * Many of them, like those in the woods of America, are mere squatters ; but the attempt to disturb them is much the same as to disturb a hornet's nest. Conscious that there is no strength but in making common cause, they are all up in arms at any attempt to dislodge any of them."

Horses are reared in great numbers in the New Forest. They are of a diminutive breed, and are supposed to be descended from the Spanish jenets driven ashore on the coast of Hampshire in the dispersion of the Armada. They are often seen feeding together in herds of twenty or thirty, and have a very picturesque appearance amid the forest scenery. Great numbers of them are annually taken and sold. They are useful for any kind of employment, and are remarkable for the hardiness of their nature, and for their agility and sureness of foot. The forest abounds also with red and fallow deer. It likewise contains a breed of hogs, which have about them several of the characteristic marks of the wild boar. Besides these wild hogs there are many of the domesticated breed in the New Forest, who are turned out to feed on acorns and beechmast during the " pannage" month, which begins about the end of September, and lasts for six weeks. The curious mode by which they are collected and managed is described by Gilpin in his Forest Scenery, and is too well known to require to be quoted here. The New Forest is a district of great interest both to the sportsman and the naturalist, as it abounds in birds of almost every species and in winter its shores are thronged by aquatic birds. Its extensive tracts of heath render the forest a favourite resort of the honey-bee, which everywhere covers the surface of it, and is frequently a source of considerable profit to the cottagers.

The various roads by which the New Forest is traversed, including that part of the railway from Southampton to Dorchester, which traverses the forest to Ringwood, are all accurately delineated in the chart which accompanies this description. The tourist may, therefore, choose for himself the route which he will pursue, according as his time may permit, or his taste incline. We shall briefly point out such objects as are deserving of especial notice. The visitor who wishes thoroughly to explore this interesting district would do well to take some of the forest towns, such as Lymington, Lyndhurst, Christchurch, &c. as central points, and from these places as his head-quarters make excursions in various directions.

Taking Southampton as the point of departure, the road passes the pretty village of Millbrook, the churchyard of which contains a monument to Pollok, the author of the " Course of Time," who died at Shirley, near this place, in 1827, at the age of twenty-nine. A mile farther on is Redbridge, at the head of Southampton Water, a place of great antiquity, which enjoys a considerable trade in corn, coal, timber, &c. A little beyond a road leads off on the left to Lyndhurst, the little capital of the Forest, distant about 9 or 10 miles from Southampton.

A little farther on the road passes Totton, near which is Testwood House, the seat of Miss Bourne. Proceeding onward the tourist reaches Cadnam Park, distant between 9 and 10 miles from Southampton. From this place a pleasant excursion may be made along the valley of the Avon to Fording bridge; whence the tourist may proceed to Ringwood, a distance of six miles, by Blackford Green, and the village of Ibbesley. A short way beyond, to the right of the road, is Rufus's stone, formerly described, and to the left is Castle Malwood. Proceeding onward we reach Stoney Cross, a place much visited in summer by large parties from Southampton, Winchester, and the neighbouring towns. A little to the left is the sequestered hamlet of Minstead, which stands in one of the finest parts of the forest. "On one side," says W. Howitt, "are open knolls and ascending woodlands, covered with majestic beeches, and the village children playing under them; on the other, the most rustic cottages, almost buried in the midst of their orchard trees, and thatched as Hampshire cottages only are—in such projecting abundance—such flowing lines. * * The whole of the cottages thereabout are in equal taste with the roof, so different to the red staring square brick houses of manufacturing districts. They seem, as no doubt they are, erected in the spirit and under the influence of the *genius loci*. The bee-hives in their rustic rows, the little crofts, all belong to a primitive country. I went on, now coming to small groups of such places, now to others of superior pretensions, but equally blent with the spirit of the surrounding nature—little paradises of cultivated life. As I advanced heathery hills stretched away on one hand, woods came down thickly and closely on the other, and a winding road, beneath the shade of large old trees, conducted me to one of the most retired and peaceful of hamlets. It was Minstead. * * * Herds of red-deer rose from the fern, and went bounding away, and dashed into the depths of the woods; troops of those grey and long-tailed forest horses turned to gaze as I passed down the open glades; and the red squirrels in hundreds scampered away from the ground where they were feeding. * * * Delighted with the true woodland wildness and solemnity of beauty, I roved onward through the wildest woods that came in my way. Awaking as from a dream, I saw far around me one deep shadow, one thick and continuous roof of boughs, and thousands of hoary boles standing clothed as it were with the very spirit of silence. I admired the magnificent sweep of some grand old trees as they hung into a glade or ravine, some delicious opening in the deep woods, or the grotesque figure of particular trees, which seemed to have been blasted into blackness, and contorted into inimitable crookedness, by the savage genius of the place." Minstead Manor House is the property of H. C. Compton, Esq.

Returning to the road, and passing Bolderwood Lodge, a little to the left, we shortly after reach Picked Post, and a short distance beyond it is the pleasant village of Ringwood, seated on the banks of the Avon, which spreads near the town into a large sheet of water full of little islands. Ringwood existed during the Roman occupation of Britain, and was a place of some importance in the Anglo-Saxon times. It contained in 1861, 3751 inhabitants, who are chiefly employed in the manufacture of woollen cloths and stockings, and in brewing ale and strong beer, for which the town has acquired a considerable name. The country around the town is rather flat. The roads from Southampton to Poole, and from Salisbury to Christchurch pass through Ringwood. At the distance of nine miles from Ringwood is the town of Christchurch. There are two roads parallel to each other which lead to it, with the river Avon flowing between them. The road on the left bank of the river passes by Kingsbar, Bistern Park (H. C. Compton, Esq.) Avon, Sopley, and Staple's Cross. In the vicinity of the latter are the mansions of Hinton House, Hinton Admiral, and High Cliff. The country between Ringwood and Christchurch is flat, and the lanes close and woody. The town of Christchurch takes its name from its church and priory, founded early in the Saxon era for a dean and twenty canons of the order of St Augustine. William Rufus bestowed the church and convent upon Ranulph Flambard, Bishop of Durham, who rebuilt the church upon a more superb scale, and its revenues were greatly augmented by Richard de Rivers, Earl of Devon, to whom the manor was given by Henry I. At the dissolution, the annual income was L.544, 6s. Some fragments of the priory walls are still standing. The church, which is in the form of a cross, is a very interesting specimen of the Norman style, though modern additions have been made to it. Within the church, there are some curious ancient monuments ; and the tower commands a delightful and extensive prospect. The town is supposed to have been of Roman origin, and in Saxon times was called Tweonea, or " the place between the rivers." Near Christchurch are Heron Court (Earl of Malmesbury) and Sandhills (W. Rose, Esq.) It returned two members to Parliament since the reign of Elizabeth ; but the number was reduced to one by the Reform Act. The population in 1861 of the parliamentary borough was 9368.

The rivers Stour and Avon, after uniting about $1\frac{1}{2}$ miles below the town, flow into Christchurch bay, which is spacious, but shallow and dangerous. " There is a curious circumstance peculiar to this harbour and the neighbouring port of Poole in Dorsetshire,—that of the tide producing two high waters ; a phenomenon quite inexplicable from the general laws of tides, and only to be accounted for by the situation of this coast as regards the Isle of Wight, and from the contraction of the channel by the jutting out of the point of land on which Hurst Castle stands."*

In the neighbourhood of the town are the remains of a camp and entrenchments, with several tumuli and barrows.

Christchurch is about 20 miles distant from Lymington. The intervening district is flat, cultivated, and enclosed. The road is parallel to the coast the whole of the way. A little to the right of the road is a large house built by Lord Bute. It stands on a cliff directly opposite to Cherbourg, from which it is about 60 miles distant. This cliff, which is termed Hordle Cliff, rises about 150 feet above the level of the sea. The flatness of the scenery is a little diversified by various hollows or narrow dells, through each of which a small rivulet finds its way to the sea. The most remarkable are those of Chuton, Ashley, and

* Gilpin's Forest Scenery, Vol. ii. p. 146.

Efford. About two or three miles farther along the coast, stands Hurst Castle, built at the extremity of a remarkable natural causeway, which runs two miles into the sea, forming, between the castle and the Isle of Wight, a narrow channel, which, at high water, scarcely exceeds 200 yards in breadth. The castle was erected in the time of Henry VIII. Here Charles I., after being removed from the Isle of Wight, was confined for some time previous to his trial and execution. Between Hurst Castle and Lymington is the small village of Millord, which commands fine views of Alum Bay and the neighbouring part of Wight. Three miles farther on is the town of Lymington, agreeably situated on the right bank of the river of the same name. It is 9 miles from Lyndhurst, 19 from the Southampton station, and about 90 south-west from London in a straight line. Lymington is a neat well built town, and pleasantly situated. It is a corporate town and Parliamentary borough, and has returned two members to Parliament since the reign of Elizabeth. The parish church, dedicated to Thomas à Becket, contains many handsome monuments. The population of the town and parish in 1861 was 4098, and of parliamentary borough, 5179.

Lymington is subordinate to the port of Southampton. Its foreign trade is unimportant, and the coasting trade is on the decline. Considerable improvements have, of late years, been made in the town with the view of affording accommodation to visitors during the bathing season. The chief manufacture in the neighbourhood is salt.

Near Lymington is Cadlands, the seat of A. R. Drummond, Esq., and Wallhampton, the seat of Sir G. Burrard, Bart. About two miles from Lymington is the village of Boldre, for above twenty years the scene of the pastoral labours of the Rev. William Gilpin, author of "Forest Scenery," and various other works on the picturesque. He built ana endowed two schools here out of the profits of the sale of his drawings, and lies buried in Boldre churchyard. The church, which is an ancient and primitive looking structure, stands on the summit of a thickly wooded eminence, and commands a variety of interesting views.

Midway between Lymington and Lyndhurst is Brockenhurst, a pleasant forest village, of Saxon origin, and recorded in the Doomsday Book by the name of Broceste. Part of the church was erected before the Conquest, and the font is a very antique and curious piece of workmanship. Near the village are Brockenhurst Park and Watcombe House. The latter was, for three years, the residence of the philanthropic Howard. To the south-west of Brockenhurst there is a heath called Sway Common, over which various tumuli are scattered. The road from Brockenhurst to Lyndhurst passes through a very interesting part of the forest. Near Lyndhurst stands Cuffnells (Sir Edward Poore, Bart.) on a rising ground embosomed in trees, and most delightfully situated in the very heart of the forest. It was the property of the late Sir Thomas Tancred, of whose heirs it was purchased by the late Sir George Rose, who made very considerable additions to the mansion. The situation of Lyndhurst is very beautiful. It has been considered as the capital of the New Forest ever since the era of its formation, and the forestal courts are still held here. An ancient stirrup is preserved in the hall of the King's House, the official residence of the Lord Warden, which is said to have been that used by William Rufus at the time he was shot by Sir Walter Tyrrel.* Opposite to the King's House stands a large square building called the King's Stables. A fine prospect of the forest may be obtained from the tower of the church. Lord Lyndhurst derives his title from this place. Population of parish 1522.

From Lyndhurst to Southampton is a distance of between 9 and 10 miles. The road joins that which leads to Stoney Cross at the village of Rumbridge.

Before closing our description of the forest we may direct the attention of the tourist to an interesting excursion which may be made to Beaulieu Abbey. This spot may be reached by crossing Southampton water to Hythe, and proceeding from thence to Beaulieu, a distance of 5 miles. The river Beaulieu is a mere forest stream till near the abbey, when it expands into a lake covering many acres. The Abbey of Beaulieu was founded by King John in 1204 for monks of the Cistertian order. The wall which surrounded the precincts of the abbey is nearly entire in several parts, and is finely mantled with ivy. Of the buildings of the abbey considerable parts remain. The abbot's lodge was converted, after the dissolution, into a family seat. The ancient kitchen and the refectory, and a long building supposed to have been the dormitory, are still standing. The refectory is now turned into a parish church, and was repaired some years ago at the expense of the late Lord Montagu, uncle of the Duke of Buccleuch. Beaulieu Abbey possessed the privilege of sanctuary, and it afforded a temporary protection to Margaret of Anjou, Queen of Henry VI., and her son Prince Edward, on her return from the continent, at the time of the Battle of Barnet. It also afforded shelter to Perkin Warbeck after the failure of his attempts in the west of England. At the dissolution, the manor of Beaulieu was granted to Thomas Wriothesley, afterwards Earl of Southampton. In the reign of William III. this estate became the property of Ralph, Lord, afterwards Duke of, Montagu, by his marriage with the heiress of the Wriothesleys. His son John, second Duke of Montagu, transmitted it to his daughters, Isabella and Mary, from whom, by intermarriages, the manor has descended to the Duke of Buccleuch.

At Beaulieu was also an Hospital of Knights Templars. The ruins of the hospital, which are now converted into farm buildings, stand about half a mile distant from the water, on a rising ground which commands extensive views.

The tourist may vary his route back to Southampton by sailing down the Beaulieu or Exe river to Exbury,—a distance of rather more than 3 miles, and proceeding from thence across the country to Calshot Castle, about 4½ miles

* "And still in merry Lyndhurst hall
Red William's stirrup decks the wall,
Who lists the sight may see;
And a fair stone in green Malwood
Informs the traveller where stood
The memorable tree."—*Red King*

from Exbury. From Calshot he may proceed by Fawley to Hythe, and cross the water at that spot, or proceed to Dibden and Eling, and there cross to Southampton.

ISLE OF WIGHT.

Southampton is a most convenient spot from which to make an excursion to the Isle of Wight. The passage from Southampton to Cowes, the usual landing-place in Wight, is performed by regular steam-boats in little more than an hour. The passage from Portsmouth seldom exceeds half that time.

The Isle of Wight (the Vecta or Vectis of the Romans) is separated from Hampshire by a beautiful channel, called the Solent Sea, the breadth of which varies from four to six miles, but at one point, near Hurst Castle, its breadth is only one mile. In this channel, though it contains no harbour of importance, there are many places of perfect security, where ships may ride at anchor. The best of these is Spithead, the great rendezvous of the British fleet in time of war. The form of the island is an irregular ellipsis, measuring 23 miles from east to west, and 13 miles from north to south. Its circumference is about 60 miles, and its superficial contents have been variously estimated at from 105,000 to 130,000 acres, of which a great portion is highly productive. It is said to have been formerly covered with woods, but to have been in a great measure denuded by its vicinity to Portsmouth, and the great demand of that naval arsenal for timber.

"The face of the country may be rather described as undulating than as hilly, though there is a range of hills, or rather downs, running from east to west through the island, with a few points of considerable elevation. There is a great variety of rural scenery, adorned with a great diversity of foliage; and though there are few or no woods, yet, as the fields are enclosed within hedge-rows, among which fine trees, and especially stately elms, grow most luxuriantly, these, added to the beauty of the verdant fields, present to the eye of the traveller a succession of most pleasing prospects. The two sides of the island present each a peculiar character. The northern side is marked by every thing that is rich, lovely, and picturesque; the southern, or the part called the *Back of the Island*, abounds in bold wild rocks, precipitous projections, ravines, fearful chasms, and other features of the imposing, and a few even of the sublime. In some parts, these opposite characters are greatly mingled. There is a peculiar scenery on the south side of the island, which is so striking to all strangers, as to require a special notice. It is a continued sinking of a tract of land, about seven miles in length, and from a-half to a-quarter of a mile in breadth. This singular district consists of a series of terraces, formed by fragments of rocks chalk, and sandstone, which have been detached from the cliffs and hills above and deposited upon a substratum of white marl. This whole *undercliff*, for such is its common name, is completely sheltered from the north, north-west, and west winds, by the range of lofty downs or hills of chalk or sandstone, which rise boldly from the upper termination of these terraces, on elevations varying from four to six and seven hundred feet in height. The two extremities of the range are indeed higher, as St Boniface Down is 800 feet above the level of the sea, and St Catherine's Hill on the west nearly 900 feet. The protection afforded by this mountain barrier is greatly increased, by the very singular and striking abruptness with which it terminates on its southern aspect. This, in many places, consists of the bare perpendicular rock of sandstone; in others of chalk, assuming its characteristic rounded form, covered with a fine turf and underwood."*

The river Medina, which, rising at the foot of St Catherine's Down, falls into the Solent Channel, at Cowes, divides the island into two hundreds of nearly equal extent, called respectively East and West Medina, the former comprehending 14, the latter, 16 parishes.

The population of the Isle of Wight is 55,362. Previously to the passing of the Reform Bill, the boroughs of Newport, Newton, and Yarmouth, returned each two members to Parliament, but Newton and Yarmouth are now disfranchised, and one member is returned for the county, and two for the borough of Newport.

The Isle of Wight was first invaded by the Romans, A. D. 43, in the reign of the Emperor Claudius, and they retained possession of it till 495, when it was reduced by Cedric the Saxon. It suffered severely during the wars of the Saxon heptarchy, and was also frequently plundered and devastated by the Danes. It was on various occasions invaded by the French, but in almost every attack they were beaten and driven back to their ships by the islanders, who had made systematic preparations for their defence. After the naval superiority of Britain was established, this island was completely secured from the calamities of foreign invasion, and during the civil war between Charles I. and his Parliament, the inhabitants enjoyed comparative freedom from the prevailing commotions.

The Lordship of the Isle of Wight was conferred by William the Conqueror on William Fitz-Osborne, who is known in English history under the title of the Earl of Hereford, and for more than two centuries the island continued to be governed by its independent lords. But in 1293, Edward I. purchased the regalities for the sum of L.4000 from Isabella de Fortibus, Lady of Wight, and, since that time, the island has been governed by wardens, appointed by the Crown. The office has now become a sinecure, and it is understood that the present governor, Viscount Eversley, does not receive any salary.

In the year 1644, the weak and unfortunate Henry VI. conferred the title of king of Wight on Henry Beauchamp, Duke of Warwick, and crowned him with his own hands; but the empty title expired with the nobleman who first bore it.

The Isle of Wight derives additional interest from the fact of its having been of late years the frequent place of residence of the Queen, as in 1844 Her Majesty and the Prince Consort purchased the mansion of Osborne, with its park, and the adjoining estate of Barton. Osborne House is situated in the immediate neighbourhood of East Cowes, and near the north coast of the island. Since it has been in the possession of Her Majesty and the Prince, the original man-

* Encyc. Brit. vol. xxi. p. 82.

sion has been greatly enlarged by the addition of a new wing, at the south-west corner of which is a massive tower which forms a conspicuous object for miles around, and the summit of which commands a magnificent and varied prospect. Population of Cowes, 5482. *Hotel:* The Gloster.

On landing at Cowes, the tourist may proceed by a pleasant road, 4½ miles in length, to

NEWPORT,

the capital of the island, a neat and thriving town, situated in a pleasant valley chequered with gardens and groves, and well-watered on the east and west by copious streams. Newport is the most ancient as well as the largest existing town of the island, and contained in 1861 a population of 7934 souls. The parish church is a large plain structure, originally erected in the year 1172. It has, however, been frequently repaired. Here was discovered, in 1793, the coffin of the Princess Elizabeth, who died a prisoner in Carisbrook Castle, about a year and seven months after the execution of her father, Charles I. It was asserted that Cromwell had caused her to be poisoned, but Clarendon declares this accusation false. The other places of worship in Newport are, several Episcopal chapels, with a Roman Catholic, and other Dissenting chapels. The Grammar School, erected in 1619, is an object of some interest, as the place chosen for the memorable conference between Charles I. and the Parliamentary Commissioners, which goes by the name of the Treaty of Newport. One of the best public buildings in Newport is a public library, called the Isle of Wight Institution, which was built by subscription in 1811, and is now well furnished with books and periodical publications. There are also two assembly rooms in the town, a Mechanic's Institution, and other societies for the promotion of science and education.

In the immediate vicinity of Newport is the picturesque village of Carisbrook, once the capital of the island under the independent Lords of Wight. The church is of great antiquity, and is supposed to stand upon the site of a Saxon church, built some centuries before the Conquest. Adjoining the church are the remains of a priory of Cistertian Monks, founded by Fitz-Osborne, Earl of Hereford, but now converted into sheds and stables. Opposite to it, on a steep hill of nearly a circular form, stand the romantic ruins of Carisbrook Castle. Its ivy-clad towers and battlements have an eminently picturesque appearance. At the north-east angle, on a mount raised much higher than the other buildings, stands the Keep, the original fortress, supposed to have been built by the Saxons as early as the sixth century. In the eleventh century, the castle was considerably enlarged by Fitz-Osborne, who surrounded the whole with a fosse. Various additions were made to it at different times, the last by Queen Elizabeth, when the outer walls, which still remain, were made to enclose about twenty acres of ground.

Among the curiosities pointed out to strangers is a well 300 feet deep, from which water is drawn up by means of a wheel turned by an ass. Another well, in the centre of the Keep, said to have been 310 feet deep, has been partially filled up.

The most memorable incident in the history of Carisbrook Castle, is the confinement of Charles I., who took refuge here after his flight from Hampton

Court, 5th November 1647. The Governor, Colonel Hammond, at first treated him as a guest, and placed no restriction on his movements. He was afterwards, however, subjected to close imprisonment, during the course of which he made several unsuccessful attempts to escape. The apartments in which he was confined are now ruinous, but a window is still pointed out as that by which he made the attempts to regain his liberty.

After Charles's execution, his two youngest children, the Duke of Gloucester and the Princess Elizabeth, became inmates of Carisbrook Castle. The latter died here, and the former, about two years after the death of his sister, was liberated by the influence and advice of Cromwell.

The old hunting-forest, called Parkhurst, which extended over nearly 4000 acres, and came close up to Newport and Carisbrook, is now so completely cut down, that scarcely any thing remains but brushwood. The walks through it are, however, still extremely pleasant.

A delightful excursion may be made from Newport to the north-east, in the direction of Fernhill and Wotton Bridge. The mansion at Fernhill was built by the late Duke of Bolton, when he was governor of the island. Behind it there is a plantation of noble trees, and the grounds are laid out in excellent taste. Wotton Bridge is a remarkably pretty village, on the left bank of the river Wotton, about 3½ miles from Newport. About two miles from Wotton Bridge, on the shore of the Solent Strait, there is a place called King's Key, where King John is said to have landed when he came to the Isle of Wight, after signing Magna Charta on the field of Runnymede. He remained three months in concealment in this neighbourhood, devising means to subvert the provisions of that charter. In the fine season of the year, a passage-boat goes and returns every day between Wotton Bridge and Portsmouth. At no great distance from this village is Osborne House, the residence of Her Majesty and the Prince Consort, and near it, Norris Castle, and East Cowes Castle (Earl of Shannon)

Crossing the river Wotton, and passing a beautiful mount called Kite Hill, a delightful walk of 1½ miles will bring the tourist to the ruins of Quarr Abbey. This once famous establishment was erected in the twelfth century by Baldwin de Rivers and Richard his son, who were both buried within its walls. It was dedicated to St Mary Magdalen, and the monks were of the Cistertian order. The abbey derived its name from the stone quarries in its neighbourhood, which furnished a great part of the stone employed in building Winchester Cathedral. Of the abbey scarcely any part now remains except some of the outer walls, which are said to have enclosed thirty acres of ground, and a very small portion of the abbey offices, which have been converted into barns and other farm-buildings. After the dissolution, Quarr Abbey was purchased by a Mr Mills of Southampton. His son sold it to the Lord Chief Justice, Sir Thomas Fleming, with whose descendants it still remains.

From Quarr Abbey, a pleasant footpath leads to the church-yard of Binstead; and a little farther on is the town of Ryde, which, eighty years ago, was only a fishing-village, but is now a considerable and beautiful town, surrounded with groves, villas, and cottages. The views from the town and neighbourhood are very fine. East of Ryde, are Ryde House, St John's, St Clare's, Fairy Hill, and the Priory. A little farther on, near the mouth of Brading Haven, is the pretty village of St Helen's, built round a green near the sea. Striking inland, a pleasant road will convey the tourist to the village of Brading, picturesquely situated on the slope of a hill at the bottom of Brading Haven. The church, which is supposed to occupy the site of the first church erected in the island in 704, is an interesting building, and contains some antique tombs. Close to the village stands the old mansion of Nunwell, the seat of Sir H. Oglander, Bart., the representative of the oldest existing family in the island, whose founder, Richard Okelandro, came over with William the Conqueror. Their family chapel and burying-place are in the church of Brading. Population of Ryde, 9269.

A short distance from Brading is the neat village of Yaverland, where there is a curious little church of great antiquity. From this point the tourist may return to Newport by Sandham Heath, Alverstone, and Ashey Down, from the summit of which there is one of the finest views in the island.

Another excursion, frequently made from Newport, is to Appuldurcombe (Earl of Yarborough), the finest seat in the Isle of Wight, and Ventnor Cove. Proceeding by Carisbrook the tourist, about 3 miles from Newport, reaches Gatcombe, a handsome modern mansion, pleasantly situated. It was formerly the seat of one of the Worsleys. About three miles farther on is the populous village of Godshill. The church, a large and venerable pile, stands in a very picturesque situation, on the summit of a steep hill that rises in the centre of the village, and commands an extensive and beautiful prospect. This church was one of the six in the island which Fitz-Osborne, Earl of Hereford, bestowed along with the Priory of Carisbrook on the great Abbey of Lyra, in Normandy. In the interior of the church are the monuments of the Worsleys, from the fifteenth, to the nineteenth century, together with the monuments of some of the Leighs of Derbyshire and the Wight, whose daughters transferred by marriage these possessions to the Worsleys, ancestors of Lord Yarborough. In the village of Godshill is a grammar-school, founded above 200 years ago by one of the Worsley family. About a mile to the south of the village is Appuldurcombe, which has long been the seat of this ancient and honourable family. It stands on the site of a very old manor-house, and was begun in 1710 by Sir Robert Worsley, and finished by his grandson Sir Richard. The mansion has four regular fronts of the Corinthian order, and a handsome colonade facing the south. It contains a large collection of paintings, drawings, and statues, some of which were in the old manor-house for many generations. The sculptures and drawings were collected by Sir Richard, the last Baronet, during the course of an extensive tour through Egypt, Turkey, Italy, and Greece, during the years 1785-7. The grounds, which are extensive, are laid out in admirable style, and adorned with fine beech trees and venerable oaks. On the most elevated point, there is an obelisk 70 feet high, erected to the memory of Sir Robert Worsley the founder of the present mansion. The ruins of a castle, called Cooks' Castle, stand on the summit of a rocky hill about a mile distant. Sir Richard Worsley, the last Baronet, died here in 1813, and his niece, by her marriage, carried th mansion and estates to the first Earl of Yarborough.

It was in Appuldurcombe that Worsley's History of the Isle of Wight was written. It was begun by Sir Robert, who died in 1747, continued by his son Sir Thomas, and finished and published by his grandson Sir Richard in 1781.

Appuldurcombe can be visited only by tickets, to be had at the office of the steward, in the town of Newport; and the days for strangers viewing it are Tuesdays and Fridays between the hours of 11 and 4 o'clock.

A short distance from Appuldurcombe is the Undercliff* and the village at Ventnor Cove, which, so late as 1830, was little more than a hamlet, but has now become a populous village, in consequence of being greatly resorted to as a winter residence for invalids. The scenery in the immediate neighbourhood is very delightful. Ventnor Cove is well deserving of a visit, on account of its picturesqueness and beauty. A little to the south-west of the Cove is Steephill, and about a mile and a half farther on, the romantic village of St Lawrence, which contained the smallest church in Great Britain, it being only 25 feet long and 12 wide; but an addition of 15 feet was made to the length a few years ago, so that the building is now 40 feet long. From the heights behind the village, the beauties of the Undercliff are seen to great advantage. A pleasant road leads along the coast through Mirables to Sand Rock, where there is an excellent hotel. A romantic path leads from the hotel to a chalybeate spring, situated in the face of a bold gloomy cliff, about 130 feet above the level of the sea. Over the spring there is a pretty cottage, erected by Mr. Waterworth, a surgeon of Newport, who discovered its virtues in 1809. According to the analysis of Dr. Marcet, the Sand Rock spring contains a larger proportion of alum and iron than any other mineral water yet discovered. It has been found very useful in the cure of those disorders which arise from nervous affections and debility. A short distance from the spring is Black-Gang Chine, a gloomy fissure in the rock, formed by the action of a stream of water, running seaward from the interior of the island. In some places the cliffs on either side of it are 500 feet high. The rocks are almost black in colour. There is scarcely a trace of vegetation and the scenery is wild

* The Undercliff is a strip of land about six miles long and from a quarter to half a mile in breadth, which seems to have settled down and slipped towards the sea, exhibiting a jumble of rocks, overturned and broken mounds of earth, deep hollows, and numerous springs, forming falls of water, collecting into pools, and hurrying to the sea. (M. Simond). It appears that the Undercliff has been formed by a succession of landslips. One of these took place in the year 1799, when a large tract of the high cliff, extending to from 80 to 90 acres, near Niton, was, on a sudden, seen sinking and sliding towards the sea. Another of these landslips happened in the winter of 1810—1811, close to Bonchurch, and there was another in 1818. Sir James Clark is of opinion, that Torquay, in Devonshire, and the Undercliff, in the Isle of Wight, are the two places on the English coast best suited to persons threatened with consumption.

and sublime. A large and commodious hotel stands immediately at the head of the chasm. A short distance from this is the pretty village of Niton, at the foot of St Catherine's Down, where there is a comfortable little inn, which may serve as a resting place and centre of observation for days, as all the most beautiful and striking scenes of the island are within short distances.

Returning to Ventnor, a short distance to the east, is Bonchurch, a lovely spot abounding in tasteful villas. The little parish church is of Saxon or early Norman construction. The Undercliff commences at Bonchurch, and the tract between this place and Niton is by far the most interesting part of the island. A short way far on is Luccombe Chine, and about a mile beyond it is Shanklin Chine,* the most beautiful and most frequently visited of all those curious ravines, which form one of the most characteristic features of the coast of this island. Its appearance from below is as if the solid cliff had been rent in twain from top to bottom. The sides of the chasm present a striking contrast,—the one is almost perpendicular, with comparatively little vegetation,—the other is more shelving, and is shaded with tall trees or wild brushwood, and enlivened by some cottages most picturesquely situated. The descent to the Chine is by a rude winding path in the sea-cliffs, near a quiet little inn. Population of Ventnor, 3208.

To vary the road the tourist may return to Newport by the villages of Newchurch and Arreton. On the Downs of Arreton are two large sepulchral barrows, which are generally referred to the period of the Danish invasion.

Another delightful excursion, and the last we shall notice, is to the north-west of the island, in the direction of Freshwater Bay and the Needles.†

About four miles from Newport is a beautiful spot called Park Cross, which combines some of the finest features of a gentle rural landscape. A mile farther on is Swainston, the fine country seat of Sir John Simeon, Bart. which occupies the site of an ancient palace of the Bishops of Winchester. A little beyond is the small village of Calbourne, with its antiquated little church, and near it is Westover, the fine mansion of the Hon. W. H. A. A'Court Holmes. Passing through a succession of shelving downs and quiet valleys we reach the river Yar, on the opposite bank of which is Freshwater village, the birth-place of the celebrated philosopher, Dr. Robert Hooke. At the western extremity of the singular peninsula formed by the Yar are the Needles, and the stupendous rocks and cliffs of Scratchell's, Alum and Tolland Bays. The Yar takes its rise just behind a creek called Freshwater Gate, in the centre of Freshwater Bay, and running due north, right across this end of the island, falls into the Solent Strait at Yarmouth. Near Freshwater is Norton Lodge, the seat of Admiral Sir G. E. Hamond, Bart., G.C.B. In Freshwater Bay there are two very remarkable isolated rocks —one

* Sir Richard Worsley says the term "chine" is applied to the backbone of an animal, which forms the highest ridge of the body. Hence the word chine may be thought peculiarly expressive of a high ridge of land cleft abruptly down.

† The word Needles is supposed to be a corruption of *Nieder fels*, and signifies Undercliff, thus showing that precisely the same process took place with regard to the Needles that is now going on at St Catherine's Point—that these rocks were originally a landslip which has been washed by the action of the sea into its present shape.

of rather a conical form, and the other a bold rugged arch, which is now nearly 600 feet from the cliffs of the island, of which it once formed a solid part. Freshwater Cave is a romantic cavern, about 120 feet in depth. The view from the interior, looking seaward, is at once curious and beautiful. A little beyond it are three other caves of less magnitude. Scratchell's Bay is often visited by tourists. Its towering chalk precipices of the most dazzling whiteness are very remarkable for their narrow streaks of black flint, which make them resemble "a ruled sheet of paper." The great object of attraction, however, is an immense cave, which is entered by a magnificent arch 150 feet in height. The cliffs on this part of the coast are, in many places, 400 feet high, and afford shelter to the sea-fowl, which congregate here in prodigious numbers. Scratchall's Bay is bounded on the north by the celebrated Needle rocks, which are five in number, though only three of them now stand boldly out of the water. They have been formed by the action of the sea on the sharp point of land at the western end of the island. They are white, with a black base, and curiously streaked with the alternate strata of flints. The tallest of these rocks, which was about 120 feet high, disappeared in the year 1764, its base having been worn through by the continual action of the sea. It is evident, that, from the operation of the same cause, the present Needles will, at no distant period, wholly disappear, and that others will be formed in their stead out of the narrow extremity of the island. A lighthouse is built on the highest point of this western part of the island, at an elevation of 715 feet above the level of the sea. At the Needles the tide rises only eight feet, while at Cowes it rises fifteen feet. Northward of the Needles is Alum Bay, which derives its name from the circumstance of that mineral being frequently picked up on the beach. This bay presents one of the most striking scenes on this coast. The cliff on one side consists of a vast precipice of chalk ; on the other it is beautifully variegated by a succession of strata of different coloured sands and earths,—white, black, red, blue, and yellow ; in some parts pure and unbroken, and in others blending into every variety of tint.

A very interesting voyage may be made round the island, and the magnificent scenery just noticed is seen to much greater advantage from the sea than from the land. The order in which the various places along the coast present themselves in the course of this trip, may be learned by consulting the chart which accompanies this description.

PORTSMOUTH.

From Cowes the tourist may proceed to Portsmouth. The passage between these places seldom exceeds half an hour. Portsmouth is 73 miles from the General Post Office, London, by the old mail road; and 18 miles from Southampton. It stands on an island, divided from the mainland by a small creek or arm of the sea. This island, called Portsea, is about fifteen miles in circumference and contains nearly 5100 acres of land of great fertility. The Romans had a station at Porchester, on its northern shore ; and it is supposed that the Roman name for a harbour, Portus, has been transmitted to the modern Portchester, Portsea, Portsmouth, Portsdown, and Gosport. Portsmouth is first noticed in the Saxon Chronicle, A. D. 501. Its favourable situation as a naval arsenal led at an early period to the works that have since distinguished it. Richard I. granted a charter to the town ; and it has lately been ascertained that there was a naval station here in the reign of John. Portsmouth was burnt by the French in the time of Richard II. It was fortified by Edward IV., Richard III., and Henry VII. ; and in the reign of Henry VIII. became the principal station of the English navy. During the great civil war, the town was garrisoned for the Parliament. Great additions have been made to its fortification, especially in the reigns of Charles II., William III., and George III. ; and it is now believed to be impregnable. The ruins of Porchester Castle are fine (See p. 36.)

One of the great advantages of this place is that very fine anchorage known by the name of Spithead, which lies about half-way between the mainland and the Isle of Wight, but nearer to the latter. It is protected by the high land of the island from southerly winds, and from northerly and easterly winds by the main land. The entrance to the harbour of Portsmouth is very narrow, but with sufficient depth of water for the largest ships. The channels by which vessels approach the mouth of the harbour are commanded by batteries of such power that an enemy's fleet, however strong, would be annihilated before it could reach even the entrance. Within the narrow gut at the entrance, on one side of which is Portsmouth, and on the other side Gosport, the water spreads out into a wide basin, in which those ships of war that are under repair or preparing for sea are riding. About a mile and a-half from the entrance, the water branches off in various directions, and, by the help of the tide, is navigable to Farnham and to Porchester Castle, a pile of antiquity that will reward the curiosity of a visitor.

As the town of Portsmouth is surrounded with walls, the streets are, for the most part, narrow, and consist of houses of inferior appearance. Some of the buildings are of ancient date: one especially, in the High Street, is worthy of notice, as being the dwelling in which Villiers, Duke of Buckingham was assassinated by Felton in the reign of Charles I. The walls which surround the town are shaded by trees, and afford a good promenade for the inhabitants.

The parish church is a venerable object, and is said to have been originally erected in 1220 ; but the chancel is the only part left of the original building. Its interior is very beautiful. At the west end is the tower, added in 1693, which is 120 feet in height. The walls of the church are adorned with a variety of handsome monuments. In the parish register is to be seen the registration of the marriage of King Charles II. with the Infanta of Portugal, 22d May 1662.

Portsea stands to the north of Portsmouth, and contains the dockyard and the principal establishments connected with it. It is considerably larger than Portsmouth, and, like it, is strongly fortified. Outside the fortifications are Sandport and Southsea, extensive suburbs, containing some handsome houses.

The dockyard at Portsmouth may be regarded as the grand naval arsenal of Britain, and the head-quarters or general rendezvous of the British fleet. The dockyard, accordingly, is the largest in the kingdom, covering nearly 120 acres, and every possible attention is paid to its extension and improvement. On the land side it is completely separated from the town by a wall 14 feet high; and along the harbour it has a wharf-wall of nearly three-quarters of a mile. Strangers are admitted to the dockyard without any formal introduction.

In the centre of the wharf-wall, facing the harbour, is the entrance into the great basin, the dimensions of which are 380 by 260 feet, and its area 2¼ acres. Into this basin open four excellent dry docks; and on each side is another dry dock, all capable of receiving ships of the largest class. Besides these, there is a double dock for frigates. There are also six building-slips, two of which are capable of receiving the largest vessels. The dockyard contains all the offices necessary for the construction and equipment of vessels. The block machinery invented by the late Sir Marc Isambart Brunel (the engineer of the Thames Tunnel) is especially deserving of notice. The machinery, which is impelled by steam, is capable of producing 1400 blocks daily, and supplies the whole of the British navy. The number of men employed in Portsmouth dockyard during the war was considerably above 4000, of whom about 1500 were shipwrights and caulkers, the remainder were joiners, smiths, sawyers, sailmakers, ropemakers, &c. On the eastern extremity of the dockyard are the houses and gardens of the Commissioner and principal officers of the yard, the chapel, the Royal Naval College, and the School of Naval Architecture. The dockyard has several times suffered considerable injury from fire. In 1776, it was set on fire by the notorious incendiary, Jack the Painter, who was executed for the crime at Winchester in 1777. The gun-wharf, adjacent to the dockyard, is an immense arsenal, consisting of various ranges of buildings for the reception of military and naval stores and artillery. The small armoury which contains upwards of 20,000 stand of arms, is a spacious building, and the great object of admiration. The victualling department has recently been removed to the opposite side of the harbour. The expense of this depository is said to have amounted to half a million of money. The storehouses are of vast dimensions. A special object of curiosity at this establishment, is the machinery substituted for manual labour in making biscuit. A fine new steam corn-mill, recently built at an expense of L.76,000, is also an object worthy of attention. On the same side of the harbour is the noble building for the reception of sick and wounded seamen.

Portsmouth and Portsea, with their suburbs, contain nine places of worship in connection with the Establishment; and those of Protestant Dissenters are still more numerous. There are also a Roman Catholic chapel and a Jewish synagogue.

Portsmouth enjoys a considerable foreign and coasting trade. The gross amount of custom's duty collected in 1861 was £26,565.

The earliest known charter of the borough was conferred by Richard I., but the corporation is said to have been established by Henry I. It first returned members to Parliament 23d Edward I. The borough limits formerly included the town and parish of Portsmouth, but they were greatly extended by the Reform Act. The enlarged borough returns two members to Parliament.

The population of Portsmouth in 1831 was 8083 ; and of Portsea, 42,306 ; together, 50,389. In 1841, 53,058, and in 1861, 94,799.

On the western side of Portsmouth harbour is the market-town of Gosport. Early in 1840, a floating bridge was established, which plies across the harbour between these places every half hour. The distance is about a mile, and the passage is made under ten minutes. A second bridge is intended to be established. The population of the town of Gosport is 7789.

The tourist may return to London either by the branch railway from Gosport, which joins the South-Western Railway at Bishopstoke, or by the South Coast Railway, by way of Brighton. (See chapters xxxiv. and xxxv.)

At the distance of 17¾ miles from Portsmouth is the city of

CHICHESTER,

an Episcopal residence, and a place of very great antiquity. Chichester is situated about seven miles from the western extremity of the county of Sussex. Its distance from London is 62 miles, south-west by south. It is placed near an arm of the sea, on a gentle eminence, nearly surrounded by the little river Lavant. Its site is supposed to be identical with that of the Roman Regnum. At the period of the Conquest, it was conferred on Roger de Montgomery, Earl of Alençon, who built a castle within the city walls. This fort was demolished in the first year of Henry I., and no traces of it now remain but an artificial mount of moderate height. During the great civil war, Chichester was held for the King by Sir Edward Ford, High Sheriff of the county ; but it was taken by Sir William Waller in 1642, after a siege of ten days. The cathedral and bishop's palace, together with several of the churches, suffered severely from the ravages of the Parliamentary soldiers. The city remained in the hands of the Parliament during the remainder of the war ; and Algernon Sidney was governor in 1645.

The city consists principally of four spacious streets, named after the four cardinal points, and meeting in one common centre, at which is an ancient octangular cross, one of the most elegant structures of the kind in England. Chichester is surrounded by an ancient stone wall, for the most part in a state of excellent repair. Two public walks, planted with fine trees, have been formed on the artificial mound of earth thrown up within the walls. The cathedral was erected in the twelfth century, but has undergone frequent repairs. It is adorned with a beautiful steeple, and contains portraits of all the kings of England down to George I., and of the bishops of Selsea and Chichester till the Reformation

Here are also to be seen some finely carved oak stalls; the chantry of St. Richard, an exquisite specimen of Gothic workmanship; and a monument, by Flaxman, to the memory of the poet Collins, who was born in this city in 1720 or 1721, and died here in 1756. Chillingworth, famed for doubting, was chancellor of this diocese, and was buried in the cloisters in 1644. The other buildings worthy of notice are, the Bishop's Palace, the Deanery erected by Bishop Sherlock, the Council-room, the Guildhall, formerly the chapel of a monastery, and the Theatre. Chichester has seven parish churches, several meeting-houses, and charitable institutions. The present corporation is established under a charter of James I., but it has been a borough from time immemorial. It has sent two representatives to Parliament since 23d Edward I. A.D. 1295. Population, 8059.

At a short distance from Chichester is Goodwood, the splendid seat of the Duke of Richmond. It is of an oriel form, consisting of a centre and two wings. The principal front is 166 feet long, and each of the wings 106 feet. The park is nearly six miles in circumference, and is adorned with fine trees. Races are annually held here in July, and much resorted to. The course is singularly picturesque. The house contains a collection of valuable paintings and statues. The views from different parts of the grounds are rich and extensive.

Within the demesnes of Goodwood were lately the ruins of Halnaker House, an interesting structure of considerable antiquity; but of late years it fell so fast into decay, that it became unsafe to visit parts of the ruins, and the greater part of these have now been taken down and sold. Half a mile to the south of Halnaker are the ruins of the Priory of Boxgrove, founded by Robert de Haia in the reign of Henry I. The church and the refectory are the only remains of the conventual buildings.

About nine miles from Goodwood is the pleasant watering-place of Bognor.

Twelve miles from Chichester, on the London Road, is Midhurst, pleasantly situated near the Arun. It was an ancient borough by prescription, having returned representatives to Parliament since 4th Edward II. Since the Reform Bill, it has returned one member to Parliament. The population of the Parl. borough in 1851 amounted to 7021. Near the town, in the midst of a beautiful and extensive park, are the ruins of Cowdray House, once the magnificent seat of the noble family of Montagu. It was destroyed by fire 24th September 1793. The eighth Lord Montagu perished about the same time in the falls of Lauffen in Switzerland; and his only sister and heir married the late W. S. Poyntz, Esq., who erected a new house in the park, about a mile from the ruins. The latter is now in possession of the Earl of Egmont. From Midhurst a road leads by Haslemere, Godalming, Guildford, and Kingston to London.

About 6½ miles east of Midhurst, 12 north of Arundel, 14 north-east from Chichester, and 49 south-west from London, is the town of Petworth, situated on a branch of the Arun. The church contains the remains of many of the Percies, Earls of Northumberland. Close beside the town is Petworth House, the magnificent mansion of Gen. Wyndham, erected by the proud Duke of Somerset. The

CHICHESTER CATHEDRAL.

interior contains one of the finest collections of books, pictures, statues, and busts in the kingdom. Several of the rooms are hung with tapestry. Here is preserved the sword used by Hotspur at the Battle of Shrewsbury. The park wall is about twelve miles in circumference. The enclosure is beautifully undulated and graced with trees of the noblest growth. In front of the mansion is a sheet of water of considerable extent.

Eleven miles from Chichester is the town of Arundel, situated on the southern declivity of the South Downs, at the base of which runs the river Arun. It is 56 miles distant from London, and 21 from Brighton. The town was incorporated by charter of Elizabeth, and has returned members to Parliament since the reign of Edward I. The Reform Bill took away one of its representatives. Arundel is a place of great antiquity, and is mentioned in the will of Alfred the Great. At the Conquest, the earldom of Arundel was conferred upon Roger Montgomery, who made it his place of residence. From the Montgomerys it passed into the possession of the family of Albini ; from them to the Fitzalans ; and from them, by marriage, to the Howard family, its present possessors. The principal object of attraction is the splendid baronial castle, the residence of the Duke of Norfolk. It is of very remote antiquity, and must have existed in the Saxon times, as *Castrum Harundel* is assessed in Doomsday Book. It is a quadrangular Gothic building, enclosing about five acres and a-half of ground, the walls being from five to twelve feet in thickness, and the ground plan very nearly resembling that of Windsor Castle, with a circular keep in the middle, raised on a mount 110 feet in height from the fosse below on the outside. It proudly overlooks the whole castle, and is a conspicuous object from the surrounding country. It is in perfect preservation, but is almost entirely overgrown with ivy. The castle has undergone various sieges, during the last of which, in 1643–4, it suffered so severely from the Parliamentary troops under Sir William Waller, that it ceased to be the residence of its noble possessors till the time of Charles, eleventh duke, by whom it was restored to its ancient magnificence. Its internal arrangements and decorations are eminently calculated to exhibit the talent and taste of that nobleman. Among the many specimens of the arts with which it is adorned, are several curious paintings of the Howard family ; a large window of painted glass in the dining-room ; and the Baron's Hall, ornamented with a painted window of the signing of Magna Charta. Arundel Castle enjoys the peculiar privilege of conferring the dignity of earl on the possessor without any patent or creation from the Crown ; a privilege not enjoyed by any other place in the kingdom. The Church of St Nicholas, a handsome Gothic edifice, contains some splendid monuments of the Earls of Arundel. A noble town-hall has lately been erected by the Duke of Norfolk. The river Arun is famous for the rich and delicate mullet which it produces. It is connected with Portsmouth by means of the Porstmouth and Arundel Canal. Arundel is a bonding port. The trade is principally in timber, coal, and corn. The population is 2498. It returns one M.P.

South-east from Arundel, on the coast, is the watering-place of Worthing, which, from an obscure village, has within the space of a few years risen to great popularity as a sea-bathing place. It is 10 miles west of Brighton, 20 east of Chichester, and 57 south of London. It possesses the advantage of a fine, firm, level sand, affording the utmost facility for bathing, even in the most tempestuous weather; and opportunities for exercise, either on horse or foot, for several miles. The climate is so mild, that myrtles and fig-trees grow in it to great perfection. The scenery in the neighbourhood is remarkably picturesque. The town contains a chapel-of-ease and four dissenting chapels. The houses, though not large, are commodious; and it is well supplied with libraries, baths, and other accommodations for visitors. Population, 5805.

A few miles to the east of Worthing is the borough of New Shoreham, at the mouth of the Adur. It has the best harbour on this part of the coast, and carries on an extensive foreign and coasting trade. A noble suspension-bridge was built over the Adur in 1833, at the expense of the Duke of Norfolk, which has considerably shortened the distance between Worthing and Brighton. The church is an ancient and interesting building, supposed to have been erected in the twelfth century: it was repaired and beautified in 1822. The proportions and decorations of its interior are particularly elegant and graceful. The borough returned two members to Parliament from 23d Edward I. till 1770, when an act passed extending the right of election to all persons possessing freehold property to the annual value of L.2 within the rape of Bramber, except what is included in the borough of Horsham. New Shoreham is six miles distant from Brighton, with which town it is connected by the South Coast Railway. The population, in 1861, of the parl. borough was 32,622.

About six miles to the north of New Shoreham is Steyning, at the foot of a hill near the Adur. It was a borough by prescription, and returned two members to Parliament from the 26th Edward I., but is now disfranchised. The town has been recently much improved, both in buildings and in general appearance. The church is very ancient, and is considered a fine specimen of Norman architecture. In 1861 the population was 1620. In its immediate vicinity is the insignificant borough of Bramber, now also disfranchised. Here are some remains of a castle which seems to have once been a place of great strength and size.

About ten miles from Steyning is the town of Brighton.

ON RIGHT FROM LOND.	From Portsm.		From London.	ON LEFT FROM LOND.
	44½	From London Bridge to Brighton (p. 23).	50½	
		Tunnel under Windmill Hill, 200 yards.		
	43¾	Hove St.	51¼	
Portslade; on the Downs to the northward is the Devil's Dyke, a vast natural amphitheatre in the hills, much resorted to by visitors from Brighton, 5 miles distant. The summit of the adjacent hill commands a most extensive, splendid, and varied prospect.		The line here runs on an embankment, with a view of the English Channel on the left.		Ruins of Aldrington church, probably the site of the Roman *Portus Adurni*.
	40¼	Southwick St.	54¾	
Portslade House. Kingston House. Buckingham **House, H. C. Bridger, Esq.**	39½	Kingston St.	55½	**Kingston has a wharf, with some trade, and exhibits an active appearance.**
		The line here runs along the north side of the inlet which forms Shoreham harbour.		
Bramber, 3 miles distant, on the east bank; and, 1 mile beyond, Steyning, on the west bank, of the river Adur.	38½	Shoreham St.	56½	
		cr. river Adur.		
Sompting.	36¼	Lancing St.	58¾	
Broadwater.				
Cisbury Hill, 2½ miles distant, is the site of a Roman encampment.	34	**WORTHING** (p. 77).	61	
Highdown Hill, 4 miles to the north-west of Worthing (on the summit of which is the tomb of an eccentric miller), deserves a visit, on account of the beautiful prospect which it commands, and which includes Chanctonbury Ring, also the site of a Roman camp.		The station is but a short distance from the town. The entrance into the latter is remarkably pleasing.		**Heene.**
Castle Goring, Sir G. R. Brooke Pechell, Bart.	31½	**Goring St.**	63½	**Goring.** **East Preston.**
Michelgrove Park. Poling	29	Angmering St.	66	**Rustington.**

ON RIGHT FROM LOND.	From Portsm.		From London.	ON LEFT FROM LOND.
Badworth Park.	26½	Arundel and Littlehampton St.	68½	Littlehampton is a retired and pretty watering-place at the mouth of the Arun : it is 4 miles distant by road from Arundel.
The town of Arundel is 2 miles distant from the station, to and from which passengers are conveyed by omnibuses (see p. 77).		cr. river Arun.		
Arundel Castle (Duke of Norfolk).	25	Ford St.	70	
Tortington.				
Madehurst Lodge, 3½ miles.	23½	Yapton St.	71½	Barnham.
				Arundel and Portsmouth Canal.
Walberton House, R. Prime, Esq. Slindon Lodge, Countess of Newburgh. Dale Park, J. Abel Smith, Esq. Avisford House.				
	21	Bognor St.	74	
Aldingbourne House, R. Hasler, Esq.		Bognor, 3 miles distant, is a retired watering-place, frequented during the bathing season.		At Bognor is Arran Lodge.
Oving.				
Boxgrove Priory, 2½ miles.				
Halnaker House, 3 miles,				
Goodwood Park, 3 miles, Duke of Richmond (see p. 76).	18	Drayton St. (The point of departure for Goodwood).	77	
Rumbold's Wyke.				
Salt Hill, F. Smith, Esq.; Northlands; Oakwood, J. Baring, Esq.; Stoke House, Sir Henry Roper; 6 miles distant, West Dean House, Rev. V. Harcourt.	16	CHICHESTER (p. 75).	79	Fishbourne.
				Chichester Harbour.
Funtington.	13	Bosham St.	82	
Racton.				The village of Emsworth is situated on the north side of an extensive inlet of the coast, partly occupied by Thorney and Hayling Islands, the latter of which is resorted to by visitors during the summer.
Westborne;—1½ mile beyond, Woodlands, and Stanstead House.				
	9	Emsworth St.	86	

ON RIGHT FROM LOND.	From Portsm.		From London.	ON LEFT FROM LOND.
Warblington.	7	Havant St.	88	
Bedhampton. Farlington. Purbrook House. Two and a-half miles beyond Havant is branch railway (by Cosham) to Fareham, on the Gosport Junction line (see below).		Havant is a small and neat market town. Population, 2470. Along north side of Langston Harbour.		Adjacent to Portsmouth on the south-east is Southsea, resorted to as a bathing-place during the summer season.
Hillsea. Kingston.		Enter Portsea Island.		
Portsmouth Harbour. Porchester Castle, ruins.		PORTSMOUTH.	95	

XXXV. LONDON TO PORTSMOUTH (GOSPORT), BY SOUTH WESTERN RAILWAY, 90 Miles.

ON RIGHT FROM LOND.	From Gosport		From London.	ON LEFT FROM LOND
The railway between Bishopstoke and Gosport traverses a richly wooded and varied tract of country, adorned with numerous seats and villages.	16	From Waterloo Road to Bishopstoke St. (p. 56).	74	Leave main line to Southampton. Allington.
		Cross valley of Itchen by Allington viaduct.		Durley.
		⌒ cr. river Hamble.		
Botley.	10	Botley and Bishop's Waltham St.	80	Bishop's Waltham, 3½ miles (p. 40).
Funtley.		Tapnage Tunnel, 200 yards.		Wickham, ½ m. (p. 37); near it, Park Place, and Rookesbury, W. Garnier, Esq.
Blackbrook. Heathfield.		⌒ cr. Titchfield riv. Fareham Tunnel, 600 yards.		Uplands House. J. Beardmore, Esq.—Roche Court, Sir J. B. W. Smythe Gardiner, Bart.
Titchfield, 2 miles.	5	Fareham St. (p. 37).	85	From Fareham a branch railway proceeds eastward to Portsmouth, passing (by Porchester and Cosham) along the base of Portsdown, and round the east side of Portsmouth harbour. The distance from Fareham to Portsmouth by this route is 9 miles, making the total from London 94 miles.
Foxbury. Rowner. Alverstoke.		Along west side of Portsmouth Harbour.		
Haslar Hospital, for the reception of sick and wounded seamen: it is capable of accommodating 2000 men at one time.		GOSPORT. On opposite side of harbour is PORTSMOUTH.	90	Fleetland House; and, on opposite side of harbour, Cams House, H P. Delmé, Esq.

XXXVI. LONDON TO GUILDFORD AND FARNHAM, BY SOUTH-WESTERN RAILWAY, 41½ Miles.

ON RIGHT FROM LOND.	From Farnm.		From London.	ON LEFT FROM LOND.
Leave main line to Winchester and Southampton.	16½	From Waterloo Road to Woking St. (p. 51).	25	Village of Woking, 1½ miles. Ripley, 4 miles; near it, Ockham Place, Earl of Lovelace.
Worplesdon.		Cross small feeders of river Wey.		Send, 2 miles; near it, Sutton Place.—Stock Pl. Clandon Park, Earl Onslow, 2 miles.
	11	GUILDFORD (p. 34).	30½	Branch to Godalming, 4m.
Henley Park.		The line between Guildford and Ash is also used as part of the Reading, Guildford, and Reigate line (see p. 185).		Line of chalk hills, forming part of the North Downs, here called the Hog's Back, on the top of which runs the coach road between Guildford and Farnham. Near this road
Branch to Reading, passing by Farnborough St. on the South Western line (see p. 185).	4½	Ash St.	37	is Hampton Lodge (H. L. Long, Esq.)
		Cross coach road from Guildford to Farnham.		Poyle Park. Near Farnham is Moor Park (see p. 37, 38), and 1¾ mile distant, Waverley Abbey, the seat of the late
Farnham Castle, Bishop of Winchester.		FARNHAM (p. 37).	41½	Lord Sydenham.

XXXVII. LONDON TO SALISBURY, BY SOUTH-WESTERN RAILWAY, 96 Miles.

ON RIGHT FROM LOND.	From Salisb.		From London.	ON LEFT FROM LOND.
	22	From Waterloo Road to Bishopstoke St. (p. 56).	74	Leave main line to Southampton.
Hursley Park, Sir W. Heathcote, Bart., 2 miles. Amfield Wood.	20	Chandler's Ford St.	76	Chilworth, 1½ miles; near it, Chilworth House. Baddesley House.
Timsbury.		cr. Andover Can.		
Michaelmarsh. Mottisfont, Rev. Sir J. Barker Mill, Bart.	15	Romsey St.	81	For account of Romsey, see p. 104.
East and West Tytherley; near the latter, Tytherley House: beyond,		cr. river Anton, which continues to the right of the line for some distance.		
Norman Court, C. B. Wall, Esq.	11	Dunbridge St.	85	
East Grimstead.		Enter Wiltshire.		East Dean.
Clarendon Lodge, Sir F. H. H. Bathurst, Bart. (see p. 42).	7	Dean St.	89	West Grimstead. Alderbury House. Longford Castle (Earl
Laverstock House, a lunatic asylum.		SALISBURY (p. 42).	96	of Radnor), 1½ mile; and near it, New Hall.

ON RIGHT FROM LOND.	From Dorch.		From London.	ON LEFT FROM LOND.
Bannister House. Freemantle Park, Sir G. H. Hewett, Bart.	61	From Waterloo Road to Southampton (p. 56). Pass along shore of Southampton Water.	80	On opposite bank of Southampton Water, Marchwood House.
Shirley House, Sir C. H. Rich, Bart. Millbrook.	59	Blechynden St. cr. head of Southampton Water at mouth of river Test.	82	
Testwood House, Miss Bourne.	56	Redbridge St. Enter New Forest (see p. 58).	85	Eling.
Lyndhurst, 2¼ m. (p.63).	53	Lyndhurst Road St.	88	
	50	Beaulieu Road St. cr. Lymington Water.	91	Ashurst Lodge. Beaulieu (Duke of Buccleuch), 4 m. (p. 64). Brockenhurst Park.
Lyndhurst, 3¾ miles. Wilverley House.	45	Brockenhurst St. Cross Lymington and Ringwood turnpike road.	96	Lymington, 4 miles. Wallhampton, Rev. Sir G. Burrard, Bart.
Burley Park.	41	Christchurch Road St. Leave New Forest.	100	Christchurch, 7½ miles (p. 62), and near it Sand hills, W. Rose, Esq., and Heron Court, Earl of Malmesbury.
Uddings, E. H. Greathed, Esq.; and 2 m. beyond, Gaunt's House, Sir R. P. Glyn, Bart.; further to right, Horton Park.	35	Ringwood St. (p. 61). cross river Avon, and 3 m. beyond, enter Dorsetshire. cr. river Stour.	106	Holmesley Lodge.
Wimborne Minster, 1 m. distant, is a market-town of great antiquity, situated on the banks of the river Stour. A nunnery was established here in the beginning of the 8th century, on the site of which the minster, or collegiate church, was afterwards built. Ethelred, brother of King Alfred, was buried here. Pop. 1861, 2271. 2 m. beyond is Kingston Lacy. Merley House.	26	Wimborne St. Lytchet Common.	115	Canford Magna. Canford House, Sir I. B. Guest, Bart.
Henbury House, 2½ m. Lytchet Minster, Sir C. E. Scott, Bart. South Lytchet House. Charborough House, J. S. W. S. E. Drax, Esq., 6 m.	20	Poole Junction St. Pass along shore of Wareham Harbour. cr. river Piddle.	121	Branch to Poole, 2 m. and 5 m. from Poole, Studland, in the Isle of Purbeck.
	15	WAREHAM ST. Wareham is a small and ancient borough, situated between the rivers Frome	126	Corfe Castle, 4½ m. distant, is a small town situated in the district called the Isle of Purbeck. The

ON RIGHT FROM LOND.	From Dorch.		From London.	ON LEFT FROM LOND.
Stokeford.		and Piddle, across each of which is a bridge. It had formerly 8 churches, now reduced to 3. Here was formerly a priory, founded in the 8th century. Much of the clay dug in the Isle of Purbeck is brought to this place and forwarded to Poole, to be shipped for the Staffordshire potteries. Wareham returns one M.P. Pop. of Parl. bor., 6694.		castle from which its name is derived is now in ruins. The inhabitants are chiefly employed in the neighbouring clay-works and stone quarries. Corfe Castle is now included in the borough of Wareham. Pop., 1900. Near Corfe Castle is Encombe, a seat of the Earl of Eldon.
		Along valley of river Frome.		Holme. Isle of Purbeck. Bindon Abbey. Lulworth Castle, J. Weld, Esq., 3 miles.
	10	Wool St.	131	Weymouth, 10½ miles.
Moreton. Woodsford. Ilsington House. Kingston House. Stinsford.	5	Moreton St.	136	West Knighton. Whitcombe. Came Abbey.
		DORCHESTER (p. 44).	141	

XXIX. HASTINGS TO ASHFORD, CANTERBURY, AND MARGATE, BY RAILWAY, 71 Miles.

ON RIGHT FROM HAST.	From Margate.		From Hastings.	ON LEFT FROM HAST.
Fairlight. Bromham Park, Sir A. Ashburnham, Bart. Guestling. Icklesham.		Hastings		In the distance, Beauport, Sir C. Lamb, Bart., and beyond, Crowhurst Park.
Winchelsea Castle, in ruins.	62	WINCHELSEA St. (p. 29).	9	Udimore.
East Guldford.	60	RYE St. (p. 29).	11	Leesham House, and beyond, Church Place. Playden.
Snargate and Brenzatt.	53	Appledore St.	18	

ON RIGHT FROM HAST.	From Margate.		From Hastings.	ON LEFT FROM HAST.
Warehorn.				Kenardington.
	50	HAM STREET St.	21	Orlestone.
Mersham Hatch, Sir N. Knatchbull, Bart.				
	44	ASHFORD St.	27	Kingsworth.
		Here join the South Eastern Railway, and proceed to		
		MARGATE, as in p. 10.	71	

XL. HASTINGS TO BRIGHTON, CHICHESTER, SOUTHAMPTON, AND DORCHESTER, BY RAILWAY, 157 Miles.

ON RIGHT FROM HAST.	From Dorches.		From Hastings	ON LEFT FROM HAST.
Branch to Hayward's Heath, on the Brighton line (p. 24).	132½	From Hastings (St Leonards) to Lewes, as in p. 26.	24½	
Lewes and Hastings turnpike road.		The line between Lewes and Brighton passes between the ranges of chalk hills, with several deep cuttings.		Kingston.
Lewes race course.		Kingston Tunnel, 90 yards.		
Falmer.	128½	Falmer St.	28½	

ON RIGHT FROM HAST.	From Dorches.		From Hastings	ON LEFT FROM HAST.
Stanmer Park, Earl of Chichester.		Falmer Hill Tunnel, 502 yards.		
		Cross Brighton and Lewes turnpike road.		
The viaduct by which the Hastings branch joins the main line is deservedly admired: it consists of 27 arches, of which that which crosses the London road is elliptical, with a span of 50 feet, and at a height above the ground of 73 feet. The other arches are semicircular, and of 30 feet span. The total length of the viaduct is 400 yards.		Ditchling Road Tunnel, 60 yards.		
		Cross London road by curved viaduct, 330 yards long, and enter		Brighton Barracks.
	124½	BRIGHTON.	32½	
		Thence by South Coast Railway, past Worthing, Arundel, and Chichester, to		
Bedhampton, and Belmont Castle.	87	Havant St. (p. 81).	70	2½ miles beyond Havant, line to Portsmouth branches off (see p. 81).
Farlington. Purbrook House, 1 mile.		The line here runs along the base of Portsdown, 447 feet high (see p. 36).		Langston Harbour. Portsea Island.
	83	Cosham St.	74	Portsmouth, by road, 3½ miles.
Wimmering. Southwick Park, T. Thistlethwayte, Esq., 2 miles.	81	Porchester St.	76	Portsmouth Harbour. Porchester Castle, probably the site of a Roman station (see p. 73).
Nelson's Monument, on top of Portsdown.	78	Fareham St.	79	Cams House, H. P. Delmé, Esq.
		From Fareham to Bishopstoke (as in p. 81).		
Branch to Salisbury, 22 miles (see p. 82).	67	Bishopstoke St.	90	
	61	SOUTHAMPTON, (p. 56).	96	
		Thence to Dorchester, as in pp. 83-84.		
Slinsford.		DORCHESTER.	157	Came Abbey.

XLI. PORTSMOUTH (OR GOSPORT) TO SALISBURY, BY RAILWAY, 42 or 38 Miles.

ON RIGHT FROM PORTS.	From Salisb.		From Portsm.	ON LEFT FROM PORTS.
Railway to Chichester, 13 miles.	38	From Portsmouth to Cosham St.	4	Portsmouth Harbour.
	33	Thence to Fareham St. (p. 81).	9	Junction of line from Gosport, 5 miles.
	22	Thence to Bishopstoke St. (p. 81)	20	
		Thence to SALISBURY (p. 82).	42	
		(or by Gosport branch).	38	

XLII. LONDON TO RICHMOND, STAINES, AND WINDSOR, BY SOUTH WESTERN RAILWAY, 26 Miles.

ON RIGHT FROM LOND.	From Windsor.		From London.	ON LEFT FROM LOND.
	26	From Waterloo Road		
In the distance, Chelsea Hospital, on the further bank of the Thames. Battersea Park.	24	to Vauxhall St. (p. 50.)	2	A short distance before Wandsworth station, leave main line to Southampton. Handsome and extensive almshouses of the Fishmongers' Co. Wandsworth.
River Thames, and beyond, villas of Lady Shelley, Rt. Hon. L. Sulivan, &c.	21	Wandsworth St. Viaduct across river Wandle, 1000 feet.	5	
Putney College, lately used as a school for engineers, but now empty.	20	Putney St.	6	
On the opposite side of the Thames, Fulham Palace (Bishop of London.)		Putney, which is connected by a wooden bridge with Fulham, on the opposite bank of the Thames, was the birth-place of Thomas Cromwell, and also of Gibbon the historian. Pop. of parish, 6481		Putney Park, Earl of Ripon, and beyond, Wimbledon Common and Wimbledon Park, (Earl Spencer.) now subdivided for villas.
Barnes Elms Park. Barnes, ½ mile distant, is a pleasant village on the banks of the Thames.		Across Barnes Common to		East Sheen. Roehampton, 1 mile. The Priory (Rt. Hon. Sir J. L. Knight Bruce).
	19	Barnes St.	7	

ON RIGHT FROM LOND.	From Windsor.		From London.	ON LEFT FROM LOND.
Kew Gardens, 120 acres in extent, contain a choice collection of exotic plants, and are laid out with much taste. The conservatory is the largest in the empire. They are open to the public, and form a favourite place of resort to the people of the metropolis. Here are also a royal palace, the favourite residence of Geo. III., and an observatory.		A loop line here branches off on the right, and, crossing the Thames, rejoins the main line near Hounslow, after passing by Chiswick, Kew, Brentford, and Isleworth.		Sheen common; and, beyond, Richmond Park. In the latter are White Lodge, occupied by H. R. H. the Prince of Wales, and Pembroke Lodge, held for life by Lord John Russell.
Kew, 1½ mile.	17	Mortlake St.	9	
Kew Park.	16	RICHMOND, noted for the beauty of the surrounding scenery; the view from Richmond Hill is probably the finest in the vicinity of London. Here the Star and Garter Hotel occupies a remarkably fine situation, and is famous alike for the prospect it commands, and the dinners it affords. The view from the windows extends over a country almost unequalled in beauty, and rendered classic by Pope, and Thomson, and Horace Walpole. Richmond Park, one of the most charming of the Royal domains, is much resorted to by Londoners. This Park is 8 miles in circuit, and contains 2253 acres. Pop. of Richmond 7423.	10	Here the line skirts Richmond Green and the remains of the old palace of Richmond. Queensberry Villa, Sir J. B. Dundas, Bart.
Twickenham Park. St. Margaret's.		cr. river Thames, and enter Middlesex.		Richmond Bridge, and, beyond, on the Surrey side, Queensberry House
Isleworth and Sion House (Duke of Northumberland), 1¼ mile. Whitton Dean House. Kneller Hall. Whitton Park. Two miles beyond Twickenham station, the loop line from Barnes rejoins the main line. Hounslow, 1 mile distant (see p. 97). Population, 5760. Hounslow Heath.	14½	Twickenham St. Twickenham, a village on the Middlesex bank of the Thames, presents some pretty scenery, and possesses interest from having been the residence of Pope, whose villa has, however, been taken down; the grotto which he constructed in the grounds still remains, with an obelisk which he erected to the memory of his mother. Pope was buried in Twickenham church, and there is a monument to him in one of the galleries. Here too is Orleans House, occupied for some time by the late King of the French while Duke of Orleans, and first a refugee in this country. It is again the property of the Orleans family. Pop. of parish 8077.	11½	(Duke of Buccleuch.) Marble Hill, General Jonathan Peel. To Hampton Court, through Bushy Park 3½m. On the farther bank of the river, opposite Twickenham, is Ham House (Earl of Dysart). Bushy Park was occupied by his late Majesty, William IV., when Duke of Clarence, and afterwards by his widow, the late Queen Dowager. It contains a magnificent avenue of horse-chesnut trees, planted under the direction of William III. Strawberry Hill, 1 mile, once the residence of Horace Walpole (Earl of Orford), whose celebrated collection of paintings, sculptures, and various objects of interest, was dispersed by public auction in 1843, at the instance of the 7th Earl Waldegrave.
	11	Feltham St.	15	Hanworth Park, 1 mile. Kenton Park, 2 miles.

VIEW FROM RICHMOND HILL.

ON RIGHT FROM LOND.	From Winds.		From London	ON LEFT FROM LOND.
East Bedfont. Stanwell, $1\frac{3}{4}$ m.; and Stanwell Place, Sir J. Gibbons, Bart.				Feltham Park.
	8	Ashford St.	18	Ashford Lodge.
		Over Shortwood common.		
Staines is a market town on the banks of the Thames, near the western boundary of Middlesex. An ancient stone near the church, which bears the date of 1280, marks the limit of the jurisdiction possessed by the corporation of London over that portion of the Thames which is to the westward of the metropolis. Population of town, 2584.	$6\frac{3}{4}$	STAINES.	$19\frac{1}{4}$	Laleham, Earl of Lucan. Duncroft House. On the opposite side of the Thames is Egham, and near it the famous Runnemede; a short distance beyond which is an island in the river (called Magna Charta Island), where the great charter was signed in 1215.
		cr. river Coln, and enter Buckinghamshire.		
	4	Wraysbury (or Wyrardisbury) St.	22	Old Windsor.
Horton. Ditton Park, Duke of Buccleugh.	2	Datchet St.	24	The village of Datchet is situated amongst beautiful meadows. The admirer of Shakspeare will naturally associate with this place the immortal poet's matchless delineation of the amorous Falstaff, and the humorous retaliation of the "Merry Wives of Windsor."
		cr. river Thames.		
Eton, (see pp. 90 and 98.)		WINDSOR.	26	

Windsor is an ancient borough situated on the south bank of the Thames, 16 miles east of Reading, and 22 miles distant from London by the road through Brentford, Hounslow, and Colnbrook. It possesses an ancient church, a theatre, barracks, and a good free school, and returns two members to Parliament. The town has no manufactures, and possesses in itself little to interest the stranger; but the attractions of the adjacent castle make it the frequent resort of visitors, especially since the facility of communication afforded by the opening of the railways. Population, 9520.

Windsor Castle has been the principal seat of British royalty for nearly eight centuries. The Saxon kings had a palace at Old Windsor long previous to the Conquest. The present castle was founded by William the Conqueror, but was almost rebuilt by Edward III., with the assistance of the celebrated William of Wykeham, who was made clerk of the works. Great alterations were made by Sir Jeffry Wyatville during the reign of George IV. St George's Chapel is a splendid specimen of florid Gothic architecture. It contains the stalls of the Knights of the Garter; and here the ceremony of installation takes place. At the east end of the chapel is the royal vault, where the remains of George III. and his Queen, George IV., the Princess Charlote, the Duke of Kent, the Duke of York, William IV. and his Queen, &c., are deposited. Edward IV. and his Queen, Henry VI., Henry VIII. and Jane Seymour, and Charles I., are also interred here. The monument to the Princess Charlotte is particularly fine, and the tombs of the Beaufort family are very gorgeous. The keep or round tower in the centre of the castle is perhaps the most remarkable part of the building. Here James I. of Scotland was confined. The terrace is supposed to be the noblest walk of its kind in Europe. A fine flight of steps leads from the east terrace to the new garden, a beautiful spot, adorned with many statues, both of bronze and marble. The little park which extends round the east and north sides of the castle is about four miles in circumference. Here is the tree supposed to be "Herne's Oak," immortalised by Shakspeare. The great park is situated on the south side of the castle, and includes the beautiful avenue of trees, nearly three miles in length, called the Long Walk. It is terminated by the colossal equestrian statue of George III., in bronze, by Westmacott. The drive through the park to Virginia Water is exceedingly striking. The interior of the Castle is remarkably magnificent. The corridor or gallery, 520 feet in length, which leads along the south and east sides of the court, and is richly adorned with bronzes, marbles, pictures, &c., excites great admiration. The state-rooms are fitted up in a very superb style, and the different apartments are adorned by a great number of paintings by the most eminent masters. These can be seen by any one possessing an order, which is easily procurable in London, at the shop of Messrs. Colnaghie, printsellers, Pall-Mall, East. Her Majesty's private apartments can only be seen during the absence of the Court from Windsor, by virtue of a special order from the Lord Chamberlain.

Half a mile from Windsor is Frogmore, the favourite residence of Her late Majesty Queen Charlotte, and of Her Royal Highness the late Duchess of Kent. Six miles distant is Ascot Heath, where races are held annually in June, under the especial patronage of royalty.

Opposite to Windsor, on the north side of the Thames, is Eton, celebrated for its college, which was founded in 1440, by Henry VI., for the education of 70 scholars. Besides these, there are generally several hundreds of the sons of the nobility and gentry receiving their education there. The total number has usually amounted to about 500. The chapel is a fine old Gothic structure, containing a monument to Sir Henry Wotton, who was long provost of the college. At the west end of the ante-chapel there is a beautiful marble statue of the founder, Henry VI., in his royal robes; and there is another statue of the founder, in bronze, in the centre of the principal court. The library contains a curious and valuable collection of books, an excellent assortment of Oriental MSS., and some beautifully illuminated missals. Eton was until lately the scene of a curious triennial pageant, called the Eton Montem, which is now abolished. Amongst other great men who were educated at Eton, may be enumerated Sir Robert Walpole, Harley Earl of Oxford, Lord Bolingbroke, Earl Camden, the famous Earl of Chatham, Outred the mathematician, Boyle the philosopher, Lord Lyttelton, Gray, Horace Walpole, West, Waller, Fox, Canning, the Marquis of Wellesley, Hallam the historian, and the Duke of Wellington. Pop. of parish (including the college) 3122.

XLIII. LONDON TO BATH THROUGH MAIDENHEAD, READING, NEWBURY, MARLBOROUGH, and DEVISES, 107½ Miles.

ON RIGHT FROM LOND.	From Bath.		From London.	ON LEFT FROM LOND.
Hyde Park, site of the Crystal Palace. Kensington Palace (p. 40.)	105¾	Kensington.	1½	Old Brompton.
Holland House, Lord Holland, (p. 40).	103¼	Hammersmith.	4	
Gunnersbury House, the Baron Rothschild.	102¼	Turnham Green.	5	Chiswick House, Duke of Devonshire. Here the famous horticultural fetes were held.
Sion Hill House, and Boston House. Wyke House. Osterley Park, Earl of Jersey.	100¼	Brentford. Here are the enormous distilleries of the late Sir Felix Booth, Bart.	7	Richmond, 2½ miles distant. (See p. 88.) Sion House, Duke of Northumberland, lies low, but is a very massive and extensive building. Its enormous size conveys an idea of grandeur, which excites a peculiar feeling of respect. The park and grounds are laid out with great taste, and ornamented with a profusion of wood and water. The house is said to contain 365 windows, to equal in number the days in a year.
Spring Grove.	98¼	Smallbury Green.	9	
	97½	Hounslow. (The road here leads to Staines on the left).	9¾	Worton House. Whitton Dean. Whitton Park.
Heston and Heston House. Cranford Park.	95	Cranford Bridge.	12¼	Sunbury, 3½ miles. Hatton.
Harlington. Sipson. Harmondsworth.	93½	The Magpies.	14	Heath Row. Stanwell Place, Sir J. Gibbons, Bart.
	92	Longford. cr. river Coln.	13½	
Iver Grove. Langley Lodge, J. Jackson, Esq. Langley Marsh, and at a little distance, Langley Park.	90¼	Colnbrook. To Windsor by Datchet, 3¼ miles.	17	Ditton Park, Duke of Buccleugh. Datchet.
Wexham. Stoke Place. Baylis House (Lord Godolphin) once the seat of Philip Dormer, Earl of Chesterfield. It is now used as a Roman Catholic School.	86¾	Slough. 1 mile distant is Stoke Poges, where the poet Gray is buried, and a monument is erected to his memory in Stoke Park, one of the finest seats in Bucks, and the property of the Rt. Hon. H. Labouchere. It formerly belonged to the descendants of Wm. Penn of Pennsylvania.	20½	Upton. Chalvey Grove. Burnham Grove. Eton and Windsor.

ON RIGHT FROM LOND.	From Bath.		From London.	ON LEFT FROM LOND.
Farnham Royal. Burnham. Hitcham. Taplow. Taplow House, and at a distance, Formosa Place, Sir G. Young, Bart; Hedsor Lodge, Lord Boston, and Dropmore.	86¼	**Salt-Hill,** the scene of the Eton Montem till its suppression in 1848. **cr. the Thames.**	21	Dorney. Weston. Bray. From Maidenhead Bridge may be seen Cliefden, a seat of the Duke of Sutherland. The first Cliefden House was built by Villiers, Duke of Buckingham. Both it and its successor were destroyed by fire.
4½ m. distant is Hurley Place, an ancient mansion, in a vault below which the principal papers which produced the Revolution of 1688 were signed. Stubbings, H. Skrine, Esq Hall Place, Sir G. E. C. East, Bart. Bear Hill. Bear Place.	80¼	MAIDENHEAD. At the Greyhound Inn in this town, Charles I. took leave of his family. Pop. 3895. **Maidenhead Thicket.**	27	St. Ives Place. Henden House. Holyport. Braywick Lodge. Shottesbrook Park, A. Vanisittart, Esq. Waltham Place. St. Lawrence, Waltham.
Wargrave. In its church is the monument of T. Day, author of Sandford and Merton.	75¼	**Hare Hatch.**	32	
	73¼	**Twyford.** Here is a small part of Wilts. **cr. river Loddon.**	34	
Shiplake House, J. Phillimore, Esq. Holme Park, Robert Palmer, Esq.				Stanlake. Whistley Park. Hurst Park. Bulmershe Court, J. Wheble, Esq.
Caversham Park. An elegant modern mansion, which formerly belonged to Earl Cadogan, stood in this park, was burned down a few years ago. The present mansion, built for Mr. Crawshay, surpasses either of its predecessors. Charles I. was confined in Old Caversham House, after the affair of Holmby. Prospect Hill.	68¼	READING, the capital of Berks, is situated on the Kennet, and carries on a considerable trade in flour. Arch. Laud, Merrick the poet, and Belgrave the mathematician, are natives of Reading. It returns two M.P.'s. Pop. 25,045. **cr. river Kennet.** Roads here lead to Wallingford on the left, and to Basingstoke on the right.	39	White Knights, a beautiful seat which belonged to the Duke of Marlborough, has now disappeared, but the American Gardens remain. Maiden Erlegh, E. Golding, Esq. Whitley Park. Coley Park, J. B. Moncke, Esq. 7 m. dist. Strathfieldsaye, Duke of Wellington. Southcot. 12 m. Bramshill Ho., Rev. Sir W.H. Cope, Bart.
Tilehurst.	65¾	Calcot Green.	41½	
Calcot Pa., J. Blagrave, Esq. Englefield House, R. P. Benyon de Beauvoir, Esq.	63¼	Theale.	44	Sulhampstead House; and 3 miles distant, Oakfield.

ON RIGHT FROM LOND.	From Bath.		From Lond.	ON LEFT FROM LOND.
Benham House.	62	Jack's Booth.	45¼	Sulhampstead Bannister. Padworth,
Benham. Woolhampton House, Viscount Falmouth. Midgham House.	58	Woolhampton. Midgham.	49¼	Aldermaston Park, W. Congreve, Esq. Wasing House. Crookham House.
Dunstan Park.	54¼	Thatcham.	53	Greenham House, J. A. Croft, Esq.
Shaw was the head-quarters of Charles I. at the last battle of Newbury. In the wainscot of one of the rooms is a hole, said to be that of a musket-shot fired through one of the windows at the King, while standing near it. Near Speen, Donnington Castle, famous for its resistance to the Parliament, and for being the residence of Chaucer during the latter part of his life.	51¼	NEWBURY. This town was formerly famous for its woollen manufactures, which gave celebrity to John Winchcomb, commonly called Jack of Newbury. It was the scene of two dreadful actions between Charles and the Parliament, the King commanding in person on both occasions. Population, 6161.	56	Church Speen. Benham Place. Hampstead Park,
Fleet Park. Avington. Denford House, G. H. Cherry, Esq. Chilton Lodge.	47¼	Halfway House. cr. river Kennet.	60	Kintbury. Barton Court, Admiral J. W. D. Dundas.
Chilton House, To Oxford, 30 miles.	42¾	Hungerford is situated on the Kennet, and carries on a considerable trade by means of that river and the Avon canal. In the Town-hall is preserved the Hungerford horn, given along with a charter by John of Gaunt to this town. cr. Kennet and Avon Canal.	64½	Hungerford Park. Inglewood House.
Somerset Hospital, so called from its founder, the Duchess of Somerset, for the accommodation of the widows of 30 clergymen, and of 20 laymen.	39¾	Froxfield, Wilts.	67½	
	38¼	Cross Ford.	69	Little Bedwin.
Littlecott Park, E. W. L. Popham, Esq. Ramsbury Manor, Sir R. Burdett, Bart.	35½	Savernake Forest, at the extremity of which, on the left, is Tottenham Park, Marquess of Aylesbury, who is also the proprietor of the forest, remarkable as the only one in the kingdom belonging to a subject. In the park was erected in 1781 by Thomas, Earl of Aylesbury, a column in honour	71¾	Great Bedwin, 2¾ miles, a small town, of very ancient origin. The church is an ancient and curious structure, and contains many interesting monuments. Pop., 2263.

ON RIGHT FROM LOND.	From Bath.		From Lond.	ON LEFT FROM LOND.
		of his uncle, Charles, Earl of Aylesbury, from whom he inherited the estate.		
To Wootton Basset, 17 m. To Swindon, 11 m.	$32\frac{3}{4}$	MARLBOROUGH, an ancient town on river Kennet, and consisting principally of one street. It is chiefly supported by its market and road trade. Its remarkable buildings are, St Mary's Church, St Peter's, the Market House, and a commodious prison, employed as a county bridewell and gaol. The Castle Inn, (on site of the Castle, was once the residence of the Earl of Hertford, and in its grotto, Thomson composed his Seasons. It now constitutes a portion of the building of Marlborough College, incorporated by Royal Charter in 1845. Marlborough returns two M.P. Pop. 4893.	$74\frac{1}{2}$	To Andover, $23\frac{1}{4}$ m. Manton. Rainscombe House. Oare House, Rev. M. Goodman. Stowell Lodge,
	$30\frac{1}{4}$	Fyfield.	77	Lockeridge House.
		Overton.		Kennet House.
	$27\frac{1}{2}$	West Kennet.	$79\frac{3}{4}$	
	$26\frac{3}{4}$	Silbury Hill. Here are the remains of a British barrow: it is 170 feet high, its diameter at the base is 500 feet, at the top 105 feet. Near this place also, (at Avebury) there are the remains of one of the most gigantic Druidical monuments in the world.	$80\frac{1}{2}$	
Calne is an ancient borough, returning 1 M. P. Pop. 5128. Two miles distant is Bowood, the noble mansion of the Marquis of Lansdowne. 2 m. from Calne, in a different direction, is Compton Basset, the seat of G. H. W. Heneage, Esq.	26	Beckhampton Inn. A road here leads to Bath, through Calne, and Chippenham, $24\frac{3}{4}$ m.	$81\frac{1}{4}$	Four miles from Chippenham is Corsham House, the seat of Lord Methuen, celebrated for its choice collection of pictures.
	$22\frac{1}{2}$	Wansdyke.	$84\frac{3}{4}$	Bishop's Cannings. South Broom House, R. Parry Nisbet, Esq.
Roundway Park, Edward Colston, Esq. To Chippenham, $10\frac{1}{4}$ m. Rowde.	$18\frac{1}{2}$	DEVIZES is a borough of considerable antiquity, situated in the centre of Wiltshire. The church of St. John's is interesting on account of its various specimens of architecture. Devizes returns two M. P. Pop. 1851, 6554.	$88\frac{3}{4}$	Potterne. Eastwell, T. H. Grubbe, Esq. To Ludgershall, 20 m. To Salisbury, 22 m. To East Lavington, 4 m. and beyond, West Lavington, Lord Churchhill. Poulshot.

ON RIGHT FROM LOND.	From Bath.		From London.	ON LEFT FROM LOND.
		cr. Kennet and Avon Canal.		
Bromham. Sloperton Cottage, the residence of Thomas Moore.	15½	Summerham Bridge.	91¾	
To Chippenham, 7¼ m. Between Melksham & Chippenham is Laycock Abbey, the seat of W. H. Fox Talbot, Esq.	11¼	**Melksham** consists of one long street, and the houses are chiefly constructed of freestone. In the vicinity are two mineral springs, whose waters have attracted much popularity.	96	**Seend.** Seend Lodge, W. H. Ludlow Bruges, Esq. To Bradford, 6 m.
		Shaw Hill.		Shaw House. Cottles House.
Neston, J. B. Fuller, Esq.	7¾	Atford.	99½	Monkton Farleigh.
Box. Shockerwick.	4¼	**Kingsdown Hill.**	103	
	3¼	Bathford, Somerset. A little farther on right, the Roman road to Cirencester.	104	Warleigh House, H. Skrine, Esq. Bathford House. Claverton, and Claverton Ho., G. Vivian, Esq.
Swainswick. Charlcombe.		**Bath Easton.**		Bathampton.
		BATH.	107¼	Bathwick.

Bath, a city in Somersetshire, is noted for the beauty of its buildings. These, consisting almost entirely of stone, present a finer appearance than those of any other city in England. The river Avon runs through the midst of it. There is an elegant bridge over the river, and it has been made navigable as far as Bristol. Bath owes its celebrity to its medicinal springs. These must have been discovered very early, as we find that the Romans had fixed a station, and erected baths here A.D. 43. Many of these have been discovered in a very perfect state. Their reputation has continually increased since the middle of the 16th century, and invalids now resort to them from all quarters.* The principal springs are those called the King's and Queen's. The temperature of the coolest is 97°, of the warmest, 117° of Fahrenheit. The medicinal properties in all are nearly the same. Bath is also frequented by great numbers for pleasure as well as health. For these the numerous public buildings and hotels afford ample accommodation. Of the former the pump-room, beside the King's Bath, and the Assembly Rooms, said to be the best adapted for the purpose of any in the kingdom, are the most conspicuous. The Abbey Church, or Cathedral, is a fine building. It was founded by Bishop King in 1495, but not finished till 1582. It suffered much on the dissolution of religious houses, but was restored by Bishop Montague in 1606. It has lately been repaired. In the east end of the church Prior Birde's chapel presents a beautiful specimen of tracery. Amongst the numerous monuments, with which in fact the church is encumbered, are those of Sir W. Waller,

* Pepys, with all his peculiar quaintness, describes a visit he paid to Bath in 1668. See Diary, vol. iv., pp. 468-474. Ed. 1851.

the Parliamentary General, and his wife; Quin the actor; Beau Nash, styled king of Bath in his day, and the great improver of the place;* and Dr. Haweis, one of the founders of the Church Missionary Society, claim attention. In a cemetery formed out of his own grounds, lies William Beckford, the author of Vathek. The Guildhall, situated in the High Street, is a noble building. Close to it is the market, which is abundantly supplied with provisions of every kind, but especially with fish. In Bath there are twenty-four churches and chapels, belonging to the Established Church, and sixteen Dissenting chapels. There are several hospitals, alms-houses, and charity schools. There is a well managed theatre also. Four newspapers are published here. The city is divided for municipal purposes into seven wards, and is governed by a mayor, fourteen aldermen, and forty-one councillors. It returns two members to Parliament. Bath and Wells form a diocese extending over the county of Somerset, and containing 388 parishes. The Thames and Severn are united by a canal called the Kennet and Avon, which passes from Bath to Newburgh. Population, 52,528.

About 8 miles from Bath is Bradford, the inhabitants of which are chiefly engaged in the manufacture of fine broad cloths. The church is an ancient edifice containing several handsome monuments. Pop. 4291. About three miles farther is Trowbridge, of which Crabbe the poet was rector. There is a monument to his memory in the church. It is celebrated for the manufacture of the best kerseymeres in the kingdom. Population, 9626.

Five miles from Trowbridge, and 14¼ from Bath, is Westbury, a town of considerable antiquity, with a venerable church containing monuments. Pop. of parl. bor., 6495. Some distance beyond Westbury is Erle Stoke Park, the seat of Lord Broughton. Nine miles from Trowbridge, in another direction, and 13 from Bath, is the large and populous town of Frome, situated on the river of the same name. It is noted for its ale. The inhabitants are chiefly employed in the woollen manufacture. It returns one member to Parliament. Near Frome is Marston Hall, the seat of the Earl of Cork and Orrery. Pop. of town, 9522.

Nearly 12 miles from Frome, and 18¾ from Bath, is Shepton Mallet, which carries on an extensive manufacture of knit-stockings and woollen goods. The market cross, erected in 1500, is a curious structure, consisting of five arches supported by pentagonal columns, and adorned with sculpture. Population, 4868.

About 4½ miles from Shepton Mallet, 18 from Bath, and 17 from Bristol, is the ancient city of Wells, forming a bishop's see jointly with Bath. It derived its origin from a collegiate church erected in 704. The cathedral is a spacious Gothic structure, and is reckoned one of the most splendid specimens of this order of architecture in England. The west front, in particular, is much admired. The Cathedral is open to the public. In the Episcopal palace Bishop Kidder and his lady were killed by a portion of the building falling in during the great storm in 1703. The chapter house and St. Cuthbert's Church are also worth notice. Wells returns two members to Parliament. Annual races are held here. Pop. 4648

* See Oliver Goldsmith's Life of Nash.

About 5½ miles from Wells is the town of Glastonbury, where stood the famous Abbey of that name, one of the richest and most powerful monastic institutions in England. The last abbot was hanged on account of his refusal to surrender the Abbey to Henry VIII. The ruins of the monastery contain the ashes of King Arthur, King Edgar, and many illustrious nobles and prelates, but there are now no remains of their monuments. The only parts of the monastery in tolerable preservation are the chapel of St. Joseph, and the abbot's kitchen. The old cross in the centre of the town has been replaced by an elegant structure. The church of St John is a handsome building, surmounted by a beautiful tower, and that of St Benedict is a venerable edifice erected by Abbot Beer. On a hill north-east of the town is the Tor or St Michael's Tower, the only remaining portion of a church and monastery which formerly stood there. The George Inn was formerly an hospital for pilgrims to the shrine of St Joseph. Population 3496

XLIV. GREAT WESTERN RAILWAY TO BATH AND BRISTOL, 118¼ Miles.

ON RIGHT FROM LOND.	From Bristol.		From London.	ON LEFT FROM LOND.
Proceeding from the terminus, the traveller passes the beautiful grounds of the Kensal Green Cemetery, enclosing a space of 50 acres. Here the Duke of Sussex and the Princess Sophia, two of Sir Walter Scott's daughters, Sydney Smith, Allan Cunningham, Tom Hood, Joseph Hume, &c., are buried.		Paddington Station is situated near the end of Praed Street. It is every way suited for the purpose to which it is appropriated; and, from its proximity to the canal, affords every facility for conveying goods to the Thames.		Kensington Gardens and Palace. Acton, a suburban parish. Berrymead Priory. About a mile from the station, and upon the left, is Ealing, a suburban outwork of the metropolis.
There is a tower on Hanger Hill which commands a most extensive and charming view. Hanwell Park.	112¾	Ealing Station. At some distance from the station is the Wharncliffe Viaduct, so called in compliment to Lord Wharncliffe, Chairman of Committee of House of Lords on the Incorporation Act. The erection is over the Brent, and is 900 feet long.	5½	Ealing Park. The Middlesex Lunatic Asylum is a magnificent building, remarkable both for the convenience of its arrangement and the enlightenment of its system.
	111	Hanwell Station.	7¼	Heston, 2 miles. Brentford, 3 m. Here Edmund Ironside defeated the Danes in 1016. The Chapel of Ease for New Brentford reckoned among its former incumbents the celebrated philologist, John Horne Tooke. Pop. 9521.
Southall Park.	109¼	Southall Station. The railway now crosses the Grand Junction Canal.	9	Hounslow, famous for being the scene of a tournament preparatory to the obtaining of Magna Charta. Also for being the spot where the forces of Charles I. and those of the Parliament frequently encamped. Pop. 5760.
Hayes, and beyond, Hillingdon House (The Count De Salis).				

ON RIGHT FROM LOND.	From Bristol.		From London.	ON LEFT FROM LOND.
At a distance on the right is Uxbridge, an ancient borough, and polling place for Middlesex. It is famous for its corn-market. It gives the title of Earl to the Marquis of Anglesey. Pop. 3815.	105¼	**West Drayton Station.** On the right Iver Court and Iver Grove.	13	Near Arlington are some remains of D'Oyley House, the seat of the famous Henry St. John Viscount Bolingbroke. Staines. At Runnemede, near Egham, Magna Charta was forced from King John in 1215.
Chalfont St. Giles where Milton finished Paradise Lost.	102¼	Langley Station.	16	Colnbrook, a small ancient market-town.
Stoke, Pa. Rt. Hon. H. Labouchere. Stoke Pogis, the spot where Gray finished several of his poems. Here Sir Ed. Coke entertained Elizabeth in 1601, and presented her with jewels to the amount of £1000. And at a distance Beaconsfield, the residence of Waller and Edmund Burke. Dropmore Lodge. Hedsor Lo. Ld. Boston.	100	Slough Station. Slough is distinguished as the residence of Sir John Herschell, whose father, the late Sir William Herschell, also made many of his most important discoveries here. (See also p. 91.)	18¼	Ditton Park, (Duke of Buccleugh.) famous for its ancient oaks. Eton.* (See also p. 90). Windsor, to which a branch line, 3 miles in length, is now opened. (See p. 89.)

* Eton College was founded in 1440, by Henry VI., for the education of 70 scholars. Besides these, there are generally several hundreds of the sons of the nobility and gentry receiving their education there. The total number has usually amounted to about 500. The chapel is a fine old Gothic structure, containing a monument to Sir Henry Wotton, who was long Provost of the College. At the west end of the ante-chapel is a beautiful marble statue of the founder, Henry VI. and in the centre of the principal court is another in bronze. The library contains a curious and valuable collection of books, an excellent assortment of Oriental MSS., and some beautifully illuminated missals. Eton was till lately the scene of a curious triennial pageant, called the Eton Montem. It has been discontinued since 1848. Among the many great men who were educated at Eton may be mentioned, Sir Robert Walpole, Harley Earl of Oxford, Lord Bolingbroke, Earl Camden, the famous Earl of Chatham, Outred the mathematician, Boyle the philosopher, Lord Lyttelton, Gray, Horace Walpole, West, Waller, Fox, Canning, the Marquis Wellesley, Hallam the historian, and the Duke of Wellington. Pop. 2840.

Two m. from Slough Station is the town of Windsor, on the Thames, having an ancient church, a theatre, barracks, and a good free school. It returns 2 M.P. Pop. 1861, 9520.

Windsor Castle has been the principal seat of British Royalty for nearly eight centuries. The Saxon kings had a palace at Old Windsor long previous to the Conquest. The present castle was founded by William the Conqueror, but was almost rebuilt by Edward III., with the assistance of the celebrated William of Wykeham, who was made clerk of the works. Great alterations were made by Sir Jeffry Wyatville during the reign of George IV. St. George's Chapel is a splendid specimen of florid Gothic architecture. It contains the stalls of the Knights of the Garter; and here the ceremony of installation takes place. Beneath it are the remains of Edward IV. and his Queen, Henry VI., Henry VIII. and Jane Seymour, Charles I., George III. and Queen, George IV., the Princess Charlotte, Duke of Kent, Duke of York, William IV., &c. The keep or round tower in the centre of the castle is perhaps the most remarkable part of the building. Here James I. of Scotland was confined. In the little park is a tree supposed to

ON RIGHT FROM LOND.	From Bristol.		From London.	ON LEFT FROM LOND.
Burnham Grove. Taplow.				Burnham Abbey.
At a distance of 10 miles is High Wycombe, the handsomest town in Buckinghamshire. It has sent 2 members to Par. since Edward I. It gives the title of Earl and Baron to the Marquis of Lansdowne. Wycombe Park, Sir G. H. Dashwood, Bart.; and Wycombe Abbey, Lord Carington. Haywood Lodge. Shottesbrook, A. Vansittart, Esq.	95¾	**Maidenhead Station.** Maidenhead is a market-town in Berks. It was anciently called South Arlington, and subsequently Maidenhithe. Besides the Great Western viaduct over the Thames, there is a magnificent bridge of 13 arches, erected at an expense of £20,000.	22½	Bray, famous for its vicar. This worthy gentleman's conscience possessed in a peculiar degree the quality of accommodating itself to circumstances. He changed his religion three times. On being reproached as a turncoat, he used to say, "Nay, nay, I always keep to my principles, which are these—to live and die Vicar of Bray." Stubbings, H. Skrine, Esq.; and beyond, Hall Place, Sir G. E. C. East, Bart.
White Waltham, the birth-place of Hearne the antiquary. Two miles distant is Wargrave, and 3 miles beyond it is Henley-upon-Thames, a place of considerable antiquity, and famous as the place whence the adherents of Charles I. were driven out by Earl of Essex.	87½	**Twyford Station.** Stanlake House. Woodley Green. Bulmarshe Court, J. Wheble, Esq. White Knights, formerly a seat of the great Duke of Marlborough, now demolished.	30¾	
Holme Park, R. Palmer, Esq. Archbishop Laud, Merrick the Poet, and Blagrave the mathematician, were natives of Reading; and here Milman the poet, and the late Sir Thomas N. Talfourd, author of Ion, &c. were educated. Caversham Park (G. Crawshay, Esq.) Here	82½	**Reading Station.** Reading, a market, borough, and county town in Berks. It is a place of great antiquity, having existed in the time of the Saxons. It was frequently taken and retaken during civil wars in 1643. The earliest charter extant is that of Henry III. It has returned two members since 23d of Edward I.	35¾	Reading is famous on many accounts. It was taken by the Danes in the ninth century, after they had defeated Alfred the Great. It acted a prominent part in the expulsion of John, Charles I. and James II. Pop. 25,045 Some of the houses in Reading are constructed of timber, but greater part of the old town is of brick. In the suburbs are many handsome houses. Here are some remains of an abbey for Benedictines, founded by Henry I. in 1112. Reading is well furnished with charitable and religious institutions. Whitley Park. Three-mile-Cross.

be "Herne's Oak," immortalised by Shakspeare. The great park is situated on the south side of the castle, and includes the beautiful avenue of trees, nearly three miles in length, called the Long Walk. It is terminated by the colossal equestrian statue of George III., in bronze, by Westmacott. The drive through the park to Virginia Water is exceedingly striking. The interior of the castle is magnificent. The corridor or gallery, 520 feet in length, leading along the south and east sides of the court, is richly adorned with bronzes, marbles, pictures, &c. The state-rooms are gorgeously fitted up, and contain many paintings by the most eminent masters. Tickets to view these rooms may be had in London of Messrs. Colnaghi, Pall-mall East. Her Majesty's private apartments can only be seen during the absence of the Court from Windsor by virtue of a special order from the Lord Chamberlain.

Half a mile from Windsor is Frogmore, the favourite residence of her late Majesty Queen Charlotte, and of the late Duchess of Kent. Six miles distant is Ascot Heath, where races are annually held in June

ON RIGHT FROM LOND.	From Bristol.		From London.	ON LEFT FROM LOND.
stood Caversham House, where Charles I. had an interview with his children in 1647. Maple Durham. Maple Durham House, Michael Blount, Esq., a fine Elizabethan building.				Coley Park, J. B. Moncke, Esq. Southcot House. Callcot Park. Tilehurst. Northcot. Belle-isle House. Purley Hall.
Hardwick House, H.P. Powys, Esq. Purley. Whitchurch. Combe Lodge, S. W. Gardiner, Esq. Basildon. Gathampton.	77	**Pangbourne Station.** Pangbourne is a place of great antiquity. Roman remains have been found here. It is united to Whitchurch on other side of the Thames.	41¼	Basildon Pa., Charles Morrison, Esq. South Bridge.
Near Goring, the Roman way called Icknield Street crosses the Thames. Mineral spring, formerly much frequented for cure of cutaneous diseases. Three miles from Wallingford St. is the borough of that name, returning 1 M.P. One of its churches contains the tomb of Blackstone, author of the Commentaries. His grandson represented this town in the parliament dissolved 1852. Population 7794.	73¾	**Goring Station.** Goring had formerly a nunnery for Augustines, founded in the reign of Henry II. of which some remains are still visible. **South-Stoke village,** in Oxfordshire, united by a bridge over Thames to Moulsford in Berks. The Railway, by a viaduct, crosses the Thames for the last time near Little Stoke.	44½	Goring is united by a bridge over the Thames to Streatley in Berks. The road to Oxford passes through Wallingford.
Cholsey.	70¾	**Wallingford Road St.**	47½	Aston Tirrold. North Moreton. Satwell. Brightwell.
Hagbourne.	65½	**Didcot Station.**	53	Ardington. In the church is a monument to Vernon, the founder of the Vernon Gallery.
Milton. Four miles to the right is Abingdon, a borough returning one M.P. It carries on an extensive corn-trade. It gives the title of Earl to the family	62¼	**Steventon Station.**	56¼	Wantage, celebrated as the birth-place of Alfred the Great; and also of Bishop Buller. Pop. 3064.
		☞ cross Wilts and Berks Canal.		
of Bertie. Population of Parl. bor. (1861) 5680. Near it is Nuneham Courtenay, the seat of G. G. Vernon Harcourt, Esq.	58¼	**Wantage Road Station.**	60	Uffington Castle, supposed to be the work of the Britons, afterwards occupied by the Romans. At a short distance is the celebrated figure of a white horse cut in the chalk hill. Wayland Smith's forge is also in the neighbourhood.
The old Faringdon mansion-house held out to the very last in favour of Charles I. The modern house is an edifice of considerable beauty. Beckett Park, Viscount Barrington.	54½	**Faringdon Road St.** Faringdon is noted for its trade in bacon and hogs, about 4000 of the latter being slaughtered every year. Pop. of Great Faringdon 2943.	63¾	Compton House, and beyond Ashdown Park (Earl Craven). Bourton.

ON RIGHT FROM LOND.	From Bristol.		From London.	ON LEFT FROM LOND.
Highworth, a market-town. Pop. of par. 4372. It is situated on an eminence near the vale of the White Horse. On Blunsden Castle Hill are the remains of a Roman encampment. Near Highworth is Coleshill, a fine mansion belonging to the Earl of Radnor.	47	**Shrivenham Station.** Here the line proceeds parallel to the Wilts and Berks Canal.	71¼	
	41¼	**Swindon Junction St.** Swindon is a market town in Wilts, pleasantly situated.	77	Swindon Lawn, A. L. Goddard, Esq., is a modern seat, with a fine lawn attached to it.
Branch Railway to Cirencester, Stroud, Gloucester, and Cheltenham Stratton. Lydiard Park, Viscount Bolingbroke. Ivy House. Brinkworth. Dauntsey. Christian Malford. Langley Burrell.	35½	**Wootton Basset St.** Wootton Basset sent two members to Parliament from the 25th of Henry VI. till the passing of the Reform Bill, when it was disfranchised. Here is an inclined plane 1 mile 30 chains long.	82¾	Tockenham. Lyneham. Foxham. Kellaways. Bremhill. Monkton House.
10 m. to the right from Chippenham is Malmesbury, famous as the birthplace of William of Malmesbury, the historian, and Hobbes the philosopher. Huish Park.	24¼	**Chippenham Station.** Chippenham is a borough by prescription, incorporated by Queen Mary, and has returned 2 M.P.'s since the time of Edward I. Pop. 7075.	93¾	Six miles to the left, on the Marlan, is the ancient borough of Calne, which returns one M.P. The church is an ancient building with a beautiful carved roof. Here, in 977, the celebrated Synod was held to settle the dispute concerning celibacy. Pop., 5179.
Corsham, the birthplace of Sir Richard Blackmore. Corsham House, the seat of Lord Methuen, contains a splendid collection of paintings.	20	**Corsham Station.** **Box Station.**	98¼	
Bath-Easton. The tower of its Gothic church contains twelve bells.	16½	**Box Tunnel,** the first on the line, from London a distance of 96 miles. Its length is 1¾ miles; height, 30 feet; width, 30 feet. Box has a neat Gothic church. Here is a medicinal spring.	101¾	Bowood Park, Marquis of Lansdowne. Compton House, G. H. Walker Heneage, Esq.
At a distance, Marshfield, and beyond, Dodington Park, C. W. Codrington, Esq. Farther off, near Acton Turville, and 10 miles from Chippenham, is Badminton, the noble seat of the Duke of Beaufort.	11½	**Bath Station.**	106¾	Prior Park once the favourite resort of Pope, and the property of Bishop Warburton, now a Roman Catholic Coll. Midford Castle.
	10¼	**Twerton Station.**	108	Newton Park, W. H. P. Gore Langton, Esq.
	7½	**Saltford Station.**	110¾	
Kelston Park, Joseph Neeld, Esq. Hanham, formerly a Roman station. Bitton, famous for its iron ore.	5	**Keynsham Station.** **Brislington Tunnel,** five eighths of a mile in length. We next reach the Grand Tunnel, 330 yards long, 50 feet high, and 30 wide. BRISTOL.	113¼	In Twerton is the cottage of Fielding, in which Tom Jones is supposed to have been written. Keynsham is supposed to derive its name from Keynee, daughter of a prince of Brecknockshire, who is said to have founded the town in a wild forest.

Bristol lies partly in the county of Somerset, partly in that of Gloucester, and was by Edward III. erected into an independent city and a county of itself. The rivers Avon and Frome run through it. The ground on which the city stands is very unequal. It is nearly 8 miles in circumference, and is supposed to cover about 1600 acres. The city, with its suburbs, contains between 700 and 800 streets, squares, and lanes, 10 markets for various commodities, and upwards of 400 licensed public houses. Bristol is a city of great antiquity. It is supposed to have been an inhabited place so early as the time of the Roman Invasion. About the time of the Norman Conquest, a strong fortress was erected there by the Earls of Gloucester, which, after it had stood about six centuries, was demolished by orders of Oliver Cromwell. During the Civil wars, it was garrisoned for the Parliament, but was stormed by King Charles, July 24, 1643. After the defeat of Charles at Naseby, Bristol surrendered to Fairfax after a siege of twenty-one days. During the excitement created by the Reform Bill, Bristol was the scene of a violent tumult, in which many lives were lost, and property destroyed to the value of nearly £70,000.

Bristol contains upwards of 20 churches and chapels of ease, besides a considerable number of chapels belonging to various bodies of Dissenters. The cathedral was originally a monastery dedicated to St Augustine. The only vestige of the original structure is a beautiful gateway. Bristol was erected into a bishop's see by Henry VIII., who annexed to its jurisdiction the whole of Dorsetshire, part of Gloucestershire, and three churches formerly in the see of Wells. In 1836, the sees of Gloucester and Bristol were conjoined. Secker, Butler, Newton, and other eminent men have held the office of Bishop of Bristol. Bishop Warburton was once Dean of this cathedral, as was also Dr. Josiah Tucker, the politico-economical writer. It was in the church of St Mary Radcliffe, that Chatterton pretended to have found the papers which he endeavoured to pass off as the MSS. of Rowley. The Exchange, erected in 1740-41, cost nearly £50,000. The city abounds in public schools and in hospitals, alms-houses, and other charitable institutions. Bristol carries on a considerable foreign trade to the West Indies, America, Newfoundland, and also to Spain and Portugal. The net amount of customs' duties for the year 1857, was £1,211,035. A considerable quantity of foreign produce is conveyed to Bristol coastwise under bond. Bristol has also a considerable inland trade, especially with the western counties, and with North and South Wales. The principal manufactures of Bristol are, glass, sugar, iron, brass, copper, lead, zinc, floorcloth, leather, earthenware, tobacco, &c.

The Bristol Docks were formed in 1804-9, by changing the course of the rivers Avon and Frome, and placing gates or locks at the extremity of the old channel. They were materially improved in 1849, and the accommodation will admit of any extension which the increase of trade may require. The works were formed by a proprietary body, at an expense of £600,000, but in 1848 they were transferred to the corporation. Amount of Dock dues collected in 1849, £28,699 : 5 : 8.

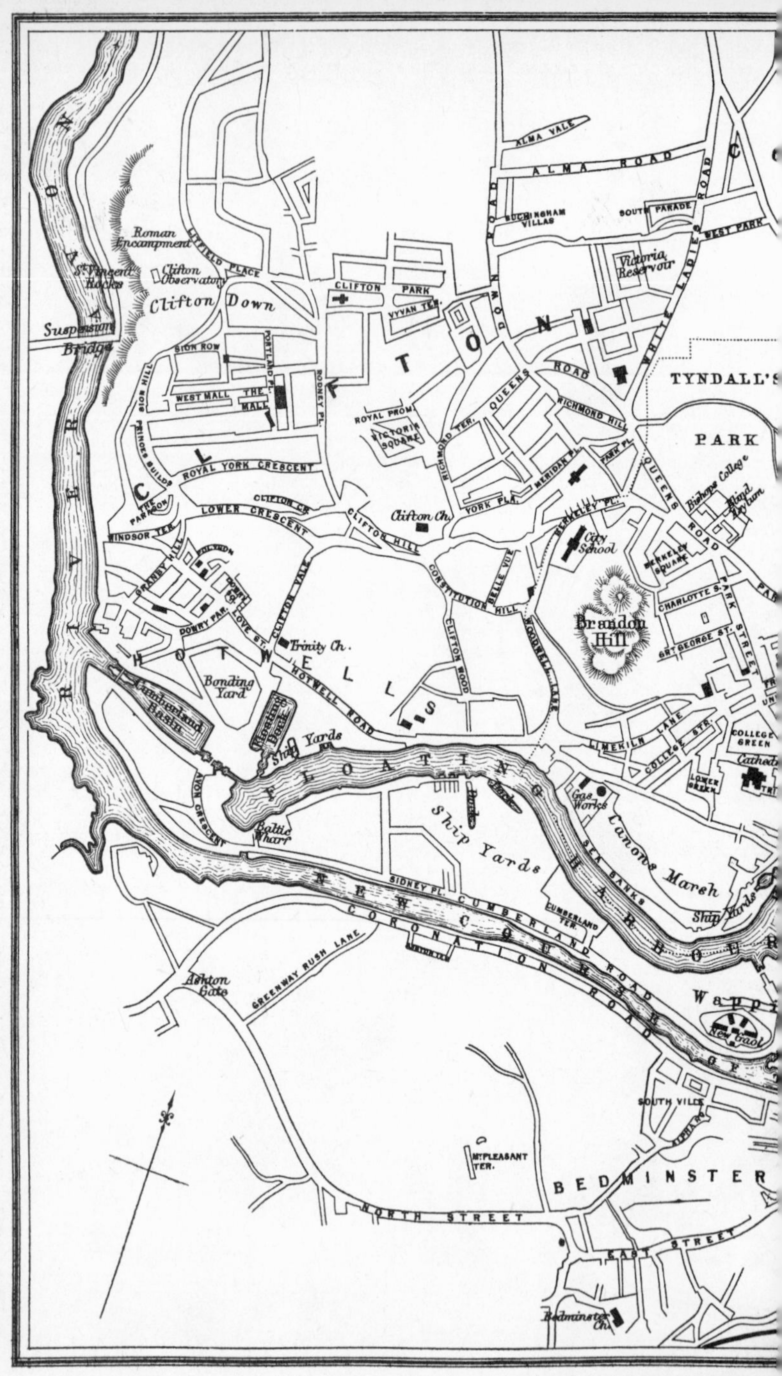
RIVER AVON
Roman Encampment
St. Vincent's Rocks
Clifton Observatory
Clifton Down
Suspension Bridge
LITFIELD PLACE
CLIFTON PARK
VYVAN TER.
ALMA VALE
ALMA ROAD
BUCKINGHAM VILLAS
SOUTH PARADE
WEST PARK
Victoria Reservoir
DOWN ROAD
WHITE LADIES ROAD
CLIFTON
SION ROW
SION HILL
PORTLAND PL.
RODNEY PL.
WEST MALL
THE MALL
PRINCES BUILDS
ROYAL YORK CRESCENT
ROYAL PROM.
VICTORIA SQUARE
RICHMOND TER.
QUEENS ROAD
RICHMOND HILL
PARK PL.
MERIDAN PL.
YORK PL.
TYNDALL'S PARK
Bishops College
Blind Asylum
THE PARROW
CLIFTON CR.
LOWER CRESCENT
WINDSOR TER.
CLIFTON HILL
Clifton Ch.
BERKELEY PL.
City School
GRANBY HILL
POLYGON
DOWRY SQ.
DOWRY PAR.
LOVE ST.
CLIFTON VALE
CONSTITUTION HILL
BELLE VUE
CLIFTON WOOD
WOODWELL LANE
BERKELEY SQUARE
CHARLOTTE S.
PARK STREET
GRT. GEORGE ST.
Brandon Hill
HOTWELLS
Trinity Ch.
Bonding Yard
HOTWELL ROAD
Cumberland Basin
Floating Dock
Ship Yards
LIMEKILN LANE
COLLEGE STR.
COLLEGE GREEN
LOWER GREEN
Cathedral
FLOATING HARBOUR
Gas Works
Canons Marsh
SEA BANKS
Ship Yards
AVON CRESCENT
Baltic Wharf
Dock
Ship Yards
SIDNEY PL.
NEW CUT
CUMBERLAND ROAD
CUMBERLAND TER.
CORONATION ROAD
GREENWAY BUSH LANE
Ashton Gate
Wapping
New Gaol
SOUTH VILLE
MT. PLEASANT TER.
BEDMINSTER
NORTH STREET
EAST STREET
Bedminster Ch.

A. &

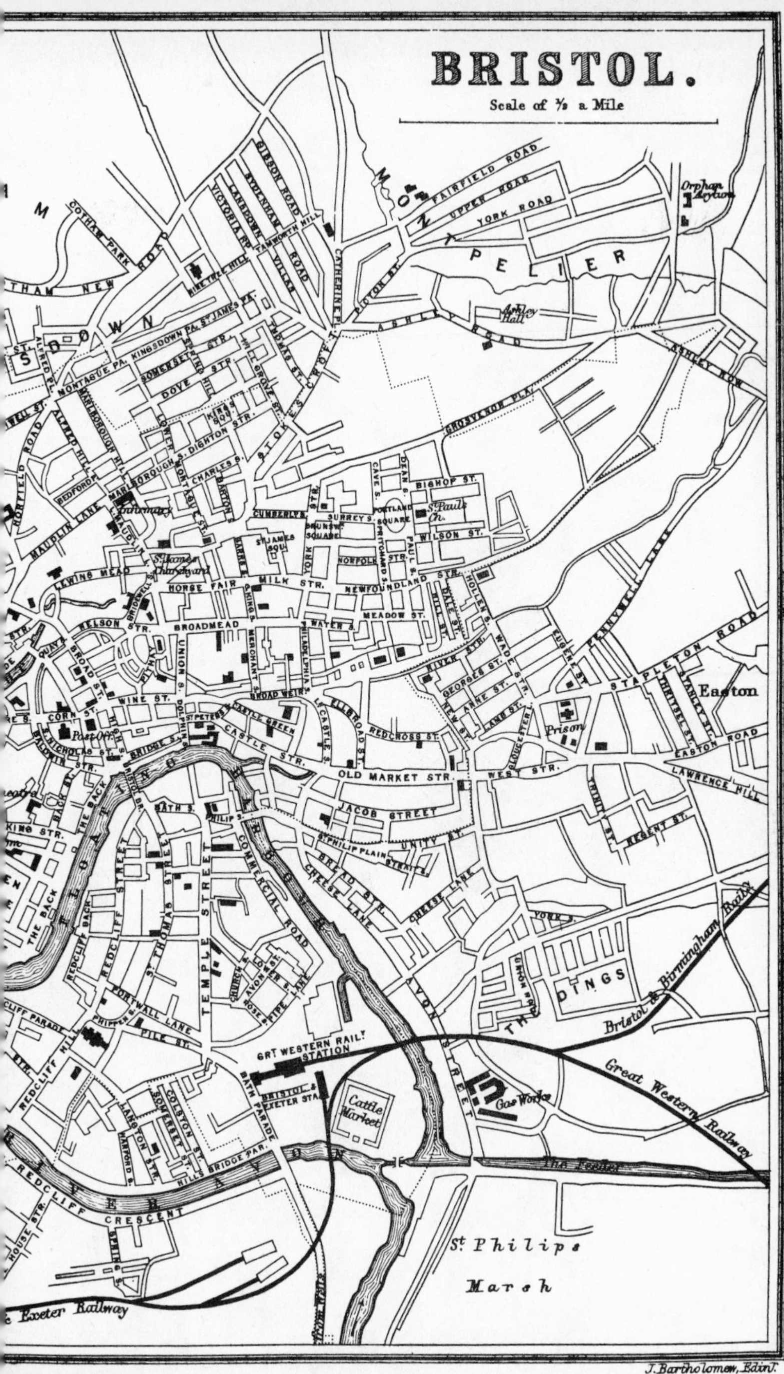

J. Bartholomew, Edinr.

burgh.

CLIFTON.

Bristol is divided, for municipal purposes, into ten wards, and its government is vested in a mayor, 16 aldermen, and 48 councillors. It returns two members to Parliament. The population, in 1831, amounted to 117,016, and in 1861, to 154,093. About a mile from Bristol is Clifton, a beautiful suburb of the city. Here are baths, springs, hot wells, assembly rooms, &c. In the neighbourhood of Bristol there are a number of fine mansions.

XLV. BATH TO SOUTHAMPTON THROUGH SALISBURY, 61 Miles.

ON RIGHT FROM BATH.	From South.		From Bath.	ON LEFT FROM BATH.
	59	South Stoke.	2	Prior Park. Midford Castle, C. T. Conolly, Esq.
	56	Charterhouse Hinton.	5	
	54	Norton St Philip.	7	Farleigh Castle, J. T. Houlton, Esq.
		cr. Frome Canal.		
Orchardleigh, and Hardington Park, Lord Poltimore. Berkeley House.	51	Beckington.	10	
	50	Standerwick.	11	Standerwick Court, H. E. Edgell, Esq. Charlcott House.
Longleat, the magnificent seat of the Marquis of Bath. To Shaftesbury, 15 m. To Mere, 10 miles; near it is Maiden-Bradley, a seat of the Duke of Somerset.	44½	WARMINSTER, a town of great antiquity on the Willey, carrying on a considerable trade in corn. Pop. 1851, 4220.	16½	
	40½	Heytesbury.	20½	Heytesbury Park, Lord Heytesbury.
	39	Upton Lovell.	22	
Ashton House.	37¼	Codford St Peter.	23¾	
Stockton House, H. Biggs, Esq.				
	34¼	Deptford.	26¾	Two miles distant, Yarnbury Camp, an ancient fortification.
	32¼	Steeple Langford.	28¾	
	30¼	Stapleford.	30¾	
	28	South Newton.	33	
To Wilton, 1½ mile (see p. 43.) Wilton House, the celebrated seat of the Earl of Pembroke. It was formerly an abbey for Benedictine nuns; but at the dissolution the site and buildings were granted to Sir W. Herbert, afterwards created Earl of Pembroke.	26	St. Peter. Fugglestone.	35	
	23¼	SALISBURY (see p. 42.)	37¾	The College, J. Campbell Wyndham, Esq. Laverstock House, now a lunatic asylum.
Moat House. Longford Castle, Earl of Radnor.	20¼	Alderbury.	40¾	Clarendon Park, Sir F. H. H. Bathurst, Bart., beyond which is Norman Court.

ON RIGHT FROM BATH.	From South.		From Bath.	ON LEFT FROM BATH.
Alderbury House. Two miles distant, Trafalgar House, Earl Nelson.	19¼	**Whaddon.**	41¾	**Brickworth House.**
To Southampton by Shoe Inn, Plaitford, 15¼ miles. To Lymington by Cadnam, 24¾ miles.	15¼	**White Parish.**	45¾	
	14¼	**Cowsfield.**	46¾	Cowsfield House, and Sherfield House, beyond which is Mottisfont Ho., Sir J. B. Mill, Bart.
Melchet Park, Hon. and Rev. F. Baring.	17	**Sherfield English.**	49½	
Broxmore Park, R. Bristowe, Esq. Embley Park, W. E. Nightingale, Esq.; Ower Paulton's, Wm. Sloane Stanley, Esq. Broadlands, Viscount Palmerston.	7½	ROMSEY (*Hants*), a large and ancient town, watered by the Test or Anton. Sir W. Petty was born here. The church, formerly attached to a nunnery, is a venerable edifice, adorned with several monuments. A large sum has lately been expended in its restoration. Pop. 2116.	53½	To Stockbridge, 9½ m. To Andover, 18 m. To Winchester, 11 m.
Lee Park.				Chilworth House, J. Fleming, Esq. Upton Lodge.
		cr. Andover Canal.		
Testwood House, Miss Bourne; Testwood Lodge, Sir H. C. Paulet, Bart.;	4	Nursling.	57½	
Shirley House, Sir C. H. Rich, Bart. and 1 mile farther, Fremantle, Sir G. H. Hewett, Bart.	2¼	Shirley.	59¾	
		Junction of the Road.		
		SOUTHAMPTON. (See p. 56).	61	Bannister Lodge. Portswood House. Bellevue.

XLVI. BATH TO POOLE THROUGH WARMINSTER, SHAFTESBURY, BLANDFORD, 56¾ Miles.

ON RIGHT FROM BATH.	From Poole.		From Bath.	ON LEFT FROM BATH.
	40¼	TO WARMINSTER, *Wilts.* (P. 103).	16½	
Longleat, Marquis of Bath.	38¼	Crockerton.	18½	
	36¾	Longbridge, Deverill.	20	
Clouds House. To Wincanton, 11 m. To Sherborne, 16 m. Pensbury House.	30¼	East Knoyle.	26½	3 miles distant, Fonthill Abbey, Marquis of Westminster. Pyt House, Vere Fane Bennett, Esq.
Motcombe Ho., Marquis of Westminster.	25¼	SHAFTESBURY, *Dorsetshire.* (P. 43).	31½	To Salisbury, 20 miles.
Iwerne House, T. B. Bower, Esq.	21¼	Fontmell Magna.	35½	
Shroton House.	20½	Sutton Waldron.	36¼	
Ranston House, Sir E. B. Baker, Bart.	19½	Iwerne Minster.	37¼	Hanford House, H. K. Seymer, Esq.
Steepleton House.	16½	Stourpain.	40¼	

ON RIGHT FROM BATH.	From Poole.		From Bath.	ON LEFT FROM BATH.
Bryanstone House, Lord Portman. Down House, Sir John James Smith, Bart. To Dorchester, 16 miles.	14	Blandford, see page 43.	$42\frac{3}{4}$	To Salisbury, 22 miles. Langton House,
		cr. river Stour.		
	12	Charlton Marshall.	$44\frac{3}{4}$	
Charborough House, J. S. W. S. E. Drax, Esq.	11	Spetisbury.	$45\frac{3}{4}$	
Lower Henbury House. Coombe Almer.	$5\frac{1}{2}$	Corfe Mullen.	$51\frac{1}{4}$	2 m. dist. Kingston Hall, W. J. Bankes, Esq. Merley House.
Higher Henbury House, W. G. Paxton, Esq.				
	$2\frac{1}{4}$	Junction of the road.	$54\frac{1}{2}$	To Wimborne Minster, $3\frac{1}{2}$ miles.
On Brownsea Island, Brownsea Castle.		POOLE.	$56\frac{3}{4}$	

Poole derives its name from the pool or bay on the north side of which it is situated. The harbour is reckoned the best and safest in the channel, and will admit vessels of 14 feet draught. Formerly, the principal branch of business was the Newfoundland fishery, but the inhabitants are now largely engaged in the import and export trade to the Baltic, America, Portugal, &c. Poole has an ancient church, several meeting-houses, free and charity schools, besides charitable institutions. It returns 2 members to Parliament. Pop. 1861, 9759. Midway between Poole and Christchurch is the new watering-place of Bournemouth.

XLVII. FROM BATH TO WEYMOUTH THROUGH FROME, $62\frac{3}{4}$ Miles.

ON RIGHT FROM BATH.	From Weym.		From Bath.	ON LEFT FROM BATH.
	$62\frac{3}{4}$	BATH.		
	$52\frac{3}{4}$	From Bath to Beckington, see page 103.	10	
		cr. river Frome.		
Marston House, Earl of Cork and Orrery.	$49\frac{1}{4}$	FROME is a large and populous town, the inhabitants of which are chiefly employed in the woollen manufacture. One M.P. Pop., 9522.	13	
				Westcombe House,
To Shepton Mallet, 7 m.	$39\frac{3}{4}$	Bruton. The objects most worthy of notice are the church, a curious ancient hexagonal cross in the market-place, the market-house, the hospital, and the free school. Pop. of par. 2232	$23\frac{3}{4}$	To Warminster, $16\frac{1}{2}$ m. To Amesbury, $15\frac{1}{4}$ m. To Hindon, $13\frac{3}{4}$ m. To Wincanton, $4\frac{3}{4}$ m., thence to Sherborne, 9 m.

ON RIGHT FROM BATH.	From Weym.		From Bath.	ON LEFT FROM BATH.
Hadspen House,	37½	Pitcombe.	25¼	At a distance, Redlynch Park, Earl of Ilchester. To Shaftesbury, 15½ m.
Cadbury House.				
To Castle Cary, through Sparkford, 11½ m., and to Yeovil, 5¼ m.	26¼	Sherborne,*(*Dortsetsh.*)	36½	
		cr. river Frome.		
	8¼	DORCHESTER, p. 44.	54½	
Maiden Castle, one of the strongest and most extensive British camps in England. It consists of a hill enclosed by two, and, in some places, three ditches, and the enclosed area contains upwards of 160 acres.	5¾	Monkton.	57	Came Abbey.
	½	MELCOMBE REGIS. Pop. of Parl. bor. of Melcombe and Weymouth, 1851, 9458.	62¼	Herringston Lodge, E. W. Williams, Esq.
		cr. riv. Wey.		
		WEYMOUTH, (See p. 44.)	62¾	Lulworth Castle, J. Weld, Esq., 16 m. from Weymouth, is frequently visited by strangers.

* Sherborne is situated on a branch of the Yeo, which divides it into two parts, called Sherborne and Castleton. In the latter are the ruins of a castle, the last place that held out for King Charles. The principal object of attention is the church, which was a cathedral till the see was removed to Old Sarum in 1075. It was then converted into an abbey church, and is now one of the finest in the west of England, containing specimens of various styles of architecture, from the time of the Normans to that of Henry VII. In the south transept is a splendid monument to the memory of John, Earl of Bristol, who died in 1698. Near this is a tablet with lines by Pope, to the memory of a son and daughter of William Lord Digby. Here also Sir Thomas Wyatt the poet was buried. The abbey is now occupied as a silk manufactory. Pop. 1861, 5523. Adjoining the town is Sherborne Castle, the seat of Lord Digby. The centre was built by Sir Walter Raleigh, whose family were robbed of the estate by James I.

XLVIII. BATH TO BRIDPORT THROUGH SHEPTON MALLET, ILCHESTER, AND CREWKERNE, 54¾ Miles.

ON RIGHT FROM BATH.	From Bridp.		From Bath.	ON LEFT FROM BATH.
	50¼	Dunkerton.	4	Combhay.
Camerton Park, J. Jarrett, Esq.	46¾	Radstock.	7½	

ON RIGHT FROM BATH.	From Bridp.		From Bath.	ON LEFT FROM BATH.
Chilcompton, and 2 miles distant, Stone Easton, Sir J. S. Hippesley, Bart.	43¾	Stratton on the Fosse.	10½	Down Side.
	40¾	Oakhill.	13½	Ashwick Grove, R. Strachey, Esq.
To Wells, 5½ miles, to Glastonbury, 9 m.	38¾	SHEPTON MALLET carries on an extensive manufactory of knit-stockings, and woollen goods. Its principal curiosity is the market-cross, erected in 1500. Pop., 4868.	15½	To Frome, 12 m.
Pylle House.	36	Street on the Fosseway.	18¼	
3 miles dist. King's Weston House, F. H. Dickinson, Esq.	30½	West Lydford.	23¾	
		cr. river Brue.		
		cr. river Yeo.		
To Yeovil, 4½ m.	24	ILCHESTER, on the south bank of the Ivel, is a place of considerable antiquity, having been fortified in the time of the Romans. Pop. 781. (See p. 48).	30¼	
	18¾	Junction of the road to Crewkerne.	35½	
Hinton St George, Earl Poulett. To Crewkerne, 9¾ m.	13½	CREWKERNE, in a valley watered by the Axe and the Parret. The church is a noble Gothic structure, richly adorned with carved work. Pop. 3566.	40¾	To Chard, 8 m. To Ilminster, 8 m. To Axminster, 13½ m. To Lyme Regis, 16 m.
	12¼	Misterton.	42	
	10¼	Mosterton, *Dorsetsh.*	44	
Parnham, Sir H. Oglander, Bart. To Axminster, 14 m.	6¼	BEAMINSTER. a town of considerable antiquity, on the banks of the Brit. It has several manufactories for sail-cloth. Its church is adorned with curious carving, and contains several monuments. Pop., 2614.	48	To Dorchester, 17½ m.
	1¼	Bradpole.	53	
		BRIDPORT, see p. 44.	54¼	

XLIX. BATH TO EXETER THROUGH SHEPTON MALLET, ILMINSTER, AND HONITON, 75 Miles.

ON RIGHT FROM BATH.	From Exeter.		From Bath.	ON LEFT FROM BATH.
				Combhay.
	71	Dunkerton.	4	Woodbarrow House.
Camerton Park.	67½	Radstock.	7½	

ON RIGHT FROM BATH.	From Exeter.		From Bath.	ON LEFT FROM BATH.
				Stratton House.
	63¾	Stratton on the Fosse.	11¼	
	60½	Oakhill.	14½	Ashwick Grove, R. Strachey, Esq.
		cross the Mendip Hills.		
	59½	SHEPTON MALLET, (p. 107.)	16½	
	57½	Cannard's Grave Inn.	17½	
East Pennard Park.	55¾	Street on the Fosseway.	19¼	
	54¼	Wraxhall.	21¾	
3 m. distant, King's Weston House, F. H. Dickinson, Esq.	50¼	West Lydford.	24¾	
		cr. river Brue.		
	43¾	ILCHESTER, (p. 107.)	31¼	
	31½	ILMINSTER.	43½	
	16½	HONITON, (p. 48.)	58½	
		EXETER, (p. 110.)	75	

L. BATH TO EXETER THROUGH BRIDGEWATER, AND TAUNTON, 81¼ Miles.

ON RIGHT FROM BATH.	From Exeter.		From Bath.	ON LEFT FROM BATH.
Camerton Park.	74¼	Dunkerton.	4	Prior Park. Fielding laid the scene of the early years of Tom Jones at this place; and its former occupant, Mr Allan, is the Allworthy of his novel.
	73¾	Radstock.	7½	To Frome, 7½ miles. Woodbarrow House. Ammerdown, J. T. Jolliffe, Esq., and near it Hardington Park, Lord Poltimore.
2 miles distant, Stone Easton Park, Sir J. S. Hippesley, Bart.	70¾	Chilcompton.	10½	Norton Hall. Stratton House.
	69¼	Old Down Inn.	12	
2 m. distant, Chewton Priory. Haydon Seat.	68¾	Emborrow.	12½	Masberry Castle.
		cr. Mendip Hills, which command fine views.		
To Bristol, 21 miles.	63	WELLS, (p. 96.)	18¼	To Shepton Mallet, 5 m.
1½ m. distant is Wokey Hole, a romantic cavern, the approach to which is remarkably picturesque.	57½	GLASTONBURY, (p. 97.)	23¾	To Shepton Mallet, 8½ m.
	55¼	Street.	25¾	To Somerton, 7 miles.

ON RIGHT FROM BATH.	From Exeter.		From Bath.	ON LEFT FROM BATH.
Sharpham Park, the birthplace of Fielding.	54	Walton.	27¼	
	52¾	Piper's Inn.	28½	
Shapwick House.	51¾	Ashcott.	29½	
	45¾	Over Polden Hill to Bawdrip.	35½	
		cr. river Parret.		
	41¾	BRIDGEWATER, p. 117.	39½	
2 m. dist. Halsewell Ho. C. J. K. Tynte, Esq.	38¼	North Petherton.	42¾	
	36	Thurloxton.	45¼	
Walford House. Hestercombe House.	35	Walford Bridge.	46¼	To Bath through Glastonbury and Wells, 41½ m.
	32½	Bath Pool.	48¾	
1 m. dist. Pyrland Hall, Sir W. W. Yea, Bart.		cr. river Tone.		
To Minehead, 23 m. To Wiveliscombe, 12 m.	30¾	TAUNTON, p. 118.	50½	Batts House, Sir G. A. Robinson, Bart. 2 m. dist. Amberd House.
	29	Bishop's Hull.	52¼	
	28¾	Rumwell.	53½	
Heatherton Park, A. Adair, Esq.	24¾	Chilson.	56½	
To Milverton, 4 miles.	23¾	WELLINGTON (See also p. 118) has manufactories of earthenware, serges, and druggets. The church, a handsome building of Gothic architecture, contains the monument of Sir John Popham, a liberal patron of this town, whose house was garrisoned for the Parliament army in the time of Charles I. It is from this place that the Duke of Wellington derives his title; and in his domain is a lofty stone column on Blackdown Hill overlooking the town, erected to commemorate his victories. Pop. 3689.	57½	
Holcombe Co., P. Bluett, Esq.	22¾	Rockwell Green.	58½	
	19¼	Maiden Down (*Devon*).	62	
	17¼	South Appledore.	64	Bridwell House.
	13¾	Welland.	67½	Bradfield, B.B. Walrond, Esq.
To Tiverton, 5½ miles.	12	CULLOMPTON, (See also p. 118) on the Culme, carries on a considerable woollen manufacture. The church is an ancient and venerable structure, consisting of three aisles, one of which is a beautiful specimen of Gothic architecture. Near the font are two curiously carved pieces of oak. Pop. 2205.	69¼	To Honiton, 10½ miles.
	9	Bradninch.	72¼	

ON RIGHT FROM BATH.	From Exeter.		From Bath.	ON LEFT FROM BATH.
				Spraydown House.
Killerton Park, Sir T. D. Acland, Bart., M.P.	4½	Broad Clist.	76¾	Poltimore House, Lord Poltimore.
	2¼	Langaton.	79	
		EXETER.	81¼	Wear House, (Sir J. T. B. Duckworth, Bart.,) near Topsham.

Exeter, the capital of Devonshire, on the banks of the Exe, is a large city, extending about three miles in circumference. It is intersected by four principal streets, which meet in the centre. A handsome bridge has been thrown over the river at an expense of L.20,000. The cathedral of St Peter is a magnificent structure, and contains numerous monuments of its bishops and of the Bohun and Courtenay families. Its western window is much admired, and the Bishop's Throne is remarkable for its height and elaborate carving. The north tower contains a clock curiously ornamented, and an immense bell (the great Tom of Exeter), weighing 12,500 lbs., both the gifts of Bishop Courtenay. Near the cathedral (and south-east) is the Bishop's Palace, a venerable building. On the north-east of the city are the ruins of Rougemont Castle, said to have been erected in the time of Julius Cæsar, and formerly the residence of the West Saxon kings. The guildhall, in High Street, rebuilt in 1464, contains several valuable portraits. A commodious custom-house has been erected on the quay. Northernhay, a public garden, well wooded and beautifully laid out, is the fashionable promenade, and commands a series of fine prospects. Formerly, Exeter was the emporium of thin woollen goods, such as serges, &c., spun and woven in the neighbouring towns, but finished in the city previous to exportation. The invention of machinery has, however, nearly destroyed these branches of trade, with the exception of that to India, which is still considerable. As Exeter is a kind of metropolis for Devon and Cornwall, it receives the produce of these counties in exchange for foreign commodities. The country around Exeter is very fertile, affording good pasture, corn, dairy, and fattening land, and abounding in fruit, especially apples, which yield plenty of the best cider. The river Exe is so far navigable, that by means of locks, vessels of 150 tons burden can come up to the city ; those that are larger remain at Topsham, and the largest at Exmouth ; the mouth of the river three miles lower. The diocese includes nearly the whole of Devon and Cornwall. In Exeter, there is a considerable number of churches belonging to the Establishment ; several chapels of ease, and a few dissenting meeting-houses ; numerous charitable institutions, and a neat theatre. The city is divided, for municipal purposes, into six wards, and is governed by a mayor, twelve aldermen, and thirty-five councillors. It returns two members to Parliament. The markets are held on Tuesday and Friday, and there is a good fish-market daily. The population in 1841 amounted to 31,312, and in 1861 to 41,749.

From Exeter to Tiverton is 13 miles—Crediton, 7½—Chulmleigh, 21½—South Molton, 29½—Barnstaple, 37¾—Bideford, 39½.

Crediton is an ancient and populous town situated on the Creedy, between two hills. It has twice suffered severely from fire. The church is an elegant Gothic structure, in which is a beautiful altar-piece. Population, 4048. Near Crediton are Downes (J. W. Buller, Esq.), Creedy House (Sir H. R. Ferguson Davie, Bart.), and Fulford Park B. Fulford, Esq.)

South Molton is an ancient market and borough-town situated on an eminence near the west side of the river Mole. It has a guildhall, a spacious church containing several monuments and a good altar-piece, a free school, a charity school, &c. Population, 3830. Between South Molton and Barnstaple is Castle Hill, the splendid mansion of Earl Fortescue, Lord-Lieutenant of the county. Barnstaple is an ancient place situated on the Taw, and is one of the neatest towns in Devonshire. Previous to the Conquest, it was a royal demesne, and is said to have been constituted a borough by King Athelstan, who built a castle here, of which nothing now remains except a high artificial mound. The woollen trade, which the town once possessed, has declined, but it still carries on a trade in timber, baize, silk stockings, and waistcoats. It has a spacious church, a guildhall, a theatre, charity, national, and free grammar-schools. The poet Gay was born in the vicinity, and received his education at the grammar-school here. Barnstaple returns two members to Parliament. Population, 10,743. A few miles from Barnstaple is Tawstock Court, the seat of Sir B. P. Wrey, Bart. beautifully situated and surrounded by extensive woods and grounds. The church contains a number of handsome monuments. Eight and a half miles from Barnstaple is Bideford, pleasantly situated on the banks of the Torridge, over which is an ancient bridge of twenty-four arches. The view above the bridge is remarkably picturesque. Bideford has greatly increased in importance within a few years, and now carries on an extensive trade. Population 5742. Near the town is Moreton House, L. W. Buck, Esq. Thirteen miles and a half from Bideford is Hartland, a small sea-port town, bleakly situated on a neck of land called Hartland Point. Pop. of par. 1916. The church, a large and handsome structure, forms a landmark to mariners. About 6½ miles from Bideford, and 45 from Exeter, is Torrington, a populous and flourishing town, finely situated on the east bank of the Torridge. A bowling-green now occupies the site of the ancient castle. The views from the two bridges in the vicinity of the town are extremely picturesque. Pop. of par. 3298. Ten miles and a half from Torrington, and 28 from Exeter, is Hatherleigh, an ancient but inconsiderable market and borough town, situated on a branch of the Torridge. The manor anciently belonged to the Abbot of Tavistock. Population, 1645. About 21 miles from Hatherleigh, and in Cornwall, is Stratton, famous as the place where the Parliamentary forces under the Earl of Stamford were defeated by the Cornish Royalists under Sir Beville Granville. Two miles from Stratton is Bude, a considerable watering-place. Five miles from Stratton is Kilkhampton, where there is a fine old church containing several ancient monuments, among others, one to the memory of Sir Beville Granville, who was killed at the battle of Lansdown. The church-yard was the scene of Hervey's "Meditations among the Tombs."

LI. EXETER TO TEIGNMOUTH, TORQUAY, AND DARTMOUTH.

ON RIGHT FROM EXET.	From Teignm.		From Exeter.	ON LEFT FROM EXET.
	14	Alphington.	2	
	12	Exminster.	4	
	9	Kenton.	7	Powderham Castle (Earl of Devon), a noble mansion, containing numerous paintings. The park and plantations are about 10 miles in circumference.
Staplake House, and, 3 miles distant, Mamhead, Sir L. Newman, Bart.	7	Star-Cross.	9	
		Cockwood.		Cockwood House.
	4¼	Shutton Bridge.	11¾	
1½ m. distant is Luscombe Castle.	3	Dawlish. Pop. 1851, 2671.	13	Dawlish, one of the most fashionable watering-places in the county.
The villas in the immediate vicinity of Teignmouth are very numerous. On the opposite side of the river is the village of Shaldon, much frequented in summer.		TEIGNMOUTH. Another road leads from Exeter to Teignmouth by Haldon Hill; but it is one mile longer than the present route.	16	Teignmouth is a town of great antiquity, and one of the most fashionable watering places on the coast, the climate being very temperate. There is a public promenade, commanding varied and beautiful views. Pop., 6022.

Eight miles from Teignmouth is the much admired and rapidly-increasing watering-place of Torquay, beautifully situated on the north side of Torbay. Kent's Hole, a cavern scarcely a mile from the town, is interesting to geologists on account of its ossiferous remains. Close to the town is Tor Abbey, the seat of R. S. S. Cary, Esq., and in the vicinity is Bishopstowe, a seat of the Bishop of Exeter.

Twelve miles from Torquay is Dartmouth, a considerable sea-port town, situated at the mouth of the Dart, which here forms a spacious harbour, capable of accommodating 500 sail. The Parish Church, of great antiquity, contains a curiously painted screen and pulpit. One of the doors is remarkably quaint. The bay is one of the most beautiful on this beautiful coast—the banks consisting of lofty wooded hills shelving down to the water. The Dart is navigable from this place to Totness, a distance of 10 miles, and a sail from the one point to the other will charm any lover of fine scenery. The town returns one member to Parliament. Pop. 1861, 4444. In the immediate vicinity of Dartmouth is Mount Boone, the seat of Sir H. P. Seale, Bart.

Five miles from Dartmouth is the busy fishing town of Brixham, remarkable as the landing-place of William III. in 1688. 4½ miles from Dartmouth, near Galmpton, is Lupton House, the beautiful seat of Lord Churston.

47 Miles.

ON RIGHT FROM EXETER.	From Totness.		From Exeter.	ON LEFT FROM EXETER.
Peamore, S. T. Kekewich.	45	**Alphington.** The church has a curious Norman font and screen.	2	Kenbury.
	43	**Kenford.**	4	Oxton House. Haldon Hill, 1818 feet above level of the sea. It commands a fine view of Exeter and other places in the neighbourhood, and of Haldon House, (Sir L. V. Palk, Bart.) Here is Castle Lawrence, built in honour of the late Gen. Lawrence. Lyndridge.
Ugbrooke House (Lord Clifford), a superb mansion of a quadrangular form, situated in a very beautiful park. It contains a good library and a valuable collection of pictures.	35	Sandy-Gate.	12	To Teignmouth, 9 m.
		cr. river Teign.		To Teignmouth, 6 m.
Ogwell House, Col. Taylor.	32½	Newton. To Chudleigh, 6 miles. To Ashburton, 7½ miles.	14½	Ford, and beyond, Haccombe House, Sir W. P. Carew, Bart.
	30½	Two-Mile Oak.	16½	
Dartington Ho., Henry Champernowne, Esq., prettily situated on the right bank of the river above Totness. In the hall are some good paintings. There is another road leading from Totness to Plymouth by Wonton, 5½ m., New Br. 1 m., Venn-Cross, 1½ m., Bittaford Br. 2½ m., Ivy Br. 2 m., thence to Plymouth, as on p. 115.	28½	Bow-Bridge. cr. river Dart.	18½	The picturesque ruins of Berry Pomeroy Castle, the property of the Duke of Somerset, encircled by wood, and overlooking a beautiful vale. Close to it is Loventor House, Sir G. Baker, Bart.
	24½	TOTNESS, a very ancient town, finely situated. Here are the remains of a castle erected in the time of William the Conqueror. The church is a handsome structure. The town returns two M.P.'s. Pop., 4001.	22½	The village of Pomeroy contains a fine old church, with quaint monuments to the Pomeroy and Seymour families. To Dartmouth, 10 miles. Gatcombe House; Follaton House (G. Stanley Cary, Esq.), 1 mile Weston House.
	18	New-Bridge. cr. river Avon.	29	2½ miles from Totness, on the Dart river, Sharpham (famous for its echoes and its beauty), R. Durant, Esq.
Venn.	16½	**Venn-Cross.**	30½	North Hewish. Butterford. Fowelscombe.
Modbury, an ancient town, consisting principally of four streets. Many of the inhabitants are employed in the woollen trade. Pop. 1622	13	**Modbury.** Another road leads from Totness to Modbury through Ingleburn, Luckbridge, and Brownstone—distance equal.	34	At Modbury may be seen the remains of a priory, and of Modbury House, formerly inhabited by the Champernownes, who lived here from the time of Edward II. till the end of the 17th century.
	10½	Sequers Bridge. cr. river Erme.	36½	Fleet House (Lady Elizabeth Bulteel), a fine old Hall of Elizabeth's time, and may be seen by order of the agent in Plymouth.
Lyneham.		cr. river Yealm.		Puslinch, Rev. J. Yonge. Membland House.
	7	Yealmpton.	40	Kitley, E. R. P. Bastard, Esq

ON RIGHT FROM EXETER.	From Totness.		From Exeter.	ON LEFT FROM EXETER.
One mile beyond, Saltram House, Earl of Morley. It contains a choice picture-gallery. Close to the house in Chelson Meadow is a pretty course used for Plymouth races.	5½	Brixton.	41½	Coffleet.
	3½	Elburton.	43½	
		Plymstock.		Radford, Col. Harris.
		cr. Laira Br.		
		PLYMOUTH.	47	

Plymouth, a sea-port town, lies 192 miles in a direct line west-south-west of St. Paul's, London, 216 miles from the General Post Office, London, by the nearest mail road, and 247 miles by railway from Paddington. It derives its name from the river Plym, which here meets the Tamar, forming by their junction an excellent harbour, divided into three parts. The town was incorporated by charter in 1438, in the reign of Henry VI. In the reign of Elizabeth a new charter was bestowed on the corporation, on the solicitation of Sir Francis Drake, who also brought water to the town from Dartmouth, by a winding channel 24 miles in length. Plymouth suffered much from the plague in A.D. 1579 and 1581. It again broke out in 1626, and carried off two thousand persons. In the civil wars Plymouth embraced the Parliamentary side, and was several times besieged by the royalists, but without success. The town is ill laid out, and the streets are narrow and inconvenient, except those near the public promenade called the Hoe. The principal buildings are, the noble Ionic structure in George Street, containing the Theatre, Assembly Rooms, and the Royal Hotel; the Athenæum, the Public Library, the Custom-house, the royal baths, the new hospital, the Guildhall, the Freemasons' Hall, the Mechanics' Institute, &c. The church of St. Andrew is spacious, containing, among other monuments, one to the memory of Charles Matthews the comedian. Here are also numerous meeting-houses, and charitable and educational institutions. Plymouth is one of the principal sea-ports in England, and is defended by a citadel and fortifications on the mainland, as well as on Drake's Island, &c. The harbour comprehends the Sound and its various arms. The estuary of the Tamar forms the harbour for the ships of war, and is called Hamoaze. This noble basin is four miles long, has moorings for nearly 100 sail of the line, and is usually studded with ships of war. The estuary of the Plym, called Catwater, forms another harbour, chiefly used for merchant vessels, and is capable of containing 1000 sail. An Act of Parliament was obtained, in 1840, for the erection of a pier in Mill Bay for the accommodation of the largest class of steam-ships at all times of the tide. The breakwater, commenced in 1812, is one of the most stupendous works of modern times. Its base is about a mile long, and the top forms a promenade, at the end of which there is a lighthouse 68 feet above the level of the breakwater. Plymouth carries on a considerable trade with the West Indies, the Baltic, and the Mediterranean, and coastwise with London and other places; and there is an active fishery, especially of whiting and hake. The imports are timber and West India produce; the exports, manganese to Scotland, wool to Hull, and lead to London and Bristol. The customs revenue of the port in 1861 was £160,042. The manufactures are sail-cloth, glass, soap, starch, and sugar-refining.

Races are held twice a-year on Chelson Meadow, and there is an annual regatta in the Sound. In August, the scenery on the rivers Tamar, Tavey, St. Germans, and Yealm, is charming beyond description, and several weeks may be most agreeably consumed in excursions from Plymouth. Eddystone Lighthouse is 14 miles from the town, and is visible in clear weather. Plymouth returns two members to Parliament. Pop. in 1861, 62,599. (See also Devonport, p. 116.)

LIII. EXETER TO PLYMOUTH AND DEVONPORT THROUGH ASHBURTON, 45 Miles.

ON RIGHT FROM EXETER.	From Devon.		From Exeter.	ON LEFT FROM EXETER.
	43	Alphington.	2	Peamore, S. T. Kekewich, Esq.
	41½	Shillingford.	3½	
Haldon Ho., Sir L. V. Palk, Bart.	41	Clopton Bridge.	4	Kenbury.
		cross river Ken.		
One-half mile distant is Chudleigh Rock, a singular and romantic cliff, in which is a curious cavern.	36	Over Hall-down to Chudleigh. Here was formerly a Benedictine monastery, and a palace of Bishop of Exeter.	9	Chudleigh is a small neat town, surrounded by beautiful scenery. The church contains some monuments of the Courtenay family. Ugbrooke House, Lord Clifford.
Canonteign (Viscount Exmouth) 2 m.	34	Knighton.	11	
Culver House.	33	Jews Bridge.	12	
		cross river Teign.		Stover Lodge, Duke of Somerset.
		Hey-Tor-Railroad.		
Ashton House.	30	Bickington.	15	To Newton-Bushel, 3 miles.
Two m. distant, Bagtor House and Sandridge Park, Lord Cranstoun.		Love-Lane.		Ingsdon House.
To Tavistock, 19 m.	26½	ASHBURTON is a neat town, with a handsome church, formerly collegiate. At one time it sent 2 M.P.'s. but now only 1. In the vicinity are tin and copper mines. Pop. 3062.	18½	To Totness, 8 miles.
Buckfast Abbey.		cross. river Dart.		
At a distance Spitchwick.	24	Buckfastleigh.	21	
Buckland, E. R. P. Bastard, Esq., and Holne Chase, a beautiful hunting seat of Sir B. P. Wrey, Bart. The drive from Ashburton round the chase affords a fine view of sylvan scenery.	22½	Dean-Prior.	22½	Dean Church.
	21	Brent, Harberton-ford.	21	
	19	South Brent.	26	
		cross river Avon.		To Modbury, 5 miles.
	18	Cherston.	27	
	15¾	Bittaford Bridge.	29¼	
Stowford, situated at the foot of a hill called the West Beacon, from the summit of which there is an extensive and beautiful prospect.	13½	Ivy Bridge, beautifully situated in a romantic dell, derives its name from a bridge, with one arch covered with ivy, which here stretches across the river Erme.	31½	
		Woodland		

ON RIGHT FROM EXETER.	From Devon.		From Exeter.	ON LEFT FROM EXETER.
Blachford, Sir Frederic Rogers, Bart.		**Cadleigh.**		
Goodamoor, P. O. Treby, Esq.	11	cr. river **Yealm.** **Lee Mill.**	32	
Beechwood, R. Rosdew, Esq. Hemerdon Hall, G. Woolcombe, Esq.				
Chaddlewood, Mrs Symons.	7	Ridgeway,	38	Four miles distant, at Brixton, Kitley, E. R. P. Bastard, Esq.
Newnham Park, G. Strode, Esq.		Or to Plympton-Earle, 38½ miles.		
Great Efford, E. Clark, Esq.	5¾	cr. river Plym.	39¼	Saltram, Earl of Morley. See p. **114.**
	2	PLYMOUTH.	43	
		To Saltash, by the Ferry, 4½ miles.		
		DEVONPORT.	45	

Devonport owes its present importance to a naval arsenal established here in the reign of William III., and called Plymouth Dock till 1824. It was first fortified in the reign of George II.; but the fortifications have since been considerably enlarged and improved. A wall twelve feet high defends the town on the north-east and south-west; and the heavy batteries on Mount Wise protect the entrance from the sea. Devonport is well built, and contains several Episcopal chapels, meeting-houses, and schools, a town-hall, a small theatre, an assembly-room, a large mechanics' institute, a beautiful promenade, called Richmond Walk, &c. The dockyard is one of the finest in the world, and comprises an area of seventy-one acres. It contains many objects of great interest, such as the blacksmith's shop, containing a huge steam hammer, the rigging-house, the boiling-house, the mast-house, the mast-pond, and the rope-houses. Thirty-two telegraphic stations connect this place with the Admiralty in London, but the electric telegraph has almost superseded them. The victualling-yard at Stonehouse, completed in 1835, is on a gigantic scale, and cost a million and a half. The steam-dock yard lately formed by Government at Morricetown, is most capacious, and will repay a visit. Devonport returns 2 M.P. Pop. 64,783.

Beyond the Crimble Passage is Mount Edgcumbe, the seat of the Earl of that name, a magnificent mansion, finely situated, and commanding most beautiful and varied prospects. Every Monday, during the summer months, the grounds attached to this charming place are thrown open to the public, but strangers can obtain admission at any time on application. On the Devonport side most extensive views of the Sound and surrounding country may be obtained from the Blockhouse, an old fortification, or from the top of Devonport column. Looking across the Hamoaze may be seen Thanks (Lord Graves), and Anthony Park (W. H. P. Carew, Esq.) At this point a steam-floating bridge connects the counties of Devon and Cornwall.

ON RIGHT FROM BRIST.	From Plym.		From Bristol.	ON LEFT FROM BRIST.
Long-Ashton. In the church is a carved screen, and some monuments of the Chokes family. Ashton Court, an old house, with a front by Inigo Jones. Has a large portrait gallery. 2 m. distant, Leigh Court, W. Miles, Esq., and Coombe House.		A mile from Bristol the Bristol and Exeter Railway branches off from the Great Western on the right. Pass through a tunnel, 100 yards in length.		Bedminster. Dundry, with its beacon, 700 feet above the level of the sea, and commanding one of the most extensive and beautiful prospects in the west of England. Barrow Gurney.
Flax-Bourton. The church has a fine doorway.	120½	**Nailsea Station.**	8	Farley Castle. Chelvey.
At a little distance from the station is Charleton House. Branch to Clevedon, 4 miles, a village on the shores of the Bristol Channel. The Church contains interesting monuments.	116½	**Yatton Clevedon Junction Station.** The line, nearly as far as Bridgewater, lies along the shore of Bristol Channel, abounding in beautiful and romantic scenery.	12	Brookley. Opposite Yatton station is Wrington. The church is a fine old building. John Locke was born in a house which adjoins the churchyard. In the churchyard is the tomb of Hannah More.
Worle.		cr. the river Yeo.		
In Banwell church are some brasses, a stone pulpit, and an octagonal font. It is in the later English. Banwell Court was built in 1584 by Bishop Godwyn, on the site of a monastery of the time of Alfred.	113	**Banwell Station.**	15½	On the left lie the Mendip Hills, with the bone caves of Banwell, and springs of Cheddar.
	110	**Weston Super Mare Station.** A branch, 1½ m. on the right, runs off to the watering place of Weston-Super-Mare.	18½	Locking. Hutton.
Breane. Berrow. Burnham, the scenery of which is much admired.		cr. the river Axe.		Bleadon has remains of a Pictish camp, where coins have been found.
Branch to Glastonbury and Wells. Wells is 5 m. from Shepton Mallet. to which place there is a branch railway, from the Wilts, Somerset, and Weymouth Railway.	101½	**Highbridge, near Burnham Station.** cr. river Brue, running from Glastonbury to the sea.	27	Lympsham. East-Brent. South-Brent.
Huntspill. Pawlett.				Puriton. Bawdrip.
	95½	**Bridgewater Station.** Bridgewater is situated on the river Parret. It was incorporated as a borough by King John, who built a castle here. It has a good coasting trade, and returns two members to Parliament.	33	The Duke of Monmouth was proclaimed King at Bridgewater, and lodged some time in the castle. He was defeated by the royal army on Sedgmoor, near Weston, 3 miles distant, where

ON RIGHT FROM BRISTOL	From Plym.		From Bristol.	ON LEFT FROM BRISTOL.
North Petherton, and 2 miles distant, Halswell House, C. J. K. Tynte, Esq. North Newton. St. Michael Church. Durston. West Monkton. Hestercombe. Cheddon Fitzpaine.		The church is a handsome spacious structure, and the spire the loftiest in the county. Pop., 11,320. cross river Parret. Approach the river Tone, and then ascend its valley to Taunton.		1000 were killed, and 1500 taken prisoners. Dunwear. The scenery of the river Tone, which runs on the left of the railway for above 8 m., is very interesting, and in some places romantic. North Curry. Rushton.
Staplegrove. Norton Fitzwarren. Hillfarrance. Nynehead.	83¾	**Taunton Station.** Taunton, a town of great antiquity, and one of the principal in Somersetshire. There are some remains of a castle, supposed to have been erected about 700 A.D. One of its churches is an edifice of great elegance and splendour, and has a beautifully carved desk and pulpit. The interior of the roof is very curious. Pop. 14,667.	44¾	Taunton sends two members to Parliament, and has a weekly market on Wednesday and Saturday. It was the scene of many iniquitous executions in the time of James II. under the direction of Kirk and Jefferies. Bishop's Hull. Bradford. Heatherton Park, W. Adair, Esq.
	76¾	**Wellington Station.** Wellington is a neat town, and contains many good houses. Through the interjacent country runs the Prætorian highway, called Watling Street. The inhabitants are chiefly employed in working coal and lime. (See p. 109). About 4 miles from the station we enter Devonshire, and pass through the principal tunnel on the line, five-eighths of a mile in length. We then descend through a deep cutting into the valley of the river Culme.	51¾	Burlescombe. Uffculme.
Branch to Tiverton on the right 5 miles. Tiverton is a town of considerable antiquity, pleasantly situated on the slope of a hill. The principal buildings are the castle, church, and free grammar school. The church is an interesting structure, containing several costly monuments. The view from the church-yard is strikingly picturesque. There is an important lace manufactory in the town. Tiverton returns two members to Parliament Pop. 10,447	67¾	**Tiverton Junction Station.**	60¾	We now descend the Culme, famous for its trout and eels.
Collumpton is a market-town of great antiquity. It was a demesne of the Saxon kings, and bequeathed by Alfred the Great to his son Ethelward. The church is a large and venerable structure, consisting of three aisles. Near the font are two curiously carved pieces of oak. The tower is a beautiful building, 100 feet high.	65½	**Collumpton.** The principal trade is the woollen manufacture. (See p. 109).	63	Welland.

ON RIGHT FROM BRIST.	From Plym.		From Bristol.	ON LEFT FROM BRIST.
Bradninch, an old town, formerly of considerable note. Pop. 1796.		The line still continues in the valley of the Culme.		Killerton, Sir T. D. Acland, Bart.
Silverton. Thorverton.	61½	Hele Station.	67	Broad Clist, 1½ mile beyond, Poltimore, Lord Poltimore.
Alphington has an ancient cross. In the church is a Norman font. Shillingford Abbot, 2 miles, and Kenbury Ho. Exminster, pleasantly situated on the Exe, before it swells out into an estuary.	53	Exeter Station. EXETER (p. 110). cr. river Exe, and continue along its right bank.	75½	Topsham, on the opposite bank of the Exe, is situated at the confluence of the little river Clist. It has a spacious and commodious quay, and ship-building is carried on to some extent. Pop. 1861, 2772. The estuary of the Exe is here above a mile broad. 2 m. from Topsham is Nutwell Court, Sir T. T. F. E. Drake, Bart.
Powderham Castle, Earl of Devon (p. 112). Kenton. Staplake House.				Courtland, Sir T. H. Roberts, Bart.
Mamhead, Sir L. Newman, Bart., 2 miles. Luscombe, 1½ miles.	44¼	Starcross Station.	84¼	Marpool Hall. Exmouth (p. 49). The Sea.
Cockwood.		Continue along sea-shore to		
	40¾	Dawlish St. (p. 112).	87¾	
Haldon Hill, 1818 feet, (see p. 113).		Continue along shore to		
Bishopsteignton.	37¾	TEIGNMOUTH (p. 112).	90¾	
Lyndridge. Ugbrooke House (Ld. Clifford), 2½ m. (see p. 113), and beyond Canonteign (Viscount Exmouth).		The line throughout from Exeter to Teignmouth, affords the Tourist an endless variety of excursions. The peeps of the sea and of the surrounding country, are beyond description fine. After reaching Teignmouth the line continues nearly along the north bank of the river Teign (here from one-half to three-quarters of a mile wide), which it crosses before reaching		Estuary of the Teign, the bridge at the mouth of which is the longest in the kingdom. It is 1671 feet in length, and consists of 34 arches, made partly of wood and partly of iron. A swing bridge opens in the centre to permit the passage of vessels.
Newton Bushel, a small market town.	32¾	Newton St.	95¾	

ON RIGHT FROM BRISTOL.	From Plym.		From Bristol.	ON LEFT FROM BRISTOL.
Stover Lodge, Duke of Somerset, 2½ m.		One mile beyond, on the left, is a branch to Torquay, 5 miles.		
Woolborough.				
Abbot's Kersewell.				Kingskerswell.
Ipplepen.				Cockington, 2 miles.
Broad Hempston.				
Staverton.				Berry Pomeroy Castle Duke of Somerset, (p. 113).
Dartington House, H. Champernowne, Esq.		cross river Dart.		Little Hempston.
	24	TOTNESS ST. (p. 113).	104½	Dartmouth, 8 miles (see p. 112).
		The line here turns westward, and approaches the elevated region of Dartmoor Forest.		Follaton House, G. Stanley Cary, Esq.
Rattery. Dean Prior, 1¾ miles.				Lisburne.
	17	Brent St.	111½	South Brent. Moreleigh.
Butterton Hill, one of the highest points of Dartmoor, 1203 feet.		cross river Avon.		
	15	Kingsbridge Road St.	113½	Kingsbridge, 9 miles distant, is a small market-town, situated at the head of an estuary, which affords a harbour for boats. Pop., 1585.
Harford. Stowford House.		The line skirts the south-east extremity of Dartmoor.		
	11¾	Ivy Bridge St.	116¾	Ivy Bridge (see p. 115).
Cornwood, and beyond, Blachford, Sir F. Rogers, Bart.		Viaduct across the river Erme. Seen from below, this has a very imposing effect.		
Goodamoor, P. O. Treby, Esq.				Chaddlewood.
Newnham Park, G. Strode, Esq.		cr. river Yealm.		
Elfordleigh.				
Boringdon Park, Earl of Morley, and beyond, Maristow, Sir Massey Lopes, Bart.	5	Plympton St.	123½	Plympton-Earle, one mile distant, is a small market-town, with a well endowed free school. Sir Joshua Reynolds was a native of this place, and his portrait, painted by himself, is contained in the guildhall. Plympton was disfranchised by the Reform Bill, previous to which it returned 2 members to Parliament. Pop. 900.
Egg Buckland.				
Whitleigh.				
Manadon House.				
		cr. river Plym.		
A portion of the line of railway between Exeter and Plymouth was originally worked on the atmospheric system; but this has for some time been abandoned.		Cross Dartmoor railway.		
		PLYMOUTH (p. 114).	128½	Saltram House (Earl of Morley).

ON RIGHT FROM EXET.	From Truro.		From Exeter.	ON LEFT FROM EXET.
Holcombe Burnell.	81	Pocomb Bridge.	2½	Perridge.
Culver House.	79½	Longdown-End.	4	Moreton - Hampstead is situated on an eminence; has a handsome church, and the remains of two castles, and in the vicinity are a rocking-stone, a cromlech, and the ruins of a Druidical temple.
	76½	Dunsford.	7	
Dartmoor Forest is an extensive waste, comprising upwards of 80,000 acres, part of the Duchy of Cornwall, the property of the Prince of Wales. It contains many eminences, from 1500 to 1800 feet in height.	72½	Moreton-Hampstead.	11	
	69½	Wormhill.	14	
		Entrance of Dartmoor Forest.		
	64½	Newhouse.	18	Tor Royal House, and in the distance, Prince Town, and near it Dartmoor Prison. Here, during the war, French prisoners were confined. In 1850, a large convict establishment was placed here, under a military guard. The convicts are employed in cultivating the moor.
		cr. East Dart.		
		cr. Cherrybrook.		
	59½	Two Bridges.	24	
		cr. the West Dart.		
To Okehampton, 17 m.	55¾	Merrivalle Bridge.	27¾	To Plymouth by Harrow Bridge, 12½ miles, which will save about 3 miles.
Near Tavistock is a tunnel, 1¾ mile in length, cut through a hard rock, for the passage of a canal. Six miles from Tavistock, near Milton Abbot, is Endsleigh, a charming seat of the Duke of Bedford.	51¾	TAVISTOCK is a neat town, pleasantly situated on the Tavy. It had formerly a rich and beautiful abbey, the remains of which are in many places still visible. It was founded in the tenth century by an Earl of Devonshire. The church contains several handsome monuments. The Duke of Bedford takes his title of Marquis from this place. Tavistock sends two members to Parliament. Pop. 8857.	31¾	To Beer Alston, 6 m.
Luscomb.		Gulworthy.		Calstock. Harewood House, Sir J. S. Trelawny, Bart. Near this is Cotele House, Earl of Mount Edgcumbe. The furniture is of the time of Mary and Elizabeth, and was chiefly collected by the late and present Earls. The hall contains an extensive collection of ancient armour, and the chapel is well fitted up. There is some noble timber on the estate. It is said that Charles II. spent several nights here. Beyond these is Buckland Abbey (Sir T. F. E. Drake, Bart.), and below Cotele is Pentillie Castle (A. Coryton, Esq.), overhanging a sudden curve of the ever-winding Tamar.
	48¼	New Bridge.	35¼	
Park Lodge.		cr. the riv. Tamar, and enter Cornwall.		
King Arthur is said to have had a palace, and kept his court at Callington. Whitford House, Sir W. B. Call, Bart.	42¾	CALLINGTON OR KELLINGTON, was constituted a borough in the 27th of Elizabeth, when it obtained the privilege of sending two members to Parliament, but is now disfranchised. Pop. 2202. Between Callington and Saltash, on the banks of the Tamar, is the church of Landulph, in which was interred in 1636, Theodore Paleologus, a descendant of the last Christian emperors of Greece.	40¾	Saltash is 9 miles from Callington. Saltash returned 2 M.P. prior to the Reform Act, when it was disfranchised. Near it are the curious and very perfect remains of Trematon Castle, held by the Earl of Cornwall, temp. of Wm. Rufus.
To Launceston, 11½ m.				

ON RIGHT FROM EXET.	From Truro.		From Exeter.	ON LEFT FROM EXET.
	41¼	New Bridge. cr. river Lynher or St Germans.	42¼	**Newton Park.**
	38¾	St Ive. cr. river Tidi.	44¾	To Devonport by Torpoint, 16½ m.
2 miles north of Liskeard is St. Cleer, the church of which has a round Saxon doorway. In the vicinity is St. Cleer's well and a stone cross. At some distance beyond is the Cheese Wring, one of the principal sights of Cornwall, a natural pile of rude rocks, 32 feet in height, the general outline resembling a child's top, the smallest end being at the base. How such enormous masses of granite assumed their present apparently insecure, but really immovable position, it is difficult to say. On an eminence at some distance is the Cromlech or Trevethy stone.	36½	Pengover.	47	To Saltash, 14 m.
		LISKEARD, an ancient and irregularly built town, partly situated on rocky hills, and partly in a vale. The church is a handsome building, erected in 1627. The town formerly returned 2 M. P. but now only 1. It carries on a considerable trade in tanning. Pop. 1861, 6585. 4 m. N.W. of Liskeard is St Neot, having one of the finest parish churches in the kingdom. It is of date 1480, and occupies the site of a monastery that stood there in the time of Edward the Confessor.	48¾	To St Germans, 9 m. The church of St Germans was once the cathedral of the bishoprick of Cornwall. It contains the original prebendal stalls, and several monuments to members of the Eliot family. In the immediate vicinity, and almost attached to the church, is Port Eliot, the seat of the Earl of St Germans, on the site of an ancient priory. On the coast, 10 miles from Liskeard, are the small towns of East and West Looe, chiefly remarkable for their picturesque appearance. Near the former
	32¼	Dobwalls.	51¼	is Trenant Park, H. T. Hope, Esq.
To Bodmin, 7½ m.	27¾	Tap-house. cr. river Fowey.	55¾	Boconnoc, seat of the late Lord Grenville, containing some very curious furniture. In the grounds is an obelisk to the memory of Sir Richard Lyttleton. Boconnoc was formerly the property of the grandfather of the great Earl of Chatham. The church dates its erection from the time of Henry VI.
To Bodmin, 6 m. **1 m. dist. Penquite, and on the Fowey river, Restormel House, J. Hext, Esq.**, and the ruins of Restormel Castle, once a royal residence, and one of the principal seats of the Earls of Cornwall. The great Lord Erskine was Baron of Restormel, but had no land in the county. Beyond this is Lanhydrock, T. J. Agar Robartes, Esq.	22	LOSTWITHIEL, an ancient town, on the beautiful river Fowey, has a considerable woollen-trade. The parish church, erected in the fourteenth century, is adorned with a fine spire. It was used as a barrack by the parliament army, and was injured by an explosion of gunpowder. It contains a curious font. To the south of the church are the ruins of a building called the palace, said to have been the residence of the Dukes of Cornwall, but now a Stannary prison. The borough formerly returned 2 M. P., but is now disfranchised. Pop. 1017.	61½	**Pelyn 5½ m. dist. is the** fishing town of Fowey, in a highly romantic situation. The surrounding scenery is very beautiful. It was once a place of importance. The contingent to the fleet of Edward II. on the expedition to Calais, from Fowey was greater in ships than that of any other port in the kingdom. Near it is Menabilly (W. Rashleigh, Esq.), containing a most valuable collection of minerals. Prideaux, Sir J. C. Rashleigh, Bart., 1 m dist.

ON RIGHT FROM EXET.	From Truro.		From Exeter.	ON LEFT FROM EXET.
	18½	St Blayzey.	65	
Trevarrick. St Mewan. The church of this parish is very old. Here is a hill called Mewan Beacon, crowned with a singular mass of crags.	14½	**St Austell** stands almost in the centre of the county, and has several tin mines and quarries of porcelain earth in its neighbourhood. The church is a handsome fabric, and its tower is fancifully ornamented. Pop. 3825.	69	Tregerrick. 2 m. dist. Duporth. Penrice.
Mevagissey is one of the Cornish fishing towns, most noted for the capture of the pilchard.		To Mevagissey, 7 m.		3 m. dist. Trenarran, J. Hext, Esq. Trewhiddle.
		cr. river Vinnick.		
	12	High Sticker.	71½	Heligan, J. H. Tremayne, Esq. To Tregony, 4½ miles.
Garlinnick.				Penzance.
	7¾	Grampound has an old chapel, and an ancient cross of granite. Pop. 573.	75¾	Trewithan. 3 m. dist., on river Fal, Trewarthenick, the seat of G. W. F. Gregor, Esq.
Lemellion, and 2½ m. distant, Carines, J. Hosken, Esq.	5½	**Probus.** The tower of the church of Probus is very elegant. 1¾ mile further a road leads off to Tregony, 3¾ m. distant. Here are the remains of an old castle, said to have been erected in the reign of Richard I. In the church is an ancient font.	78	About 10 m. from Tregony is the disfranchised borough of St Mawes. The castle was built by Henry VIII. Opposite St Mawes is Pendennis Castle, of the same period. These two castles occupy very elevated and strong positions
Tresillian House	3¼	Tresillian. Here the royal army surrendered to Fairfax in 1646.	80¼	commanding the entrance to Falmouth Harbour. Pendennis contains a small depot of arms, and is garrisoned by a company of soldiers.
Trehane E. late W. Pendarves, Esq. Penare.	2	Kiggon Mill.	81½	Pencalenick. Lambeson.
Tregolls, the seat of Sir S. T. Spry. At a distance, Liskis. Cheveyla. Croft West.		**TRURO.** Thence to Land's End by route, p. 127.	83½	Park. 3 miles from Truro, on the river Fal, is Tregothnan House, Viscount Falmouth.

LVI. EXETER TO LAUNCESTON, BODMIN, TRURO, PENZANCE, AND LAND'S END, 123¼ Miles.

ON RIGHT FROM EXET.	From L. End.		From Exeter.	ON LEFT FROM EXET.
Cleave House.				Barley House. Willow-Hayes.
Hallswood.	121	Adderwater.	2¼	Hurston

ON RIGHT FROM EXET.	From L. End.		From Exeter.	ON LEFT FROM EXET.
	117	Lilly Bridge.	6¼	
	116	Tap House.	7¼	Great Fulford, (B. Fulford, Esq.) which has been the property of the Fulford family since the time of Richard I.
The neighbourhood of Crockernwell is finely wooded, and the banks of the river Teign are peculiarly attractive.	114¾	Cheriton Cross.	8½	
	112¼	Crockernwell. Here is a moving-stone and a cromlech.	11	Hockworthy.
	108¼	Merry-Meet.	15	
	105¼	South Zeal.	18	Ramsley.
		cr. the river Taw.		
	104½	Sticklepath.	18¾	
Okelands. About a mile south-west of the town, are the ruins of the castle dismantled by Henry VIII.	101	Okehampton, a town of considerable antiquity. It formerly returned 2 M. P., but is now disfranchised.	22¼	Okehampton Park.
Place House.		cr. the river Okement.		Lower Bowden.
Millaton.	95	Over Sourton Down, to Bridestow.	28¼	Leawood, C. P. Hamlyn, Esq. Great Stadon.
Bidlake.				Lower Stadon.
Lewcross.				Down House. Lew Trenchard.
Stowford.				
Hayne, C. A. Harris, Esq.				Portgate, and farther off Sydenham, J. H. Tremayne, Esq.
Lifton Down.	86	Lifton.	37¼	Lifton Park. In the distance Endsleigh, Duke of Bedford.
	85	Cadron.	38¼	
		cr. the river Tamar, and enter Cornwall.		
One mile from Launceston is Werrington House, Duke of Northumberland, a fine mansion, beautifully situated on the river Tamar. 14½ miles distant is Camelford, which, before the Reform Act, returned two M. P. Here, according to tradition, King Arthur was mortally wounded in battle, with his nephew, Modred. Six miles distant, on		LAUNCESTON is situated on an eminence, on the summit of which are the ruins of its castle, an ancient fortress, supposed to have been erected by the Britons. The church is a handsome building, ornamented with some curious carving. The town returns one member to Parliament. Pop. 5140.	40¾	Launceston is 11½ miles from Tavistock, and 10¼ miles from Callington. Almost adjoining Launceston is the disfranchised borough of Newport. The whole village is the property of the Duke of Northumberland.

ON RIGHT FROM EXET.	From L. End.		From Exeter.	ON LEFT FROM EXET.
a precipitous and rugged headland, are the ruins of Tintagel, King Arthur's castle; and near it the small fishing town of Bossinney, which, before the Reform Bill, returned two M. P. Three miles from Tintagel is the singularly romantic little town of Boscastle. To Stratton, 18 miles.				
Tregadillick.		Trebursey.		Trebursey House, W. A. H. Arundell, Esq.
	76½	Trerithick Bridge.	46¾	At a dist. Trebartha Hall, F. Rodd, Esq.
		cr. Penpont Water.		
	74¾	Five Lane's Inn.	48½	
	73¼	Trewint.	49	
	71¾	Palmer's Bridge.	51½	
		Jamaica Inn.		
This cross, which has been ornamented with scrolls, is now much defaced by age.		Four Holes Cross.		The road now crosses Bodmin moor.
		cr. the river Fowey.		
The manor here once belonged to the Knights Hospitallers.	67½	Temple.	55¾	
3 miles distant is Pencarrow, seat of Rev. Sir H. H. Molesworth, Bart. Colquite, D. Hoblyn Petre, Esq. Boscarne. To Camelford, 12 m. To Wadebridge, 8 m. (Near it are nine enormous stones called the Sisters.) In the vicinity of Camelford two battles were fought, one between the Saxons and the Britons, the other between King Arthur and Mordred, his nephew.	61½	BODMIN was formerly a place of considerable importance, and contained a priory, cathedral, and 13 churches. Of these only one remains, a very handsome building, containing a curious antique font. The principal trade of Bodmin is in wool. It returns 2 M.P. Pop. 1851, 6337.	61¾	On a down in this neighbourhood are some monumental stones, supposed to be the remains of a Druidical temple. Lanhydroc, T. J. Agar Robartes, Esq. To Lostwithiel, 6 miles.
	59½	Lanivet Ford.	63¾	At Lanivet are the remains of an ancient monastic building.
14 miles distant is the seaport town of Padstow, at the mouth of the Camel. It has a considerable trade in herrings, pilchards, and slates, and manufactures serges. Dr Prideaux was a native of this town.	53½	Junction of the road. St Columb, Major. 3¼ miles to the right. St Columb is 246 miles from London.	69¾	St Columb derives its name from its church, St Columba. At a distance Trekenning.
	52½	Fraddon.	70¾	
St Enoder.	49½	Summer Court.	73¾	
	44¾	Trespen.	78½	St Michael, an inconsiderable, disfranchised borough. Though consisting

ON RIGHT FROM EXETER.	From L. End.		From Exeter.	ON LEFT FROM EXETER.
Penmount.	44¼	St. Erme.	79	of only four farms, it once had the privilege of returning two M.P.
Rose Dale.	42	Buckshead.	81¼	
To Redruth, 8½ miles. Redruth is situated on a bleak and exposed spot in the very bosom of the mining district. It is of very remote origin, but did not rise to any importance till the discovery and working of the copper mines, which have been the means of increasing its population six-fold during the last century. **3 miles north-west of Redruth is Tehidy Park, the seat of late Baroness Basset, formerly of her father, the late Lord De Dunstanville, who organized and headed the miners of Cornwall to relieve Plymouth when threatened by the combined French and Spanish fleets in 1779.**	41	TRURO is considered the capital of Cornwall. It is situated at the conflux of the Kenwin and the St. Allen. It carries on a considerable trade in tin and copper ore, and has works for converting tin into bars and ingots. It returns 2 M.P. Pop. 1861 11,337 The Parliament of the Lord Warden of the Stanneries, and the Vice-Warden's Courts, are held here. At a short distance is the church of St. Michael Penkivel, in which the gallant Admiral Boscawen is interred. Lord Truro takes his title from this town.	82¼	Bodrean. To Grampound, 7½ m. To Tregoney, 7 miles. Bosvigo House. Comprigny. Foote the comedian and Lord Vivian, were natives of Truro; and Henry Martyn, Sir H. Davy, Admiral Viscount Exmouth, Polwhele, &c., were educated here. 3 m. distant is Tregothnan, the seat of Viscount Falmouth, standing on an eminence, and commanding some fine views. At a distance Killiganoon, late Admiral Spry; Trelissick, R. A. Daniell, Esq.
Killiow.	39¾	**Calenick.**	83½	At a little distance Carclew, the seat of Sir Ch. Lemon, Bart., one of the finest mansions in Cornwall.
Tregolls, Sir S. T. Spry. Higher Polleau.	36	Perranwell.	87¼	Beyond Carclew is Enys, J. S. Enys, Esq.; and 3 miles from it is Penryn, on an eminence, formerly defended by a castle. It unites with Falmouth in returning 2 M.P
Tretheage.	32	Tregolls.	91¼	
Helston is a populous town on the east side of the river Cober, in the immediate vicinity of the mining districts. It was first incorporated by Richard Cœur de Lion. A curious festival, called the Fury or Flora Dance, is held on the 8th of May. Pop. 1861, 8497. Helston once possessed an hospital of St. John. A bowling-green is kept on the site of the ancient castle. It returns one M.P.	29½	Buttris.	93¾	Falmouth, two miles distant, is a considerable sea-port, having a commodious harbour. The entrance to the harbour is defended by the Castles of Pendennis and St. Mawes. Pendennis Castle endured a siege of six months, in the Royal cause, during the civil wars. It joins with Penryn in returning 2 M.P. Pop. of Penryn and Falmouth 1861, 14,485. 3 miles S.E. of Helston are Mawgan and Trelowarren, Sir R. R. Vyvyan, Bt.
	28½	Polgreen.	94¾	
	27	Meneby.	96¼	
	26	Trevennen.	97¼	
	24	HELSTON, cr. river Loe.	99¼	
In Breage is the celebrated copper and tin mine of Huel Vor. In this parish, too, are the remains of Pengerswick Tower.	21	St. Breage.	102¼	Penrose, Rev. J. Rogers. In the ground is a large sheet of water, called Looe Pool, surrounded by beautiful scenery. 2 m. from Penrose, and near

ON RIGHT FROM EXET.	From L. End.		From Exeter.	ON LEFT FROM EXET.
		Germoe.		Mawgan, is Trelowarren, Sir R. R. Vyvyan, Bart.
Godolphin Park, Duke of Leeds. Beyond, at some distance, is Crowan, the church of which contains many memorials of the ancient family of St Aubyn. Their ancient seat, Clowance, was unfortunately burned by accident, but is now rebuilt.	18	**Chywoon.**	105¼	
		Perran.		Acton Castle.
Marazion enjoys a peculiar degree of salubrity from its situation at the foot of a hill on Mount's Bay, by which it is completely sheltered from cold winds. At a short distance is St Michael's Mount, an isolated rocky promontory, which, together with the tower of the chapel erected on its summit, rises to the height of 250 feet above the level of the sea. The view from the top is inexpressibly grand.	17¼	Marazion, or Market-Jew, is supposed to be the oldest town in the county, being situated near the great mart for tin, the ancient Ictis, at St Michael's Mount. It is said to have flourished most during the pilgrimages to Mount St Michael.	107¾	
St. Michael's Mount was the property of the late Sir J. St Aubyn, Bart., whose family made improvements on it. It now belongs to J. St Aubyn, Esq. Here Lady Catherine Gordon, wife of Perkin Warbeck, took refuge; and many families secured themselves during the rebellion of the Cornish men in the reign of Edward VI. Population, 1545.	11½	PENZANCE.* Here you may proceed to Sennen, 8½ miles; thence to Land's End, 1¾ miles; or to Newlyn, 1½ miles; Trevelloe, 1¾ miles; St Buryan, 2¾ miles; Trebear, 1½ miles; Trevescan, 2¾ miles; thence to the Land's End, ¾ mile: making altogether, from Penzance, 11 miles.	111¾	Penzance is the most westerly town in England. It enjoys a very mild atmosphere, and the soil around is extremely fertile. It carries on a considerable trade in the exportation of tin and pilchards. The new market house, the geological museum. and St. Paul's church, are its most handsome edifices. In its vicinity are several natural curiosities, such as Logan Rock, Lamorna Cove, and Lanyon Quoit. At the distance of five miles is a Druidical circle, called the Merry Maidens. Pop of Penzance 1861, 9414. The town stands in the parish of Madron, of which the late Sir Humphry Davy was a native.
2 miles from Penzance, Trengwainton, Sir C. D. Price, Bart.		LAND'S END,	123¼	

a promontory at the western extremity of the English coast. About a mile from the promontory are a number of rocks, called the Long Ships. On the largest of these is erected a light-house, 112 feet above the level of the sea.

WALES.

LVII. TOUR FROM BRISTOL ALONG THE COAST OF WALES THROUGH NEWPORT, CARDIFF, SWANSEA, CAERMARTHEN, PEMBROKE, HAVERFORDWEST, ST DAVID'S, CARDIGAN, ABERYSTWITH, &c.

The tourist having crossed the Severn by the new passsage will find no place

* Eight miles from Penzance is the populous fishing town of St. Ives. Its harbour is defended by a pier, erected by the celebrated engineer Smeaton, and is capable of accommodating 200 vessels. The town depends chiefly on the coast trade and pilchard fishery. One M.P. Pop. 10,353. Tregenna Castle, the seat of H. L. Stephens, Esq., occupies a lofty eminence not far from the town, and commands a noble prospect.

worthy of notice till his arrival at Caerwent. Its ruins indicate its former extent and magnificence under the Romans, but it has now dwindled into a village. On the left is Llanwern, the mansion of the Rev. Sir C. J. Salusbury, Bart., commanding an extensive view. Near the 13th mile-stone is the neat village of Christchurch, with its white-washed cottages. At a short distance to the right is Caerleon, a town of great antiquity, situated on the river Usk. The walls are in some places 14 feet high and 12 feet broad, and the shape of the town seems to have been that of an oblong square, three sides straight and the fourth curved. There is here ample scope for the researches of the antiquary, and numerous coins found near it have enriched the cabinets of the curious. In this neighbourhood there are many Roman encampments. Two miles from Caerleon is Llantarnam House, once a seat of a considerable branch of the Morgan family. The site of this structure was a rich Cistertian Abbey of six monks. Some traces of the ancient fabric still remain. Between Caerleon and Newport is St Julian's, once the residence of the celebrated Lord Herbert of Cherbury. Part of it has been converted into a farm-house, but other parts remain in their original state. Near it is an old barn which once formed part of St Julian's Abbey. Further on is Newport Castle, built apparently for the defence of the river, which is commanded by three strong towers. Close to Newport a stone bridge, consisting of five arches, has been thrown over the Usk, at an expense of £10,165. The town itself presents little that is interesting to the traveller, excepting a church exhibiting architecture of various ages. The churchyard commands an extensive view of the surrounding country—the Severn and Bristol Channel. It is a sea-port and a place of considerable trade, chiefly in iron and coal. Its prosperity has greatly increased of late years. By means of canals and railways, Newport communicates with various parts of South Wales, while boats and sloops, besides two steam packets, daily sail between that town and Bristol. The road from Newport passes Tredegar House, with its extensive and well-planned grounds and noble trees, the property of Sir C. M. R. G. Morgan, Bart., and next the village St. Mellons, where the upper and lower roads from Newport to Cardiff unite. Here there is a small encampment surrounded by a deep trench. Three miles from St. Mellons is Rhymney Church, an edifice not less than 180 feet from the chancel to the tower, which is ornamented with battlements and Gothic pinnacles. Having crossed the river Rhymney, which separates England from Wales, the tourist enters CARDIFF, the capital of Glamorganshire. It is a well-built sea-port and borough town, at the mouth of the river Taff, over which there is a bridge consisting of five arches. The castle was founded by Robert Fitz-Hamon, a Norman Baron, towards the end of the eleventh century, but the modern improvements seem incongruous with the appearance of the ruins. The keep, which is still very perfect, is of an octagonal shape. From the mound enclosed by it, and also from the ramparts, charming views of the surrounding country are obtained. In the castle are several excellent portraits. Robert Duke of Normandy was confined twenty-six years in Cardiff Castle after he had been deprived of his sight and inheritance by his younger brother, Henry I The place of his confinement is still pointed out. The castle belongs to the

Marquess of Bute, and gives him the title of Baron Cardiff, as heir general of Sir Wm. Herbert, Earl of Pembroke, K.G., brother-in-law of Henry VIII. The tower of the church is extremely elegant, but there is nothing in the inside worthy of notice. In this town, Robert, Earl of Gloucester, founded a priory of White Friars and another of Black. By means of railway and canal, iron is brought from the works at Merthyr Tydvil, and sent to English and foreign markets. The numerous improvements on the town and its neighbourhood, particularly the docks commenced by the second Marquess, and opened in 1839, and the railways connecting it with London, have already wonderfully increased the prosperity of Cardiff. Upwards of 750,000 tons of coals were shipped at Cardiff in 1853. Pop. (1851) 18,351; (1861) 32,954.

About two miles from Cardiff is Llandaff, now only an inconsiderable village. The object most deserving attention is the ancient cathedral, the remains of which are very beautiful. The Bishop's palace was destroyed by Owen Glendower in the reign of Henry IV. Resuming the route—6 miles from Cardiff are the village and church of St. Nicholas; here a road on the left leads to Duffryn House (J. B. Pryce, Esq.) About half-way between these two places are some ancient monuments, supposed to be Druidic. The largest of these is supported by five stones, forming a room 16 feet long, 15 feet wide, and from 4½ to 6 feet high, and open toward the south. At the east side are three stones closely set together. The contents of the largest are 324 square feet. Near Duffryn House there is another cromlech, but of dimensions inferior to the former. It is supposed to have received its present name from the Christians having in contempt converted it into a dog kennel. Between Duffryn House and the sea is Wenvoe Castle (R. F. Jenner, Esq.) On regaining the turnpike the beautiful and picturesque grounds of Cottrell (Admiral Sir G. Tyler) next attract attention. Near the gate grows a magnificent Wych-elm, one of the largest in the kingdom. Llantrithyd Park, the beautiful domain of Sir T. D. Aubrey, Bart., abounds in romantic spots. The house is supposed to have been built in the time of Henry VI. The windows are very large, one of them being twelve feet square. The road now enters a down, and a fine prospect opens to view. The town of Cowbridge—at the bottom Llanblethian, with its hill, church, and castle beyond, and the boldly situated Castle Penlline (John Homfray, Esq.) form a scene of grandeur much admired by travellers. Cowbridge, or Port-vaen, is a neat borough and market-town, divided by the river Ddau. It was formerly surrounded by walls, of which one gate, a bold Gothic structure, alone remains. The free grammar school, partly endowed by Sir Leoline Jenkins, a Secretary of State in the reign of Charles II., is in considerable repute. Pop. 1861, 1094. The chapel, which contains several handsome monuments, is singularly constructed, and at a distance appears like an embattled fortress. In a field near it are a large tumulus, and the remains of a Druidic temple. Cowbridge unites with Cardiff and Llantrissant in returning a member to Parliament. At a short distance north-east from Cowbridge is Aberthin, a neat rural village, and near it a large elm-tree, which measures 28 feet in circumference. It is hollow, with an entrance like a Gothic doorway, and capable of containing thirty-six full-grown persons. The route from Cowbridge to Neath frequently passes through rich pastures and meadows, adorned with plantations and villas, hamlets and villages, none of which deserve particular notice. About 6 miles from Cowbridge is Bridgend, a small irregular town on the river Ogmore. The hamlet of Oldcastle stands on one side of the town, and Newcastle on the other. One of the bridges over the river is an elegant structure. The church-yard affords a fine prospect of the surrounding country. Five miles to the south is Ewenny Abbey, (R. T. Turbervill, Esq.) one of the most perfect specimens of the ancient monastery now extant. Its embattled walls and towers seem to have been intended for defence rather than for devotion. The church is of a cruciform shape, very massive, and in the Norman style of architecture. Onwards the well-wooded hill of Margam presents a fine appearance. It is 1099 feet high, and covered from base to summit with magnificent oak trees, the value of which has been estimated at £60,000. It is the property of C. R. M. Talbot, Esq., of Margam Park. Here is a remarkably fine orangery, which, it is said, had this singular origin. A vessel, conveying from Portugal, to Mary, Queen of William III., a present of orange and lemon trees, was stranded, and the cargo became the property of Sir Thomas, afterwards Lord Mansel. The late T. Mansel Talbot, Esq., in 1787, built for their reception a superb green-house, 327 feet in length, with a handsome palladian front, adorned with statues, vases, and other antique curiosities. In the pleasure ground adjoining is a bay tree, upwards of 60 feet high, and supposed to be the largest in the world. A little farther is the village of Margam, delightfully situated at the verge of the above-mentioned forest, and abounding in monastic antiquities. Here are some very interesting ruins of an abbey, founded by Robert, Earl of Gloucester, in 1147. At the dissolution it was purchased by one of the Mansel family, and is now the property of C. R. M. Talbot, Esq. his representative. While repairing the parish church in 1810 several curious remains were discovered. On the wall of one of the houses, in the village, is a curious ancient cross, and in the adjoining grounds are various monumental stones with inscriptions. On a hill in the neighbourhood, are a large rude stone, 14 feet high, and an entrenched Roman camp. About a mile from Margam was a convent, called Eglwys Nunyd, or Nun's Church, now a farm-house, and near it is a Roman monument 4 feet high. This neighbourhood abounds in coal, iron ore, and limestone. At Aberavon very extensive copper works are carried on. Pop. 7754. The climate in this part of Wales is very mild. Briton Ferry, on the bank of the river Neath, is surrounded by scenery of remarkable beauty. Near it is Baglan House (H. Gwyn, Esq.) Baglan Hall, the property of Griffith Llewellyn, Esq., commands varied and extensive views of the river and the adjacent surrounding country. The tourist may either cross the ferry, and proceed to Swansea (5 miles), or continue the pleasing route along the bank of the Neath to the town of that name. There is a broad-gauge railway from Neath to Merthyr Tydvil. The Neath canal, 14 miles in extent, terminates at Giant's Grave, where 60,000 tons of coal are shipped annually. Further on there is a single stone monument, called Maen Llythyrog, reckoned one of the remotest relics of antiquity. Gnoll, situated on the summit of a hill, commands a very extensive prospect. Its hanging woods, shady walks, and picturesque cascades, are much admired. NEATH or Nedd, the Nidum of Antoninus, is seated on the eastern bank of the river Neath. It is one of five contributary boroughs which returns a member to Parliament. The population in 1851 amounted to 5841. It possesses some trade, as a sea-port, in coals, iron, and copper, for which it is considerably indebted to its canal, which communicates between Aberdare and Briton Ferry. Neath Castle is now an inconsiderable ruin. About one mile west of the town are the ruins of the abbey. The site of the refectory, the chapel, the hall, and several other rooms may still be traced. It was established for monks of the Cistertian order by Richard de Granville, an ancestor of the Duke of Buckingham and Chandos. In this abbey Edward II. sheltered himself after his escape from Caerphilly Castle, and was recaptured. Near the ruins are some very extensive works for the manufacture of iron and copper. Here are two immense blast furnaces, an iron foundry, and an engine manufactory. From Neath to Brecon is 27 miles, to Merthyr Tydvil about 25. The direct road from Neath to Swansea is 8½ miles in length, and by railway they are but 8 miles apart, but there is a very pleasant bridle-road by Briton Ferry.

SWANSEA,

(anciently Aber-tawy), is situated at the confluence of the river Tawe with the Bristol Channel, and near the centre of a beautiful bay. The population is 41,606. Swansea is a favourite resort in the summer for bathing. A very flourishing pottery has long been carried on here; also, an iron foundry, roperies, extensive breweries, and much shipbuilding. One mile and a half distant are extensive copper works. At one of them, it is said that not less than 40,000 tons of coal are consumed annually. Swansea is, with the exception of Cardiff, the most considerable sea-port in Wales, and employs much shipping, but has no foreign trade. It is accessible from London by the Great Western Railway to Bristol or Gloucester, and thence by the South Wales Railway. Packets sail regularly to Dublin, Waterford, and Cork; twice or thrice a-week to Ilfracombe; and to Bristol, four times a-week. Swansea Castle, the property of the Duke of Beaufort, was erected A.D. 1099 by Henry de Beaumont, who conquered Gowerland from the Welsh. The habitable parts are now converted into a poor-house and gaol. St. Mary's Church contains some very ancient monuments. St. John's Church was formerly a chapel belonging to the Knights of Jerusalem. As a watering-place this town has the advantage of a fine level sandy shore, and the vicinity affords a great number of agreeable walks and rides. There is a mineral spring here. A large tract of country north of Swansea abounds with coal, and copper-works. From Swansea, an excursion may be made to the district of Gower or Gwyr, the south-west of which is inhabited by a colony of Flemings who settled there in the reign of Henry I. They do not understand the Welsh language, are distinguished by their dialect and provincial dress, and rarely intermarry with the Welsh. The most interesting objects in this district are Oystermouth Castle, five miles from Swansea, a majestic ruin, commanding a delightful prospect, with the Mumbles Point close at hand—the rocky scenery of Caswell Bay—a huge cromlech called King

Arthur's Stone, upon a mountain called Cwm Bryn, near Llanrhidian—the picturesque ruins of Penrice Castle, so called after the family of Pēnrice, who settled here in the reign of Edward I.—a modern villa, of the same name, the seat of C. R. M. Talbot, Esq.—Oxwich Bay—the neat village of Cheriton—the bold promontory of Wormshead, &c. Boating excursions to Oxwich, Penrice, Wormshead, and other places on the shores of the promontory of Gower, are sometimes undertaken by parties of pleasure from Swansea during the summer months.

From Swansea to Pont-ar-Dulais is 9 miles—Neath, 8—Briton Ferry, 5—Cardiff, 39—Caermarthen, 26.

The upper road from Swansea to Caermarthen then leads by Melin Cadleg, 3½ miles; Corseinon, with its elegant and beautiful churches, 5 miles; (on the right to Neath, 10 miles); Pont-ar-Dulais, 8½; Cenbrenlwyd, (Caermarthenshire). 10¼; Bryn-y-Maen, 11; Llannon, 13½; Pontyferem, 17; Llangyndeyrn, 21. The lower road lies through Llanwelly and Kidwelly, 9 miles from Caermarthen. The castle of Kidwelly was formerly of great extent, and to it King John retired when at war with the barons. It is said to have been built soon after the Conquest by William de Londres, a Norman adventurer, (A. D. 1094,) who conquered Glamorganshire. The gateway is very fine, and the whole a magnificent remain. It is now the property of the Earl of Cawdor.

CAERMARTHEN

is one of the most wealthy towns in Wales, elevated above the navigable river Towy. It commands a view of one of the most beautiful vales in the principality. This town was the site of the Roman station Maridunum. Here the Welsh held their parliaments, and established their chancery and exchequer. In the 38th of Henry VIII. it was created a borough. Caermarthen carries on a foreign and considerable coasting trade. The Towy is famed for its salmon. It conveys ships of 250 tons up to the bridge. Here are established the Cambrian and a Cwmreigyddion society. Here also are a handsome town-hall, market-house, free grammar-school, an institution called the Presbyterian college, several meeting-houses, national, Lancastrian, and Sunday schools. The remains of the castle have been converted into the county gaol. At the west end of the town there is a column to the memory of General Sir T. Picton, who represented the borough in Parliament. The Ivy Bush Inn was once the property of Sir Richard Steele, who was interred in St Peter's Church. In the neighbourhood of this town he wrote the comedy of the Conscious Lovers. The famous magician, Ambrose Merlin, was a native of Caermarthen. Here also was born Lewis Bailey, Bishop of Bangor, and author of the Practice of Piety. Pop. 1861, 9993. It joins with Llanelly in returning one M.P. About two miles from Caermarthen is an eminence called Merlin's Hill, near the brow of which is Merlin's Chair, where superstition says the famous prophet used to sit when he uttered his prophecies.

A number of interesting objects are to be seen on the road from Caermarthen to Llandilo Vawr about 15 miles distant. The first object of notice is Abergwilli Palace, the noble mansion of the Bishop of St David's, with its highly ornamented grounds; then Grongaer Hill, the spot to which the poet Dyer has given so much celebrity. At some distance to the right is Middleton Hall, (E. H. Adams, Esq.), a very splendid mansion. Nearly opposite Rhiw-yr-Adar is Golden Grove, the property of the Earl of Cawdor, inherited from his maternal ancestors the Vaughans. Beyond this is Dynevor Castle, seated upon a lofty hill clothed with venerable oaks, once the regal seat of the ancient Cambrian monarchs. The last prince who inhabited it was Rhŷs ap Tew Dwr Mawr, an ancestor of its present possessor, Lord Dynevor. The forces of Henry I. besieged it in 1226, but were defeated with the loss of 2000 men, by Llywelyn Prince of North Wales. Newton Park (Lord Dynevor,) the view from the summit of Golwg-y-byd, the British fortress on the rugged eminence of Careg Cennen, and the ruins of Drŷslwyn Castle will also be found well worthy of attention.

About 12 or 13 miles from Caermarthen are the ruins of Laugharne Castle, built or rebuilt by Sir Guido de Brian in the reign of Henry III. The town of Laugharne is one of the cleanest and best built towns in South Wales. Dean Tucker was a native of this place. The neighbouring heights command grand and extensive sea views. One mile distant is another ruin called Roche's Castle, but supposed to have been a monastery. A few miles from Laugharne is the village of Llanddowror, on the south bank of the Taff; the scenery is highly beautiful. Five miles distant from Laugharne is a place called Green Bridge, consisting of a natural excavation through which runs a small rivulet, and there disappears till it mingles its waters with the ocean.

About 27 miles from Caermarthen is Tenby, a fashionable sea-bathing place, delightfully situated on a rock facing Caermarthen Bay. The shore is well adapted for bathing, and the sands afford delightful promenades. Here are all the usual conveniences and amusements of a watering place. The trade of Tenby consists of coal and culm, and the oyster and trawl fisheries. Here are some remains of a castle supposed to have been erected by the Flemings. The ancient walls of the town are still sufficiently perfect to show its former strength and extent. The religious establishments of the town and suburbs have been numerous. The church is a spacious structure, with a spire 152 feet high ; the interior contains some fine old monuments. Many pleasant excursions may be made from Tenby ; among others, to the Isle of Caldy, 3 miles from the shore. The tower of its ancient priory is still standing.

About 4 or 5 miles from Tenby are the ruins of Manorbeer Castle, once the property of the Barri family, supposed to have been erected about the time of William Rufus. It was the birth-place of Giraldus de Barri, commonly surnamed Cambrensis, the celebrated historian of Wales. It has evidently been a place of great strength and importance. A little farther on are the ivy-mantled walls of Carew Castle, and about 3 miles from Pembroke the ruins of Lamphey, once the residence of the bishops of St David's, afterwards a seat of the great Lord Essex. Ten miles from Tenby is

PEMBROKE,

the capital of Pembrokeshire, pleasantly situated on a navigable creek of Milford Haven. It was formerly surrounded by a wall, some parts of which are still visible. It carries on but little trade, and owes its chief importance to its Royal dockyard. In 1861, the town contained 15,071 inhabitants. It unites with Tenby, Wiston, and Milford, in returning one M. P. On an eminence west of the town are the remains of a castle which ranks among the most splendid monuments of antiquity in South Wales. It was the birth-place of Henry VII., and is famous for the brave defence made by its garrison in favour of Charles I. The natural cavern called the Wogan lies immediately under the chapel, and opens with a wide mouth toward the sea. Pembroke gives the title of Earl to the senior branch of the Herbert family—Earls of Pembroke and Montgomery.

To the south of Pembroke is Orielton, the seat of Sir John Owen, Bart., and beyond it Stackpole Court, the baronial mansion of the Earl of Cawdor, placed on the west side of the pool on a fine eminence at the edge of a bold declivity. It bore originally a castellated form, and during the civil wars was garrisoned for the king. It came into the possession of Sir A. Campbell, ancestor of the Earl of Cawdor, by his marriage with Miss Lort, the heiress of this extensive domain. In the vicinity is Bosherston Mere, a remarkable cleft through which, during heavy gales from the south-west, the sea is forced up from beneath in a column 30 feet in height. A short distance east of Bosherston Mere is a curious hermitage called St Govan's chapel. Carew Castle (T. G. W. Carew, Esq.), 4 miles from Pembroke, is well worthy of a visit. The road lies through rich and picturesque scenery. A little to the north a fine view of Milford may be obtained. A great part of Carew Castle is in a state of excellent preservation, and it ranks among the most beautiful and interesting ruins in the principality. It was one of the royal demesnes of the princes of South Wales, and with seven others, was given as a dowry with Nêst, daughter of Rhŷs ap Tew Dwr, to Gerald de Windsor, an ancestor of the Carew family. Henry VII. is said to have been entertained here in his progress to Bosworth Field. In 1644, it was garrisoned for the king, and held out a long siege. Half-a-mile to the south-east of the castle is the church of St John the Baptist, a large and venerable structure. Within this parish are Freestone Hall, J. Allen, Esq.; and Wilsdon, on the site of which Cromwell took up his quarters when besieging Pembroke Castle.

The tourist is usually conveyed from Pembroke to Milford Haven in a boat. The entrance to the haven is remarkably fine, and the extent and smoothness of the water give it the appearance of a lake. The harbour is said to be one of the best in Europe, and is capable of holding all the navy of England in perfect security. At the upper end of the haven is MILFORD, a remarkable neat well built town. Its trade is small and has decreased since the dockyard was removed to Pembroke. Steam-packets sail daily to Waterford. The church is a very elegant building, with stained glass windows and a lofty tower at the west end. The custom-house, quay, observatory, and hotel, also deserve notice. The scenery around Milford is very picturesque. On a fork of land, formed by the confluence of the two rivers Cleddy and Cleddeu, stands Rose Castle, an ancient seat of the Owens, and higher up on the estuary of the Cleddeu is Picton Castle, the seat of the late Lord Milford, and now the residence of J. H Philipps, Esq.

The ancient style of grandeur in which the mansion was built is somewhat incongruous with the modern alterations made on it. The castle commands a fine view towards Landshipping, where the two rivers meet, and jointly form Milford Haven. Close to Picton Castle is Slebech, once an ancient commandery of the Knights of Jerusalem.

About 8 miles from Milford Haven is Haverfordwest. On the road is Steynton, where Sir William Jones was a scholar.

HAVERFORDWEST,

a sea-port, market, and borough-town, is beautifully situated on an eminence above the navigable river Cleddy. It was the capital of the possessions of the Flemings, granted to them in the time of William Rufus and his son Henry. Its public buildings are three churches, a handsome guildhall, and the gaol, originally the keep of an ancient castle, an extensive fortress erected by Gilbert de Clare, first Earl of Pembroke. In the civil wars, this castle was garrisoned for the King. Haverfordwest unites with Fishguard and Narberth in returning one M.P. Population, 7019. From Haverfordwest to Pembroke by water is 15 miles, by the road, 10, to Cardigan, 28½. About 10½ miles from Haverfordwest is Narberth, a small neat town, with the picturesque ruins of a castle. Population of borough, 1209. On the road to St. David's, at the distance of about 6 miles, are the ruins of Roche Castle, commanding a most extensive view by sea and land. It sustained a siege against the Parliamentary forces during the civil wars.

ST DAVID'S,

sixteen miles from Haverfordwest, is an ancient but almost deserted city though still exhibiting indications of past splendour in its ecclesiastical remains. The cathedral is a venerable Gothic structure, displaying much ornamental architecture. It contains a variety of ancient monuments, and the bishop's throne is of exquisite workmanship. Near the cathedral are the ruins of the Episcopal palace, formerly a magnificent building, founded by Bishop Gower in the fourteenth century, and a chapel, the only relic of St Mary's College, which was founded by John of Gaunt and Blanche, his wife. David, the national saint of Wales, with the consent of his nephew, King Arthur, is said to have removed the metropolitan see from Caerleon to Menevia, afterwards named St David's. He was the first of 26 Archbishops of Menevia, and died here about the year 1544, after he had filled the metropolitan chair of Wales for sixty years, and was interred in his own cathedral. About 500 years after his death, he was canonized by Pope Calixtus II. His successors exercised the archiepiscopal power down to the time of Bishop Bernard, (consecrated in 1115,) who, by command of Henry I. resigned this power to the see of Canterbury. St David's had once seven suffragans included within its metropolitan pale, viz. Worcester, Hereford, Llandaff, Bangor, St Asaph, Llanbadarn, and Margam. It has had a greater number of prelates than any other see in the kingdom, and has numbered among its bishops Bull, Lowth, Horsley, Burgess, &c. At present Bishop Thirlwall, the historian of Greece, presides over this see. The shrine of St David's, in ancient times, acquired the highest celebrity, and in the list of monarchs who resorted to it are to be included the names of William the Conqueror, Henry II., Edward I., Eleanor, his queen, &c. Population of parish, 2199. One mile west from St. David's is the shell of St. Stephen's Chapel, commanding an extensive view of Whitsand Bay, in which stand six dangerous rocks called the Bishop and his Clerks.

About 15 miles from St. David's is Fishguard, situated on a bay of St. George's Channel, forming an excellent harbour. In this and the adjoining parish are extensive quarries of excellent slate. Population of borough, 1593. About 6½ miles from Fishguard is Newport, where are the ruins of a castle. In the vicinity are several Druidical remains. About 10 miles from Newport is the town of Cardigan, one mile before which are the ruins of St. Dogmell's Priory. The village of St. Dogmell's is a remarkably picturesque object.

CARDIGAN,

the county-town of Cardiganshire, is situated near the mouth of the Teifi. It carries on a considerable coasting trade. The principal buildings are, the church, a venerable structure; the town hall; the gaol; and an ancient bridge of seven arches. On a low cliff, at the foot of the bridge, are the ruins of the castle, once a strong fortress, but destroyed in the civil wars. A mansion has been erected, by Mr. Bowen, on the site of the keep, the dungeons of which serve for cellars. Cardigan joins with Aberystwith, Adpar, and Lampeter, in returning one M.P., and gives the title of Earl to the family of Brudenell. Population in 1861, 3543. The Teifi is celebrated for the richness of its scenery, particularly between Cardigan and Kilgerran Castle.

From Cardigan to Haverfordwest is twenty-six miles, Narberth, twenty-six, Newcastle Emlyn, ten.

About twenty-two miles from Cardigan is Aberaeron, a neat little sea-port, pleasantly situated at the mouth of the river Aeron, a stream celebrated for its trout and salmon. The scenery of this vale is particularly beautiful. Sixteen miles from Aberaeron is Aberystwith, whence the tourist may proceed by Machynlleth, Dolgelly, &c. See p. 139.

LVIII. A TOUR THROUGH WALES.

ON RIGHT FROM BRIST.	From Beachley		From Bristol.	ON LEFT FROM BRIST.
	859¼	From Bristol, Gloucestershire, to St. Arvan's, Monmouthsh.	19	
	855¼	Llanfihangel Tor-y-mynydd.	23	

ON RIGHT FROM BRIST.	From Beachley.		From Bristol.	ON LEFT FROM BRIST.
		2¾ m. farther a road leads on the right to Monmouth 8½ m., and on the left to Usk, 4 m.		
To Monmouth, 7¾ m. Clytha, W. Jones, Esq.	350¼	Ragland, famous for the ruins of the ancient castle of the Somersets, Earls of Worcester, now Dukes of Beaufort. It was almost entirely destroyed during the civil wars, after a siege of ten weeks, when garrisoned for the royal cause. Lord Raglan takes his title from this place.	28½	Usk is a place of great antiquity, situated on a tongue of land formed by the confluence of the Olna and Usk. It has an ancient church, and the ruins of a priory. But the chief object of attention is the ruins of its castle. The Usk abounds with salmon. Pop of par. 2112. To Usk, 5¼ m.
	347	Clytha House. Junction of the road.	31¾	Clytha Castle, situated on an eminence, is a mausoleum that was erected to the memory of the heiress of the house of Tredegar.
Coldbrook House, F. H. Williams, Esq.				
	341¼	ABERGAVENNY,	37¾	

an ancient town situated at the junction of the Gavenny with the Usk. The ruins of the castle, which is in a very dilapidated state, form a very picturesque object. The church of St Mary was the chapel belonging to the priory, and contains many ancient monuments. The free grammar-school was founded in the reign of Henry VIII. The trade of the place has greatly declined, but during summer it is much frequented by visitors. Near Abergavenny is the Sugar-loaf mountain, 1852 feet above the level of the sea. The ascent is easy, and the summit commands an extensive and beautiful prospect. This place gives the title of Earl to the Neville family. Pop. 4621.

To Hereford, 24 m. Hill Ho.	339¾	Pentre Inn.	39¼	Glan Usk Park, Sir J. Bailey, Bart.
	337½	Enter South Wales.	41½	
Gwernvale, J. Gwynne, Esq. More Park.		Crickhowell, a small but pretty town on the Usk. To the east of the town are the ruins of the castle. Pop. of par. 1516.		To Merthyr Tydvil, 14 miles.
Here are the picturesque ruins of Tretower Castle.	333	Tretower.	46	Buckland, J. P. Gwynne Holford, Esq.
	321¼	BRECKNOCK or BRECON.	57¾	

is delightfully situated at the confluence of the Honddu with the Usk; hence the British name of the town Aberhonddu. The objects chiefly deserving of attention are the ruins of the castle, consisting of some remains of the "Keep" called "Ely-Tower," so named from Dr. Morton, bishop of Ely, who was confined here by Richard III., and the scene of the conference of the bishop with Stafford Duke of Buckingham: the scanty remains of the priory founded in the reign of Henry I.: the Church of St John, at the end of which is a beautiful Saxon stone font: St Mary's Church, with a steeple 90 feet in height: St David's Church, on the north bank of the Usk; and Christchurch College, once a Dominican priory, attached to which is a free grammar-school. There are also several meeting-houses and charitable institutions. The ancient mansion called Brecknock Priory, is the property of the Marquis Camden. Mrs Siddons was a native of Brecon. One M.P. Pop. 5639.

ON RIGHT FROM BRIST.	From Beachley.		From Bristol.	ON LEFT FROM BRIST.
4 m. dist. is Aberedwy, one of the most picturesque villages in Wales.	305	BUILTH, a small town, delightfully situated on the Wye. At the east end of the town are the vestiges of a castle of great strength. About a mile distant are the Park Wells, much frequented.	$73\frac{3}{4}$	
		cr. river Wye.		
Welfield, E. D. Thomas, Esq.		Keep the river Wye on the left.		
		cr. river Ithon.		
	291	Rhayader.	$87\frac{3}{4}$	Noyadd.
Dderw.		cr. river Wye.		
	$289\frac{3}{4}$	Cwm. Ystwith (*Cardiganshire.*)	99	Hafod, late Duke of Newcastle. The grounds are remarkably beautiful. Near this spot are extensive lead mines.
		cr. the Ystwith.		
	$286\frac{3}{4}$	Pentre Brunant.		
		Fountain Inn.	102	
	$272\frac{3}{4}$	Devil's Bridge, a singularly romantic spot, where a deep cleft in the rocks is crossed by two arches, one above the other, beneath which the rapid river Mynach descends in terrific cascades. The lower arch is said to have been built by the monks of Strata-Florida Abbey, in reign of William Rufus, and the upper arch was thrown over it in 1753. The Hafod Hotel, Devil's Bridge, is an entire renovation of the old Hafod Arms Hotel. The extensive alterations and improvements have been effected by a company to whom the property now belongs.	106	
	$269\frac{3}{4}$	Eskynald.	109	Crosswood, Earl of Lisburne.
	$261\frac{1}{4}$	ABERYSTWITH,	$117\frac{1}{2}$	Caermarthen, $46\frac{1}{2}$, Cardigan, $37\frac{1}{2}$.

a sea-port, borough, and market-town, situated at the mouths of the Rheidol and the Ystwith. It is the largest town in the county. It was once fortified with walls, a portion of which still remains on the shore. The castle, situated west of the town on a rock projecting into the sea, was founded in 1109 by Gilbert De Strongbow. It was afterwards destroyed, but was rebuilt in 1277 by Edward I. It was a fortress of great strength, and once the residence of Cadwallader,

It was finally destroyed by Cromwell. The ruin was the property of the late Duke of Newcastle. The town contains two churches and several meeting-houses, assembly rooms, a chalybeate spring, a library, baths, a theatre, &c. The castle house was built by the late Sir Uvedale Price of Foxley, Bart., after designs by Nash. Aberystwith has a considerable coasting trade in corn, lead, oak, bark, and butter. It is much frequented for sea-bathing. Extensive walks have been formed in the vicinity. There are several lead mines in this neighbourhood, so rich in silver that the district is called by the Welch Potosi From the Gogerddan mines, at present unworked and little known, Sir Hugh Middleton accumulated the wealth which he expended in his great undertaking of bringing the New River to London. Aberystwith unites with Cardigan, Adpar, and Lampeter, in returning one M.P. Pop. 1861, 5641. About 3 miles distant is Nanteos, W. E. Powell, Esq., and Gogerddan, Pryse Loveden, Esq.

ON RIGHT FROM BRIST.	From Beachley.		From Bristol.	ON LEFT FROM BRIST.
From Machynlleth you may cross to Shrewsbury through Welsh-Pool.	243¼	Machynlleth (*Montgomeryshire,*) a very ancient market-town and borough, beautifully situated at the confluence of the Dulas and Dyfi. It forms the centre of the woollen trade in this part of the country. Here is an ancient structure to which Owen Glyndwr is said to have summoned the nobility and gentry of Wales in 1402. Pop, 1640.	135½	
Forward to Dinas Mowddwy, 13 miles.		cr. the river Dyfi.		
	242¼	Junction of the road.	136½	To Towyn, 11 miles.
	239¼	Esgairgeiliog. Enter Merionethsh.	139½	
	235¼	Junction of the road.	143½	
To Dinas Mowddwy, 6½ miles.	231¼	Dinas Mowddwy road.	147½	
	228¼	DOLGELLY,	150½	

situated in a fertile valley on the river Wnion, surrounded by mountains, and greatly celebrated for its beautiful scenery. It is much frequented by persons making excursions of pleasure, and there is perhaps no place in the principality whence so many excursions may be advantageously made. Those mostly taken are to Machynlleth, the waterfalls, Barmouth, Cader Idris, Dinas Mowddwy, thence to Bala, over the mountains, and back through the vale in which the Dee rises. Owen Glyndwr assembled his Parliament at Dolgelly in 1404. Some Roman coins have been found in this vicinity, bearing this inscription, IMP. CÆSAR TRAIAN. A considerable trade in coarse cloth is carried on at Dolgelly. Pop. 1861, 2217. Near Dolgelly is Cader Idris, in height the second mountain in Wales. The summit is 2850 feet above the town,

Its ascent is much easier than that of Snowdon, and its summit, in a clear day commands a view more than 400 miles in circumference. Two miles from Dolgelly is Nannau, once the residence of Hawel Lele, an inveterate enemy of Owen Glyndwr. It was the ancient seat of the family Nanney of Nannau, but now through marriage, is that of Sir R. W. Vaughan, Bart. In the upper part of the park are the remains of a British fort. Ten miles distant from Dolgelly is Barmouth, one of the most frequented watering-places in Wales. The intervening scenery is remarkably grand. From Dolgelly to Bala, 18 miles; to Harlech, 18 miles.

ON RIGHT FROM BRIST.	From Beachley.		From Bristol.	ON LEFT FROM BRIST.
		cr. river Wnion.		
	226¾	Llanelltyd.	152	To Barmouth, 10 miles. To Harlech, 17 miles.
Llwyn. Tynycoed.				
	215¼	Trawsfynydd.	163½	
2 miles distant is the village of Festiniog, situated in a most enchanting vale. Near it are the falls of the Cynfael, and between them a singular rock called Hugh Loyd's pulpit.	210¼	Maentwrog, remarkable for the picturesque scenery by which it is surrounded.	168½	
	209¼	Tan-y-Bwlch Inn.	169½	Plas-Tan-y-Bwlch. W G. Oakeley, Esq. The grounds are extensive and interesting. To Criccieth, 11¼ m., to Caernarvon by Llanllyfni 25 miles.
	202¾	Pont-Aberglaslyn is a single stone arch built over a rapid mountain torrent that divides the counties of Merioneth and Caernarvon.	176	The surrounding scenery is remarkably sublime and picturesque.
The summit of Snowdon is 3571 feet above the level of the sea. It is about 5 or 6 yards in diameter, and is surrounded by a low wall. In a clear day, part of England, Scotland, Ireland, and the Isle of Man may be distinctly seen.	201¼	Beddgelert (*Caernarvonshire.*) Here guides may be procured to ascend Snowdon, the summit of which is 6 miles distant,	177½	Persons wishing to ascend Snowdon from Caernarvon should proceed to the village of Dol Bedarn, and there procure a guide.
Plas-y-Nant, Sir R. B. Williams Bulkeley, Bart., Lord-Lieutenant of the County.	194¼	Bettws-Garmon.	184½	
	189¼	CAERNARVON, an ancient town, situated partly on the Menai strait, partly on the estuary of the Seiont. It was the only station the Romans possessed in this part of Cambria.	189½	To Pwllheli, 22 miles, to Nevin, 21 miles. Coed Helen.

Some fragments of the walls of the ancient city still remain. Near the Seiont was a strong fort, long the residence of the British princes. The principal object of interest is the castle erected by Edward I. The external walls are nearly entire, and are from 8 to 10 feet thick. This castle was the birth-place of Edward II. The room in which he was born is still shown. It was taken and re-

CAERNARVON CASTLE.

taken during the civil wars. It was held by the late Field-Marshal the Marquis of Anglesey as constable. On the outside of the town walls, a spacious terrace extends from the quay to the north end of the town. There is a fine view from the summit of the rock behind the Caernarvon Hotel. In the vicinity are numerous Druidical circles and ancient monumental stones. It is surrounded by the wildest of Snowdonian scenery. Caernarvon gives the title of Earl to a branch of the Herbert family. Pop. (1861) 8512. It joins with Conway, Criccieth, Pwllheli, Bangor, and Nevin, in returning 1 M.P.

ON RIGHT FROM BRIST.	From Beachley		From Bristol.	ON LEFT FROM BRIST.
	186¼	Llanfair.	192½	Plas Llanfair. Bryntyrion. Vaynol House.
	181¼	Menai Bridge (p. 182)	197½	
	178¾	BANGOR (p. 182).	200	Treborth.

From Bangor you may proceed by Pen Maen Mawr to Aberconway, and return through the vale of Llanrwst to Cerniogau Mawr, and thence to Capel Curig (see pp. 180-181), or proceed through St Asaph and Holywell to Chester. The tourist may return to Bristol by Chirk, Oswestry, Welsh-Pool, Montgomery, Weobley, Hereford, and Monmouth. For a description of the road from Bangor to Oswestry, see pp. 180-181.

Porkington, W. Ormsby Gore, Esq.	113½	Oswestry.	265½	To Shrewsbury, 17½ m.
Broom Hall.	110	Llynclys.	268½	To Ellesmere, 7½ m.
To Bala, 26 miles.	107¾	Llanymynech.	271	To Shrewsbury, 16 m.
To Llanfyllin, 8 miles.		cr. riv. Vyrnwy, & enter Montgomeryshire.		To Shrewsbury, 15¼ m.
	104½	Junction of the road. About a mile farther, a road leads off on the right to Welsh-Pool by Guilsfield, 7 miles.	274½	
One mile distant is Powis Castle, the seat of the Earl of Powis.	100¾	New Quay.	278½	1 m. distant, on the opposite side of the Severn, is Buttington, where, in 894, the Danes were routed by the generals of King Alfred.
Leighton Hall. To Newtown, 9 m., to Llanfair, 12 m. Gunley, Rev. R. H. M. Pryce.	97¾	WELSH-POOL is one of the chief marts for Welsh flannel. Pop. 1851, 4434. To the north of the town, on Moel-y-Golfa, is an obelisk erected in commemoration of Lord Rodney's victory over the French fleet in 1782.	281	Llwynderw.
Nantcribba, Viscount Hereford.	95½	cr. the Severn.	283	
To Newtown, 8½ miles.	93¼	Forden.	285½	
Llanfair, 12 miles.	89½	MONTGOMERY.	289½	

The church is a venerable cruciform structure, containing an exquisitely carved screen and rood-loft, removed from the priory of Cherbury at the dissolution of that establishment. In the south transept is a sumptuous monument to the memory of the father of the celebrated Lord Herbert of Cherbury. The latter was born at Eyton in Shropshire in 1581. Montgomery was formerly surrounded by walls, and possessed a castle supposed to have been founded by Baldwin, lieutenant of the marches, to William the Conqueror. This fortress seems to have been held by the ancestors of Lord Herbert of Cherbury and was the principal residence of that family, and a branch of the Herbert family, Earls of Pembroke and Montgomery, derives the latter title from this place. During the civil wars, it was garrisoned for the King by Lord Herbert, who surrendered on the approach of the Parliamentary army. The Royalists attempted to take it, but were completely defeated. Only a few fragments of the building now remain. Not far from the castle, situated on a hill, is a very extensive British fort. Montgomery unites with Llanidloes, Welsh-Pool, Llanfyllin, Newtown, and Machynlleth, in returning one M.P. Pop. of Montgomery borough 1861, 1276. About two miles south-west stood Blackhall, once the hospitable residence of the Herbert family. It was consumed by fire. At a short distance is Lymore Park, one of the seats of the Earl of Powis. At the distance of 2½ miles, on the Shrewsbury road, stands the priory of Cherbury, founded in the reign of King John. About 5 miles from Montgomery is the long mountain or Cefn Digol, celebrated as the spot where, in 1294, the last battle took place between the Welsh and the English.

ON RIGHT FROM BRIST.	From Beachley		From Bristol.	ON LEFT FROM BRIST.
Mellington.	85¼	Red-Court House.	293½	To Bishop's Castle through Churchstoke, 7 m.
	82½	Bishop's Moat.	296¼	
Three m. distant, Walcot Hall, Earl of Powis, and near it are the remains of several encampments.	80½	BISHOP'S CASTLE (*Salop.*) The Bishops of Hereford had formerly a castle here, which, however, has long since been destroyed. The town prior to the Reform Act, which disfranchised it, returned two M.P. Pop. of par. 2083.	298¼	Oakley House, and beyond Linley Hall. To Ludlow by Onibury, 18 m., by Barford Gate, 17 m.
		cr. river Clun.		
	75	Clun.	303¾	
		cr. river Teme.		To Ludlow, 17 m.
Knighton unites with New Radnor, Presteign, Rhayader, Cefn Llys, and Knuclas in returning one M.P.	68	KNIGHTON (*Radnorsh.*) or in Welch Tref-y-Clawdd, derives its name from its situation on the earthen rampart raised by Offa as a separation between the British and Saxons. A castle formerly stood here, but no traces of it are now visible. Pop. 1655.	310¾	Two miles distant Stanage Pa., E. Rogers, Esq.
	65	Norton.	313¾	Three m. dist. Brampton Park.
To New Radnor 7½ m.		cr. river Lug.		
	63¾	PRESTEIGN, situated partly in Radnor and partly in Hereford. It has a church, a town-hall, where the assizes are held, and a free school. To the north of the town there is a circular hill, ornamented with plantations and delightful walks. Pop. of par. 2383.	315¾	Boultibrook. To Ludlow, 16 m., Hereford, 28 m., Tenbury, 18 m., Leominster, 14¼ m.

ON RIGHT FROM BRIST.	From Beach.		From Bristol.	ON LEFT FROM BRIST.
		cr. river Endwell.		
To New Radnor, 7¼ m.	61¾	Rodd (*Herefordshire*).	317	Staunton Park, (J. K. King, Esq.) and beyond Shobdon, (Lord Bateman.)
Eywood. At a distance Harpton Court, Rt. Hon. Sir T. F. Lewis, Bart.	60	Titley.	318¾	Titley Co.
	56¾	KINGTON (*Herefordsh.*) carries on a considerable clothing business, and a trade in iron and nails. Mrs Siddons first acted in a barn in this town.	322¾	Whittern,
	54½	Lyonshall (*Herefordsh.*)	324¼	Moor Court.
Newport House.	51½	Woonton.	327¼	
Two m. distant is Lady Lift, an eminence commanding an extensive prospect.	49¾	Sarnesfield.	329	Sarnesfield House.
Garnstone, S. Peploe, Esq.	47¾	WEOBLEY. a small town, noted for its malt liquor. Here stood an ancient castle, which was taken from the Empress Maud by King Stephen.	331	
Foxley.	44½	Wormesley.	334¼	
In the distance Garnons, Sir G. H. Cotterell, Bart., and beyond Moccas Court, Sir V. Cornewall, Bart.	42½	Brinsop Court.	336¼	
	41¼	Tillington.	337½	Tillington Co Burghill Co.
	38½	Cross Elms.	340¼	
	37¼	White Cross.	341½	
	36¼	HEREFORD (see p 145.)	342½	
	18½	MONMOUTH (see p. 144.)	360¼	
		Beachley.	378¾	

LIX. BRISTOL.—CHEPSTOW.—MONMOUTH.—HEREFORD.—LUDLOW.—SHREWSBURY.—CHESTER.—LIVERPOOL.—158¼ Miles.

ON RIGHT FROM BRIST.	From Liverp.		From Bristol.	ON LEFT FROM BRIST.
Redland Court, Sir Richard Vaughan. Redland House.	155¼	Westbury.	3	Stokehouse and Leigh Court, W. Miles, Esq. Cole House.
Overcourt and Knole Park, W. C. Master, Esq.	151¾	Compton Green-Field.	6½	2 m. dist. King's Weston, P. W. S. Miles, Esq.
	140½	Aust or Old Passage.	11¾	Holly House.
		cr. river Severn. The old passage has now been greatly improved.		
Sedbury Park, G. Ormerod, Esq.	145½	Beachley.	12½	Beachley Lodge,

ON RIGHT FROM BRIST.	From Liverp.		From Bristol.	ON LEFT FROM BRIST.
On the other side of the Wye, Hardwicke House. St Lawrence.		cr. river Wye.		
About a mile from Chepstow is Piercefield, a noble mansion, celebrated for the views obtained from its walks, which extend along the banks of the Wye for 3 miles. The ruins of Tintern Abbey, 4 miles from Chepstow, belonging to the Duke of Beaufort, form a remarkably beautiful and picturesque object. The monastery was founded in the year 1131 by Walter de Clare. At the dissolution, the site was granted to Henry second Earl of Worcester, ancestor of its present possessor. The ruins are seen to great advantage from a spot about half a mile down the river.	141¼	CHEPSTOW, *Monmouth.* Chepstow carries on a considerable trade in timber, coals, grindstones, iron, and cider. The most interesting object is the ruins of the castle, situated on the edge of a lofty precipice overhanging the Wye. The ruins are covered with ivy, and present a very picturesque appearance. Here Henry Martin, one of the regicides, was confined for more than twenty years. The oldest portions of the building were erected about 800 years ago by William Fitzosborne, Earl of Hereford. The church, which was formerly the chapel of a Benedictine Priory, contains the monument of Henry second Earl of Worcester, and the gravestone of Henry Martin. Pop. 3364.	17	The tide rises here to a great height (on some occasions over 50 feet), and very suddenly.
	139¼	St Arvans.	19	To Monmouth by the old road through Trelleck, 14 miles.
	138¼	Wyndcliff.	20	The view from the summit of Wyndcliff extends into nine counties, and is considered one of the most beautiful in England.
	135¼	Tintern.	23	
	133¼	Llandogo.	25	
Clearwell Castle, Earl of Dunraven and Mountearl.		Bigswear, Iron Bridge.		
		cr. river Wye, and enter Gloucestershire.		
	128¾	Redbrook.	30½	
		Enter Monmouthshire.		
		cr. river Wye.		
The rides and walks in the vicinity of the town are peculiarly romantic. From the summit of Kymin hill, where a monument to Nelson has been erected, there is a prospect of remarkable extent and beauty. To Mitchel Dean by Coleford, 13 m. To Ross, 10½ m.	126¼	MONMOUTH. Monmouth, the capital of the county, is pleasantly situated at the confluence of the Monnow and the Wye. The principal objects are the town hall, the county gaol, the free school, St Mary's church, St Thomas's church, the ruins of the once celebrated castle, the remains of the ancient walls, &c. The inhabitants are chiefly employed in the iron and tin works in the neighbourhood. Monmouth, together with Usk and Newport, returns one M. P. to Parliament. Pop. of borough 1861, 5783. Henry V. and Geoffrey of Monmouth, the historian or chronicler, were natives of this town	32	One mile and a half from Monmouth is Troy House, (Duke of Beaufort,) once famous for its gardens, which have been converted into orchards. Here are shown the cradle of Henry V., and the sword which he bore at Agincourt. To Abergavenny by Dingestow and Tregare, 16½ m., by Ragland, 17 m. To Usk by Ragland, 13 m.

TINTERN ABBEY FROM THE WYE.

ON RIGHT FROM BRIST.	From Liverp.		From Bristol.	ON LEFT FROM BRIST.
	123¼	Welsh Newton, (*Herefordshire.*)	35	
Harewood, Sir H. Hoskyns, Bart.	119¼	St Weonards.	39	Treago, P. R. Mynors, Esq.
Lyston House, Henry Whittaker, Esq.	115¾	Wormelow Tump.	42½	Bryngwyn, J. Phillips, Esq., and 1 m. distant, Mynde Park, T. G. Symons, Esq.
Near Callow are the remains of Roman Camps. In the distance Holme Lacy, Sir E. F. Scudamore Stanhope, Bart.	113¼	Callow.	45	Allensmore Park, E. B. Pateshall, Esq.
		cr. river Wye.		
2 m. dist. Rotherwas Park, C. Bodenham, Esq.	109¼	HEREFORD.	49	

The principal building is the cathedral, refounded in the time of William I. It contains numerous sepulchral monuments as far back as the eleventh century. The library contains a great number of MSS., among which is Wycliffe's Bible. The cathedral was much injured by the fall of the west front in the year 1786, which has been since rebuilt, though with little regard to consistency of architecture. Two of the five churches of the city were destroyed during a siege in 1645. The other buildings worthy of notice are the court-house, the Bishop's Palace, the College inhabited by the vicars choral, the county gaol, the Theatre, of which the Kemble family had for many years the direction, the ruins of a monastery of Blackfriars, &c. The principal manufactures are those of gloves, leather, and flannels. The county has long been celebrated for cider. A triennial meeting is held here of the three choirs of Hereford, Worcester, and Gloucester, for the performance of oratorios, and the profits are appropriated to charitable purposes. Guillim the Herald, Nell Gwynne, and Garrick, were natives of Hereford. It affords the title of Viscount to the Devereux family. The borough returns two M.P. Pop. 15,585.

To Ledbury, 15¼ m. To Worcester, 25¾ m. Bromyard, 14 m.				To Hay, 19¾ m. To Kington by Yazor, 28¾, by Weobley, 29¾ m.
Race Course.	107½	Holmer.	50¾	
	106½	Pipe.	51¾	
Moreton House,	105½	Moreton.	52¾	
	104	Wellington.	54¼	
Hampton Court, (J. Arkwright, Esq.) said to have been built by Henry IV. It belonged at one time to Baron Coningsby, the General of William III.	100½	Hope under Dinmore.	57¾	Winsley, Sir J. V. B. Johnstone, Bart.
	99	Wharton.	59¼	
		cr. river Arrow.		Ryelands, R. Lane, Esq.
Leominster has various meeting-houses, free and national schools, and cha-	96½	Leominster. This town carries on a considerable trade in hats,	61¾	The river Lugg flows on the east and north sides of Leominster, and two

ON RIGHT FROM BRIST.	From Liverp.		From Bristol.	ON LEFT FROM BRIST.
ritable institutions. Races are held in August. It returns two M.P. Pop. 5658. To Tenbury, 11 m. To Ludlow, 12¾ m. To Bromyard, 11½ m.		wheat, wool, cider, hops, &c. The principal objects are the church, rebuilt at the commencement of last century,—the Butter cross, a singular building of timber and plaster, erected about the year 1633,—the market-house, the gaol, and the House of Industry, which was part of a priory. This town gives the title of Baron to the Earls of Pomfret. cr. river Lugg. Two roads lead from Leominster to Ludlow, the one by Stockton Cross 1½ m. Ashton 2¼, Brimfield 2¼, Ashford Bowdler 1¾, Ludlow 2¼. in all 10 m., or by		smaller streams pass through the town. It is of ancient date, and many of the timber and plaster houses are ornamented with curious and grotesque carvings. To Kington, 21 m. To Presteign, 14¾ m. Eyton Hall, E. Evans, Esq.
Berrington, Lord Rodney.	94	Luston.	64¼	Highwood House.
	91	Orleton.	67¼	
	89¾	Richard's Castle.	68½	The Haye Park, J. Salwey, Esq.
Moor Park, J. Salwey, Esq., and beyond Ashford Hall.	88	Overton, (*Shropshire.*)	70¼	The Lodge, J. Salwey, Esq.
The Sheet. 2¼ m. distant, Henley Court. To Cleobury Mortimer, 11¼ m. To Bridgnorth, 19¼.	86½	LUDLOW	71¾	Ludford Park, E. L. Charlton, Esq. To Presteign, 16¼.

is a populous and very ancient town, situated on an eminence at the junction of the rivers Corve and Teme. Here are the ruins of a castle which was long the residence of royalty, and afterwards of the Lords Presidents of the Welsh marches. Prince Arthur, the brother of Henry VIII., held his court, and died in this castle, and Milton's Mask of Comus was first performed here under the direction of the Earl of Bridgewater. In one of the towers, Butler wrote a part of Hudibras. The church contains a number of curious antique monuments and inscriptions. Two M. P. Pop. 6033.

To Much Wenlock, 18 miles.	84½	Race Course.	73¾	Oakley Park, Lady Windsor.
In the distance Stanton Lacy, and beyond Downton Hall, Sir C. H. R. Boughton, Bart.	83¾	Bromfield Church.	74½	
	81¼	Onibury.	77	Stone Ho. Earl of Powis.
	79¼	Stokesay.	79	Sibdon Castle and at a

ON RIGHT FROM BRIST.	From Liverp.		From Bristol.	ON LEFT FROM BRIST.
				little distance, Walcot Pa. Earl of Powis.
	78	Halford.	80¼	To Bishop's Castle, by Lydbury North, 9½ miles.
	76½	Stretford.	81¾	
	75¼	Felhampton.	83	**Wistanston.**
Acton Scott Hall.	72¼	Little Stretton.	86	
	70¾	Church Stretton.	87½	
To Much Wenlock, 12¾ miles.	69½	All Stretton.	88¾	Here are the traces of Watling Street, one of the finest specimens of a Roman road in the kingdom. It is formed of large stakes, with wattles woven between them. It commences at Dover, and terminates at Cardigan.
1½ mile distant is Caer Caradoc or Cradock, at the top of which the remains of an old British camp are still visible.	66½	Lee Botwood.	91¼	
Longnor Hall. To Wellington, 17 miles. Three miles distant Acton Burnell Castle, Sir C. F. Smythe, Bart.	65¾	Longnor.	92½	
To Wellington, 14 miles. Condover, E. W. S. Owen, Esq.	64¼	Dorrington.	94	**Lyth Hill.**
	60¼	Baiston Hill.	98	
		cr. the Leol brook.		
Longner Hall, and beyond Attingham Hall, Lord Berwick.	57¾	SHREWSBURY.	100½	

Shrewsbury is situated on two eminences, and surrounded on three sides by the Severn. The streets are narrow and steep. It was formerly surrounded by a wall, defended by several towers, of which scarcely any vestige now remains. Its castle has now become private property, and part of it has been formed into a mansion. Shrewsbury and its neighbourhood have been the scene of various interesting events. The town itself has sustained many severe sieges; and, four miles distant, at Battlefield Church, is the spot where the famous battle took place, in 1403, between Henry IV. and Hotspur. Shrewsbury has on various occasions, for short periods, been the residence of royalty, and Parliaments have also been held within its walls. The town contains many public buildings worthy of notice, among which may be mentioned the different churches, the town-hall, the market-house, the county-hall, the infirmary, the gaol, the free grammar-school, founded by Edward VI., and raised into great repute by Bishop Butler; the theatre, said to have formed part of an ancient palace, &c. There are two handsome bridges over the Severn, and a delightful promenade on its banks, called St Chad's Walk, or the Quarry. Shrewsbury is the chief mart for Welsh webs, which are made in Montgomery, and dressed here. This town is also famous for its brawn and cakes. It returns two members to Parliament. Pop. 1861, 22,163. Four miles from the town are the interesting ruins of Haughmond Abbey, founded in the year 1100, by William Fitzallan. Of the abbey church the nave only remains, having a roof of fine oak. Speaker Onslow, Dr Burney, and many other eminent men, were natives of this town. From Shrewsbury to Newport is 18 miles; to Wellington, 11 miles; to Drayton, 18 miles; Oswestry, 18 miles; Bishop's Castle, 20 miles; Montgomery, 21½ miles; Welsh-Pool, 19 miles. Shrewsbury is connected by railway with all parts of the kingdom.

ON RIGHT FROM BRIST.	From Liverp.		From Bristol.	ON LEFT FROM BRIST.
About one mile from Shrewsbury is a column, surmounted by a statue of General Viscount Hill, erected in 1816. At a distance Sundorne Castle, A. W. Corbet, Esq. To Wem, 4¾ miles.	54¼	Albrighton.	104	2 miles beyond Shrewsbury is Shelton, celebrated for an immense oak, 44 feet 3 inches in circumference.
	52	Harmer Hill.	106¼	
	50¼	Middle.	108	
	48¾	Burlton.	109½	Petton Hall.
	46	Cockshut.	112¼	
To Whitchurch, 11½ m. To Wem, 9½ miles.	42½	cross Ellesmere canal.	115⅞	
Oteley Park, and beyond Bettisfield Park, Sir J. Hanmer, Bart., and Gredington Hall, Lord Kenyon.	41½	Ellesmere. Pop. 3643	116¾	Hardwicke House, Sir J. R. Kynaston, Bart. To Oswestry, 7¾ miles. To Llangollen, 15 miles.
Ellesmere has a considerable trade in malting and tanning. The site of the castle, now a bowling green, commands a delightful prospect.	36½	Overton, (*Flintshire.*)	121¾	Overton Lodge. Rose Hill.
¾ m. beyond Overton is Bryn-y-Pys, F. R. Price, Esq.; and Maesgwaylod Lodge, near which is Gwernhayled, and, three miles distant, Emral Park, Sir R. Pulestone, Bart.		Eyton, (*Denbighshire.*)		In the distance Wynnstay, Sir W. W. Wynn, Bart., and beyond Ruabon.
To Whitchurch, 13 m.	31½	Marchwiel.	126¾	Erddig, S. Yorke, Esq.
Cefn Hall. To Whitchurch, 15¾ m. To Holt, 6 miles; thence to Chester, 8 miles.	29¼	WREXHAM is a populous and well-built town, noted for its fairs. The church is a splendid building, of the fifteenth century. The interior is richly adorned, and contains a superb altar-piece, besides a number of beautiful monuments. Pop. 7562.	129	To Ruthin, 16 miles. To Mold, 12 miles.
Acton Park, (Sir R. H. Cunliffe, Bart.) the birth-place of Judge Jeffreys.				Gwersyllt Hall, and Gwersyllt Hill.

ON RIGHT FROM BRIST.	From Liverp.		From Bristol.	ON LEFT FROM BRIST.
Horseley Hall.		Gresford Road.	133	Gresford Lodge, Sir H. A. Johnson, Bart.
Netherleigh House.				
Trefalen.		cross river Alun.		
Eaton Hall, Marquis of Westminster.	23	Pulford, (*Cheshire.*)	135¼	
Eccleston.				
		cross river Dee.		
	17½	CHESTER.	140¾	

Chester is an ancient and populous city situated on a rocky eminence. The houses are singularly constructed. They have porticoes running along the front, affording a covered walk to pedestrians, and beneath these are shops and warehouses on a level with the street. The castle is said to have been erected in the reign of William the Conqueror. A part of the original building has been repaired, and part of it was demolished, and a range of magnificent buildings has been erected on its site. They consist chiefly of an armoury containing nearly 30,000 stand of arms, barracks, court of justice, county gaol, the shire hall, the offices of the palatinate, and a curious ancient chapel. The cathedral was the church of the dissolved abbey of St Werburgh. It contains curious monuments, and a neat choir. The bishop's throne was formerly the shrine of St Werburgh. The chapter-house, a beautiful edifice on the east side of the cloisters, appears to have been erected in the time of Randle, the first Earl of Chester, whose remains, together with those of his uncle and several of his successors, were deposited here. St John's Church, on the east side of the city, without the walls, is supposed to have been founded by Ethelred in 689. In Trinity Church lie the remains of Matthew Henry the commentator, and of Parnell the poet. Sir J. Vanbrugh was a native of Chester. Chester contains various other churches, several meeting-houses, charitable institutions, public libraries, &c. Chester was formerly a Roman station, and abounds with antiquities. Its ancient walls, which are still standing, are about two miles in circumference, and form a delightful promenade, commanding fine views. There are four gates in the city walls. Races are held in spring and autumn on a fine course called the Roodee. Here Edward of Caernarvon received the submission of the Welsh in 1300. It was besieged and taken by the Parliamentary forces in 1645. It returns two M.P. Pop. 1861, 31,110. Eaton Hall, a seat of the Marquis of Westminster, situated on the banks of the Dee, about 3½ miles from Chester, is a superb mansion, rebuilt in the Gothic style, from designs by Mr Porden in 1813, and is fitted up with great splendour. It contains West's two fine paintings of Cromwell dissolving the Parliament, and the landing of Charles II. From Chester to Holywell is 18½ miles; to Great Neston, 10¾; to Parkgate, 12; to Frodsham. 11; to Tarporley, 10¼.

ON RIGHT FROM BRIST.	From Liverp.		From Bristol.	ON LEFT FROM BRIST.
Hoole House.				
		cr. Ellesmere canal.		
Chorlton.				Moston Hall.
Backford Hall, B. Glegg, Esq.	14¼	Backford.	144	Mollington Hall.
Hooton Hall.	10¾	Great Sutton.	147½	Three miles distant Puddington Hall, and Burton Hall.
	8	Eastham.	150¼	Thornton Hall. Sutton Hall.
Bromborough Hall.	6¾	Bromborough.	151½	Poulton Hall.
	4½	Lower Bebington.	153¾	
	2	Tranmere.	156¼	
	1	Woodside Ferry.	257¼	
Birkenhead Priory, a fine picturesque ruin. It was founded about 1150.		cross river Mersey		Birkenhead (see p. 246.)
		LIVERPOOL. (See p. 221.)	158¼	

LX. BRISTOL TO GLOUCESTER, WORCESTER, AND KIDDERMINSTER, 80¼ Miles.

ON RIGHT FROM BRIST.	From Kidder.		From Bristol.	ON LEFT FROM BRIST.
Stoke Gifford Park, Duke of Beaufort.	78	Horfield.	2¼	Henley House.
	76½	Filton.	3¾	Pen Park.
	74¼	Patchway House.	6	Over Court.
	73¼	Almondsbury.	7	Knole Park, W. C. Master, Esq. Tockington.
Alveston Lodge.	71	Alveston.	9¼	
	70¼	Ship Inn.	10	1 mile dist. is Thornbury, an ancient town, with an elegant church, and the ruins of a castle, erected by the Duke of Buckingham who was beheaded by Richard III.
Cromhall Park, Earl of Ducie.	67¼	Junction of the road.	13	
Tortworth Court, Earl of Ducie.	65½	Falfield.	14¾	Hill Court House, H. Jenner Fust, Esq.
	64¼	Stone.	16	
	62½	Newport.	17¾	
To Dursley, 3 miles.	61¼	Berkeley Heath.	19	1½ mile dist. is Berkeley, the birth place of Dr Jenner, the discoverer of vaccination. Here is Berkeley Castle, the ancient baronial

BRISTOL & BIRMINGHAM RAILWAY.

(BIRMINGHAM TO WORCESTER, CHELTENHAM, GLOUCESTER & BRISTOL.)

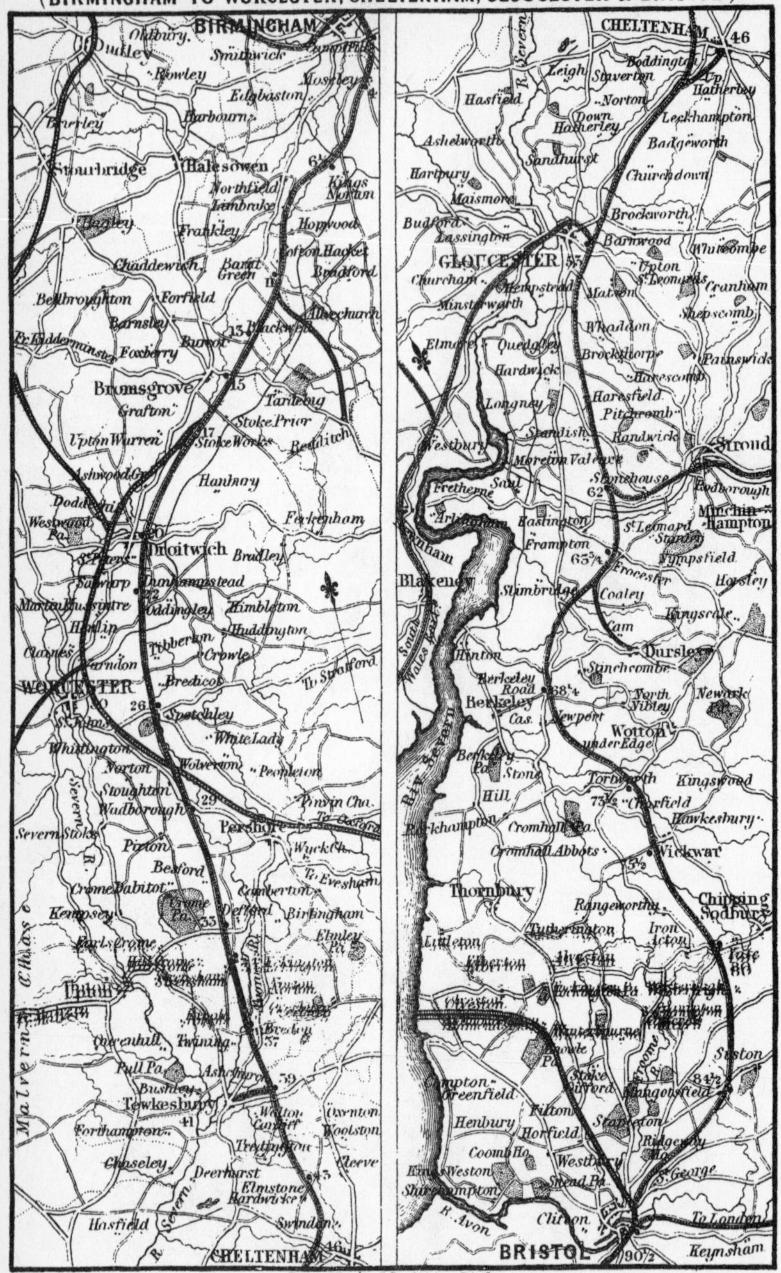

Drawn & Eng.d by J. Bartholomew, Edin.r

Published by A. & C. Black, Edinburgh.

ON RIGHT FROM BRIST.	From Kidder.		From Bristol.	ON LEFT FROM BRIST.
				residence of the Berkeley family, and now the seat of Admiral Sir M. Berkeley. It was founded soon after the Conquest, and has been the scene of various historical events, among others of the murder of Edward II. The castellated form of the mansion is still preserved, and it contains a large collection of portraits.
1 mile distant the Leaze, Mrs P. Hickes. Alkerton, H. Purnel Hickes, Esq. In the distance, Spring Park, Earl of Ducie.	57¼	Cambridge Inn.	22¾	Gossington Hall. Frampton Court, H. C. Clifford, Esq. 3 miles distant Fretherne Lodge.
		cr. the riv. Stroud, and the Thames and Severn Canal.		
In the distance, Standish Park.	53¼	**Moreton Valence.**	27	
	51¼	Hardwicke.	29	**Hardwicke Court, T. J. L. Baker, Esq.** Quedgeley House, J. C. Hayward, Esq.
To Painswick 6½ miles. Cirencester, 17 miles. To Cheltenham, 9 miles. To Tewkesbury, 10½ m.	46¾	GLOUCESTER. (See p. 156.)	33½	Hempstead Court, Rev. S. Lysons.
		cr. riv. Severn, and the Gloucester Canal.		
Pull Court, W. Dowdeswell, Esq.	35½	Division of the roads.	44¾	
Ham Court.	28½	Longdon, (*Worcestershire.*)	51¾	To Ledbury 10 miles, Great Malvern, 8 miles. New Ho. Earl Coventry.
To Pershore, 8¼ miles.	25½	Upton.	54¾	5 miles from Upton is Madresfield Court, the seat of Earl Beauchamp.
		5½ miles beyond Upton are Malvern Wells, situated at the foot of the Malvern hills; and, 2½ miles further is Great Malvern, a village of considerable antiquity, and the principal place of accommodation for those who visit the wells. Its church, erected in the reign of Henry VII., contains several curious monuments. Behind the village the Malvern Hills rise 1300 feet above the level of the Severn.		
3 miles distant Croome Court, Earl Coventry.	24½	Hanley Castle.	55¾	Blackmore Park, T. C. Hornyold, Esq.
The Rhyd, Sir E. H. Lechmere, Bart. Severn End.	21¼	Rhyd Green, (To Great Malvern, 4 m.)	59	

ON RIGHT FROM BRIST.	From Kidder.		From Bristol.	ON LEFT FROM BRIST.
	16¾	Powick.	63½	Powick Court,
		cr. the river Teme.		
Spetchley, R. Berkeley, Esq.	14¾	St John's.	65½	Boughton House, and, beyond, Crow's Nest.
		cross river Severn.		
To Tewkesbury, 15¼ m. To Pershore, 9 To Evesham, 16 To Alcester, 16 To Droitwich, 6¾	14¼	WORCESTER.	66	

Worcester, the capital of the county of that name, is nearly in the centre of England. It is finely situated on a gradual ascent from the left bank of the Severn, over which there is an elegant stone bridge. The circumference of the city is four miles, and on the east side it is sheltered by a range of hills. The streets are in general well built, and the chief one, the Foregate, is very handsome. The cathedral is an elegant fabric, of the thirteenth and fourteenth centuries, restored in 1830. It is 394 feet in length, 78 feet in breadth, and 162 in height. The tower contains eight bells, the largest weighing 6600 lbs. The interior of the cathedral is a splendid specimen of architecture. The choir is magnificent, the pulpit is octagonal, and consists of stone. The monuments are numerous; that of King John is the most ancient royal monument extant in England. The statues of Bishops Wulstan, Oswald, and Hough, and the tomb of Prince Arthur, son of Henry VII., a curious piece of antique workmanship, in the Gothic style, claim attention. The cloisters where the monks formerly resided are now occupied by the dignitaries of the cathedral. Adjoining is the chapter-house, appropriated to the King's school, but used also at the triennial meetings of the choirs of Worcester, Hereford, and Gloucester. The other public buildings worthy of notice are the Episcopal palace, close to the Severn, the residence of George III. and his Queen during their stay at Worcester in 1788; Edgar's Tower, a curious specimen of antiquity; the guildhall, a handsome edifice (in the Foregate); the town-hall, county gaol, the market-house, and infirmary. There are numerous churches and chapels in Worcester, and several places of worship for Dissenters. There are also many hospitals and charitable institutions, a library, theatre, race-ground, &c. Formerly Worcester carried on a considerable trade in woollen cloths and carpets, but that has given place to the manufacture of gloves and porcelain, the latter more remarkable for the beauty of the work than for the extent to which it is carried on. The trade by the river is very considerable consisting partly in colonial produce, supplied by Bristol and Liverpool, and partly in culinary salt brought from the brine springs of Droitwich, six miles distant, and carried to some of the western counties of England, and some parts of South Wales. The hop market of Worcester is one of the largest in the kingdom. The country around the city is highly fertile, and the markets held on Wednesday, Friday, and Saturday, are well supplied. The Severn affords abundance of fresh-water fish. Here Charles II. was defeated by Cromwell in 1651. Worcester gives the title of Marquis to the Duke of Beaufort. It returns two members to Parliament, and is divided for municipal purposes into six wards. It is governed by a mayor, twelve aldermen, and thirty-six councillors. It is connected by railway with Bristol and Birmingham, and thus with all parts of the kingdom. Latterly a portion of the Oxford, Worcester, and Wolverhampton line, has been opened to Evesham. Population 31,227.

ON RIGHT FROM BRISTOL	From Kidder.		From Bristol.	ON LEFT FROM BRISTOL.
Perdiswell, Sir O. P. Wakeman, Bart.	10¾	Droitwich Canal.	69½	
Westwood Park, Rt. Hon. Sir J. S. Pakington, Bart.		cr. river Salwarpe.		
To Droitwich, 4½ miles.	8¾	Ombersley.	71¾	Ombersley Court, Lord Sandys. In the distance, Witley Court (Lord Ward), and beyond, Stanford Court, Sir T. E. Winnington, Bart.
Hill Grove. Oakland, H. Talbot, Esq.	4½	Hartlebury.	76	To Stourport, 2 miles, Bewdley, 6 miles. Hartlebury Castle (Bishop of Worcester).
Greenhill, G. Talbot, Esq.		KIDDERMINSTER.	80¼	Blakebrook House, J. Best, Esq. Lea Castle, J. P. B. Westhead, Esq. Broomfield House.

Kidderminster is a large and populous town on the Stour, famous for the manufacture of carpets. The old church is a noble Gothic pile, containing numerous monuments. The walks in the churchyard command fine views of the town and its vicinity. The town possesses several charitable institutions. It returns one member to Parliament. Pop. 1861, 15,399. The Staffordshire and Worcester canal, which passes through Kidderminster, opens a communication with Hull, Liverpool, Bristol, Manchester, &c. In the vicinity are the remains of an ancient castle, the vestiges of an encampment at Warsal Hill, and a chalybeate well at Sandburn. Richard Baxter was for many years vicar at Kidderminster, and Baskerville the printer was born in the vicinity.

From Kidderminster to Bewdley is 3 miles, to Stourport 4 miles, to Tenbury 16 miles, to Leominster 27 miles, to Ludlow 24 miles, to Bridgenorth 13¾ miles, to Stourbridge 6¾ miles. Bewdley on the Severn is chiefly supported by its navigation, and has a considerable trade in tanning leather. Pop. 7084. It unites with Stourport in returning one M.P. Stourbridge is a handsome town, noted for the manufacture of glass. The canal, which passes the town, communicates with the adjacent counties, and contributes greatly to its prosperity. Pop. 8166.

Two miles and a quarter from the town is Hagley, the famous mansion erected by the first Lord Lyttelton. It contains a valuable library and a numerous collection of paintings. The grounds command varied and extensive views. In Hagley church is the mausoleum of the Lyttelton family. Near Stourbridge also, but in Staffordshire, are Himley Hall, the seat of Lord Ward, and Enville Hall, the seat of the Earl of Stamford and Warrington, the latter a spacious and elegant mansion, with grounds laid out by the poet Shenstone, to whose memory a small chapel is dedicated. Ten miles from Kidderminster is Hales Owen, a neat town, formerly celebrated for its monastery, some remains of which still exist. The church, which is admired for its beautiful spire, contains several interesting monuments, one in memory of the poet Shenstone, who was educated in the free grammar-school, and buried in the adjacent cemetery. In the vicinity is the Leasowes (M. Attwood, Esq.,) a beautiful seat, indebted for much of its elegance to the taste of the poet Shenstone, who was born here. Hales Owen is 7½ miles from Birmingham.

LXI. LONDON TO GLOUCESTER AND CHELTENHAM (by Railway), 121 Miles.

ON RIGHT FROM LOND.	From Cheltm.		From London.	ON LEFT FROM LOND.
Rodborne-Cheney. Moredon. Little Blunsdon. Cricklade, 2 miles. It is a borough by prescription, and has returned members to Parliament since the reign of Edward I. The Town-Hall was built in 1569. Pop. 36,893.	44	From London to Swindon St. (*Wiltshire*). P. 101. The town is pleasantly situated on an eminence, and commands an extensive view of the three counties of Wilts, Berks, and Gloucester. Pop. 4167.	77	Wootton Bassett, at a considerable distance. Pop. 1896. Lediard Tregaze, Viscount Bolingbroke. Lediard Mellicent. Purton.
	39¾	Purton Station.	81¼	
		Enter Gloucestershire.		
Leigh. Somerford Keynes. Oaksey. Poole Keynes. Kemble.	35¾	Minety Station.	85¼	Minety. Charlton Park (Earl of Suffolk and Berkshire).
		Re-enter Wiltshire.		Ewen.
South Cerney, on the banks of the Churn. Here is the famous spire of All Saints Church, an ancient and curious building. Behind it is Ampney Down, with a manor-house built in the time of Henry VIII. by the Hungerford family. Branch to Cirencester, 9¾ miles. Cirencester has returned 2 M.P.'s since the 13th of Elizabeth. The church is a handsome Gothic build-		Enter Gloucestershire.		Cirencester, an ancient borough market-town, derives its name from the river Churn, on which it is situated. Canute the Great held a Parliament here. Here was formerly a castle and a Saxon monastery for prebendaries. Pop. 1861, 6336. The chief manufacture of Cirencester is of cutlery. There are also carpet and woollen manufactories,

ON RIGHT FROM LOND.	From Cheltm.		From London.	ON LEFT FROM LOND.
ing, one of the finest in the kingdom, and contains numerous sepultural brasses and monuments.	30	**Tetbury Road Station.**	91	and two breweries. Many antiquities, both Roman and Saxon, have at different times been discovered in this town and neighbourhood.
Coates. Oakley Grove, Earl Bathurst.		cr. the Roman Way.		
Rodmarton, supposed to have been a Roman station, because here, in 1436, were found a number of Roman coins. Samuel Lysons, joint author of Magna Britannia, was born here. Sapperton. Its church contains several ancient monuments, and here in 1759, a great quantity of silver and brass coins was discovered.		cr. river Frome, and pass through a tunnel of considerable length.		
Chalford. The scenery in its neighbourhood is extremely beautiful. Bisley. The principal manufacture is of coarse clothing, but owing to the unfavourable situation of the town, the market is thinly attended.	21¾	**Brimscomb Station.**	99¼	**Minchin - Hampton,** pleasantly situated on the Frome, is supposed to be the place where Alfred the Great defeated the Danes in 879. In the church-yard is interred James Bradley, who discovered the aberration of light, and the nutation of the earth's axis. Pop. 4890. Hyde Court. Bownham House. Hill House.
Lyppiatt Park. Misserden Court (late Sir E. B. Sandys, Bart.) Stratfords House. Randwick. Standish Ho. Lord Sherborne. Pitchcomb. Painswick, a market-town, irregularly built on the banks of the Slade Water. It is chiefly inhabited by clothiers. The spire of St Mary's church is 174 feet	19½	**Stroud Station.** Stroud is situated near the confluence of the Frome and the Slade. It is a market and borough town, and may be considered the centre of the clothing manufacture of this part of the country. It returns 2 M. P., and is a polling place of the county. Canton, the natural philosopher, and White, Arabic Professor at Oxford, were natives of Stroud. Pop. 35,517.	101½	Rodborough, and, a little to the left, King Stanley, said to have been the residence of one of the Mercian Kings, and where there are some remains of a Roman camp. Leonard Stanley was much destroyed by fire in 1686, and has not since recovered its former importance. The church is an ancient building, in form of a cross. The priory kitchen of a monastery for Benedictines still remains. Frocester is a pretty village, and commands a fine prospect. The Earl of Ducie has a seat here, where Elizabeth passed a night, in 1574, on her progress through this county.

ON RIGHT FROM LOND.	From Cheltm.		From London.	ON LEFT FROM LOND.
in height, and contains a fine peal of bells. Painswick House, W. H. Hyett, Esq. Lower Haresfield. Harescomb. Its church contains some curious old monuments. Brockthrop. Whaddon. Matson. Here is a delightful eminence called Robin's Wood Hill, in the shape of a cone, and covered with almost continual verdure.	17¼	Stonehouse Station.	103¾	Haresfield Court, D. J. Niblett, Esq. Hardwicke Court, T. J. L. Baker, Esq. Quedgeley House, J. Curtis Hayward, Esq. Tuffley.
Churchdown. Badgeworth possesses a mineral spring of the same qualities as those of Cheltenham and Gloucester. Leckhampton. Its church contains some curious monuments, particularly the effigies of a knight, cross-legged, and his lady. The manor is supposed to be as old as the time of Henry VII.	7	Gloucester Station.	114	Hempstead Court, Rev. S. Lysons. Sandhurst. Down Hatherley. Norton. Staverton. Boddington.
2 m. dist. Southam Ho. (Earl of Ellenborough.)		Cheltenham.	121	

Gloucester, the capital of the county from which it derives its name, gave his title to H. R. H. the late Duke of Gloucester. It is situated in a beautiful valley on the bank of the Severn, and is sheltered on the east by a range of hills. The city is intersected by four principal streets which meet in the centre. They are broad, clean, well-paved, and lighted. The principal building is the cathedral, begun in 1047, and enlarged at subsequent periods. It is 420 feet in length, 144 feet in breadth, and surmounted by a tower 129 feet in height. The interior is impressive, the stalls are said to be scarcely inferior to those at Windsor; the choir is richly ornamented, and there is a whispering gallery. The eastern window is the largest in England. The Cathedral is adorned by several monuments, of which those of Robert Duke of Normandy, Edward II., Bishop Warburton, and Dr Jenner, chiefly claim attention. The bishopric of Gloucester was first constituted by Henry VIII., and was joined to Bristol in 1836, so that the Bishop takes his seat in Parliament under the title of Bishop of Gloucester and Bristol. There are various parochial churches, several meeting-houses, a gaol, constructed on the plan of Howard, a town-hall, custom-house, assembly rooms, theatre, &c. The new bridge over the Severn is a handsome structure, 87 feet span. The principal trade of Gloucester consists in the manufacture of pins, iron, flax, and hemp. A considerable inland trade is carried on with the counties through which the Severn flows. There is also a small quantity of wine, spirits, and West Indian produce imported. The river admits sloops and brigs up to the city, but for larger vessels, a canal and basins have been recently formed with depth of water sufficient to admit vessels of 500 tons burden. For municipal purposes, the city is divided into three wards, and is governed by a mayor, six aldermen, and eighteen councillors. It has returned two members to Parliament since temp. Edward I. Gloucester was the birth-place of Robert of Gloucester the chronicler, John Taylor the water poet, George Whitfield the famous Methodist, and R. Raikes the founder of Sunday schools. Markets are held on Wednesdays and Saturdays, and the supply is abundant. Pop. 1861, 16,512. About 3 miles beyond Gloucester is Highnam Court, erected from a design by Inigo Jones. Gloucester is connected by railway with all parts of the kingdom, but unfortunately the two main lines meeting at this city are of different guages.

Cheltenham is situated on the River Chelt, which flows into the Severn. Its situation is healthy and picturesque, and it is sheltered on the north by the Cotswold hills. It owes its celebrity to its mineral waters, which were first discovered in 1716. The waters are cathartic and chalybeate, resembling those of Harrowgate. Every accommodation has been provided for those who use them. The well walk is a magnificent promenade, shaded by ancient elms. St. Mary's Church is a large elegant building in the form of a cross with a lofty octagonal spire. It contains a curious font, and near it is an ancient stone cross. Besides this there are Trinity Church, numerous new churches, and a few places of worship for Dissenters. There are also some charitable establishments, assembly rooms, good hotels, billiard rooms, and a theatre. Cheltenham returns 1 M.P. Pop. 1861, 39,693. Two miles distant is Southam House (Earl of Ellenborough.)

LXII. BIRMINGHAM AND GLOUCESTER RAILWAY, 52½ Miles.

ON RIGHT FROM GLO'ST.	From Birmin.		From Glo'st.	ON LEFT FROM GLO'ST.
	53	From Glo'ster Station. GLOUCESTER.		
Montpelier Lodge (Lord De Saumarez). Prestbury. Southam House (Earl of Ellenborough).	46	CHELTENHAM.	7	Staverton. Boddington. Elmstone Hardwick. Stoke Orchard.
Bishop's Cleeve, and at a distance Winchcomb, near which are the ruins of Sudely Castle; and beyond is Toddington House, Lord Sudeley.	43	Cleeve Station.	10	Tredington.
Oxenton. In the meadows near Tewkesbury, a dreadful conflict took place in 1471 between the adherents of the Houses of York and Lancaster, in which the latter were totally defeated. The spot still retains the name of the Bloody Field.	39	Ashchurch. Tewkesbury Branch, 2 Miles. TEWKESBURY is pleasantly situated at the junction of the Severn and the Avon. Here was formerly an abbey founded by the Saxons, the church of which still remains, and is a stately structure in the form	14	Walton Cardiff. Walton House. Tewkesbury has a considerable trade in malting, and manufactures cotton stockings and nails. It returns two M.P. Pop. 1861, 5876 It affords the title of Baron to the Earl of Munster.

ON RIGHT FROM GLO'ST.	From Birm.		From Glo'st.	ON LEFT FROM GLO'ST.
		of a cathedral. It contains the monuments of many distinguished persons. From the summit of the tower there is a delightful prospect. The gateway, which once formed the entrance to the abbey, still remains, and behind the church are vestiges of the cloisters.		Across the Severn, Pull Co., J. E. Dowdeswell, Esq.
Kemerton and Kemerton Court. Overbury Park.	37	**Bredon Station.**	16	Across the Avon, Strensham Court, J. Taylor, Esq.
Elmley Pa., T. H. H. Davies, Esq. Wooller's Hill, C. E. Hanford, Esq.	34	**Eckington Station.** cr. the Avon.	19	Strensham, the birthplace of Butler the poet. At a distance, Upton.
	33	**Defford Station.**	20	Line to Worcester, Droitwich, Stourbridge, &c., branches off here. At a distance, Upton. Severnstoke.
	29	**Wadborough Station.**	24	Besford Court, Sir T. G. Saunders Sebright, Bart.
Line to Pershore, Evesham, &c., branches off here. At a short distance is Pershore, a handsome well-built town. Here are the ruins of the Abbey House. The scenery of the vicinity is picturesque. Pop. 2905.	28	**Abbots Wood Junction.**	25	Croome Park (Earl Coventry,) and beyond the Rhyd, Sir E. H. Lechmere, Bart.
	26	SPETCHLEY Station.	27	Spetcheley Park, R. Berkeley, Esq.
Stoulton. Peopleton. Crowle and Crowle House. Huddington. Himbleton.	22	**Dunhampstead Station.**	31	
Bradley. Hanbury Hall, a spacious mansion, erected about 1710. The hall and staircases are painted with allegorical subjects by Sir Godfrey Kneller. The church contains several monuments of the Vernon family.	20	DROITWICH Road Station. Droitwich is a place of very considerable antiquity, famous for its salt springs. It was a very populous place in the time of William the Conqueror. Its salt, produced from brine springs, is esteemed the best in Europe. It returns one member to Parliament. Pop. 7086.	33	Whittington. Warndon. Tibberton, and beyond Hinlip Hall, Viscount Southwell. Oddingley. Hadzor House, J. H. Galton, Esq. Westwood Park, Right Hon. Sir J. S. Pakington, Bart. M.P., and beyond Ombersley Court, Lord Sandys.
	17	**Stoke Works Station.**	36	Upton Warren. Grafton House (Earl of Shrewsbury) in ruins
	15	BROMSGROVE Station.	38	Bromsgrove, on the Sal-

ON RIGHT FROM GLO'ST.	From Birm.		From Glo'st.	ON LEFT FROM GLO'ST.
At Barnet Green are a chalybeate spring and a petrifying well.	13	Blackwell Station.	40	warpe, consists principally of one street, in which are many old houses curiously ornamented. The inhabitants are employed in the manufacture of nails, needles, and linens. The church contains a number of handsome monuments, particularly of the Talbots, Earls of Shrewsbury, and has a highly ornamented tower and spire. Pop. 5262.
Hewell Grange, Lady Windsor. This seat has belonged to the family of the Earls of Plymouth and their representatives since 1341. Bordesley Park, and beyond Beoley Hall. Coston Hackett. Coston Hall. Northfield.	11	BARNET GREEN Station.	32	Chaddesley Corbett. Bell Broughton. Frankley.
King's Norton.	6½	KING'S NORTON.	46½	
	4	MOSELEY Station.	49	
	2	Camphill.	51	Harborne.
Moseley Hall, J. A. Taylor, Esq.		Birmingham, (see p. 203).	53	Edgbaston, Lord Calthorpe.

LXIII. LONDON TO GLOUCESTER THROUGH MAIDENHEAD, FARINGDON, AND CIRENCESTER, 107½ Miles.

ON RIGHT FROM LOND.	From Glo'st.		From Lond.	ON LEFT FROM LOND.
Cliefden, Duke of Sutherland.	81¼	From Hyde Pa. Corner to Maidenhead, Berks, (see pp. 91, 92.)	26	
	79¼	Junction of the road. ☞ cr. river Thames and enter Oxfordshire.	28	To Reading, 11 miles. Park Place, Henerton House.
To Great Marlow, 7½ m. Fawley Court, W. P. W. Freeman, Esq., and beyond, Stonor Park, Lord Camoys.	72¼	HENLEY ON THAMES has a considerable trade in corn, flour, malt, and beechwood. The church is a handsome structure, containing several interesting monuments. Pop. of par. 3419.	35	To Reading, 8 miles. Bolney Court. Grey's Court, Hon. and Rev. Sir F. J. Stapleton, Bart., and beyond, Crowsley Park.
	67¼	Nettlebed.	40	
About 3 miles distant is Chalgrove Field, where Hampden fell, on the 18th of June 1643. A monument in commemoration of this event was erected in 1843, and its completion celebrated on the two-hundredth anniversary of the day.	61¼	Bensington or Benson.	46	Near Wallingford, Mongewell House.
	58¼	Dorchester was formerly a Roman station. The windows of the church present some curious paintings. The font is very ancient and curious.	49	
Nuneham Courtenay, G. G. Vernon Harcourt, Esq.	56½	Burcott.	50¾	

ON RIGHT FROM LOND.	From Glo'ster.		From Lond.	ON LEFT FROM LOND.
		cr. river Isis, and enter Berks.		Milton House.
To Oxford, $6\frac{1}{2}$ miles. 2 miles distant, Radley House. Sir G. Bowyer, Bart. Oakley House.	$51\frac{1}{2}$	ABINGDON, an ancient town, communicating by a cut with the Thames. It has two ancient churches, several meeting-houses, and charitable institutions, a handsome market-house, a gaol, corn-mills, and manufactories of sail-cloth. One M.P. Pop. 5680.	$55\frac{3}{4}$	To East Ilsley, 11 m. Newbury, $21\frac{1}{2}$ miles. Wantage, 10 miles. Hungerford, 24 miles.
	$50\frac{1}{2}$	Shippon.	$56\frac{3}{4}$	
Buckland House, Sir R. G. Throckmorton, Bart.	$44\frac{3}{4}$	Kingston Inn.	$62\frac{1}{2}$	Pusey House, P. Pusey, Esq.
Farringdon House, W. Bennett, Esq.	$36\frac{3}{4}$	FARRINGDON. The church contains several curious monuments. Near this town are the remains of a camp supposed to be of Danish origin. Pop. 2943.	$70\frac{1}{2}$	Buscot Park, late P. Loveden, Esq.
		cr. the Isis, and enter Gloucestershire.		
	$31\frac{3}{4}$	LECHLADE.	$75\frac{1}{2}$	
Fairford Park, J. R. R. Barker, Esq., and 2 miles distant Williamstrip Park, Sir M. E. Hicks Beach, Bart. Ampney Park, and beyond Barnsley Park, Sir J. Musgrave, Bart.	$27\frac{3}{4}$	FAIRFORD. The church, erected towards the close of the fifteenth century, by John Tame, a merchant, for the reception of some painted glass which he had captured at sea, is a very interesting building, and contains a number of curious monuments, amongst which is that of the founder and his son, Sir E. Tame. cr. river Coln.	80	
The Abbey was granted to the family of Master by Queen Elizabeth in 1564.	18	CIRCENCESTER, p. 154. in Trewsbury Mead, about 2 miles distant, is a spring called Thames Head, the primary source of that river.	$89\frac{1}{4}$	Oakley Park, (Earl Bathurst,) formed by Lord Bathurst, the friend of Pope. To Cricklade, $6\frac{3}{4}$ miles. Malmesbury, $11\frac{1}{2}$ miles.
Cerney House. Cotswold House. Rencombe Park, Sir J. W. Guise, Bart. Birdlip Hill commands a very extensive prospect.	$7\frac{1}{4}$	Along the Roman road to Birdlip.	100	Charlton Park, Earl of Suffolk and Berkshire. Minchinhampton, 10 m. Stroud, 11 m. Misserden Castle, (late Sir E. B. Sandys, Bart.) Whitcomb Park. Prinknash Park, T. J. Howell, Esq. This place formerly belonged to the Abbots of Gloucester.

ON RIGHT FROM LOND.	From Glo'ster.		From Lond.	ON LEFT FROM LOND.
To Cheltenham, 5 m.	4¾	Division of the road.	102½	Bowden Hall.
				Barnwood Court, and Barnwood Ho.
		GLOUCESTER, see p. 156.	107¼	

LXIV. LONDON TO OXFORD THROUGH MAIDENHEAD AND HENLEY, 58 Miles.

ON RIGHT FROM LOND.	From Oxford.		From Lond.	ON LEFT FROM LOND.
Cliefden (Duke of Sutherland).	32	From London to Maidenhead (see pp. 91-92).	26	
Pinkneys. Temple House, T. P. Williams, Esq., and beyond Bisham Abbey, A. A. Vansittart, Esq. Culham Court. Remenham.				Hall Place, Sir Gilbert East, Bart.
		☞ cross the Thames, and enter Oxfordshire.		Park Place, a noble mansion, beautifully situated, containing a good library, and a choice collection of pictures.
Fawley Court, W. P. Williams Freeman, Esq. This place suffered much in the civil wars, from a troop of horse in the interests of Charles I. who tore the books in the library to pieces, and burned many valuable manuscripts and title-deeds of the estate.	23	HENLEY UPON THAMES. The scenery around is extremely beautiful. The town carries on a considerable trade in corn, flour, and malt. In one of the inns (Red Lion) of this place Shenstone wrote his poem, "On an Inn." Pop. of Parish, 3419.	35	3 miles distant Crowsley. The park is well stocked with deer, and contains a quantity of fine timber. Rotherfield Grays. Blounts Court.
Henley Pa.	21	Assington Cross.	37	Grey's Court, Hon. and Rev. Sir F. J. Stapleton, Bart.
Bixbrand, and beyond Stonor Park, Lord Camoys.	20	Bix Turnpike.	38	
	18	Nettlebed.	40	Joyce Grove,
2 m. distant, Swincombe House, and beyond Watlington Park. At a distance Watlington, a small town, carrying on but little traffic of any nature. Lace-making forms the principal employment of the females. A weekly market has been held here since the time of Richard I. Beyond Watlington is Sherbourne Castle (Earl of Macclesfield).	16½	Nuffield Heath.	41½	Braziers House, J. S. Manley, Esq. Ipsden Ho. J. Reade, Esq. Crowmarsh.

ON RIGHT FROM LOND.	From Oxford.		From Lond.	ON LEFT FROM LOND.
				Castle Priory, W. S. Blackstone, Esq.
Brightwell House, W. F. Lowndes Stone, Esq. Chalgrove, where Hampden fell.	12	Bensington.	46	Wallingford, formerly of great importance, is situated on the Thames, over which there is a bridge of 19 arches. It returns 1 M.P. Pop. of par. bor. 1851, 8064.
Warborough.	10	Shillingford.	48	
		cross the Thames.		
Drayton.	8	Dorchester.	50	Little Wittenham. Clifton Hampden.
Chiselhampton. March Baldon, and Baldon House, Sir. H. P. Willoughby, Bart.	$5\frac{1}{4}$	Nuneham Courtenay.	$52\frac{3}{4}$	Nuneham Park, G. G V. Harcourt, Esq. The house is handsome, and contains a choice collection of pictures.
Balden Toot, and beyond Cuddesden Palace, Bishop of Oxford.	$3\frac{1}{4}$	Sandford.	$54\frac{3}{4}$	Radley House, Sir G. Bowyer, Bart.
		Littlemoor.		
	$2\frac{1}{2}$	Cowley.	$55\frac{1}{2}$	
Horsepath.		OXFORD.	58	South Hinksey.

Oxford, the capital of the county to which it gives its name, and the seat of one of the most celebrated universities of Europe, is pleasantly situate upon a gentle eminence in a valley at the confluence of two small rivers, the Isis and Cherwell. It is a place of very remote antiquity, but the first fact connected with it that is known with certainty is, that in the reign of Alfred, who at one time resided at Oxford with his three sons. the place was noted for a monastery which was founded in the year 727. Oxford was twice set on fire, and otherwise suffered severely from the Danes. Edmund Ironside was murdered there. Canute frequently resided at Oxford, and Harold Harefoot, his son and successor, was crowned and died there. In the year 1067, the town was stormed by William the Conqueror, and a castle was built by him, now partly occupied by the county gaol and the house of correction. During her contest with Stephen, the Empress Maude was closely besieged in Oxford Castle by her rival, but escaped in the night with only three attendants; and the castle surrendered next morning. In the reign of Richard II. the lectures of Dr John Wycliffe, the warden of Canterbury College, occasioned a great excitement, and afterwards produced very important results. Henry II. resided at Oxford during the greater part of his reign, and here his valiant son Richard Cœur de Lion was born. In the reign of Edward III. the university and town suffered much from a pestilence which carried off a fourth part of the students. In the martyrdoms of Mary's reign, Latimer, Ridley, and Cranmer were burnt at Oxford in front of Balliol College. During the civil wars, Oxford, after once or twice changing masters, became the head-quarters of the King. After the battle of Naseby, it surrendered to the parliamentary army under Fairfax. During the reign of James II. the university firmly resisted an illegal command of that prince to elect a Roman Catholic to the presidency of Magdalen College. James proceeded thither in person and expelled the contuma-

OXFORD UNIVERSITY.

cious members, whom, however, when alarmed by the preparations of the Prince of Orange, he afterwards restored. The origin of the University of Oxford, like that of the town, is involved in obscurity. The first places of education here appear to have been schools for the instruction of youth. The earliest charter of privileges to the University as a corporate body is of the 28th Henry III. In 1603, the University obtained from James I. the privilege of sending two representatives to Parliament. Oxford University contains nineteen colleges and five halls.

UNIVERSITY COLLEGE is said to have been founded by Alfred; but this is believed on good grounds to be a mistake. The college, as such, was erected from funds bequeathed by William of Durham, Rector of Wearmouth, who died in 1249. The funds of this college have been augmented by different benefactors—and especially by Dr. Radcliffe. The chapel contains a fine monument, by Flaxman, to the memory of Sir W. Jones, the distinguished Orientalist, a curious altar-piece after Carlo Dolce, burnt in wood, &c. The common room contains Wilton's fine bust of King Alfred.

BALLIOL COLLEGE received its foundation about the year 1263 from Sir John Balliol of Barnard Castle (father of John Balliol, King of Scotland), and his wife Devorgilla. The library was formerly considered one of the best in the University, and previously to the Reformation was particularly rich in manuscripts. Wycliffe was of this College.

MERTON COLLEGE was founded about the year 1264 by Walter de Merton, Lord Chancellor, and afterwards Bishop of Rochester. Its chapel, rebuilt about the beginning of the fifteenth century, is a remarkably fine specimen of Gothic workmanship, and contains an altar-piece of the Crucifixion, supposed to be by Tintoretto, and monuments to Sir Thomas Bodley and Sir Henry Saville. The Library is the oldest in the kingdom.

EXETER COLLEGE was founded in 1314 by Walter de Stapledon, Bishop of Exeter, Lord Treasurer of England, and Secretary of State to Edward II. It has a handsome hall and chapel, and a good library.

ORIEL COLLEGE was founded about the year 1326, nominally by Edward II. but really by Adam de Brome, his almoner. The architectural beauty of the library is striking. Among the plate are two cups, one given by Edward II. and the other by Bishop Carpenter.

QUEEN'S COLLEGE derived its name from Philippa, Queen of Edward III. by whose confessor, Robert de Eglesfield, it was founded in 1340. This college has been particularly patronized by the Queens of England. The existing buildings, with the exception of the library, were chiefly erected during the last century. The chapel has a painted ceiling of the Ascension by Sir James Thornhill, and for an altar-piece a copy by Cranke of Correggio's "Night." The library contains about 20,000 volumes, and, among other curiosities, a very ancient portrait on glass of Henry V., and another of Cardinal Beaufort.

NEW COLLEGE owes its establishment in 1380, to William of Wykeham, Bishop of Winchester, and Lord High Chancellor, in the reign of Edward III. The buildings were completed in 1387, the same year in which Wykeham began his collegiate establishment at Winchester. This is one of the wealthiest colleges in Oxford, and possesses the most beautiful chapel in the university. Among the curiosities preserved in this chapel is the superb and costly crosier of the founder.

LINCOLN COLLEGE was founded about the year 1427, by Richard Flemmyng, Bishop of Lincoln. John Wesley, founder of the Methodists, was of this college.

ALL SOUL'S COLLEGE was founded in the year 1437, by Henry Chichelé, Archbishop of Canterbury. The library of this college, the foundation stone of which was laid by Dr. Young, author of the "Night Thoughts," was erected by Colonel Codrington, and contains perhaps the largest room appropriated to the purpose in England. In the chapel is a fine statue of Judge Blackstone by Bacon, and the college hall contains numerous paintings; among others, one of the Finding of the Law, by Sir J. Thornhill.

MAGDALEN COLLEGE was founded by William of Waynflete, Bishop of Winchester, in the year 1457. It is bound by its statutes to entertain the Kings of England, and their sons, when at Oxford. The chapel contains a picture of Christ bearing the cross, said to be by Guido, the Last Judgment painted on glass, &c.

BRAZEN NOSE COLLEGE was founded in the year 1509, by William Smyth, Bishop of Lincoln, in conjunction with his friend, Sir Richard Sutton, Knight. Its singular name is said to have arisen from the circumstance of its having been erected on the site of two ancient halls, one of which was called Brazen Nose Hall, on account of an iron ring fixed in a nose of brass, and serving as a knocker to the gate. The chapel is fine, and the hall is embellished with portraits.

CORPUS CHRISTI COLLEGE was founded in 1516, by Richard Fox, Bishop of Winchester. The library, which is particularly rich in printed books and manuscripts, contains a statue of the founder in his pontifical robes. In the hall are a few portraits, and in the chapel an altar-piece by Rubens.

CHRIST CHURCH COLLEGE, the largest and most magnificent foundation at Oxford, owes its origin in 1524 to Cardinal Wolsey. Its chapel is the cathedral church of the bishopric of Oxford. The hall is one of the finest in the kingdom, and boasts a very extensive collection of portraits. The library is very rich in manuscripts, prints, and coins. In Peckwater Quadrangle there is a collection of pictures bequeathed to the college by General Guise in 1765, and since enlarged. The bell called Great Tom weighs nearly 17,000 lbs.

TRINITY COLLEGE was originally founded and endowed by Edward III., Richard II., and the priors and bishops of Durham. Being classed with religious houses at the Reformation, it was suppressed, and Sir Thomas Pope, having purchased the site and buildings, endowed a new foundation in 1554.

ST. JOHN'S COLLEGE was founded in 1555, by Sir Thomas White, Alderman and Lord Mayor of London. Its gardens are much admired; the library is one of the largest and best furnished in the university, and possesses a curious piece of tapestry representing our Saviour and disciples at Emmaus.

JESUS COLLEGE was founded in 1571, by Queen Elizabeth at the suggestion of Hugh ap Rice. D.C.L., for the more especial benefit of his countrymen, the natives of Wales. This was the first college founded by a Protestant. The library has a good collection of books and some curiosities, among which is a silver bowl capable of containing ten gallons, a metal watch, given by Charles I., and a huge stirrup said to have been used by Queen Elizabeth. In the hall there is a portrait of Charles I. by Vandyke, and in the chapel a copy of Guido's "Michael triumphing over Satan."

WADHAM COLLEGE, founded in 1613, by Nicholas and Dorothy Wadham, is remarkable as having given rise to the Royal Society, the first meeting of which was held in a room over the gateway. The chapel and hall are fine.

PEMBROKE COLLEGE, originally Broadgate Hall, was in 1624 converted into a college by the joint munificence of Thomas Tesdale and the Rev. Richard Wightwick. Dr. Samuel Johnson was of this college, and in the hall there is a bust of him by Bacon, a portrait of Charles I., and other paintings.

WORCESTER COLLEGE was founded in 1714, from funds bequeathed by Sir Thomas Cookes, Bart. It possesses handsome gardens, chapel, and a library containing a valuable collection of architectural books and manuscripts.

Besides the colleges, there are five halls at Oxford—that is, establishments not endowed with estates, but simply under the government of a principal for the education and residence of students. These are, St Alban Hall, which derived its name from Robert de Sancto Albano, a burgess of Oxford, in the reign of King John; St Edmund Hall, said to be so called from St Edmund, Archbishop of Canterbury, in the reign of Henry III.; New Inn Hall, founded by William of Wykeham; St Mary Hall, founded by Edward II.; and St Mary Magdalen Hall, the most considerable of the whole number, originally founded as a grammar school in 1480, by William Waynflete, the founder of Magdalen College.

The chief public establishments connected with the University are—

THE SCHOOLS containing the Pomfret statues and the Arundelian marbles.

THE BODLEIAN LIBRARY, founded by Sir Thomas Bodley at the close of the sixteenth century, on the remains of one established by Humphrey, Duke of Gloucester. This library contains, perhaps, the most valuable collection of books and manuscripts in Europe.

THE PICTURE GALLERY.

THE THEATRE, built by Gilbert Sheldon, Archbishop of Canterbury, and Chancellor of the University in 1664-1669, at the expense of L.15,000. It was designed and completed by Sir Christopher Wren.

CLARENDON ROOMS, erected in 1711, with the profits of the sale of Clarendon's "History of the Rebellion," the copyright of which was presented to the University by his Lordship's son. They are used for offices and lecture rooms.

THE ASHMOLEAN MUSEUM, built at the charge of the University in 1682, by Sir C. Wren, for the reception of the collections of Ashmole, the antiquary.

RADCLIFFE'S LIBRARY, one of the most imposing architectural ornaments of Oxford, founded by Dr. Radcliffe, who, besides other sums, bequeathed L.40,000 for the erection of the building. The building was designed and executed between 1737 and 1749 by Gibbs of Aberdeen.

THE RADCLIFFE OBSERVATORY, erected out of the funds of Dr Radcliffe, by the trustees of his will, at an expense of L.30,000. Besides these buildings there is a botanic garden, containing about five acres.

THE NEW UNIVERSITY PRINTING OFFICE erected 1826-7.

The total number of electors (doctors and masters of arts) upon the books of the different colleges and halls of Oxford is above 3450.

Oxford contains fifteen parish churches. The other buildings most worthy of notice are, the town-hall, the city bridewell, where is preserved the door of the prison in which Cranmer, Ridley, and Latimer were confined, the county gaol, the Radcliffe Infirmary, &c. There are several meeting houses belonging to dissenting bodies. Races are held annually in Port Meadow, a short distance from the city. Oxford returns two M.P. Pop. 27,560.

At Stanton Harcourt, 4½ miles distant, are some remains of a mansion that belonged to the Earls Harcourt, now extinct. In one of the rooms, Pope passed a portion of two summers in translating Homer. The church contains several monuments of the Harcourt family. In the vicinity are three large monumental stones called the Devil's Quoits.

LXV. LONDON TO GLOUCESTER THROUGH OXFORD AND CHELTENHAM, 103 Miles.

ON RIGHT FROM LOND.	From Glo'ster.		From London.	ON LEFT FROM LOND.
	49	From Hyde Pa. Corner to Oxford, (see p. 188.) cross river Isis.	54	
Wytham Abbey, Earl of Abingdon	47¼	Botley Hill, (*Berks.*) cross river Isis.	55¾	Cumner.
Ensham Hall (Earl of Macclesfield), and beyond Blenheim (Duke of Marlborough), see p. 189.	43¼	Ensham, (Oxon). cr. riv. Windrush.	59¾	
	38¼	WITNEY. famous for its blankets and other thick woollens. The principal buildings are, the church, a spacious Gothic structure, with several ancient monuments; the town-hall, and the Staple or Blanket-Hall. Pop. 3458.	64¾	Cockthorpe Park.
The Priory, W J. Lenthall, Esq. To Chipping Norton, 10 m. To Stow on the Wold, 10 miles.	31	BURFORD formerly carried on a large manufacture of linen cloths and malt. The church contains a monument to the memory of Chief Baron Sir L. Tanfield.	72	2½ miles distant, Broadwell Grove, and near it is Filkins Hall.
Barrington Grove, C. Greenaway, Esq. Barrington Park, Lord Dynevor. Sherborne Castle, Lord Sherborne.		Enter Gloucestershire.		To Faringdon, 10 miles. Eastington Park.

ON RIGHT FROM LOND.	From Glo'ster.		From London.	ON LEFT FROM LOND.
	21¾	NORTHLEACH, formerly remarkable for its clothing trade, which has now declined. It has a free grammar school. The church is a handsome structure, and contains numerous brasses and other monuments.	81¼	Stowell Park.
Salperton Park, J. Browne, Esq. Sandywell Park, W. L. Lawrence, Esq.	15	Frogmill Inn. The hill beyond this commands a fine prospect, including the vale of Evesham, Cheltenham, Tewkesbury, Worcester, and the Malvern Hills.	88	Compton Abdale. To Gloucester by Seven Wells, 14½ miles.
	9	CHELTENHAM, (p. 157.)	94	Charlton Pa.
		GLOUCESTER, (p. 156.)	103	Hempstead House.

LXVI. LONDON TO HEREFORD THROUGH GLOUCESTER AND LEDBURY, 136 Miles.

ON RIGHT FROM LOND.	From Heref.		From London.	ON LEFT FROM LOND.
	33	London to Gloucester.	103	To Ross, 15½ miles; to Mitcheldean, 11 miles; to Newnham, 11 miles.
		cr. riv. Severn, and enter Aldney Island.		
		cross river Severn.		
Maisemore Lodge.				Highnam Court, Sir J W. Guise, Bart.
Maisemore Court,				Hartpury Court, R. Canning, Esq.
To Upton, 10 miles.	26	Junction of the road.	110	
	23½	Staunton, *Worcestersh.*	112½	
Down House, G. Dowdeswell, Esq.				
		Enter Herefordshire.		Haffield House.
Bromesberrow Place, O. Ricardo, Esq. 1 mile distant Eastnor Castle, the magnificent seat of Earl Somers. Hope End. To Malvern by Little Malvern and Malvern Wells, 8 miles; thence to Worcester, 8 miles.	16	LEDBURY carries on a considerable manufacture of ropes, lines, and sacks. The church is of Saxon origin, and contains several monuments. Large quantities of cider are made in the vicinity. This town formerly sent two members to Parliament. Pop. 3263.	120	To Ross, 13½ miles.
Mainstone Court, J. Johnstone, Esq.; and, 4 miles distant, Herefordshire Beacon an immense fortress, of British origin	12	Trumpet. This spot commands a fine view of the Herefordshire beacon.	124	
	9¾	Tarrington.	127¼	Stoke Edith Park Lady Emily Foley.

ON RIGHT FROM LOND.	From Herefo.		From London.	ON LEFT FROM LOND.
	6	Dormington.	130	About 4 miles from Dormington is Holme Lacy, the ancient seat of the Scudamore family, where Pope wrote the "Man of Ross." The mansion and grounds are very interesting. The present possessor is Sir E. F. Scudamore Stanhope, Bart.
		cross river Frome.		
New Court.	3	Lugwardine.	133	
		cross river Lugg.		
		HEREFORD, (see p. 145.)	136	

LXVII. LONDON TO HEREFORD THROUGH GLOUCESTER AND ROSS, 134 Miles.

ON RIGHT FROM LOND.	From Herefo.		From London.	ON LEFT FROM LOND.
	31	Lond. to Glo'st. (p. 167.)	103	
		cr. river Severn and Glo'ster Canal.		
Highnam Court (Sir J. W. Guise, Bart.), erected from a design by Inigo Jones, and containing, among other original portraits, those of Cromwell and Algernon Sidney.				High Grove,
	23¼	Huntley.	110¾	Huntly Court, and beyond Flaxley Abbey, Sir M. H. C. Boevey, Bart.
	20	Longhope.	114	To Mitchel Dean, 2 m.
		Enter Herefordshire.		
	16	Weston.	118	
About 5 miles from Ross are the massy ivy-covered ruins of Goodrich Castle. There was a castle here before the Conquest. The keep, which is the most ancient part, is in the Saxon style. During the civil war it was a scene of desperate contention, being repeatedly taken and retaken. It was the last castle in England, except Pendennis, that held out for the King. It was afterwards destroyed by order of the Parliament. There is a remarkably fine view from the battlements of one of the towers.	14	ROSS, situated on a rock elevated above the east bank of the Wye. Here the celebrated "Man of Ross" Mr J. Kyrle lived, and was interred in Ross church, where a monument has been erected to his memory. The church also contains several monuments of the Rudhall family, one of whom defended Hereford against Cromwell. The churchyard and the contiguous prospect ground laid out by Mr Kyrle are celebrated for their beautiful views. Ross is a favourite resort for summer parties visiting the Wye. Pop. 3715.	120	A little below the town, on the right bank of the river, stand the ruins of Wilton Castle, which, at one time, belonged to Thomas Guy, the founder of Guy's Hospital in London. The estate of Wilton was left by him to that establishment. Near Ross is Goodrich Court, the seat of the late Sir S. R. Meyrick, containing a celebrated collection of armour. It is freely shown on application.
		cr. river Wye.		
	13	Wilton.	121	
To Hereford through Little Dew Church, 12 m. Pengethly. Harewood, Sir H. Hoskyns, Bart.	11	Peterstow.		To Monmouth, 10½ m. Bryngwyn, J. Phillipps, Esq. Mynde Park, T. G. Symons, Esq.
In the distance Holme Lacy, Sir E. F. Sardamore Stanhope, Bart.	4	Callow.	130	Allensmore, E. B. Pateshall, Esq.
		cr. river Wye.		
		HEREFORD.	134	

ON RIGHT FROM LOND.	From St David's.		From London.	ON LEFT FROM LOND.
	80¼	From Hyde Park Corner to LLANDOVERY (*Caermarthenshire*, p. 171.)	187¼	Two m. distant Henllys.
Dolau Cothi, J. Johnes, Esq.	70¼	Pumsant.	197¼	
		⁂ cr. river Teivy.	204¾	
To Aberystwith through Aberaeron, 29 miles, Tregaron, 11 miles.	62¼	LAMPETER (*Cardiganshire*,) a small town on the west bank of the Teivy, which is noted for its salmon. The church is an ancient building, with a square tower. Here is a college founded by Bishop Burgess for the education of Welsh clergymen.	205¼	To Caermarthen, 22 m. Lampeter forms one of the Cardigan district of burghs, returning one M.P. Pop. of Lampeter 989.
	53¾	Allt Yr Odyn Arms.	213¾	Allt Yr Odyn.
	52¼	Rhydowen.	215¼	
	42¼	NEWCASTLE EMLYN (*Caermarthenshire*), delightfully situated on the banks of the Teivy. The ruins of a castle, occupied by the Royalists during the civil war, stand on an eminence commanding a fine prospect.	225¼	To Kilgarron, 8 miles. At this place are the ruins of a castle occupying the summit of a naked rock rising from the bed of the Teivy. The surrounding scenery is very interesting.
	33½	Llangoedmore.	234	Llangoedmore Place. Castle Maelgwn.
To Aberystwith, 39½ m.	32¼	CARDIGAN, (p. 136.)	235¼	To Haverfordwest, 26½ miles.
	31	St Dogmell's *Pembrokeshire.*	236½	Here are the remains of an abbey, standing in a beautiful situation.
	21¾	NEWPORT, (p. 136.)	245¾	
	14¾	FISHGUARD, (p. 136.)	252¾	To Haverfordwest, 13 m. Glynammel.
	8¾	Mathry.	258¾	
	7	Penlan.	260½	
Cryglas.	2	Hendra.	265½	
Trevacwm.		ST DAVID'S, (p. 135.)	267½	

LXIX. LONDON TO HAVERFORDWEST AND MILFORD, BY OXFORD, GLOUCESTER, ROSS, MONMOUTH, BRECON, AND CAERMARTHEN, 255½ Miles.

ON RIGHT FROM LOND.	From Milford.		From London.	ON LEFT FROM LOND.
To Hereford, 12½ miles.	134½	From Hyde Pa. Corner to Wilton, *Herefordsh.* (p. 168.)	121	
Goodrich is remarkable for the ruins of its castle, one of the most picturesque objects on the banks of the Wye It was alternately	130½	Goodrich.	125	Goodrich Court (seat of the late Sir S. Meyrick) is an admirable imitation of the antique, and by far the most perfect thing of its kind in England.
	129½	Whitchurch.	126¼	Near Whitchurch is Sy-

ON RIGHT FROM LOND.	From Milford.		From London.	ON LEFT FROM LOND.
possessed by the Parliament forces and the Royalists during the civil wars. To Hereford, 18 miles; Abergavenny by Rockfield and Llanvapley, 15 m.	124¾	MONMOUTH, (p. 144.)	130¾	mond's Yate, a lofty rock, surmounted by an encampment, and commanding a fine prospect. To Gloucester by Mitchel Dean, 27 m., Chepstow, 15¼ miles
	122	Wonastow.	133½	Troy House, Duke of Beaufort.
	121	Dingestow.	134½	Dingestow Court, S. Bosanquet, Esq. To Usk, 7 miles.
	118¼	Tregare.	137¼	At a distance the ruins of Ragland Castle.
	117	Bryngwyn.	138½	Clytha, W. Jones, Esq.
	113¼	Llanvihangel.	142¼	
Coed Morgan.	112¼	Llangattock.	143¼	Llanover House, Sir B. Hall, Bart.
Coldbrook House, F. H. Williams, Esq. Hill House.	108¼	ABERGAVENNY, (p. 137.)	147¼	To Pontypool, 9 miles; Newport, 17; Usk, 10. Near Abergavenny is the Sugar Loaf mountain, 1850 feet high.
Pentre Ho.	106¾	Pentre.	148¾	
	106	Llanwenarth. 1¾ miles farther enter South Wales. cr. river Grwyney.	149½	
	104	Enter Brecknockshire.	151½	
Gwernvale, J. Gwynne, Esq. More Park. Penmyarth.	102	CRICKHOWELL, (p. 137.)	153½	To Merthyr Tydvil, 14 miles. Dany Park. Glanusk, Sir J. Bailey Bart.
Here are the picturesque ruins of Tretower Castle.	99¾	Tretower.	155¾	
To Hay, 15 miles.	96½	Bwlch.	159	Buckland House, J. P. Gwynne Holford, Esq.
	94¼	Llansaintfraed.	161¼	
Skethiog House.	92¾	Skethiog.	162¾	
Peterstone Court, and in the distance Tregoyd, Viscount Hereford.	91½	Llanhamlach.	164	
To Hay, 15¼ miles; Builth, 6¼ miles.	88¼	BRECON,* (p. 137.) cross river Usk.	167¼	Neath, 27 miles.
	86	Llanspyddyd.	169½	
Penpont House.	83	Penpont. cross river Usk.	172½	
	79¾	Rhyd Brue.	175¾	
	77½	Trecastle. Here is a good inn.	178	
	76½	Llywel. Enter Caermarthensh.	179	

* About 18 miles from Brecon is the market-town and borough of Merthyr Tydvil, situated

ON RIGHT FROM LOND.	From Milford.		From London.	ON LEFT FROM LOND.
To Builth, 23 miles; Lampeter, 18 miles. Ten miles from Llandovery are the chalybeate springs of Llanwrtyd, similar to those of Harrowgate. They are much frequented in summer. Maesllydan. Blanoes, D. Jones, Esq., 3 miles distant Llwyny-wormwood, Rev. Sir E. H. G. Williams, Bart.	68¼	LLANDOVERY, a small town on the Bran, on the west bank of which are the ruins of a castle. A considerable quantity of woollen stockings are made here. Pop. of Borough 1855.	187½	Another road leads from Llandovery to Llandilofawr, through Llangadock.
Llwynybrain.	67	Llandingat. cross river Towey.	188½	
Taliaris	56¼	LLANDILOFAWR, a neat well built town, on the west bank of the Towey. The river abounds with salmon, trout, and eels. Pop. of parish 5440.	199¼	Manoravon, D. Pugh, Esq. Tregib. Beyond Llandilofawr is Dynevor Castle, in ruins, and Newton Park, one of the finest seats in Wales, the property of Lord Dynevor, p. 133. Golden Grove, Earl of Cawdor. Grongar Hill, celebrated by Dyer, and the ruins of Dryslyn Castle, on an eminence, commanding a fine view of the vale of Towey, p. 132.
Pantglas, D. Jones, Esq.	51¼	Cross Inn.	204¼	
	47¾	Cothy Bridge.	207¾	Middleton Hall, E. H. Adams, Esq.
	45	White Mill.	210½	
Near Abergwili is Merlin's Cave, shown as the scene of the magician's incantations; and, at a short distance is the spot where he is said to have been buried.	43½	Abergwili.	212	Abergwili Palace, (Bishop of St David's) rebuilt in 1830.
	41½	CAERMARTHEN, (p. 132)	224	
	18¼	NARBERTH, (p. 135.)	237¼	
	7½	HAVERFORDWEST, (p. 135.)	248	
		MILFORD, (p. 134.)	255½	

in Glamorganshire, at the head of the vale of Taff, celebrated for its rich and thick veins of coal, as well as for its romantic beauty. Merthyr Tydvil is famous for the number and extent of its iron works, the most remarkable of which are those of Dowlais and Cyfartha, the former belonging to Sir John Guest and Co., the latter to the Messrs Crawshay. Near Merthyr Tydvil is Dowlais House, the seat of Sir I. B. Guest, Bart. The trade of this town has been greatly benefited by the construction of both a canal and a railway to the seaport of Cardiff, distant about 24 miles. The Vale of Neath Railway connects Merthyr with Swansea. One M.P. Population of parish 49,794.

About 3 miles north of Merthyr Tydvil are the scanty remains of the ancient castle of Morlais, said to have been the seat of the kings of Brecon. It was demolished by the parliamentary army during the civil wars.

LXX. LONDON TO ABERYSTWITH THROUGH OXFORD, GLOUCESTER, AND HEREFORD, 210¾ Miles.

ON RIGHT FROM LOND.	From Aberyst.		From London.	ON LEFT FROM LOND.
		From Tyburn Turnpike to HEREFORD, (p. 145.)	134	
	71¾	Creden Hill.	139	Two miles distant the site of the Roman station of Kenchester.
Mansell Lacy House. Foxley House.	69¾	Mansell Lacy.	141	
Garnstone.	68¼	Yazor.	142½	
To Weobley, 2½ miles.	66¾	Norton Canon.	144	
To Leominster, 10 miles. 2 miles distant is Lady Lift, an eminence commanding a splendid prospect.	63¾	Sarnesfield.	147	To Hay, 12½ miles.
	61¾	Woonton.	149	3 miles distant Newport House.
	58½	Lyonshall.	152¼	The Court.
Whittern, and 2 miles distant, Eywood Park, late Earl of Oxford, and Mortimer, and Titley Court.	57½	Penrhôs.	153¼	
		cr. the river Arrow.		
To Presteign, 6 miles.	56	KINGTON, p. 143.	154¾	5 miles beyond, Harpton Court, Rt. Hon. Sir G. C. Lewis, Bart.
Downton Hall.	48¾	NEW RADNOR *(Radnorshire.)*	161	
	46¾	Llanvihangel Nant Melan.	164	About a mile from this place is a celebrated waterfall called Water-break-its-neck.
	41¾	Llandegley.	169	
Pen-y-bont Court.	39¾	Pen-y-bont.	171	Pen-y-bont Hall, J. C. Severn, Esq. 5 miles to the left are the mineral springs of Llandrindod, much frequented in summer.
	35¾	Nantmel.	175	Llwynbaried.
Dderw	29¾	RHAYADER.	181	
		cr. river Wye.		
	18¾	CWM YSTWITH *(Cardiganshire.)*	192¼	
		cr. river Ystwith.		
	15½	Pentrebrunant.	195¼	To Tregarron, 15 miles, Lampeter, 26 miles.
	11½	Devil's Bridge, (p. 138.)	199¼	
	8½	Eskynald.	202¼	
		ABERYSTWITH, (p. 138.)	210¾	

LXXI. LONDON TO WORCESTER THROUGH HIGH-WYCOMBE, OXFORD, AND PERSHORE, 111 Miles.

ON RIGHT FROM LOND.	From Worces.		From London.	ON LEFT FROM LOND.
Glympton Park. Kiddington House, (Lord Vaux.)	49	From London to Woodstock, see p. 189.	62	Blenheim, Duke of Marlborough. Ditchley Park, Viscount Dillon, and beyond Cornbury Park, Lord Churchill.
	42	Enstone.	69	

ON RIGHT FROM LOND.	From Worces.		From London.	ON LEFT FROM LOND.
Heythrop Park, Earl of Shrewsbury, and 1½ m. to the right Great Tew Park.	37½	CHIPPING NORTON, an ancient town, with a free grammar school and an old church rebuilt, and rich in mon. brasses. There is a manufactory of coarse woollen cloth here. This borough sent members to Parliament in time of Edward I. and III., but has not since possessed that privilege. Pop. 3137.	73½	To Burford, 10 m. Sarsden House, J. H. Langston, Esq.
The four shires contiguous are Worcester, Warwick, Glos'ter, and Oxford. A battle was fought here between the English and the Danes, in which the latter, under Canute, were totally defeated.	31	Four Shire Stone.	80	Cornwell. Daylesford House. Adlestrop, Lord Leigh.
Batsford Park, Lord Redesdale. Northwick Park, Lord Northwick. Farncombe Abbey.	29¼	Moreton in the Marsh, *Gloucestershire.*	81¾	Toddenham, Sir P. Pole, Bart. Sezincote Park, Sir C. R. Rushout, Bart. Springhill, General Earl Beauchamp. Middlehill, Sir T. Phillipps, Bart.
	21	Broadway, *Worcestersh.*	90	In the distance Somerville Aston, Lord Somerville.
	15¾	Bengeworth.	95¼	
Evesham was formerly noted for its abbey, the tower of which still remains. One of its churches is adorned with a beautiful Gothic window. It has lately been connected with Worcester by railway, the line between these two places forming the first instalment of the Oxford, Worcester, and Wolverhampton. 1 M.P. Pop. 4680.	10½	EVESHAM.	99½	
		cr. river Avon.		Great Hampton. 2½ miles distant, Elmley Park, T. H. Davies, Esq. Avon Bank, T. B. Marriott, Esq.
	9	PERSHORE. The principal trade of this town is the manufacture of stockings. Here may be seen some ruins of the Abbey House, the only remains of an extensive monastic establishment. The situation of the town is very beautiful, and the surrounding scenery is picturesque, particularly at a place called Aylesborough, 1 mile from the town. Pop. 2905.	102	Wyck Hill House, C. Pole, Esq. 2 m. dist. Besford Court, Sir T. G. Saunders Sebright, Bart. Birlingham Court, and 3 m. dist., Croome Park, Earl Coventry.
	4¾	Stoulton.	106¼	Caldwell House.
	2¼	Whittington.	108¾	Spetchley Park, R. Berkeley, Esq.
White Ladies. Here Charles II. sought shelter after his defeat at Worcester.		cr. Worcester and Birmingham Canal.		
		WORCESTER, see p. 152.	111	

LXXII. LONDON TO ABERYSTWITH THROUGH WORCESTER AND LEOMINSTER, 207¾ Miles.

ON RIGHT FROM LOND.	From Aberyst.		From London.	ON LEFT FROM LOND.
		From Tyburn Turnpike to		
To Droitwich, 7 miles, Kidderminster, 14½ miles.	96¾	WORCESTER, (p. 173.)	111	To Tewkesbury, 16¼ m. To Evesham by railway, 14 m.
		cr. river Severn.		Crow's Nest.
	92¾	Cotheridge.	115	Cotheridge House.
	90¾	Broadwas.	117	
Whitbourne Court,	89¾	Doddenham Lane.	118	
To Tenbury, 15 miles.	88	Knightsford Bridge.	119¾	Gaines, J. Freeman, Esq.
		cr. river Teme, and enter Herefordshire.		
Brockhampton House, J. Barneby, Esq. To Kidderminster, 22¾ miles, Tenbury, 10 miles. Buckenhill.	82¾	BROMYARD, a small town, with a church of Saxon architecture. Pop. of parish, 2927.	125	To Ledbury, 13½ miles, Hereford, 14 miles.
Bredenbury House.	79½	Bredenbury.	128¼	
	78½	New Inn.	129¼	
	77¾	Batchley Green.	130	
	76	Docklow.	131¾	Buckland, W. G. Cherry, Esq.
Henner House	74¾	Steens Bridge.	133	3 miles distant Hampton Court, the magnificent seat of J. Arkwright, Esq., erected in the time of Henry IV. One of the apartments is in the same state as when occupied by William III., who here visited Baron Coningsby. In the library is preserved the handkerchief applied to the wound he received at the Battle of the Boyne.
	73¾	Trumpet.	134	
	71¾	Eaton Bridge.	136	
		cr. river Lug.		
To Tenbury, 11 miles, Ludlow, 12¼ miles. At a distance Berrington.	70¾	LEOMINSTER, (p. 145.)	137	To Hereford, 13 miles.
At a distance Eyton Hall, E. Evans, Esq.	68¼	Cholstry.	139½	To Kington by Pembridge, 13 miles.
	67¼	Cobden Ash.	140½	
	66½	Kingsland.	141¼	
Two miles distant Croft Castle. Near the N. W. extremity of the park there is a British camp, with a double ditch and rampart. Four miles from Mortimer's Cross are the ruins of Wigmore Castle.	64½	Mortimer's Cross. On this spot is a pedestal erected in commemoration of the battle which took place here, and settled Edward IV. on the throne	143¼	
		cr. Kingston Canal.		
Shobden Court, Lord Bateman.	62¾	Shobden.	145	At a dist. Stanton Pa.
To Tenbury, 15 miles.	60¾	Byton Lane.	147	To Hereford by Pembridge, 18¾ miles.
Kinsham Court.	58¾	Cwm.	149	
		cr. river Endwell, and enter Radnorshire.		
At a distance, Brampton Park, late Earl of Oxford and Mortimer.	56½	PRESTEIGN, a neat town on the small	151¼	Eywood (late Earl of Oxford and Mortimer). Titley Court.

ON RIGHT FROM LOND.	From Aberyst.		From London.	ON LEFT FROM LOND.
To Ludlow, 16½ miles, Knighton, 7 miles, thence to Shrewsbury, 33 miles.		river Lug. Near it is a circular hill, much visited, called the Warden, with plantations and delightful walks. Pop. of par. 2383. (See p. 142.)		To Kington, 7 miles.
	54½	Beggar's Bush.	153¼	Newcastle.
Grove Hall.	51½	Kinnerton.	156¼	Downton, and beyond Harpton Court, Rt. Hon Sir G. C. Lewis, Bart.
	48¾	NEW RADNOR.	159	
		ABERYSTWITH, (p. 138.)	207¾	

LXXIII. LONDON TO SHREWSBURY THROUGH AYLESBURY, KIDDERMINSTER, AND MUCH-WENLOCK, 160¼ Miles.

ON RIGHT FROM LOND.	From Shrews.		From London.	ON LEFT FROM LOND.
		From Tyburn Turnpike to Uxbridge.		
Chalfont House, J. N. Hibbert, Esq. Newlands. Newplace.	145¼	Middlesex (see p. 188.) cross river Coln, and enter Bucks.	15	In the distance, Bulstrade Park (Duke of Portland.)
The Vache, G. Palliser, Esq.		Chalfont, St Giles's, remarkable as having been the residence of Milton while the plague raged in London, in 1655. Here he finished Paradise Lost.		
	134¼	AMERSHAM. is an ancient town, which manufactures large quantities of black lace and cotton. It has a spacious church, containing several monuments, and a town-hall, built, in 1642, by Sir W. Drake. Pop. 3550.	26	Shardeloes, T. T. Drake, Esq. Little Missenden Abbey. 3 m. distant is Hampden House (Earl of Buckinghamshire), formerly the seat of the celebrated John Hampden, and the place where he is interred. The spot of land on which the ship-money was levied is situated a short distance south of the avenue to the house.
Great Missenden Abbey, G. Carrington, Esq. Halton House, Sir G. H. Dashwood, Bart. and beyond Aston-Clinton.	129¼	Great Missenden was the seat of a rich Abbey. Part of the cloisters still remain.	31	
2 miles from Aylesbury is Hartwell House (John Lee, Esq.), which was for many years the asylum of Louis XVIII.	124¾	WENDOVER. The inhabitants sre supported by lace making. It formerly returned 2 M.P. The Chiltern Hills pass by Wendover. Pop. of parish 1932.	35½	Chequers, Lady Frankland Russell. 3 m. dist. Great Kimble, Sir F. B. Morland, Bart.
Lillies, late Lord Nugent. Creslow Pastures (Lord Clifford), tenanted by R. Rowland, Esq.	119¾	AYLESBURY. (see p. 191.) cr. river Thame.	40½	To Thame 9¾ miles; to Bicester, 16¾ miles. Oving House.
	116	WHITCHURCH.	44¼	

ON RIGHT FROM LOND.	From Shrews.		From London	ON LEFT FROM LOND.
4 miles distant Whaddon Hall (W. Selby Lowndes, Esq.)	109½	WINSLOW. 6 miles distant is Stukeley, the church of which is one of the most perfect Saxon buildings in the kingdom. Pop. of parish, 1890.	51	3 miles distant, Claydon House, Sir H. Verney, Bart. Addington House.
		cr. river Ouse.		
To Brackley, 7¼ miles, thence to Banbury, 8½ miles.	102½	BUCKINGHAM (see p. 192).	57¾	
Morton House. Stowe, Duke of Buckingham (see p. 192).	98½	Finmore (*Oxon*).	61¾	Shelswell, J. Harrison, Esq., and beyond Tusmore House.
Evenley Hall, Hon. P. S. Pierrepont.	94¾	Enter Northamptonshire.	65½	
	91¼	Aynho on the Hill.	69	Aynho Hall, and beyond, North Aston, Earl of Clonmel.
		cr. riv. Charwell, and the Oxford Canal, and re-enter Oxon.		
Astrop Hall, W. Willes, Esq.	88¼	Adderbury. The church is a Gothic building, containing several monuments.	72	Adderbury House, W. Chamberlin, Esq. At a short distance stood the residence of the notorious John Wilmot, second Earl of Rochester.
To Warwick through Southam, 22¼ m., to Daventry, 17½ m. 1½ m. beyond, Banbury; to Warwick through Gaydon, 17½ m.	84¼	BANBURY (see p. 192).	75½	To Chipping Norton, 12 m. Broughton Castle, Lord Saye and Sele. Wroxton Abbey, Earl of Guilford.
	82¾	Drayton.	77½	Upton House, Captain J. Russell.
	81¾	Wroxton.	78½	Radway, E. S. Miller, Esq. Lower Eatington Hall, E. J. Shirley, Esq.
	77½	Upton (*Warwickshire*).	82¾	
		Edgehill (see p. 192).		
At a distance, Walton Hall, Sir C. Mordaunt, Bart.		cr. River Avon.		
Charlecote, G. Lucy, Esq. To Warwick, 8 m. Alveston House, Sir T. G. Skipwith, Bart. Clopton House.	65¼	STRATFORD ON AVON (see p. 190).	95	
Kinwarton. Coughton Court, Sir R. G. Throckmorton, Bart.	57¼	ALCESTER, at the confluence of the Alne and Arrow, is supposed to have been a Roman station. It has a neat church, a market hall, and a free grammar school. About 600 persons are employed in the manufacture of needles. Pop. 2128.	103	Ragley Park (Marquis of Hertford), built by Lord Conway about the middle of last century, but since improved under the direction of Wyatt. The grounds are extensive and beautiful, and abound in fine trees.
	50¾	Enter Worcestershire.	109½	
2 m. dist. Bordesley Pa. Hewell Grange (Robt. Clive, Esq.) a noble mansion, which has belonged to the same family since 1541.	47¼	Tardebigg.	113	Grafton House (Earl of Shrewsbury).
		cr. Worcester Canal.		
	44	BROMSGROVE contains many old houses, curiously ornamented. The inhabitants are chiefly em-	116¼	

ON RIGHT FROM LOND.	From Shrews.		From London.	ON LEFT FROM LOND.
		ployed in the manufacture of nails, needles, and coarse linen. It has a free grammar school, and a church, an elegant Gothic edifice, adorned with some stained glass, and several ancient monuments, particularly of the Talbots, Earls of Shrewsbury. Pop. 5262.		
Park Hall. Sion Hill.	34½	KIDDERMINSTER, (see p. 153.)	125¾	On the road to Bewdley, Spring Grove, A. Skey, Esq.
		cr. river Stour and the Stafford and Worcester Canal.		
Coton Hall.	27¼	Enter Shropshire.	133	
				Dudmaston, W. W. Whitmore, Esq.
Aldenham House, Sir J. E. E. Dalberg Acton, Bart	20¾	BRIDGENORTH is divided into two parts by the river Severn, over which there is a handsome bridge of seven arches. Many of the cellars are cut out of the rock, and are covered by gardens and footpaths. Bridgenorth, besides its traffic on the river, carries on a considerable trade in cloth, stockings, iron tools, &c. Near the town is a terrace more than a mile long, commanding a very extensive prospect. Two M.P. Pop. 7699.	139½	
		cr. river Severn.		
At a distance, Willey Park, Lord Forester. To Shiffnal, 10½ miles.	12½	MUCH-WENLOCK. Here are the remains of a Cluniac monastery. It was a very magnificent building. The remains consist chiefly of the church, which is a fine specimen of the Gothic style, and part of the chapter-house. Here are extensive limestone quarries. Two M.P. Pop. 21,590.	147¾	Morville Hall. To Ludlow, 19¾ miles. To Church Stretton, 12½ m.
Belswardine, and beyond Buildwas Park, W. Moseley, Esq.	10½	Harley.	149¾	
Attingham Hall, Lord Berwick.	8½	Cressage.	152	Cound Hall. Eaton.
		cr. river Severn.		
				Berrington.
		SHREWSBURY, (p. 147)	130¼	

Six miles before reaching Shrewsbury, a little to the left of the road, is the village of Wroxeter, the site of the Roman city of Uriconium.

LXXIV. LONDON TO SHREWSBURY THROUGH AYLESBURY, KIDDERMINSTER, BROSELEY, AND COLEBROOK-DALE, 161¼ Miles.

ON RIGHT FROM LOND.	From Shrews.		From London.	ON LEFT FROM LOND.
Stanley Hall, Sir H. Tyrwhitt, Bart. Apley Park, T. C. Whitmore, Esq. on the other side of the Severn.	21¾	From London to Bridgenorth, (see p. 177.)	139½	Willey Park, Lord Forester.
2 miles distant, Hay.	15¼	BROSELEY is a large and populous town, situated on the Severn. The inhabitants are chiefly employed in the iron and coal mines in the vicinity. There is also a manufactory of coarse earthenware and tobacco pipes. Pop. of par. 4724.	146	Caughley.
Madeley Wood House.		cr. river Severn over the famous iron-bridge, consisting of one arch 100½ feet in span, and weighing 378 tons 15 cwt.		
	13¾	COLEBROOK-DALE, a beautiful winding glen, celebrated for its numerous iron works, steam-engines, forges, &c.	147½	
	12¼	Buildwas, famous for the ruins of a Cistertian Abbey, founded in 1135, and for an elegant iron bridge over the Severn.	149	Buildwas Park, W. Moseley, Esq.
Attingham Hall, Lord Berwick.		SHREWSBURY, (p. 147.)	161¼	

LXXV. LONDON TO SHREWSBURY THROUGH COVENTRY AND BIRMINGHAM, 153¼ Miles, THENCE TO HOLYHEAD, 260½ Miles.

ON RIGHT FROM LOND.	From Holyhd.		From London	ON LEFT FROM LOND.
	151	From London to Birmingham, (see p. 199.)	109½	Edgbaston, Lord Calthorpe.
Aston Pa., J. Watt, Esq. erected about the beginning of the seventeenth century, by Sir T. Holt, who entertained Charles I. here shortly before the battle of Edgehill. Sandwell Park, Earl of Dartmouth.	149½	(Soho, *Staffordshire.*) Messrs Boulton and Watt's manufactory of plated goods, steam-engines, &c. is considered the first establishment of its kind in the world.	111	Soho, M. Boulton, Esq.
To Walsall 3 miles. Bescot Hall.	143	WEDNESBURY.	117½	

Wednesbury is a market-town of great antiquity, distinguished for its numerous manufactures of cast iron works of every kind, guns, &c. The old church, supposed to have been erected in the eighth century, is an elegant Gothic structure, with a lofty and beautiful spire. The interior is adorned with some exquisite carving, and contains several monuments of the ancestors of the families of the Earls Harcourt (extinct) and of Lord Ward. Some vestiges of an ancient fort built by the Saxons may still be traced. Coal is obtained here in great abundance, and of superior quality. Here also is found that peculiar species of iron ore, called " blond metal," and some spots abound with a red earth called hip, employed in glazing vessels. Pop. 15,298.

ON RIGHT FROM LOND.	From Holyhd.		From London.	ON LEFT FROM LOND.
	140½	Bilston, one of the most extensive villages in this country. Here are manufactories of japanned and enamelled goods, and in the vicinity are coal mines, stone quarries, iron forges, and slitting mills. Pop. of town and chapelry 24,364. cr. Birmingham Canal.	120	At Bradley there is a fire in the earth which has been burning for many years in spite of every endeavour to extinguish it.
To Walsall 7 m. to Stafford by Carnock 18¼ m., and by Penkridge, 16¼ m.	137¾	WOLVERHAMPTON. (See p. 237.) cr. Staffordshire and Worcestershire Canal.	122¾	To Dudley 7 miles, and to Himley Hall, Lord Ward, 5 m.; to Stourbridge 10 m., to Kidderminster 15½ m., to Bridgenorth, 14 m.
5 m. distant is Boscobel House, which afforded an asylum to Charles II. after the battle of Worcester.	135¾	Tettenhall. The Church contains an antique carved font, and a painted window. Enter Shropshire.	124¾	Wrottesley Hall, Lord Wrottesley; 2¼ m. farther. Patshull, Sir Robert Pigot Bart. Hatton Grange, R. A. Slaney, Esq.
Chillington Park, T. W. Giffard, Esq. Tong Castle, adorned with a fine collection of paintings; and beyond Weston Park, Earl of Bradford. Aston Hall, G. A. Moultrie, Esq.; and beyond Drayton Lodge. Decker Hill, W. Botfield, Esq.	125¼	SHIFFNAL. The church is a spacious building, containing several monuments, one of which is in memory of W. Wakely, who lived to the age of 124 years, under the reigns of eight different Kings and Queens. Pop. of Par. 5,923. cr. Shropshire Canal.	135¼	Shiffnal Manor, Lord Stafford. To Shrewsbury by Colebrook-Dale, 20 miles. To Much-Wenlock, 10½ miles. To Bridgenorth, 16½ m. To Newport, 8 miles.
Prior's Leigh Hall, ½ m. distant is Wellington, a small town about 2 miles from the base of the Wrekin. The inhabitants are chiefly employed in working coals and lime. There are also iron-works. Pop. of par. 11 169. Orleton, Miss Cludde.	119½	Ketley Iron-Works. Watling Street, one of the finest specimens of Roman road in the kingdom. A line of road has been surveyed from Wellington to Chirk, by which 7 miles would be saved in going from Watling Street to Chirk, instead of going by Shrewsbury and Oswestry.	141	The Wrekin, 1320 feet high. The summit, occupied by an ancient fortification, commands an extensive prospect.

ON RIGHT FROM LOND.	From Holyhd.		From London.	ON LEFT FROM LOND.
		cr. river Tern.		
Attingham, Lord Berwick.	111¼	Atcham.	149¼	Chilton Grove, J. Vaughan, Esq.
		cr. river Severn.		
Longner, R. Burton, Esq.	108½	Lord Hill's column.	152	
Sundorne Castle, A. W. Corbet, Esq., 3 m. To Drayton, 18 miles. To Wem, 11 m. Thence to Whitchurch, 9 m. To Ellesmere, 17 miles.	107¼	SHREWSBURY (p. 174.)	153¼	
		cr. river Severn.		
Berwick House, Hon. H. W. Powys.	105¼	Shelton.	155¼	
Great Berwick.	102¾	Montford Bridge.	157¾	Preston Hall.
Great Ness, J. Edwards, Esq.		cr. river Severn.		Breidden Hill, and the pillar erected in honour of Lord Rodney.
Boreatton Hall, R. Hunt, Esq.; and Boreatton Park.	98¾	Nesscliff.	161¾	
	93¼	At the Queen's Head, a turnpike road passes on right through Whittington to Gobowen, which is one mile shorter than that through Oswestry.	167¼	Knockin Hall, Hon. C Bridgeman. Aston Hall, W. Lloyd, Esq. Sweeney Hall. Porkington, W. O. Gore, Esq.
Pradoe, T. Kenyon, Esq. Tedsmore, T. B. Owen, Esq. Halston Hall. Whittington Castle, in ruins, situated on the borders of a lake, and shaded by fine old trees. To Ellesmere, 8 miles. To Whitchurch, 19 m.	89¼	OSWESTRY.	171¼	To Welsh Pool, 15 m. To Llanfair, 19¼ m. To Llanfyllin, 14 m. To Bala, 25 m.

Oswestry was formerly surrounded by walls, which, together with its four gates, were all taken down about 1782. Of its castle, which appears to have been erected in the reign of King Stephen, the only portion existing is on a lofty artificial mount at the west end of the town, commanding a rich and extensive prospect. Oswestry has two churches (one a venerable building, its tower covered with ivy,) a free grammar school, a town hall, a theatre, several meeting houses, and charitable institutions. It formerly carried on a considerable trade in Welsh woollens. Pop. 5414.

Belmont, J. V. Lovett, Esq. At a dist. Brynkinalt, Viscount Dungannon.	88½	cr. riv. Ceiriog, & enter Denbighshire. CHIRK.	177	Pentrepant, T. G. W. Carew, Esq. Chirk Castle, R. Myddelton Biddulph, Esq.

Chirk, a populous village, celebrated for the beauty of the surrounding scenery. The church contains a number of ancient monuments of the Myddelton family; and in the churchyard are several aged yews. In 1165, Chirk was the scene of a severe contest between the English and the Welsh. About two miles distant, on the road to Ruabon, is a landscape of remarkable beauty.

To the left is Chirk Castle, (R. Myddelton Biddulph, Esq.), an ancient and noble castellated mansion, situated on an eminence, which commands a prospect, it is said, into 17 counties. About three miles beyond Chirk is the aqueduct of the Ellesmere canal, constructed by Mr Telford, in 1805. It consists of 19 stone arches, supporting an iron trough, 1007 feet long, and is a wonderful effort of ingenious contrivance.

Montague Stanley W Miller

SNOWDON
from Capel Curig.

ON RIGHT FROM LOND.	From Holyhd.		From London.	ON LEFT FROM LOND.
At a distance Wynnstay, Sir W. W. Wynn, Bart. The ruins of Caer Dinas Bran, or Crow Castle, a Welsh fortress of great antiquity, situated on a conical mountain, and almost inaccessible on all sides. At a short distance from Llangollen is the site of the palace of Owen Glendower.	$76\frac{3}{4}$	LLANGOLLEN. Llangollen Vale is greatly celebrated for its beauty. 2 m. distant from Llangollen, on the road to Ruthin, are the beautiful and picturesque remains of Valle Crucis Abbey, founded in 1200. They are covered with ivy, and shaded by lofty ash trees; and near the ruins is Elliseg's Pillar, erected by Concenn, in memory of his ancestor, Elliseg, who was killed fighting against the Saxons, in 607.	$183\frac{3}{4}$	Plas Newydd, originally the retreat of Lady Eleanor Butler and Miss Ponsonby.
		cross river Dee.		
On the opposite side of the river, on the summit of a hill, is a British encampment, once the retreat of Owen Glendower.	69	Enter Merionethshire.	$191\frac{1}{2}$	Beyond Corwen is the citadel of the Druids, to which Caractacus retreated after his defeat at Caer Caradock.
5 miles from Corwen is the beautiful cascade of Pont-y-Glyn; and, a little beyond, the charming vale of Edeirnion.	$66\frac{1}{2}$	CORWEN, a neat small town, much resorted to by anglers, as the river abounds with trout, grayling, and salmon. The church is an ancient building, romantically situated; and in the churchyard is an old stone pillar, called the sword of Glendower.	174	Glyn Dyffryn, with a bridge and waterfall.
	$56\frac{1}{2}$	Cerrig-y-Druidion, Denbighshire.	204	
	$53\frac{1}{2}$	Cernioge-Mawr.	207	To Bala, $11\frac{3}{4}$ miles.
The whole of the scenery along the Conway, as far as Bettws, is of a very beautiful description.		cross the Conway by Waterloo Bridge. The arch is 105 feet in span		To Caernarvon by Maentwrog, $38\frac{1}{4}$ miles; thence to Menai Bridge, 9 miles.
Voelas Hall, C. W. G. Wynne, Esq.	44	Bettws-y-Coed, (*Caernarvonshire,*) has a curious bridge across a stream amidst rocky scenery.	$216\frac{1}{2}$	
	39	Capel Curig, a romantic place near several lakes abounding with fish. From this place the traveller may take a guide to visit Snowdon, the pass of Llanberis, &c. The road now proceeds along the Ogwen lake, and through a defile of the grandest description to	$221\frac{1}{2}$	
	$30\frac{1}{2}$	Tyn-y-Maes Inn.	230	Snowdon, 3571 feet high.
Penrhyn Castle, Hon. E. G. Douglas Pennant.	$25\frac{3}{4}$	Llandegai.	$234\frac{3}{4}$	
	24	BANGOR (See p. 182.)	$236\frac{1}{2}$	
	$21\frac{1}{2}$	Menai Bridge.	239	Treborth; and beyond, Vaynol, T. A. Smith, Esq.

Llandegai. The church contains a handsome monument in memory of a Lord and Lady Penrhyn. On the left is a celebrated slate quarry, of immense extent. A railroad, constructed at the expense of L.170,000, leads from the mountain to Port Penrhyn, from which between 500 and 600 tons are shipped every week. On the right is Penrhyn Castle, (Hon. E. G. Douglas Pennant), an elegant mansion built in the reign of Henry VI., on the site of an ancient palace belonging to Roderick Molwynog, grandson to Cadwallader, the last King of the Britons. It has lately been improved by Wyatt, and is surrounded by beautiful grounds. In this castle is preserved an elegant specimen of the *Hirlas*, or ancient drinking horn.

BANGOR, a neatly-built city, lying in a narrow valley between two ridges of rock, with the beautiful bay of Beaumaris to the north. It possesses a cathedral, containing monuments of several Welsh princes, &c.; a Bishop's palace, the residence of the Bishop of Bangor, a free grammar school, and several charitable institutions. The surrounding scenery is peculiarly magnificent. Pop. of bor. 1851, 6338. On a rocky eminence ¼ m. east of Bangor, formerly stood a castle, built by Hugh Lupus, Earl of Chester, during the reign of William II. Beaumaris is distant 4 miles. Bangor is one of the Carnarvon district of burghs.

Menai Bridge. The foundation of the Bridge over the Menai Strait was laid August 10, 1819, by Mr Telford, engineer. It was opened January 30, 1826. The height of the roadway above the surface of high water is 100 feet. The main opening of the bridge is 560 feet between the points of supension, and the roadway is 30 feet in breadth. South of this is another and more stupendous work, the Britannia tubular bridge, which conveys the railway from Caernarvonshire to Anglesea. (See account of it, p. 250). There is frequent steam communication during the summer months between Menai Bridge, Bangor, Beaumaris, and Liverpool. From Menai Bridge an entirely new road has been made through the Island of Anglesea, crossing the main ridge at 160 feet below the level of the old road. It is broad, smooth, and well-paved; and, by crossing the Stanley Sands, the circuity by the Four-mile-bridge is avoided, and the line to Holyhead rendered very direct.

ON RIGHT FROM LOND.	From Holyhd.		From London.	ON LEFT FROM LOND.
2 m. from Menai Bridge, on the summit of a rocky eminence, called Craig-y-Dinas, is a column erected in 1816 in honour of the Marquis of Anglesey; and, 6 m. N.E., Beaumaris and Baron Hill, Sir R. Bulkeley, Bart.	19½	Llanfair.	241	Plas Newydd (Marquis of Anglesey), formerly one of the principal groves in Anglesea sacred to Druidic worship; Plas Gwyn; and, 3 m. distant, Plas Coch, W. B. Hughes, Esq.
	15	Pentre Berw.	245½	
	13¼	Llangristiolus Church.	246¾	
2 m. dist. Hirdrevaig.	12	Caean-Mon, or Mona.	248½	To Aberffraw, 6 miles, a small fishing port, at the mouth of the river Aber. Pop. 1238.
	4¾	Ceirchiog Inn.	255¾	
		Junction of the old Holyhead Road.		
	2¼	Cross Stanley Sands by the embankment.	258¼	
Penrhos Hall, Lord Stanley of Alderley.		HOLYHEAD. (See p. 249).	260½	

ON RIGHT FROM LOND.	From Hungerf.		From London.	ON LEFT FROM LOND.
Leave main line of G. W. R. Prospect Hill. Tilehurst. Calcot Park, J. Blagrave, Esq.	25½	From Great Western Railway Terminus to Reading, pp. 92, 99. The whole course of the line is through the valley of the Kennet.	35¾	Town of Reading. Coley Park, J. B. Monck, Esq. Branch line to **Basingstoke** (see p. 187). River Kennet.
Theale. Englefield House, R. P. B. de Beauvoir, Esq.	20¼	Theale St.	41	Sulhampstead House. Ufton. Padworth.
Bradfield Hall, 2½ miles. Benham House. Benham Lodge. Midgham.	16¾	Aldermaston St.	44½	Aldermaston Park, W. Congreve, Esq., 1½ m. Wasing, and Wasing House.
Woolhampton House. Bucklebury, 3 miles. Dunstan Park.	14¾	Woolhampton St. Nearly along the banks of the Kennet and Avon Canal, here running close to the river.	46½	Brompton. Crookham House. Crookham End House.
Thatcham. Shaw (see p. 93).	12	Thatcham St. cr. river Kennet and Avon Canal, and continue along south bank of river.	49¼	Crookham Heath. Greenham House, J. A. Croft, Esq.
To East Ilsley, 9½ miles. To Abingdon, 20 miles. 1 mile distant, Donnington Castle, and Donnington Grove. (See p. 93.) Church Speen and Speen Hill. Benham Place. Elcot Park.	8½	**NEWBURY** (see p. 93).	52¾	Sandford Priory, and beyond, Highclere Park (Earl of Carnarvon.) To Andover, 16 m.; to Whitchurch, 12 m. Enborne. Hampstead Park.
Barton Court, Admiral J. W. D. Dundas. Avington. Denford House, G. H. Cherry, Esq. Chilton Lodge and Chilton House.	3	Kintbury St.	58¼	West Woodhay, 2¼ miles; and beyond, Walbury Hill, the site of an ancient encampment; near it is Inkpen Beacon, 1011 feet, the highest of the chalk hills which form the North Downs.
Edington.		**HUNGERFORD.** (See p. 93.) Thence to Marlborough, by coach, 10 miles. To Devizes, 24¼ miles (see p. 94).	61¼	Hungerford Park.

ON RIGHT FROM LOND.	From Westb.		From London.	ON LEFT FROM LOND.
		From Great Western Railway terminus to		
	15½	Chippenham St. (p. 101).	93¾	2½ miles beyond Chippenham, leave main line of G. W. R.
Corsham House, Lord Methuen. Monk's Park. Neston Park, J. B. Fuller, Esq. Shaw House. Atworth, 3 miles.		Along valley of river Avon to		Notton House. Lackham. Laycock Abbey, W. H. F. Talbot, Esq. Bowden Hill. Spye Park (J. B. Starky, Esq.), 3 m. To Devizes, 7½ miles.
	9½	Melksham St. (see p. 95).	100	
Broughton Gifford. Great Chalfield.		Population of Melksham, 6236.		Whaddon.
Staverton. Woolley. Bradford, 1½ mile (see p. 96).		[bridge] cr. river Avon. [bridge] cr. Wilts and Berks Canal.		Hilperton.
Upper Studley. N. Bradley.	5½	Trowbridge St. (see p. 96).	105½	Rowde Ashton, W. Long, Esq. Heywood House, H. G. G. Ludlow, Esq.
Frome, 6 miles (p. 96), and beyond Marston Park, Earl of Cork and Orrery.		WESTBURY (p. 96). The line from Chippenham to Westbury forms part of the Wilts, Somerset, and Weymouth Railway, which was intended to extend to Dorchester and Weymouth on the one hand, and to Salisbury on the other, with branches to Sherborne and Bridport, and also to the main line of the G. W. R. near Bridgewater.	109½	To Longleat Park (Marquis of Bath), 8 m. About two miles from Westbury the figure of a horse is cut out of the chalk ridge, and forms a prominent object for some miles round. A few yards above is an oval trench or fosse, attributed to the Danes in the time of Alfred. The locality is called Bratton Castle, from Bratton, a village one mile distant.

LXXVIII. DOVER AND FOLKESTONE TO READING AND BRISTOL, BY RAILWAY, 195½ Miles.

ON RIGHT FROM DOVER.	From Bristol.		From Dover.	ON LEFT FROM DOVER.
		From Dover, by South Eastern Railway, to		
Leave line of Brighton Railway, by Croydon, to London.	128½	Reigate Junction St (pp. 8-10.)	67	Leave line to Brighton.

ON RIGHT FROM DOVER.	From Bristol.		From Dover.	ON LEFT FROM DOVER.
Clandon Park, Earl Onslow.		Thence, by Reading, Guildford, and Reigate line, to		Wonersh Park, Lord Grantley. 1 mile before reaching Guildford, leave branch to Godalming (p. 34).
Sutton Place, J. J. W Weston, Esq.	107½	Guildford (p. 32).	88	Loseley Place.
	101½	Ash St.	94	Leave branch to Farnham (p. 37).
Ash Common.		cr. Basingstoke Canal.		
		cr. river Blackwater, and enter Hampshire.		
		Cross main line of South Western Railway.		Farnborough Place.
Frimley. Chobham Hills in the distance.	97½	Farnborough St.	98	
	95½	Blackwater St.	100	
Sandhurst College, 1 mile.	96	Sandhurst St.	101½	
The Royal Military College at Sandhurst, for the instruction of officers for staff appointments, and of cadets for the army, is a plain edifice with a Doric portico, calculated to afford accommodation to 430 students. A chapel, an observatory, and a riding school are attached to the college.		cr. river Blackwater, and enter Berks. The railway crosses the "Devil's Causeway," a line of ancient Roman road.		Village of Sandhurst. Finchampstead, 1 mile. Barkham, 1¾ mile.
Bagshot, 4 miles. Hennikins Lodge. Luckley House. Easthampstead Park (Marquis of Downshire), 2¼ miles. Buckhurst Hill, ¾ mile. Hurst and Hurst Grove.	89½	Wokingham St. Wokingham (or Oakingham) is a market town situated within the precincts of Windsor Forest. It has an extensive market for poultry: the inhabitants are principally engaged in the malting and flour trades, in throwing silk, and in the manufacture of boots and shoes. It is a corporate town, with an alderman and eleven burgesses. Population, 2404.	106	Bear Wood Park, John Walter, Esq. Maiden Erlegh, E. Golding, Esq. White Knights (the house of John Duke of Marlborough) is demolished, but a portion of his garden remains. (See p. 92.)

ON RIGHT FROM DOVER.	From Bristol.		From Dover.	ON LEFT FROM DOVER.
Bulmershe Court, G. Wheble, Esq.		cr. feeder of Loddon.		
Early Park.		cr. river Loddon.		
		Join line of G. W. Railway, and reach		
Caversham Park (p. 99).	82½	READING (see pp. 92-99) Thence to	113	7 m. distant, Strathfieldsaye, Duke of Wellington.
		BRISTOL, as in pp. 100-101.	195½	

LXXIX. LONDON TO OXFORD, BY RAILWAY, 63 Miles.

ON RIGHT FROM LOND.	From Oxford.		From London.	ON LEFT FROM LOND.
		From Great Western Railway terminus to		
	10	Didcot St. (p. 100).	53	Leave main line of G. W. R.
Long Wittenham.				
Appleford.		cr. river Thames and enter Oxfordshire.		Sutton Courtney, 1½ miles.
	7	**Abingdon Road St.**	56	Town of Abingdon, 2½ miles (pp. 100, 160).
		cr. Thames again, and re-enter Berkshire.		Radley House, Sir G. Bowyer, Bart.
The Thames, and beyond, Nuneham Park, G. G. V. Harcourt, Esq., much visited by Oxonians.				Sunningwell, 2 miles.
Sandford.		The line for some distance runs parallel with the Thames, or more properly the Isis, since it does not acquire the former name until after its junction with the Thame, some distance lower down.		Bagley Wood.
				South Hinksey.
Iffley.				3 miles distant is the village of Cumnor, rendered classic ground by the genius of Scott. In a field adjoining the churchyard some remains of the ancient manor-house of Cumnor Hall are still visible, but most of the ruins, which were in a dangerous state, were pulled down in 1810.
Junction of the Cherwell with the Isis.				
		OXFORD (pp. 162-166 and 187).	63	

ON RIGHT FROM SOUTH.	From Oxford.		From South.	ON LEFT FROM SOUTH.
Leave main line of S. W. R. to London.		From Southampton, by South Western Railway, to		
Sherfield, and Archer Lodge.	42¼	Basingstoke St. (p. 52).	32	The Vine, W. L. Wiggett Chute, Esq. One of this family (John Chute) was the friend and correspondent of Horace Walpole.
Strathfieldsaye, 2½ miles, the seat of the Duke of Wellington, and beyond, Heckfield Place, Viscount Eversley.		Leave Hants, and enter Berkshire.		Bramley. Silchester, the site of a Roman station, probably the Calleva Atrebatum of the Itinerary. Numerous antiquities are found here. The remains of an amphitheatre are discernible outside the walls.
Hunters' Park. Moor Place.	34¾	Mortimer St.	39½	Mortimer Strathfield. Mortimer Hill. Oakfield House. Burghfield.
		cr. river Kennet, and join Hungerford branch of G. W. Railway.		
	27¼	READING St. (pp. 92, 99).	47	
		Thence, by Didcot, as in preceding route, to OXFORD (see also pp. 162-166).	74¼	

Oxford has now become an important centre of railway communication by the completion of the various lines in connection with it, of which the two most important are the Oxford and Rugby, and the Oxford, Worcester, and Wolverhampton. The Oxford and Rugby line runs through the valley of the Cherwell, by Banbury, and, entering Warwickshire, passes near Southam, and joins the London and North Western Railway at Rugby ; thus opening a communication with the midland and northern districts. The Oxford, Worcester, and Wolverhampton Railway extends from Oxford in a general north-westerly direction as far as Worcester, passing a short distance to the west of Woodstock, and by Moreton-in-the Marsh, Chipping-Campden ; and Evesham; from Worcester its course is chiefly northward by Droitwich (where a branch connects it with the line of the Birmingham and Gloucester Railway), Kidderminster, Stourbridge, and Dudley, to Wolverhampton, near which town it joins the northern section of the London and North-western line.

LXXXI. LONDON TO BIRMINGHAM BY OXFORD, WOODSTOCK, AND STRATFORD ON AVON, 116½ Miles.

ON RIGHT FROM LOND.	From Birmin		From London.	ON LEFT FROM LOND.
Friars Place.	115½	From Tyburn Turnpike to Bayswater.	1	Kensington Palace (see p. 40). Holland House, Lord Holland. (See p. 40.)
Hanger Hill, and beyond, Twyford Abbey. Hanwell Park.	111½	Acton. cr. river Brent.	5	The Priory. Ealing Park. Osterley Park, Earl of Jersey.
	107¼	Southall.	9¼	Southall Park.
Hayes End Park.	104	Hayes End.	12¼	Park House.
	102¾	Hillingdon.	13¾	
Hillingdon House, Count de Salis.	101½	UXBRIDGE.	15	Delaford Park, Langley Park, and Iver Grove.
		cr. river Coln and Grand Junction Canal, and enter Bucks.		
Denham. Chalfont House, J. N. Hibbert, Esq.	97½	Gerard's Cross.	19	Bulstrode, Duke of Portland.
Wilton Park, C.G. Dupre, Esq.	93½	BEACONSFIELD. The church contains the remains of the Rt. Hon. Edmund Burke, and the poet Waller is interred in the churchyard. Pop. of parish 1662.	23	Hall Barn, built by the Rt. Hon. Edmund Burke, and beyond, Dropmore Lodge (Lady Grenville), and Cliefden (Duke of Sutherland).
To Amersham, 7 miles. Brands House, J. Newman, Esq.	87½	HIGH-WYCOMBE, the finest town in the county It has a handsome	29	To Great Marlow, 5 miles. Wycombe Abbey, Lord Carington.

ON RIGHT FROM LOND.	From Birmin.		From London.	ON LEFT FROM LOND.
Hughenden Manor, Rt. Hon. B. Disraeli.	84¾	town-hall, erected in 1757, by John, Earl of Shelburne, a free grammar school, and an ancient church, ornamented with a fine altar piece, and a superb monument to Henry Petty, Earl of Shelburne, and Sophia, the first wife of the first Marquis of Lansdowne. The Wycombe stream turns fifteen paper and corn-mills. Two M.P. Pop. 8373.	31¾	
Plummers' Hill, and 3 miles distant, Bradenham House, late I. D'Israeli, Esq.		West-Wycombe. Here is a handsome mausoleum, erected by the late Lord Le De Spencer.		Wycombe Park, Sir G. H. Dashwood, Bart.
	80¼	Stoken Church (*Oxon*).	36¼	Sherbourne Castle, (Earl of Macclesfield,) containing two libraries, an armoury, several fine specimens of painting and sculpture, and among other portraits an original of Catherine Parr, Queen to Henry VIII.
Aston House, near which is Kingston. Thame Park, The Baroness Wenman.		Wycombe Park, Sir G. H. Dashwood, Bart.		
Rycot Park.	74¼	Tetsworth.	42¼	Nethercote House, Sir R. P. Jodrell, Bart.
Holton Park.	69	Wheatley Bridge.	47½	Adwell House. Cuddesden Palace, Bishcp of Oxford.
		cr. river Thame.		Shotover House.
Headington House.		cr. river Cherwell.		
	62½	OXFORD.	54	
	60	Wolvercote,	56½	
Adjoining the church is a grammar school, founded and endowed in 1586 by Mr Cornwell, a native of this place.	54½	WOODSTOCK is famous for its manufacture of gloves and other leathern articles, but that of polished steel has declined. It has a handsome town hall, erected from a design of Sir W. Chambers, at the sole expense of the Duke of Marlborough, and is celebrated in history as the occasional residence of Henry I. and II., and of fair Rosamond. One M.P. Pop. of Parl. borough 7827.	62	Blenheim, the magnificent seat of the Duke of Marlborough, erected in the reign of Queen Anne for the great Duke. Sir J. Vanbrugh was the architect employed, and half a million was granted by Parliament for the erection. The interior is splendidly adorned, and contains a valuable collection of pictures, a library of more than 17,000 volumes, and an elegant chapel. The gardens are extensive, the park, consisting of about 2700 acres, is richly wooded, and the grounds are laid out with great taste.
Kiddington House (Lord Vaux.)				
Heythrop Park, Earl of Shrewsbury.	47½	Enstone has a church dedicated to St Keneim.	69	Ditchley Park,* Viscount Dillon; and beyond, Cornbury Park, Lord Churchill.
2 miles distant are the Roll-rich Stones, the most curious memorial of antiquity in the county, supposed to be of Druidical origin.	43¾	Chapel House.	72¾	
	40¼	Compton Hill, (*Warwickshire.*)	75¾	
Weston House. Sir George R. Phillips, Bart.	39½	Long Compton.	77	Tidmington Hall.
	33½	SHIPSTON, (*Worcesters.*)	83	3½ miles dist. Foxcote House, P. H. Howard, Esq.

* See Scott's Woodstock.

ON RIGHT FROM LOND.	From Birmin.		From London.	ON LEFT FROM LOND.
Honnington Hall, the Rev. H. Townsend.	31½	**Tredington.**	85	
Lower Eatington Hall, E. J. Shirley, Esq.	29½	Newbold. cr. river Stour.	87	
Alveston House, Sir T. G. Skipwith, Bart.	27½	Alderminster.	89	Alscot Park, J. R. West, Esq.
Alveston Villa, and beyond Charlecote House, G. Lucy, Esq.		Re-enter Warwicksh. cr. river Avon.		
	22½	STRATFORD ON AVON.	94	

Stratford on Avon, celebrated as the birth-place of Shakspeare. The house in which he was born is situated in Henley Street. It has lately been purchased by subscription, and will be carefully preserved for the inspection of future generations. The approach to the church, which is delightfully situated on the banks of the Avon, is by an avenue of lime-trees. In the chancel is the celebrated bust of the poet, in front of which he and his wife are buried. The town-hall in High Street was erected in 1768, the year before the Jubilee. A good statue of Shakspeare stands at the north end of the building. The interior is adorned with portraits of Shakspeare, Garrick, and the Duke of Dorset. In the High Street also are the remains of an ancient cross, and adjoining them is the guildhall, a portion of which is occupied as a grammar school, where it is said Shakspeare received his education. By railway, the Oxford, Worcester, and Wolverhampton line now connects Stratford with all parts of the kingdom. Pop. of township, 3672.

ON RIGHT FROM LOND.	From Birmin.		From London.	ON LEFT FROM LOND.
Clopton House, and beyond, Welcombe Lodge. Wooton Hall, Sir C. F. Smythe, Bart.	15	HENLEY-IN-ARDEN. In the market-place are vestiges of an ancient cross.	101½	Beaudesert House, and beyond Oldberrow Court.
Here was the ancient forest of Arden. To Warwick 10 miles.	10	Hockley House.	106½	Umberslade Park.
Packwood House.		cr. river Thame.		
		BIRMINGHAM. (see p. 204.)	116½	Edgbaston (Lord Calthorpe.)

LXXXII. LONDON TO BIRMINGHAM BY AYLESBURY, BUCKINGHAM, BANBURY, AND WARWICK, 115¾ Miles.

ON RIGHT FROM LOND.	From Birmin.		From London.	ON LEFT FROM LOND.
	114½	From Tyburn Turnpike to Paddington.	1¼	To Kensal Green.
1½ m. Belsize House, M. Forster, Esq., and beyond, Rosslyn House. Hendon Place, (Lord Tenterden.)	112½	Kilburn. cr. river Brent.	2¾	Brandesbury House. At a distance, Wembley Park.

ON RIGHT FROM LOND.	From Birmin.		From London.	ON LEFT FROM LOND.
Forward to St Albans through Elstree, 10½ m.	107¼	Edgeware.	8	Cannon's Park, once the seat of the Dukes of Chandos.
Crabtree. Grove.	105	**Stanmore.**	10¼	Bentley Priory, Marquis of Abercorn. Hill House.
Bushey Grove, S. Marjoribanks, Esq., and beyond Aldenham Abbey, W. Stuart, Esq.	102	Bushey (*Herts.*) cr. river Colne.	13¼	Moor Park, Lord Ebury.
To St Albans, 3 miles. Watford Place. Nascott. Russell Farm. Cecil Lodge.	100½	WATFORD. The church contains several fine monuments. Here are mills for throwing silk and making paper. Pop. 4385. (See p. 200.) cr. river Gade and Grand Junction Canal.	14¾	To Rickmansworth, 3 miles. Cashiobury Park, Earl of Essex. The Grove, Earl of Clarendon. The chief portion of Lord Chancellor Clarendon's fine collection of pictures is to be seen here.
Langley House. To Hemel Hempstead, 2¼ miles, and beyond, Gadesbridge Park, Sir Astley P. Cooper, Bart., and Gorhambury, (Earl of Verulam).	95½	King's Langley.	19¾	Langley Bury.
	93¼	Two Waters.	22	This place is famous for its paper mills.
	92	Box-Moor.	23¼	Box Moor Hall.
Berkhampstead Castle. To Dunstable, 11 miles.	89	BERKHAMPSTEAD.	26¼	Westbrook Hay, Hon. G. D. Ryder.
Northcote Court, and Ashridge Park (late Earl of Bridgewater, now (1855) Earl of Brownlow). A monastery was erected here about 1283, which, after the dissolution, became the seat of royalty, and was frequently the residence of Queen Elizabeth when Princess. The conventual buildings were nearly all pulled down during the present century by the late Duke of Bridgewater.	87¾	North Church.	27½	Ashlyns Hall, J. Smith, Esq. Champneys.
	84	TRING.	31¼	Tring Park.
	81	Aston-Clinton (*Bucks.*	34¼	Aston Clinton.
Weedon House. Lillies, the seat of the late Lord Nugent. Creslow Pastures, Lord Clifford, Whaddon Hall, (W. S. Lowndes, Esq.) 5 miles.	77	AYLESBURY, a town of great antiquity, is situated nearly in the middle of the county, on an eminence in the fertile tract called the Vale of Aylesbury. The church is an ancient and spacious structure, with a large churchyard. Here is a town-hall, county-gaol, and a market-house. The inhabitants of this town and its vicinity rear a great number of early ducklings, which are sent to the London market. Two M.P. Pop. of Parl. bor. 27,090. cr. river Thame.	38¼	To London through Wendover, 40¼ miles; to Thame, 9¾ miles; to Bicester, 16¼ miles. Green End, W. Rickford, Esq. Two miles from Aylesbury is Hartwell House, (J. Lee, Esq.,) for many years the residence of Louis XVIII. as Count de Provence, and of the Duke and Duchess D'Angouleme. On the road to Bicester, Wotton House, (Marquis of Chandos.)
Swanbourne House, (Rt. Hon. Sir T. F. Fremantle, Bart.)	73½	Hardwicke.	41¾	Oving House.
	72¼	Whitchurch.	43	
Stukeley 6 m., the church of which is one of the most perfect Saxon buildings in England.	66½	WINSLOW. cr. river Ouse.	48¾	Three miles distant Claydon House, Sir H. Verney, Bart.

ON RIGHT FROM LOND.	From Birmin.		From London.	ON LEFT FROM LOND.
Three miles distant is Stowe, the magnificent seat of the Duke of Buckingham, celebrated by the muse of Pope, and, until lately, enriched by a choice collection of valuable works of art, including plate and furniture of the most costly description a fine gallery of paintings, a library of 10,000 vols., and an extensive collection of MSS. Owing to the pecuniary embarrassments of the noble owner, these were all disposed of by public auction in 1848. Morton House, Rev. W. Andrewes. Morton Lodge, H. Smith, Esq.	59¾	BUCKINGHAM, an ancient and irregular built town on the Ouse. The inhabitants are chiefly employed in agriculture and lace-making. The church is an elegant building, erected in 1780 on an artificial mount formerly occupied by a castle. The altar is adorned with a copy of Raphael's transfiguration, presented by an ancestor of the present Duke of Buckingham. The other public edifices are the town-hall, new gaol, free grammar school, meeting-house, and the remains of the chapel of St John and Thomas á Becket. This town suffered greatly by fire in 1725. It returns two M.P. Pop. 7626.	55½	To Banbury, 18 miles. Five miles from Buckingham is Chetwode, in the church of which is some fine stained glass, of great antiquity. Chetwode Priory, H. Branbridge, Esq. Two miles from Buckingham, on road to Stoney Stratford, the remains of a Roman villa were discovered in 1837. Evenley Hall, Hon. P S. Pierrepont.
Biddlesdon Park, G. Morgan, Esq.	55	Westbury.	60¼	To Oxford, 20¾ miles.
To Towcester, 11 miles. Farthinghoe. Thenford Hall, J. M. Severne, Esq.	52½	BRACKLEY (*Northamp.*) is one of the oldest boroughs in England, and still contains many remnants of its pristine greatness. It has a handsome market-house, two churches, a free school, and the ruins of an hospital, said to have been erected by the Zouche family Pop. 2239.	62¾	
		cr. Oxford Canal.		
To Warwick through Southam, 22¼ miles.	44	BANBURY (*Oxon.*) on the Cherwell. is famous for its malt liquor, its cheese, and the cakes which are called by its name. Here was formerly a castle of great strength, which sustained two severe sieges during the civil wars. The only remains now in existence are a small portion of the wall. Pop. 10.216. One M.P.	71¼	Broughton Castle, Lord Saye and Sele. To Chipping Norton, 12 miles. To Deddington, 6¾ m.
	42	Drayton.	73¼	
	41	Wroxton.	74¼	Wroxton Abbey, Earl of Guilford. Alkerton, where Lydiat the astronomer and mathematician was buried.
	36¾	Upton, (*Warwicksh.*)	78½	Upton House, Captain J. Russell. To Stratford on Avon, 12¾ miles.
	36	Edgehill, remarkable as the spot where the first battle between Charles I. and the Parliament was fought.	79¼	Radway Grange, F. S. Miller, Esq.

ON RIGHT FROM LOND.	From Birmin.		From London.	ON LEFT FROM LOND.
	31¾	KINETON. The castle formerly existing here is said to have been built by King John.	83½	5 miles distant is the village of Tysoe. Opposite its church is a hill, on the side of which was cut the figure called the Red Horse, which gives name to the adjacent vale.
Compton Verney, Lord Willoughby De Broke.	29¾	Compton-Verney.	85½	Walton Hall, Sir C. Mordaunt, Bart.
Newbold Park.		cr. Roman Way.		To Stratford on Avon, 5 miles.
	27½	Wellesbourne Hastings.	87¾	Charlecote, G. Lucy, Esq. and beyond, Alveston House, Sir T. G. Skipwith, Bart.
The Hill.	23¾	Barford.	91½	
		cr. river Avon.		
Warwick Castle, Earl of Warwick.	20¾	WARWICK.	94½	Grove Park, Lord Dormer.

Warwick is situated nearly in the centre of the county. It stands on a rocky hill, having a somewhat abrupt acclivity, watered by the Avon. This town is believed to be of Saxon origin, and was formerly surrounded with walls. It has three churches, of which St Mary's is the most remarkable. It has a lofty square tower, supported by piers, between which carriages may pass. The interior is richly adorned, and contains a number of ancient and curious monuments. Beauchamp chapel, a beautiful specimen of the Gothic style, contains a monument to the memory of Richard Beauchamp, Earl of Warwick, the founder of the Lady chapel. This chapel is considered the most splendid in the kingdom, with the exception of that of Henry VII., in Westminster Abbey. Here is also a monument to Dudley, Earl of Leicester, Elizabeth's favourite. The other public buildings are, the county hall, the court house, gaol, bridewell, theatre, market house, free grammar school, the county asylum, public library and news-room, and several meeting houses. The races are held twice a-year on a plain near the west end of the town. Warwick returns two M.P. Population, 1861, 10,570. Several manufactures are carried on here, particularly those of combing and spinning long wool.

Warwick Castle, the magnificent residence of the Earl of Warwick, is situated at the south-east end of the town, on a rock washed by the Avon. The date of its original erection is unknown. Cæsar's tower, the most ancient part of the structure, is 147 feet high. Guy's tower, 128 feet high, was erected in 1394. The approach to the grand front exhibits three stupendous towers, and the entrance is flanked with embattled walls covered with ivy. The interior is remarkable for splendour and elegance. The principal suite of apartments extends 333 feet in a straight line, and is adorned with valuable paintings and curious specimens of ancient armour. In the green-house is a beautiful antique vase, well known as the Warwick vase, found at Tivoli, and capable of containing 168 gallons. About a mile from Warwick is Guy's Cliff, the retreat of the famous Earl Guy, and where he and his

Countess are supposed to be interred. Blacklow hill, opposite, is the spot where Piers Gavaston was beheaded in 1312

Two miles from Warwick is LEAMINGTON, or LEAMINGTON PRIORS, one of the most fashionable spas in the kingdom. It is pleasantly situated on the Leam, which is crossed by a handsome bridge. The waters are used, both internally and for the purpose of bathing, and are found very efficacious in many chronic disorders, in diseases of the skin, and visceral obstructions. The principal buildings are the new pump-room and baths, which are supposed to be the most elegant in Europe; the assembly-rooms, concert and ball-rooms, the reading-rooms and library, the billiard-room, the Regent Hotel, the museum and picture gallery, the theatre, &c. The Ranelagh and Priory Gardens form delightful promenades. Leamington possesses also two churches, an Episcopal chapel, a meeting-house, a Roman Catholic chapel, an institution for the gratuitous supply of baths to the poor, national schools, several libraries, &c. The rides and walks in the vicinity are interesting and attractive; and very delightful excursions may be made to Warwick Castle, Kenilworth, Stratford, &c. Pop. 17,958.

KENILWORTH is five miles distant from Leamington, and about the same distance from Warwick and from Coventry. Its name is said to have been derived from Kenulph, a Saxon King of Mercia, and his son Kenelm. In Queen Elizabeth's time it was called Killingworth; but the original and correct designation is now restored. The ruins of its magnificent castle form one of the most splendid and picturesque remains of castellated strength to be found in the kingdom. It was founded by Geoffrey de Clinton, Lord Chamberlain and Treasurer to Henry I., but it shortly passed to the Crown. Henry III. granted the castle to the famous Simon de Montfort, Earl of Leicester, and Eleanor his wife, for their respective lives; and when the Earl took up arms against the King, it was the great place of resort for the insurgent nobles. After the defeat and death of the Earl of Leicester, his eldest son, Simon de Montfort, continued to shelter himself in this fortress. He shortly afterwards withdrew to France, but his adherents held out the castle for six months against all the forces the King could bring against it, and they ultimately capitulated upon highly favourable terms. In the time of Edward I. it was the scene of a splendid and costly tournament. Edward II. was kept a prisoner in this castle before his removal to Berkeley Castle, where he was ultimately murdered. In the reign of Edward III., Kenilworth passed into the possession of John of Gaunt, Duke of Lancaster, who made large additions to it. When his son, Henry Bolingbroke, became King, it again became the property of the Crown, and so continued till the reign of Elizabeth, who conferred it on her favourite, Robert Dudley, Earl of Leicester. This nobleman expended enormous sums in adorning and enlarging this structure. The following description of the appearance of the castle at this period is given by Sir Walter Scott in his novel of "Kenilworth:"—"The outer wall of this splendid and gigantic structure enclosed seven acres, a part of which was occupied by extensive stables, and by a pleasure-garden, with its trim arbours and parterres, and the rest forming the large base-court or outer yard of the noble castle. The lordly structure itself, which rose near the centre of this spacious enclosure, was composed of a huge pile of magnificent castellated buildings, apparently of different ages, surrounding an inner court, and bearing, in the names attached to each portion of the magnificent mass, and in the armorial bearings which were there blazoned, the emblems of mighty chiefs who had long passed away, and whose history, could ambition have bent ear to it, might have read a lesson to the haughty favourite who had acquired, and was now augmenting, this fair domain. A large and massive keep, which formed the citadel of the castle, was of uncertain though great antiquity. It bore the name of Cæsar, probably from its resemblance to that in the Tower of London so called. * * * The external wall of this royal castle was, on the south and west sides, adorned and defended by a lake, partly artificial, across which Leicester had constructed a stately bridge, that Elizabeth might enter the castle by a path hitherto untrodden, instead of the usual entrance to the northward, over which he had erected a gatehouse or barbican, which still exists, and is equal in extent, and superior in architecture, to the baronial castle of many a northern chief. Beyond the lake lay an extensive chase, full of red deer, fallow deer, roes, and every species of game, and abounding with lofty trees, from amongst which the extensive front and massive towers of the castle were seen to rise in majesty and beauty."

Elizabeth visited Leicester at Kenilworth in the years 1566, 1568, and 1575. The last visit, which far eclipsed all other "Royal Progresses," has been immortalized by Scott. A reference to the ground plan of the castle, and some extracts from the inventory of Leicester's furniture, in the appendix to Scott's "Kenilworth," will afford some idea of the enormous extent of the place, and the costliness of its decorations. After Leicester's death Kenilworth was seized by the crown, and was ultimately granted by Cromwell to certain officers of his army, who demolished the splendid fabric for the materials. After the Restoration, Charles II. gave the property to Sir Edward Hyde, whom he created Baron Kenilworth and Earl of Clarendon. For a long period the castle was left to ruin; but the present Earl of Clarendon has manifested a praiseworthy anxiety to arrest its decay. The only remaining part of the original fortress is the keep or Cæsar's Tower, the walls of which are in some places sixteen feet thick. The remains of the additions made by John of Gaunt, Duke of Lancaster, are termed Lancaster buildings. In the latter are to be seen the relics of the great hall, a fine baronial room, 86 feet in length, and 45 feet in width. Although the erections of Leicester are of the most recent date, they have the most ancient and ruined appearance, having been built of a brown friable stone, not well calculated to stand the weather. "We cannot but add," says Sir Walter Scott, "that of this lordly palace, where princes feasted and heroes fought, now in the bloody earnest of storm and siege, and now in the games of chivalry, where beauty dealt the prize which valour won, all is now desolate. The bed of the lake is now a rushy swamp, and the massy ruins of the castle only serve to show what their splendour once was, and to impress on the musing visitor the transitory value of human possessions, and the happiness of those who enjoy a humble lot in virtuous contentment."

ON RIGHT FROM LOND.	From Birmin.		From London.	ON LEFT FROM LOND.
Priory. Guy's Cliff, Hon. C. B. Percy.		Resuming the route to Birmingham, cr. Warwick and Birmingham Canal.		Stank House. Grove Park, Lord Dormer.
The learned Dr Parr was perpetual curate of Hatton.	17¾	Hatton.	97½	To Birmingham through Hockley, 17 miles.
	14¾	Wroxhall.	102½	Wroxhall Abbey, C. Wren Hoskyns, Esq., the representative of the celebrated Sir C. Wren. The mansion stands on the site of a nunnery, erected by Hugh de Hatton in the time of King Stephen.
Springfield. Temple Balsall.	10	Knowle. The church is a handsome building, containing some curious carving.	105¼	
	7½	Solihull.	107¾	Malvern Hall.
Olton House.	1½	Spark Brook.	113¾	
		BIRMINGHAM.	115¼	

LXXXIII. LONDON TO BIRMINGHAM BY ST ALBANS, DUNSTABLE, DAVENTRY, AND COVENTRY, 108¾ miles.

ON RIGHT FROM LOND.	From Birmin.		From London.	ON LEFT FROM LOND.
	108¾	From Hicks's Hall to Islington.	1¼	
	105½	Highgate.	4	Caen Wood, Earl of Mansfield. While occupied by the great Lord Mansfield it narrowly escaped destruction by the Gordon Rioters; and Fitzroy Farm.
	100½	Whetstone.	9	
Oak Hill, Sir P. H. Clarke, Bart. The Grove. Beech Hill Pa. Trent Pa. R. C. L. Bevan, Esq. Wrotham Park, Earl of Strafford. Tittenhanger Park Earl of Hardwicke. At a distance Hatfield House, the princely seat of the Marquis of Salisbury, erected at the commencement of the 17th century. It belonged to James I., and was exchanged by him for Theobalds. Charles I. was a prisoner here. Two miles beyond is Brocket Hall, the seat of Viscount Palmerston.	98½	BARNET is a neat town, situated on the top of a hill, and celebrated for the battle which took place, in 1471, between the houses of York and Lancaster, in which the great Earl of Warwick lost his life. An obelisk has been erected on the spot.	11	Totteridge Park. Derham Park. Clare Hall.
	94¾	South Mimms. Ridge Hill, (*Herts.*)	14¾	
	91¼	London Colney.	17½	Colney Ho.
		cross river Colne.		
	88½	ST ALBANS.	21	

St Albans is a town of very great antiquity, having derived its origin from the ruins of the Roman *Verulamium.* An immense number and variety of antiquities have been discovered here at different times, and some vestiges of the ancient town may still be seen at a little distance from St Albans. Here was formerly a magnificent abbey and monastery for Benedictine monks, of which the fine old abbey church and a large square gateway are now the only remains. The abbey was founded by Offa, King of the Mercians, in honour of St Alban. The church was made parochial in the reign of Edward VI. It has all the appearance of a cathedral, and its interior exhibits the various styles of several ages of architecture, and is adorned with numerous rich screens and monuments. Its appearance from the hill, on the Watford Road, is very striking. The town contains three other churches, in one of which—the church of St Michael—the fine monument to the great Lord Bacon may be seen. St Albans has also a new town-hall, several meeting-houses, and charitable institutions. Two battles were fought here during the wars of the Roses; the first, in 1455, when Richard Duke of York obtained a victory over Henry VI.; the second, in 1461, when Margaret of Anjou defeated the king-maker Earl of Warwick. St Albans returned two members to Parliament till 1852, when it was disfranchised. Population in 1861, 7675. Sir John Mandeville, the traveller, was a native of this town, and there is a monument to his memory in the abbey church. There is one also to the good Duke Humphrey of Gloucester.

ON RIGHT FROM LOND.	From Birmin.		From London.	ON LEFT FROM LOND.
To Hatfield, 5 miles; to Luton, 10¼ miles. Gorhambury, (Earl of Verulam. In the park are the ruins of the Old House, the residence of the Lord Keeper and his illustrious son, Lord Bacon.	84¼	Redbourn.	25¼	To Watford, 8 miles. Childwick Bury, J. Lomax, Esq. Beechwood Park, Sir T. G. S. Sebright, Bart.
Rothampsted. Market Cell, and 2 miles distant, Luton Hoo, J. G. Leigh, Esq. Four miles distant is Chalgrave, the church of which is very old, and contains several monuments; and 1 mile beyond, is the church of Toddington, in which are tombs of the Cheyne and Strafford families.	76	DUNSTABLE, *Bedfordsh.* famous for its manufacture of straw-plait bonnets and baskets, and for the size of its larks, great numbers of which are sent to London. The church is an ancient and interesting building, a part of it having been formerly attached to a celebrated priory in the time of Henry I. Charles I. slept at the Red Lion Inn on his way to Naseby. Pop. 4470.	33½	About 1½ mile distant are the remains of a British fortification, called Maiden Bower; not far from which are still to be seen vestiges of another named Tottenhal Castle. Here is the Roman Watling Street.
To Woburn, 4¼ miles. Milton Bryant.	72¼	Hockliffe.	37¼	To Leighton Buzzard 3½ miles. Hockliffe Grange, R. T. Gilpin, Esq.
Battiesden Park, Sir E. H. P. Turner, Bart.; and beyond, Woburn Abbey, Duke of Bedford.	66¼	Brickhill (*Bucks*).	43¼	Stock Grove.

ON RIGHT FROM LOND.	From Birmin.		From London.	ON LEFT FROM LOND.
		cr. Grand Junction Canal.		Great Brickhill House, P. D. P. Duncombe, Esq.
	64½	Fenny Stratford.	45	In the distance, Whaddon Hall, W.S., Lowndes, Esq.
Wolverton House. Wolverton Park.	57¼	STONY STRATFORD is built on the Watling Street. It suffered greatly from fire in 1742.	52¼	
		cr. riv. Ouse and the Grand Junction Canal.		
Cosgrove Hall, J. C. Mansel, Esq. Cosgrove Priory. Stoke Park.	56½	Old Stratford, (*Northamptonshire.*)	53	Denshanger, and, 3 miles distant, Wicken Park. Wakefield Lodge, Duke of Grafton. Whitlebury Forest.
Easton Neston, Earl of Pomfret. To Northampton, 9 m. Pattishall House.	49½	TOWCESTER, (p. 202.)	60	**To Brackley, 11 miles.**
		cross river Tow.		
	47	Foster's Booth.	62½	
	41½	Weedon Beck.	68	At a distance, Everdon Hall, and Fawsley Pa. Sir C. Knightley, Bart., and beyond is Canons Ashby, Sir H. E. L. Dryden, Bart., representative of the Poet Dryden.
To Northampton, 8 m.		cr. Grand Junction Canal.		
2 miles distant is Norton Hall, (B. Botfield, Esq.), and, 2 miles farther to the right, Whilton. Welton Place, R. T. Clarke, Esq. To Lutterworth, 16 m.	37¼	DAVENTRY carries on a considerable manufacture of silk stockings, shoes, and whips. On an adjacent eminence, called Danes' or Borough Hill, are some of the most extensive encampments in England. Pop. 4124.	72¼	Drayton Grange, (Lord Overstone); and, 4 miles distant, Catesby House. Beyond is Shuckburgh Park, Sir F. Shuckburgh, Bart. To Southam, 10½ miles. To Banbury, 16½ miles.
At a distance Ashby St Leger, containing a small room in which the gunpowder plot was concocted. The house belonged to Catesby, one of the conspirators. (See p. 202.)	34½	Braunston. Here is a handsome church and a curious stone cross.	75	
		cr. Oxford Canal, at the commencement of the Grand Junction Canal.		
Ashby Lodge, G. H. Arnold, Esq.	32¾	Willoughby, (*Warwickshire.*)	76¾	
Dunchurch Lodge. Bilton Grange. Bilton Hall. **To Rugby, 2½ miles.**	29½	Dunchurch.	80	**To Southam, 8 miles.**
		Dunsmoor Heath.		1½ mile distant, Bourton House; and Birbury Hall, Sir T. Biddulph, Bart.
	24½	Black Dog Inn.	85	

ON RIGHT FROM LOND.	From Birmin.		From London.	ON LEFT FROM LOND.
	24¼	Knightslow Cross.	85¼	
¾ m. distant is Wolston House, and, on the other side of the river Dove, Brandon House; and, 2 miles further, on the right, Combe Abbey, a seat of Earl Craven. The present noble mansion stands on the site of a Cistercian monastery. Several of the apartments are very fine, and contain many valuable portraits.	22¾	Ryton.	86¾	**Ryton House.** 1 mile beyond Ryton to Southam, 9¼ miles.
		cr. river Avon.		
	20	Whitley Bridge.	89½	Whitley Abbey, Viscount Hood. Here Charles I. is supposed to have fixed his station when he unsuccessfully summoned the city of Chester in 1642. Styvichall, A. F. Gregory, Esq.
Pinley House. The Charter House. Hawkesbury Hall.		cr. river Sow.		
To Lutterworth, 15½ m. To Nuneaton, 8¼ miles. To Tamworth, 18½ m.	18¼	COVENTRY is a city of great antiquity, with very narrow streets. The churches, St Mary's Hall, and several private houses, present interesting subjects for the study of the antiquarian. By means of canals, Coventry carries on a considerable trade, and there is an extensive manufacture of watches and ribbons. Two M. P. Pop. 41,647.	91¼	To Kenilworth 5 miles, thence to Warwick 5¼ m. To Stoneleigh Abbey, Lord Leigh, 5 m.
	15½	Allesley.	94	Allesley Park, E. V. Neale, Esq.
Meriden Hall.	12	Meriden.	97½	
Berkswell Hall, Sir J. E. Eardley Wilmot, Bart. To Warwick, 14 miles.	9¾	Stone Bridge.	99¾	Packington Hall, Earl of Aylesford. To Coleshill and Coleshill Park, Lord Digby, 4 miles.
Elmdon Hall, A. Spooner Lillingston, Esq.	5½	Wells Green.	104	
		BIRMINGHAM, p. 203.	109½	

ON RIGHT FROM LOND.	From Birmin.		From London.	ON LEFT FROM LOND.
A line of railway now connects the Camden Town Station with the East and West India Docks, passing round the north and east sides of the metropolis.		**London Terminus, Euston Square.** The new entrance hall, completed in 1849, at a cost of £150,000, is a fine specimen of decorative architecture. The railway passes through a deep excavation to		
		Camden Town Station, the grand depot for the goods and locomotive departments of the company. Primrose Hill Tunnel, 1220 yards long.		Kensal Green Cemetery, one of the prettiest resting places near London. Branch to Kensington. Twyford Abbey.
Kilburn, Willesden, and beyond Hampstead. The hill commands a charming and varied prospect.	109½	Kilburn Station.	3	
Brandesbury House.	106¼	Willesden Station.	6¼	
Wembley Park.	104¼	Sudbury Station.	8¼	Sudbury.
To Stanmore, 3½ miles, Edgeware 4½, Barnet 10½. Cannons. Bentley Priory. Bushey.	101	Harrow Station. **Harrow on the Hill.** It is situated upon one of the loftiest hills in Middlesex, commanding extensive and delightful views. Pop. of parish, 5525.	11½	Harrow on the Hill, 1 mile, famous for its school and the eminent men, such as Byron and Sir R. Peel, who have been educated there.
	99	Pinner Station.	13½	Eastbury House.
	96¼	Bushey Station.	16¼	At a distance, Moor Park, Lord Ebury.
To St Albans, 7 miles.	94¾	Watford Station (*Herts*) Three-quarters of a mile distant is Watford, a populous and well-built market-town, almost surrounded by the Coln, on which are mills for throwing silk, and making paper. The church contains numerous brasses and tombs of ancient date. **Watford Tunnel,** 1 mile, 170 yards in length.	17¾	To Rickmansworth 4 miles, Amersham, 10 miles, High Wycombe, 17 miles. Cashiobury Park, Earl of Essex, and Grove Park, Earl of Clarendon, containing a collection of pictures, part of that formed by Lord Chancellor Clarendon.* Hunton Bridge.
Abbot's Langley. Booksellers' Provident Institution.	91½	King's Langley St. ☞ cr. Grand Junction Canal.	21	Grand Junction Canal and river Gade.
1½ m. distant is Hemel-Hempstead. The church appears to be of Norman origin, but has subsequently undergone various alterations. The interior is highly ornamented. Pop. of par. 1861, 7948. Beyond is Gorhambury (Earl of Verulam), and Gadesbridge, Sir A. P. Cooper, Bart.	88	Boxmoor Station. Recross the Grand Junction.	24½	Two Waters, so called from Junction of the Gade with Bulbourn Brook, is famous for its paper-mills. Westbrook Hay, Hon. G. D. Ryder.
	84½	Berkhampstead St.	28	To Chesham, 6 miles. To Amersham, 12 m.

* See description of the Portraits, by Lady Theresa Lewis, in her "Friends and Contemporaries of Lord Chancellor Clarendon."

ON RIGHT FROM LOND.	From Birmin.		From London.	ON LEFT FROM LOND.
To Dunstable, 11 miles. Three miles distant is Ashridge Park, the seat of the late Duke of Bridgewater, and afterwards of the late Earl of Bridgewater, occupies the site of an ancient building, formerly a monastery, which, after the Reformation, became the seat of royalty, and was the frequent residence of Queen Elizabeth when Princess. In 1602, it passed to the Lord Chancellor Ellesmere, an ancestor of the Bridgewater family. This fine estate is now held by the Earl of Brownlow.		In Great Berkhampstead, Bishop Kenn and Cowper the poet were born. Here are the remains of a castle, formerly the residence of the kings of Mercia. The church contains numerous brasses and other monuments. Pop. 3631.		Ashlyn's Hall, A. Smith, Esq.
		North Church Tunnel, 360 yards in length.		
To Ivinghoe, $2\frac{1}{2}$ miles; Dunstable, 9 miles. Tring is $1\frac{3}{4}$ miles distant from the station. It is a very ancient place, and is supposed to be of Roman origin. It has a fine church with carved roof, and several monuments. Pop. 3130.	$80\frac{3}{4}$	TRING STATION. From Tring, an elevated ridge of ground, called the Chiltern Hills, extends to Oxfordshire. To suppress the banditti who formerly infested this place, an officer, called the Steward of the Chiltern Hundreds, was appointed by the Crown. The duties have long since ceased; but the office is retained to enable any member of Parliament to resign his seat.	$31\frac{1}{4}$	To Aylesbury, 9 miles. To Wendover, 6 miles. Tring Park, a beautiful seat, adorned with pleasing scenery.
	$76\frac{1}{4}$	**Cheddington Junction Station.**	$36\frac{1}{4}$	Here is the junction of the Aylesbury with the Birmingham Railway.
Ivinghoe.	72	**Leighton Junction St.**	$40\frac{1}{2}$	Mentmore, the Baron Meyer de Rothschild.
To Dunstable, 9 miles. To Dunstable, 7 miles. To Ampthill, 18 miles. To Bedford, 26 miles.		LEIGHTON BUZZARD.		To Wing, $5\frac{1}{2}$ miles. Liscombe Park, H. W. Lovett, Esq.

Leighton Buzzard is half a mile from the station, and is situated in the north-eastern extremity of the county of Bedford, on the banks of the Ouzel. Here is a pentagonal cross of curious architecture. The church is a very old building, containing a font, stone-stalls, &c. The Grand Junction Canal passes close to the town. Pop. of township, 1861, 4330. Seven miles from the station is Woburn, a small but neat town. It is a place of some antiquity, and has been twice destroyed by fire. The church is a venerable building, entirely covered with ivy. It contains several monuments, and an altar-piece by Carlo Maratti. The inhabitants of Woburn are chiefly employed in lace-making. Woburn Abbey, the seat of the Duke of Bedford, is a magnificent quadrangular building, and contains a splendid collection of paintings, statues, busts, &c. The park is 12 miles in circumference, and is well stocked with deer.

Battlesden Park, Sir E. H. Page Turner, Bart.		**Linslade Tunnel,** 290 yards in length. Enter Bucks.		Stoke Hammond, and Great Brickhill Manor, P. D. P. Duncombe, Esq.

ON RIGHT FROM LOND.	From Birming.		From London.	ON LEFT FROM LOND.
Fenny Stratford. Newport Pagnell, 4 miles. Olney, 9 miles	$65\frac{3}{4}$	Bletchley Junction St.	$46\frac{3}{4}$	Branches to Banbury, $31\frac{1}{4}$ m.; and to Buckingham and Oxford, $31\frac{1}{2}$ m.
	60	WOLVERTON St. This is the company's central station, where they have extra engines, workshops, &c. Ten minutes are usually allowed at this station. Here are female attendants,* and refreshments and every accommodation may be obtained.	$52\frac{1}{2}$	Stony Stratford, 2 m. Buckingham, 9 miles. Stony Stratford is situated on the Ouse. Many of the inhabitants are employed in lace making. Four miles distant from Stony Stratford, but in Northamptonshire, is Wakefield Lodge, the seat of the Duke of Grafton.
Linford House, and beyond, Gayhurst Park, Lord Carington. Castle Thorpe. Hanslope House.		cross Wolverton Viaduct, 660 feet in length. Enter Northamptonshire.		Wolverton House. Stoke Park, and beyond, Easton Neston, a seat of the Earl of Pomfret, which formerly contained a splendid collection of ancient paintings and marbles, given by a Countess of Pomfret, in 1755, to the University of Oxford. The adjoining church contains several curious and interesting monuments.
	$52\frac{1}{2}$	ROADE Station.	60	
Courteen Hall, Sir C. Wake, Bart. To Northampton, 4 m. Market Harborough, 21 miles.	$49\frac{1}{2}$	Blisworth Junction St. Bugbrook Suspension Bridge. Stowehill Tunnel, 500 yards in length.	63	1 mile from the latter is Towcester, situated on the ancient Watling Street, near the river Tow. The church contains a monument in memory of Wm. Sponne, who founded a college in this town in the time of Henry VI. Pop. 2417.
To Northampton, $7\frac{3}{4}$ m. Brockhall, T. R. Thornton, Esq. At a distance Althorp (Earl Spencer). There is a fine picture gallery, and a still finer library here.	$42\frac{3}{4}$	WEEDON Station. Weedon has handsome and extensive barracks, garrisoned by a regiment of the line, and a demi-field battery of artillery. It has also an extensive powder magazine, and is a depot of arms.	$69\frac{3}{4}$	To Towcester 4 miles. Everdon Hall. To Daventry, 4 miles, near which are the very perfect remains of Roman field works on Watling Street; Southam, 14 miles; Leamington, 21 miles; Warwick, 23 m. $1\frac{1}{2}$ mile distant is Stowe Nine Churches, containing a beautiful monument to the memory of Elizabeth, daughter of Lord Latimer. The sculptor of this exquisite work being unknown.
		cross Birmingham and Holyhead road.		
$1\frac{1}{2}$ mile distant is the village of Crick. The hill through which this tunnel is carried forms a portion of the high ground which sepa-	$37\frac{1}{4}$	Crick Station. Crick is the choice "meet" of the Pytchley hunt. Kilsby Tunnel, 1 mile 640 yards in length, 24 feet wide, and 22 feet in	$75\frac{1}{4}$	Norton Hall, B Botfield, Esq. Ashby St Leger, in the church of which is a monument to Sir W. Catesby, beheaded at Leicester after the battle of Bosworth Field (see p. 198).

* Females are also in attendance at the London, Watford, Rugby, Coventry, and Birmingham Stations.

ON RIGHT FROM LOND.	From Birmin.		From London.	ON LEFT FROM LOND.
		height above the rails, and cost upwards of £300,000.		
rates the waters of the Avon from those of the Ouse and Nen.		Enter Warwickshire.		
Stamford line branches off.		☞ cross Oxford and Coventry Canal.		
To Lutterworth, 7 m.; to Market Harboro', 19 m. Midland Railway joins.	29¾	RUGBY Junction St.	82¾	Hill Moreton.

One mile distant is Rugby, a market-town in the county of Warwick, famous for its grammar-school, founded in the reign of Elizabeth by Lawrence Sheriff. The school is now considered one of the best in the kingdom. The late celebrated scholar, Dr. Arnold, author of the History of Rome, &c., was one of its head masters. Adjacent to the town is an eminence called Castle Mount, from its having originally been the site of a castle supposed to have been erected in the time of King Stephen. The Midland Counties, the Trent Valley, the Stamford and the Leamington Railways commence here. Pop. of Rugby 1861, 7818. One mile and a half from Rugby is Bilton Hall, remarkable as having been the residence of Addison. In the garden is a long avenue called Addison's Walk, this having been his favourite promenade. To Dunchurch, three miles.

Trent Valley line joins. Newbold Grange. Newbold Hall, Sir T. G. Skipwith, Bart. Holbrook Grange, T. Caldecott, Esq.				Branch to Leamington.
Wolston. At a distance, Combe Abbey (Earl Craven).	23¼	Brandon Station.	89¼	Brandon Hamlet.
		Sowe Viaduct.		Whitley Abbey, Viscount Hood.
Branch to Nuneaton.	18½	COVENTRY (see p. 199).	94	Branch to Warwick. To Southam, 13 miles. To Kenilworth, 5 miles.
Allesley Park, E. V. Neale, Esq.	15	Allesley Gate Station.	97½	
Berkswell Hall, Sir J. E. Eardley Wilmot, Bart.	13½	Dooker's Lane Station.	99	
At a distance, Packington Pa., Earl of Aylesford.		☞ cr. Woonton Green Viaduct.		
The Birmingham and Derby Junction branches off here.	9¼	Hampton Junction St.	103¼	
	6	Marston-Green Station.	106½	Elmdon Hall, A. Spooner Lillingston, Esq.
	3½	Stechford Station.	109	
		BIRMINGHAM St.	112½	

Birmingham, a large commercial and manufacturing town, is situated in the north-east corner of Warwickshire. It is seventy-nine miles south-east from Liverpool, and the same distance north-east from Bristol, both in a straight line. As Birmingham is nearly in the centre of England, its situation is elevated. The soil around it is light, but has lately been much improved. The appearance of the city itself is mean—a great multitude of the houses being inhabited by workmen. St. Martin's church is the only building of great antiquity. Its exterior is poor, having in 1690 been cased with a covering of bricks to preserve it from falling. The spire alone remains in its original state, a graceful monument of olden architecture. The interior is grand and imposing, though disfigured by a coating of plaster and by tawdry ornaments. St. Philip's Church is an elegant building, and, in the opinion of many, forms the chief architectural ornament of the city. Besides these two, there are upwards of 12 churches and chapels belonging to the Established Church, and forty-five Dissenting chapels, several of them elegant in form. Till lately, Birmingham possessed few public buildings worthy of notice, but the citizens are adding to their number. The town-hall is a splendid edifice of the Corinthian order, the material being Anglesea marble. Its length is 166 feet, breadth 104 feet, and height 83 feet. The saloon, 140 feet long, 65 feet wide, and 65 feet high, contains one of the largest organs in Europe. The grammar-school is a fine Gothic edifice, designed by Mr. Barry, and erected at an expense of L.4000. The theatre, the banks, the libraries, Society of Arts, &c. are also worthy of notice. The schools in Birmingham are numerous and flourishing. Among these may be mentioned the free grammar school founded and chartered by Edward VI. Its income derived from land is L.3000 per annum; the Blue Coat School and the Protestant Dissenter's charity school are supported by subscriptions. There are several associations for moral and intellectual improvement, such as a mechanic's institution with a library of more than 1500 volumes, the Society of Arts, and a philosophical institution. The old library contains above 30,000 volumes, and the new library above 5000. The savings banks, and provident institutions and societies, are numerous and highly beneficial. There are also many charitable institutions well supported. The Dispensary, Humane Society, and Magdalen Institution merit great praise. From a very early period Birmingham has been renowned for its manufactures in steel, iron, &c. This trade is now carried on to an extent elsewhere unequalled. The principal branches of it are, plate and plated wares, ornamented steel goods, jewellery, japannery, papier maché, cut-glass ornaments, steel-pens, buckles and buttons, cast-iron articles, guns and pistols, steam-engines, toys, &c. Birmingham is connected with London and various places by means of canals, and forms a centre of railway communication with every part of the kingdom. The railway from London to Birmingham, which was opened in 1837, is now amalgamated with the Grand Junction line, the two forming the London and North Western Railway. Birmingham returns two M.P. The population in 1831 was 110,914; including the suburbs, 138,252. In 1841 it was 182,922 in 1851, 232,841; and in 1861, 296,076.

The journey is performed in 2 hours 45 minutes. Omnibuses leave the following offices in London and Birmingham for the railway stations. London offices:—Spread Eagle, Gracechurch Street; Cross-Keys, Wood Street; Bolt-in-Tun, Fleet Street; Swan with Two Necks, Lad Lane; George and Blue Boar, Holborn; Spread Eagle, Regent Circus; Golden Cross, Charing Cross; and Green Man and Still, Oxford Street. Birmingham offices:—Swan, Castle, Hen and Chickens, Albion, and Nelson.

LXXXV. LONDON TO DENBIGH THROUGH BIRMINGHAM, NEWPORT, WHITCHURCH, WREXHAM, AND MOLD, 206½.

ON RIGHT FROM LOND.	From Denbig.		From London.	ON LEFT FROM LOND.
	206½	From Hicks's Hall to		
Aston Park, once the residence of James Watt.	97	Birmingham, (p. 199.) cr. the Warwick Canal.	109½	Edgbaston Hall, Lord Calthorpe.
	95¾	Hockley Brook. Enter Staffordshire.	110¾	
				Soho, M. R. Boulton, Esq.
	94¾	Handsworth.	111¾	Sandwell Park, Earl of Dartmouth.
Perry Hall, J. Gough, Esq.		cr. the river Tame.		Hampstead Hall.
Great Barr Hall, Sir F. E. Scott, Bart.	91¼	Snail's Green.	115¼	
2 miles distant Aldridge Lodge. To Lichfield, 9½ miles.	88½	WALSALL has a fine and spacious church, and three others, a town hall, a subscription library, several meeting houses, and other dissenting chapels, a free grammar, English Blue Coat, and Sunday schools. The inhabitants are principally employed in manufacturing hardware used in saddlery. 1 M.P. Pop. 37,760.	118	2 miles distant Bentley House. To Wolverhampton, 6½ miles.
		cr. the Essington and Wirley Canal.		
	85¾	Bloxwich.	120¾	
Forward to Cannock, 1 mile. To Castle Bromwich, 15 miles.	81¾	Church Bridge.	124¾	**Hilton Hall.**
	79¾	Four Crosses Inn.	126¾	To Wolverhampton, 7½ miles, Brewood, 2¼ miles.
Hatherton Hall, and beyond, Teddesley Hall, Lord Hatherton.				2 miles distant Somerford Hall.
2 miles distant Stretton Hall.	77½	Spread Eagle.	129	
		London and North Western Railway.		
1 mile south of Ivetsey Bank is Boscobel House, where the Penderells lived who concealed Charles II. after the battle of Worcester. In a field near the house is the Royal Oak,	72¼	Ivetsey Bank.	134¼	
	70¼	Weston under Lizard.	136¼	**Weston Hall, Earl of Bradford.**

ON RIGHT FROM LOND.	From Denbigh		From London.	ON LEFT FROM LOND.
planted on the original spot from an acorn of the tree in which Charles was sheltered. The existing representatives of this family had a small pension granted to them a few years ago.	67¼	Bloomsbury. Enter Shropshire.	139¼	To Shiffnal, 4½ miles.
	66¾	Woodcote.	139¾	**Woodcote Hall,** John **Cotes,** Esq. The ruins of Lilleshall Abbey, belonging to the Duke of Sutherland, one of the finest vestiges of Norman architecture in the kingdom. 2½ miles distant Lilleshall, Duke of Sutherland. To Wellington, 8½ miles, thence to Shrewsbury, 18 miles. Longford Hall, R. M. Leake, Esq.
Aqualate Hall, Sir T. F. F. Boughey, Bart. To Stafford, 12¾ miles. To Eccleshall, 9¼ miles. Newport affords the title of Viscount to the Earls of Bradford.	64½	NEWPORT, a small town near the Roman Watling Street, possesses an old church, (part of which has been rebuilt in such a style as totally to destroy its venerable character,) and several other places of worship. The humorous poet, Tom Brown, is said by some to have been born here; but others affirm that Shiffnal was his birth-place. Pop. 2856.	142¼	
Chetwynd Park, B. Borough, Esq.	62¾	Chetwynd.	143¾	
	60¼	Stanford Bridge.	146¼	
To Drayton, 4½ miles.	58½	Hinstock.	148	
	56¼	Shakeford.	150¼	
	54¼	Sutton Heath.	152¼	
		cr. river Tern.		
To Drayton, 3 miles. Buntingsdale Hall, J. Tayleur, Esq.	52¼	Tern Hill.	154¼	To Shrewsbury, 16 m., Wellington, 14½ miles.
To Whitchurch by Ightfield, 8 miles. 2 miles distant, Cloverly Hall, J. W. Dod, Esq.	51	Bletchley.	155½	
Sandford Hall.	48¼	Sandford.	158¼	2 miles distant Hawkestone (Viscount Hill), celebrated for its combination of natural and artificial beauties. In the grounds there is an obelisk surmounted by a statue of Sir R. Hill, first Protestant Lord Mayor of London.
	44¾	Great Ash.	161¾	
		cr. the Ellesmere Canal.		
To Newcastle under Lyme, 22 m.,—Nantwich, 11 m.,—Chester, 20 m.,—Malpas, 5 miles. At a distance, Combermere Abbey, Viscount Combermere.	43¼	WHITCHURCH is pleasantly situated on an eminence, at the summit of which stands the church, a handsome edifice rebuilt in 1722, on the site of a more ancient structure. It contains several effigies of the Talbots, one of which is to the memory of the famous Earl of Shrewsbury, "the English Achilles." Here are also a house of industry, a free school, meet-	163¼	

ON RIGHT FROM LOND.	From Denbig.		From London.	ON LEFT FROM LOND.
		ing-houses, charity schools, and alms-houses. Pop. of town, 3704.		
Iscoed Park.	$39\frac{1}{4}$	Little Green.	$167\frac{1}{4}$	1 mile distant Hanmer Hall, Sir J. Hanmer, Bart.
Emral Park, Sir R. Puleston, Bart.	$32\frac{1}{4}$	Bangor Iscoed, (*Flintshire.*) cr. the river Dee.	$174\frac{1}{4}$	Gredington, Lord Kenyon, and Bettisfield Park, Sir J. Hanmer, Bart.
Cefn.	$30\frac{3}{4}$	Marchwiel, (*Denbighshire.*) The church contains several monuments, and a stained glass window, executed by Eggerton.	$176\frac{3}{4}$	To Ellesmere, 10 miles. Erthig, S. Yorke, Esq.
To Chester by Holt 14 miles, by Pulford $11\frac{3}{4}$ m. 1 mile distant, Acton Park, (Sir R. H. Cunliffe, Bart.) the birth-place of the infamous Judge Jeffreys, beyond, — Hoseley Hall.	$27\frac{1}{2}$	WREXHAM, a flourishing town, noted for its fairs. The principal object is the church, a noble structure of the fifteenth century, surmounted by a tower of great beauty. The interior is highly ornamented, and contains a superb altar piece, besides a number of monuments of peculiar beauty. Pop. of Parl. bor. 1861, 7562. Both Wrexham and Ruthin are included in the Denbigh district of burghs. (See also p. 148.)	179	To Oswestry, 15 m.,—Llangollen, 12 miles,—Ruthin, 16 miles. Another road, 24 miles in length, leads from Wrexham by Ruthin, $3\frac{1}{2}$ miles shorter than the road by Mold. Ruthin is situated on the declivity of a hill in the vale of Clwyd. The principal objects are the church, the town-hall, the free school which has produced many eminent scholars, and the remains of the castle. Pop. of Parl. bor. 1861, 3372. 2 m. from Ruthin is Pool Park, Lord Bagot.
Gwersyllt Hall.	$22\frac{1}{2}$	Caergwrle, (*Flintsh.*)	184	
Plas Issa. There is another road from Mold to Denbigh by Allen Kilken, Llangwyfan, Llandyrnog, and Whitchurch, $3\frac{1}{2}$ miles shorter than the route described.	$15\frac{1}{2}$	MOLD, a small neat town, with a church containing some good monuments. In the vicinity are cotton-mills. On an eminence called the Moel Fammau is a monument, erected in honour of the Geo. III. jubilee. Pop. of Par. bor. 1861, 3735. It forms one of the Flint district of burghs.	191	Leeswood, J. W. Eyton, Esq., and beyond Nerquis Hall Tower. To Ruthin, 8 miles.
Llwynegrin. Gwysaney Hall, P. D. Cooke, Esq. Kilken Hall. Halkyn Castle, Marquis of Westminster. To Caerwys, 1 mile.	$9\frac{1}{2}$	Nannerch.	197	Rhual. Rhual Issa. Penbedw. Moel-y-Gaer mountain, 1280 feet high. The summit has upon it some fine remains of a military work.

ON RIGHT FROM LOND.	From Denbigh		From London.	ON LEFT FROM LOND.
Bryn Bella, (Sir J. S. Piozzi Salusbury,) once the residence of Madame Piozzi, friend of Dr Johnson, while Mrs Thrale. She bequeathed this property to the present owner, a relative of her last husband.	4¼	Bodfari.	202¼	3 miles distant, Glanywern, J. Madocks, Esq.
	3¼	Pont Ryffyth. ☞ cr. the river Clwyd. and enter Denbighshire.	203¼	Near this bridge is Lleweny Hall, containing a fine Gothic hall, fitted up as an armoury. At a short distance
Llanerch Park.	1	Whitchurch.	205½	are extensive bleaching works, established by the late Hon. T. Fitzmaurice.*
		DENBIGH.	206½	

Denbigh, the capital of Denbighshire, is pleasantly situated on a rocky eminence in the beautiful vale of Clwyd. The castle, now in ruins, was founded in the reign of Edward I. It underwent a siege during the civil wars, and after the Restoration of Charles II. was blown up with gunpowder and rendered completely untenable. The ruins cover the summit of the craggy hill, and the prospect through the broken arches and frittering walls is extensive and beautiful. Denbigh has been compared to Stirling in Scotland, and has a very imposing aspect from a distance, with the ruinous castle crowning the summit of the hill. The parish church is situated at Whitchurch, one mile from the town, but is seldom used by the inhabitants, who generally attend divine worship at the ancient chapel of St Hilary. In the porch of the parish church, partly ruinous, are the effigies in brass of Richard Middleton of Gwaenynog, and Jane, his wife. He was governor of Denbigh Castle in the reigns of Edward VI., Mary, and Elizabeth. William, his third son, was a sea captain, and a poet; Thomas, fourth son, became Lord Mayor of London, and founder of the family of Chirk Castle; Hugh, the sixth son, expended an immense fortune in bringing the new river into London. An ancient priory for Carmelites existed at Denbigh, but the conventual church, now converted into a malt-house, is all that remains of the institution. Denbigh had formerly a considerable manufactory of gloves and shoes. It unites with Holt, Ruthin, and Wrexham, in returning one M.P. Pop. of Par. bor. 1861, 5946. The vicinity abounds with beautiful and interesting scenery. It gives the title of Earl to the Fielding family.

* Mr Fitzmaurice was brother of the first and uncle of the present Marquis of Lansdowne, and having married Mary third Countess of Orkney in her own right, was grandfather of the present Earl. In order to encourage his tenantry in Ireland, and promote the national manufacture of linens, he erected a bleaching establishment here at an expense of L.2000, in which, under his own superintendence, 4000 pieces were bleached yearly. It is said he usually travelled in his coach to Chester, and when there stood behind a counter.

ON RIGHT FROM LOND.	From Holyhd.		From London.	ON LEFT FROM LOND.
To Kettering, 13¾ m.; Wellingborough, 11 m.; 1½ m. distant, Abington Abbey (a lunatic asylum), and beyond Overstone Park, Lord Overstone.	274	From Hicks's Hall to		
	208	NORTHAMPTON, p. 224.	66	To Daventry, 12 miles. 2 miles distant Upton Hall.
To Market Harborough, 15½ m.; 1½ m. distant, Boughton House, R. W. Howard Vyse, Esq,	206½	Kingsthorpe.	67½	Kingsthorpe House, and Althorp Park, Earl Spencer. (See p. 202.)
Brampton House. Spratton House. Cottesbrooke House, Sir J. H. Langham, Bart.	203¾	Chapel Brampton.	70¼	
Thornby Hall; and, 2 miles distant, is Naseby, where the decisive battle was fought between Charles I. and the Parliamentary forces under Cromwell. The village is considered the centre of England, and the highest ground in it. 3 rivers, the Welland, Nene, and Avon, take their rise in this parish.	200¼	Creaton. To the left of this place is Holmby House, where Charles I. was imprisoned.	73¾	Teeton House. Hollowell and Guildsborough Hall, W. Z. L. Ward, Esq.
Sulby Abbey, G. Payne, Esq.	196¾	Thornby.	77¼	
To Leicester, 16 miles. At a distance, Bosworth Hall, G. F. Turville, Esq. Misterton Hall. To Leicester, 12½ m.	193½	Welford.	80½	3 miles distant Stanford Hall, (the Baroness Braye.)
		cr. river Kilworth, and enter Leicestersh.		
	190¼	North Kilworth.	83¾	
	187	Walcote.	87	
	185	LUTTERWORTH, on the Swift, has a considerable stocking trade. The church is a large handsome building, and contains several tombs of the Feildings, and a carved oak pulpit, the top of which is said to have formed part of that from which Wyckliffe delivered his discourses. The chair in which he expired is also shown. He was buried here in 1387; but, in 1428, his body was taken up and burnt, and his ashes cast into the Swift. Pop. 2289.	89	To Rugby, 8 miles; to Coventry, 13¼ miles. Coton Hall.
Ullesthorpe House. Claybrooke Hall.	184	Bitteswell.	90	
	181	Claybrooke.	93	
	179	High Cross (on Watling Street). Here two Roman roads, the Fosse and	95	Newnham Paddox Earl of Denbigh.

ON RIGHT FROM LOND.	From Holyhd.		From London.	ON LEFT FROM LOND.
		Watling Street, cross each other.		
	178	Smockington.	96	
	175½	Burbage.	98½	
To Ashby de la Zouch, 16¼ miles; Market Bosworth, 7 miles. Lindley Hall.	174½	HINCKLEY, noted for its ale and manufacture of hosiery, has a church with an oak roof, curiously ornamented, a very ancient town-hall, &c. Pop. of town, 1861, 6344. In the vicinity is a spring called the Holywell, formerly dedicated to the Virgin.	99½	To Nuneaton, 5 miles. Weddington Hall, Nuneaton, and 3 miles beyond, Arbury Park, C. N. Newdegate, Esq. Ansley Hall, Sir J. N. Ludford Chetwode, Bart.
	167½	Witherley.	106½	2 m. distant, Caldecote Hall. Oldbury Hall. Mancetter House, Mancetter Hall, and Mancetter, a Roman station.
		cr. river Anker, and enter Warwickshire.		
Atherstone Hall, C. H. Bracebridge, Esq. 2¾ m., Grendon Hall, Sir G. Chetwynd, Bart., and 4 m. dist., Gopsall Hall, (Earl Howe.) To Burton upon Trent, 20 miles; to Tamworth, by Grendon, 9 miles.	166½	ATHERSTONE carries on a considerable trade in hats. In a meadow north of the church the Earl of Richmond encamped previous to the battle of Bosworth Field.	107½	Merevale Hall, W. S. Dugdale, Esq.; and 2 miles beyond, Baxterly Hall.
	162½	Hall End.	111½	To Coleshill, 9¾ miles, Sutton Coldfield, 7¼ m.
1½ mile distant, Pooley Hall.	161	Wilnecote. Enter Staffordshire.	113	Drayton Manor, Sir R. Peel, Bart.
To Ashby de la Zouch, 13 m.; Burton upon Trent, 15 miles. Tamworth Castle. Wigginton Lodge.	158½	TAMWORTH, (p. 357.)	115½	Bonehill, and beyond Middleton Hall, Lord Wenlock. Hint's Hall, W. H. C. Floyer, Esq.
		cr. river Tame and Grand Junction Canal.		Swinfen Hall, J. Swinfen, Esq.
Camberford Hall. Packington Hall. Stowe Hall.	156¼	Hopwas.	117¾	Freeford Hall, R. Dyott, Esq., Maple Hayes and Pipe Grange.
	150½	LICHFIELD	123½	

is finely situated on a branch of the river Trent. It is divided by a sheet of water into two parts, the city and the close, the latter being fortified. The cathedral, erected chiefly in the twelfth and thirteenth centuries, is the most interesting object in the town, and, from its elevated situation, visible at a great distance. It is 491 feet by 153, and surrounded by a wall. It suffered much in the famous siege which it underwent during the Parliamentary war, but has since been twice thoroughly repaired. The exterior is almost unrivalled for the elegance of its architecture, and the interior corresponds in splendour and magnificence. Of the numerous monuments, those of Dr. Johnson and Garrick, the former a native of the town, chiefly merit attention. There are also monuments to Lady Mary Wortley Montagu and Miss Seward, and the celebrated work of Chantrey representing two sleeping children. The other places deserving notice are, the house in Bacon Street, where Dr Darwin wrote his Zoonomia, and the house on the west side of the Market Place, the birth-place of Dr Johnson, a statue of whom now adorns the same street. This statue is 19 feet high, in a sitting position, and on the pedestal are three bas reliefs illustrative of the doctor's life. Also the market-house, the town-hall, the Hospital of St. John, the spot where Lord Brooke fell during the siege of the cathedral, indicated by a pavement of white pebbles, and an inscription recording the event, and the free school of St John, where Ashmole, Addison, Johnson, Garrick, Wollaston, Hawkins Browne, and many other eminent men received the rudiments of their education. Lichfield contains three parochial churches, several chapels and meeting-houses, charitable institutions, a theatre, library, &c. The city is a county in itself, with exempt jurisdiction. and sends two members to the House of Commons. It affords the title of Earl to the Anson family. There is little trade except with the interior by means of canals and railway. The brewing of ale also yields considerable profit. The markets are held on Tuesdays and Fridays. Pop. 6893.

ON RIGHT FROM LOND.	From Holyhd.		From London.	ON LEFT FROM LOND.
To Ashborne, 24 miles; Abbot's Bromley, 10½ miles.				To Birmingham, 16¾ miles, Walsall, 9 miles.
Elmhurst Hall, C. J. Smith, Esq., Liswis Hall and Haunch Hall.	147¼	Longdon Green.	126¾	Beaudesert (Marquis of Anglesea,) a noble building in a noble park.
	146½	Longdon.	127½	
Armitage Park, J. H. Lister Esq.; Lea Hall.				
In the vicinity of Rugeley, the Grand Trunk Canal is carried over the Trent by means of a noble aqueduct.	144½	Brereton.	129½	
To Stone 12¼ miles. Colton Hall, Bishton Hall, and beyond, Blithfield House, (Lord Bagot.) Shugborough, (Earl of Lichfield), the birth-place of the famous Lord Anson, celebrated for its natural as well as sculptural beauties.	143	RUGELEY carries on a considerable trade in hats, and has several mills and iron forges. The church has been rebuilt, but has an old tower at the west end. About 2 miles north of the town on Cannock Chase is a famous spring. Pop. 4362.	131	Hagley Park, the Baroness de la Zouche. Stoke House.
	140¾	Wolseley Bridge.	133¼	Wolseley Hall, Sir C. Wolseley, Bart. Haywood House.
Tixall Hall, Sir T. A. C. Constable Bart. Ingestre Hall, Earl of Shrewsbury, and beyond, Sandon Hall, Earl of Harrowby.	137	Milford.	137	Brockton Hall, W. Chetwynd, Esq. Brockton Lodge. Milford Hall.

ON RIGHT FROM LOND.	From Holyhd.		From London.	ON LEFT FROM LOND.
	135¼	Weeping Cross.	138¾	To Walsall, 15 miles.
		cr. the Stafford and Worcester Canal, and the river Penk.		
		cr. the river Sow.		
To Stone, 7¼ miles; Sandon, 5 miles.	133¼	STAFFORD,	140¾	To Newport, 10 miles.

the capital of the county of that name, is situated on the north bank of the river Sow, about three miles above its junction with the Trent. The situation of the town is low but pleasant, the streets being in general regular, and built of stone. A castle, erected here at a very early period, was several times demolished and rebuilt, but finally destroyed during the Parliamentary war. Its ruins now occupy the summit of a neighbouring hill. The county-hall is an elegant and spacious edifice in the centre of the town. Near it is the market-place, well adapted to the purpose intended. There are also four churches, (the most remarkable of which, St. Mary's, is cruciform, and contains a curious font), several Dissenting places of worship, a free school founded by Edward VI., a county infirmary, county jail, and lunatic asylum. The inhabitants are chiefly employed in the manufacture of boots and shoes, cutlery, and the tanning of leather. Isaak Walton was a native. There is also considerable traffic with the neighbouring counties by means of railways and canal. The town returns two M.P., and has done so since the reign of Edward I. It gives the title of Marquis to the Dukes of Sutherland, and that of Baron to the Jerningham family. Population, 12,532.

				Creswell Hall. Seighford Hall, F. Eld. Esq.
	130	Great Bridgeford.	144	
		cr. the river Sow.		
	128¼	Walton.	145¾	
Johnson Hall.	126¼	ECCLESHALL,	147¼	Acton Hall. Eccleshall Castle, Bishop of Lichfield and Coventry.

a neat and pleasant town, situated on the banks of a small stream that flows into the Sow. In its church Bishop Halse concealed Queen Margaret when she fled from Muckleston. It contains a few monuments of the Bosville family. Eccleshall Castle, the residence of the Bishops of Lichfield and Coventry, was founded at a very early period, and rebuilt in 1310, in consequence of damage received in the civil wars, was repaired in 1695.

To Stone, 6 miles. Charnes Hall, W. Yonge, Esq., and Broughton Hall, Sir H. D. Broughton, Bart.	123	Croxton.	151	To Newport, 9 miles Sugnall Hall.
	121	Broughton.	153	

ON RIGHT FROM LOND.	From Holyhd.		From London.	ON LEFT FROM LOND.
To Newcastle-under-Lyme, 10½ miles.	117¼	Muckleston.	156¾	To Drayton, 4 miles. Muckleston Hall, Oakley Hall, Sir J. N. L. Chetwode, Bart. Adderley Hall, and beyond, Shavington, Earl of Kilmorey.
		Enter Shropshire.		To Drayton, 8 miles.
	114½	Dorrington.	159½	Dorrington Old Hall. To Whitchurch, 13½ m.
	113¾	Woore.	160¼	Drayton, 7 miles.
To Newcastle-under-Lyme, 8¼ miles.		Enter Cheshire.		
	111¾	Bridgemore.	162¼	
Hough House.	108¾	Walgherton.	165¼	Doddington Hall, Sir H. D. Broughton, Bart.
Crewe Station, and beyond, Crewe Hall, Lord Crewe.		Stapeley.		Stapeley House, Rev. Jas. Folliott.
To Newcastle, 15 m.				To Whitchurch, 10 m.
	104¾	NANTWICH	169¼	Drayton, 12¾ miles.

stands in a low flat situation on the east bank of the Weaver. The houses are for the most part old, and built of timber and plaster. The church is large and cruciform, with stalls, stone pulpit, and an octagonal tower. The Dissenters have several meeting-houses, and there are several ranges of alms-houses. The prosperity of the town was formerly owing to its brine springs and salt-works, which were of great antiquity and celebrity, but only one spring is now worked. The chief manufactures are of shoes, cheese, gloves, and cotton goods. The Chester, the Ellesmere, the Liverpool, and Birmingham Junction canals, and the Middlewich Branch canal unite in the neighbourhood of the town, and the Grand Junction canal passes at no great distance. The Crewe station, a great focus of railways, is close to Nantwich. Pop. of township, 6225.

ON RIGHT FROM LOND.	From Holyhd.		From London.	ON LEFT FROM LOND.
Two miles distant, the Rookery.				Dorfold Hall. 7 miles distant, Combermere Abbey (Viscount Combermere) an ancient Cistercian abbey. It is beautifully situated.
		cr. river Weaver.		
	103¾	Acton.	170¼	6 m. distant is Cholmondeley Castle (Marquis of Cholmondeley), to whom Nantwich gives the title of Baron.
Pool Hall (F. E. Massey, Esq.) was built in the 16th century, and is one of the most venerable specimens of domestic architecture in the county.	102½	Hurleston.	171½	
	101¼	Barbridge.	172¾	
Calveley Hall, E. D. Davenport, Esq., and 4 m. to the right, Darnhall, T. G. Corbett, Esq.				Haughton.
		cr. Chester Canal.		

ON RIGHT FROM LOND.	From Holyhd.		From London.	ON LEFT FROM LOND.
Tilstone Lodge, J. Tollemache, Esq.	98¾	Highway Side.	175¼	Two miles distant are the ruins of Beeston Castle, erected by Randle Blundell, Earl of Chester, in 1220. It was dismantled during the civil wars by orders of the Parliament. This fortress stands on the slope and summit of a sandstone rock, which forms on one side an almost perpendicular precipice of great height. The outer court encloses an area of about 5 acres. The walls are prodigiously thick, and have several round towers. A deep ditch, sunk in the solid rock, surrounds the keep, which was entered by a drawbridge opposite two circular watch-towers still remaining. Camden speaks of a draw-well bored to the base of the rock, a depth of 90 yards, and communicating with a brook in the vale below.
To Northwich, 10 miles. The Bank, and 2 miles farther to the right, Oulton Hall, Sir P. De Malpas Grey Egerton, Bart.	95¾	TARPORLEY is pleasantly situated, cleanly and neatly built, and is noted for its annual fox-hunt. The church is an ancient structure, containing several monuments with inscriptions, interesting to the antiquary, and some armorial bearings in windows of coloured glass. The inhabitants are chiefly employed in the manufacture of stockings and leather breeches. In 1642, a battle was fought at this place between Sir W. Brereton and the Royalists from Chester, who, on this occasion, were victorious. Pop. 1212.	178¼	
	94	Clotton.	180	
	93	Dudden.	181	
3 miles distant Aston Hayes, Grey Booth, Esq. To Frodsham, 7¾ miles, Northwich, 12 miles.	91½	Tarvin.	182½	
	90	Stamford Bridge.	184	
To Frodsham, 9½ miles.	88¼	Vicar's Cross.	185¾	Littleton Hill.
		cr. Chester Canal.		
Hoole House.	86¾	Boughton.	187¼	To Whitchurch, 19 m. Boughton Hall.
To Frodsham, 11 miles; Liverpool across the Ferry, 18; Park Gate, 12.	85½	CHESTER (p. 149.)	188½	Eaton Hall (Marquis of Westminster). To Wrexham, 10½ m.
		cr. the river Dee.		
		cr. Ellesmere Can.		
	81	Bretton (*Flintshire.*)	193	
Hawarden gives the title of Viscount to the Maude family.		HAWARDEN, a well-built town, with the ruins of an ancient castle. Many of the inhabitants are employed in the collieries and in the manufacture of earthen-ware. Pop. of township, 652.		To Mold, 6½ miles. Hawarden Castle, Sir S. B. Glynne, Bart. Hawarden Hayes.
Aston Hall. The picturesque ruins of Ewloe Castle are delightfully situated in a sylvan dingle, in which the forces of Henry II. met with a signal defeat from the sons of Owen Gwynedd.	76	Ewloe.	198	Northop Hall.
To Flint, 3 miles.	73½	Northop.	200½	To Mold, 3 miles. Lower Saughton, Middle Saughton, and Upper Saughton.

ON RIGHT FROM LOND.	From Holyhd.		From London.	ON LEFT FROM LOND.
	70¾	**Halkin.**	203¼	Halkyn Castle, Marquis of Westminster.
To Flint, 2½ miles. Three miles beyond is Downing, formerly the residence of the celebrated topographer, T. Pennant, Esq., and one mile beyond it, near the sea, Mostyn Hall, Lord Mostyn, and farther along is Talacre, Sir P. Mostyn, Bart.	67	HOLYWELL derives its name from a spring called St Winifred's Well. In the vicinity are extensive lead mines, and numerous manufactories of paper, snuff, copper, and cotton. It joins with 7 other Flint boroughs in returning 1 M.P. Pop. of Parl. Bor. 5335.	207	Brynfoed.
	61¼	Brick Kiln.	212¾	1½ mile dist. Bryn Bella, Sir J. S. Piozzi Salusbury, the heir of Madame Piozzi.
		cr. river Clwyd.		
The see of St Asaph was founded so early as 543, and comprises parts of the counties of Flint, Montgomery, Denbigh, Merioneth, and Salop. Bodhyddan, W.S. Conwy, Esq.; farther to the right Pengwern, Lord Mostyn.	57	ST ASAPH, a small but pleasant and very ancient city, situated between the Clwyd and Elwy. The cathedral is a neat plain structure, and the east window has painted glass. This see has numbered among its bishops the excellent Dr. W. Beveridge. In the churchyard is the tomb of Bishop Isaac Barrow, who was tutor to the great mathematician and divine, Dr Isaac Barrow, his nephew. The Episcopal palace, recently rebuilt, is a commodious residence, and the scenery of the Clwyd is particularly beautiful. It affords the title of Viscount to the Earls of Ashburnham. Pop. 1861, 2063. This is one of the Flint dist. of burghs.	217	Llanerch Park and Bronwylfa, General Sir Henry Browne, K.C.H. Wygfair and Cefn. Three miles distant Plas Heaton, J. Heaton, Esq.; and beyond, Faenol, one of the best old houses in the county of Flint. To Denbigh, 3¾ miles.
		cr. the river Elwy.		
Bodelwyddan, Sir J. H. Williams, Bart.	52¼	Llan St Sior or St George (*Denbighshire.*)	221¾	
Kinmel Park, H. R. Hughes, Esq.	50	ABERGELE is much frequented in the bathing season, there being excellent sands, and the scenery in the vicinity beautiful. Near it is a huge calcareous rock called Cefn-yr Oge, in which are several natural caverns. Pop. of parish 3308.	224	Dyffrynaled, P. W. Yorke, Esq. Three miles distant Coed Coch, J. L. Wynne, Esq.; farther to the left Garthewin, B. H. Wynne, Esq.
Gwrych Castle, L. H. B. Hesketh, Esq.; Bryndulas, J. Hesketh, Esq. Marle. Bodyscallan.	47¾	Llandulas.	226¼	
		cr. river Conway.		Brynsteddfod, J. C. Jones, Esq.
	38½	ABERCONWAY (*Caernarvonshire*)	235½	

ON RIGHT FROM LOND.	From Holyhd.		From London.	ON LEFT FROM LOND.
Gloddaeth.				To Llanrwst, 12 miles.
To Beaumaris across the Lavan Sands and Ferry, 5¼ miles, but this route is by no means safe, as the sands frequently shift.	29¼	Over Penmaen Mawr. Mountain to Aber.	244¾	
Penrhyn Castle, Hon. E. G. Douglas Pennant. Lime Grove.	25¾	Llandegai.	248¼	Snowdon in the distance.
	24	BANGOR (p. 182).	250	
	21½	Menai Bridge. (See p. 182.)	252½	Treborth, and beyond Vaynol, T. A. Smith, Esq.
To Beaumaris, 4 miles, and Baron Hill, Sir R. B. W. Bulkeley, Bart.		[ferry] cr. the Menai Strait, and enter Anglesea.		To Llangefni, 6¾ miles.
		HOLYHEAD (p. 249).	274	

LXXXVII. FROM LONDON TO CHESTER THROUGH NEWPORT AND WHITCHURCH, 183½ Miles,—Continued to PARKGATE, 195½ Miles.

ON RIGHT FROM LOND.	From Parkgate		From London.	ON LEFT FROM LOND.
	32	From Hicks's Hall to Whitchurch, p. 206.	163½	
		Enter Cheshire.		
	30	Grindley Bridge.	165½	
Combermere Abbey, Viscount Combermere. About 2½ miles distant is Cholmondeley Castle (Marquis of Cholmondeley), an elegant mansion, adorned with a library and a fine collection of paintings.	25½	Hampton Guide Post.	169¾	1½ mile distant is Malpas, a well built town, situated on an eminence near the Dee. The church is a handsome building, containing a vault of the Cholmondeley family. Bishop Heber was a native of this town.
Bolesworth Castle.	23	Broxton.	172½	Carden Hall, (J. H. Leche, Esq.)

ON RIGHT FROM LOND.	From Parkgate		From London.	ON LEFT FROM LOND.
	19¾	Handley.	175½	Aldersey Hall, S. Aldersey, Esq.
	18¾	Golbourn Bridge.	176½	Eaton Hall, Marquis of Westminster.
	17	Higher Hatton.	178¼	Rowton Boughton Hall.
Hoole Hall.	13¼	Boughton.	182	
Bache Hall.	12	CHESTER, p. 149.	183¼	
Mollington Hall, J. Ffeilden, Esq. Moston Hall.	9½	Mollington.	185¾	
	6¾	The Yacht.	188½	Puddington Hall Burton Hall, R. Congreve, Esq.
	2¼	Enderton.	193	
To Liverpool, by Wood side Ferry, 10¾ miles.	1¼	GREAT NESTON.	194	
		PARKGATE.	195¼	

Parkgate is much resorted to for sea-bathing. It is also noted as a station from which packets sail for Ireland.

LXXXVIII. LONDON TO LIVERPOOL THROUGH DUNSTABLE, COVENTRY, LICHFIELD, STONE, KNUTSFORD, AND WARRINGTON, 206 Miles.

ON RIGHT FROM LOND.	From Liverp.		From London.	ON LEFT FROM LOND.
Packington Hall, Earl of Aylesford.	106¼	From Hicks's Hall to Stone Bridge, Warwickshire (p. 199).	99¾	To Warwick, 14 miles; to Birmingham, 9¾ miles.
3 miles distant is Maxstoke Castle (T. Dilke, Esq.), a considerable part of which remains in the same state as when erected by Edward III. Here also are the remains of a priory built by the same monarch. Blyth Hall (W. S. Dugdale, Esq.), formerly the property of Sir W. Dugdale, author of the Monasticon. Hams Hall, C. B. Adderley, Esq.	102¼	COLESHILL. The church is a fine specimen of Gothic architecture, containing numerous monuments, particularly of the Clinton and Digby families, and two of cross-legged knights. It affords the title of Viscount to the Earls Digby.	103¾	Coleshill Park, Lord Digby.

ON RIGHT FROM LOND.	From Liverp.		From London.	ON LEFT FROM LOND.
	100¼	Curdworth Bridge.	105¾	
		cr. river Tame.		
		cr. Birmingham Canal.		
Moxhul Hall, B. P. G. C. Noel, Esq. Middleton Hall, Lord Wenlock.	98¼	Wishaw.	107¾	
		Enter Staffordshire.		
To Tamworth, 5 miles. Canwell Hall, Lord Wenlock.	94¼	Basset's Pole.	111¾	To Sutton Coldfield, 2¼ miles, and beyond Sutton Park.
Hints Hall, W. H. C. Floyer, Esq.	91¼	Weeford.	114¾	Thickbroom Cot.
Swinfen Hall, J. Swinfen, Esq. Freeford Hall, R. Dyott, Esq.	89½	Swinfen.	116½	Shenstone Pa., E. Grove, Esq., and beyond, Fotherley Hall.
		cr. Wyrley and Essington Canal.		
To Derby, 23¾ miles; Abbot's Bromley, 11½ m. Stowe House. Elmhurst Hall, J. Smith, Esq.	87¼	LICHFIELD.* (See p. 210.	114¾	To Birmingham, 15¾ m. Walsall, 9 miles. Pipe Grange. Maple Hayes.
Armytage Park.	83¼	Longdon.	122¾	Beaudesert Park (Marquis of Anglesea; a magnificent mansion, surrounded by fine trees.
	81¼	Brereton.	124¾	
	79¾	RUGELEY carries on a considerable trade in hats, and has several mills and iron forges, an ancient church, &c. Pop. of town, 4362. (See p. 211.)	126¼	The Grand Trunk Canal is here carried over the Trent by a noble aqueduct. Hagley Park, the Baroness De la Zouche. Two miles distant, on Cannock Chase is a famous spring.
Bellamore House. Colton Hall, Bishton Hall.	77½	Wolseley Bridge.	128½	Wolseley Hall, Sir C. Wolseley, Bart.
		cr. river Trent and Grand Trunk Canal.		
Blithfield House, (Lord Bagot.)	76¾	Colwich. The church contains a number of monuments of the Ansons and Wolseleys.	129¼	
	75¼	Great Haywood.	130¾	Shugborough (Earl of Lichfield), the birth-place of the great Lord Anson. Tixall Park, Sir T. A. C. Constable, Bart. Ingestre Hall, Earl
	72¾	Shirleywich.	133¼	

This road to Lichfield is 4¾ miles nearer than that through Northampton and Lutterworth.

ON RIGHT FROM LOND.	From Liverp.		From London.	ON LEFT FROM LOND.
				of Shrewsbury. This seat has belonged to the same family since the time of Edward III.
	72	Weston.	134	
Sandon Hall, Earl of Harrowby; and beyond Chartley, Earl Ferrers, and the ruins of Chartley Castle.	69½	Sandon.	136½	To Stafford, 4¼ miles.
	66¼	Stoke.	139¾	
To Leek, 16½ miles; to Cheadle, 10 miles. Stone Park, Earl Granville.	65¼	STONE has a handsome modern church, a free school, and other charities. Pop. of township, 4509. cr. Grand Trunk Canal and the Trent.	140¾	To Stafford, 7 miles; to Eccleshall, 5½ miles.
Meaford Hall, Viscount St Vincent.	63¾	Darlaston.	142¼	Darlaston Hall, S. S. Jervis, Esq.; and beyond, Swinnerton Park, T. Fitzherbert, Esq.
Barlaston, R. Adderley, Esq.	61¾	Tittensor Mill.	144¼	
		cr. river Trent.		
	60	Trentham Inn.	146	Trentham Park, (Duke of Sutherland), surrounded by beautiful and extensive grounds.
	59¼	Hanford.	146¾	
Fenton Hall; and 1½ mile distant is Stoke upon Trent.				Butterton Hall. Clayton. Keele Hall, R. Sneyd, Esq.
Etruria Hall.	56¼	NEWCASTLE-UNDER-LYME, p. 221.	149¾	
To Burslem, 2 m.	54½	Chesterton.	151½	
Glough Hall.	51½	Talk-on-the-Hill.	154½	Linley Wood.
		cr. Grand Trunk Canal. Enter Cheshire.		
	50	Church-Lawton.	156	Lawton Hall, C. B. Lawton, Esq. Rode Hall, R. Wilbraham, Esq.
Moreton Hall.	47	Moreton.	159	
	45½	Astbury.	160½	
Buglawton Hall. Eaton Hall, G. C. Antrobus, Esq.	44	CONGLETON, a neat town near the banks of the Dane, having manufactures of silk, ribands, cotton, and leather. Pop. 12,344.	162	Somerford Park, Sir C. W. Shakerley, Bt., and beyond Brereton Park. Somerford Booth's Hall, C. Swetenham, Esq., and Swettenham Hall, T. J. W. Swettenham, Esq. Hulme Walfield.
		cr. river Dane.		
	40¼	Marton.	165¾	
Thornvcroft Hall.	39¼	Siddington.	166¾	Capesthorne Hall, E. D. Davenport, Esq.

ON RIGHT FROM LOND.	From Liverp.		From London.	ON LEFT FROM LOND.
Henbury. Birtles, and Alderley Park, Lord Stanley of Alderley.	34¾	Chelford.	171¼	Astle Park. Withington Hall, J. Glegg, Esq., and 3 miles distant, Over Peover, Sir H. M. Mainwaring, Bart.
Norbury Booth's Hall, P. Legh, Esq.	31¾	Ollerton Gate.	174¼	Toft Hall, R. Leycester, Esq.
Tatton Park, W. T. Egerton, Esq., M.P.	29½	KNUTSFORD is said to have derived its name from Canute or Knut passing the ford here with his army. Many of the inhabitants are engaged in the manufacture of cotton. Annual races are held here in July. Pop. of town 3575.	176½	Tabley Hall, seat of Lord de Tabley, a handsome edifice of the Doric order, containing a fine picture gallery. Within the grounds is the old hall of Tabley, a venerable structure covered with ivy, standing on an island in a lake which adorns the park.
	26¾	Mere.	179¾	Mere Hall, P. L. Brooke, Esq.
High-Legh Hall, G. C. Legh, Esq. West Hall, E. Legh, Esq. Outhrington Hall, T. Trafford, Esq., 2 m.; and	24½	High Legh.	181½	Two miles distant Arley Hall.
Dunham Massey Park, Earl of Stamford and Warrington, 3 m.	20¾	Duke of Bridgewater's Canal.	185¼	Appleton Hall.
Thelwall Hall and Statham Lodge.	19	Latchford. cr. river Mersey, and enter Lancashire.	187	
To Manchester, 18 m. Fairfield Hall and Orford Hall.	17¾	WARRINGTON. (see p. 238.)	188¼	
Bank Hall, J. W. Patten, Esq. Bewsay Hall, Lord Lilford.	16½	Sankey Bridge.	189½	
		cr. Sankey Navigation.		
	15½	Sankey.	190½	
Bold Hall, Sir H. Bold Hoghton, Bart.	11	Rainhill.	195	Halsnead Hall, R. Willis, Esq.
Two m. dist. Sherdley House and Sutton Lodge. Knowsley Park, the magnificent seat of the Earl of Derby: and one mile to the right Eccleston Hall.	8	PRESCOT, noted for its manufacture of watch-tools and movements. At Ravenhead are celebrated plate-glass works. Pop. of town, 6066.	198	In Prescot was born the celebrated actor, J. P. Kemble. The Hasles, Sir T. B. Birch, Bart. Roby Hall. Childwall Hall, Marquis of Salisbury.
Croxteth Park, Earl of Sefton.	4	Knotty Ash.	202	
		LIVERPOOL, p. 221.	206	

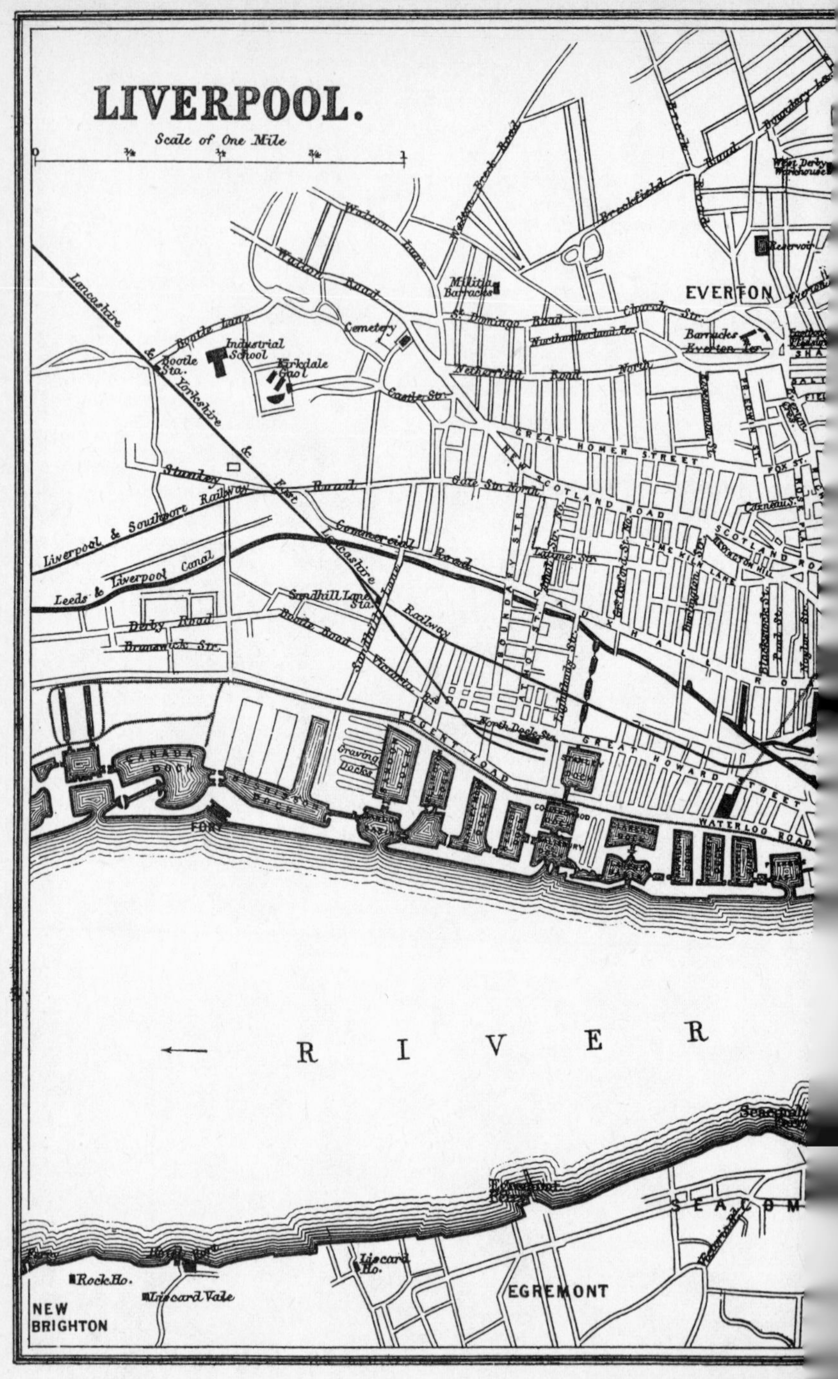
LIVERPOOL.
Scale of One Mile
0
1/4
1/2
3/4
1
EVERTON
Militia Barracks
St. Domingo Road
Northumberland Ter.
Barracks
Everton Ter.
Netherfield Road North
Cemetery
Industrial School
Kirkdale Gaol
Bootle Sta.
Bootle Lane
Walton Lane
Walton Road
Breckfield Road
Castle Str.
Great Homer Street
Church Str.
Lancashire & Yorkshire & East
Stanley Road
Gate Str. North
Liverpool & Southport Railway
Commercial Road
Leeds & Liverpool Canal
Derby Road
Brunswick Str.
Sandhill Lane Sta.
Bootle Road
Lancashire Railway
Scotland Road
Latimer Str.
Lime Kiln Lane
Vauxhall Road
Boundary Str.
Regent Road
North Dock Str.
Great Howard Street
Waterloo Road
Canada Dock
Huskisson Dock
Fort
Graving Docks
Stanley Dock
Fox St.
Reservoir
West Derby Workhouse
RIVER
SEACOMBE
EGREMONT
Liscard Ho.
Rock Ho.
Liscard Vale
NEW BRIGHTON
A. & C.

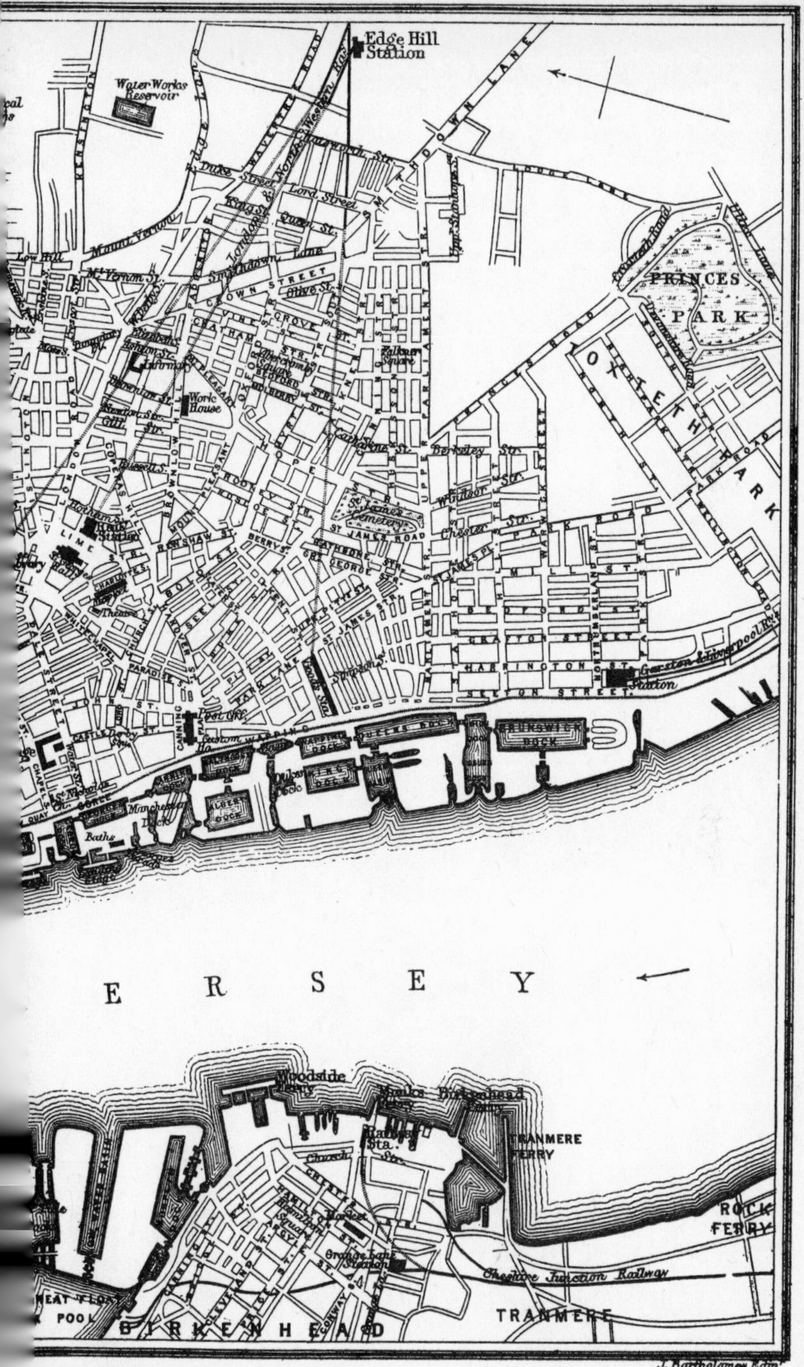

Edge Hill Station
Water Works Reservoir
PRINCES PARK
TOXTETH PARK
Work House
St. James Cemetery
BRUNSWICK DOCK
M E R S E Y
Woodside Ferry
Birkenhead Ferry
TRANMERE FERRY
ROCK FERRY
Cheshire Junction Railway
TRANMERE
BIRKENHEAD
Grange Lane Station
J. Bartholomew, Edin.

NEWCASTLE-UNDER-LYME is a place of considerable antiquity, and a corporate town so early as the reign of Henry VI. A castle was built here during the reign of Henry VII.; but no vestiges of it remain, except a portion of the mound on which it was built. The town has an old church, several meeting-houses, and a range of alms-houses, founded by the second Duke of Albemarle. The chief manufacture is that of hats. There are several silk mills, a paper and a cotton mill; a few of the inhabitants are engaged in the potteries. Two M.P. Pop. 12.938.

STOKE-UPON-TRENT is one of the new Parliamentary boroughs created by the Reform Act. This borough has this peculiarity, that instead of comprehending one principal town and its suburbs, it consists of a considerable district, extending 7½ miles in length, and about three miles in breadth, and including the market-towns of Burslem, Hanley, Lane-End, Stoke, Tunstall Court, &c. This district is commonly termed the "Potteries," and is the chief seat of the earthen-ware manufacture in England. In the borough, or in its immediate neighbourhood, a very large proportion of the population is engaged in the manufactory of earthenware. Coals, marl, and potter's clay are dug in the vicinity. At Etruria is the superb mansion erected by the late Josiah Wedgwood, the great improver of the earthen manufacture of the district. Stoke-upon-Trent returns two M. P. Pop. of Parliamentary borough, 1861, 10,207. It is connected by railway with all parts of the kingdom.

LIVERPOOL, now second only to London, is situated on the right side of the Mersey. A castle is said to have been built here by Roger of Poictiers, which was demolished in 1659. St. George's Church now stands on the site. During the civil wars, Liverpool held out against Prince Rupert for a month, but at last it was taken, and many of the garrison and inhabitants were put to the sword. The town was very soon after retaken by Colonel Birch, and continued to remain true to the popular cause. Liverpool was merely a chapelry attached to the parish of Walton till the reign of William III., and in 1650 but 15 ships belonged to the port. It was at one time deeply engaged in the African slave trade; and in 1764, more than half this trade was carried on by the merchants of Liverpool. Since the great extension of the cotton manufacture it has become the port where the great bulk of the raw material is received, and whence the exports of manufactured goods are chiefly made to all parts of the world. It also enjoys a very large proportion of the trade between England and Ireland, the value of Irish produce imported in 1844 having been £4,618,957. Liverpool is supposed to possess one-tenth part of the shipping of Great Britain; one-third part of the foreign trade; one sixth part of the general commerce; and more than one-half as much trade as the port of London. The customs dues amounted in 1857 to £3,621,409; and the cotton imported to 2,250,500 bales. The imports are about thirty millions in value, the exports exceeding that sum by a tenth, and it is calculated that more than 1600 tons of goods pass daily between Liverpool and Manchester. Nearly one-third of the tonnage inwards and outwards is engaged in the trade with the United States. Considerable traffic is carried on also with Africa, the West India Islands, with Brazil, and other parts of South America, and with the East Indies. Its intercourse with Ireland is greater in amount than that kept up with all the other ports in Great Britain. The inland trade of Liverpool is much assisted by means of canals and railways and it has benefited more than any port in the kingdom, (London alone excepted) by the application of steam power to navigation. The docks are constructed on a most stupendous scale. They consist of wet, dry, and graving docks, and are connected with wide and commodious quays, and immense warehouses. The wet docks occupy an aggregate area of about 174 acres, and the quays measure 14 miles in length. The dry docks occupy an area of twenty acres.

Till the beginning of the present century, the streets of Liverpool were narrow and inconvenient, and the buildings devoid of architectural beauty, but successive improvements have given to the town an elegance not to be met with in any other commercial port in the kingdom. The most important public buildings are, the Town-hall, the Exchange buildings, the Custom-house, and St George's Hall. The town-hall is a handsome Palladian building, surmounted by a dome, which is crowned by a statue of Britannia. It contains a number of portraits and a statue of Roscoe by Chantrey, and on the landing of the staircase there is a statue of Canning by the same artist. The interior of the town-hall, besides the rooms on the basement story, contains a saloon, two drawing-rooms, two ball-rooms, a banqueting-room, and a refectory, the whole elegantly fitted up. The exchange buildings form three sides of a square, in the centre of which is a group of statuary, in memory of Nelson, executed by Westmacott in 1813. The new custom-house, a very fine building, both in magnitude and architectural execution, contains also the post-office, the excise-office, the stamp-office, the dock-treasurer's and secretary's offices, the board-room, and offices of the dock committee. The finest building in Liverpool is that allotted to the assize courts, and includes a noble apartment called St George's Hall. The whole cost about L.192,000. At the junction of the London road and Pembroke Place, there is an equestrian statue of George III. by Westmacott. St James's cemetery was once a quarry of red stone, and consists principally of catacombs. On the summit of the rock near the entrance is a beautiful chapel, containing some good sculpture. Here the late Mr. Huskisson was interred, and a monument to his memory has been placed over the spot, with a statue of fine white marble, habited in a toga. Liverpool contains thirty-five places of worship connected with the Establishment, and seventy belonging to Dissenters of various denominations. There are in Liverpool numerous Sunday, evening, and day schools, with many medical as well as provident and religious charities. There are also several literary institutions and places of public amusement. Among the literary institutions may be mentioned the Royal Institution, formed in 1814, by Mr. Roscoe—the Literary, Scientific, and Commercial Institution, set on foot in 1835—the Mechanics' Institution, opened in 1837—the Liverpool Institution of the Fine Arts—the Atheneum—the Lyceum—the Collegiate Institution, &c. Liverpool has ten prisons.

The markets of Liverpool are very remarkable structures; that of St John occupies nearly two acres of ground, the whole being under one roof, and supported by 116 cast-iron pillars.

The zoological gardens comprise ten acres of ground, and are laid out with a good deal of taste. Its attractions have recently been increased by the munificence of the late Earl of Derby.

The manufactures of Liverpool are not important. There are several sugar refineries, some small founderies, a good deal of ship-building in wood and iron, a manufactory of steam-engines for vessels, and manufactories of anchors, chain cables, and similar articles naturally in demand in a large port.

The value of the corporation estates is estimated at three millions of money, and the annual income derived from dock dues alone, amounted in 1850, to L.242,989:14:9. A great proportion of this income has been devoted to the improvement of the town, including the building of churches and other public edifices. The sum expended in these objects and in widening the streets, between 1786 and 1838, amounted to L.1,668,300.

The site of Liverpool is low and unhealthy. According to the Registrar-General's return of births and deaths, the deaths and marriages are double, while the births are little more than half, the number of the average of all England.

In 1700 the population of Liverpool was only 4240; in 1861, it amounted to 443,938. It returns two members to Parliament.

The country around Liverpool abounds in every direction with fine residences. Of these, the most important are, Knowsley Hall (Earl of Derby); Croxteth Park (Earl of Sefton); Ince Blundell, the seat of the Blundell family; Childwall Hall (Marquis of Salisbury); Speke Hall (R. Watt, Esq.); Hale Hall (J. T. Blackburne, Esq.); Woolton Hall, &c.

At Everton is the cottage where Prince Rupert established his head quarters when he besieged the town in 1644.

LXXXIX. LONDON TO MANCHESTER THROUGH ST ALBANS, NORTHAMPTON, LEICESTER, DERBY, MACCLESFIELD, AND STOCKPORT, 186 Miles.

ON RIGHT FROM LOND.	From Manch.		From London.	ON LEFT FROM LOND.
Milton Bryant. Woburn Abbey, Duke of Bedford, see p. 201.	148¾	From London to Hockliffe, *Bedfordsh.* (p. 196-197)	37¼	Hockliffe Grange, R. T. Gilpin, Esq. Battlesden Park, Sir E. H. P. Turner, Bart.
Wavendon Hall, H. C. Hoare, Esq.	144½	WOBURN, (p. 201).	41½	
		Enter Buckinghamsh.		
		cr. river Ouse.		
Horton House, Sir R. H. Gunning, Bart.	136	NEWPORT PAGNELL, an ancient town on the banks of the Ouse, formerly famous for its lace trade. Cowper the poet lived many years at Olney in the vicinity. Pop. 3476.	50	Gayhurst Park. A room in this mansion was the retreat of Sir Everard Digby, one of the Guy Fawkes conspirators.

ON RIGHT FROM LOND.	From Manch.		From London.	ON LEFT FROM LOND.
2 m. distant is Castle Ashby, the seat of the Marquis of Northampton.	$127\frac{1}{2}$	Horton Inn, *Northamptonshire.*	$58\frac{1}{2}$	3 miles distant, Courteen Hall, Sir C. Wake, Bart.
Delapre Abbey, E. Bouverie, Esq.	122	Queen's Cross, one of those crosses erected by Edward I. in memory of Queen Eleanor.	64	2 miles distant, Upton Hall.
To Kettering, $13\frac{3}{4}$ m. To Wellingborough, 11 miles. Abington Abbey, now a Lunatic Asylum.	120	NORTHAMPTON, p. 226	66	To Daventry, 12 miles.
Boughton House, R. W. Howard Vyse, Esq.; and beyond Overstone, Lord Overstone.	$118\frac{1}{2}$	Kingsthorpe.	$67\frac{1}{2}$	Kingsthorpe House, To Welford, 13 miles; thence to Lutterworth, $8\frac{1}{2}$.
Pitsford Hall and Moulton Grange.	$113\frac{3}{4}$	Brixworth.	$72\frac{1}{4}$	
Lamport Hall, Sir C. E. Isham, Bart.	$111\frac{1}{2}$	Lamport.	$74\frac{1}{2}$	At a distance Cottesbroke Park, Sir J. H. Langham, Bart.
	$109\frac{3}{4}$	Maidwell.	$76\frac{1}{4}$	
	$107\frac{3}{4}$	Kelmarsh.	$78\frac{1}{4}$	Kelmarsh Hall, Lord Bateman.
Arthingworth Hall, Rev. H. R. Rokeby.	105	Oxendon Magna.	81	
		cr. river Welland, and enter Leicestersh.		
Dingley Hall, H. H. H. Hungerford, Esq	$102\frac{1}{2}$	MARKET HARBOROUGH, a small town carrying on a trade in carpets. It is supposed to be of Roman origin, and there are traces of a Roman camp in the vicinity. Charles I. fixed his head quarters here immediately previous to the battle of Naseby. Pop. 2302.	$83\frac{1}{2}$	To Lutterworth, 13 m.
Carlton Curlieu Hall, Sir J. H. Palmer, Bart.	97	Kibworth.	89	Wistow Hall, Sir H. Halford, Bart.
Nosely Hall, Sir A. G. Hazlerigg, Bart.	$94\frac{1}{2}$	Great Glen.	$91\frac{3}{4}$	
Stretton Hall, Rev. Sir G. S. Robinson, Bart. Staughton Grange.	$91\frac{1}{2}$	Oadby.	$94\frac{1}{2}$	
	88	LEICESTER, (p. 354.)	98	
Birstal House. Wanlip Hall, Sir G. J. Palmer, Bart.	$86\frac{1}{4}$	Belgrave.	$99\frac{3}{4}$	
		cross river Soar.		
Quorndon Hall.	81	Mountsorrel, (p. 352.) originally called Mount Soar Hill, from its situation on the banks of the Soar.	105	Bradgate Park. Rothley Temple, T. Babington, Esq. Swithland Hall, Earl of Lanesborough. Quorndon House, E. B. Farnham, Esq.
To Nottingham, $15\frac{1}{4}$ m. 3 miles distant Prestwold Ha. C. W. Packe, Esq., and Burton Hall.	77	LOUGHBOROUGH, (p. 352)	109	Garendon Park, C. M. Phillipps, Esq.
	71	Kegworth.	115	To Ashby de la Zouch, 12 miles. Whatton House.

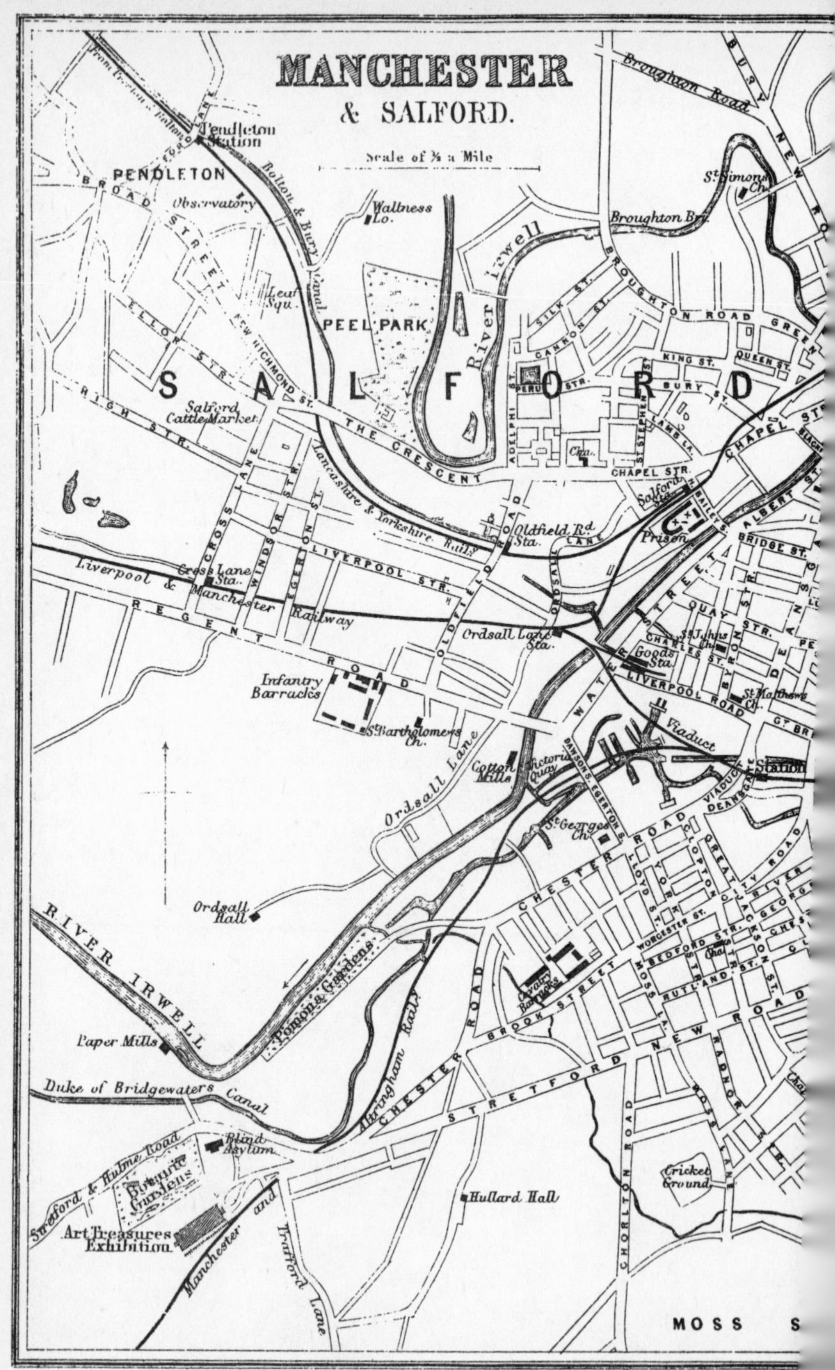
MANCHESTER
& SALFORD.
Scale of ¼ a Mile
Pendleton Station
PENDLETON
BROAD STREET
Observatory
Bolton & Bury Canal
Waltness Lo.
ELLOR STR.
Leaf Squ.
NEW RICHMOND ST.
PEEL PARK
River Irwell
Broughton Road
Broughton Br.
St. Simons Ch.
SILK ST.
CANNON ST.
BROUGHTON ROAD
KING ST.
QUEEN ST.
S A L F O R D
HIGH STR.
Salford Cattle Market
THE CRESCENT
PERU STR.
BURY ST.
ADELPHI ST.
ST. STEPHEN ST.
LAMBS LA.
Cha.
CHAPEL STR.
CHAPEL ST.
Salford Sta.
Prison
ALBERT
BAILEY S.
BRIDGE ST.
CROSS LANE
WINDSOR STR.
EGERTON ST.
Lancashire & Yorkshire Railw.
Oldfield Rd. Sta.
OLDFIELD ROAD
LIVERPOOL STR.
Liverpool & Manchester Railway
Cross Lane Sta.
REGENT ROAD
ORDSALL LANE
Ordsall Lane Sta.
WATER STREET
QUAY STR.
St. Johns Ch.
CHARLES ST.
BYRON STR.
Goods Sta.
LIVERPOOL ROAD
St. Matthews Ch.
Infantry Barracks
St. Bartholomews Ch.
Viaduct
Ordsall Lane
Cotton Mills
Victoria Quay
DAWSON S.
EGERTON S.
Station
VIADUCT
DEANSGATE
St. Georges Ch.
CHESTER ROAD
LLOYD ST.
YORK ST.
CLOPTON ST.
GREAT JACKSON ST.
CITY ROAD
Ordsall Hall
RIVER IRWELL
Pomona Gardens
WORCESTER ST.
BEDFORD STR.
RUTLAND ST.
Cha.
Cavalry Barracks
BROOK STREET
NEW ROAD
Paper Mills
Altringham Railw.
CHESTER ROAD
STRETFORD NEW ROAD
RADNOR
MOSS LANE
Duke of Bridgewaters Canal
Blind Asylum
Stretford & Hulme Road
Botanic Gardens
Art Treasures Exhibition
Manchester and
Trafford Lane
Hullard Hall
CHORLTON ROAD
Cricket Ground
MOSS S

A. & C.

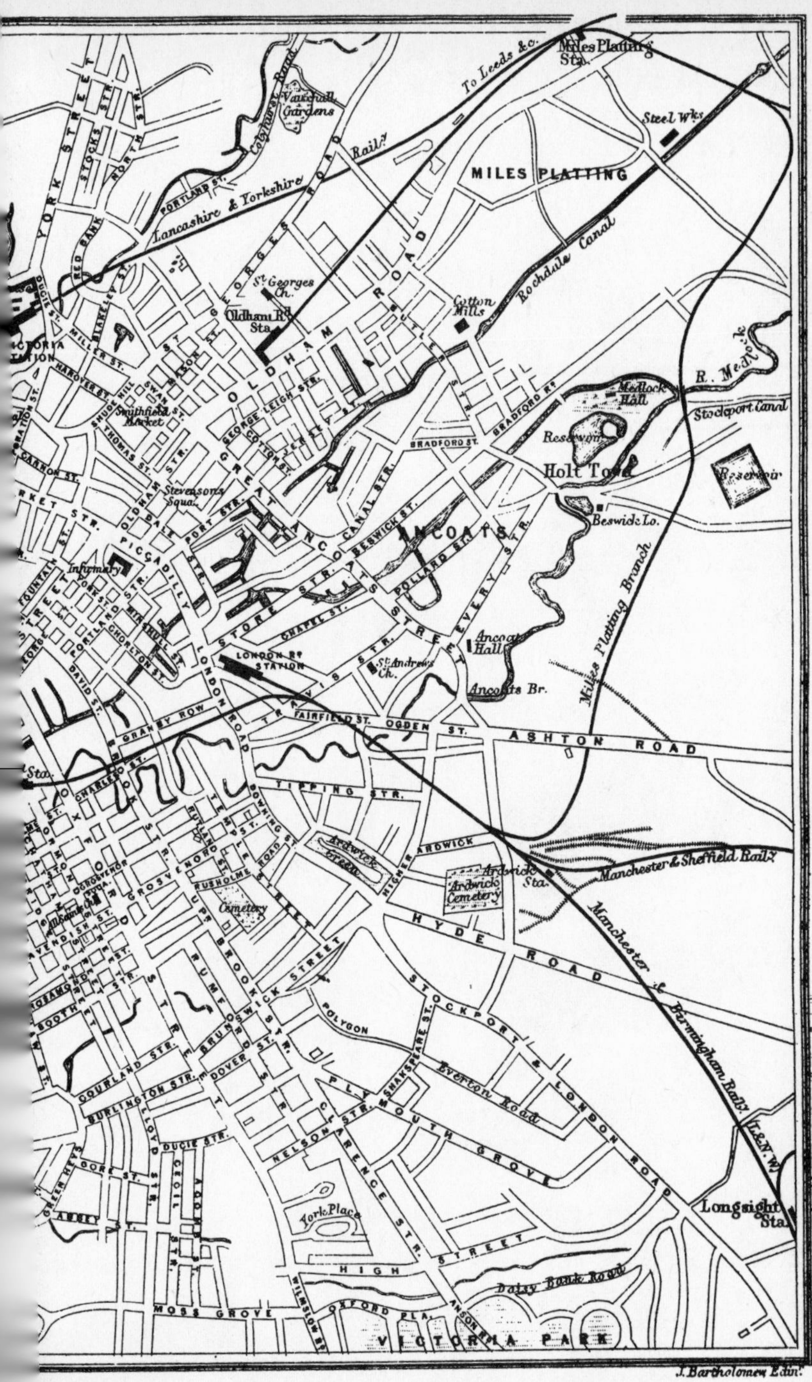

J. Bartholomew, Edin.

gh

ON RIGHT FROM LOND.	From Manch.		From London.	ON LEFT FROM LOND.
		cr. river Trent, and enter Derbyshire.		Donnington Park, Marquis of Hastings.
Thurlston Hall.	63	Elvaston.	123	
Elvaston Castle, Earl of Harrington. To Nottingham, 16 m.; Mansfield 22 m.; Alfreton 15½ m.; Chesterfield, 23¾ m.; Belper, 8½ m.; Matlock, 17½ m.; Wirksworth, 14 m.; Buxton, 31¾ m.	60	DERBY, (p. 355.) About ½ mile from Derby, on the banks of the river, is Little Chester, the Derventio of the Romans.	126	Osmaston Hall, Sir R. E. Wilmot, Bart. To Burton-upon-Trent, 11¼ miles. To Uttoxeter, 18¾ m. Radborne Hall, E. S. Chandos Pole, Esq.
Kedleston, Lord Scarsdale. Bradley Hall. Ashbourne Hall, once a seat of the Boothbys, and where the Pretender spent a night in 1745. A short distance from Ashbourne is the picturesque village of Tissington, celebrated for the annual custom of "Well dressing" on Holy Thursday.	46¾	ASHBOURNE is noted for its cattle fairs. Many of the inhabitants are employed in the cotton manufacture. The church is a good specimen of early English, and has various brasses and tombs to the Boothbys, &c. Pop. 3501.	139¼	Longford Hall, Hon. E. K W. Coke. At Mayfield, near Ashbourne, is the cottage in which Moore composed "Lalla Rookh." 6 miles distant is the romantic vale of Dovedale.
Tissington Hall, Sir W. Fitzherbert, Bart. Sandy Brook Hall, Sir M. Blakiston. Okeover Park.		cr. river Dove, and enter Staffordshire.		Mayfield Hall, and 2 m. distant, Calwich Hall, C. Granville, Esq. To Uttoxeter and Doveridge Hall (Lord Waterpark), 10¼ m.
Ilam Hall, (J. W. Russell, Esq.), noted for its picturesque scenery. On the grounds is a grotto in which Congreve wrote the "Old Bachelor."	37	Winkhill Bridge. cr. the riv. Hamps.	148	Wooton Hall, and beyond, Alton Towers, (Earl of Shrewsbury), a noble seat.
To Bakewell, 18 miles. To Buxton, 12 miles. Ball Hay. The Abbey.	31¾	LEEK, p. 227.	154¼	Ashenhurst Hall. Westwood House. To Cheadle, 10¾ miles. To Burslem, 9¼ miles. To Newcastle-under-Lyme, 11½ miles.
Highfield House. Horton Hall.	30¼	Pool End.	155¾	
Rudyard. 2 m. distant, Swithamley Hall.	27	Rushton Marsh. cr. river Dane, and enter Cheshire.	159	Reservoir of the Trent and Mersey Canal. East Cliff Hall.
Foden Bank.	25¾		160¼	
To Buxton, 11 miles; to Chapel-en-le-Frith, 12½ miles. Hurdsfield House, J. Brocklehurst, Esq., jr. Titherington Hall	18¾	MACCLESFIELD, p. 227.	167¼	Gawsworth, Earl of Harrington. Park House. To Knutsford, 11 m. Birtles, and beyond, Alderley Park, Lord Stanley of Alderley.
	15¼	cr. river Bollin. Butley.	170¾	

ON RIGHT FROM LOND.	From Manch.		From London.	ON LEFT FROM LOND.
Two miles dist. Styperson Park. Shrigley Hall.				Adlington Hall, C. R. B. Legh, Esq.
Two miles distant Lyme Park, T. Legh, Esq.	12½	Hope Green.	173½	Two m. distant Mottram St. Andrew, L. Wright, Esq.
Poynton Hall, Lord Vernon.	11½	Poynton.	174½	
	10½	Norbury.	175½	Two m. dist. Bramall Hall, W. Davenport, Esq.
Two m. beyond, Marple Hall, T. B. Isherwood, Esq.	9½	Bullock Smithy.	176½	
To Barnsley, 33 miles; Huddersfield, 38 miles. Woodbank.	6¾	STOCKPORT, p. 227.	179¼	
		☞ cr. river Mersey, and enter Lancashire.		
	5¼	Heaton Norris.	180¾	
	4	Levenshulme.	182	
	2	Ardwick Green.	184	Trafford Park, Sir H. De Trafford, Bart.
		MANCHESTER, p 229.	186	

NORTHAMPTON is situated on the north bank of the Nen. It is a place of considerable antiquity. During the wars of the Roses, a great battle was fought near the town (July 10th 1460,) in which the Lancastrians were defeated by the Kingmaker, Earl of Warwick, and Henry VI. taken prisoner. In the civil wars of Charles I., Northampton was taken by Lord Brooke, and fortified for the Parliament. The principal objects deserving of notice are, All-Saints Church; St Peter's, a remarkably fine and curious specimen of enriched Norman architecture; St Sepulchre's, supposed to have been erected by the Knights-Templars about the beginning of the twelfth century; St. Giles', adorned with several curious monuments; the Castle Hill meeting-house, which contains a tablet to the memory of Dr Doddridge, who exercised his ministry, and conducted an academy for the education of ministers, in this town for more than twenty years; the Baptist meeting-house, in which is a monument to John Ryland; the town-hall; the county-gaol; the county-hall; sessions-house; new corn-exchange, &c. Of the several religious houses which existed before the Reformation, the Hospitals of St Thomas and St John yet remain. Of the castle, which was near the west bridge, there are only the earth works, and of the town walls there are no traces. The principal branch of trade carried on in Northampton is boot and shoe-making. Considerable business is done in currying leather, and some stockings and lace are made. It has also several iron foundries; and its horse-fairs are much frequented. It is connected by railway with all parts of the empire. It returns two members to Parliament. Pop. 1861, 32,813. Six miles distant is Althorp, the seat of Earl Spencer, containing numerous fine pictures, and a very extensive library * of curious and scarce books, chiefly collected at great expense by the second Earl, one of the greatest bibliopoles of his day.

* See Dr Dibdin's description of it.

LEEK is an ancient town, possessing extensive manufactories of silks, twists, buttons, ribands, shawls, &c. There is in the churchyard a curious pyramidal cross, the origin of which is involved in obscurity. It is about 10 feet high, and is decorated with imagery and fretwork. Here are the remains of Dieu la Croix Abbey. The scenery surrounding the town is peculiarly romantic. Pop. 10,045. To Congleton, 5½ miles.

MACCLESFIELD is situated on the edge of a dreary district called Macclesfield Forest. It is now the principal seat in the island of the silk throwing trade, and is connected by railway with all parts of the empire. It is likewise the chief place for the manufacture of silk handkerchiefs, and possesses extensive copper and brass-works. The most important factories are situated on the Bollen. Macclesfield has a church founded in 1278 by Eleanor, Queen of Edward I. but since restored. There are two chapels adjoining this church, one belonging to the Marquis of Cholmondeley, the other to the Legh family of Lyme. An ancestor of the latter family served under Edward III. and his son the Black Prince, during all their wars in France, and the estate of Lyme was given him for recovering a standard at the battle of Cressy. Besides St Michael's, there are four other churches in the town and suburbs, various meeting-houses, a Roman Catholic chapel, town-hall, assembly-rooms, a subscription library, containing upwards of 20,000 volumes, a mechanics' institute, a free grammar-school, with an annual revenue of L.1300, and more than fifty schools of all kinds. When the Factory Commissioners visited Macclesfield, it was found that, of the children in the employment of the manufacturers, 96 per cent could read. Macclesfield returns two members to Parliament. It affords the title of Earl to one of the noble families of Parker. Pop. 36,101.

STOCKPORT, situated on the Mersey, is a town of great antiquity, famous for its manufactures of cotton and hats. By means of a canal, this town has water communication with the rivers Dee, Ribble, Trent, and Severn, and thus with the greater part of the kingdom. It is also a focus of railways. The trade which it carries on is very extensive. It contains three churches, several meeting-houses, a Catholic chapel, a theatre, a library and news-room, a free grammar-school, and other charitable institutions. It returns two members to Parliament Pop. 1861, 54,681. Stockport is 176 miles from London by the nearest road.

XC. LONDON TO MANCHESTER THROUGH BUXTON AND STOCKPORT.

182½ Miles.

ON RIGHT FROM LOND.	From Manch.		From London.	ON LEFT FROM LOND.
	56½	From Hicks's Hall to DERBY, p. 225.	126	
Bradley Hall. Ashbourne Hall, formerly a seat of the Boothbys.	43¼	ASHBOURNE, p. 225.	139½	
Sandy-Brook Hall, Sir M. Blakiston, Bart.	42¼	Sandy-Brook.	140¼	
	40¾	Bentley.	141¾	Ilam Hall, J. W. Russell, Esq.
Tissington Hall, Sir W. Fitzherbert, Bart.	38	New Inn.	144½	
	34¼	Newhaven Inn.	148½	To Haddon Hall, (Duke of Rutland), 9 m. and beyond Chatsworth, (Duke of Devonshire).
	29½	Hurdlow House.	153	
	28½	Over Street.	154	
	22¾	BUXTON.	159¾	
To Tideswell, 7 miles.				To Leek, 12 miles; Congleton, 16 miles; Macclesfield, 10 miles.
Bank Hall.	20	White Hall.	162½	
	16¼	Whaley Bridge, p. 232.	166¼	Lyme Park, T. Legh, Esq.
	6¾	STOCKPORT, p. 227.	175¾	
		MANCHESTER, p. 229.	182½	Trafford Park, Sir H. De Trafford, Bart.

Buxton is situated on the lower part of a deep valley surrounded by bleak hills and extensive tracks of moorland. The old town stands upon much higher ground than the new, and has the remains of a cross in the market-place. Buxton is celebrated for its waters, which annually attract from 12,000 to 14,000 visitors. They are of the calcareous class of mineral waters, and have long been celebrated for their medicinal virtues. Their temperature is lower than those of Bath, and they are more agreeable for bathing. They are administered internally to persons in whom the digestive organs are feeble, and are found very efficacious in the cure of gout and rheumatism. The Crescent at Buxton is an extensive and elegant structure, comprising two hotels, a library, an assembly-room, &c. The stables, which are of very great extent, are built in a circular form, and have a covered ride 160 yards round. This immense pile of building was erected by the 5th Duke of Devonshire at a cost of L.120,000. Near the Crescent is the Old Hall, built in the reign of Elizabeth by the Earl of Shrewsbury, in whose custody Mary Queen of Scots was placed. Here are still shown the apartments which the unfortunate Queen occupied in one of her visits to Buxton. The public baths at Buxton are very numerous, and are fitted up with every attention to the convenience of the visitors. St. Ann's Well is remarkable, because, by means of a double pump, either hot or cold water may be obtained within a few inches of each other. The church at Buxton is an elegant edifice built in 1812 by the late (sixth) Duke of Devonshire. Here are also places of worship for Presbyterians, Independents, and Wesleyan Methodists. The public walks at Buxton are laid out with much taste, and the environs abound with natural curiosities and romantic scenery. Half a mile distant is Poole's Hole, a cavern of considerable dimensions, containing among other curious objects an immense congelation, called the "Flitch of Bacon," and a large mass of stalactite called the "Queen of Scots Pillar," from having been visited by Mary during her sojourn at Buxton. Two miles from Buxton is the Diamond Hill, where the Buxton diamonds are found, close to which there is a tower built by the Duke of Devonshire. Four miles distant is Chee Tor, a huge mass of limestone, which rises above 300 feet perpendicular from the river Wye. There are various other places in the vicinity, which deserve a visit, such as Miller's Dale, Cresbrook, Monsal Dale, Ashford, Axe Edge, from which on a favourable day the mountains of North Wales may be seen, the Marvel Stone, &c. About five miles from Buxton, on the road to Castleton, is a spring called the "Ebbing and Flowing Well." Pop. of Buxton 1877.

MANCHESTER, as its name shows (Man-castra) was a Roman station, and is supposed to have taken its rise in the reign of Titus. Under the Saxons, it became the abode of a Thane. After the Norman Conquest, William gave the place to William of Poictou. The barony descended to the Gresleys, and the De la Warres, and at length the manorial rights became vested in the family of Moseley. In the civil wars, Manchester ranged itself on the side of the Parliament, and sustained a siege conducted by Lord Strange, afterwards Earl of Derby. Manchester was distinguished for its manufactures so early as the times of Henry VIII. and Edward VI. At first the woollen was its chief branch of trade; but since the middle of last century, cotton has taken the lead, and Manchester has now become the great centre of that manufacture. Of late, the spinning and weaving of silk have been introduced, and the printing and dyeing of silk are also extensively carried on in this city. The manufacture of machinery has risen to great importance and perfection in Manchester, and it has also manufactures of linen, small-wares, hats, umbrellas, &c. Its commerce is greatly aided by its communications with almost every part of England, by means of railways and canals. The district in which the city stands contains some of the best coal strata in England; a circumstance to which the place is indebted in no small degree for its prosperity. One of the most interesting buildings in Manchester is the collegiate church (now the cathedral), a noble Gothic building, containing several chapels and chantries, a richly ornamented choir, a number of monuments, &c. It was built in 1422. The reputed founder was Thomas Lord De la Warre, but several other persons assisted in building it. Considerable additions were made in the sixteenth century and many alterations and additions are of recent origin. Of the numerous chapels all but one are private property. The chapel of the Derby family is that which possesses the greatest share of historic interest. St Mary's chapel contains several interesting monuments of the family of the Chethams; and there is a marble statue of Humphry Chetham, erected by one who in early life was an inmate of Chetham's Hospital; and the Trafford chapel, in addition to the memorials of the ancient family from which it takes its name, possesses a very handsome monument to the memory of Dauntsey Hulme, Esq., a distinguished philanthropist. There is an Independent College in Manchester, and the Wesleyans have a College at Didsbury, four miles from Manchester. There are about 50 churches in Manchester, besides the cathedral; and a church-building society has been formed to promote additional church accommodation. The Dissenters have also numerous places of worship, and Manchester has been long distinguished as possessing a greater dissenting population than most other towns in the kingdom. The ecclesiastical government of Manchester was formerly vested in the warden and four fellows of the collegiate church, but it has recently been erected into a bishoprick, and the collegiate church consequently elevated to the rank of a cathedral. The first bishop was consecrated in 1847. The free grammar-school of Manchester was founded in the early part of the fifteenth century by Hugh Oldham, Bishop of Exeter, and is very richly endowed, but is far from effecting the good which its splendid resources might produce. Chetham's Hospital, or the College, was originally founded by the De la Warres, in the reign of Henry VI. After the dissolution, it became the property of the Derby family, and was purchased from the celebrated Countess of Derby, in compliance with the will of Humphry Chetham, an eminent merchant, for the purpose of forming a Blue-coat hospital and library. This institution provides for the education and support of eighty poor children. The library consists of upwards of 25,000 volumes, and there is an annual provision for its augmentation. The inhabitants of the town are allowed free access to it under certain regulations. The educational institutions in Manchester were long defective both in number and quality, but great exertions have been, and are now making to extend the benefits of instruction to all classes of the commnnity. One of the results of this commendable spirit is the Swinton School for poor children; a model of its kind. There are two Mechanics' Institutions in the town, several Lyceums, an institution called the Athenæum, a Literary and Philosophical Society, numerous charitable institutions, &c. The other public buildings worthy of notice are, the Exchange, the Infirmary, the Society of Arts or Royal Institution, the Town-Hall, the two Theatres, the new Museum of Natural History, the New Bailey Prison, the Chamber of Commerce, the Free Trade Hall, Free Library, Owen's College, &c &c. A Botanic Garden was formed here in 1830, and there are three Public Parks, the Peel, Phillips', and Queen's. There are six railways diverging from Manchester, which furnish the city with the greatest facilities for extending its trade—viz. the Liverpool and Manchester, the Manchester and Leeds, the Bolton and Bury, the Manchester and Birmingham, the Manchester and Sheffield, and the Manchester and Bowden lines. The immense mills, workshops, and foundries, well deserve a visit from the tourist. Manchester returns two M.P. Pop. 357,979. The Manchester races are held twice a-year at Lower Broughton.

Salford is separated from Manchester by the river Irwell. It is a large and populous town, returning one M.P. Here has been erected a monument to Sir R. Peel. Pop. 102,449.

ON RIGHT FROM LOND.	From Manch.		From London.	ON LEFT FROM LOND.
	61	From Hicks's Hall to DERBY.	126	Mark Eaton Hall, F Mundy, Esq.
	57¾	Kedleston Inn. In the church are several monuments of the Curzons, Lords Scarsdale.	129¼	Kedleston, the magnificent seat of Lord Scarsdale. The grounds are about 5 miles in circumference. In the park is a spring nearly allied in its qualities to the waters of Harrogate. The house may be seen every day from 11 o'clock, A.M. till 3 P.M.
Allestree Hall, W. Evans, Esq.	54¾	Weston Underwood Inn.	132¼	
	52¼	Cross-hands Inn.	134¾	
	50¼	The Black Swan.	136¾	
	48¾	Bateman Bridge.	138¼	
	47¼	Wallbrook Bridge.	139¾	
Wigwell Hall.	47	WIRKSWORTH, p. 232,	140	Hopton Hall.
Haddon Hall, (Duke of Rutland.)	43	Matlock.	144	
Chatsworth, the noble seat of the Duke of Devonshire.	34¼	Bakewell.	152¾	To Ashbourne, 15 miles.
2 miles distant, Hassop Hall, Countess of Newburgh. To Sheffield, 17 miles	32½	Ashford.	154½	Ashford Hall, Hon. G. H. Cavendish. In passing from Ashford to Wardlow, a view is obtained of Monsal Dale, one of the most delightful scenes in Derbyshire.
		cross River Wye.		
	31½	Little Longstone.	155½	
	29¼	Wardlow.	157¾	
To Castleton, 4½ miles.*		½ mile distant from the		At Whestone, one mile

* Castleton.—This town derives its name from a castle, the remains of which are situated on a steep rock. It is supposed to have been erected by William Peveril, the natural son of the Conqueror. It has been held at different times by various distinguished individuals; among others, by Simon de Montfort, and John of Gaunt. Owing to its situation, it was almost impregnable. This castle has given its title to Sir Walter Scott's Peveril of the Peak, and forms the scene of a considerable portion of the events of that popular novel. The vicinity of Castleton abounds in wild and romantic scenery. For centuries the only accessible road to Buxton and Chapel-en-le-Frith was by a deep descent called the Winnets or Windgates, from the stream of air that always sweeps through the chasm. Dark, rugged, and perpendicular precipices are seen on each side of the road. At one of the sudden turns of the road to the left, a most beautiful view of Castleton vale opens to the eye. Among the curiosities in the vicinity are the Peak Cavern or Devil's Cave, a magnificent and extraordinary work of nature, situated about 100 yards from the village. The mine called the Speedwell Level; the waterfall in the navigation mine which falls 30 yards; Mam-Tor, or the Shivering Mountain, 800 feet above the level of the valley, the summit exhibiting traces of a Roman encampment and of two barrows; the ancient lead mines of Odin, at the southern foot of Mam-Tor; Eldon Hole, 3 miles distant, between 70 and 80 yards in depth; Bradwell cavern, remarkable for the beauty and richness of the stalactites it contains, and the Blue John mine, situated on the side of Tree Cliff, opposite Mam Tor, the only mine in which this beautiful material is found in masses of sufficient size for working. Its recesses are supposed to be connected with a series of caverns extending over an area of many square miles, and including Eldon Hole, Peak cavern, Speedwell, and Bagshaw's cavern at Bradwell. The charge for exploring the mine is, for one person, 2s.; for three, 4s. 6d.; for four, 5s.; and 1s. per head for every additional person. The guides make an additional charge if a Bengal light be used. The churchyard of Hathersage, 6 miles from Castleton, is the reputed burial-place of Little John the companion of Robin Hood. The

ON RIGHT FROM LOND.	From Manch.		From London.	ON LEFT FROM LOND.
		road is Tideswell, a small town, situated in a valley amid bleak naked hills. The church, a fine building erected about the beginning of the 14th century, contains some curious monuments. The ebbing well, which is supposed to have given a name to the town, has ceased to flow.*		from Tideswell, there is an ancient cross of rather elegant design.
	20	CHAPEL-EN-LE-FRITH, a neat small town, supported by the manufacture of cotton.	167	Bank Hall. Horridge, T. G. Gisborne, Esq.
	17	Whaley Bridge.	170	Taxall Lodge.
		cr. river Goyt, and enter Cheshire.		
	$13\frac{3}{4}$	Disley.	$173\frac{1}{4}$	Lyme Park, T. Legh, Esq.
	12	Hoo Lane.	175	
Marple Hall, T. B. Isherwood, Esq.	$9\frac{1}{2}$	Bullock Smithy.	$177\frac{1}{2}$	Poynton Hall, Lord Vernon. Bramall Hall, W. D. Davenport, Esq.
Wood Bank.	7	STOCKPORT, or by the new road, which avoids the steep and disagreeable passage through the town.	180	
		cr. river Mersey.		Trafford Park, Sir H. De Trafford, Bart.
		MANCHESTER.	187	

WIRKSWORTH is a place of great antiquity, and the capital of the lead-mine district. The church is a handsome Gothic structure of the fourteenth century, and contains some interesting monuments and tombs. The lead-mines afford the chief means of employment, but there are cotton, hosiery, hat, and some other manufactories, in the neighbourhood.

The Barmote Courts for determining disputes among the miners, and offences against their ancient laws, are held here twice a-year; and here is deposited the ancient brass dish used as a standard for measuring the ore. Sir John Gell, the

road passes through Hope-Dale, a beautiful vale, in which is a very ancient village where a church existed before the Conquest.

* 4 miles from Tideswell is the pleasant village of Eyam, remarkable as the spot where the devotedness of Monpesson and his wife was exhibited during the great plague of 1666 The disease, which was conveyed by a box of cloth, spread with an astonishing rapidity, and carried off 250 persons out of a population of 330. Mr. Monpesson, who then held the living of Eyam, resisted all solicitations to desert his flock. To prevent as much as possible the effects of contagion, he closed the church, and preached to the people in a narrow dell, called Cucklett-dale, at a little distance from the town. For seven months, during which the pestilence continued its ravages, this devoted pastor watched over Eyam. He retained his health, but his wife fell a victim to the fury of the disease, and was buried in the churchyard, where her tombstone yet remains. Miss Seward was born at Eyam, of which her father was the rector. At a place on Eyam Moor, known as Wet-withins, is a druidical circle, consisting of sixteen stones, enclosing a space about ninety feet in diameter.

Parliamentary general, resided at Hopton, in this parish, but the ancient family seat is now pulled down. Pop. of town 2592.

Two miles from Wirksworth is Cromford, situated in a deep valley, enclosed on three sides by lofty limestone rocks. This town owes its prosperity to the cotton manufacture. The late Sir Richard Arkwright, the inventor of the spinning frame, erected here a spacious cotton-mill, now occupied by Messrs R. and P. Arkwright, who employ about 800 persons. To the left, after passing through Scarthin-Nick (a perforated rock), near Cromford, is Willersley Castle, a spacious mansion erected by Sir R. Arkwright, and now possessed by his grandson. The gardens and grounds are open on Mondays and Thursdays. Two miles from Cromford is the village of Matlock on the Derwent, a favourite summer resort for invalids and tourists. Matlockdale, in which the village stands, extends for two miles north and south, and is bounded on each side by steep rocks, whose naked sides rise to the height of about 300 feet. The Derwent flows through the dale, and its banks are lined with trees, except where the rocks rise almost perpendicularly from the water. Of these the most striking is the High Tor, which rises to a height of 396 feet. Opposite to it is Masson, a rock of greater elevation than the Tor, but inferior to it as a picturesque object. The mineral springs and beautiful scenery of Matlock have caused a great influx of visitors, for whose accommodation excellent inns, lodging-houses, and bathing establishments have been erected. The buildings are grouped in a singular manner up the mountain side. Matlock is not only a place full of interest in itself, but is also the centre of a district every part of which has its attractions. The usual amusement of strangers consists in visiting the caverns and mines, the petrifying wells and the rocks. Of the caverns, the Rutland cavern is the largest, and, when lighted up, has a very magnificent appearance. The Cumberland cavern is the most interesting to the geologist. The Devonshire cavern is remarkable for its flat roof and perpendicular sides. The Fluor cavern is the one from which the fluor spar is obtained. The Speedwell mine contains fine stalactites and spars; and in the Side-mine is a grotto, in which are to be found crystallizations of calcareous spar of unequalled beauty and richness. At the museums, the mineralogical productions are on sale, formed into vases and ornamental designs, and specimens of spars, fossils, &c. may be purchased.

The walks in the neighbourhood of Matlock are very delightful. The summit of Masson commands most attractive views over a vast extent of country. Two miles from Matlock, on the Wirksworth road, are the crags of Stonehouse, commanding a magnificent prospect. About the same distance is Bonsall, a picturesque mining village, with an ancient church and a curious old cross. The village of Old Matlock, two miles from Matlock-Bath, is inhabited chiefly by persons employed in the lead-mines and in the cotton manufacture. The "Romantic Rocks" are a very interesting series of masses and fragments, which appear as if just torn asunder, the angles exactly corresponding, so that if the spectator could by any possibility move them back, they would fit with the greatest nicety. Altogether, at Matlock the tourist, the geologist, and the mineralogist, may enjoy advantages which few other places can afford.

Eight miles north-west by west is Haddon Hall, the seat of the Duke of Rutland, situated on a bold eminence on the east side of the Wye, and affording a complete picture of an ancient baronial residence. No part of the building is of a date later than the sixteenth century. The tower over the gateway on the east side of the upper quadrangle is supposed to have been built in the reign of Edward III. The chapel is of the time of Henry VI.; and the tower at the north-west corner, on which are the arms of the Vernons, &c. is nearly of the same period. The gallery was erected in the reign of Queen Elizabeth. All the principal rooms, except the gallery, were hung with loose arras, a great part of which still remains. The doors were concealed behind the hangings, but there were great iron hooks by which the tapestry could be held back, to avoid the inconvenience of lifting it up every time of passing in and out. The workmanship of these doors is very rude and ill-fashioned. The chaplain's room is an interesting old place, and contains a number of objects calculated to convey an idea of the mode of living two centuries ago. The park was ploughed up and cultivated about sixty years since; but in the vicinity of the mansion there is still a sweeping group of luxuriant old trees. The gardens are composed of terraces ranging one above another, each having a sort of stone balustrade. The prospects from the leads and the watch-tower are extremely fine.

Haddon was, soon after the Conquest, the property of the Avenells, from whom it came to the Vernons. The last male heir of this family, Sir John Vernon, was commonly called the King of the Peak, on account of his hospitality and magnificent mode of living. He died in the seventh year of Elizabeth, and Haddon passed by marriage with one of his daughters into the possession of the family of Manners, then Earls of Rutland, and was their principal seat till the beginning of the last century, when it was superseded by Belvoir Castle in Leicestershire. In the reign of Queen Anne, the first Duke of Rutland maintained seven score servants in this ancient seat of old English hospitality.

The Duke of Rutland has a shooting seat at Stanton Woodhouse, in Darley Dale, a short distance from Haddon.

Twelve miles north by west of Matlock is Chatsworth, the magnificent mansion of the Duke of Devonshire. The public entrance to the domain is near the pretty village of Edensor, where there is an excellent inn for the accommodation of visitors. Chatsworth was among the domains given by William the Conqueror to William Peveril, his natural son;* but in the reign of Elizabeth, it was purchased by Sir W. Cavendish, who commenced a mansion house here, which, after his death, was completed by his widow, the famous Countess of Shrewsbury. The present building was nearly completed by the first Duke of Devonshire previous to 1706, but a wing was added by the late (sixth) Duke. It is composed of four nearly equal sides, with an open quadrangular court within. The middle of the court is occupied by a marble statue of Orion, seated on the back of a dolphin, round which the water of a fountain is continually playing. The rooms of this palace are spacious and lofty, some of them hung with tapestry, and adorned with beautiful carvings, executed by Gibbons and Watson. The pictures are not numerous, but there is a valuable col-

* See Scott's Peveril of the Peak, chap. i. p. 1.

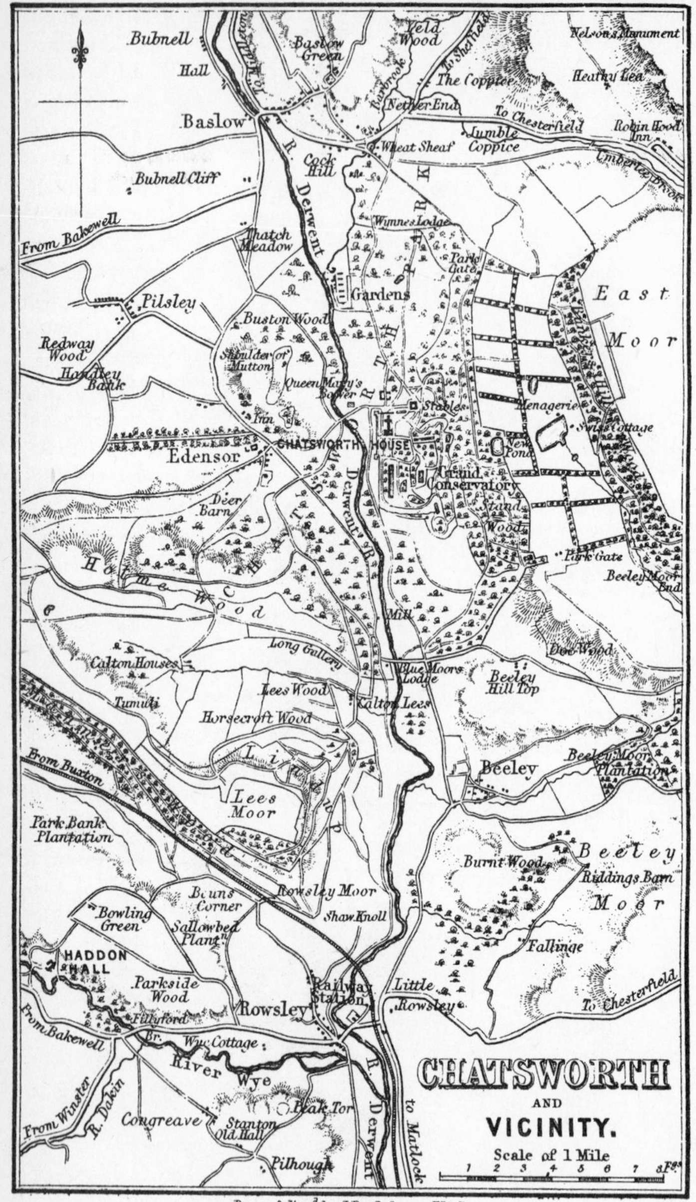

Drawn & Engd. by J. Bartholomew, Edinr.

Published by A. & C. Black, Edinburgh.

lection of books, and many exquisite works of sculpture by Canova, Thorwaldsen, Chantrey, Wyatt, Westmacott, &c. Chatsworth gardens are among the most celebrated in the kingdom. The grand conservatory is 300 feet long by 145 feet wide, and comprises an area of about an acre, in the centre of which is a carriage road. Nothing of the kind was ever before planned on so gigantic a style; but the late Duke of Devonshire was fortunate in the possession, as his servant, of Sir Joseph Paxton, now of Crystal Palace notoriety. To the south and south-east of the mansion are some curious water-works, formerly much celebrated. The park is about nine miles in circumference, and is beautifully diversified with hill and dale. The prospect from different parts of it are exceedingly fine. The old House of Chatsworth was for thirteen years the prison of Mary Queen of Scots,—a circumstance which caused her name to be given to a suite of apartments in the building, which are supposed to correspond in situation with those which she inhabited. It was here also that Hobbes, the philosopher, passed many of his days.

Four miles from Chatsworth is Bakewell, a place of great antiquity, much resorted to by anglers, as the river abounds with trout, grayling, &c. The manor of Bakewell originally belonged to William Peveril, natural son of William the Conqueror. It is now the property of the Duke of Rutland. In the town there is a cotton manufactory established by the late Sir R. Arkwright, and in the vicinity are marble works and lead mines. The church, an ancient cruciform structure, exhibits the styles of three different periods of architecture, and contains several curious monuments of the Vernon and Manners families. In the church-yard is an ancient cross. On Stanton manor, four miles distant, are rocking-stones and a Druidical circle.

A delightful excursion may be made from Matlock to Dove Dale,* distant 13 miles. The scenery of this far-famed spot is of the most romantic description. In the vicinity is the town of Ashbourne, the church of which contains numerous monuments, including a beautiful specimen of sculpture by Banks, to the memory of a daughter of a former Sir Brook Boothby. Ashbourne Hall, till lately the mansion of this family, is situated in the vicinity. Here the Pretender spent a night in 1745. At Mayfield, near Ashbourne, is the cottage in which Moore composed "Lalla Rookh." On the Staffordshire side of the Dove is Ilam Hall, the mansion of Jesse Watts Russell, Esq. Ilam church is a venerable ivy-covered edifice, and contains an interesting monument by Chantrey.

Pleasing excursions may also be made from Matlock to the Druidical remains at Arbor Low,—the Router Rock,—Robin Hood's Stride,—the masses of rocks bearing the name of Bradley Tor, which are all within a short distance, and are objects of attraction to the antiquarian, the artist, and the lover of remarkable and picturesque scenery.

Winfield Manor House, Hardwick House, and Newstead Abbey, formerly the property of Byron, and now that of Colonel Wildman, are frequently visited by parties from Matlock, and will amply repay the notice of the tourist.

* See description of the Dove in Walton and Cotton's Angler, Major's Edition, p. 277, &c.

BY RAILWAY, 97¼ Miles.

ON RIGHT FROM BIRM.	From Liverp.		From Birmin.	ON LEFT FROM BIRM.
	97¼	From Birmingham to		
Perry Hall, J. Gough, Esq.	93¾	Perry Bar St.	3½	Hampstead Hall.
	90¾	Newton Road St.	6½	Sandwell Park, Earl of Dartmouth.
Great Bar Hall, Sir F. E. Scott, Bart.		cr. river Tame.		Charlemont. Darlaston is ¾ m., and Bilston, 2½ miles distant.
2 m. distant is Walsall.	87¾	Bescot Junction St.	9½	
	85½	Willenhall St.	11¾	
Bentley Hall, the house in which King Charles lay concealed after the battle of Worcester. Moseley Court. Hilton Hall.	83	WOLVERHAMPTON. p. 237, (126¼ miles from London.)	14¼	To Wrottesley Hall, (Lord Wrottesley) 5 m. Dunstall Hall, H. Hordern, Esq. Oxley Hall, A. Hordern, Esq.
	77¼	Four Ashes St.	20	Somerford Hall.
Hatherton Hall, Lord Hatherton.	75¾	Spread Eagle St.	21½	2 miles distant, Stretton Hall, and beyond Weston Park, Earl of Bradford.
Teddesley Hall, Lord Hatherton.	73¼	Penkridge St.	24	
Tillington House.	68	STAFFORD, p. 211. Here the Trent Valley line joins.	29¼	
3½ miles distant is Stone, on the line of the North Staffordshire Railway, which branches off at the Norton Br. station.	62¼	Norton Bridge St.	35	Seighford Hall, F. Eld, Esq. 2½ m. distant is Eccleshall, in the church of which Bishop Halse concealed Queen Margaret after her escape from Mucklestone. Near it is Eccleshall Castle, (Bishop of Lichfield,) founded at a very early period, and rebuilt 1510. (See p. 12.)
Swinnerton, T. Fitzherbert, Esq., and beyond, Darlaston Hall, S. S. Jervis, Esq., and Meaford Hall, Viscount St Vincent. Trentham Park, Duke of Sutherland.	58¾	Standon Bridge St.	38½	
Whitmore Hall, E. Mainwaring, Esq. Butterton Hall.	54¼	Whitmore, (from London, 155¾ miles.) Newcastle-under-Lyme is 4½ miles distant, and Stoke upon Trent 6½ miles distant. This station is fixed here as an accommodation to the potteries.	43	

ON RIGHT FROM BIRM.	From Liverp.		From Birm.	ON LEFT FROM BIRM.
To Newcastle-under-Lyme, 5½ miles; Potteries, 7 miles.	51½	Madeley St.	45¾	To Woore, 3½ miles, Audlem, 8 miles distant.
Betley Hall, C. Tollet, Esq.	43¼	Crewe Junction St. (from London 166½ m.)	54	Crewe has now become an important centre of railway communication; lines to Chester, Manchester, Lancaster, and the Potteries, unite here, and there are extensive refreshment rooms, with every accommodation for passengers.
Crewe Hall, Lord Crewe.	41¾	Coppenhall.	55¼	
Manor Hall.	39	Minshull Vernon St.	58¼	
Stanthorne Hall.	36¾	Winsford St.	61	
2 miles distant is Northwich, the inhabitants of which are chiefly employed in the manufacture of salt, which is obtained from brine springs in the vicinity. Pop. 1368.	32	HARTFORD St.	65¼	Winsford village is celebrated for its salt-works.
Winnington Hall, Lord Stanley of Alderley. Marbury Hall, J. H. S. Barry, Esq.	29¼	Acton St.	68	Vale-Royal (Lord Delamere), erected on the site of an ancient abbey.
Wincham Hall.	25	Preston Brook St.	72	Aston Park, Sir A. J. Aston, G.C.B.
Belmont Hall, J. Leigh, Esq.	22½	Moore St.	74	Norton Priory, Sir R. Brooke, Bart.
Arley Hall (R. E. Egerton Warburton, Esq.) in the distance.	19	WARRINGTON, (and 190¼ m. from London.)	78	Bewsay Hall, Lord Lilford.

WOLVERHAMPTON (122 miles N. W. by W. of London, and 14 miles N. W. of Birmingham) is a place of great antiquity, and the most populous town in Staffordshire. A monastery was erected here about the tenth, and refounded in the sixteenth century, but no remains of it now exist. Of its numerous churches, St. Peter's (the collegiate church) is the most remarkable. It is an ancient Gothic edifice, containing many brasses and other monuments, a curious font, and a stone pulpit, more than 800 years old, cut out of one block. In the church-yard is an ancient cross, covered with a profusion of rude sculpture. The chief manufacture of the town consists in locks and keys, japanned goods, and other articles of hardware. Two M.P. Pop. of parl. borough, 147,670.

Two miles distant is Tettenhall, the church of which contains a carved font, and a curious painted window.

Three miles distant from Stafford is Ingestre Hall, Earl of Shrewsbury; near which are Tixall Hall, Sir T. A. C. Constable, Bart.; Sandon Hall, Earl of Harrowby, and Shugborough, Earl of Lichfield. The latter was the birth-place of the celebrated naval commander and circumnavigator, Lord Anson.

The Crewe and Chester Railway commences at Crewe (166 miles from London), and leads by Nantwich, 4 miles; Calveley, 7¾ m.; Beeston, 10¼ m.; Tattenhall, 14 m.; Waverton, 18 m.; to Chester, 21 miles; thence to Birkenhead. 15 miles. Distance from Chester to Holyhead by railway, 85 m., and thence to Dublin per steamer, 60 miles. A steam-boat leaves George's Pier Head, Liverpool, for Monk's Ferry, 20 minutes before the train starts from Birkenhead, and returns to Liverpool on the arrival of the trains from Chester.

WARRINGTON is one of the principal stations on the line, being midway between Liverpool and Manchester. About half a mile from the station is the large and populous town of Warrington, on the north bank of the Mersey in Lancashire. It is one of the oldest towns in Lancashire, and was a Roman station. A bridge was built here over the Mersey by the Earl of Derby, for the purpose of enabling Henry VII. to pay him a visit with greater convenience. The principal manufactures are cottons, shoes, and fustians, and in the vicinity are pin, glass, and iron-works. Vessels of 70 or 80 tons burthen can come up the river to within a short distance of the town. The church is of Saxon origin, and erected before the Conquest, but the injuries which it received during the civil wars have destroyed most of the traces of its antiquity. It contains some curious monuments, especially one to the memory of Sir Thomas Boteler and his lady. There are also chapels of ease, meeting-houses, free schools, &c. During the Civil Wars, Warrington was the scene of several severe conflicts. From the press of this town, the first newspaper ever published in Lancashire was issued, and it was also the first town in the country from which a stage-coach was started. Howard's work on Prisons was printed at Warrington, as were also the most of Mrs Barbauld's poems, the earlier writings of the late Thomas Roscoe, the works of Dr Ferrier, Gibson, and many others. In 1757, an academy was established here, which rapidly rose into celebrity, under the direction of Dr Aikin, Dr Priestley, Dr Taylor, Dr Enfield, and the Rev. Gilbert Wakefield, but the establishment was unfortunately broken up in 1783, and from its fragments a college was formed at York, which has been recently transferred to Manchester. Bradley Hall, in the neighbourhood of Warrington, is supposed to occupy the site of one of the castles of the Haydocks, a powerful family in Lancashire during the time of the Plantagenets. One M.P. Pop. of parl. borough 1861, 26,947. Warrington affords an earldom to the Grey family, Earls of Stamford and Warrington.

About two miles and a half from Warrington station is WINWICK, which (with the exception of Doddington in Cambridgeshire) possesses the richest rectory in the kingdom, the patronage of which has been lodged in the hands of the Stanley family since the reign of Henry VI. According to tradition, this place was the favourite residence of Oswald, King of Northumbria, and near the church is pointed out the spot where he fell fighting against the pagans of Mercia, A.D. 642. St Oswald's Well, about half a mile to the north of the church, was originally formed, according to Bede, by the piety of pilgrims who visited the spot. The earth and water are supposed to be possessed of peculiar sanctity, and from it all the neighbouring Roman Catholic chapels are supplied with holy water. The church, a large irregular structure, of very remote antiquity, contains a number of interesting monuments and curious brasses. There are no less than thirty-seven endowed charities in the parish.

Two miles and a quarter from Winwick is NEWTON JUNCTION STATION, (84 miles from Birmingham, 196½ from London,) where the Grand Junction Railway terminates, and the journey to Manchester or Liverpool is continued on the Liverpool and Manchester Railway.

This Railway was opened September 15, 1830, and cost nearly L.1,000,000 sterling. The principal station is in Lime Street, Liverpool.

ON RIGHT FROM LIVER.	From Manch.		From Liverp.	ON LEFT FROM LIVER.
		Lime St. Station.		Newsham House.
Childwall Hall, Marquis of Salisbury.	28	Broad Green St.	3½	Croxteth Park, Earl of Sefton.
Roby Hall.	26¼	Roby St.	5¼	The Hasles, Sir T. B. Birch, Bart., and beyond Knowsley Park, Earl of Derby.
Halsnead Hall, R. Willis, Esq.	26	Huyton St.	5½	
	24½	Huyton Quarry St.	6½	Prescot, noted for its manufacture of watch tools and movements. In the vicinity are numerous collieries. Pop. 6066.
	22½	Rainhill St.	9	
	21¼	Lea Green St.	10¼	
Bold Hall, Sir H. Bold Hoghton, Bart.	19¾	ST HELEN'S JUNCTION ST. (90 m. from Birmingham 202½ m. from London.)	11¾	Eccleston Hall. Shirley Hall. St Helen's. Here are copper and glass works. A coal railroad leads to Runcorn. The manufactory of plate-glass at Ravenhead is the largest establishment of the kind in the kingdom. Pop. of St Helens 18,396.
	18	Collin's Green.	13½	
At a distance Bewsay Hall, Lord Lilford.		cr. Sankey Viad.		
	16¾	Warrington Junction Station.	14¾	
Winwick Hall.	15¾	NEWTON STATION. Here the Grand Junction Railway joins.	15¾	At a distance Gareswood Hall and New Hall, Sir R. T. Gerard, Bart.
	15¼	Preston Junction St.	16	Haydock Lodge, and Golborne Park, T. Legh, Esq.
	15	PARKSIDE ST. (85¾ miles from Birmingham, and 198¼ from London.) There is a tablet erected near the spot where Mr Huskisson was killed on the day of the opening of this railway. The North Union Railway branches off here to Wigan and Preston.	16½	At Newton there is an old hall, said to have been formerly the residence of royalty. ¾ of a mile distant there is an ancient barrow covered with very old oaks.
	12¾	KENYON JUNCTION STATION. Here the Bolton and Leigh Railway joins.	18¾	Pennington and Pennington Hall.
	10¾	Bury Lane St.	20¾	
		Flow Moss. The Railway here crosses Chat Moss, which, until the formation of the railroad, was a most dangerous and treacherous bog, in some places 30 feet deep.		
	8½	Astley St.	23	
Trafford Park, Sir Humphery De Trafford, Bart.	7¾	Barton Moss St.	23¾	
	5	Patricroft St.	26½	Worsley Hall, the noble residence of the Earl of Ellesmere.
	4	Eccles St.	27½	

ON RIGHT FROM LIVER.	From Manch.		From Liverp.	ON LEFT FROM LIVER.
	3	Weaste Lane St.	28½	
	1¾	Cross Lane St.	29¾	
		MANCHESTER. 85 m. from Birmingham; 188½ m. from London.	31½	

XCIV. BIRMINGHAM TO MANCHESTER, BY RAILWAY, DIRECT, 85 Miles.

ON RIGHT FROM BIRM.	From Manch.	From Birmingham on the Grand Junct. Rail.	From Birm.	ON LEFT FROM BIRM.
Crewe Hall, Lord Crewe.	31	CREWE St. (p. 247.)	54	
Brereton Hall, and beyond, Somerford Park, Sir C. Shakerley, Bart.	26¼	SANDBACH ST.	58¾	
	22¾	HOLMES CHAPEL.	62¼	Peover Hall, Sir H. M. Mainwaring, Bart.
	17	CHELFORD ST.	68	
Davenport Hall, and Swettenham Hall.	13¾	Alderley St.	71¼	To Altringham, or Altrincham, 8 miles, a market town, which has some manufactories of yarn, worsted, and cotton. It is connected with Manchester by a railway 7¾ miles in length. Pop. 6628.
	12	Wilmslow St.	73	
Withington Hall, Astle Park.	10½	Handforth St.	74½	
Alderley Park, Lord Stanley of Alderley.	8¾	Cheadle St.	76¼	
Mottram Hall. Poynton Park, Lord Vernon.	5¼	STOCKPORT ST.	79¾	
Branch to Macclesfield, 9 miles.	5¼	Seaton, Norris St.	79¾	
	4½	Heaton, Chapel St.	80½	
	3	Levenshulme St.	82	
	1¾	Longsight St.	83¼	
		MANCHESTER.	85	

This railway commences at a spacious station in London Road, Manchester, which is to be used jointly by this and the Manchester and Sheffield Railway Company. The railway is conducted through Manchester upon a viaduct, in which occurs an extraordinary skew arch, crossing Fairfield Street at an angle of only 24½ degrees. The span of the bridge is about 128 feet 9 inches. It is considered to be one of the finest specimens of iron-bridge building ever executed. The viaduct, at the Manchester end of the line, contains considerably more than 100 arches. At Stockport is an immense viaduct, which crosses the Mersey at an elevation of 111 feet measured to the top of the parapet. Soon after leaving this viaduct the railway enters a deep cutting, in which occurs a short tunnel 297 yards long, the only one on the line. On the remaining portion of the line are several extensive viaducts. The Bolling viaduct consists of 11 arches, of 49 feet span. The Peover viaduct, crossing the river of that name, consists of 9 or 10 arches of about 40 feet span, and 70 feet high. The Dane viaduct consists of 23 arches of 63 feet span, and crosses the river Dane at an elevation of about 95 feet from the surface of the water to the top of the parapet.

This railway was opened throughout the whole line on the 10th of August 1842.

ON RIGHT FROM LOND.	From Liverp.		From London.	ON LEFT FROM LOND.
Midland Railway, to Leicester and Derby (chap. cxxvii.). Newbold. Harborough Magna.	118¼	From London to RUGBY, (pp. 199-203). cr. riv. Avon. cr. Oxford Canal.	82¾	Leave main line of N. Western Railway. Holbrook Grange. Oxford Canal.
Newbold Revel, Sir T. G. Skipwith, Bart. Monks Kirby, 2 m. and beyond, Newnham-Paddox, Earl of Denbigh. Withybrook.	113¾	Stretton St. Stretton is on the Fosse Way, an ancient line of Roman (or probably British) road.	87¼	Brinklow, and beyond, Combe Abbey, Earl Craven, 8 miles.
	110½	Shilton St.	90½	To Coventry, 6 miles. Anstey Hall.
	108¼	Bulkington St. cr. Ashby de la Zouch Canal, and enter valley of R. Anker, a tributary of the Trent.	92¾	Coventry, 6 miles. Bedworth, 2 miles. Arbury Park, C. N. Newdegate Esq., 2 miles. Chilvers Coton.
Hinckley, 4 m. (see p. 210). Weddington Hall and Lindley Hall. Caldecote Hall. Line of ancient Watling St.	104½	Nuneaton St. Nuneaton is a considerable and well-built market town, 8½ miles from Coventry, and 23 m. from Birmingham. The ribbon manufacture is carried on here, and abundance of coal is procured in the neighbourhood. Population, of town, 4645.	96½	Stockingford, 2 miles. Ansley Hall, Sir J. N. L. Chetwode, Bart., 3½ miles. Oldbury Hall. 1 m. before Atherstone is Mancetter, the site of the Roman *Manduessedum.* Mancetter House. Bentley Park.
Gopsall, Earl Howe, 5 m. To Ashby de la Zouch, 13¾ miles. Grendon Hall, Sir G. Chetwynd, Bart.	99¼	Atherstone St. (see p. 210). Cross Watling Street. cr. Coventry Canal twice. cr. riv. Anker.	101¾	Baxterley Hall, 2½ m. To Coleshill, 10 miles Merevale Park, W. S. Dugdale, Esq. Coventry Canal parallel.
Shuttington. Amington Hall, C. H. W. A'Court, Esq.	95¾	Polesworth St. cr. riv. Anker. Cross Birmingham and Derby Railway.	105¼	Pooley Hall.
Railway to Derby, 24 miles. Wiggington. Camberford Hall. Fisherwick	91½	TAMWORTH ST. Enter Staffordshire. cr. riv. Tame, (an affluent of the Trent), and Coventry Canal, which for some distance runs parallel to the former.	109½	Railway to Birmingham, 17 miles. Drayton Manor, Sir R. Peel, Bart. Wiggington Lo. Whittington. Swinfen Park, J. Swinfen, Esq., 2 miles. Freeford Hall, R. Dyott, Esq., 1 mile

ON RIGHT FROM LOND.	From Liverp.		From London.	ON LEFT FROM LOND.
Burton on Trent, 11½ m. The road between Lichfield and Burton is part of the Icknield St., an ancient British way. Kings Bromley, 2½ m.	85¼	Lichfield St. Cross line of S. Staffordshire Railway.	115¾	Town of Lichfield, 1½ mile (see p. 210). Stow House and Stow Hill. Elmhurst Hall. Haunch Hall.
Abbots Bromley, 6 m. distant, is a market-town, Pop. 1508.	80¾	Armitage St. cr. Grand Trunk Canal, and riv. Trent.	120¼	Longdon. Armitage, 1 mile. Beaudesert Park, Marquis of Anglesey. Armytage Park.
Colton Hall. Colton, and beyond, Blithfield Hall, **Lord** Bagot. Bishton Hall.	77½	Rugeley St. (see p. 211). Proceed along valley of riv. Trent. North Staffordshire line branches off to right, shortly before reaching	123½	Hagley Park, Baroness de la Zouche. Wolseley Hall. Wolseley Park, Sir C. Wolseley Bart.
Shugborough **Park,** Earl of Lichfield. Tixal Park, Sir T. A. C. Constable, Bart., and beyond, Ingestre **Hall,** Earl of Shrewsbury and **Talbot.**	74½	Colwich St. cr. riv. Trent, and along valley of small riv. Sow. cr. Stafford and Worcester Canal, and riv. Penk.	126½	Milford Hall. Baswick.
Queensbury Lo.		Rejoin main line of N. Western Railway shortly before reaching		
	68½	STAFFORD ST. Thence to	132½	Branch to Shrewsbury, 29 miles (total from London to Shrewsbury by this route, 161½ miles).
Crewe Hall, (Lord Crewe). Branch from Crewe to Manchester, as in p. 240, 31 m.;—making the total from London to Manchester, by this route 188½ miles.	43¾	CREWE, as in pp. 236, 7. From Crewe, by Warrington, to	157¼	Branch from Crewe, by Chester, to Birkenhead, 36½ m., making the total distance from London to Birkenhead by this route, 193½ miles.
Knowsley Park, Earl of Derby. Croxteth Park, Earl of Sefton.	13¾	Newton Bridge (on the Liverpool and Manchester line, p. 233). Thence to	187¼	
		LIVERPOOL (p. 239).	201	Childwall Hall, Marquis of Salisbury.

XCVI. LONDON TO WARWICK AND LEAMINGTON, BY RAILWAY,

97¾ Miles.

ON RIGHT FROM LOND.	From Leamin.		From London.	ON LEFT FROM LOND.
		From London, by North Western Railway, to		
Leave main line to Birmingham, 18½ miles.	9¼	COVENTRY (p. 203). The railway here turns to the southward.	86½	Whitley Abbey, Viscount Hood, 1½ miles.
Kenilworth Castle, 1 mile (see p. 194). Leek Wootton.	4¼	Kenilworth St.	93½	Baginton Hall, 2 m. Stoneleigh Abbey, Lord Leigh, 2 miles. Stoneleigh Park, Lord Leigh, 1½ m. Ashow.
Milverton. Warwick Castle, Earl of Warwick, 1½ mile (p. 193).		cr. river Avon. A short distance to the right of the line is Guy's Cliff, and, near it, Blacklow Hill (see p. 194). LEAMINGTON.	97	Town of Leamington, ¾ mile (see p. 194).

XCVII. LONDON TO SHREWSBURY, THROUGH BIRMINGHAM, BY RAILWAY

156¼ Miles.

ON RIGHT FROM LOND.	From Shrewsb.		From London.	ON LEFT FROM LOND.
	43¾	From London to Birmingham (p. 203).	112½	
Leave main line to Liverpool and Manchester.	29½	Thence to Wolverhampton St. (p. 236).	126¾	In the distance Himley Hall, Lord Ward.
Bilbrook House.	28½	Stafford Road St. cr. Stafford and Worcester Canal.	127¾	Dunstall Park. Tettenhall. The Wergs.
Chillington Pak, T W. Giffard, Esq., 1¼ mile.	25	Codsal St. Enter Shropshire.	131½	Wrottesley Park, Lord Wrottesley, 1 mile, and beyond, Patshull Park, Sir R. Pigot, Bart., 1½ m.
Donington. Tonge, and Tonge Castle; beyond, Weston Park, Earl of Bradford, 2¾ miles.	22	Albrighton St.	134¼	Albrighton Hall. Boningale, 1¼ mile. Hatton Hall, R. A. Slaney, Esq. 1½ mile.

ON RIGHT FROM LOND.	From Shrewsb.		From London.	ON LEFT FROM LOND.
Aston Hall. Decker Hill. Priors Leigh.	17¼	SHIFFNAL, (see p. 179) a large market town, formerly a great thoroughfare for coach traffic. Population of parish, 5923	139	Shifnal Manor, Lord Stafford. Colebrook Dale, 6 miles (p. 178). New Dawley.
Wombridge.		Through Oakengates Tunnel.		
Hadley.	13¼	Oakengates St. Oakengates, a small place on the line of Watling St., is the *Uxacona* of the Roman Itineraries.	143	Ketley Iron Works.
Junction of branch from Stafford, 29 miles. Admaston.	10¼	Wellington St. (see p. 179).	146	Colebrook Dale, 4¾ m. The Wrekin, 1320 feet high.
Allscot.		Admaston Street.		Orleton Hall.
	6¼	Walcot St.	150	Wrockwardine. Uppington, 1½ mile.
Withington.		cr. river Tern and Shrewsbury Canal.		
	3¾	Upton Magna St.	152½	Attingham Park, Lord Berwick.
Uffington, and beyond Sundorne Castle, A. W. Corbet, Esq.		cr. Shrewsbury Canal.		Longner Castle.
		cr. river Severn.		Longner Hall.
		SHREWSBURY (p. 147).	156¼	

XCVIII. SHREWSBURY TO CHESTER AND BIRKENHEAD, BY RAILWAY, 57½ miles.

ON RIGHT FROM SHREWS.	From Birkenh.		From Shrewsb.	ON LEFT FROM SHREWS.
Green Fields. Preston Gubbals, 1 mile, and beyond, Hardwick Grange, Viscount Hill, and Acton Reynald Hall, Sir V. R. Corbet, Bart.	53¼	From Shrewsbury to Leaton St.	4¼	Berwick Hall, Hon. H. W. Powys. Beyond river Severn, Ross Hall, and further on, Isle Park.

RIGHT FROM SHREW.	From Birkenh.		From Shrewsb.	ON LEFT FROM SHREW.
Middle, 2 miles.	50	Baschurch St.	7½	Walford.
Weston Lullingfields. Bagley. Woodhouse, 1½ mile.		cr. river Perry, a small affluent of the Severn.		Ruyton, 2¼ miles. Boreatton Hall. Boreatton Park. Pradoe, T. Kenyon, Esq., 1½ mile
To Ellesmere, 6 miles.	44½	Rednall St.	13	Tedsmore Hall, E. B. Owen, Esq., 1 mile.
Halston Hall.		cr. Llanymynech branch of Ellesmere Canal.		Aston Hall, W. Lloyd, Esq., 1¾ mile.
		Cross high road from London to Holyhead.		
Whittington Castle, in ruins. Ellesmere, 5¾ miles (see p. 148).	41½	Whittington St.	16	Oswestry, 2 miles (see p. 180).
Belmont.	39½	Gobowen St.	18	Branch to Oswestry, 2¼ miles; near Oswestry, Porkington, W. O. Gore, Esq.
	37¾	Presgwyn St.	19¾	
		cr. Ellesmere Canal, and river Ceriog, and enter Wales.		Aqueduct of Ellesmere Canal.
Chirk Bank. Brynkinalt, Viscount Dungannon.	36¾	Chirk St. (see p. 180).	20¾	Chirk Castle, M. Biddulph, Esq.
Vale of Llangollen, celebrated for the beauty of its scenery.	35½	Llangollen Road St.	22¼	Llangollen, 5 miles. Corwen, 14 miles.
		Viaduct across valley of Dee.		
Bellan Place. Wynnstay Park, Sir W. W. Wynn, Bart.	34	Cefn St.	23½	Pont-y-Cyssyllte aqueduct, by which the Ellesmere Canal is carried across the river Dee, a fine specimen of engineering skill.
Overton, 5 miles.	32¾	Ruabon St.	24¾	The scenery in the neighbourhood of Ruabon is of the most romantic and striking description.
Hafod.	30¾	Rhos St.	26¾	
Erthig. Acton Park, Sir R. H. Cunliffe, Bart.	27½	WREXHAM St. (see pp. 148, 207). Pop. of par. 1851, 15,520.	30	Pentrebychan. Mold, 11 miles. Gwersylt Hall. Gwersylt Hill.
		cr. river Alen.		
Gresford Lodge, Sir H. A. Johnson, Bart. Trefalen Hall.	24½	Gresford St.	33	Mount Alyn.
	23	Rossett St.	34½	

RIGHT FROM SHREW.	From Birkenh.		From Shrewsb.	ON LEFT FROM SHREW.
Darland Hall.		cr. Pulford Brook, and enter Cheshire.		
Eaton Hall, 1¾ mile, Marquis of Westminster (see p. 149).	21¼	Pulford St.	36¼	Doddleston.
	17½	Saltney St.	40	
		Join Chester and Holyhead line, and cr. river Dee.		
Branch from Crewe, 21½ miles, joins here.	15½	CHESTER (see p. 149).	42	Chester Lunatic Asylum.
Moston Hall.		cr. Dee and Mersey Canal.		
Backford. Stanney Wood. Great Sutton. Sutton Hall.	12½	Mollington St.	45	Mollington Hall, F. Ffielden, Esq.
	8½	Sutton St.	49	Capenhurst. Burton Hall, 3 miles. Puddington Hall, 2¾ m.
Hooton Hall, 1¼ mile.	7½	Hooton St.	50	Willaston, 1¼ mile.
Bromborough Hall.	6½	Bromborough St.	51	Poulton Hall.
	4½	Spital St.	53	
Derby House.	3½	Bebington St.	54	Bebington.
	2½	Rock Lane St.	55	
River Mersey, and on opposite side, LIVERPOOL. (See p. 221.)	1½	Tranmere St.	56	Tranmere.
		BIRKENHEAD.	57½	Leasowe Castle, Major-General Hon. Sir E. Cust, 4 miles.

From an insignificant village, Birkenhead has, within the space of a few years, grown into an important and flourishing seaport town. According to the census of 1831, it contained at that time only 2599 inhabitants, which number had in 1861 increased to 51,649. The astonishing rapidity with which it progressed for some time has not however been maintained more recently. Extensive docks, of sufficient capacity to receive vessels of the largest class, have been constructed here, and a variety of public works undertaken; and the town altogether promises to become in time a rival in importance to its gigantic neighbour on the opposite side of the Mersey.

ON RIGHT FROM LOND.	From Holyhd.		From London.	ON LEFT FROM LOND.
		From London, by North Western Railway (Trent Valley line), to		
Crewe Hall, (Lord Crewe). Leave main line to Liverpool and Manchester.	105¾	CREWE (p. 242). Thence, by Chester and Crewe line, cr. river Weaver.	157¼	At Crewe are extensive refreshment and waiting rooms, with every convenience for the accommodation of passengers.
	102	Nantwich St.	161	Nantwich, 3¾ miles (see p. 213).
Wettenhall, 2½ miles.		cr. Middlewich branch of Ellesmere and Chester Canal.		Worleston, and beyond, the Rookery. Poole Hall. Wardle.
Calveley Hall, E. D. Davenport, Esq.	97½	Calveley St.	165½	Haughton Hall, and in the distance Cholmondeley Castle, Marquis of Cholmondeley.
4 miles distant, Oulton Hall, Sir P. De G. Egerton, Bart. Tilstone Fearnall.		cr. Ellesmere and Chester Canal, The course of which the line follows nearly the whole way to Chester.		Bunbury.
Tilstone Lodge, J Tollemache, Esq. Tarporley, 2 miles (see p. 214), and ½ mile beyond, to the right, Eaton Banks.	95¼	Beeston St.	167¾	Beeston Castle, in ruins, 1½ mile. Burwardsley, 2 miles; beyond Bolesworth Castle.
Hargrave. Waverton.	91¼	Tattenhall St.	171¾	Tattenhall, 1½ mile.
	88¼	Waverton St.	174¾	Hatton Hall. Saighton. Boughton.
Rowton Heath. Christleton.		cr. Ellesmere and Chester Canal.		
	84½	CHESTER.	178½	Eaton Hall, Marquis of Westminster, 4 miles (see p. 149).
Chester and Birkenhead line, 15¼ miles. River Dee, here running in a straight line, in an artificial channel.		The railway passes round the city on the northern and western sides, and, bending southward, crosses the river Dee, nearly along the south bank of which it runs to		Two miles beyond Chester, enter Wales. Branch line to Mould, 9 miles (p. 207). Broughton.
	77½	Queen Ferry St.	185½	Hawarden, and Hawarden Castle, Sir S. R. Glynne, Bart. 1½ m. (p. 214).
Estuary of the Dee, which changes with the state of the tide from a magnificent arm of the sea, more than three miles in width, to a dreary expanse of sand and ooze, in which the river forms an insignificant and narrow channel.		Along south side of estuary of Dee to		Aston Hall. Welsh mountains. Northop, 3½ miles.
	72	Flint St. Flint is a borough and seaport town, the inhabitants of which are chiefly employed in the coal	191	Halkyn Castle, Marquis of Westminster.

ON RIGHT FROM LOND.	From Holyhd.		From London.	ON LEFT FROM LOND.
Ruins of Flint Castle. Richard II. was a prisoner here, and the castle was besieged and taken by the Parliamentary army during the civil wars.		works and lead mines in the vicinity. It has extensive wharfs, accessible to vessels of 300 tons burden. It is also a bathing place. Conjointly with St. Asaph, Holywell, Mold, and four other small burghs, Flint returns 1 M.P. Pop. 3428.		
	193	Bagillt St.	77	
	67¾	HOLYWELL St.	195¼	Holywell, 1¼ mile (see p. 215). Greenfield Hall, R. Richardson, Esq. Downing, 1 mile.
Point of Air, with lighthouse on its summit.	64½	Mostyn St. Two miles beyond, leave the shore; again approach the sea, before reaching	198½	Mostyn Hall, Lord Mostyn. Gronant. Talacre, Sir P. Mostyn, Bt. Llanasaph.
	58¼	Prestatyn St.	204¾	
Rhyl Hall. After leaving the estuary of the Dee, the sea is visible on the right hand nearly the whole way.	54½	RHYL St. cr. river Clwyd.	208½	Rhuddlan, 2 miles. The old castle is an object of great interest. St Asaph, 5½ miles (see p. 215.) Kinmel Park, late Lord Dinorben.
Llandrylloyn Rhos. Bryn Dinarth. Llangwystenin. Marl. Boddyscallan. Gloddaeth, Lord Mostyn.	50¼	Abergele St. Penmaen Rhos Tunnel.	212¾	Gwrych Castle, L. H. B. Hesketh, Esq. Llandulas. Bryndulas, J. Hesketh, Esq. Moranedd, Bronywendon, and Tangrallt. Coed Coch, 2½ miles. Colwyn village. Minydon, Mrs. Clough. Glanyden, H. Hesketh, Esq. Groesyneirion. Mochdre.
	44½	Colwyn St. 6½ miles beyond, leave the shore, which stretches out, and terminates in the promontory of Great Orme's Head. Cross mouth of river Conway by tubular bridge.	218½	Brynsteddfod, Archdeacon Jones. Pwll-y-Crochan, Lady Erskine. Llansaintfraid, 1½ m. Pendyffryn.
Mouth of river Conway, and beyond, Great Orme's Head, a mass of hard limestone, which contains copper ore, 673 feet high.	39¼	Conway St. (p. 250.) Penbach Tunnel.	223¾	Llanrwst, 12 miles distant, is a small town on the east bank of the river Conway, situated in a beautiful valley. It was formerly celebrated for the manufacture of Welsh harps. Close to it is Gwydyr House, Lord Willoughby d' Eresby.
Lavan Sands, and entrance to Menai Strait.	34½	Penmaenmawr St.	228½	Penmaen Mawr Mountain, 1540 feet high.
Penrhyn Castle, Hon. E. G. Douglas Pennant. Lime Grove.	30¼	Aber St. Leave the shore, and proceed inland to	232¾	Llanfair, and, in the distance, the mountains of Caernarvonshire. Llanllechid.
Bangor (see p. 140).	25	BANGOR St.	238	Caernarvon, 9 miles (see p. 140).

ON RIGHT FROM LOND.	From Holyhd.		From London.	ON LEFT FROM LOND.
Menai Suspension Bridge (see p. 182).	22¾	**Three miles after Bangor, cross Menai** Strait by BRITANNIA* TUBULAR BRIDGE,	240¼	
Beaumaris, 4½ miles. Beaumaris, the county town of Anglesea, is pleasantly situated on the Menai Strait. A castle was erected here about the close of the thirteenth century, by Edward I., the remains of which are included within the domains of Sir R. B. W. Bulkeley Bart. Beaumaris is much resorted to during the summer months, and has of late been much improved. It was once surrounded with walls, which in some places are still entire. The town-hall is an elegant modern building. The church contains a curious monument, and in the vestry were deposited the remains of Lady Beatrix Herbert, daughter of the celebrated Lord Herbert of Cherbury. In the neighbourhood of Beaumaris is Baron Hill, the seat of Sir R. B. W. Bulkeley, Bart., commanding beautiful prospects; and about 4 miles from the town are the remains of Penmon Priory, consisting of the refectory, the dormitory, and the church. Beaumaris unites with Amlwch, Holyhead, and Llangefni, in returning 1 M.P. Pop. 2558	21	**and reach Llanfair St**	242	The island of Anglesey is rich in mineral produce. The copper mines in the Parys mountain (situated near Amlwch, on the N. coast of the island), which were discovered in 1768, produced at one time as much as 3000 tons of metal annually, but they have now greatly declined. Lead ore and asbestos have also been found, and coal is worked. Anglesey was formerly a principal seat of Druidical superstition, and contained sacred groves, which were cut down by the Romans under Suetonius Paulinus, A. D. 61. It was subjugated with the rest of Wales, by Edward I., and made a county by Henry VIII.
		Thence, through the Isle of Anglesey, by Gaerwen, Bodorgan, and Tycroes Stations, to		
		HOLYHEAD.	263	
		At a short distance is Penrhos, a seat of Lord Stanley of Alderley.		
		Holyhead is a place of very remote antiquity, and appears, from the vestiges of military works still to be seen, to have been an important Roman station. The principal trade of this port consists in the importation of agricultural produce from Ireland; and the town is greatly increased and improved		

in consequence of its being the most convenient place of embarkation for Dublin. Steam-packets leave Holyhead for that city thrice daily, in connection with the express and mail trains which leave London at 9-30 A.M., 5 P.M., and 8-45 P.M., and which arrive at Holyhead at 5-15 P.M., 12-35 A.M., and 5-45 A.M. The distance to Kingstown is about 60 miles, and the voyage is performed in 4½ hours, the packets arriving at Kingstown at 10 P.M., 6-30 A.M., and 11 A.M. respectively; the whole distance between London and the Irish metropolis being thus accomplished in less than 14 hours. Communication is besides constantly kept up by submarine electric telegraph between the sister kingdoms. A religious house is said to have been erected at Holyhead in the latter part of the sixth century; but the house for canons regular, called the College, appears to have been founded about 1137. The church, which is a handsome building, was erected about the time of Edward III. Holyhead contains also an assembly room, baths, a light-house, an extensive harbour, and a pier. The promontory of the head is an immense precipice, hollowed by the ocean into magnificent caverns, affording shelter to falcons and sea-fowls. In the neighbourhood a harbour of refuge on a great scale, is in the course of formation. Pop. 6193.

* See account of it, p. 250.

Conway, or Aber-Conway, was formerly surrounded by high and massive walls, strengthened by twenty-four towers, which, with four gateways, still remain in tolerable preservation. The principal object is the remains of the magnificent castle erected by Edward I. It is seated on a rock, washed on two sides by the Conway, and is of an oblong form, flanked by eight embattled towers. During the civil wars it was garrisoned for the King, but was taken by the Parliamentary army. It remained entire, however, till it was granted by Charles II. to the Earl of Conway, who dismantled it for the sake of the timber, iron, lead, &c. It is now the property of the Marquis of Hertford, to whom it gives the title of Baron Conway. Over the river is a fine suspension bridge, erected from designs by Telford. The church contains several monuments of the Wynne family. In Castle Street is a very old structure, called the College, inhabited at present by a few poor families. Near the market-place is a very large antique building, erected in 1585, by Robert Wynne, Esq. of Gwydy It is now the property of Lord Mostyn. Aberconway unites with Caernarvon. Bangor, Nevin, Pwllheli, and Criccieth, in returning one M.P. Pop. of bor 2523.

The railway between Chester and Holyhead is rendered pre-eminently remarkable by those stupendous and wonderful triumphs of modern engineering, the Conway and Britannia tubular bridges, by which the line is respectively carried across the estuary formed by the mouth of the river Conway, and across the Menai Strait. These hollow rectangular tubes, sustained in their position by no other power than that which they derive from the strength of their materials, and the manner in which these are combined, consist of plates of wrought iron from ½ to ¾ of an inch in thickness, firmly rivetted together, so as to form a single and continuous structure,—one tube (or connected series of tubes) serving for the passage of the up, and the other of the down, trains. To attempt any description of these great works would be out of place here; but the following particulars with reference to the larger structure, that which crosses the Menai Strait, will not be uninteresting. In this, the Britannia Bridge, the total length of each line of tube (regarded as a whole) is 1513 feet, which is made up by the union of four separate lengths of tube—two of longer, and two of shorter, dimensions. The two main lengths of tube, each measuring 472 feet, pass from the towers constructed respectively at high water mark on the Caernarvon and Anglesey shores, to the Britannia tower,—a structure of solid masonry, raised in the middle of the strait to the height of 210 feet, and based on a little rock formerly covered at high water. The shorter portions of tube connect the land-towers on either side with the abutments which terminate the embankments upon which the line of railway is carried, and by which the shores of the strait are approached. The total weight of *each tube* (regarded as a whole, in its entire length,) is nearly 5000 tons, and the whole structure is elevated to a height of 100 feet above the level of the water, so as to admit of the unimpeded passage of large vessels beneath it. In the construction of the tubes and towers as many as 1500 workmen were employed. The tubes were formed on the ground, upon the Caernarvon shore, and afterwards floated by means of pontoons, and subsequently raised to the required elevation by the use of powerful hydraulic presses. The Conway bridge, the construction of which preceded that of the larger structure, but which is similar in principle, consists of only one span of 400 feet, from shore to shore, and two abutments of masonry. Its height above the level of the water is only 18 feet. The tubes of which it is composed (each weighing 1300 tons) were built on the adjacent shore, and thence floated and raised in the same manner as described in reference to the Britannia Bridge.

ON RIGHT FROM LOND.	From Carlisle.		From London.	ON LEFT FROM LOND.
	168	From London, by N. Western Railway (Trent valley line), to STAFFORD (p. 242). Thence, by Warrington, to	132½	Junction of lines from Birmingham, 29¼ m., and Shrewsbury, 29 miles.
To Manchester, 16¼ m.	112¼	Newton Bridge St. on Liverpool and Manchester line (p. 238). Thence, by North Union Railway, to	188¼	To Liverpool, 14¾ m.
Heley Hall, Lord Kingsdown. Ince Hall.	111½	Golborne St.	189	Golborne Hall. and Haydock Hall, T. Legh, Esq. New Hall, Sir R. T. Gerard, Bart.
* Haigh Hall, rendered classic by Sir Walter Scott, the ancient seat of the Bradshaigh family, has descended by marriage to the Earl of Crawfurd and Balcarres. It contains a fine collection of pictures.	105¼	WIGAN St. (see p. 253).	195¼	Winstanley Hall, M. Bankes, Esq. Standish Hall, C. Standish, Esq. 7 m. distant is Lathom House (Lord Skelmersdale), occupying the site of the ancient house, which, under the command of the heroic Countess of Derby, successfully resisted the Parliamentary forces during a siege of 3 months.
Adlington Hall, R. C. B. Clayton, Esq.	102	Standish St.	198½	
Duxbury Hall, W. S. Standish, Esq. Gillibrand Hall. Astley Hall, Sir H. B. Hoghton, Bart.	99¾	Coppull St.	200¾	
	96¼	EUXTON.	204¼	Euxton Hall, W. J. Anderton, Esq. Shaw Hall, containing a museum of natural history, and some curious frescoes brought from Herculaneum.
	94¼	Leyland St.	206¼	
Cuerdon Hall, R. Townley Parker, Esq.	92½	Farrington Gate.	208	Penwortham Priory, L. Rawstone, Esq.
	90¼	PRESTON (see p. 254).	210¼	Branch to Fleetwood, 20 miles. Trenchwood. Ashton Lodge, J. Pedder, Esq.
Barton Lodge.	85½	Broughton St.	215	Newsham Hall. Myerscough Hall.
Claughton Hall, T. F. Brockholes, Esq.	82¾	Brock St.	217¾	Myerscough House. Kirkland Hall.

* See Introduction to Scott's "Betrothed," pp. 8-10.

ON RIGHT FROM LOND.	From Carlisle.		From London.	ON LEFT FROM LOND.
Barnacre. Lower Wyersdale. Cleveley.	80¾	**Garstang,** seated on the left bank of the Wyer, which abounds with trout, gudgeon, &c. The church of the parish once belonged to the Abbey of Cockersand. In the vicinity are several cotton factories, and the ruins of Greenhalgh Castle, which the Earl of Derby garrisoned for Charles I. in 1643. It was subsequently dismantled by the Parliament. Pop. of parish 7221.	219¾	
Quernmoor, 2 miles.	77½	Scorton St.	223	
		cr. river Wyer		
	75	Bay Horse St.	225½	Forton Lodge. Cockerham Hall.
	73¾	Galgate St.	226¾	Ellel-Grange.
To Hornby, 9 miles. To Ingleton, 18½ miles. 2½ miles distant, Quernmore Park, and Halton.	69	LANCASTER, (See p. 254.) Thence, by Lancaster and Carlisle Railway, cr. river Lune, by viaduct of 9 arches—3 of wood and 6 of stone.	231½	Thurnham Hall. Ellel-Hall. Ashton Hall, Duke of Hamilton and Brandon. Stodday Lodge.
	66	Hest Bank St.	234½	
	65	Bolton-le-Sands St.	235½	
Borwick Hall.	63½	Carnforth St.	237	Yealand Village and Leighton Hall.
	58¼	Burton and Holme St.	242¼	Beetham Village.
	55½	Milnthorpe St. cr. Lancaster and Kendal Canal.	245	Levens Hall, a mansion rich in oak carvings. The gardens also are much admired. Sizergh Hall, (W. Strickland, Esq.), the ancient seat of the Stricklands. One apartment in it called the "Queen's Room," is said to have been occupied by Catharine Parr.
Benson Knott, 1098 feet above the level of the sea.	50	Kendal Junction. cr. river. Mint by viaduct of 6 arches, each 50 feet span.	250½	Here the Kendal and Windermere Railway branches off; Kendal is 2 miles distant, Windermere, 10½.
	41½	Low Gill St.	259	

ON RIGHT FROM LOND.	From Carlisle.		From London.	ON LEFT FROM LOND.
	37	Tebay and Orton St. Alternate embankments, and cuttings in solid granite over Shap Fells. The depth of cutting ranges between 50 and 60 feet, and width at base 30 feet.	263½	
3 miles distant, the village and township of Reagill.	29½	Shap St.	270½	Shap Wells, a saline spa, a few hundred yards from the line after emerging from the cutting. One mile distant are the remains of Shap Abbey, which at the time of the dissolution belonged to the ancestors of Hogarth the painter.
Brougham Hall, Lord Brougham, surrounded by fine woods; and Brougham Castle, supposed to occupy the site of a Roman station.	22	Clifton Moor St. Clifton Moor was the scene of a skirmish between the Royal troops under William, Duke of Cumberland, and those of the Pretender, in 1745.	278½	Lowther Castle, the seat of the Earl of Lonsdale, a splendid modern structure, standing in a park of 600 acres.
	19½	cr. river Eamont by viaduct of 5 arches 50 feet in span, and 70 in height.	280½	
2 miles from Penrith, Edenhall, Sir G. Musgrave, Bart. 6 miles north-east of Penrith stands a Druidical circle 350 yards in circumference, formed of 67 stones, some of them 10 feet high, known by the name of Long Meg and her daughters. Long Meg—an unhewn block of red freestone, 15 feet in circumference and 18 in height—stands a little apart from the circle.	17½	Penrith St. Penrith, an ancient market town. Its church has been rebuilt, but the walls of the old castle remain. The town had a population in 1851 of 6668.	283½	4 miles north-west of Penrith, Greystoke Castle, H. Howard, Esq.
	13	Plumpton St.	287½	Hutton Hall, Sir H. R. F. Vane, Bart.
Newbiggen Hall.	7	Southwaite St.	293½	Wreay Village.
	3	Brisco St.	297½	Upperby Village and ch.
Railway to Newcastle, and 4 miles distant Corby Castle, P. H. Howard, Esq.		CARLISLE.	300½	Railway to Maryport.

Wigan is an ancient town, situated near the little river Douglas, on the banks of which the Saxons were defeated by King Arthur. It is noted for its manufacture of cotton goods, and its large brass and pewter works. The vicinity also abounds with cannel coal. Wigan has two churches, of which All-Saints is old, and contains tombs of the Bradshaigh family, ancestors of the Earl of Crawford and Balcarres. It has also a town-hall, several dissenting chapels and meeting houses, free blue coat and national schools, and various literary and charitable institutions. There is a monumental pillar here in honour of Sir T. Tyldesley, who was killed at the battle of Wigan Lane, in 1651, when the Royalists under the Earl of Derby were routed by Colonel Lilburne. Wigan was visited by the Pretender in 1745. In the vicinity is a sulphurous spring, with a neat building for the accommodation of visitors. Two M.P. Pop. 37,658.*

PRESTON is a town of great antiquity, on the north bank of the Ribble. There were formerly two monastic institutions in Preston, one called the Hospital of St Mary Magdalene, the other a monastery of Greyfriars The last was occupied as a prison until about fifty years ago, and traces of it yet remain. During the civil wars Preston was first occupied by the Royal party, but was quickly taken by the Parliamentary forces, and the mayor killed in the assault. It was afterwards retaken by the Earl of Derby, who demolished the defences. At Ribbleton Moor, near Preston, the Duke of Hamilton was defeated, in 1648, by Cromwell; and, in 1715, the friends of the Pretender were routed by Generals Willes and Carpenter at the same spot. Preston contains five churches and one chapel, belonging to the Established Church, and numerous chapels belonging to dissenting bodies. It has also a guild-hall, a town-hall, a corn exchange, a cloth and a market-hall, assembly rooms, a theatre, &c. What are called the "Guilds" of Preston are held every twenty years, when the trades meet with banners and music, form a procession, and hold a jubilee at considerable cost to the town. Preston is well provided with schools of all descriptions. About 10,000 Sunday scholars are gratuitously educated. Preston is a port—vessels of 150 tons ascending nearly to the town, and the customs duties amounted in 1850 to L.76,295:8:6. Sir Richard Arkwright was born at Preston in 1732; and here, in 1768, he commenced, in connection with a mechanic named John Kay, some of his improvements in the cotton-spinning mechanism. The chief manufacture is cotton, but there is also a good deal of flax-spinning executed here. Two M.P. Pop. of borough, 82,985.

The N. Western Railway connects Preston with all parts of the empire, and a line 20 miles in length, connects it with the mouth of the Wyre, where is situated the new watering-place of Fleetwood, with an excellent hotel, erected by Sir P H. Fleetwood, Bart. As a bathing-place it possesses very superior attractions. Pop. 1851, 3048. From Preston a canal leads to Kendal, through Lancaster.

LANCASTER is situated on the Lune, at some distance from its entrance into the sea. The principal object is the castle, a strong fortress, erected in the reign of Edward III. by John of Gaunt. It stands upon the summit of a hill, and forms a very striking feature in the general view of the town. It is now converted into the county gaol. The county courts now attached to this venerable building

* Some interesting traditions regarding Wigan are recorded by Mr Roby in his "Traditions of Lancashire." A small volume on similar subjects by a young author of great promise has also been recently published at Wigan. See also Introduction to Scott's "Betrothed," pp 8-10.

are chiefly of a modern date, and are extremely commodious. On the north of the castle stands St Marys, the old church, which is later English, and contains carved stalls, screen, and monuments. A town-hall, lunatic asylum, theatre, assembly rooms, several alms-houses and an excellent grammar-school are among the other public buildings of the town. Lancaster has a considerable trade, the river being navigable (though with difficulty) for vessels of between 200 and 300 tons. Cotton and hardware manufactures constitute the principal exports. A large trade in coal and limestone is carried on by means of the canal, which is carried over the Lune by an aqueduct erected in 1797, at an expense of L.48,000. Lancaster affords the title of Duke to the Prince of Wales. Two M.P. Pop. 16,005.

CARLISLE is an ancient city, pleasantly situated on an eminence nearly enclosed by three streams, the Eden, the Caldew, and the Peteril. It is supposed to be of British origin, and there is reason to conclude that it was a Roman station. It appears to have been first fortified about the time of Agricola; the erection of its castle is attributed to William Rufus. Carlisle was taken by David, King of Scots, and afterwards besieged unsuccessfully by Robert Bruce in 1312. It suffered severely during the civil wars, having declared for Charles I. In 1745, it surrendered to Prince Charles Stuart, and on being retaken by the Duke of Cumberland, was the scene of many cruel severities upon the conquered. After the junction of the kingdoms it sank into decay, but has made great progress since the commencement of the present century. The principal business of the town consists in its manufactures of cotton goods and ginghams, and in a coasting trade. There is a canal from Carlisle to the Solway, and some traffic arises also from its lying on the North Western line of Railway from London to Edinburgh, Glasgow, &c. Before the Reformation, there were several ecclesiastical establishments in the city. It was erected into a see by Henry I. in 1133. Dr Paley was Arch-Deacon of Carlisle, and is buried in the cathedral, where a monument has been recently erected to his memory. The cathedral is an ancient building of red freestone, some parts of which are assigned to the Saxon times. It has however suffered much from neglect and the lapse of time, and contains a few monuments of interest. There are numerous other churches in Carlisle, several meeting-houses, a Roman Catholic chapel, a Mechanics' Institute, a theatre, a grammar-school founded by Henry VIII. and forty-seven other schools of various kinds. The court-houses were built at an expense of L.100,000. A considerable portion of the old castle still remains, comprising the keep, a lofty and massive tower, in which is a very deep well. The whole has been restored and is a striking feature of the town. Towards the north were the apartments in which Mary Queen of Scots was confined on her flight to England, after the battle of Langside. Carlisle gives the title of Earl to a branch of the Howard family. Two M.P. Pop. 1861, 29,417. Excellent hotels at the railway station, Carlisle.

CI. CARLISLE TO GLASGOW (105 Miles) AND EDINBURGH (101 Miles) BY CALEDONIAN RAILWAY.

ON RIGHT FROM CARL.	From Glasgow.	From Edinb.		From Carlisle.	ON LEFT FROM CARL.
Railway to Newcastle.	105	101	From Carlisle.		Railway to Maryport and Whitehaven.
	101	97	cr. river Eden to Rockcliffe St.	4	Mouth of river Eden, and Solway Firth.
			cr. river Esk.		
	96½	92½	Gretna Junction.	8½	
			cr. small river Sark, and enter Scotland.		
			The line is continued through the valleys of the Annan and Clyde, by		
	85	81	Ecclefechan.	20	Hoddam, Admiral Sharpe.
	79	75	Lockerbie.	26	
	65½	61½	Beattock.	39½	
	47	43	Abington, and	58	
	38½	34½	Symington, to	66½	
	31½	27½	Carstairs Junction, where it divides, the left hand branch passing through Clydesdale to	73½	Carstairs House, H. Monteith, Esq.
			GLASGOW, and the right hand branch, by Midcalder, to	105	
			EDINBURGH.	101	

CII. CARLISLE TO DUMFRIES, BY RAILWAY, 32½ Miles.

ON RIGHT FROM CARL.	From Dumfr.		From Carlisle.	ON LEFT FROM CARL.
		From Carlisle, by Caledonian Railway, to		
In the distance, Netherby, Right Hon. Sir Jas. Graham, Bart.	24	Gretna Junction.	8½	
		Thence, along north side of Solway Firth, by		
	15	Annan, to	17½	Kelhead.
		DUMFRIES.	32½	

ON RIGHT FROM LOND.	From Maccles.		From London.	ON LEFT FROM LOND.
	38½	From London to Colwich St. on Trent valley line of North Western Railway, (p. 242.)	127	Leave Trent valley line to Stafford. Great Haywood. Shugborough Park, Earl of Lichfield. Tixall Park, Sir T. A. C. Constable, Bart. Ingestre Hall and Park, Earl of Shrewsbury. Weston Hall.
Chartley Hall, Earl Ferrers, 2 miles.	34	Along valley of river Trent to Weston St.	131½	Grand Trunk Canal, and river Trent.
Sandon Hall, Earl of Harrowby.	31½	Sandon St.	134	Stafford, by road, 5 m.
Milwich, 2¼ miles. Hilderstone, 3 miles, and Hilderstone Hall. Near Stone is Stone Hall, Earl Granville.	27	Stone Junction St. Stone is a small market town, 6 miles north of Stafford, on the banks of the Trent, and near the Grand Trunk Canal. A considerable manufacture of shoes is carried on here. Pop. 4509.	138½	Branch to main line of North Western Railway, which it joins at Norton Bridge. Darlaston Hall, S. S. Jervis, Esq. Meaford Hall, Viscount St Vincent. 2 miles distant, Swinnerton Park, T. Fitzherbert, Esq.
Barlaston Hall, R. Adderley, Esq.	24½	Continue along Grand Trunk Canal to Barlaston St.	141	
Lane End, 2 miles.	23	Trentham St.	142½	Trentham Park, Duke of Sutherland.
Longton Hall. Fenton Hall.		Enter the district of "the Potteries" (see p. 221.)		Stoke Lodge.
Branch by Lane End to Uttoxeter, and thence to Birmingham and Derby Railway, which it joins at Burton and Willington.	20	Stoke St. (see p. 221.) cr. Grand Trunk Canal.	145½	Newcastle-under-Lyne, 2 miles; beyond, Keele Hall. Wolstanton.
Etruria Hall.	18¾	Etruria St.	146¾	
Tunstall. Clough Hall.	17¾	Burslem St.	147¾	Chesterton, supposed to be the site of a Roman station, perhaps the *Mediolanum* of the seventh Itinerary. Talk-on-the Hill.
	13¾	Harecastle Junction St.	151¾	Branch railway to Crewe 8¼ miles. Church Lawton, and Lawton Hall.

ON RIGHT FROM LOND.	From Maccles.		From London.	ON LEFT FROM LOND.
		cr. Macclesfield Canal, and enter Cheshire.		Rode Hall, R. Wilbraham, Esq. Macclesfield Canal.
Mow Cop, or Mole Cop, Hill, on the borders of Cheshire and Staffordshire, 1091 feet high.	11¼	Mow Cop St.	154½	Ramsdill Hall. Astbury.
Congleton Edge.	8¼	Congleton St.	157½	Congleton, ¾ mile (see p. 219), and beyond, Somerford Park, Sir C. P. Shakerley, Bart.
Bosley.		cr. Macclesfield Canal.		Buglawton Hall.
Churnet Valley line to Leek and Uttoxeter branches off here. Sutton St James.	4¾	North Rode St.	160¾	North Rode Hall. Gawsworth, Earl of Harrington.
		MACCLESFIELD (see p. 227).	165½	From Macclesfield a branch railway extends to Cheadle Station on the Manchester and Birmingham branch of the London and North Western line.

CIV. MANCHESTER TO BOLTON AND PRESTON, BY RAILWAY, 31 Miles.

ON RIGHT FROM MAN.	From Preston.		From Manch.	ON LEFT FROM MAN.
Salford (see p. 230).		From Salford Station, Manchester, to Oldfield Road St., and Pendleton St.		Trafford Park, Sir H. De Trafford, Bart.
River Irwell; and beyond, Kersall Hill, Irwell House, and Heaton Park, Earl of Wilton.	29¼		1¾	Pendlebury.
Branch to Bury and Haslingden.	26½	Clifton Junction.	4½	Clifton Hall, and beyond, Worsley Hall, Earl of Ellesmere.
Clifton House, and beyond, Stand Hall.		Dixon Fold.		
	24	Stone Clough St.	7	Kearsley Moor.
Kearsley Hall. Darley Hall.		Halshaw Moor.		Farnworth and Kearsley.
Darcy Lever, 1 m., and Bradshawe Hall, T. Bradshawe Isherwood, Esq., representative of President Bradshawe, temp. Chas. I.	22½	Moses Gate St.	8½	Great Lever. Bolton Moor.
Smithills Hall, P. Ainsworth, Esq., 2 m. Halliwell Lodge; beyond, Moss Bank. Lostock Park.	20¾	BOLTON (see p. 259).	10½	Deane. Hulton Park, W. Hulton, Esq., 2 m. Aspull

ON RIGHT FROM MANC.	From Preston.		From Manch.	ON LEFT FROM MANC.
	16½	Lostock Lane St.	14½	
Horwich.		Red Moss.		Haigh Hall, Earl of Craufurd and Balcarres, 2¼ miles. (See p. 251.
	14½	Horwich and Blackrod St.	16½	
Anderton Hall; beyond, Rivington Pike, and Rivington Hall, 1¾ m.				Adlington Hall, R. C B. Clayton, Esq., 1½ m.
		cr. river Douglas.		
	12¼	Adlington St.	18¾	Ellerbeck Hall.
		cr. Leeds and Liverpool Canal.		Duxbury Park, W. S. Standish, Esq. Gillibrand Hall.
6½ m. from Chorley, on the road to Blackburne, is Hoghton Tower, formerly a splendid mansion, and, for several generations, the principal seat of Sir H. B. Hoghton's family, but now in a ruinous condition. The eminence on which it stands commands an extensive view of the surrounding country.	9	CHORLEY, see p. 260.	22	Astley Hall, Sir H. Bold Hoghton, Bart.
Shaw Hall.	6	Euxton St. where the line joins the North Union Railway to	25	Euxton Hall
Cuerdon Hall, R. T. Parker, Esq.		PRESTON (see p. 254.)	31	

BOLTON, or Bolton-le-Moors, is said to be of Saxon origin. The principal trade is the cotton manufacture and its subsidiary branches, as bleaching, calico-printing, machine-making, &c. There are above thirty coal-mines in the parish. Blackrod contains a sulphur spring. The country, for six miles round Bolton, has undergone very considerable improvement within the last few years; villages have sprung up where there was not a dwelling, and hamlets have become the seat of a dense population. Within six years, five new churches have been erected in the neighbourhood of Bolton, and besides these two or three others are projected. Bolton has a town-hall, a theatre, and assembly-rooms, numerous churches and meeting-houses, a free grammar-school, &c. Between Bolton and Wigan are found large quantities of cannel-coal, which is often manufactured into snuff-boxes, candlesticks, &c. Bolton suffered severely in the civil wars, especially during the great siege, when Prince Rupert and the Earl of Derby stormed the town, and dislodged the Republican troops. In consequence of this achievement, the latter was beheaded in Bolton after the battle of Worcester Bolton returns two M.P. Pop. in 1861, 70,395. The Manchester, Bolton, and

Bury Canal was begun in 1791, and completed soon after. About one and a half mile N.E. of Bolton, President John Bradshawe, one of the regicides, had a seat at Bradshawe Chapel. At a place called Hall-in-the-Wood, one mile from Bolton, Samuel Crompton invented the machine called the "Mule." A railway leads from Bolton to Leigh, and thence to the Liverpool and Manchester Railway, joining it at Kenyon. Leigh is seven miles from Bolton. It enjoys a considerable share of the cotton, and a portion of the silk trade. In the church there is a private chapel of the Tyldesley family, which contains the remains of Sir Thomas Tyldesley, the distinguished royalist, who fell at the battle of Wigan-lane. Pop. 10,621.

The first mile of the railway between Bolton and Preston, from its junction with the Manchester and Bolton Railway, is considered a fine specimen of engineering skill. It runs through the south-west side of the town in a curve, and crosses nine streets under as many bridges. The construction of the roofs of the bridges is much admired. They consist of cast-iron beams and present a flat surface to the eye of the spectator underneath.

CHORLEY is situated on the banks of the Chor, whence it takes its name. A family of the same name held the manor of Chorley from a very early period. The staple manufactures are cotton fabrics, muslins, jaconets, and fancy articles. There are five coal-mines in the neighbourhood, and a lead-mine at Anglezarke. The old church is an ancient building. There is a grammar-school, and several churches, meeting-houses, and charitable institutions. Pop. 15,013.

CV. LIVERPOOL TO PRESTON, THROUGH ORMSKIRK, BY RAILWAY, 26½ Miles.

ON RIGHT FROM LIVER.	From Preston.		From Liverp.	ON LEFT FROM LIVER.
Everton. Kirkdale.		From terminus in Great Howard Street, Liverpool, to Bootle Lane St.		River Mersey.
		cr. Leeds and Liverpool Canal.		
Walton. Walton Hall, and beyond, Croxteth Park, Earl of Sefton. Knowsley, Earl of Derby. Branch line to Wigan and Bolton.	25	Walton Junction St.	1½	Branch line to Southport, 16 miles, a small watering place situated on the south side of the entrance to the estuary of the Ribble, which has been of late years much resorted to during the summer. Broad and level sands extend along the whole coast between this place and Liverpool.
Fazakerley		cr. Leeds and Liverpool Canal.		Bootle. Orrell. Stand Park.

ON RIGHT FROM LIVER.	From Preston.		From Liverp.	ON LEFT FROM LIVER.
	21¾	Aintree St.	4¾	
		cr. river Alt, and Leeds and Liverpool Canal.		Netherton. Crosby Hall, W. Blundell, Esq. Ince Blundell Hall, T. Weld Blundell, Esq.
Moor Hall.	20	Maghull St.	6½	Lydiate and Aughton.
		Town Green St.		
To Wigan, 11 miles.	15½	ORMSKIRK, a market town, 12 miles north of Liverpool, has two large annual cattle-fairs. The church contains the burial place of the Earls of Derby. Pop. 6426.	11	To Southport, 8½ m. Scarisbrick Hall, C. Scarisbrick, Esq., 3 m.
Lathom House, Lord Skelmersdale, 1½ mile (see p. 251).				
	13	Burscough St.	13½	
St. John's.		cr. Leeds and Liverpool Canal.		
		cr. Douglas Navigation.		
	9½	Rufford St.	17	Rufford Hall, Sir T. G. Hesketh, Bart.
		cr. river Douglas.		
Chorley, 7 miles. Eccleston, 2 miles.	7½	Croston St.	19	Bank Hall. Bretherton.
		Farrington Moss. Charnock Moss.		
Leyland. Farrington. Walton-le-dale.		6 miles beyond Croston, join North Union Railway and proceed by it to		Longton. Hutton Hall, 2 miles. Howick Hall, 2 miles. Penwortham Lodge.
		PRESTON (p. 254).	26½	Penwortham Hall, L. Rawstone, Esq.

CVI. CARLISLE TO WHITEHAVEN, BY RAILWAY, 40 Miles.

ON RIGHT FROM CARL.	From Whiteh.		From Carlisle.	ON LEFT FROM CARL.
		From Carlisle.		
		cr. river Caldew.		
	35½	Dalston St.	4½	Dalston, ¾ mile. Rose Castle, Bishop of Carlisle, 1 mile.
		cr. river Wampool.		
Thursby, ¾ mile.	32¾	Curthwaite St.	7¼	
Crofton Hall, Sir W. Brisco, Bart.		Along valley of river Wampool.		
Micklethwaite.		Cross coach road from Carlisle to Whitehaven.		

ON RIGHT FROM CARL.	From Whiteh.		From Carlisle.	ON LEFT FROM CARL.
Waverton.	28¼	WIGTON St. Wigton is a small market town, in which some manufacture of cotton is carried on. About a mile distant, at Old Carlisle, are the remains of a Roman station. Pop. 4011.	11¾	Hesket Newmarket, 10 miles distant, a small but neatly built market town, on the banks of the river Caldew. Pop. of parish, 1983.
		Cross coach road.		
Bromfield, 1½ mile. Langrigg.	24½	Leegate St.	15½	
	21¾	Brayton St.	18¼	Brayton Hall. Allhallows, 3 miles.
Aspatria.	19¾	Aspatria St. Along valley of the river Ellen, which the line crosses several times.	20¼	Plumbland. Gilcrux.
	18¾	Arkleby St. Cross road from Allonby to Cockermouth.	21¼	
Allonby, 2 miles distant, situated on the coast, is much resorted to for bathing during the summer season. It commands an extensive view of the Solway Firth, with the opposite shores of Scotland.	16¼	Bulgill St.	23¾	To Cockermouth, 7 m. (see p. 330). Tallentire Hall, W. Browne, Esq., 3¼ m. River Ellen.
Cross Canonby.	14½	Dearham St. cr. river Ellen.	25½	Dearham, 1 mile.
Netherhall, J. P. Senhouse, Esq. River Ellen. Shortly after leaving Maryport, the railway approaches the sea, and continues close along the shore, with the sea on the right, nearly the whole way to Whitehaven.	12	MARYPORT, a small seaport town, at the mouth of the river Ellen. It carries on considerable trade in the export of coals to Ireland, and has increased in size of late years. Pop. 6037.	28	Ellenborough, a Roman station, gives title of Earl to the Law family. Cockermouth, 6 miles.
	10	Flimby St.	30	Flimby is a small place, much frequented for bathing during the summer season.
Workington, situated on the south bank of the Derwent, near its mouth, has a good harbour, and carries on a considerable trade in coals and iron, the produce of the mines in its neighbourhood. There is also an extensive salmon fishery. Pop. 1851, 5837. On the east side of the town is Workington Hall, H. Curwen, Esq., beautifully situated on an elevation near the	7	WORKINGTON St. cr. river Derwent near its mouth. Near Workington the line recedes inland, but again approaches the shore 1 mile before reaching	33	Railway to Cockermouth, 8½ miles, running throughout along the valley of the river Derwent, which it crosses several times.
	4½	Harrington St.	35½	Distington, 2 miles; near it, Lilly Hall and Hays Castle.
		cr. Lowca Beck.		
	1¼	Parton St.	38½	Moresby, near which is the site of a Roman sta-

ON RIGHT FROM CARL.	From Whiteh.		From Carlisle.	ON LEFT FROM CARL
banks of the Derwent. It is a large quadrangular structure, of considerable antiquity. Mary Queen of Scots took refuge here on landing in England, after the battle of Langside; and the apartment which she occupied is still distinguished as the Queen's Chamber.	1½	Along the foot of the cliffs of new red sandstone which here line the coast, to	38½	tion, probably the *Arbeja* of the Notitia.
		WHITEHAVEN (p. 289).	40	Whitehaven Castle, Earl of Lonsdale.

CVII. LONDON TO WHITEHAVEN, BY PRESTON, FLEETWOOD, AND RAVENGLASS, 293½ Miles.

ON RIGHT FROM LOND.	From Whiteh.		From London.	ON LEFT FROM LOND.
		From London, by North Western Railway, to		
	83¼	PRESTON (p. 251).	210¼	River Ribble; and, on opposite bank, Penwortham Lodge, and Penwortham Hall.
Leave railway to Lancaster and Carlisle.		Thence, by Preston and Wyre Railway, to		Ashton, and Talketh Hall.
Lancaster Canal. Cottam.	80¼	Lea Road St.	213¼	Clifton. Newton.
Salwick.	77½	Salwick St.	216	Ribby Hall.
Treales. Greenhalgh. Singleton, and near it, Bankfield.	75½	Kirkham, a market town, 19 miles south by west of Lancaster, is a small but improving place. It has some manufacture of cotton; sail cloth and cordage are also made, as well as coarse linens. Pop. 3380.	218	Branch to Lytham, 4 miles, a small watering place, pleasantly situated on the north side of the estuary of the Ribble. Near it is Lytham Hall, T. Clifton, Esq. Great Plumpton. Hardhorn.
Poulton is called Poulton-le-Fylde, to distinguish it from another place of the same name, known as Poulton-le-Sand, also in Lancashire, and situated further to the north, on the shore of Morecambe Bay.	68½	POULTON, a small market town, two miles distant from the west bank of the Wyre.	225	Branch to Blackpool, 3½ miles, which is much frequented as a summer bathing place. It extends about a mile along the shore, in front of a fine sandy beach. Near it is Rakes Hall.
Thornton. Mouth of river Wyre.		Across west side of estuary of Wyre to		
	63	FLEETWOOD (see p. 254).	230½	Rossall Hall, Sir P. Hesketh Fleetwood, Bt.

ON RIGHT FROM LOND.	From Whiteh.		From London.	ON LEFT FROM LOND.
		From Fleetwood, by steamer, across Morecambe Bay, 12½ miles, to		
	50½	Piel Pier.	243	Piel I. and Castle (in ruins), Foulney I., Roe I., and Walney I.
Rampside.				
Leece.				
		Thence, by railway, to		
To Ulverstone, by railway 6½ or by road 5 miles (see p. 278).	45	Furness Abbey Junction St.	248½	Furness Abbey in ruins, the property of the Earl of Burlington, (see p. 279.)
				Estuary of the Duddon, and Duddon Sands; beyond, Black Combe, 1919 feet.
		Along east bank of river Duddon to		
Swarthmore, Conishead Priory, and Bardsea Hall, T. R. G. Braddyll, Esq.	38½	Kirkby St.	255	
Broughton Tower.	35	Broughton St.	258	
		Broughton is a small market-town, situated at the head of the estuary of the Duddon, which divides Lancashire from Cumberland. Pop. of parish 1250.		Millom Castle Black Combe.
	31	Under Hill St.	262½	
	29½	Holborn Hill St.	264	
	28	Silecroft St.	265½	
	21	Bootle St.	272½	
Muncaster Castle, (Lord Muncaster.)	18	Eskmeals St.	275½	
Irton, and Irton Hall, S. Irton, Esq.	16½	RAVENGLASS.	277½	
	14½	Drigg St.	279½	
Gosforth, 3 miles. Ponsonby Hall, E. Stanley, Esq.	12½	Seascales St.	281	The railway hence runs along the sea-shore as far as St Bees.
Calder Abbey.		cr. river Calder.		
Calder Bridge, 2 miles.	11	Sellafield St.	283	

NEWCASTLE & CARLISLE
AND NORTH-SHIELDS & TYNEMOUTH, RAILWAYS.

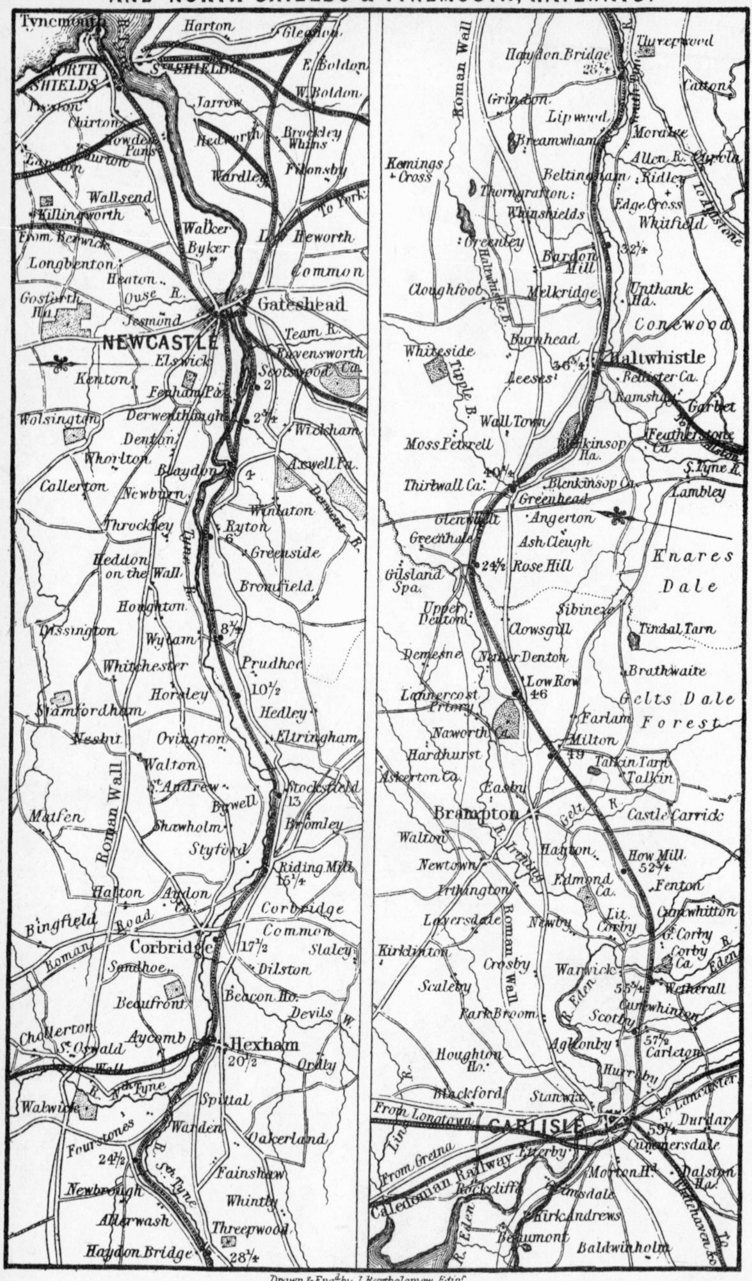

Drawn & Engd. by J. Bartholomew, Edinr.

Published by A. & C. Black, Edinburgh.

ON RIGHT FROM LOND.	From Whiteh.		From London.	ON LEFT FROM LOND.
		cr. river Ehen.		
Beckermet.	8½	Braystones St.	285	St Bees Head, on the summit of which is a light-house, is a fine bluff promontory of new red sandstone, 222 feet in height.
Egremont, 2 miles (see p. 326.)	7	Nethertown St.	286½	
Linethwaite.	4	St Bees St. (see p. 291.)	289½	
Hensingham.		Thence proceed inland, through a beautiful valley to		Rotington.
Whitehaven Castle, Earl of Lonsdale.				St Bees Lighthouse.
		WHITEHAVEN. (p. 289.)	293½	Sandwith.

From London to Whitehaven, by way of Lancaster, Carlisle, and Maryport (by railway), is 337¾ miles.

CVIII. CARLISLE TO NEWCASTLE, BY RAILWAY, 59¼ Miles.

ON RIGHT FROM CARL.	From Newcas.		From Carlisle.	ON LEFT FROM CARL.
Wetheral. Here are the ruins of a priory, and a very curious cavern.	57¾	Scotby St.	1½	Warwick Hall.
	55¾	Wetheral St.	3½	Edmond Castle, Sir S. Graham, Bart.
Corby Castle, (P. H. Howard, Esq.) a very fine mansion with beautiful grounds, which are open to the public.	52¾	How Mill St.	6½	Brampton, a very ancient place, surrounded by hills, and supposed to have been the Roman Bremeturacum. The Castle-hill commands a very extensive prospect. About 2 miles from the town, on a rock overhanging the Gelt, is the celebrated Roman inscription noticed by Camden. Pop. 2379.
	49	Milton St.	10¼	
	46	Low Row St.	13¼	Naworth Castle, formerly the baronial mansion of the Dacres of the North. It is now the property of the Earl of Carlisle.
	42¼	Rose Hill St.	17	Ruins of Lanercost Priory.
At a distance, Featherstone Castle; ruins of Bellister Castle.				Gilsland Spa, a much frequented watering-place, situated in the romantic vale of Irthing. Here Sir Walter Scott first met Miss Charpentier, afterwards Lady Scott.*
	40¼	Greenhead St.	19	

* See Lockhart's Life of Scott p. 74.

ON RIGHT FROM CARL.	From Newcas.		From Carlisle.	ON LEFT FROM CARL.
				Ruins of Thirwall Castle.
Unthank Hall.	37	HALTWHISTLE ST. (See p. 408.)	22¼	Blenkinsopp Hall, J. B. Coulson, Esq.
Ridley House.		Haltwhistle Tunnel, 201 yards in length.		
	32¼	Bardon Mill St.	27	
Ruins of Langley Castle, and Threapwood.	28¼	Haydon Bridge St.	31	High Wardon, J. Errington, Esq.
	24¾	Four Stones St.	34½	
Spital, J. Kirsopp, Esq.	20¾	HEXHAM ST.	38½	The Hermitage.
Beacon House. Oakerland.		pleasantly situated on the south side of the river Tyne. It is supposed to have been a Roman station. Here are the remains of an abbey of vast extent and extraordinary magnificence. The church exhibits a mixture of the Gothic and Saxon styles of architecture. There are various leather, hat, and glove manufactories in the town. Pop. 1851, 4601.		Beaufront. Dilston Castle in ruins, the seat of the Earl of Derwentwater, which was forfeited in the rebellion of 1715. Ovingham, in the churchyard of which lies Bewick.
	17½	Corbridge St.	41¾	Styford. Bywell Hall, W. B. Beaumont, Esq.
	15¼	Riding Mill St.	44	
	13	Stocksfield St.	46¼	
Ruins of Prudhoe Castle.	10½	Prudhoe St.	48¾	
Bradley Hall.	8¼	Wylam St.	51	Wylam Hall, C. Blackett, Esq.
Stella Hall.	6	Ryton St.	53¼	Close House, C. Bewicke, Esq.
Axwell Park, Sir W. A. Clavering, Bart.	4	Blaydon St.	55¼	
In the distance Ravensworth Castle, Lord Ravensworth.	3	Scotswood St.	56¼	Benwell Lodge.
Swalwell, celebrated for its iron-works, established near the close of the seventeenth century, by Mr A. Crawley.		NEWCASTLE. (See p. 391.)	59¼	Elswick, J. H. Hinde, Esq.

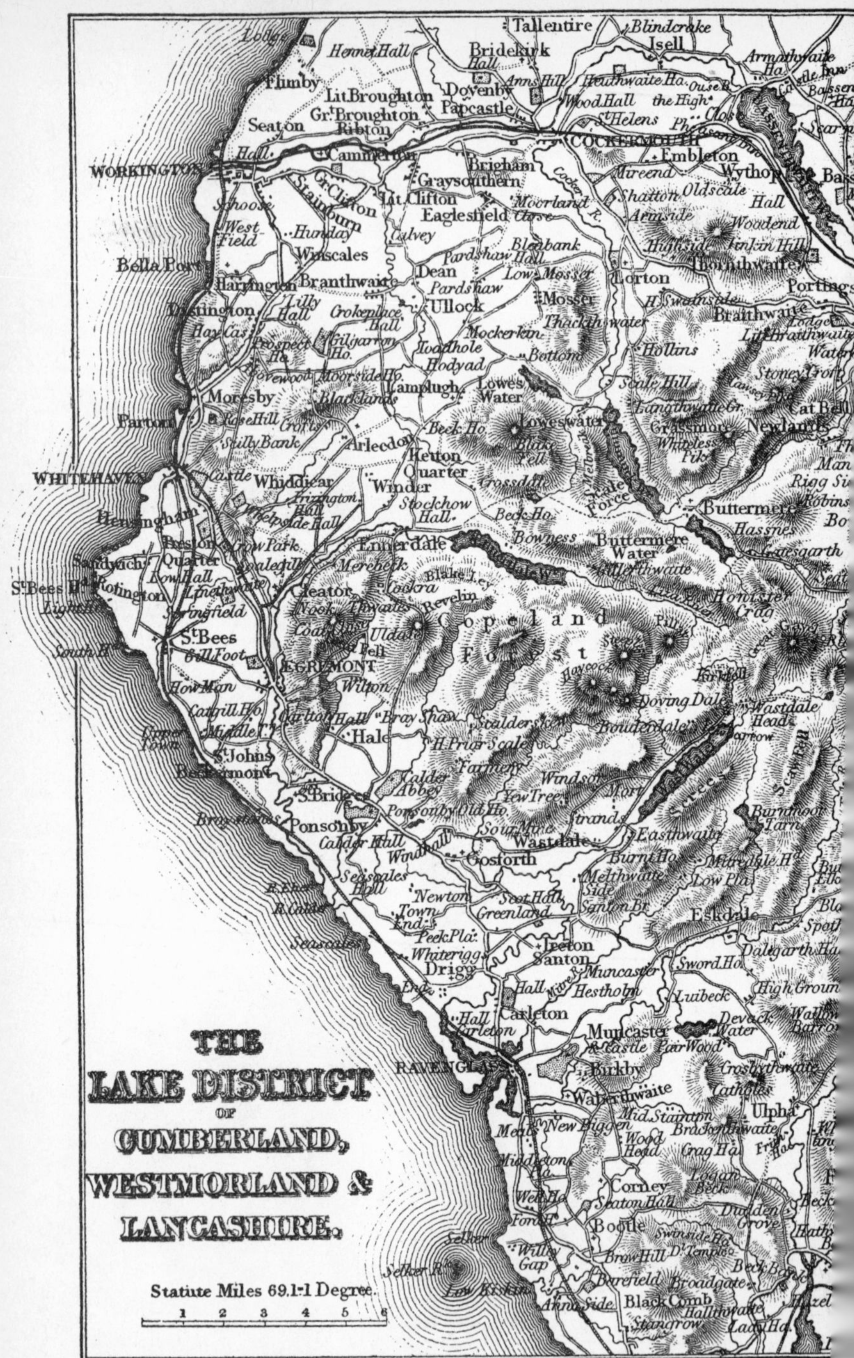
THE LAKE DISTRICT
OF
CUMBERLAND,
WESTMORLAND &
LANCASHIRE.
Statute Miles 69.1=1 Degree
1 2 3 4 5 6
Tallentire
Blindcrake
Isell
Bridekirk
Hennet Hall
Flimby
Lit. Broughton
Gr.t Broughton
Dovenby
Papcastle
Seaton
Ribton
WORKINGTON
Cammerton
Brigham
COCKERMOUTH
Embleton
Wythop
Graysouthern
Lit. Clifton
Gr. Clifton
Stainburn
Eaglesfield
Winscales
Bella Port
Harrington
Branthwaite
Distington
Dean
Pardshaw
Ullock
Lorton
Mosser
Braithwaite
Portinscale
Thornthwaite
Moresby
Lamplugh
Lowes Water
Loweswater
Arlecdon
Parton
WHITEHAVEN
Whiddicar
Winder
Hensingham
Ennerdale
Buttermere
Buttermere Water
Newlands
Sandwich
St. Bees Hd.
St. Bees
Rotington
Cleator
EGREMONT
Copeland Forest
Wastdale Head
Hale
St. Johns
Beckermont
St. Bridget
Ponsonby
Calder Abbey
Gosforth
Wastdale
Eskdale
Seascales
Drigg
Santon
Irton
Muncaster
Carleton
RAVENGLASS
Birkby
Waberthwaite
New Biggen
Corney
Bootle
Ulpha
Black Comb
Selker Rks.
Selker

Edinburg

Engraved by S. Hall Bury Str. Bloomsbury.

y A. & C. Black.

THE LAKE DISTRICT.

For the accommodation of strangers about to make the Tour of the Lake District, and who are in doubt, from the number of routes, which, and in what order to take them, we have drawn up an abstract of four Tours, which it is supposed commence and terminate at each of the four principal towns lying upon the edge of the district, viz., Kendal, Ulverston, Penrith, and Whitehaven. By consulting the map of the Lake District, and charts, Tourists will be able to vary the Tours according to their convenience; and by reference to the Index, the reader will find the page of the volume, in which the objects mentioned in the abstract are described at length.

ABSTRACT OF TOURS.

I. KENDAL.

KENDAL—BOWNESS—WINDERMERE—AMBLESIDE—TROUTBECK Excursion—CONISTON—ascend the OLD MAN—Circuit of CONISTON LAKE—AMBLESIDE—LANGDALE Excursion—Excursion round GRASMERE and RYDALMERE—WYTHBURN—ascend HELVELLYN—THIRLEMERE—KESWICK—Circuit of DERWENTWATER—VALE of ST. JOHN—ascend SKIDDAW—BASSENTHWAITE Excursion—BORROWDALE—BUTTERMERE—SCALE HILL—Excursion to ENNERDALE WATER—EGREMONT—STRANDS at the foot of WAST WATER—ascend Scawfell Pike—KESWICK by way of Sty Head—PENRITH—Excursion to HAWES WATER—Excursion to ULLESWATER—PATTERDALE—AMBLESIDE, by HAWKSHEAD and ESTHWAITE WATER to BOWNESS—KENDAL.

II. ULVERSTON.

ULVERSTON—Coniston Lake—Waterhead Inn—ascend the OLD MAN—AMBLESIDE—Circuit of WINDERMERE—TROUTBECK Excursion—LANGDALE Excursion, in which Langdale Pikes may be ascended—Excursion to RYDAL, GRASMERE and Loughrigg Tarn—Grasmere—Wythburn—ascend HELVELLYN—Thirlmere—KESWICK—Circuit of DERWENTWATER—Excursion into the VALE of ST JOHN—ascend SKIDDAW—Circuit of BASSENTHWAITE LAKE—Excursion through BORROWDALE to BUTTERMERE—CRUMMOCK WATER—SCALE HILL—ENNERDALE WATER—EGREMONT—Strands—ascend SCAWFELL PIKE—WAST WATER—over Sty Head to KESWICK—PENRITH—Excursion to HAWES WATER—Excursion to ULLESWATER—PATTERDALE—AMBLESIDE—HAWKSHEAD—ESTHWAITE WATER—ULVERSTON—Excursion by Broughton into DUNNERDALE and SEATHWAITE.

III. PENRITH.

PENRITH—Excursion to HAWES WATER—ULLESWATER—PATTERDALE—ascend HELVELLYN, by Kirkstone, to AMBLESIDE—TROUTBECK Excursion—Circuit of WINDERMERE—LANGDALE Excursion—ascend LANGDALE PIKES—Coniston—Circuit of CONISTON LAKE—ascend the OLD MAN—return to AMBLESIDE—Excursion round GRASMERE and RYDALMERE—WYTHBURN—THIRLEMERE—KESWICK—ascend SKIDDAW—Circuit of DERWENTWATER—Excursion into the Vale of St John—Circuit of BASSENTHWAITE WATER—BORROWDALE—BUTTERMERE—SCALE HILL—Excursion to ENNERDALE WATER—EGREMONT—STRANDS at the foot of WAST WATE—ascend Scawfell Pike—KESWICK by way of Sty Head—PENRITH.

IV. WHITEHAVEN.

WHITHAVEN—Excursion to Ennerdale Lake—EGREMONT—WAST WATER—ascend SCAWFELL PIKE—by Sty Head, and through Borrowdale, to KESWICK—Circuit of Keswick Lake—ascend SKIDDAW—Excursion to the VALE of ST JOHN—Circuit of BASSENTHWAITE WATER—PENRITH—Excursion to HAWES WATER—ULLESWATER—PATTERDALE—ascend HELVELLYN—AMBLESIDE by Kirkstone—Circuit of WINDERMERE—TROUTBECK Excursion—CONISTON—ascend the OLD MAN—Circuit of CONISTON LAKE—HAWKSHEAD—BOWNESS—AMBLESIDE—LANGDALE Excursion, in which LANGDALE PIKES may be ascended—Excursion round GRASMERE and RYDALMERE—Grasmere—Wythburn—Thirlemere—KESWICK—BORROWDALE—BUTTERMERE—SCALE HILL—WHITEHAVEN.

THE LAKE DISTRICT.

THE section of England, known by the name of the Lake District, occupies a portion of the three counties of Cumberland, Westmorland, and Lancaster, and extends over an area, the greatest length and breadth of which are not more than forty-five miles. The picturesque attractions of the district are probably unequalled in any other part of England; and although some of the Scottish lochs and mountains must be admitted to present prospects of more imposing grandeur, it may safely be said, that no tract of country in Britain combines in richer affluence those varied features of sublimity and beauty which have conferred upon this spot so high a reputation.

For the lover of nature, no tour could be devised of a more pleasing character than that which these lakes afford. "We penetrate the Glaciers, and traverse the Rhone and the Rhine, whilst our domestic lakes of Ullswater, Keswick, and Windermere exhibit scenes in so sublime a style, with such beautiful colourings of rock, wood, and water, backed with so stupendous a disposition of mountains, that if they do not fairly take the lead of all the views of Europe, yet they are indisputably such as no English traveller should leave behind him."*

Nor is it only to the admirer of external nature that this district presents attractions. It is no less interesting to the antiquarian, the geologist, and the botanist. The remains of three Abbeys,—Furness,—Calder, and Shap,—of numerous castles,—of one or two Roman stations,—and of many Druidical erections,—afford ample scope for the research of the antiquarian; whilst the rich variety of stratified and unstratified rocks, forming a complete series from the granitic to the carboniferous beds;—and many rare plants, with ample facilities for observing the effect produced upon vegetation by the varying temperature of the air at different altitudes, yield to the students of geology and of botany abundant matter for employment in their respective pursuits. A further interest is imparted to the locality from its being the spot with which many of our great modern poets have been more or less intimately connected, and from which many of their finest poems have emanated.

The district may be traversed by many routes, the selection of which will depend upon the tourist's convenience and taste, but especially upon the point

* CUMBERLAND.

from which he enters it. But as the Lancaster and Carlisle Railway is now, undoubtedly, the great avenue of approach, both from the north and south, and, by means of the Kendal Junction Line, brings Tourists directly to Kendal and the shores of Windermere, we conceive that we shall best consult his accommodation by commencing with the description of these places.

KENDAL.

[*Hotels:*—King's Arms; Commercial; Crown.]

KENDAL, otherwise Kirkby-in-Kendal, the largest town in Westmorland, is situate in a pleasant valley on the banks of the river Kent, from which it derives its name. It contained in 1861, 12,029 inhabitants, and is a place of considerable manufacturing industry, having a large trade in woollen goods. The woollen manufacture was founded as early as the fourteenth century, by some Flemish weavers, who settled here at the invitation of Edward III. The town is intersected by four leading streets, two of which, lying north and south, form a spacious thoroughfare of a mile in length. The river is spanned by three neat stone bridges; it is of no great width, though subject to sudden floods by its proximity to the mountains. The houses, built of the limestone which abounds in the neighbourhood, possess an air of cleanliness and comfort,—their white walls contrasting pleasingly with numerous poplars, which impart a cheerful rural aspect to the town.

The barony of Kendal was granted by William the Conqueror to Ivo de Taillebois, one of his followers, in which grant the inhabitants of the town, as villein (*i. e.* bond or serf) tenants, were also included; but they were afterwards emancipated, and their freedom confirmed by a charter from one of his descendants. The barony now belongs, in unequal portions, to the Earl of Lonsdale and the Hon. Mrs. Howard, both of whom have extensive possessions in Westmorland. By the Municipal Corporations Reform Act, the government of the borough is vested in a mayor, six aldermen, and eighteen common councillors, six of whom are elected by each of the three wards into which it is divided. By the Reform Act, which disfranchised Appleby, the county town, Kendal, has the privilege of returning one member to Parliament.

The Parish Church, a spacious Gothic edifice, dedicated to the Holy Trinity stands in that part of the borough called Kirkland. The tower is square, and possesses an altitude of 72 feet. Like most other ecclesiastical structures of ancient date, it contains a number of curious monuments and epitaphs. There are two other churches in the town, both lately erected, and forming handsome edifices; that which stands at the foot of Stricklandgate is dedicated to St Thomas, the other near Stramondgate Bridge to St George. In addition to the churches of the establishment, the Dissenters have upwards of a dozen places of worship. The Roman Catholics have recently erected a beautiful new Chapel, on the New Road near the Natural History Society's Museum. This Museum contains a collection of specimens illustrating local and general natural history and antiquities. The Whitehall Buildings, at the head of Lowther Street, form a handsome pile. They contain a news-room, ball-room, auction-room, billiard-room, &c. The Lancaster and Carlisle Railway passes within a short distance to the east of the town, and the Kendal and Windermere Railway forms a junction with the Lancaster and Carlisle at Oxenholme, two miles from Kendal. On the east of the town is the termination of the Lancaster and Preston Canal, which affords great facilities for the conveyance of coal to and from Kendal.

The ruins of KENDAL CASTLE, of which only four broken towers, and the outer wall, surrounded by a deep fosse, remain, crown the summit of a steep elevation on the east of the town.* The remains of this fortress are well worthy of a visit, on account of the views of the town and valley which the hill commands. This was the ancient seat of the Barons of Kendal, and the birth-place of Catherine Parr, the last Queen of Henry VIII., a lady, who (as Pennant quaintly remarks,) "had the good fortune to descend to the grave with her head, in all probability merely by outliving her tyrant." Opposite to the castle, on the west side of the town, is Castle-how-hill, or Castle-low-hill, a large circular mount of gravel and earth, round the base of which there is a deep fosse, strengthened with two bastions on the east. It is of great antiquity, and is supposed by some to have been one of those hills called *Laws*, where in ancient times justice was administered. In 1788, a handsome obelisk was erected on its summit in commemoration of the Revolution of 1688.

About a mile to the south of the town, at a spot where the river almost bends upon itself, and hence called Water Crook, are the scarcely perceptible remains of the Roman Station, *Concangium*, formerly a place of some importance, judging from the number of urns, tiles, and other relics of antiquity discovered there. It is believed that a watch was stationed at this point for the security of the Roman posts at Ambleside and Overborough. In the walls of a farm-house in the vicinity are two altars, a large stone with a sepulchral inscription, and a mutilated statue.

* "A straggling burgh, of ancient charter proud,
And dignified by battlements and towers
Of some stern castle, mouldering on the brow
Of a green hill."—

WORDSWORTH.

One mile and a-half to the west, at the termination of a long ascent over an open moor, is the bold escarpment of limestone rock, called UNDERBARROW (or Scout) SCAR. It is a remarkable object, and would repay the trouble of a visit for the splendid view of the distant lake mountains, and the interjacent country, which it commands. A hill, rising abruptly on the east of the town termed Benson Knott, has an altitude of 1098 feet above the level of the sea. From the summit of this hill, an extensive prospect is also obtained.

LEVENS HALL, the seat of the Hon. Mrs Howard, five miles south of Kendal, is a venerable mansion, in the Elizabethan style, buried among lofty trees. The park, through which the river Kent winds betwixt bold and beautifully wooded banks, is separated by the turnpike road from the house. It is of considerable size, well-stocked with deer, and contains a noble avenue of ancient oaks. The gardens, however, form the greatest attraction, being laid out in the old French style, of which this is perhaps a unique example in the kingdom. They were planned by Mr Beaumont, (whose portrait, very properly, is preserved in the Hall,) gardener to King James II. Trim alleys, bowling-greens, and wildernesses fenced round by sight-proof thickets of beech, remind the beholder, by their antique appearance, of times " long, long ago." In one part a great number of yews, hollies, laurels, and other evergreens, are cut into an infinite variety of grotesque shapes.

——" a spacious plot
For pleasure made, a goodly spot,
With lawns, and beds of flowers, and shades
Of trellis-work, in long arcades,
And cirque and crescent framed by walls
Of close-clipt foliage, green and tall,
Converging walks."

White Doe of Rylstone.

The gardens, as may be imagined, harmonize well with the old Hall, the interior of which also deserves more than a passing glance. It contains some exquisite specimens of elaborate carved work—

" The chambers carved so curiously,
Carved with figures strange and sweet,
All made out of the carver's brain."

Christabel.

The work in the south drawing-room is exceedingly rich, as may be conceived from its having been estimated that, at the present rate of wages, its execution would cost L.3000. The carved chimney-piece in the Library is a curious and interesting piece of workmanship. Three of Lely's best portraits hang on the walls of different chambers, as well as other portraits of personages of consequence in bygone times. The entrance hall is decorated with relics of ancient armour of various dates, and one of the rooms is adorned with some splendid pieces of tapestry, descriptive of a tale from one of the Italian poets.

SIZERGH HALL, the seat of the ancient family of Strickland, situate three and a half miles south of Kendal, at the foot of a bleak hill facing the east, is also deserving of a visit. It is an antique fortified building, standing in an undulating park, delightfully sprinkled with wood. Only a small portion of the old Tower remains, frequent additions and repairs having given an irregular but picturesque aspect to the whole pile. It contains a considerable collection of carved oak, tapestry, portraits, and armour.

The other seats in the neighbourhood are, Abbot Hall, Kirkland (Mrs Wilson); The Vicarage, Kirkland (Rev. J. Barnes); Helm Lodge, two miles south (W. D. Crewdson, Esq.); Heaves Lodge, four miles south (James Gandy, Esq.); Sedgwick House, four miles south (John Wakefield, Esq.); Dallam Tower, seven miles south (George Wilson, Esq.); Mosergh House, four miles north (Mr. Machell); Shaw End, five miles north (Henry Shepherd, Esq.); Low Bridge House, six miles north (R. Fothergill, Esq.); Raw Head, four miles east (Mr Sleddall); Hill Top, three miles east (William Wilson, Esq.)

WINDERMERE.

Small steam-boats have within the last few years been established upon Windermere, which during the summer season make several voyages daily from one extremity of the lake to the other. Windermere is now rendered easy of access to tourists, by the railway which branches from the Lancaster and Carlisle line at Kendal, and terminates about a mile to the north of Bowness, near the shores of the lake at

BIRTHWAITE.

[*Hotels:*—Windermere.]

On the arrival of the trains, coaches leave the station at Windermere for Ambleside and Keswick, and the mail daily proceeds by this route to Cockermouth, and thence, by railway, to Whitehaven. Coaches also travel daily between the Windermere railway terminus and the towns of Hawkshead and Coniston.

We would by all means recommend those strangers who have sufficient time to circumnambulate this, which is the queen of the lakes, and largest sheet of water in the district, to do so at an early period of their visit, that the quiet scenery with which it is surrounded may not be considered *tame*, as will probably be the case if the survey be delayed until the bolder features of the country have been inspected.

Windermere, or more properly Winandermere, is about eleven miles in length, and one mile in breadth. It forms part of the county of Westmorland, although the greatest extent of its margin belongs to Lancashire. It has many feeders, the principal of which is formed by the confluence of the Brathay and Rothay shortly before entering the lake. The streams from Troutbeck, Blelham Tarn, and Esthwaite Water also pour in their waters at different points. Numerous islands, varying considerably in size, diversify its surface at no great distance from one another,—none of them being more than four and a half miles from the central part of the lake. Their names commencing with the most northerly are—Rough Holm (opposite Rayrigg), Lady Holm (so called from a chapel

WINDERMERE FROM NEAR BOWNESS

dedicated to our Lady, which once stood upon it), Hen Holm, House Holm, Thompson's Holm, Curwen's or Belle Isle (round which are several nameless islets), Berkshire Island (a little below the ferry points), Ling Holm, Grass Holm, and Silver Holm. Windermere is deeper than any of the other lakes, with the exception of Wast Water, its depth in some parts being upwards of 240 feet. It is plentifully stocked with perch, pike, trout, and char, which last, at the proper season, is potted in large quantities and forwarded to the south. It is a remarkable fact, that at the spawning season, when the trout and char leave the lake, the former fish invariably takes the Rothay, and the latter the Brathy.

The prevailing character of the scenery around Windermere is soft and graceful beauty. It shrinks from all approach to that wildness and sublimity which characterise some of the other lakes, and challenges admiration on the score of grandeur only at its head, where the mountains rise to a considerable height, and present admirable outlines to the eye of the spectator. The rest of the margin is occupied by gentle eminences, which, being exuberantly wooded, add a richness and a breadth to the scenery which bare hills cannot of themselves bestow. Numerous villas and cottages, gleaming amid the woods, impart an aspect of domestic beauty, which further contributes to enrich the character of the landscape. Around the shores of the lake there are many places which may be made the temporary residence of the tourist while exploring the beauties of the adjacent country, and probably he may find it advantageous to make several of them his abode in succession: Bowness, on the east shore, half way between the two extremities, and therefore the most eligible; Ambleside, one mile beyond the head of the lake; Low Wood Inn, a mile and a half from its head on the east shore; the Ferry Inn on the promontory over against Bowness; and Newby Bridge at its foot,—all furnish comfortable quarters for the tourist, where boats, guides, and all his other wants can be supplied.

We shall commence our perambulation at the town first named, proceeding along the west border, and returning by the east border of the water.

BOWNESS.

[*Hotels:*—Royal; Crown.]

This pretty village is placed on the edge of a large bay, opposite Belle Isle, about eight miles from Kendal, and six from Ambleside. It has two excellent hotels, which, from the delightful character of the adjacent country, and the convenient situation of the village for making excursions, are much frequented during the touring season. The Church dedicated to St Martin is an ancient structure with a square tower, and a finely painted chancel window, which originally belonged to Furness Abbey. The churchyard contains a monument erected to the memory of Richard Watson, the late learned Bishop of Llandaff, the author of "the Apology for the Bible," and other well known works. He was born at Haversham, in another part of the county, in which village his father was schoolmaster for upwards of forty years. He was interred at this place: the inscription upon his tomb is simple and unpretending. "Ricardi Watson, Episcopi Landavensis, cineribus sacrum obiit Julii 1, A.D. 1816, Ætatis 79." The interior of the church may be described in these lines, taken from "the Excursion," which have doubtless been suggested by this, or a similar structure.

"Not raised in nice proportions was the pile,
But, large and massy, for duration built;
With pillars crowded, and the roof upheld
By naked rafters, intricately cross'd
Like leafless underboughs, 'mid some thick grove,
All wither'd by the depth of shade above.
Admonitory texts inscribed the walls—
Each in its ornamental scroll inclosed,
Each also crown'd with winged heads—a pair
Of rudely-painted cherubim. The floor
Of nave and aisle, in unpretending guise,
Was occupied by oaken benches, ranged
In seemly rows ———
And marble monuments were here display'd
Thronging the walls, and on the floor beneath
Sepulchral stones appear'd with emblems graven,
And foot-worn epitaphs, and some with small
And shining effigies of brass inlaid."

The school-house has been lately rebuilt through the munificence of the late Mr Bolton of Storrs. It stands on an eminence to the east of the village, and forms a handsome edifice. The view from the front is exquisitely beautiful, comprising the whole of the upper half of the lake. The mountains round the head, into the recesses of which the waters seem to penetrate, arrange themselves in highly graceful forms, and the wooded heights of the opposite shore cast a deep shadow upon the "bosom of the steady lake." From this point Belle Isle appears to be a portion of the mainland.

In addition to the villas afterwards enumerated, there are in the neighbourhood, Holly Hill (Mrs Bellasis), The Craig (W. R. Gregg, Esq.), Birthwaite (G. Gardner, Esq.), Rayrigg (Major Rodgers,) The Wood (Miss Yates), St Catherine's (the Earl of Bradford), Elleray, Orrest Head (John Braithwaite, Esq.), Belle Grange (Mrs Curwen), Wray (Wm. Wilson, Esq.)

Several interesting walks will be pointed out to strangers, amongst which we may mention those through the parsonage-land to the Ferry Point, and to Storrs. If the tourist will take the trouble to proceed about half a mile along the road to Brant Fell, he will be rewarded by one of the finest views of the lake he can obtain. The Fells of Furness are seen across the lake, but the murmur of

——"bees that soar for bloom,
High as the highest peak of Furness Fells," *

is of course inaudible. A pleasing walk of four or five miles may be obtained

* WORDSWORTH.

thus: pursue the road to Ambleside until it enters that from Kendal (this portion of the walk will be particularized presently): turn to the right, and keep on this road for about a mile. The Wood, St Catherine's, and Elleray, are passed on the left. The last was the property of late Prof. Wilson of Edinburgh, and was at one time occupied by the late Major Hamilton, the author of Cyril Thornton, of a history of the Peninsular Campaigns, and other literary works. The house is perched upon the hill-side, having beautiful views of the surrounding scenery visible from its windows. It is thus alluded to in one of the poems of its late owner:

> "And sweet that dwelling rests upon the brow
> (Beneath its sycamore) of Orrest Hill,
> As if it smiled on Windermere below,
> Her green recesses and her islands still!"

A narrow lane branches off from the Kendal road near the Orrest Head gate, by which Bowness will be reached one mile and a-half from Orrest Head.

The more distant excursions will include the valley of Troutbeck,* the circuit of the two sections of Windermere, Esthwaite Water, and Coniston Lake. These are but a few, but an inspection of the chart will suggest others. Boating upon the lake will probably be the amusement resorted to earliest and most frequently. The various islands should be visited, especially Belle Isle, upon which strangers are allowed to land. It contains Mr. Curwen's residence, erected in 1776, in the form of a perfect cycle. The island is rather more than a mile in circumference, and contains upwards of thirty acres. It is intersected by neat walks, over which fine trees throw their massy arms. The islet to the left of it is Hen Holm, the next Lady Holm. Wansfell Pike is beheld over the former. The eminences to the right are those of the Kentmore Range, Hill Bell, and High Street. Fairfield is in full view, crowning a chain of hills terminated by Rydal Nab.

CIRCUIT OF WINDERMERE,

FROM BOWNESS.

Quitting Bowness for Ambleside, the stately woods of Rayrigg are entered three-quarters of a mile from the former place. A bay of the lake is then seen to project almost to the road. Rayrigg House stands on the left near the waters' edge; shortly before emerging from the wood, the road ascends a steep hill, and then pursues a level course, affording from its terrace a magnificent view of the lake—a view "to which," says Wilson, "there was nothing to compare in the hanging gardens of Babylon. There is the widest breadth of water—the richest foreground of wood—and the most magnificent background of mountains,

* For a description of this valley, refer to page 284.

not only in Westmorland, but—believe us—in all the world." Our old acquaintances, the two Pikes of Langdale are easily recognized. On the left is Bowfell, a square-topped hill, between which and the Pikes, Great End and Great Gable peep up. On the left of Bowfell, the summit of Scawfell Pike is faintly visible. The road is intersected two miles from Bowness by the Kendal and Ambleside road, at a place called Cook's House, nine miles from Kendal. A road proceeds into Troutbeck in a line with the one over which we have been conducting the tourist. From Cook's House to Troutbeck Bridge is almost a mile. From this place a road conducts by the west bank of the stream to the village of Troutbeck, the nearest part of which is a mile and a half distant. Continuing our progress towards Ambleside, Calgarth, embosomed in trees, is passed on the left. The late Bishop Watson built this mansion, and resided here during the latter years of his life; it is still occupied by his descendants. Two miles beyond is Low Wood Inn, which, standing pleasantly on the margin of the lake at its broadest part, is an excellent station for those who are able to devote a few days to the beauties of the neighbourhood. Most of the excursions recommended to be made from Ambleside may, with almost equal advantage, be performed from this inn. Close at hand is Dove's Nest, the house Mrs. Hemans inhabited one summer. Her description of the place, taken from her delightful letters, will not be deemed uninteresting:—"The house was originally meant for a small villa, though it has long passed into the hands of farmers, and there is, in consequence, an air of neglect about the little demesne, which does not at all approach desolation, and yet gives it something of touching interest. You see everywhere traces of love and care beginning to be effaced—rose trees spreading into wildness—laurels darkening the windows with too luxuriant branches; and I cannot help saying to myself, 'Perhaps some heart like my own in its feelings and sufferings has here sought refuge and repose.' The ground is laid out in rather an antiquated style; which, now that nature is beginning to reclaim it from art, I do not at all dislike. There is a little grassy terrace immediately under the window, descending to a small court, with a circular grass-plot, on which grows one tall white-rose tree. You cannot imagine how much I delight in that fair, solitary, neglected-looking tree. I am writing to you from an old-fashioned alcove in the little garden, round which the sweet-briar and the rose-tree have completely run wild; and I look down from it upon lovely Winandermere, which seems at this moment even like another sky, so truly is every summer cloud and tint of azure pictured in its transparent mirror.

* * * * * * *

"I am so delighted with the spot, that I scarcely know how I shall leave it. The situation is one of the deepest retirement; but the bright lake before me, with all its fairy barks and sails, glancing like 'things of life' over its blue water, prevents the solitude from being overshadowed by anything like sadness."

Wansfell Holm (J. Hornby, Esq.) is seen on the right, immediately before reaching the head of Windermere. The road for the last three or four miles has been alternately approaching to and receding from the margin of the lake, but never retiring further from it than a few fathoms. At Waterhead is the neat residence of Mr. Thomas Jackson, and further on, Waterside (Mr. William Newton,) is passed on the left.

A mile beyond is Ambleside, afterwards described, from which we continue our perambulation. Passing Croft Lodge (J. Holmes, Esq.) on the right, Brathay Bridge is crossed at Clappersgate, one mile from Ambleside, and shortly afterwards Brathay Hall, (G. Redmayne, Esq.) is seen on the left. A bay, called Pull Wyke, there makes a deep indentation; and looking across the lake, Wansfell Holm, Low Wood Inn, and lower down, Calgarth, the seat of the late Bishop Watson, are pleasing objects. Wansfell Pike and the Troutbeck Hundreds tower above them. The road to Hawkshead having deviated to the right, the village of High Wray is gained, five miles from Ambleside; and three miles beyond is the Ferry Inn. At this place the shores suddenly contract, and between the two promontories a public ferry is established, by means of which, passengers, cattle, and vehicles are conveyed across the lake at a trifling charge. About the year 1635; a marriage was celebrated at Hawkshead, between a wealthy yeoman from the neighbourhood of Bowness, and a lady of the family Sawrey of Sawrey. As is still customary in Westmorland amongst the rustic population, the married couple were attended by a numerous concourse of friends, some of whom were probably more than cheerful. In conducting the bridegroom homewards, and crossing the ferry, the boat was swamped, either by an eddy of wind, or by too great a pressure on one side, and thus upwards of fifty persons, including the bride and bridegroom, perished. While at the Ferry Inn, the tourist should not fail to visit the Station, a pleasure house belonging to Mr. Curwen of Belle Isle, standing on a spot whence fine views of the circumjacent scenery are commanded. "The view from the Station," says Professor Wilson, "is a very delightful one, but it requires a fine day. Its character is that of beauty, which disappears almost utterly in wet or drizzly weather. If there be strong bright sunshine, a 'blue breeze' perhaps gives animation to the scene. You look down on the islands which are here very happily disposed. The banks of Windermere are rich and various in groves, woods, coppice, and corn-fields. The large deep valley of Troutbeck stretches finely away up to the mountains of High Street and Hill Bell—hill and eminence are all cultivated wherever the trees have been cleared away, and numerous villas are visible in every direction, which, although not perhaps all built on very tasteful models, have yet an airy and sprightly character; and with their fields of brighter verdure and sheltering groves, may be fairly allowed to add to, rather than detract from, the beauty of a scene, one of whose chief charms is that it is the cheerful abode of social life." At a short distance from the land is Belle Isle, upon which stands—

"A Grecian temple rising from the deep."

the residence of H. Curwen Esq. The island is rather more than a mile in circumference, containing upwards of thirty acres. Neat walks, over which fine trees throw their massive arms, intersect the island, which in high floods is cut in two. Strangers are allowed to land; and as the views are extremely pleasing, they should avail themselves of the privilege. The village of Bowness is a pretty object on the east margin of the lake.* One mile and a half from the Ferry Inn, the stream called Cunsey, which runs from Esthwaite Water,

* This island was formerly the property and residence of the Philipsons, an ancient Westmorland family, who were also owners of Calgarth. During the civil war between Charles I. and the Parliament, there were two brothers, both of whom had espoused the royal cause. The elder, to whom the island belonged, was a Colonel, and the younger a Major in the royal army. The latter was a man of high and adventurous courage; and from some of his desperate exploits had acquired amongst the Parliamentarians the appellation of Robin the Devil. It happened when the king's death had extinguished for a time the ardour of the cavaliers, that a certain Colonel Briggs, an officer in Oliver's army, resided in Kendal, who having heard that Major Philipson was secreted in his brother's house on Belle Isle, went thither armed with his double authority, (for he was a civil magistrate as well as a military man—

Great on the bench, great in the saddle,
Mighty he was at both of these,
And styled of War as well as Peace,)

with the view of making a prisoner of so obnoxious a person. The Major, however, was on the alert, and gallantly withstood a siege of eight months, until his brother came to his relief. The attack being thus repulsed, the Major was not a man who would sit down quietly under the injury he had received. He therefore raised a small band of horse and set forth one Sunday morning in search of Briggs. Upon arriving at Kendal, he was informed that the Colonel was at prayers. Without further consideration he proceeded to the church, and having posted his men at the entrance, dashed forward himself down the principal aisle into the midst of the assemblage. Whatever were his intentions—whether to shoot the Colonel on the spot, or merely to carry him off prisoner—they were defeated: his enemy was not present. The congregation was at first too much surprised to seize the Major, who, in discovering that his object could not be effected, galloped up the next aisle. As he was making his exit from the church, his head came violently in contact with the arch of the door-way, which was much smaller than that through which he had entered. His helmet was struck off by the blow, his saddle girth gave way, and he himself was much stunned. The congregation, taking advantage of the confusion, attempted to seize him; but with the assistance of his followers, the Major made his escape after a violent struggle, and rode back to his brother's house. The helmet still hangs in one of the aisles of Kendal church. This incident furnished Sir Walter Scott with a hint for his description of a similar adventure in Rokeby, canto vi.

"All eyes upon the gateway hung,
When through the Gothic arch there sprung
A horseman arm'd at headlong speed—
Sable his cloak, his plume, his steed—
Fire from the flinty floor was spurn'd,
The vaults unwonted clang return'd!
One instant's glance around he threw
From saddlebow his pistol drew,
Grimly determin'd was his look,
His charger with his spurs he struck—
All scatter'd backward as he came,
For all knew Bertram Risingham.
Three bounds that noble courser gave,
The first has reach'd the central nave

is crossed. At a short distance from the place where this stream joins the lake, is the island called Ling Holm. On the opposite margin, the Storrs promontory is seen projecting into the lake. Two miles beyond is the village of Graithwaite, in the vicinity of which is Graithwaite Hall, (J. J. Rawlinson, Esq.) From this place to Newby Bridge the road passes through a woodland section of the country, consisting chiefly of coppices. As the foot of the lake is approached, it narrows rapidly and becomes truly

"Wooded Winandermere, the *river*-lake."

Landing, (John Harrison, Esq.,) is passed on the left shortly before reaching Newby Bridge, at which there is a comfortable inn. The stream which issues from the lake takes the name of the Leven. From this place to the principal towns in the neighbourhood, the distances are:—Ulverston, eight miles. Kendal, by way of Cartmell Fell, ten miles—by Levens Bridge, fifteen miles. Ambleside, by the road we have described, fifteen miles. Bowness, nine miles. On crossing the bridge, Mr Machell's neat residence is seen on the right, and further on, Fell Foot, (—— Starkie, Esq.,) is passed on the left; a short distance beyond, Town Head, (Wm. Townley, Esq.,) is near the road on the left, about two miles from Newby Bridge. The road passes under an eminence of the Cartmell Fell chain, called Gummer's How, which forms a conspicuous object in all views from the upper end of the lake. Six miles from Newby Bridge is Storrs Hall, the mansion of the late John Bolton, Esq. (now Rev. T. Stanaforth) seated amongst fine grounds which extend to the margin of the lake. It was built by Sir John Legard, Bart., but extensive additions were made by its late owner. Here Mr Canning was wont to pay frequent visits, withdrawing for a time from the cares of public life to breathe the fresh air of nature.* The road

---

The second clear'd the chancel wide,
The third he was at Wycliffe's side.
* * * * * * *
While yet the smoke the deed conceals,
Bertram his ready charger wheels—
But flounder'd on the pavement floor,
The steed and down the rider bore—
And bursting in the headlong sway,
The faithless saddle-girths gave way.
'Twas while he toil'd him to be freed,
And with the rein to raise the steed,
That from amazement's iron trance,
All Wycliffe's soldiers waked at once."—

* The following passage from Mr Lockhart's Life of Scott graphically describes one of these visits, to which the presence of Wordsworth, Southey, Scott, and Professor Wilson gave peculiar interest.

"A large company had been assembled at Mr Bolton's seat in honour of the minister—it included Mr Wordsworth and Mr Southey. It has not, I suppose, often happened to a plain English merchant, wholly the architect of his own fortunes, to entertain at one time a party embracing so many illustrious names. He was proud of his guests; they respected him, and honoured and loved each other; and it would have been difficult to say which star in the constellation shone with the brightest or the softest light. There was 'high discourse,' intermingled with as gay flashings of courtly wit as ever Canning displayed; and a plentiful allowance on all

leading from Kendal to the ferry is next crossed, and soon afterwards Ferney Green (George Greaves, Esq.), Burnside (G. A. Aufrere, Esq.), and Belle Field, (Mark Beaufoy, Esq.), are successively passed immediately before Bowness, the termination of our perambulation of twenty-nine miles is regained.

AMBLESIDE.

[*Inns*:—Salutation; Commercial; White Lion.]

Ambleside, a small and irregularly built market-town of 1603 inhabitants, is situate on steeply inclined ground, a mile from the head of Windermere, upon or near to the spot formerly occupied by the Roman Station—Dictis. Lying immediately under Wansfell, and surrounded by mountains on all sides, except towards the south-west the situation is one of great beauty, and consequently during summer it is much frequented by tourists, who make it their abode for some time. There are several inns; two of which, the Salutation and the Commercial, are excellent establishments. The chapel is a modern structure, having been rebuilt in 1812. In a field near the edge of the lake, are the indistinct remains of Roman fortifications, where coins, urns, and other relics, have been frequently discovered. Numerous excursions may be made from Ambleside; and the interesting walks in the immediate neighbourhood are still more abundant.

The valley of Ambleside, on the border of which the town stands, is well wooded, and watered by several streams; the principal river is the Rothay, which flows from Grasmere and Rydal Lakes, and joins the Brathay, shortly before entering Windermere. Upon Stock Gill, a tributary to the Rothay, there is a fine fall, or *force*, in a copsewood, about 700 yards from the Market Cross, the road to which passes behind the Salutation Inn. The fall, or rather falls, for there are four, are 70 feet in height. Portions of all four are visible from the usual stand; but the views may be pleasingly varied by descending the bank to the stream, or proceeding farther up the Gill.

Loughrigg Fell, a rocky hill which rises opposite to the town, to an elevation of 1000 feet above Windermere, commands extensive prospects of the vale and surrounding mountains, as well as of Windermere, Grasmere, and Rydal Lakes, Blelham, Loughrigg, and Elterwater Tarns, with the towns of Ambleside and Hawkshead.

sides of those airy transient pleasantries in which the fancy of poets, however wise and grave delights to run riot when they are sure not to be misunderstood. There were beautiful and accomplished women to adorn and enjoy this circle. The weather was as Elysian as the scenery. There were brilliant cavalcades through the woods in the mornings, and delicious boatings on the lake by moonlight; and the last day, Professor Wilson ('the Admiral of the Lake,' as Canning called him,) presided over one of the most splendid regattas that ever enlivened Windermere. Perhaps there were not fewer than fifty barges following in the Professor's radiant procession when it paused at the point of Storrs to admit into the place of honour the vessel that carried kind and happy Mr Bolton and his guests. The three bards of the lakes led the cheers that hailed Scott and Canning; and music, and sunshine, flags, streamers, and gay dresses, the merry hum of voices, and the rapid splashing of innumerable oars, made up a dazzling mixture of sensations as the flotilla wound its way among the richly-foliaged islands, and along bays and promontories peopled with enthusiastic spectators."

From the summit of WANSFELL PIKE, (1590 feet in height,) which stands on the east, the mountains have a highly imposing appearance, and thence may be seen the whole expanse of Windermere, with its islands ; but on account of the altitude of the spectator, the view is not so fine as that from another part of the Pike, called Troutbeck Hundreds, a little to the south.

The village of RYDAL, supposed to be a contraction of Rothay-Dale, is placed in a narrow gorge, formed by the advance of Loughrigg fell and Rydal Knab, at the lower extremity of Rydal Mere, one mile and a quarter from Ambleside. Here, in the midst of a park containing great numbers of noble forest trees,* stands Rydal Hall, the seat of Rev. Sir R. Fleming. The celebrated falls are within the park, and strangers desirous to view them, must take a conductor from one of the cottages near the Hall gates. The fall below the house is beheld from the window of an old summer house. Amongst the juvenile poems of Wordsworth there is a sketch of this cascade.—

" While thick above the rill the branches close,
In rocky basin its wild waves repose,
Inverted shrubs, and moss of gloomy green,
Cling from the rocks with pale wood-weeds between;
Save that aloft the subtle sunbeams shine
On wither'd briars, that o'er the crags recline,
Sole light admitted there, a small cascade
Illumes with sparkling foam the impervious shade;
Beyond, along the vista of the brook,
Where antique roots its bristling course o'erlook,
The eye reposes on a secret bridge,
Half grey, half shagg'd with ivy to its ridge."

The chapel, from its prominent position, arrests the stranger's notice the moment he arrives at the village. It was erected by Lady le Fleming in 1824, at her own expense.

Rydal Mount, for many years the dwelling of the poet Wordsworth, stands on a projection of the hill called Knab Scar, and is approached by the road leading to the Hall. It is, as Mrs Hemans in one of her letters describes it, " a lovely cottage-like building, almost hidden by a profusion of roses and ivy." The grounds, laid out in a great measure by the hands of the poet himself, though but of circumscribed dimensions, are so artfully, whilst seeming to be so artlessly planned, as to appear of considerable extent. From a grassy mound in front, " commanding a view always so rich, and sometimes so brightly solemn, that one can well imagine its influence traceable in many of the poet's writings, you catch a gleam of Windermere over the grove tops,—close at hand

* " The sylvan, or say rather the forest scenery of Rydal Park, was, in the memory of living men, magnificent, and it still contains a treasure of old trees. By all means wander away into those old woods, and lose yourselves for an hour or two among the cooing of cushats, and the shrill shriek of startled blackbirds, and the rustle of the harmless glow-worm among the last year's red beech leaves. No very great harm should you even fall asleep under the shadow of an oak, while the magpie chatters at safe distance, and the more innocent squirrel peeps down upon you from a bough of the canopy, and then hoisting his tail, glides into the obscurity of the loftiest umbrage "—PROFESSOR WILSON.

are Rydal Hall, and its ancient woods,—right opposite the Loughrigg Fells, ferny, rocky, and sylvan, and to the right Rydal Mere, scarcely seen through embowering trees, whilst just below, the chapel lifts up its little tower."

The walk to Rydal, on the banks of the Rothay, under Loughrigg Fell, is extremely delightful. Though more circuitous than the highway, it presents finer combinations of scenery. The tourist, intending to take this round, should pursue the road to Clappersgate for half a mile to Rothay Bridge, and having crossed the bridge, enter the first gate on the right. The road leads alongside the river, passing many handsome villas, to Pelter Bridge, 2½ miles. Rydal Hall, with its park, and Rydal Mount, will be frequently in sight. Behind, Ambleside, backed by Wansfell, has a picturesque appearance. On the right are the heights of Fairfield and Kirkstone. By crossing the bridge, the Keswick road will be gained, and the tourist can then either return to Ambleside, or proceed to Rydal, which is 300 or 400 yards further. Those who are fond of long walks ought to abstain from crossing the bridge, but, keeping to the left, pursue the road behind the farm house, called Coat How, which leads along the south-west shore of Rydal Mere. This mere being passed, the road ascends the hill side steeply for some time, until it reaches a splendid terrace, overlooking Grasmere Lake, with its single islet, and then, climbing again, joins on Red Bank the Grasmere, and Langdale road.* Here the tourist has the choice of returning to Ambleside by Loughrigg Tarn and Clappersgate, or proceeding to Grasmere village, in doing which he will pass in succession Tail End, the Wyke, and the Cottage. The village is a sweet little place, at the head of the lake, 4 miles from Ambleside. In the churchyard are interred the remains of the poet Wordsworth. An excellent hotel (The Lowther and Hollins) has recently been opened on an eminence overlooking the high road from Ambleside to Keswick Allan Bank stands on a platform of ground behind the village. This house was, for some time, the abode of Wordsworth (and subsequently of Thomas de Quincey). The house, however, in which he lived for many years,

* This is by far the best station for viewing the Lake and Vale of Grasmere. Probably it was this very view that called from Mrs Hemans her sonnet entitled

A REMEMBRANCE OF GRASMERE.

" O vale and lake, within your mountain urn,
Smiling so tranquilly, and set so deep!
Oft doth your dreamy loveliness return,
Colouring the tender shadows of my sleep
With light Elysian;--for the hues that steep
Your shores in melting lustre, seem to float
On golden clouds from spirit-lands remote
Isles of the blest;—and in our memory keep
Their place with holiest harmonies. Fair scene
Most loved by evening and her dewy star!
Oh! ne'er may man, with touch unhallow'd, jar
The perfect music of the charm serene!
Still, still unchanged, may *one* sweet region wear
Smiles that subdue the soul to love, and tears, and prayer!

and in which he composed many of his most beautiful pieces, is at Grasmere Town End.* The singularly shaped hill, called Helm Crag, is conspicuously visible from Grasmere. Its apex exhibits so irregular an outline, as to have given rise to numberless whimsical comparisons. Gray compares it to a gigantic building demolished, and the stones which composed it flung across in wild confusion. And Wordsworth speaks of

"The ancient Woman seated on Helm Crag."

The narrow valley of Easedale, a dependency of Grasmere, lying in a recess between Helm Crag and Silver How, deserves a visit for its picturesque and secluded beauty.

"The spot was made by nature for herself."

It contains a large tarn, and a small cascade, called Sour Milk Gill. The melancholy fate of John and Sarah Green, who lived in this vale, is now pretty generally known through Mr. De Quincey, who published an account of it in his "Recollections of the Lakes."

About a mile from Grasmere, on an eminence, over which the old road to Ambleside passes, and exactly opposite to the middle of the lake, is the Wishing Gate. It has been so called, time out of mind, from a belief that wishes formed or indulged there have a favourable issue. Apart from any adventitious interest, the gate is an excellent station for viewing the lake.

A pleasing excursion, of ten miles, into the retired side-valley of TROUTBECK, may be conveniently taken from Ambleside. As the latter part of the route is practicable for horsemen and pedestrians only, those who take conveyances will be compelled to return by the road they went, as soon as they arrive at the head of Troutbeck, unless they proceed by way of Kirkstone to Patterdale. The tourist must pursue the Kendal road for two miles, and take the first road on the left when he has passed Low Wood Inn. From the eminences of this road, many exquisite views of Windermere are obtained; and, perhaps, the finest view of the lake that can be had from any station, is that from the highest part of it. The mountains in the west present an admirable outline, and the whole length of the lake stretches out before the spectator,

"——— with all its fairy crowds
Of islands, that together lie
As quietly as spots of sky
Amongst the evening clouds."

* The whole valley of Grasmere, in fact, teems with memorials of Wordsworth. There is scarcely a crag, a knoll, or a rill, which he has not embalmed in verse. To this cottage at Town End, which is now partially hidden from those on the highway, by the intervention of some later built cottages, Wordsworth brought his bride in 1802. Previous to his departure to fetch her, he composed his Farewell, in which these lines occur,—

"Farewell, thou little nook of mountain ground,
Thou rocky corner in the lowest stair
Of that magnificent Temple, which doth bound
One side of our whole vale with grandeur rare;
Sweet garden-orchard, eminently fair,
The loveliest spot that man hath ever found!"

"There is not," says Professor Wilson, "such another splendid prospect in all England. The lake has much of the character of a river, without losing its own. The islands are seen almost all lying together in a cluster—below which all is loveliness and beauty—above, all majesty and grandeur. Bold or gentle promontories break all the banks into frequent bays, seldom without a cottage or cottages embowered in trees; and, while the whole landscape is of a sylvan kind, parts of it are so laden with woods, that you see only here and there a wreath of smoke, but no houses, and could almost believe that you are gazing on the primeval forests." One mile and a half from Low Wood, one extremity of the 'long vale-village' of Troutbeck is reached, at a point about a mile from Troutbeck Bridge. The rude picturesqueness of its many-chimneyed cottages, with their unnumbered gables and slate-slab porticoes, will not be passed unnoticed by the tourist, as he bends his way towards the hills. "The cottages (says the writer from whom our last extract was made) stand for the most part in clusters of twos and threes, with here and there what in Scotland is called a *clachan*—many a sma' toun within the ae lang toun—but where in all broad Scotland is a mile-long scattered congregation of rural dwellings, all dropped down where the Painter and the Poet would have wished to plant them, on knolls and in dells, on banks and braes, and below tree-crested rocks, and all bound together in picturesque confusion, by old groves of ash, oak, and sycamore, and by flower gardens and fruit orchards, rich as those of the Hesperides?" The road pursues the western side of the valley, at some distance from the lowest level, which is occupied by the stream giving its name to the village. On the opposite side, the Howe, the residence of Captain Wilson, R. N., will be observed, and further on, the chapel is perceived on the banks of the stream, near the bridge, by which the roads are connected. That on the east side is the most direct road from Bowness to the valley, but it is objectionable on account of its not conducting the traveller through the village. The road on the western flank joins the Kendal and Ambleside road at Troutbeck Bridge, keeping throughout on the banks of the stream, the meanderings of which, on its way to Windermere, round rugged scaurs and wooded banks, are continually in sight. Half a mile beyond the chapel, is the only inn in the valley, bearing the quaint title of "The Mortal Man,"—a name acquired from the lines, composed, doubtless, by some native poet, which a few years ago decorated the sign-board—

"O Mortal Man, who livest on bread,
What is't that makes thy nose so red?—
Thou silly ass, that looks so pale,
It is with drinking Birkett's ale."

Two miles beyond the inn, the tourist has immediately below him, a tongue or swelling from the bottom of the vale called Troutbeck Park, which is visible even from the surface of Windermere. Taking his station here, and turning to the north-east, the spectator has the mountains of Kentmere before him. The nearest elevation is called the Yoke, the two next, having the appearance of the humps on a dromedary's back, are Hill Bell and Froswick,—and further on is

DERWENT WATER & BASSENTHWAITE.

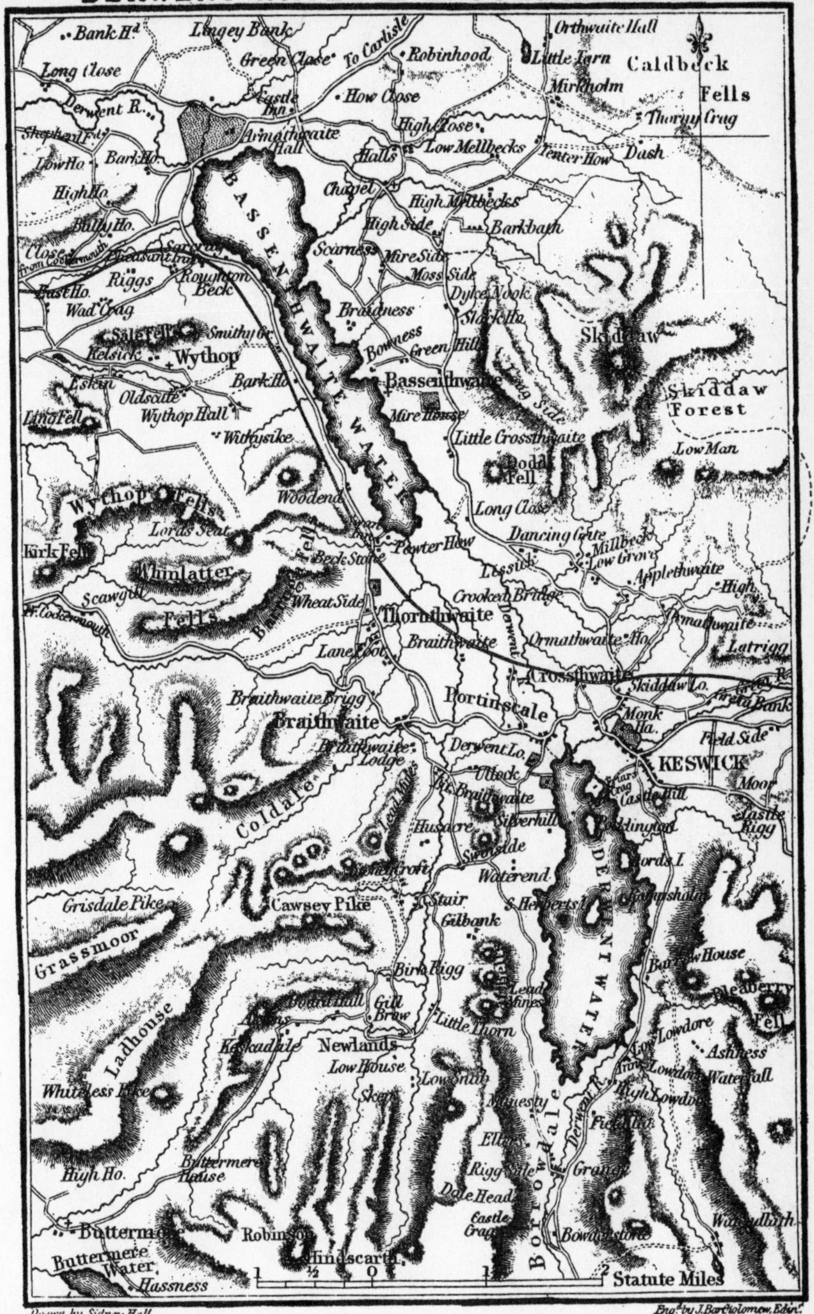

Drawn by Sidney Hall　　　Engd by J. Bartholomew, Edinr.

High Street. Having left the Mortal Man three miles behind, and climbed the side of Kirkstone for some distance, a road through the fields, on the left, will be discovered, which passes in succession three farm-houses, High Grove, Middle Grove, and Low Grove, in Stockdale, and enters Ambleside, three miles from the deviation.

A favourite excursion, with the temporary residents in Ambleside, is that through the two LANGDALES. If the object of the tourist be merely to view the vale of Great Langdale (the finer of the two) with Dungeon Gill Force, and to ascend the Pikes, he will traverse a road perfectly practicable for carriages; but if he desire to see something more of the country, by visiting Skelwith and Colwith Forces, Little Langdale and Blea Tarns, he must be content to go on horseback, in a car, or on foot. This circuit, which we shall describe, is about eighteen miles in length. With the intention, then, of visiting the two Langdales in succession, the tourist will leave Ambleside by the road to Clappersgate, winding on the banks of the Brathay, (near the source of which he will be ere long,) under the craggy heights of Loughrigg Fell. A newly-built chapel will be observed in a charming situation on the south bank of the river. "Sweeter stream-scenery," says Wilson, "with richer fore, and loftier back-ground, is nowhere to be seen within the four seas." A few hundred yards above Skelwith Bridge (three miles from Ambleside) the stream is precipitated over a ledge of rock, making a fall twenty feet in height. The cascade is not so remarkable in itself, as for the magnificent scenery around it. Langdale Pikes have a peculiarly striking appearance. By this bridge the traveller is conducted into Lancashire, in which county the road does not continue for more than a mile before it re-enters Westmorland at Colwith Bridge. A short distance above the bridge, the stream, issuing from a tarn farther up, makes a fine cascade called Colwith Force. It is in a dell close to the road, and is about 70 feet high. A stupendous mountain, called Wetherlamb, occupies a conspicuous position in a chain of lofty hills on the south-west. Proceeding, Little Langdale Tarn becomes visible on the left—on the right is Lingmoor, a hill which serves as a partition between the two Langdales. At the termination of the inclosed land, amongst a few trees, are two dwellings, called Fell Foot, seven and a-half miles from Ambleside. One of them was formerly an inn, whereat the gangs of pack-horses were refreshed previous to their ascent of the mountain passes of Wrynose and Hardknot—this being the route by which the manufactures of Kendal were transported to the western coast. Taking the road to the right, and ascending some distance between the mountains, a solitary pool of water, named Blea Tarn, is perceived in the bottom of an elevated depression.

Those magnificent objects,—

> ——— the two huge peaks
> That from some other vale peer into this,

are the two Pikes of Langdale. The more southern one is named Pike o' Stickle —the other, and higher, Harrison Stickle. Having passed the tarn, the road winds down a steep descent into the head of Great Langdale, that part of it called Mickleden, through which is the road over the Stake into Borrowdale, being right before the eye. Mill Becks, a farm-house, at which refreshment is usually taken, is soon reached. Here a guide to Dungeon Gill Force, and to the summit of the Pikes, can be obtained. The former is a fall of water, formed by a stream which runs down a fissure in the mountain's side not far above the house. A curious natural arch has been made, by a large stone having rolled from a higher part of the mountain, and got wedged in between the cheeks of rock. Over the bridge thus formed, ladies have been known, like Wordsworth's Idle Shepherd Boy, to possess the intrepidity to pass.* Two roads traverse the valley, one of which keeps under the hills on the left, the other takes the middle of the vale ;—the former is to be preferred by those unencumbered with carriages. One mile and a half from Mill Becks, is the little Chapel of Langdale, whence a road strikes up the hill-side, crossing Red Bank into Rydal, or Grasmere. A large sheet of water, lying amongst the meadows, which now comes into sight, is Elterwater Tarn, at the head of which stands Elterwater Hall. The stream feeding the tarn is crossed by a bridge, a short distance above the tarn Near the bridge are the works of Elterwater Gunpowder Company. A little further in a recess, on the flank of Loughrigg Fell, is Loughrigg Tarn, a lovely spot on which Wilson has composed some beautiful lines. Ambleside is only three miles beyond.

Ambleside abounds with villas. Among them may be named, Fox Ghyll (H. Roughsedge, Esq.), Fox Howe (Mrs Arnold), Rothay Bank (J. Crossfield, Esq.), Oak Bank (C. Robinson, Esq.), The Cottage (H. P. Lutwidge, Esq.), The Oaks (Dr Davy), The Knoll (Miss Martineau), Covey Cottage (G. Partridge, Esq.), Bellevue (M. Harrison, Esq.), Green Bank (B. Harrison, Esq.), Hill Top (T. Carr, Esq.), Brathay Hall (G. Redmayne, Esq.), Croft Lodge (J. Holmes, Esq.), Wanlass How (Mrs Brenchley), Wansfell Holme (J. Hornby, Esq.), Wray Castle (J. Dawson, Esq.), Rydal Hall (Rev. Sir R. Fleming), Rydal Mount (the residence of the late William Wordsworth, Esq.), Glen Rothay (W. Ball Esq.), Allan Bank (Thomas Dawson, Esq.), The Cottage (Mrs. Orrell).

ULVERSTON.

[*Inns:*—Sun; Braddyll's Arms.]

Ulverston, a market-town and port, containing about 6630 inhabitants, situate in that division of Lancashire, termed " North of the Sands," is supposed to derive its name from Ulph, a Saxon Lord. It is about a mile from the estuary of the Leven, with which it is connected by a canal, constructed in 1795, and ca-

* " There is a spot which you may see
If ever you to Langdale go.
Into a chasm, a mighty block
Hath fallen, and made a bridge of rock :
The gulf is deep below,
And in a basin black and small,
Receives a lofty Waterfall."

Wordsworth.

BUTTERMERE, CRUMMOCK & LOWES WATER.

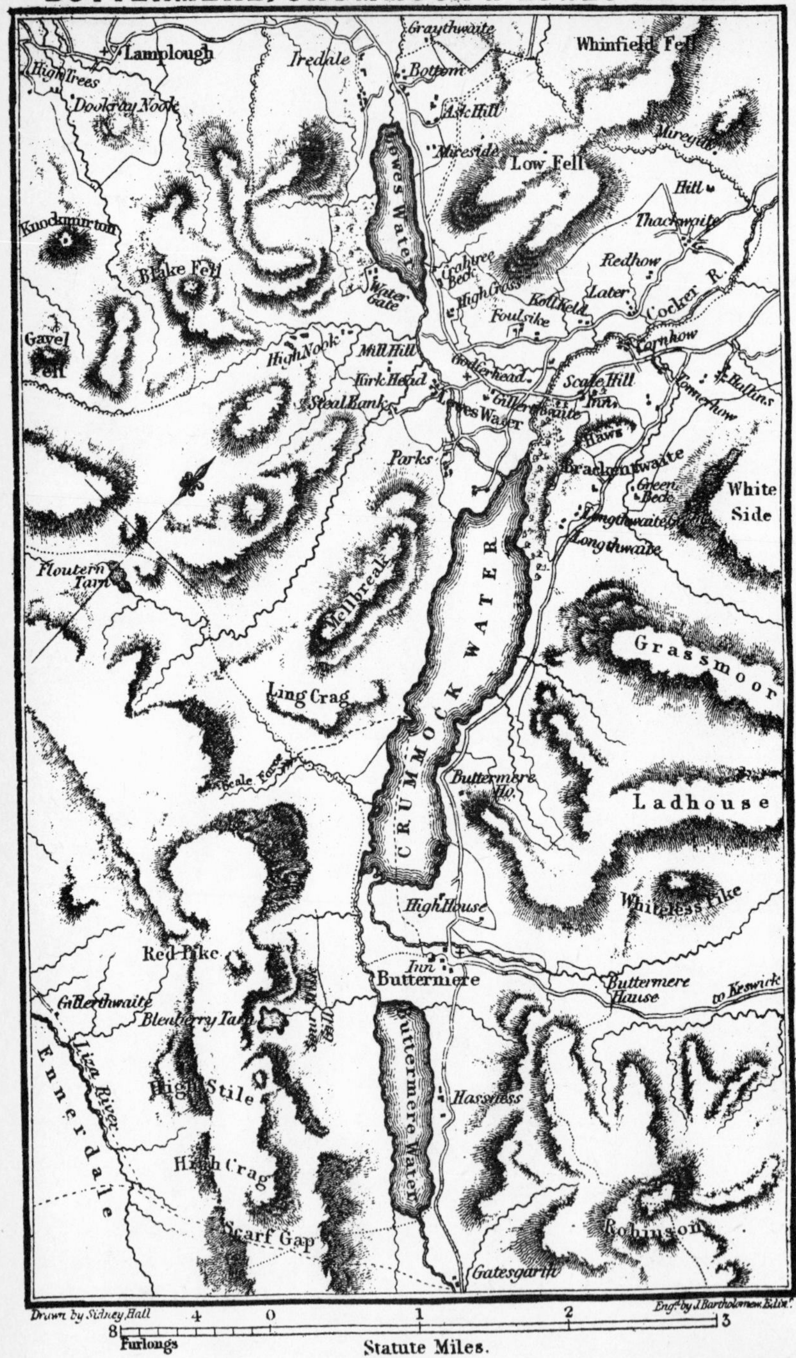

pable of floating vessels of 200 tons. The appearance of the town is neat, the greater part of the houses being of modern erection. The parish church, dedicated to St Mary, received considerable additions in 1804; but a tower and Norman doorway of the old structure still remain. From the sloping ground behind the church, a delightful view of the bay and neighbouring country may be obtained. A new and elegant church, dedicated to the Holy Trinity, was erected at the upper end of the town in 1832. Amongst other buildings of recent erection, the Savings' Bank may be noticed. The town contains a Theatre, Assembly Room, and Subscription Library, and two good Inns,—the Sun and Braddyll's Arms. Ship-building is carried on to some extent; and the manufacture of check, canvass, and hats, is a considerable branch of trade.

The Duke of Buccleuch is Lord of the liberty of Furness, of which the Manor of Ulverston forms part.

CONISHEAD PRIORY, the seat of T. R. G. Braddyll, Esq., has been termed, from its beautiful situation, "the Paradise of Furness." It is situate two miles south of Ulverston, near the sea-shore, in an extensive and well-wooded park, which is intersected, like most old parks, with public roads, forming a favourite promenade for the inhabitants of the town. The mansion, which has lately been rebuilt in a style of magnificence of which there are few examples in the north of England, occupies the site of the ancient Priory, founded by William de Lancaster, the fourth in descent from Ivo de Taillebois, first Baron of Kendal, in the reign of Henry II. Upon the dissolution of the religious houses, it fell into the hands of Henry the VIII., whose cupidity was excited by the great extent of its landed possessions. The interior of the mansion possesses some good paintings of Titian, the Carracci, Romney, Reynolds, and other celebrated painters. HOLKER HALL, a seat of the Duke of Devonshire, is placed in a noble park on the opposite shore of the Leven, about three and a half miles east of Ulverston. The noble owner has a good collection of pictures, among which are many excellent paintings by Romney.

Six miles north-east of Ulverston is the village of Cartmell, in which is an ancient church, once a priory, of unusual size and beauty, dedicated to the Virgin. A short distance from the village is a medicinal spring called Holywell. Six miles and a half to the south-west of Ulverston, in a close valley called Beckansgill, or the glen of deadly nightshade, from that plant being found there in great abundance, are the beautiful remains of FURNESS ABBEY, now belonging to the Duke of Devonshire. This abbey was founded in 1127, by Stephen, Earl of Montaigne and Boulogne, afterwards King of England; "This prince conferred the greater part of the district, excepting the land of Michael Fleming, on the Abbey of Furness, by a charter dated 1126, in which, for the first time, the name Furness 'Fudernesia' or the further ness, is found. By this institution it was held till the dissolution, when it reverted to the Crown, and became part of the duchy of Lancaster. In the year 1662, it was granted by Charles II. to the Duke of Albemarle, and his heirs, with all the rights, privileges, and jurisdictions belonging thereto. The Lordship is now held by the Duke of Buccleuch, to whom the property of the Duke of Albemarle descended by marriage. In the early part of English history, the Falls of Furness formed the boundary between Scotland and England, and in 1138, a terrible eruption from the north laid the whole peninsula desolate. The ruins of the castle of Pile of Fouldrey form a monument of that invasion." *

The ruins amply attest the former magnificence of the structure. The length of the church is 287 feet, the nave is 70 feet broad, and the walls in some places 54 feet high, and 5 feet thick. The walls of the church, and those of the chapter-house, the refectorium, and the school-house, are still in great part remaining, and exhibit fine specimens of Gothic architecture ; the chapter-house, 60 feet by 45, has been a sumptuous apartment ; the roof, which was of fret-work, was supported by six channelled pillars. The great east window, the four seats near it, adorned with Gothic ornaments, and four statues found in the ruins, are particularly worthy of notice.

By the ebbing of the tide, the sands of Morecambe Bay, lying between Lancaster (hence usually termed the LANCASTER SANDS) and Ulverston, are twice a day, to the extent of several miles, left perfectly dry, except in the channels of the rivers Kent and Leven, and may be crossed by vehicles of every description. Guides, who are remunerated by Government, are stationed at the places where the rivers flow, to conduct travellers across in safety. The whole distance from Lancaster to Ulverston is twenty-two miles. From Hest Bank, the point of entry upon the sands on the eastern shore, to Kents Bank, is a distance of eleven miles. Three miles of *terra firma* are then crossed, and three miles of sand follow, lying between the shores of the Leven estuary, from the nearest of which Ulverston is distant something more than a mile. If the proper time be chosen, (which can be easily ascertained by inquiry at Lancaster and Ulverston,) there is no danger in crossing these sandy plains, and yet few years pass in which lives are not lost. †

KESWICK.

[*Hotels:*—Royal Oak; Queen's Head, King's Arms.]

KESWICK, a market-town in the parish of Crosthwaite, and county of Cumberland, is situate on the south bank of the Greta, in a large and fertile vale, little more than a mile from the foot of Skiddaw, and half a mile from Derwentwater. It contains 2610 inhabitants, and consists of one large street. The principal manufactures are linsey-wolsey stuffs, and edge-tools, particularly the former. Black-lead pencils, made of the plumbago (or *wad*, as it is provincially called,) extracted from the mine in Borrowdale, are also a considerable branch

* BAINES' Hist. of Lancashire, Vol. iv. p. 627.

† " I must not omit to tell you that Mr Wordsworth not only admired our exploit in crossing the Ulverston Sands as a deed of ' derring do,' but as a decided proof of taste : the lake scenery, he says, is never seen to such advantage as after the passage of what he calls its majestic barrier."—MRS HEMANS' *Letters*.

of manufacture. Char, taken in Buttermere lake, is potted in large quantities during the proper season, and forwarded to the south of England. The Town Hall, erected in 1813, upon the site of the old Court House, stands in the centre of the town. The clock-bell, which was taken from a building that formerly stood on Lord's Island in the lake, has the letters and figures "H. D. R. O. 1001," upon it,—a decisive proof of its high antiquity. The parish church, an ancient structure, dedicated to St Kentigern, stands three quarters of a mile distant. A new church of elegant proportions was erected on the east of the town by the late John Marshall, Esq., who became lord of the manor by purchasing the forfeited estates of Ratcliffe, Earl of Derwentwater, from the Commissioners of Greenwich Hospital, to whom they were granted by the Crown. A manorial court is held annually in May. The two museums, kept by Messrs Crosthwaite and Hutton, deserve a visit, as they contain specimens illustrating the natural history of the neighbourhood, as well as many foreign curiosities. Minerals and geological specimens are kept on sale. Mr Flintoft's accurate model of the lake district, the labour of many years, should also be inspected. For the tourist this model possesses peculiar interest, exhibiting, as it does, an exact representation of the country through which he is travelling, with every object minutely laid down, and the whole coloured after nature. The dimensions of the model are 12 feet 9 inches by 9 feet 3 inches. There are two good hotels, the Royal Oak and the Queen's Head, besides numerous inns, at which guides, ponies, boatmen, and boats can be obtained. Tourists desiring to make a prolonged stay may also be accommodated with comfortable lodgings at many private houses.

GRETA HALL, the residence of the late Dr Southey, the Poet Laureate, is seated on a slight eminence near the town, about 200 yards to the right of the bridge across the river on the road to Cockermouth. The scenery visible from the windows has been finely sketched by himself in these hexametrical lines:

" 'Twas at that sober hour when the light of day is receding,
And from surrounding things the hues wherewith day has adorn'd them
Fade like the hopes of youth till the beauty of youth is departed:
Pensive, though not in thought, I stood at the window beholding
Mountain, and lake, and vale; the valley disrobed of its verdure;
Derwent retaining yet from eve a glassy reflection,
Where his expanded breast, then still and smooth as a mirror,
Under the woods reposed; the hills that calm and majestic
Lifted their heads into the silent sky, from far Glaramara,
Bleacrag, and Maidenmawr to Grisedal and westernmost Wythop.
Dark and distinct they rose. The clouds had gathered above them,
High in the middle air huge purple pillowy masses,
While in the west beyond was the last pale tint of the twilight,
Green as the stream in the glen, whose pure and chrysolite waters
Flow o'er a schistous bed, and serene as the age of the righteous.
Earth was hush'd and still; all motion and sound were suspended;
Neither man was heard, bird, beast, nor humming of insect,
Only the voice of the Greta, heard only when all is in stillness."

The lake sometimes called Keswick Lake, but better known by the name of

DERWENTWATER,

is about half a mile from the town. A scene of more luxuriant beauty than this lake affords can scarcely be imagined. Its shape is symmetrical without being formal, while its size is neither so large as to merge the character of the lake in that of the inland sea, nor so circumscribed as to expose it to the charge of insignificance. The admirers of nature are divided in opinion as to the respective merits of this lake and Ulleswater ; some assigning the palm of superiority to the one and some to the other. Those who are familiar with the Alpine scenery of Scotland, which so far surpasses in savage grandeur any thing within the limits of the sister country, almost uniformly give the preference to Derwentwater, while those who have not possessed opportunities of contemplating nature in her sterner moods are more deeply impressed with the more majestic attributes of her rival.

Derwentwater approaches to the oval form, extending from north to south about three miles, and being in breadth about a mile and a half, "expanding within an amphitheatre of mountains, rocky but not vast, broken into many fantastic shapes, peaked, splintered, impending, sometimes pyramidal, opening by narrow vallies to the view of rocks that rise immediately beyond, and are again overlooked by others. The precipices seldom overshoot the water, but are arranged at some distance ; and the shores swell with woody eminences, or sink into green pastoral margins. Masses of wood also frequently appear among the cliffs, feathering them to their summits ; and a white cottage sometimes peeps from out their skirts, seated on the smooth knoll of a pasture projecting to the lake, and looks so exquisitely picturesque, as to seem placed there purposely to adorn it. The lake in return faithfully reflects the whole picture, and so even and brilliantly translucent is its surface, that it rather heightens than obscures the colouring."*

The principal islands in the lake are Vicar's Isle, Lord's Island, and St Herbert's Isle. VICAR'S ISLE or DERWENT ISLE is that nearest the foot of the lake ; it contains about six acres, and belongs to Captain Henry, whose residence is upon it. LORD'S ISLAND, of a size somewhat larger than the last, has upon it the hardly perceptible remains of a pleasure-house, erected by one of the Ratcliffes with the stones of their deserted castle which stood on Castlerigg. This island was once connected with the mainland, from which it was severed by the Ratcliffes, by a fosse, over which a drawbridge was thrown. ST HERBERT'S ISLE, placed nearly in the centre of the lake, derives its name from a holy hermit who lived in the seventh century, and had his cell on this island. The remains of the hermitage are still visible. To St Cuthbert of Durham this "saintly eremite" bore so perfect a love as to pray that he him-

* So transparent is the water, that pebbles may be easily seen fifteen or twenty feet below its surface.

self might expire the moment the breath of life quitted the body of his friend, so that their souls might wing their flight to Heaven in company.

Near the ruins, the late Sir Wilfred Lawson, (to whose representative the island at present belongs,) erected a few years ago a small cottage which, being built of unhewn stone, and artificially mossed over, has a venerable appearance. There are three or four other islets, the largest of which is Rampsholm. At irregular intervals of a few years, the lake exhibits a singular phenomenon in the rising of a piece of ground, called The FLOATING ISLAND, from the bottom to the surface of the water. Its superficial extent varies in different years, from an acre to a few perches. It is composed of earthy matter, six feet in thickness, covered with vegetation, and is full of air-bubbles, which, it is supposed, by penetrating the whole mass, diminish its specific gravity, and are the cause of its buoyancy. This natural phenomenon is situate about 150 yards from the shore, near Lowdore.

The walks in the neighbourhood of Keswick are numerous and interesting. From Crow Park and Friar Crag, two places situate on the east shore, near the foot of the lake, beautiful views of the lake, vale, and surrounding mountains are obtained. From a wooded eminence called Castle Head, standing on the left of the Borrowdale road, about half a mile from Keswick, there is an enchanting prospect extending on the south into the "Jaws of Borodale," in which Castle Crag appears like a prominent front tooth. Cat Bells, on the other side of the lake, are fine objects, as well as other mountains which tower over the vale of Newlands. From a summit, called Castlerigg, one mile from Keswick on the Ambleside road, there is a most extensive view, comprising the lakes of Derwentwater and Bassenthwaite, the fertile vale through which the Derwent winds on its passage from the one lake to the other, and the heights of Skiddaw. Gray declares that, on leaving Keswick, when he turned round at this place to contemplate the scenery behind him, he was so charmed "that he had almost a mind to go back again." A walk over Latrigg, "Skiddaw's Cub," will furnish the stranger with innumerable delightful prospects; and, in fact, it is impossible to stir in the neighbourhood of Keswick, without having scenery of the finest description before the eye. One mile and a-half from Keswick, on an eminence to the right of the old road to Penrith, is a small Druidical circle, measuring 100 feet by 108, consisting of forty-eight stones, some of which are 7 feet high.

Perhaps an excursion exhibiting more beautiful prospects of rock, wood, and water, than that round Derwentwater, does not exist in the vicinity of the Lakes. It is not more than 10 miles in length, if Grange Bridge be the limit of the ride in that direction; but if the excursion be extended to Bowder Stone, two miles must be added. Leaving Keswick by the Borrowdale Road, Castle Head, Wallow Crag, and Falcon Crag, are successively passed on the left. A hollow in the summit of Wallow Crag is visible from the road. There is a tradition current in the country, that, by means of this hollow, the Countess of Derwentwater effected her escape when the Earl was arrested for high treason, carrying with her a quantity of jewels and other valuables. It has ever since borne the name of the Lady's Rake. Barrow House stands two miles from Keswick, on the left of the road. Behind the house there is a fine cascade 124 feet in height, which may be seen on application at the lodge. A mountain road strikes off at this point to the village of Watendlath, two miles from the deflection. The road, after passing the village, near which there is a tarn, re-enters the Borrowdale road a little beyond Bowder Stone. In making the ascent to the village, splendid views of the lake and Skiddaw are obtained. One mile beyond Barrow, the road having passed under Thrang Crag, is LOWDORE HOTEL, behind which is the celebrated Lowdore Waterfall. The grandeur of the rocks around the stream render the scene impressive, whatever may be the state of the weather, but the cascade is dependent in a great measure for its effect on the quantity of water. After heavy rains, the noise of the fall may be heard as far down the lake as Friar Crag. Gowder Crag rises on the left, Shepherd's Crag on the right, of the waterfall. One mile further, Grange Bridge, spanning Borrowdale Beck, is attained. Should the tourist desire to see the curious mass of rock called Bowder Stone, the road into Borrowdale must be continued for a mile further. This immense block, which has evidently rolled from the heights above, stands on a platform of ground, a short distance to the left of the road. A branch road has been made to the stone, which rejoins the Borrowdale road further on. It has been computed to weigh upwards of 1900 tons. Its summit may be gained by means of a ladder which has been affixed to it for the use of strangers.

> "Upon a semicirque of turf-clad ground,
> A mass of rock, resembling, as it lay
> Right at the foot of that moist precipice,
> A stranded ship, with keel upturned, that rests
> Careless of winds and waves."
>
> WORDSWORTH.

Close to Bowder Stone, but on the opposite side of the river, from the bank of which it suddenly rises, is an elevation clothed with wood called Castle Crag, so termed from a Roman fortification having once occupied the summit, the faint traces of which still remain. Some of the relics found here are shown in one of the museums at Keswick. Returning to and crossing Grange Bridge, the village of Grange is passed, and, one mile beyond, are a few houses called Manesty, near which is a small medicinal spring. Passing under the summit styled Cat Bells, the road enters the pretty village of Portinscale, 4¾ miles from Grange Bridge, near which are many elegant villas. Keswick is but a mile and a quarter beyond.

An agreeable excursion of thirteen miles and a half may be made from Keswick into the famed VALLEY OF ST JOHN. The Penrith road must be pursued for four miles, to the village of Threlkeld. This road, lying almost the whole way on the banks of the Greta, passes under the mountain-masses of Skiddaw and Saddleback, (more poetically called Blencathara.) In a recess of the latter mountain, deeply embosomed in huge cliffs, there lies a piece of water called Scales Tarn, which exaggerating travellers have described as an abyss of waters upon which the sun never shines, and wherein the stars of heaven may be seen at noon-day.

In the same tarn, tradition asserts that two immortal fish have their abode. Amongst the acknowledgments which the Minstrel, in his "Song at the feast of Brougham Castle," states had been made to the secret power of the good Lord Clifford, when a shepherd boy in adversity, was the following:—

"And both the undying fish that swim
In Bowscale Tarn did wait on him,
The pair were servants of his eye
In their immortality;
They moved about in open sight,
To and fro for his delight."

The old hall at Threlkeld has been long in a state of dilapidation, the only habitable part having been for years converted into a farm-house. This was one of the places of residence of Sir Lancelot Threlkeld, a powerful knight in the reign of Henry VII., and uncle to the Lord Clifford above-mentioned, who was wont to say that "he had three noble houses—one for pleasure, Crosby in Westmorland, where he had a park full of deer; one for profit and warmth, namely, Yanwith, nigh Penrith; and the third, Threlkeld on the edge of the vale of Keswick, well stocked with tenants to go with him to the wars." These "three noble houses" are now the property of the Earl of Lonsdale, and are all occupied as farm-houses.

A short distance on the Keswick side of Threlkeld, the road leading into the Vale of St John branches off on the right. A branch of the river Greta, called St John's Beck, runs through this valley, which is narrow, but extremely picturesque, being bounded on the right by Nathdale or Naddle Fell, and on the left by Great Dodd, a hill at the extremity of the Helvellyn chain. The chapel occupies a striking situation on the right, at the summit of the pass between St John's Vale and Naddle. Though standing at such an elevation, the sun never shines upon it during three months of the year. There are fine retrospective views of Saddleback, and the peculiar conformation of the summit which gives its name to the mountain may be clearly perceived. The high road to Keswick is gained four miles and a half from Threlkeld. From the end of Naddle Fell, in the Vale of Thirlspot, near to Thirlemere, some sweet glimpses of that lake may be obtained. The rock which has given celebrity to the valley stands near the extremity on the left. The resemblance to a fortification is certainly very striking. It is the scene of Sir Walter Scott's Bridal of Triermain, in which there is the following description of the appearance which the rock presented to the charmed senses of King Arthur:—

"With toil the King his way pursued
By lonely Threlkeld's waste and wood,
Till on his course obliquely shone
The narrow valley of St John.

Down sloping to the western sky,
Where lingering sunbeams love to lie.
* * * * * * *
Paled in by many a lofty hill,
The narrow dale lay smooth and still,
And, down its verdant bosom led,
A winding brooklet found its bed.
But midmost of the vale, a mound
Arose with airy turrets crown'd,
Buttress, and rampire's circling bound,
And mighty keep and tower;
Seem'd some primeval giant's hand
The castle's massive walls had plann'd,
A ponderous bulwark to withstand
Ambitious Nimrod's power,
Above the moated entrance slung,
The balanced drawbridge trembling hung,
As jealous of a foe;
Wicket of Oak, as iron hard,
With iron studded, clench'd, and barr'd,
And prong'd portcullis, join'd to guard
The gloomy pass below.
But the grey walls no banners crown'd,
Upon the watch-tower's airy round
No warder stood his horn to sound,
No guard beside the bridge was found,
And, where the Gothic gateway frown'd,
Glanced neither bill nor bow.
* * * * * * * *
——————when a pilgrim strays,
In morning mist or evening maze,
Along the mountain lone,
That fairy fortress often mocks
His gaze upon the castled rocks
Of the Valley of St John."

Keswick is nine miles and a-half from Threlkeld by way of the Vale of St John. The ridge of Castlerigg, whence there is the splendid prospect already noticed, is crossed one mile from Keswick.

A drive round the lake of BASSENTHWAITE is frequently taken by tourists whilst making Keswick their head-quarters. This lake lies three miles to the north of Derwentwater, from which it is separated by low meadows, that in wet weather are flooded to some extent; it is four miles long, and about one mile broad. The pleasant village of Portinscale is a mile and a-quarter from Keswick. Two miles beyond, the road which must be pursued quits the old Cockermouth road near the village of Braithwaite,—between the two villages the tourist has Grisedale Pike directly before him. The road then becomes elevated, forming a fine terrace whence the beautiful vales of Thornthwaite, Braithwaite, and Keswick, are beheld, with all their luxuriance of wood. Skirting the base of Lord's Seat and Barf, and after making many ascents and descents disclosing delightful views of the lake, backed by Skiddaw, Ouse Bridge is crossed nine miles and a-half from Keswick. The bridge spans the Derwent soon after it issues from the lake. A quarter of a mile beyond is Armathwaite Hall, the seat of Sir H. R. F. Vane, Bart. The Castle Inn, where refreshment may be taken, is ten miles from Keswick, which town the tourist reaches by a road eight miles in length, passing under Skiddaw. Bassenthwaite Church is seen on the right near the margin of the lake.

The last excursion from Keswick which we shall detail is that by way of Borrowdale to BUTTERMERE, CRUMMOCK, and LOWES WATER. The road has been already described as far as Bowder Stone, a little beyond which it joins the road from Watendlath. A mile below Bowder Stone is Rosthwaite, where there is a small inn. A short distance farther a road strikes off on the left through Stonethwaite to Langdale, passing over the ridge called the Stake. One mile from Rosthwaite the road into Wastdale, by the pass of Sty Head, continues up Borrowdale on the left. Near the deviation is Seatoller, the residence of Abraham Fisher, Esq., in the neighbourhood of which is the celebrated mine of plumbago, or *black lead*, as it is usually called. It has been worked at intervals for upwards of two centuries, but, being now less productive, the ore has been excavated for several years consecutively. This is the only mine of the kind in England, and there are only one or two places in Scotland where plumbago has been discovered, but the lead obtained there is of an inferior quality. The best ore procured at the Borrowdale mine sells for L. 1, 10s. a pound. In the vicinity of the lead mine are four yew trees of extraordinary size.

At Seatoller the ascent of Buttermere Haws is commenced. This hill is steep and the road rough, private carriages, therefore, should not be taken over. It is eleven hundred feet in height, and commands noble prospects of the receding valley of Borrowdale. Helvellyn may be descried over the Borrowdale Fells. The hill called Glaramara is on the left. With a little stretch of fancy the streams may be heard

"Murmuring in Glaramara's inmost caves."

On the right of the pass is the hill named Yewdale.

The road descends rapidly into the head of Buttermere dale ; Honister Crag, presenting an almost perpendicular wall of rock, rising on the left to the height of fifteen hundred feet. In the face of the rock, a considerable height above its base, large chambers have been cut, tier above tier, in which roofing-slates are excavated. The slates are shaped in the quarry, and brought down by men on wooden hurdles. These quarries belong to General Wyndham. Two miles below Honister Crag, and four from Seatoller, is a farm house near the head of Buttermere Lake, called Gatescarth, whence a mountain road crosses by the pass of Scarf Gap, into the head of Ennerdale, and reaches Wastdale Head by means of another pass called Black Sail. Hasness, the residence of General Benson, occupies a pretty situation on the left near the margin of the lake. A series of mountain summits tower over the opposite shore of the lake. The Hay Stacks, so termed from their form, are the most eastern ; then follow High Crag, High Stile, and Red Pike. A stream issuing from a small tarn which lies between the two last, makes a fine cascade, bearing the name of Sour-Milk

Gill. The village of Buttermere stands on declining ground near the foot of the lake fourteen miles from Keswick. It consists of a few scattered farm-houses, with a good inn, forming, by reason of the surrounding hills, the very picture of seclusion. " The margin of the lake, which is overhung by some of the loftiest and steepest of the Cumbrian mountains, exhibits on either side few traces of human neighbourhood ; the level area, where the hills recede enough to allow of any, is of a wild pastoral character or almost savage. The waters of the lake are deep and sullen, and the barrier mountains, by excluding the sun for much of his daily course, strengthen the gloomy impressions. At the foot of this lake lie a few unornamented fields, through which rolls a little brook connecting it with the larger lake of Crummock, and at the edge of this miniature domain, upon the road side, stands a cluster of cottages, so small and few that in the richer tracts of the island they would scarcely be complimented with the name of hamlet."* A good road of nine miles, after climbing a Haws 800 feet high, conducts the visitor through the vale of Newlands to Keswick. A small chapel has been erected at the expense of the Rev. Vaughan Thomas, by the road side, upon the site of a still smaller one. The old chapel has been thus described: —" It is not only the very smallest chapel, by many degrees, in all England, but is so mere a toy in outward appearance, that were it not for its antiquity, its wild mountain exposure, and its consecrated connexion with the final hopes and fears of the adjacent pastoral hamlet,—but for these considerations the first movement of a stranger's feelings would be towards loud laughter ; for the chapel looks not so much a miniature chapel in a drop scene from the Opera House, as a miniature copy from such a scene, and evidently could not receive within its walls more than half a dozen households." †

A footpath leading through the fields, and across the little stream connecting the two lakes, conducts to Scale Force, one of the loftiest waterfalls in the vicinity of the lakes. The road, in damp weather especially, is none of the cleanest, and therefore a boat is frequently taken, which lands the visitor about half a-mile from the fall. A mountain path, leaving Scale Force on the left and climbing the fells above it, leads into Ennerdale. Floutern Tarn, which is passed on the way, serves as a land-mark.

Extending the excursion to Scale Hill, four miles from Buttermere, the road traverses the eastern shore of Crummock Water, passing under the hills Whiteless, Grasmoor, and Whiteside. Melbreak is a fine object on the other shore. From the foot of this mountain a narrow promontory juts into the lake, the extremity of which, when the waters are swollen, becomes insulated. A short distance before Scale Hill is reached, there is a fine view into the sylvan valley of Lorton. At Scale Hill there is a comfortable inn, which for a few days might be made advantageously the tourist's residence. Boats may be had upon Crummock Lake, from which the inn is about a mile distant. Scale Force might be

* De Quincey † Ibid.

visited if not seen previously. One boating excursion at least ought to be taken for the purpose of viewing the fine panorama of mountains which enclose the lake, and which can be nowhere seen to such advantage as from the bosom of the water. Green has pointed out one station for obtaining a fine view, not only of Crummock Lake, but of Buttermere also. It is from a point two or three hundred yards above the promontory under Melbreak; Honister Crag is seen closing the prospect on the north. The lake is three miles long by about three-quarters of a mile broad; its sounded depth is twenty-two fathoms. There are three small islands at the head, but they are too near the shore to add much to the other beauties of the scenery. The small lake called Lowes Water may also be visited. It is scarcely a mile long, and the scenery at its head is tame, but that round its foot is of a magnificent description.

From Scale Hill the tourist may proceed to the town of Cockermouth, the birth-place of the poet Wordsworth, which is seven miles distant—visit Ennerdale Water by way of Lamplugh—or return to Keswick by the vale of Lorton, a distance of twelve miles. This vale, watered by the Cocker, a stream which, issuing from Crummock Lake, joins the Derwent at Cockermouth, presents many charming views. Four miles from Scale Hill, the Keswick and Cockermouth road is entered, near the Yew-tree which Wordsworth has celebrated.

> "There is a Yew-tree, pride of Lorton Vale,
> Which to this day stands single in the midst
> Of its own darkness, as it stood of yore,
> Not loth to furnish weapons for the bands
> Of Umfraville or Percy, ere they march'd
> To Scotland's heaths; or those that cross'd the sea,
> And drew their sounding bows at Agincour,
> Perhaps at earlier Cressy or Poictiers.
> Of vast circumference and gloom profound,
> This solitary Tree!—a living thing
> Produced too slowly ever to decay;
> Of form and aspect too magnificent
> To be destroy'd."

The road commences soon afterwards the long and steep ascent of Whinlatter, from the summit of which the spectator has a noble combination of objects before him,—comprehending Derwentwater, Bassenthwaite Water, Skiddaw, and Keswick Vale. The distance between Scale Hill and Keswick may be shortened by almost two miles, if the road under Whiteside and Grisedale Pike be taken. For the horseman and pedestrian the shorter route is to be preferred, as that part under the mountains forms a terrace, from which, views of Lorton Vale, or the neighbouring hills, and extending even to the Scotch mountains, may be obtained.

WHITEHAVEN.

[*Hotels:*—Globe; Black Lion; Golden Lion.]

Whitehaven is a market-town and sea-port, seated at the upper end of a small creek on the west coast in the county of Cumberland. It is situate in the parish of St Bees, and contains 18,842 inhabitants. This town has advanced rapidly from insignificance to its present state of prosperity, for in the year 1566 six fishermen's huts were all that bore the name of Whitehaven. This sudden progress in the scale of importance is to be attributed in a great measure to the munificence of the Lowther family, who, having large estates around the town, and valuable possessions in coal underneath it, have liberally come forward on all occasions, when opportunities have occurred, to promote its prosperity.

The chief manufactures are coarse linens, and articles connected with the fitting up of vessels. Ship-building is also carried on to a considerable extent. The port is the second in the county, there being upwards of 200 vessels belonging to it trading with the sea-ports of Great Britain, and with America, the West Indies, and the Baltic, as well as almost an equal number engaged in the coal trade ; large quantities of iron and lead ore, grain, and lime are exported. The harbour is spacious and commodious, having seven piers extending into the sea in different directions, and affording ample security for vessels lying within. At the entrance of the harbour there are two light-houses, and a third is situate on the promontory of St Bees Head, three miles to the south-west. A machine, called the patent-slip, erected by Lord Lonsdale, into which vessels are drawn with ease and expedition when repairs are required, deserves a visit. The bay and harbour are defended by batteries, formerly consisting of upwards of a hundred guns, but lately suffered to fall into decay. These batteries received extensive additions after the alarm caused by the descent of the notorious Paul Jones in 1778. This desperado, who was a native of Galloway, and had served his apprenticeship in Whitehaven, landed here with thirty armed men, the crew of an American privateer which had been equipped at Nantes for this expedition. The success of the enterprise was, however, frustrated by one of the company, through whom the inhabitants were placed on the alert. The only damage they succeeded in doing was the setting fire to three ships, only one of which was burnt. They were obliged to make a precipitate retreat, having first spiked the guns of the battery, so that they escaped unhurt to the coast of Scotland, where they plundered the house of the Earl of Selkirk. Since 1803 a life-boat has been stationed here,—which has been the means of saving many lives.

The streets of the town have a neat appearance, being straight as well as wide, and intersecting each other at right angles. A rivulet called the Poe runs underneath the town to the harbour. There are four churches of the establishment besides several dissenting places of worship. The schools are numerous, educating more than 1700 children, nearly 500 of whom are taught at the National School. The Theatre in Roper Street has a handsome appearance ; it was erected in 1769. The Workhouse is a large building in Scotch Street. The Harbour Office, in which the affairs of the harbour, docks, and customs are transacted, is a large structure on the West Strand. The Public Office, containing a police office, news-room, &c., stands in Lowther Street. The town now enjoys the privilege of returning a Member to Parliament.

ULLES WATER.

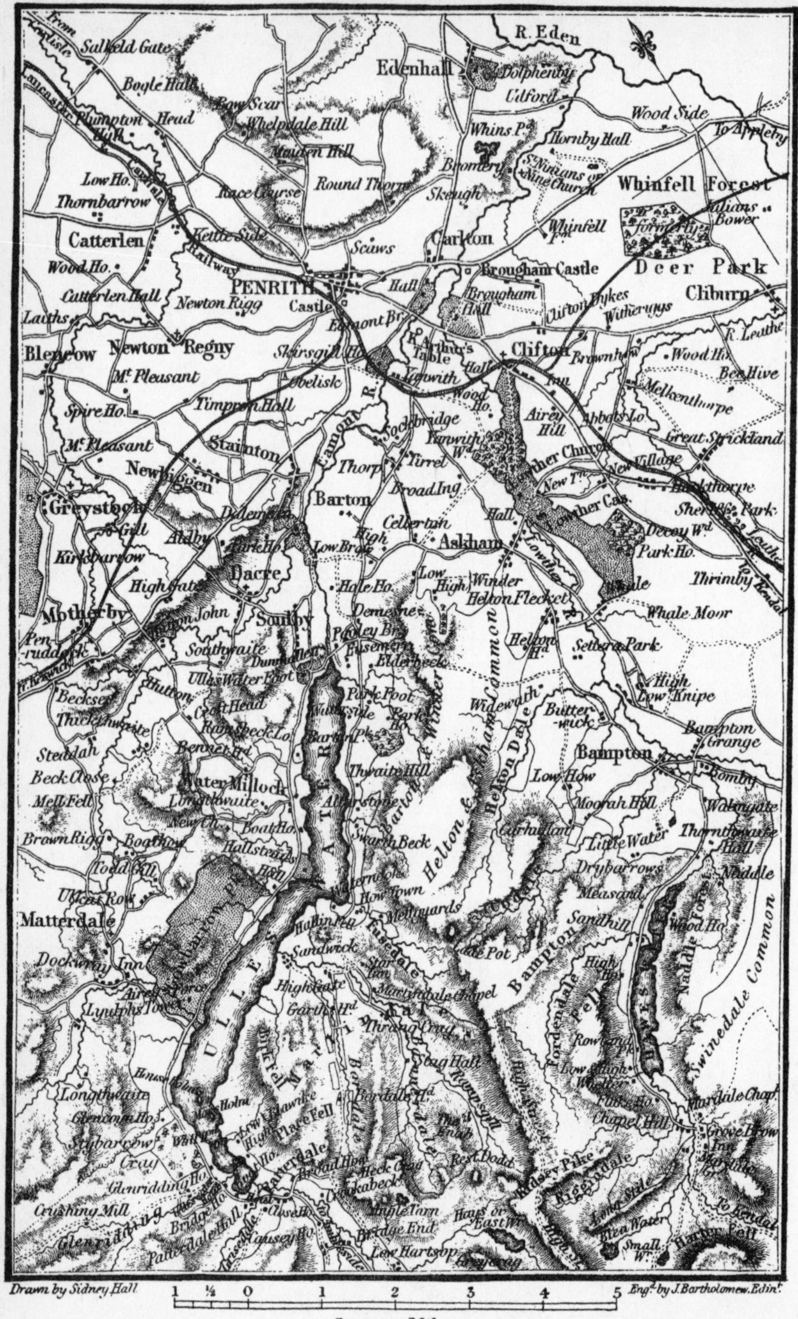

Drawn by Sidney Hall

Engd. by J. Bartholomew. Edinr.

1 ½ 0 1 2 3 4 5

Statute Miles.

The coal mines are the principal source of wealth at Whitehaven. They are, perhaps, the most extraordinary in the world, lying underneath the town, and extending a considerable distance under the bed of the sea. They are 320 yards in depth, and such vast quantities of coal have been excavated from them as to have given them the appearance of a subterranean city. At times of pressing demand, 1500 tons are frequently taken to the shore for exportation each day. The sea has not unfrequently burst into the mines, causing an immense destruction of life and property; the miners are also much annoyed with fire-damp and choke-damp. There are many short railways to convey the coal to the shore, and steam engines of great power are in continual operation for the purpose of carrying off the superfluous water. The mines have five principal entrances, called Bearmouths, three on the south side and two on the north, by all of which horses can descend.

Whitehaven is in direct communication with Liverpool, Belfast, Dublin, and Douglas in the Isle of Man, by the packets of the Steam Navigation Company. A packet sails several times a week to and from Liverpool; and as this mode of reaching Whitehaven is much more economical and expeditious than the inland one, many persons avail themselves of it for the purpose of arriving at the lake country. All information relative to the fares and times of sailing may be ascertained upon inquiry at the office of the Company, 36 King Street, or by reference to Bradshaw's Railway Guide. Railway Trains leave Whitehaven several times a-day for Workington, Cockermouth, and Maryport, in connection with the Maryport and Carlisle Railway, and for St Bees and Ravenglass, by the Furness Junction Railway. Customs dues collected in 1857, £73,201.

The residences in the neighbourhood of Whitehaven are Whitehaven Castle (Earl of Lonsdale), on the south-east of the town; Hensingham House (H. Jefferson, Esq.), one mile south; Summer Grove (J. Spedding), two miles south; Keekle Grove (Mrs Perry), three miles south; Linethwaite (G. Harrison, Esq.), three miles south; Moresby Hall (Miss Tate), two miles north, built after a design of Inigo Jones; Roseneath (Mrs Solomon); Rose Hill (G. W Hartley, Esq.).

Excursions may be made from Whitehaven to St Bees, to Ennerdale. Lake and to Wast Water.

ST BEES.

The village which gives its name to the parish of St Bees, in which Whitehaven in situated, lies in a narrow valley near the shore, four miles to the south of Whitehaven. Its appellation is said to be derived from St Bega, an Irish virgin and saint, who lived here, and founded a monastery about the year 650. The church, which was erected some time after her death, was dedicated to her, and is still in a state of excellent preservation. The tower is the only part of the Saxon edifice remaining, the rest being in the florid Gothic style. It is built of red freestone, in a cruciform shape, and possesses some fine carvings, particularly at the east end, which is lighted by three lancet-shaped windows. The nave is used as the parish church, and the cross aisle as a place of burial. Until 1810 the chancel was unroofed, but in that year it was repaired, and is now occupied as the divinity school "for the reception of young men intended for the Church, but not designed to finish their studies at Oxford or Cambridge."— "The old Conventual Church," says Wordsworth, in the preface to his poem of 'St Bees,' "is well worthy of being visited by any strangers who might be led to the neighbourhood of this celebrated spot."

The Grammar School, founded by Archbishop Grindal, stands near the church.

Ennerdale Lake is less visited than most of the other lakes, in consequence of its difficulty of access, and the want of houses of entertainment in the valley. It lies nine miles to the east of Whitehaven, from which town it is more easily reached than from any other. Its length is not more than two miles and a half, and its extreme width is about three-quarters of a mile. The stream which enters at its head is called the Liza, but the river issuing from the lake takes the name of Ehen. This stream is crossed for the first time by those approaching the lake five miles from Whitehaven, and a second time three miles further up, at the village of Ennerdale Bridge, at which is the chapel, and near it two small inns; the foot of the lake is one mile beyond. The first mile and a half of Ennerdale Water is the most picturesque part, and, therefore, carriages need not proceed further along the road than this distance, as there is no outlet for them at the upper end of the valley. The pedestrian or horseman will do well to traverse the whole length of the vale, as the mountains round its upper end are thrown into magnificent groups. Long before reaching the head of the lake the scenery becomes wild and desolate. A mile and a half beyond the extremity is the farm house of Gillerthwaite, the last habitation in the vale. Here the road for vehicles ends. A shepherd's path passes along the banks of the Liza, and two miles and a half beyond Gillerthwaite the extremity of Ennerdale is reached. Great Gable (2925 feet) is a fine object at the head; and the Pillar (2893 feet) has a striking appearance on the right. Great Gable is so called from its resembling the gable-end of a house. On the summit there was wont to be a small hollow in the rock never entirely empty of water,—"having," says Wordsworth, "no other feeder than the dews of heaven, the showers, the vapours, the hoar frost, and the spotless snow." This rock is now destroyed. The peculiar shape of the Pillar will not fail to strike the eye for some distance.

A sheep cote at the termination of the valley will be noticed. At this point a path strikes up the hill on the left, called Scarf Gap, and reaches Gatescarth in Buttermere, by a road three miles in length. Another path passes over Black Sail on the right, and winding round Kirkfell into Mosedale, having Yewbarrow on the right, reaches Wastdale Head, three miles from the sheep cote. Wastdale Head will be mentioned again in the description of our next excursion.

WAST WATER

Is most generally visited from Keswick by following the road up Borrowdale (described pages 26 and 30), and as far as Seathwaite, and from that striking across the Slyhead Pass to Wastdale Head. It may also be visited by the Furness Junction Railway from Drigg or Seascale Station, the former of which is 14½ and the latter 12½ miles from Whitehaven, or by the road which passes through the town of Egremont. Following the road, two miles and a half beyond Egremont, on the right, is the village of Beckermet. A house near this village, the residence of Joseph Hartley, Esq., bears the name of Wotobank, from the hill near which it stands. The derivation of this name is assigned by tradition to the following incident:—A Lord of Beckermet, with his lady and servants, were one day hunting wolves. During the chase the lady was discovered to be missing. After a long and painful search, her body was found on this hill or bank slain by a wolf, which was discovered in the very act of tearing it to pieces. In the first transports of his grief the husband exclaimed, "Woe to this bank!"

> "The name remains, and *Wotobank* is seen
> From every mountain bleak and valley green."
>
> MRS. COWLEY'S *Edwina.*

The road crosses Calder Bridge four miles from Egremont. There are two good inns in the village. Close at hand is Ponsonby Hall, the residence of E. Stanley, Esq., in a beautiful park. One mile above the village, on the north bank of the stream, are the picturesque remains of Calder Abbey, founded by Ranulph de Meschiens in 1134, for a colony of Cistertians who were detached from Furness Abbey. It subsequently received many valuable grants. At the dissolution it shared the common fate of the Romish ecclesiastical establishments.

In the church-yard at Gosforth, six miles from Egremont, there is an ancient stone pillar, which, until lately, was surmounted by a cross. The pretty village of Strands is four miles beyond Gosforth. It has two decent inns, at which boats on the lake may be procured. The ascent of Scawfell Pikes may be conveniently made from this place, by taking a boat to the head of the lake and landing at the foot of the mountain. Wast Water, one mile from Strands, is three and a half miles in length, and about half a mile broad. The deepest part yet discovered is forty-five fathoms. It has never been known to be iced over even in the severest winter. The mountains round this lake rise to a great altitude. The Screes hang over the south-east margin, and form an extraordinary feature in the landscape. Seatallon guards the opposite shore. The road traverses the north-western shore, and, six miles from Strands, arrives at the village of Wastdale Head, which consists merely of a few scattered homesteads and a little chapel. It would be a great accommodation to tourists if there were an inn at this place. Refreshment can, however, be obtained at one of the farm-houses, for which, of course, some remuneration will be given. The panorama of mountains surrounding this level area is strikingly grand. Standing at the head of the lake, the spectator will have Yewbarrow, like the slanting roof of a house, on his left, further up, Kirkfell, and immediately before him Great Gable,—a little on the right of which is Lingmell, a protrusion from Scawfell—the Pikes, (the highest land in England,) and Scawfell then follow.* Between Yewbarrow and Kirkfell there is the path over Black Sail into Ennerdale, before noticed. A foot road, passing round the head of the lake, and climbing the high ground between the Screes and Scawfell, descends by way of Burnmoor Tarn into Eskdale. Tourists on foot or horseback may proceed to Keswick, fourteen miles distant, by the pass of Sty Head—the highest in the lake district. The Borrowdale road is entered near Seathwaite. Great Gable is on the left of the pass, and Great End on the right. The summit, 1300 feet high, commands, as may be imagined, a most extensive view. The ascent is remarkably steep ; and if horses are taken over, great caution should be used. The notorious Baron Trenck once dashed down on horseback, leaving his astonished guide behind carefully picking his way. The fearless horseman arrived safe at the bottom, and performed in one day a journey of fifty-six miles, through steep and difficult roads, which nearly killed his horse.

PENRITH.

[*Hotels*:—Crown ; George.]

Penrith is an ancient market-town, seated at the foot of an eminence near the southern verge of the county of Cumberland. It contains 7189 inhabitants, and the appearance of the town is clean and neat. It lies in the neighbourhood of three rivers, the Lowther, Eamont, and Petterill, within the district called Inglewood Forest. The existence of Penrith may be traced back for many centuries. An army of 30,000 Scots laid it waste in the nineteenth year of Edward III., carrying away many of the inhabitants prisoners, and in the reign of Richard III. the town was again sacked. The manufactures are very trifling, consisting principally of linen goods and some woollen fabrics.

The ruins of the *Castle*, supposed to have been erected by the Nevilles, overlook the town from the west, and give it a noble appearance. It was for some time the residence of the Duke of Gloucester, afterwards Richard III., and continued in the possession of the Crown till the Revolution, when it was granted, together with the honour of Penrith, to Walter Bentinck, Earl of Portland. In the contest between Charles I. and the Long Parliament, this castle was seized and dismantled by the adherents of the Commonwealth, and the lead, timber, and other materials were sold. In 1783, the late Duke of Portland sold it, together with the honour of Penrith, including Inglewood Forest, to the Duke of Devonshire. Among the ruins is a subterraneous passage, which leads to a house in Penrith, called Dockray Hall, about three hundred yards distant.

The *Church* is a plain structure ; it was partly rebuilt in 1722, and is dedi-

* A description of the Pikes, and their ascent, is given on a subsequent page.

cated to St Andrew. It was given by Henry I. to the Bishop of Carlisle, who is still the patron of the cure.

On one of the walls is the following record of the ravages of a pestilence toward the end of the reign of Queen Elizabeth:—" A. D. M.D.XCVIII. ex gravi peste, quæ regionibus hisce incubuit, obierunt apud Penrith 2260, Kendal 2500, Richmond 2200, Carlisle 1196.

Posteri,
Avertite vos et vivite."

This memorial on brass has been substituted in the place of a more ancient inscription engraven on stone. It appears from an ancient register kept in the parish that this dreadful pestilence raged here from September 22, 1597, to January 5, 1599, a period of fifteen months!

In the church-yard is a singular monument of antiquity, called the *Giant's Grave*, the origin of which is involved in obscurity. It consists of two stone pillars, standing at the opposite ends of a grave fifteen feet asunder, and tapering from a circumference of eleven feet six inches at the base to seven feet at the top. Between these are four other stones; the whole are covered with Runic or other unintelligible carvings. Near them is another stone called the Giant's thumb. These remains are said to have once formed a monument erected to the memory of Owen Cœsarius, a giant.

On the heights to the north of Penrith is a square stone building, called *the Beacon*, well placed for giving alarm in the time of danger. From this elevation the views are at once extensive and delightfully picturesque; Helvellyn, Ulleswater, Skiddaw and Saddleback, with their attendant mountains; Crossfell (2900 feet high), and the eastern chain of hills stretching from Stanemoor in Yorkshire, through Westmorland and Cumberland into Scotland, being within the boundary of the prospect.

The antiquities in the neighbourhood of Penrith are numerous.

The remains of *Brougham Castle*, which are supposed to occupy the site of the Roman station *Brovoniacum*, occupy a striking situation near the junction of the rivers Eamont and Lowther, one mile and three-quarters from Penrith, a little to the right of the Appleby Road. The *vallum* of an encapment is still to be traced, and altars, coins, and other antiquities have often been found at the place.

A short distance beyond Brougham Castle stands the *Countess's Pillar*, erected in 1656, by Lady Anne Clifford.

Two miles below Brougham Castle, on the precipitous banks of the Eamont, are two excavations in the rock, called *Giant's Caves*, or *Isis Parlis*. One is very large, and contains marks of having been inhabited. There are traces of a door and window: and a strong column has marks of iron grating upon it. The approach to these singular remains is difficult. They are said to have been the abode of a giant called *Isis*.

A short distance on the Westmorland side of Eamont Bridge, in a field on the right of the road, about a mile and a half from Penrith, is another curious relic of antiquity, *King Arthur's Round Table,** a circular area above twenty yards in diameter, surrounded by a fosse and mound ; with two approaches opposite each other conducting to the area. As the fosse is on the inner side, it could not be intended for the purpose of defence, and it has reasonably been conjectured that the enclosure was designed for the exercise of the feats of chivalry, and the embankment around for the convenience of the spectators. Higher up the river Eamont is Mayborough, an area of nearly 100 yards in diameter, surrounded by a mound, composed of pebble stones elevated several feet. In the centre ofthe area is a large block of unhewn stone eleven feet high, supposed to have been a place of Druidical Judicature. Six miles north-east of Penrith, on the summit of an eminence near Little Salkeld, are the finest relics of antiquity in this vicinity, called *Long Meg and her daughters.* They consist of a circle, 350 yards in circumference, formed of sixty-seven stones, some of them ten feet high. Seventeen paces from the southern side of the circle stands Long Meg,—a square unhewn column of red freestone, fifteen feet in circumference, and eighteen feet high.

In a note to his sonnet on this monument, the poet Wordsworth observes,—"When I first saw this monument, as I came upon it by surprise, I might overrate its importance as an object ; but though it will not bear a comparison with Stonehenge, I must say I have not seen any other relique of those dark ages which can pretend to rival it in singularity and dignity of appearance."

At Old Penrith, five miles north-west of Penrith, are the remains of the Roman station *Brementenracum.* A military road, twenty-one feet broad, led from it to the Roman wall.

The seats of the nobility and gentry in the neighbourhood of Penrith are very numerous. The more important are—Carleton Hall, (John Cowper, Esq.,) one mile south-east. Brougham Hall (Lord Brougham), one and a-half miles south-east. Skirgill House (L. Dent, Esq.), one mile south-west. Dalemain (E. W. Hasell, Esq.) three and a-half miles south-west. Lowther Castle, (the Earl of Lonsdale,) four miles south. Greystock Castle, (Henry Howard, Esq.,) four and a-half miles west north-west. Eden Hill, (Sir George Musgrave, Bart.,) four miles east. Hutton Hall (Sir H. R. F. Vane, Bart.), five miles north-west by north. Some of these, however, deserve more particular mention.

BROUGHAM HALL, an old and picturesque building, is the seat of Henry, Lord Brougham and Vaux. It will be visited with interest, as the patrimonial inheritance

* "He pass'd red Penrith's Table Round,
For feats of chivalry renown'd :
Left Mayborough's mound, and stones of power
By Druids raised in magic hour,
And traced the Eamont's winding way,
Till Ulfo's lake beneath him lay."
Bridal of Triermain.

and occasional residence of unquestionably the first orator of the age. It stands upon an eminence not far from the ruins of Brougham Castle, commanding extensive views of the surrounding country, the mountains beyond Ulleswater closing the prospect. From its situation and beautiful prospects, it has been termed "the Windsor of the North." Having at one time belonged to a family named Bird, it was from this circumstance sometimes called *Bird's Nest.* The pleasure-grounds and shrubberies are of considerable extent and tastefully laid out. In one part is the Hermit's Cell,—a small thatched building containing furniture fitted for, and emblematic of, a recluse. Upon the table in the centre these lines are painted:—

"And may at last my weary age
Find out the peaceful hermitage,
The hairy gown and mossy cell,
Where I may sit and rightly spell,
Of every star that Heaven doth shew,
And every herb that sips the dew,—
Till old experience do attain
To something like prophetic strain."

The family of Brougham (or Burgham, as it was formerly spelt,) is ancient and respectable. The manor, which bears the same name after having been long alienated, was re-acquired, and still belongs to the Broughams.

EDEN HALL, the seat of the famous Border clan of the Musgraves, is a large and handsome edifice on the west bank of the river Eden, which, being bordered with trees, forms an elegant feature in the pleasure-grounds. In the hall there is preserved with scrupulous care an old and anciently painted glass goblet called the Luck of Edenhall, which would appear, from the following traditionary legend, to be wedded to the fortunes of its present possessors. The butler, in going to procure water at a well in the neighbourhood, (rather an unusual employment for a butler,) came suddenly upon a company of fairies, who were feasting and making merry on the green sward. In their flight they left behind this glass, and one of them returning for it, found it in the hands of the butler. Seeing that its recovery was hopeless, she flew away, singing aloud—

"If that glass should break or fall,
Farewell the luck of Eden Hall."

The Musgraves came to England with the Conqueror, and settled first at Musgrave in Westmorland, then at Hartley Castle in the same county, and finally at their present residence.

LOWTHER CASTLE, the seat of the Earl of Lonsdale, is seated in a noble park of 600 acres, on the east side of the woody vale of Lowther. It was erected by the late Earl upon the site of the old hall, which had been nearly destroyed by fire, as far back as the year 1726, after the designs of the architect Smirke. The white stone of which it is built, is in pleasing contrast with the vivid green of the park and woods. The effect of the whole pile is strikingly grand, worthy the residence of its wealthy and powerful owner. The north front in the castellated style of the thirteenth or fourteenth century, is 420 feet in length. The south front is in the Gothic Cathedral style, and has the usual number of pinnacles, pointed windows, &c. So far from the diversity of the fronts being discordant, the art of the designer has made them increase each other's effect. Surmounting the whole is a lofty tower, from the summit of which the prospect is extremely fine —the mountains of Helvellyn, Seat Sandal, Saddleback, and Skiddaw, their sides probably shadowed

" By the white mist that dwells upon the hills,"

are distinctly visible. The fitting up of the interior is in a style of grandeur corresponding with the external appearance. Heart of oak and birch occupy, in a great measure, the place of foreign woods in the furniture and carvings. The staircase which climbs the great central tower is highly imposing. Many masterpieces of the old painters hang upon the walls, and the corridors and rooms are adorned with busts from the chisels of Chantrey, Westmacott, and other sculptors. Amongst these, the bust of Queen Victoria, taken when she was about three or four years of age, will be viewed with more than ordinary interest. There is also a facsimile of the famous Wellington shield, carved in solid silver, after the designs of the late Stothard, R. A. The different compartments exhibit in a regular series, the victories which his Grace has obtained over the foes of Britain in India and the Peninsula, but as the shield was executed before the battle of Waterloo, that crowning victory is unfortunately omitted.

The capabilities of the situation which the park afforded had been publicly noticed by Lord Macartney, who, in describing a romantic scene in the imperial park at Gehol in China, observed, that " it reminded him of Lowther in Westmorland, which, from the extent of prospect, the grand surrounding objects, the noble situation, the diversities of surface, the extensive woods and command of water, might be rendered by a man of sense, spirit, and taste, the finest scene in the British dominions." How far his Lordship's views have been realized the visitor will judge. The park has been much admired for the profusion of fine forest trees which embellish its banks and braes. It is watered by the Lowther, the pellucid clearness of which fully justifies its supposed etymological derivation. The grey and tree-crowned crags, the transparent stream, and the graceful windings of its course, add greatly to the charms of its scenery. One portion bears the name of the Elysian fields. Near the Castle there is a large grassy terrace shaded by fine trees, from which the prospect is most charming.

The Lowther family is of great antiquity, the names of William de Lowther and Thomas de Lowther, being subscribed as witnesses to a grant of lands in the reign of Henry II. Sir John Lowther, first Viscount Lonsdale, distinguished himself by influencing the counties of Westmorland and Cumberland in favour of King William, at the memorable era of 1688 ; in return for which service, that king created him a Viscount, and conferred upon him many other honours. Sir James Lowther, first Earl of Lonsdale, succeeded to the three great inheritances of Mauds Meaburn, Lowther, and Whitehaven, which came to him by different branches of the family. When a commoner, he was thirty years M. P. for Westmorland or Cumberland, and in 1761 was returned for both counties. He was also Lord Lieutenant of the two counties, an alderman of Carlisle, and succeeded to the two millions left by his kinsman, Sir James Lowther of Whitehaven, 1755. Of his immense wealth, the distribution of which by will was said to give universal satisfaction, "a small portion in gold," L.50,000, was found in his houses.

Upon the death of the first Earl, the title of Viscount descended to his cousin, Sir William Lowther of Swillington, Bart., who, in 1807, was created an Earl. At his death, in 1842, he was succeeded in the possession of the title and estates by his eldest son, the present Earl.

Tourists whilst at Penrith will not fail to visit the romantic lake of

ULLESWATER,

upon which a small steamer now plies during the summer months.

The road between Ambleside and Penrith passes along the northern shore of Ulleswater; and as it is a general rule that lake scenery, in order to be seen to advantage, should be visited in a direction opposite to that in which the waters flow, it is well to observe this order of approach. Two roads conduct from Penrith to Pooley Bridge, at the foot of the lake, about six miles distant, both of which lead through a country abounding in picturesque scenery. One leaves the Keswick road two miles and a-half from Penrith, and, passing through Mr Hasell's park at Dalemain, reaches Ulleswater, three-quarters of a mile above Pooley Bridge. The other road leads along the Shap road to Eamont Bridge, shortly before reaching which, Carleton Hall is seen on the left. After crossing the bridge, by which Westmorland is entered, the first road on the right must be taken. In the angle of the field on the left at this deviation, is King Arthur's Round Table, and a little beyond on the right is Mayborough, both of which antique remains have been previously noticed. At Yanwath, two and a-half miles from Penrith, there are the ruins of an ancient Hall, formerly one of the "noble houses" of Sir Lancelot Threlkeld. The road, passing through Tirrel and Barton, ultimately arrives at Pooley Bridge, six miles from Penrith. The Eamont is crossed by a stone bridge upon issuing from Ulleswater. At "the Sun," a good hotel, boats upon the lake may be procured. On the west of the village is a steep and conical hill, clothed with wood, called Dunmallet, upon which there were formerly the vestiges of a Roman fortification. Winding walks lead to the summit, from which a fine view of the lake is commanded. About half a mile from Pooley, on the east side of the lake, is a villa named Eusemere, which for some time was the residence of the late William Wilberforce. From Pooley Bridge to Patterdale, a distance of ten miles the road traverses the west margin of Ulleswater. The lake itself is nine miles in length, and is partitioned by the mountains into three separate chambers, or *reaches*, as they are locally termed, no two of which can be seen at once from any point near the margin. Its extreme width is about three-quarters of a mile. The first reach, commencing at the foot, is terminated on the left by Hallin Fell, which stretches forward to a promontory, from the opposite side called Skelley Neb, upon which stands Mr Marshall's house, Halsteads. The middle and longest reach is closed in by Birk Fell on the left, and on the right by Stybarrow Crag, far away above which " the dark brow of the mighty Helvellyn" rises into thin air. The little island, called House Holm, spots the water exactly at the termination of this section of the lake. The highest reach is the smallest and narrowest, but the mingled grandeur and beauty which surround it, are beyond the power of the liveliest imagination to depict. Four or five islands dimple the surface, and by their diminutive size impress more deeply upon the beholder the vastness of the hills which tower above them ; Stybarrow Crag, and other offshoots from Helvellyn on one side, Birk Fell and Place Fell on the other, springing from the lake's margin almost at one bound, shut in this terrestrial paradise.

> " Abrupt and sheer the mountains sink
> *At once* upon the level brink."

Leaving Pooley Bridge by the high road, Waterfoot is passed on the right about a mile from the bridge, and Rampsbeck Lodge, on the left, about two miles from the same place. A little further is the village of Watermillock. So far the lake has lain amongst somewhat tame scenery, but here promise is given of its coming grandeur. Halsteads, the seat of Wm. Marshall, Esq., is seen on the left,—the grounds circling which are beautifully laid out. The wood at the foot of Hallin Fell, on the other shore, has a pleasing effect. A mile from Halsteads, Gowbarrow Park is entered. This park, which contains upwards of a thousand acres, must attract the attention of the most careless observer, by its " grace of forest charms decayed," and innumerable sylvan groups of great beauty still remain, round which herds of deer will be seen bounding. It belongs to Henry Howard, Esq. of Greystoke Castle, to whom it was devised by Charles, 11th Duke of Norfolk, his uncle. The Duke's predecessor erected upon an eminence in the park a hunting-box in the castellated style, which is called Lyulph's Tower ; it commands a splendid view of the lake. About five and a-half miles from Pooley Bridge, a stream is crossed by a small bridge, a mile above which, in a rocky dell, is a waterfall of considerable volume, called Airey Force. The banks of the stream, which are thickly sown with trees, become exceedingly precipitous as the cascade is approached. Two wooden bridges are thrown across the stream, one above, the other below, the fall. Glencoin Beck, issuing from Linking Dale Head, runs under the road a mile beyond Airey bridge, and forms the line of demarcation between Cumberland and Westmorland. The highest reach of the lake is now unfolded to the view. The road soon afterwards passes under Sty-narrow Crag, at which point it has been much widened,—formerly it was a narrow path between the steep mountain and the water's edge. An ancestor of the Mounseys of Goldrill Cottage acquired the title of *King of Patterdale*, from having successfully repulsed a body of Scotch moss-troopers at this place, with the aid of a few villagers. His residence was at that time Patterdale Hall, but a few years ago the patrimonial estate was sold to Mr Marshall of Leeds. The brook from Glenridding is then crossed. Helvellyn may be ascended from this valley, for which purpose a guide should be obtained at Patterdale. The path to the summit lies for a considerable distance by the side of Glenridding Beck. On the left is Glenridding House, Rev. Mr Askew; Patterdale Hall is passed on the right, and the village of Patterdale is soon afterwards reached. The Churchyard, in which lie interred the remains of the unfortunate Charles Gough, contains a yew-tree of remarkable size. There are two hotels here, one on the banks of the lake (Bownass's), the other, Gelderd's long established family hotel, at both of which excellent accommodation can be obtained. Guides may be had to the mountains in the vicinity, and boats for excursions upon the lake. There is now a steamer on the lake. A few days might be pleasantly spent at this place, in investigating the hidden beauties of the neighbourhood. There are innumerable nooks and shy recesses in the dells and by the lake,

"Where flow'rets blow, and whispering Naiads dwell."*

which the leisurely wanderer has only to see in order to admire. An afternoon might be advantageously employed in visiting the islands, of which there are four: House Holm, standing at the mouth of the highest reach, Moss Holm, Middle Holm, and Cherry Holm. Place Fell Quarry, half a mile from the inn, is a good station for viewing the lake; and the walk to Blowick, two farm-houses under Place Fell, affords many charming prospects. A ramble of five or six miles may be taken into the retired valley of Martindale; nor would the hardy pedestrian have much difficulty in making his way over the Fells to Hawes Water. The summits of Helvellyn and High Street might be visited; both of which will repay the visitor for the toil he must necessarily incur, by the extensive views they command. The latter stands at the head of Kentmere:—its name, a strange one for a mountain, it acquired from the road which the Romans constructed over it. The traces of this road are yet visible. Its height is 2700 feet.

Ambleside is ten miles from Patterdale, the road leading over the steep pass of Kirkstone. A small inn, bearing the sign of "The Traveller's Rest," has lately been erected on the highest part of the pass, breaking in, with its mean associations, upon the solemn feelings which the surrounding solitude is calculated to inspire. In descending, Windermere and the valley of Ambleside are spread out like a map before the spectator.

HAWES WATER,

three miles long by half a mile broad, lies embosomed in lofty mountains, thirteen and a half miles north of Penrith. It is the property of the Earl of Lons-

* Hartley Coleridge

dale. The road best adapted for carriages is that by way of Shap ; but the nearest and most picturesque road is that by way of Yanwath, Askham, Helton, and Bampton. The latter road quits the Penrith and Pooley Bridge road at Yanwath ; after leaving that village, it crosses what was formerly Tirrel and Yanwath Moor, to Askham, five miles from Penrith. Helton is rather more than a mile beyond, and Bampton is nearly four miles further. The grammar school at this village has been long in great repute. Shap, a straggling village on the mail road between Kendal and Penrith, is five miles distant. The road passes near the ruins of Shap Abbey, lying on the banks of the Lowther, now bare, but once occupied by a thick forest. This abbey, anciently called Heppe, was founded by Thomas, the son of Gospatrick, for monks of the Premonstratensian order, about the year 1150. It was dedicated to St Magdalen. Upon the dissolution, the abbey and manor were granted to Thomas Lord Wharton, from whose descendant, the Duke of Wharton, an ancestor of the Earl of Lonsdale, purchased them. The only part left standing is the church tower. From the vestiges of buildings yet visible, the abbey appears to have been extensive. In the vicinity of Shap are two of those rude structures to which no certain date can be assigned, and which are therefore usually referred to the primitive times of the Druids. Karl Lofts, the name of one, consists of two parallel lines of unhewn masses of granite, half a mile long by sixty or seventy feet broad, terminating at the south extremity in a small circle of similar blocks. Many of the granitic blocks have been barbarously carried off for building purposes, or some other " base use." At a place called Gunnerskeld Bottom there is a circle of large stones, thought to be a sepulchral cairn.

Returning to Bampton, the foot of Hawes Water is reached, a mile and a half beyond that village. The wild wood of Naddle Forest beautifully feathers the steeps of the east shore. Rather more than a mile from the foot of the lake, Fordendale brook is crossed near a few houses, called Measand Becks. The brook makes some pretty falls on the mountain side. A broad promontory enters the lake at this place, and approaches within 200 or 300 yards of the other margin. The mountains surrounding the head of this lake present a magnificent contour. They consist of High Street and Kidsty Pike, with their nameless dependencies. The little chapel of Mardale stands close to the road about a mile above the lake, and over against it is a neat white house, called Chapel Hill, the residence of a yeoman named Holme. The ancestor of this family came originally from Stockholm, and landed in England in the train of the Conqueror. He was rewarded with an estate in Northamptonshire, where the family were seated until the reign of King John, at which period, its head, flying from his enemies, concealed himself in a cavity (to this day called Hugh's cave) in one of the hill sides. The estate on which his descendant resides was purchased by the fugitive. Having wound round a rocky screen, a few houses, called collectively Mardale Green, (amongst which there is a small inn,) are seen thinly sown over the floor of the narrow valley. Harter Fell closes in this level area on the south—lofty mountains rise on the east and west, and contribute to make this as perfect a solitude as can well be conceived. The pedestrian will find a road over the pass of Gatescarth, which reaches Kendal by the vale of Long-sleddale, fifteen miles from Mardale Green. From Mardale the rambler might ascend High Street, or cross the Martindale Fells to Patterdale, at the head of Ulleswater.

MOUNTAINS.

The mountains best known and most usually ascended by tourists are—Scawfell, Helvellyn, Skiddaw, Coniston Old Man, and Langdale Pikes. Guides can be procured at any of the neighbouring inns, who, for a moderate compensation, will conduct strangers to the summit by the least circuitous path ; and being generally intelligent persons, will point out and name those objects most worthy of notice, which are visible on the ascent or from the highest point. Fine clear days should be selected for an expedition of this kind, as well for the advantage of having an extensive prospect, as for safety. Mists and wreaths of vapour, capping the summits of mountains, or creeping along their sides, are beautiful objects when viewed from the lowly valley ; but when the wanderer becomes surrounded with them on the hills, they occasion anything but agreeable sensations, and have not unfrequently led to serious accidents. A pocket compass will be found useful in discovering the tourist's position with reference to the surrounding scenery, and a telescope in bringing within view the more distant parts of it. A flask containing brandy, which may be diluted at the springs on the way, will be found no unnecessary burden. With these preliminary observations, we shall proceed to describe the mountains we have named above.

SCAWFELL.

The aggregation of mountains called collectively Scawfell, which stand at the head of Wastdale, form four several summits bearing separate names. The most southerly of the four is Scawfell, (3100) feet ; the next is Scawfell Pikes, (3160 feet) ; Lingmell, of considerably inferior elevation, is more to the west, forming a sort of buttress for the support of the loftier heights ; and Great End is the advanced guard on the north, having its aspect towards Borrowdale. The whole mass is composed of a species of hard dark slate. The Pikes, being the highest summit in England, is most commonly the object of the stranger's ambition; some confusion has, however, been caused by the similarity of names, and the lower elevation of Scawfell been attained, where that of Scawfell Pikes was desired. Since the trigonometrical survey, a pile of stones, surmounted by a staff, has been placed on the latter mountain summit; such mistakes, therefore, need not, except through carelessness, occur in future.

The ascent of the two higher mountains may be commenced from several valleys—from Langdale, Borrowdale, or Wastdale. Of these, the station from which the ascent may most readily be made is Strands, at the foot of Wast Water. A boat being taken up the lake, will land the pedestrian at the foot of Lingmell, which projects towards the water. The top of Lingmell being almost gained, a turn must be made to the right, and that direction persevered in for three-quarters of a mile. Deflections to the right and left in succession will place the hardy climber upon Scawfell Pikes. From Borrowdale the best course is to pursue the Wastdale road, until Sty Head Tarn is reached Leaving this tarn on the left, and bending your way towards Sprinkling Tarn, which must also be kept on the left, a turn to the right must shortly be made conducting to a pass called East Haws, having on the left, Hanging Knott, and on the right Wastdale Broad Crag. The summit of Scawfell Pikes is in view from this place, but much exertion will be required before either will be reached. Great End will have to be ascended, and continuing along the summit-ridge, some rocky eminences will be passed on the left. A considerable descent must then be made, and two small hollows crossed, from the second of which the trigonometrical station on the Pikes will be reached. The two elevations of Scawfell and Scawfell Pikes, though not more than three-quarters of a mile distant from each other in a direct line, are separated by a fearful chasm, called Mickle-dore, which compels a circuit to be made of two miles in passing from one to the other. The passage by Mickle-dore, though dangerous, is not impassable, as some of the adventurous dalesmen can testify. All vegetation but that of lichens has forsaken the summits of Scawfell Pikes and its rival; "Cushions or tufts of moss parched and brown," says Wordsworth with his usual poetical feeling, "appear between the huge blocks and stones that lie on heaps on all sides to a great distance, like skeletons or bones of the earth not needed at the creation, and there left to be covered with never-dying lichens which the clouds and dews nourish and adorn with colours of exquisite beauty. Flowers, the most brilliant feathers, and even gems, scarcely surpass in colouring some of those masses of stone."

The view from the Pikes is, of course, of a most extensive description, embracing such a "tumultuous waste of huge hill tops" that the mind and eye alike become confused in the endeavour to distinguish the various objects. The mountains having lost the shapes they possessed when viewed from beaneath, are only to be recognized by those acquainted with the locality of each; however, with the aid of his compass, map, and our directions, the enquiring gazer will be able to assign its name to most of them. Turning to the south, Morecambe Bay and the Lancashire coast to a great extent are seen, and on clear days the prospect comprehends a portion of the Welsh Highlands. Scawfell intercepts the view of Wast Water and part of the Screes. To the left Eskdale and Miterdale are seen contributing their waters to the ocean. Furness and the Isle of Walney are visible in the same direction, as well as Devoke Water, placed on an elevated moor, beyond which Black Combe is a prominent object. Still more to the east Wrynose, Wetherlam, Coniston Old Man, with the rest of the mountains at the head of Eskdale, Seathwaite and Little Langdale are conspicuous. Bowfell, obscuring Langdale, appears in the east, and beyond. part of the middle of Windermere. Far away, beyond, are the Yorkshire hills with Ingleborough, the monarch of them all, plainly visible. To the left of Bowfell, Langdale Pikes are descried, and in the east the eye rests upon Hill Bell, High Street, Wansfell. Fairfield, Seat Sandal, and Helvellyn in succession. In the north Skiddaw and Saddleback cannot be mistaken, beyond which, the blue mountains of Scotland bound the prospect. Immediately beneath the spectator he will perceive Sty Head Tarn dwindled to a little spot. Great End conceals Borrowdale, and a little to the left rises the mighty mass of Great Gable. Castle Crag, Grange Crag, and Gate Crag, shut out the greater part of Derwentwater. In the north-west are a series of hills, the principal of which are, Causey Pike, Grizedale Pike, Maiden-mawr, Hindscarth and Robinson. Then come the Buttermere and Crummock mountains, with Grasmoor conspicuously visible. Nearer are the Pillar, Hay Cock, High Style, and Red Pike. Westward the eye sinks into the depths of Wastdale, round which are piled Kirkfell, Yewbarrow, Seatallan, and Buckbarrow. The Irish sea bounds the whole western horizon, and over the extremity of the vale of Wast Water the Isle of Man can be sometimes perceived.

HELVELLYN.

This mountain is more widely known by name than any other, partly from its easiness of access, and its proximity to a turnpike road, over which a coach passes daily within a mile and a-half of the summit, and partly in connection with a melancholy accident which some years ago befel a stranger upon it, whose fate, the elegiac verses of Wordsworth and Scott have contributed to make universally lamented. It stands, the highest of a long chain of hills, at the angle formed by the vales of Grasmere, Legberthwaite, and Patterdale, about half way between Keswick and Ambleside. From its central position and its great altitude, it commands an extensive map-like view of the whole Lake district, no fewer than six lakes being visible from its summit, whilst the circumjacent mountains present themselves in fine arrangement. Its height is 3055 feet above the level of the sea, being something more than a hundred feet lower than Scawfell Pikes, and higher than Skiddaw by thirty-three feet. Its geological structure is slate in one part and in another a flinty porphyry.

The ascent of Helvellyn can be effected from several quarters. Grasmere, Legberthwaite, Wythburn, and Patterdale, severally afford advantageous points for the commencement of the escalade, the two latter, however, lying in diametrically opposite directions, are the places where it is usually begun. It may be well, perhaps, to mention, that ponies can be used for a great portion of the way if the lowland be quitted at Grasmere, a facility of which none of the other paths will admit. The ascent from Wythburn, though the shortest, is the steepest. A guide can be procured at the little inn which stands near the chapel, but as the path is easily discovered without his assistance, many persons will feel inclined to dispense with this restraint upon their motions and conversation. The path, which begins to ascend almost at the inn-door, will be pointed out by the people of the inn. A spring, called Brownrigg's Well, issuing from the ground within 300 yards of the summit, sends out a stream, which, after rushing violently down the mountain's side, crosses the highway 200 or 300 yards from the Horse's Head at Wythburn. Taking this stream as a guide, the stranger need have no fear of losing his way, for Helvellyn Man is a little to the left, at the distance we have mentioned, above its source. In the ascent, a small sheet of water, called Harrop Tarn, will be seen under Tarn Crag, a lofty precipice on the opposite side of the receding valley. The scars, seams, and ravines,

——" the history of forgotten storms,
On the blank folds inscribed of drear Helvellyn,"*

which indent the mountain on all sides, will forcibly impress upon every beholder the possible vastness of the effects of those elements whose ordinary results are so trivial.

From Patterdale, the glens of Grisedale and Glenridding may be either of them used as approaches to Helvellyn. The latter glen is to be preferred, as the stream flowing through it, which has its rise in the Red Tarn, may be taken as a guide up the mountain. This tarn lies 600 feet immediately below the highest elevation, fenced in on the south-east by a ridge of rock called Striding Edge, and on the north-west by a similar barrier, called Swirrel Edge. Catchedecam, the termination of the latter, must be ascended, and the ridge crossed, in order to attain the object of the climber's ambition. Although the path
ridge may be somewhat startling, there is no real danger to be apprehended. Sometimes, from mistake or fool-hardiness, Striding Edge is taken ; but this is at once appalling and perilous, for at one part the path is not more than two yards broad, with a tremendous precipice on either side. It was at this spot that Charles Gough met with the accident which caused his death.† The Edge be-

* Hartley Coleridge.

† This unfortunate " young lover of nature" attempted to cross Helvellyn from Patterdale one day in the spring of 1805, after a fall of snow had partially concealed the path, and rendered it dangerous. It could never be ascertained whether he was killed by his fall, or had perished from hunger. Three months elapsed before the body was found, attended by a faithful dog, which he had with him at the time of the accident.

" This dog had been through three months' space
A dweller in that savage place ;

WINANDERMERE, CONISTON & GRASMERE.

Drawn by Sidney Hall
Engd. by J. Bartholomew, Edinr.

½ ¼ 0 1 2 3 4

Statute Miles.

ing passed, little exertion is required to place the weary pedestrian by the side of Helvellyn Man—as the pile of stones on the summit is called—thence to gaze on the wonderful display of mountains and lakes which every where surround him. This Man, and that on a lower elevation, to the north, form the separating landmarks between Cumberland and Westmorland. And now, as to the view, and the multitudinous objects within its range. Northwards, Keppel Cove Tarn is perceived, having on the right Catchedecam. Beyond the extremity of the tarn Saddleback rears its huge form, a little to the left of which is Skiddaw. Between the two, and in the north-west, a portion of the Solway Firth is descried, and the extreme distance is bounded by the Scottish mountains. Turning eastwards, the Red Tarn below its "huge nameless rock," lies between Swirrel Edge on the left, and Striding Edge on the right. Beyond is the crooked form of Ulleswater, on the left margin of which are Gowbarrow Park and Stybarrow Crag, whilst the right is bounded by the dwindled precipices of Place Fell, Beck Fell, and Swarth Fell. High Street and High Bell are seen in the east over Striding Edge. Kirkstone, Fairfield, and Dolly Waggon Pike, are more to the south. A portion of Windermere is seen over the last-named hill, whilst in a clear atmosphere, Lancaster Castle can be descried beyond Windermere. Esthwaite water is directly south, and beyond is the sea in the Bay of Morecambe. In the south-west, the Old Man stands guarding the right shore of Coniston Lake. On the right is the assemblage of hills termed Coniston Fells, whilst Black Combe, beheld through Wrynose Gap, lifts its dreary summit in the distance. Bowfell and Langdale Pikes are more to the west, having on the left Scawfell Pikes and Scawfell, and on the right Great Gable. The "gorgeous pavilions" of the Buttermere mountains are pitched in the west, amongst which the Pillar and Grasmoor are prominent. Cat Bells are visible, though Derwentwater, upon the west margin of which they stand, is hidden. Our old acquaintance, Honister Crag, may be seen in a hollow, a little to the left of Cat Bells. From the lower Man views of Thirlemere and Bassenthwaite Lake are commanded, both of which are concealed by a breast of the mountain from those on the highest Man.

SKIDDAW.

As this mountain stands at the head of an extensive valley, apart from the

---

Yes—proof was plain, that since the day
On which the traveller thus had died,
The dog had watched about the spot
Or by his master's side:
How nourish'd there through such long time,
He knows, who gave that love sublime,
And gave that strength of feeling great
Above all human estimate."

Thus is this striking instance of brute fidelity commemorated by Wordsworth. Scott's lines on this accident commencing, "I climbed the dark brow of the mighty Helvellyn," are too well known to be quoted at length.

adjacent eminences, its huge bulk and great height are more strikingly apparent than those of the two former, although of inferior altitude to either of them. It is extremely easy of access, so much so, that ladies may ride on horseback from Keswick to the summit, a distance of six miles. According to the Government surveyors, its height is 3022 feet above the sea; upon one part of it granite is to be found, but the great mass of this mountain, as well as of Saddleback, is composed of a dark schistose stone. It is seldom ascended from any other place but Keswick, at which town every thing necessary for the expedition will be furnished. The Penrith road must be pursued for half-a-mile, to a bridge which spans the Greta just beyond the turnpike gate. Crossing the bridge the road passes Greta Bank House, and opposite the cottages adjoining take the road on the left which skirts Latrigg, at an elevation sufficient to command delightful views of Keswick vale. The main road which skirts Latrigg on the other side takes one very much out of the way. "This road," says Green, "is unequalled for scenic beauty in the environs of Keswick." After leaving the bridge, a small plantation is traversed in front of Greta Bank, after which the road to be taken turns to the right. Proceeding onwards a few yards only, another road leading through a gate turns abruptly to the left by the side of a fence, which is followed for a distance of three quarters of a mile, to a hollow at the foot of the steepest hill on the ascent, having on the right a deep ravine, down which a transparent stream is seen falling. The path then holds along for about a mile by the side of a wall, which it crosses, and proceeds in a direct line forward, whilst the wall diverges to the right. A large and barren plain, called Skiddaw Forest, in the middle of which there is a spring of beautifully clear water, is then traversed for a mile, leaving a double-pointed elevation, called Skiddaw Low Man, the highest summit on the left; Skiddaw Man will then be ascended.

Many persons prefer the views whch they obtain during the ascent to that from the summit, and reasonably so, if *beauty* of scenery be sought for. A view will always be indistinct in proportion as it is extensive. Nothing can exceed the charming appearance of the valley and town of Keswick, of Derwentwater and its surrounding eminences, when beheld from the mountain's side; the lake especially, with its bays and islands, is nowhere seen to such advantage. In consequence of Skiddaw being exposed to the blasts of the west wind from the Irish Channel, the visitor will not be inclined, from the intense cold, to stay long on the summit; we shall therefore proceed to run over hastily the names of the principal objects which are visible from that elevated position. In the north, beyond the lowlands of Cumberland, in which Carlisle and its cathedral are perceived, the Solway Frith is seen, on the further side of which the Scottish mountains are displayed in fine arrangement. Criffell is seen over Skiddaw Far Man, and the Moffat and Cheviot hills stretch away to the right. Dumfries is visible at the mouth of the frith. In the north-west, over High Pike and Long Brow, the vale and town of Penrith are beheld, with Cross Fell (2901 feet) beyond. Directly east is the rival summit of Saddleback, separated by the tract called Skiddaw Forest from the mountain on which the spectator is standing. Helvellyn is in the south-east; beyond, Ingleborough in Yorkshire is dimly descried. Between Helvellyn and Saddleback, Place Fell, at the head of Ulleswater, and High Street are visible. When the atmosphere is clear, Lancaster Castle may be seen in the south-east. Derwentwater is not comprehended in the view from the highest Man, being concealed by some of the other eminences of Skiddaw, but from the third man a perfect bird's-eye prospect of that lake is obtained. In the south "there is a succession of five several ranges of mountain seen out-topping each other, from a stripe of the lovely valley to the highest of the Pikes. Grisedale in one grand line stretches from the inclosures at Braithwaite to its Pike, succeeded in the second range by Barrow Stile End, and Utterside. Rising from the fields of Newlands, the third range commences with Rolling End, ascending from which are Causey Pike, Scar Crag, Top Sail, Ill Crags, and Grasmoor,—the latter lessening the Pike of Grisedale by appearing over its top. The fourth line in this wild combination is composed of Cat Bells, Maiden-moor, Dalehead, Hindsgarth, Robinson, High Crag, High Stile, and Red Pike. The fifth and last is that sublime chain of summits, extending on the south from Coniston to Ennerdale on the north ; amongst these the High Pike or Man, standing towering over the rest, has on the left Great End, Hanging Knott, Bow Fell, and the Fells of Coniston ; on the right, Lingmell Crags, Great Gable, Kirk Fell, Black Sail, the Pillar, the Steeple, and the Hay Cock, with Yewbarrow and part of the Screes through the pass at Black Sail. On the right of Grisedale Pike and Hobcarten Crag is Low Fell, succeeded by Whinfield Fell, over which, in a clear atmosphere, may be observed more than the northern half of the Isle of Man ; and on a mistless sunny evening, even Ireland may be seen. The north-west end or foot of Bassenthwaite Water is here seen, the head being obscured by Longside."* Workington can be seen at the mouth of the Derwent in the west, and more to the north the coast towns of Maryport and Allonby. The town and castle of Cockermouth are perceived, over the extremity of Bassenthwaite Lake, seated on the Cocker. Such is an outline of this wonderful panorama, which may be fitly closed with Wordsworth's fine sonnet :—

"Pelion and Ossa flourish side by side,
Together in immortal books enroll'd ;
His ancient dower Olympus hath not sold,
And that aspiring hill, which did divide
Into two ample horns his forehead wide,
Shines with poetic radiance as of old ;
While not an English mountain we behold
By the celestial Muse's glorified.
Yet round our sea-girt shore they rise in crowds ;
What was the great Parnassus' self to thee,
Mount Skiddaw ? In his natural sovereignty,
Our British hill is nobler far, he shrouds
His double front among Atlantic clouds,
And pours forth streams more sweet than Castaly."

* GREEN'S Guide

CONISTON OLD MAN.

This mountain stands at the north-west angle of Coniston Lake, from the eastern shore of which it presents a magnificent appearance. It is 2577 feet in height, forming the highest peak of the range called Coniston Fells. It is composed of a fine roofing slate, for the excavation of which there are several large quarries. The slates are carried down the lake by means of boats, and, at its termination, are carted to Ulverston. There are also some valuable copper-mines upon this mountain, belonging to Rev. Sir R. Fleming of Rydal, who is Lord of the Manor. There are three tarns upon the Old Man, called Levers Water, Low Water, and Gates Water. The first lies between that mountain and Wetherlam, a stupendous hill on the north; and the last is placed at the foot of Dow Crag. Low Water, notwithstanding its name, is the highest.

The most eligible mode of ascending the Old Man is to leave the village of Coniston by the Walna Scar road, and, pursuing the way along the common for a few hundred yards, to take a path which will be seen to climb the mountain side on the right. This path leads directly up to the Man, finely built on the edge of a precipice overhanging Low Water. There is a fine open view to the south, embracing the estuaries of the Kent, Leven, and Duddon, a long line of coast, and, in serene weather, the Isle of Man. Snowdon may be distinguished on a very clear day. It appears a little to the left of Black Combe, over Millum Park. In the home views, the eye will be attracted by Coniston Lake, the whole length of which is immediately below the spectator. A part of Windermere can be seen more to the east. On other sides, the Old Man is surrounded by high mountains, which wear an aspect of imposing grandeur from this elevation. Scawfell and Bowfell are particularly fine, and the apex of Skiddaw can be discerned in the distance.

LANGDALE PIKES.

The two peculiarly shaped hills, which stand at the head of the valley of Great Langdale, though known by the general name of Langdale Pikes, have separate names. The most southerly is termed Pike o' Stickle, and is lower by 100 feet than Harrison Stickle, which is 2400 feet in height. They are of a porphyritic structure, and, on account of their steepness, are somewhat difficult to ascend. They are conspicuous objects from the upper end of Windermere, and from the road leading from Kendal to Ambleside. They are usually ascended during the Langdale excursion, (as to which see page 277,) but pedestrians would have no difficulty in making the ascent from the Stake, or from Grasmere through Easdale. The easiest mode, however, is that from Langdale. A guide can be procured at Milbecks, where tourists commonly take some refreshment. The path pursues a peat road leading to Stickle Tarn, well known to the angler for its fine trout, which lies under a lofty ridge of rock called Pavey Ark. This tarn must be left on the right, and a streamlet which runs down the hill-side taken as a guide. The path becomes at this part exceedingly steep, but a little patient exertion will soon place the tourist on the summit of Hanison Stickle. Though of considerably inferior elevation to the other mountains we have described, the views from this spot are extremely fine. Looking eastward, Helvellyn, Seat Sandal, and Fairfield bound the prospect ; and, in the north-west and north, Skiddaw and Saddleback are seen in the distance. Stickle Tarn is immediately below the eye, guarded by the frowning heights of Pavey Ark. In the south-east are the hills around the valley of Ambleside, beyond those at the head of Troutbeck and Kentmere. In turning to the south, the eye is attracted by the valley of Great Langdale, containing Elterwater and Loughrigg Tarn, and terminated by Windermere, with Curwen's Isle and the other islands diversifying its smooth surface. Loughrigg Fell conceals a portion of the head of the lake as well as the town of Ambleside. Underbarrow Scar, near Kendal, is seen over Bowness. Esthwaite Water is seen in the south-south-east, and close at hand, towards the right, is the bluff summit of Wetherlam End. A small part of the sea is embraced in the view in this direction. Through an opening, having on the left Pike o' Bliscoe, and on the right Crinkle Crags Gatescale is presented in the north. The Old Man and the Great Carrs shut in the prospect in the south-west.

ITINERARY.

CIX. ULVERSTON—CONISTON LAKE—AMBLESIDE, 24 Miles.

ON RIGHT FROM ULVERST.	From Ambl.	ULVERSTON.	From Ulv.	ON LEFT FROM ULVERST.
		On the shore of the Leven Æstuary to		
Penny Bridge, J. P. Machell, Esq.	18½	Penny Bridge.	3½	
Bridge Field, Joseph Penny, Esq.	16	Along the left bank of the Crake to cr. Lowick Bridge.	6	The Crake issues from Coniston Lake, and enters the Leven near Penny Bridge.
The extensive iron forge of Messrs. Harrison, Ainslie, and Co.	15	Along the right bank of the Crake to	7	Here are the remains of a fine old hall, part of which is occupied by a farmer.
	14	Nibthwaite, near the foot of	8	
Two promontories extend into the lake near its foot, which have a most picturesque effect. One is terminated by steep rocks, and both become insulated when the lake is swollen.		CONISTON LAKE.		Water Park, Benson Harrison, Esq. Fine view of the mountains round the head of the lake.
Brantwood, Mrs. Copley, on the left.	8½	Along the east shore of which the road passes to	13½	From an eminence near the highest promontory, a beautiful view of the lake may be obtained. On the opposite shore, are the dark Fells of Torver.
Coniston Bank, Wm. Bradshaw, Esq., on the left.	8¼		13¾	Further up, Coniston Hall, surrounded with trees, is descried.
Tent Lodge, formerly the residence of Miss Elizabeth Smith, a lady of extraordinary acquirements.	8¼		15¾	This hall has changed owners but twice since the Conquest, most of which time it has belonged to the Flemings. Beyond are the towering Fells of Coniston. Just below, is the rocky islet, Peel.
Waterhead House, James Marshall, Esq.		Waterhead Hotel.		
This Inn is pleasingly situate on the margin of the lake; boats, post-horses, and guides, can be supplied. A few days might be spent agreeably here, as the excursions in the vicinity are numerous. The Old Man is in the immediate neighbourhood; its ascent, though a work of toil, would highly gratify the Tourist. A walk into the narrow valleys of Yewdale and Tilberthwaite, will afford many grand scenes. Newfield, in the retired vale of Seathwaite, can be reached by the Walna Scar road, which passes through Church Coniston, and under the Old Man. This road, which is very mountainous and rough, is six miles in length.	8	To Coniston Vill. 1 mile. To Hawkshead, 3 miles. To Bowness, 8 miles. On quitting Waterhead Inn, the road winds round the grounds of Waterhead House, and is on the ascent for some distance. The lake presents a striking retrospect from the summit of the ascent.	14	This lake, called also Thurston Water, is six miles long, and nearly three-quarters of a mile broad, its depth is stated to be 162 feet. Its margin is very regular, having few indentations of any magnitude. Two small islands are situate near the eastern shore. Its principal feeders are the streams from Yewdale and Tilberthwaite, and those running from the tarns on the Man Mountain. It abounds with trout and char; the latter fish is thought to be found in greater perfection here than elsewhere. The scenery at the foot is tame, but that at the upper extremity is of the grandest description.
Blelham Tarn.	4½	Borwick Ground.	17½	The Old Man, (2577 feet,) and Wetherlam, (2400 feet) are extremely majestic. The greatest portion of the lake belongs to Rev. Sir R. Fleming of Rydal Hall, who has some valuable copper mines upon the Old Man.
Pull Wyke, a bay of Windermere, here makes an advance. Wansfell Holm, J. Hornby, Esq., Dove Nest, and Low Wood Inn, are pleasing objects on the opposite shore. Wansfell Pike (1590 feet) rises above.	2½	Road to the Ferry.	19½	Fine view of the Rydal and Ambleside Mountains.
	1½	cr. Brathay Bridge.	20½	Loughrigg Fell is before the eye.
Brathay Hall.		enter Westmorland.		
As the road winds round the extremity of Loughrigg Fell, the mountains surrounding the valley of Ambleside are strikingly unfolded.		Clappersgate Vill.		Croft Lodge, James Holmes, Esq.
		cr. Rothay Bridge.		
		AMBLESIDE.	22	

ON RIGHT FROM KENDAL.	From Conist.	KENDAL.	From Kend.	ON LEFT FROM KENDAL.
Kendal must be left by the road over the House of Correction hill.	16	Turnpike Gate.	2	St. Thomas' Church.
	13¾	Over moorish and hilly ground to Crook vill.	4½	Keep to the left. the road on the right is to Ambleside.
Bowness village, half-a-mile to the right.	10½	First view of Windermere.	7½	Furness Fells in the distant foreground. Storr's Hall, Rev. T. Stanforth.
In crossing, the views up the lake, and of the mountains round the head, are extremely fine. Looking down, Gummer's How, on the east margin, is conspicuous. Bowness, with its church, school, and villas, is a pretty object.	9¾	FERRY. Between the two promontories, the lake is only 400 yards across. The Ferry boats are kept on the Lancashire side.	8¼	Berkshire Isle, and a little beyond, the Storr's Point projects. At the Ferry Inn, enquire for the Station House, whence there is a splendid view of the lake.
Belle Isle on the right. Strangers are allowed to land. It contains upwards of thirty acres. Mr. Curwen's house, of a circular shape, is upon it.	9½	Ferry Inn. Enter Lancashire.	8½	"This vagrant owl hath learn'd his cheer On the banks of Windermere; Where a band of them make merry, Mocking the man that keeps the Ferry, Hallooing from an open throat, Like travellers shouting for a boat."— *Wordsworth's Waggoner.*
From the summit of the ascent from the Ferry, Ingleborough is visible. The Old Man is in sight. This lake is two miles in length, and one-third of a mile in breadth. The scenery around it is pleasing, but destitute of any features of grandeur. A peninsula swells from the west shore, and pleasantly relieves the monotonous regularity of the margin. The stream which issues from it, is called the Cunsey; it enters Windermere a mile and a half below the Ferry. Many handsome villas enliven the banks of the lake. In a pond near the head, is a diminutive floating island, having upon it several small trees.	7	Sawrey vill. along the east shore of ESTHWAITE LAKE, and round its head to	11	Langdale Pikes are visible: on the right is the Pass of Dunmail Raise, to the east of which are Helvellyn, Seat Sandal, and Fairfield. The apex of Skiddaw is seen through Dunmail Raise gap.
	5	HAWKSHEAD. Inn, Red Lion. To Ambleside, 5 miles. To Newby Bridge, 8 miles. To Ulverston, 16 miles.	13	Hawkshead is a small but ancient market-town at the head of the valley of Esthwaite. The old hall where the Abbots of Furness held their Courts, is a farm-house, lying about a mile distant. St. Michael's Church, a structure of great antiquity, is placed on a rocky eminence immediately over the town, commanding fine views of the adjacent country. —"the grassy church-yard hangs Upon a slope above the village school."
At the termination of the ascent, the lake and vale of Coniston, hemmed in by magnificent mountains, break upon the eye with almost theatrical surprise. Waterhead House, Marshall, Esq., on the left.	1	Over elevated ground to Coniston Waterhead Inn, an excellent Hotel, beautifully situated on the margin of the lake, near its head.	17	This school was founded in 1585, by Archbishop Sandys, a member of an ancient family still seated in the neighbourhood. The poet Wordsworth, and his brother, the late Master of Trinity College, Cambridge, were educated here. In the verses of the former, allusion is frequently made to
Coniston Village lies immediately under the Man mountain, half a mile from the western margin of the lake. It has two small inns.		CONISTON VILL.	18	"The antique market village, where were passed My school-days."

From Coniston village, or the Inn at Waterhead, a mountain road, five and a half miles in length, passes through Tilberthwaite, between Oxen Fell Cross on the right, and Wetherlam on the left, and joins the Little Langdale road at Fellfoot. The pedestrian might proceed by way of Blea Tarn into Great Langdale. Another road, five miles in length, passing through Yewdale, and climbing the moor on the east of Oxen Fell, enters the road leading from Ambleside to Little Langdale, half a mile above Skelwith Bridge.

A pleasing excursion round the lake might be made by Tourists staying at the Waterhead Inn. Coniston village, one mile; Coniston Hall, formerly a seat of the Flemings of Rydal, but now a farm-house, two miles, on the left, some elevated fells are then interposed between the road and lake. Torver village, three and a half miles. A little beyond Torver Church, turn to the left, the road crosses the rivulet flowing from Gateswater, which lies at the foot of Dow-Crag on the Old Man, and approaches the lake at Oxen Houses, five and a half miles. A short distance from the foot, Bowdray Bridge over the Crake, right and a half miles. Nibthwaite village, nine miles, by the east margin to Waterhead Inn, 17 miles.

ON RIGHT FROM KENDAL.	From Ambles.	KENDAL.	From Kendal.	ON LEFT FROM KENDAL.
Kendal must be left by the road over the House of Correction Hill. St Thomas' Church.	14	Proceed by the Kendal and Windermere Railway to Birthwaite, which is 9 miles from Kendal, 2 from Bowness, and 5 from Ambleside, and where, in the summer season, coaches for all parts of the lake district wait the arrival of the trains.		Fine views on the right of the valley of Kendal. Shap and Howgill Fells in the distance.
Keep to the right. Obelisk. Tolson Hall, Mr Bateman.	12		2	Road on the left to Bowness, 8 miles from Kendal.
The valley of Kentmere diverges to the right. It is five or six miles long, and pent in by the huge mountains of Hill Bell, (2436 feet.) High Street, (2700 feet,) and Harter Fell. The remains of a Roman road, the highest in England, are still to be traced upon the two former. At Kentmere Hall, a ruined peel-tower, now occupied as a farm house, Bernard Gilpin, "the Apostle of the North," was born 1517.	10	Staveley vill. Watered by the Kent, upon which there are several bobbin, and woollen mills. From the road between the fourth and fifth milestones Coniston Fells are visible.	4	Ings Chapel was erected at the expense of Richard Bateman, a Leghorn merchant. He was a native of the township; and, being a clever lad, he was sent by the inhabitants to London. He rose by diligence and industry, from the situation a menial servant to be his master's partner, and amassed a considerable fortune. For some years he resided at Leghorn, whence he forwarded the slabs of marble with which the chapel is floored. His story is alluded to in Wordsworth's "Michael;" but his tragical end is not told. The captain of the vessel in which he was sailing to England, poisoned him, and seized the ship and cargo.
The pedestrian, after ascending High Street, which commands an extensive prospect, might descend to Haws Water, or into Martindale, proceeding thence to Patterdale.	$7\frac{3}{4}$	Ings Chapel.	$6\frac{1}{4}$	
	$6\frac{1}{4}$	Bannerigg Head.	$7\frac{3}{4}$	First view of Windermere.
Orrest Head, John Braithwaite, Esq. A mile beyond is Elleray, which belonged to the late Professor Wilson of Edinburgh. The view from the front of the house is very fine.	$5\frac{3}{4}$	Orrest Head. Road on the left to Bowness, two miles.	$8\frac{1}{4}$	From this eminence, and hence to the lake, splendid views of the mountains in the west are commanded. Langdale Pikes, from their peculiar shape, are easily known. Bowfell, a broad topped mountain, is on the south. Between the two, Great End and Great Gable are seen. On the south of Bowfell, Scawfell Pike may be seen in clear weather. Farther south are Crinkle Crags, Wrynose, Wetherlam and Coniston Old Man. To the south east of Langdale Pikes, in the foreground, is Loughrigg Fell; farther back, are Fairfield and Scandale.
		Birthwaite. Railway Terminus Windermere Hotel.	9	
St Catherines, Earl of Bradford.	5	Cook's House. Road on the left to Bowness. On the right a road leads through Troutbeck, over Kirkstone, and descends to Ulleswater.		
Road along the banks of the stream to Troutbeck vill, one and a half miles distant. At the turn of the road, a little beyond the eleventh milestone, the mountains round Ambleside vale open out in a beautiful manner.	4	cr. Troutbeck Bridge. On the margin of Windermere,	10	Calgarth Park, built by the eminent Bishop Watson. This portion of the route is eminently beautiful.
An excellent establishment on the margin of the lake. There is a fine expanse of water visible from the windows. The tourist will find employment for many days in rambling about the adjacent country, or boating upon the lake. Wansfell Holm, J. Hornby, Esq.	2	Low Wood Inn. To Bowness, 4 miles. To Hawkshead by the Ferry, 9 miles. To Newby Bridge, 12 miles.	12	Loughrigg Fell is seen on the opposite shore. At its foot, Brathay Hall, G. Redmayne, Esq. Dove Nest, a house inhabited, during one summer, by Mrs Hemans, is a short distance farther on the right.
Waterhead House Thomas Jackson, Esq.	1	Toll bar; head of the Lake.	13	Waterside, Mr Newton.
		AMBLESIDE. Inns—Salutation, Commercial, and White Lion.	14	Road to Clappersgate.

ON RIGHT FROM AMBLESIDE.	From Keswick.		From Ambleside.	ON LEFT FROM AMBLESIDE.
Green Bank, **Benson** Harrison, Esq.		AMBLESIDE.		
Fairfield, (2950 feet,) with its offshoots, closing in the vale. Behind is Wansfell Pike.	15½	cr. Scandale Beck.	½	Loughrigg Fell bounds the vale upon the left.
			1	Through the meadows on the left, the Rothay flows. A tall straight oak, growing in the wall, is called "Lord's Oak."
There is a pretty peep into the glen through which Rydal Beck runs.				Pelter Bridge. The road over it divides into two on the other side, one leads back to Ambleside, the other to Grasmere, both extremely beautiful walks.
Rydal Hall (Rev. Sir R. Fleming,) seated in large park containing some noble trees. There are two cascades within the park, shown on application at the lodge.	14½	RYDAL VILL.	1½	Loughrigg Fell here projects, and with a corresponding protrusion from Fairfield, called Rydal Knab, on the opposite side of the valley, leaves room for little more space than what is occupied by the road and the stream flowing from Rydal Mere.
		Glen Rothay, William Ball, Esq., at the turn of the road.		
Rydal Mount. Wordsworth's residence stands a little above the chapel, built by Lady le Fleming in 1824. A splendid view of the valley obtained by climbing the heights behind Rydal Mount.		RYDAL LAKE.		This lake is only about three-quarters of a mile long, by scarcely a fourth of a mile broad. It has two small islands, upon one of which there is a heronry, belonging to Rev. Sir. R. Fleming, the owner of the lake.
The Knab, a house formerly occupied by the English Opium Eater, and by Hartley Coleridge, eldest son of Samuel T. Coleridge the poet.		The towering heights of Knab Scar on the right. Loughrigg Fell on the left.		
Excavations of great size have been made here. At this place the old road to Grasmere branches off. It is shorter, and to be preferred by those on foot, for the fine views it commands of Rydal and Grasmere lakes. It leads past "The Wishing Gate."	12½	White Moss Slate Quarry.	2½	The road here winds round a projecting rock. Grasmere Lake suddenly breaks upon the view beyond the projection.
		Along the margin of GRASMERE LAKE. Brown's Lake Hotel.		This lake is one mile and a quarter in length, and one-third of a mile broad. It has a single island in the centre. The hills around are happily disposed.
One of these cottages was Wordsworth's dwelling for seven years, De Quincey afterwards resided in it for some time.	12½	Town End.	3½	
Parties staying at Grasmere or the Swan, should visit Easedale, a recess of Grasmere. It contains a lonely tarn, surrounded by lofty rocks.		Road on the left to Grasmere village, a sweet little place, near which is Allan Bank, Thomas Dawson, Esq., and the Cottage, — Mrs. Orrell.		The view from the road near the head of the lake, looking forward, is extremely fine. Silver How is seen over the south-west angle of the water; right onward, is Helm Crag, the summit of which is strewn with large blocks of stone, presenting many eccentric forms. Green thought he saw a likeness to a lion and a lamb. West, to a mass of antediluvian remains, and Otley says, that viewed from Dunmail Raise, a mortar elevated for throwing shells into the valley, is no unapt comparison. The road is seen to pass over Dunmail Raise, a depression between two hills, that on the left, is Steel Fell, the other, Seat Sandal.
"Who does not know the famous Swan?" A mile beyond the inn, a mountain road strikes off into Patterdale, climbing on the way a steep haws between Fair Field and Seat Sandal, and passing a desolate sheet of water, called Grisedale Tarn, lying between Seat Sandal, and Helvellyn.	11¾	Swan Inn, The ascent of Helvellyn is not unusually commenced here.	4¼	

ON RIGHT FROM AMBLESID.	From Keswick.		From Ambles.	ON LEFT FROM AMBLESIDE.
Seat Sandal. Fine retrospective views: from the summit, Skiddaw is visible.	10¾	Toll Bar. The road rises gradually until it attains the height of 720 feet, at the pass of	5¼	Helm Crag. Fair Field.
The tradition is, that Dunmail, King of Cumberland, was defeated here by Edmund the Saxon king, in 945. A cairn, still in part remaining, was raised as a memorial of the victory. The conqueror put out the eyes of his adversary's two sons, and gave the territory to Malcolm, king of Scotland, to preserve the peace of the northern part of the kingdom.	9½	DUNMAIL RAISE. Enter Cumberland. Steel Fell on the left. Seat Sandal on the right.	6½	"They now have reach'd that pile of stones, Heap'd over brave King Dunmail's bones, He who once held supreme command, Last king of rocky Cumberland; His bones, and those of all his power, Slain here in a disastrous hour."— *Wordsworth.* Thirlemere is in view.
The road is too near the foot of Helvellyn to allow any notion to be formed of that mountain's immense height. Armboth House, Late W. Jackson, Esq., on the west shore.	8¼	Horse's Head, Wytheburn. The village, called locally "the city," is half a mile distant on the left.	7¾	The ascent of Helvellyn from this inn is shorter, but steeper, than from any other place. Opposite the inn, is the chapel which Wordsworth describes as —"Wytheburn's modest house of prayer, As lowly as the lowliest dwelling."
Half way down the lake on the right, are some houses called Fisher's Place, near which are some pretty cascades formed by a stream flowing off Helvellyn. Pedestrians frequently cross Armboth Fell to the village of Watendlath, proceeding thence to Keswick. Splendid views of Derwentwater are obtained in the descent. Near the foot of Thirlemere, one extremity of the vale of St. John is passed. The views along it, with Saddleback beyond, are very fine. The celebrated "Castle Rock" stands at the entrance on the right. "From a field on the eastern side of the road, and a little short of the tenth milestone, the view of the vale of St. John presents a most singularly interesting assemblage of the wild and the lovely."—*Green.*		THIRLEMERE LAKE, called also Wytheburn Water and Leathes Water, washing the base of Helvellyn.		Eagle Crag is seen hanging over the upper end of the lake, a sheet of water, environed by frowning precipices, two and a half miles long, 500 feet above the level of the sea, and about 100 feet in depth. There is a small island near the shore at its foot. It is so narrow as to allow a wooden bridge to be thrown across its middle. To obtain some picturesque views, the lake should be crossed by this bridge, and the road on the west shore taken, which joins the turnpike road, a little beyond the twelfth mile-stone. Raven Crag is a fine object near the foot. This lake is the property of T. S. Leathes, Esq., whose residence, Dalehead House, is in the neighbourhood.
	6	Road on the right through St. John's Vale.	10	
	4¾	☞ cr. Smeathwaite Bridge over St. John's Beck, which issues from Thirlemere.	11¼	Shoulthwaite Moss, backed by a rocky hill called Bend.
Naddle Fell.				
Hence may be seen the three mountains, Skiddaw, Saddleback, and Helvellyn.	2	Causey Foot.	14	A farm-house on the left, shaded by wood, is named Causey Foot.
From this place, there is the view of the vale of the Derwent and its two lakes, which Gray regretted so much to leave. Skiddaw is immediately before the eye.	1¼ 1	Summit of Castlerigg. Road on right to Druid's Circle. KESWICK.	14¾ 16	When the pedestrian reaches a piece of open ground in the descent, he is advised to enter one of the fields on the left, to obtain a view of the whole expanse of Derwentwater.

CXIII. AMBLESIDE—LANGDALE—ESKDALE—EGREMONT—WHITEHAVEN, 38 Miles.

*** The whole of this route is seldom travelled continuously; but as most of it will be traversed in detached portions, it has been thought better to place the total distance under one description, from which the Tourist may select the sections he requires. In consequence of there being no inn at which post-horses are kept between Ambleside and Calder Bridge, carriages cannot pursue this route.

ON RIGHT FROM AMBLESIDE.	From Whiteh.	AMBLESIDE.	From Ambles.	ON LEFT FROM AMBLESIDE.
		cr. Rothay Bridge.		
Croft Lodge, James Holmes Esq.	37	Clappersgate vill.	1	A road on the left, leading to Hawkshead, crosses the Brathay and enters Lancashire.
Loughrigg Fell. Two miles and a half from Ambleside, a road turns into Great Langdale.		On the banks of the Brathay, Brathay Chapel.		Sweeter stream scenery, with richer fore and loftier back grounds, is no where to be seen within the four seas.—Wilson.
There is a waterfall a short distance above the bridge 20 feet in height. The views of Langdale Pikes are extremely fine. From the terrace attained soon after passing Skelwith Br. there is a superb view of Elterwater, and of Great and Little Langdale, separated by Lingmoor.	35	cr. Skelwith Bridge. Enter Lancashire. Having crossed the bridge, the road on the right leading up a steep hill must be taken.	3	Road deviates between the two bridges, passing on the east of Oxen Fell through Yewdale to Coniston.
Road into Great Langdale skirting the head of Elterwater Tarn. Lingmoor.	33½	cr. Colwith Bridge. Re-enter Westmorland.	4½	A little above the bridge in a deep dell near the road is a fine waterfall called Colwith Force, 70 feet in height. One mile beyond, Little Langdale Tarn is perceived. Wetherlam, a stupendous mountain, rises on the south of the tarn.
A road bends to the right; and, after passing Blea Tarn, enters the head of Great Langdale. Along this road the Pikes wear their boldest features.	31	Fell Foot. The road winds steeply to the summit of	7	Mountain road through Tilberthwaite to Coniston, 5 miles. The toilsome ascent of Wrynose is commenced at this place. The retrospective views are fine. Wansfell Pike is seen in the distance. The Carrs, and Coniston Fells.
At the spot where the Counties of Cumberland, Westmorland, and Lancashire unite, the Three Shire Stones are placed.	29½	WRYNOSE, (Pronounced locally *Raynus*.) Enter Lancashire.	8½	Traces of a Roman road over both Hardknot and Wrynose are yet remaining.
The ascent of Hardknot is begun; the highest part of the hill is on the right.	27½	Descend to Cockley Beck Bridge, over the Duddon. Enter Cumberland.	10½	The Duddon bends at this place; and, passing through the beautiful vale of Seathwaite, enters Morecambe Bay, near Broughton. The distance between Cockley Beck and Broughton by the road is 12 miles. The pedestrian is strongly advised to traverse this valley, unsurpassed in picturesque and retired beauty by any other in the Lake district. It may be approached from Coniston by the Walna Scar road. There is an inn at Newfield, 4 or 5 miles down the valley. The Duddon is the subject of a series of sonnets by Wordsworth.
From this summit there is a magnificent view of Scawfell Pikes and Scawfell. On the left the Irish Sea is seen; and, in clear weather, the Isle of Man. Half way down the hill, and about 120 yards from the road, are the faintly visible remains of a Roman fortification called Hardknot Castle, once a place of importance. —— that lone camp on Hardknot's height, Whose Guardians bent the knee to Jove and Mars.	25½	Summit of HARD KNOT. Descend into ESKDALE.	12½	
The mountains encircling Eskdale, are the Seathwaite Fells on the left, and projections from Scawfell on the right.	24½	cr. Esk Bridge.	13½	This beautiful vale is watered by the Esk, which, after a course of about 16 miles, enters the sea near Ravenglass. The valley is narrow at the spot where it is entered, but it widens rapidly towards the west. It contains two or three hamlets and a few scattered houses. Great numbers of sheep are pastured in it.

ON RIGHT FROM AMBLESIDE.	From Whiteh.		From Ambles.	ON LEFT FROM AMBLESIDE.
The Wool Pack, a small inn, is a short distance from the road.	23	Dawson Ground.	15	Birker Force, a fine cascade, may be seen from the road amongst the cliffs. The rocks around are very grand.
The inn is a little to the right of the road. At this place a mountain road leaves Eskdale, and passing Burnmoor Tarn, enters Wastdale Head between the Screes and Scawfell, 6 miles. The latter mountain may be ascended from Eskdale. On elevated ground, 4 miles south of Bout, there is a lonely tarn, with a rocky island in its centre, called Devoke Water. About half a mile from its foot are some ruins called Barnscar, which, according to tradition, were a Danish city. The situation is marked by several small piles of stones. No record of such a place has, however, come down to us. A number of silver coins have been found at it.	22	Bout vill.	16	At the schoolhouse a road strikes off to the left, conducting to Dalegarth Hall, now a farm house, but formerly a residence of the Stanleys of Ponsonby, at which directions will be given to a noble waterfall, called Stanley Gill or Dalegarth Force. The stream is crossed three times by wooden bridges on approaching the fall. The chasm is exceedingly grand. Returning, the Eskdale and Wastdale mountains, with Scawfell amongst them, are seen in fine outline.
	18	cr. Bridge over the Mite. Fine view of the coast from the road between the two bridges.	20	Road to Ravenglass, a small town, 19 miles from Ulverston, and 16 miles from Whitehaven, seated in an arm of the sea at the confluence of the Esk, Irt, and Mite. A small coasting trade is carried on as well as ship-building and oyster fishing. Muncaster Castle, Lord Muncaster's seat, is near it.
Here a road diverges to Strands, a small village, one mile from the foot of Wast Water. From Latterbarrow an eminence, under which the road passes, there is a fine view of the lake.	16½	cr. Santon Bridge, across the Irt, which flows from Wast Water.	21½	Black Combe, a lofty hill, 7 miles to the south of the town, commands an extensive view of the coast. The Welsh mountains, and the Isle of Man, are within the boundary of the view.
Road to Strands, four miles.	13	Gosforth vill.	25½	In the churchyard is a stone pillar of great antiquity, covered with illegible carvings. Ponsonby Hall, J.E. Stanley, Esq.
One mile above this bridge are the remains of Calder Abbey, founded in 1134, for monks of the Cistercian order. The abbey stands on the grounds pertaining to Captain Irwin's residence.	10	cr. Calder Bridge.	28	Here there are two good inns.
	6	EGREMONT.*	32	Spring Field, Robt. Jefferson Esq.
Keekle Grove, F. L. B. Dykes Esq.	3		35	Linethwaite, George Harrison, Esq.
Ingwell, Mrs Gunson. Summer Grove, Major Spedding.		WHITEHAVEN.	38	Hensingham House, Henry Jefferson, Esq.

* Egremont is a neat market town, containing about 2500 inhabitants, seated at the distance of two miles and a half from the coast, upon the banks of the Ehen, the stream which flows from Ennerdale Lake. It is stated to have been a borough at the period when Parliamentary representatives were remunerated for their services; and that, to avoid the expense of a member, the burgesses petitioned to have the burgh disfranchised, which was accordingly done. The Parish Church is an ancient edifice, dedicated to St Mary. It was granted by William de Meschiens to the Cell of St Bees. Upon an eminence to the west of the town stand the ruins of Egremont Castle, formerly a place of great strength and importance. It was built by the above named William de Meschiens soon after the Norman Conquest. In the lapse of time it passed into the possession of the Lucy family. There is a tradition, respecting the fortress whilst belonging to the Lucies, which Wordsworth has versified in some stanzas entitled, "The Horn of Egremont Castle." General Wyndham is the present owner of both the Manor and Castle of Egremont. Large quantities of iron ore are excavated in the neighbourhood, which are conveyed to Whitehaven unsmelted, and thence shipped to South Wales. St Bees, at which there is a fine Conventual Church, is two and a half miles distant. A good road, of seven miles in length, conducts to the foot of Ennerdale Lake. The distances from Egremont to the neighbouring towns are, — Ravenglass, 11 miles; Broughton, 20 miles; Ulverston, 30 miles; Cockermouth, 13 miles; Maryport, 20 miles.

ON RIGHT FROM WHITEHA.	From Keswick.		From Whiteha.	ON LEFT FROM WHITEHA.
Scilly Bank, 500 feet.		WHITEHAVEN.		A handsome freestone arch, with an entablature adorned with the arms of the Lowther family, spans the road on leaving the town for the north.
In the neighbourhood of Moresby, is the site of Arbeia, a Roman station, where various antique remains have been discovered. All marks of the station have been long defaced by the plough	24½		2½	Moresby Church: Moresby Hall, Miss Tate.
Rose Hill, Gilfrid Hartley, Esq.	24	Moresby Vill.	3	
Roseneath, Mrs. Solomon.				Parton and Harrington, two small sea-ports, are near Moresby.
Road to Lowes Water.	23¼		3¾	
Prospect, Capt. Caldecott. Gilgarron (Walker).	22	Distington Vill.	5	At the south-end of the village, are the ruins of Hayes Castle, once the residence of the Moresby family.
The road is for some miles in the vale of the Derwent. This river takes its name on issuing from Derwentwater. It subsequently enters Bassenthwaite Lake, and finally, after winding through a pleasant country, enters the sea at Workington.	20¾	Brigham Chapel on the left. The village is half a mile to the right.	6¼	Road to Workington.
A description of this town is appended to No. VII.	13	COCKERMOUTH, seated on the Derwent, at the junction of the Cocker.	14	Junction of the road from Workington to Cockermouth. These towns are eight miles from each other. The former is a sea-port, carrying on a considerable coasting trade. There are several extensive collieries in the neighbourhood, chiefly belonging to H. C. Curwen, Esq. of Workington Hall.
Sale Fell.	10	Wheat Sheaf.	17	
The valley through which the road passes, is watered by a small stream, which enters the large bay, near the foot of Bassenthwaite Water, called Peel Wyke.	8½	BASSENTHWAITE LAKE.	18½	Road to Carlisle, skirting the foot of the lake.
The opposite shore is pleasantly indented with several promontories, the three principal of which are called Scarness, Braidness, and Bowness. There is a fine breadth of cultivated land, sprinkled with hamlets and solitary houses, between the lake and the mountains.	8	Pheasant Inn.	19	This lake is approached at its widest part. It is four miles in length, about three-quarters of a mile in breadth, and seventy-two feet in extreme depth.
	6½	Smithy Green.	20½	Skiddaw on its east side, furnishes, in combination with the water, many splendid views. Beyond the head, are Wallow and Falcon Crags, backed by Bleaberry Fell and High Seat. At the foot of Skiddaw, is Dodd Fell, and in the distance Helvellyn is visible. In front of a portion of Skiddaw, called Long Side, and near the margin of the lake, stand Bassenthwaite Church and Mirehouse, the residence of J. S. Spedding, Esq.
The road traverses a thickly wooded country, at the base of Wythop Fells, Barf, and Lord's Seat. One of West's stations is at Beck Wythop, whence, says he, the whole cultivated land, between the lake and the mountains, is seen in all its beauty, and Skiddaw appears nowhere of such majestic height as from this place.		The road passes along the margin of Bassenthwaite Water.		
	3¾	Thornthwaite Vill.	23¼	
	2	cr. the stream from Newlands.	25	A road, nine miles in length, leads through Newlands to Buttermere. The lower part of the vale is picturesque, the upper, wild.
Many pretty villas adorn this little village. From eminences in the neighbourhood, views both of Derwentwater and Bassenthwaite Lake are commanded.	1¼	Portinscale Vill.	25¾	
		Long Bridge.		Grisedale Pike, a fine object.
		KESWICK. Inns, Royal Oak, Queen's Head, and King's Arms.	27	Greta Hall, the residence of the late Robert Southey

ON RIGHT FROM KESWICK.	From Cockerm.	KESWICK.	From Keswick.	ON LEFT FROM KESWICK.
	25½	Road to the Lake.	¼	
Vicar's or Derwent Isle. Lords Isle. Friar Crag projects into the lake a little beyond. Cat Bells are fine objects on the opposite shore, Grizedale, and Causey Pikes are to the left of them.	25		½	Castle Head, an eminence from which there is a beautiful view of the lake. Wallow Crag Falcon Crag.
Behind Barrow House is a cascade of 124 feet fall.	23½	Barrow House. S. Z. Langton Esq.	2	Road to the hamlet called Watendlath, placed near a tarn in a desolate and narrow vale. Thrang Crag.
The many topped Skiddaw, lifting its gigantic bulk beyond the foot of the lake, is a grand object. Crossthwaite Church will be observed lying at its base. Southey lies interred here, and a recumbent effigy of the Poet, cut in white marble, by Lough, has been erected to his memory.	22½	Lowdore Hotel.	3	The celebrated fall lies behind the hotel, on the stream running from Watendlath Tarn. Its height is 100 feet. Gowder Crag on the left, Shepherd's Crag on the right of the fall.
Grange Bridge, and the village of Grange. The road returns to Keswick by the west margin of Derwent Water.	21½		4	Grange Crag.
Borrowdale, a valley 6 miles long, and containing 2000 acres, is now entered. It is watered, in its whole length, by the river Grange, which, after it issues from Derwent Water, takes the name of Derwent. At Castle Crag the road and the bed of the river occupy all the level portion, but beyond the vale widens considerably. Above Rosthwaite the valley divides into two branches; the eastern branch is called Stonethwaite. Borrowdale formerly belonged to Furness Abbey.	20½	Castle Crag on the right. "From the summit of this rock the views are so singularly great and pleasing, that they ought never to be omitted." WEST.	5	There is a good view from this eminence. Shortly before reaching this point, a road deviates to, and passes, Bowder Stone, re-entering the main road a little beyond. This mass of rock has been likened to A stranded ship with keel upturn'd that rests Careless of winds or wave. It is 62 feet long, 36 feet high, and 89 feet in circumference. It has been estimated to weigh 1971 tons, and to contain 23,000 cubic feet. The view hence is exquisitely beautiful.
Here is a small inn. This is the widest part of the valley. The mountain Glaramara is seen in front. Scawfell Pikes, Scawfell and Great Gavel are seen over Seathwaite.	19½	Rosthwaite vill.	6	Half a mile beyond, near Borrowdale Chapel, a road diverges to the valley and village of Stonethwaite. Eagle Crag is a fine rock near the latter. A mountain path proceeds over the Stake, a lofty pass, into Langdale.
	18	cr. Seatollar Bridge.	7½	Near this bridge the road into Wastdale, by Sty Head, strikes off.
The ascent of Buttermere Haws, which rises to the height of 1100 feet above the sea, is now commenced. The retrospective views are fine. A portion of Helvellyn is seen over the Borrowdale and Armboth Fells.	17½	Seatollar. Abraham Fisher, Esq. Descend into Buttermere dale.	8	The well known black lead mine, and the immense Borrowdale Yews, are near Seatollar. The former is the only mine of the kind in England. The largest of the yews is 21 feet in girth.
Yew Crag. The upper part of this vale is exceedingly wild and uncultivated.	15½	Honister Crag.	10	Honister Crag, 1700 feet high. Here are some valuable slate quarries belonging to General Wyndham.

ON RIGHT FROM KESWICK.	From Cockerm.		From Keswick.	ON LEFT FROM KESWICK.
		Honister Crag.		
A few houses placed half a mile above the head of Buttermere Water, "under the most extraordinary amphitheatre of mountainous rocks that ever eye beheld."	13½	Gatescarth.	12	A mountain path conducts by the pass called Scarf Gap into Ennerdale. Black Sail, another pass leads into Wastdale
This lake is one and a half miles long, and half a mile broad; and at its deepest part is 90 feet deep. Char is taken plentifully. The distance between this lake and Crummock Water is about three quarters of a mile.		On the eastern margin of BUTTERMERE LAKE.		
	12½	Hasness (General Benson) on the left.	13	The lofty mountains seen above the opposite shore are Hay Stacks, High Crag, High Stile, and Red Pike. Between the two latter is a tarn, the stream running from which makes a pretty waterfall.
The Chapel has been lately rebuilt; before, it was the most diminutive in the kingdom. A road, nine miles in length, climbs a steep Haws upwards of 1000 feet high, and descending into Keskadale and Newlands, proceeds to Keswick. This lake is about three miles long by three quarters of a mile broad. Its depth is in some parts 120 feet. It abounds with char and fine trout. There are three small islands close to the shore at the head of the lake.	11½	Buttermere vill. With a good Inn. Woodhouse (R. Jopson, Esq.,) on the left. Along the eastern shore of CRUMMOCK WATER. "The mountains of the vale of Buttermere and Crummock are no where so impressive as from the bosom of Crummock Water." WORDSWORTH.	14	Scale Force, the loftiest waterfall about the lakes, is 2 miles distant to the west of Crummock Water. Its height is 156 feet. A mountain path leads by this fall, and Floutern Tarn into Ennerdale, 6 miles. Having wound round a bold promontory called Rannerdale Knott, a splendid view of the lake is presented. Melbreak is a grand object on the other margin. From its foot there juts a narrow promontory, a little above which there is a remarkably fine view. The mountains on the east shore are Whiteless Pike, Ladhouse, Grasmoor, and Whiteside.
A little before reaching Longthwaite, a few houses to the left of the road, some high ground is interposed between the road and the lake. The road afterwards passes between Haws on the left, and Whiteside on the right.	8½	Longthwaite vill.	17	Four miles from Buttermere, the road from Scale Hill to Cockermouth is entered. A turn must be made to the left.
Lowes Water, which sends a stream into Crummock Lake is about one mile and a half distant. This lake is three quarters of a mile long, scarcely one quarter broad, and about 60 feet in extreme depth. It lies between Low Fell in the south, and Blake Fell in the north. The scenery round its foot is, contrary to the general rule, finest at its foot, and here it is very grand. Melbreak forms a striking feature in the views.	7	Scale Hill. Foulsyke (Misses Skelton). To Whitehaven, 14 miles by Ullock and Moresby. To Egremont, 15 miles by Lamplugh and Ennerdale Bridge. To Calder Bridge, by the same places, 17 miles. To Keswick by Lorton and Whinlatter, 12 miles.	18½	There is a good inn at this place, where the tourist would do well to stay a few days. The village is about a quarter of a mile from the river Cocker, which flows from Crummock Water, and is here crossed by a bridge of five arches. A good prospect is obtained from an eminence in Mr Marshall's wood. The pedestrian may make his way by the stream issuing from Floutern Tarn behind Melbreak into Ennerdale, seven miles.
Road under Whiteside to Keswick which shortens the distance by two miles. For horsemen and pedestrians it is the preferable route.	6		19½	The road to Cockermouth passes through the vale of Lorton on the east bank of the Cocker. This vale presents many richly picturesque views. It is three miles in length, with many elevated hills around; but not lofty enough to cast a gloom upon the smiling aspect of the scenery. Lorton Hall, R. Bridge, Esq.
Deviation of the road through Lorton vill. to Keswick. The famous yew tree, "pride of Lorton vale," stands near the junction of this road with that from Keswick to Cockermouth.	4		21½	
	3	Enter the Keswick and Cockermouth road. 9 miles from Keswick.	22½	
		COCKERMOUTH. Inns, Globe, Sun.	25½	

Cockermouth is an ancient borough and neat market-town of 7057 inhabitants, seated at the junction of the Cocker with the Derwent, from which circumstance it derives its name. It sent two representatives to Parliament as early as the twenty-third year of Edward I., and, by the Reform Act, it has still the privilege of returning two members. The honour and castle of Cockermouth belong to General Wyndham. The ruins of this ancient fortress, formerly a place of great strength, are seated on a bold eminence which rises from the east bank of the Cocker. It was built soon after the Norman Conquest by Waldieve, first ord of Allerdale, of whose successors it was for many centuries the baronial seat. In 1648, it was garrisoned for King Charles, but being afterwards taken by the Parliamentarians, was dismantled by them, and has ever since lain in ruins, except a small part at present occupied by General Wyndham. The Gateway Tower, embellished with the arms of the Umfravilles, Multons, Lucies, Percies, and Nevilles, is a striking object. On the north side of the town is a tumulus, called Toots Hill; one mile to the west are the remains of a rampart and ditch of an encampment, 750 feet in circuit, called Fitt's Wood. On the summit of a hill at Pap Castle, a village one mile and a-half south-west of Cockermouth, are the traces of a Roman castrum. A great number of antique remains have been discovered at this place, and in the neighbourhood. The castle was subsequently the residence of the above-mentioned Waldieve, by whom it was demolished, and the materials used in the construction of Cockermouth Castle. Tickell, the poet, Addison's friend, was born at Bridekirk, two miles distant.*

The seats in the neighbourhood are—Dovenby Hall (Mrs Dykes), three miles north-west; Tallentire Hall (William Browne, Esq.), three and a half miles north; Isel Hall (Sir Wilfrid Lawson Bt.), three and a half miles north-east Woodhall (J. S. Fisher, Esq.), two and a half miles north.

The best inns are, the Globe, and the Sun. The distances to the principal towns in the neighbourhood are—Maryport, seven miles, Workington, eight miles, Keswick, by Whinlatter, twelve miles, by Bassenthwaite Water, thirteen and a-half miles, Whitehaven, fourteen miles, Wigton, sixteen miles, Carlisle, twenty-seven miles.

Cockermouth is now connected with the general railway system of the country.

* Cockermouth is the birth-place of the poet Wordsworth, who was born on the 7th April 1770.

ON RIGHT FROM KESWICK.	From Egrem.	KESWICK.	From Keswick.	ON LEFT FROM KESWICK.
		For 7½ miles the road is the same as the former No.		
	23½	cr. Seatollar Bridge.	7½	"Travellers who may not have been accustomed to pay attention to things so unobtrusive," says Wordsworth, speaking of the rude bridges of this district, "will excuse me if I point out the proportion between the span and elevation of the arch, the lightness of the parapet, and the graceful manner in which its curve follows faithfully that of the arch."
		Road to the left.		
The *wad* mine is in a recess called Gillercoom, in the side of the mountain on the right. The path crosses the stream at Far Bridge; from this place an immense mass of rock called Hanging Stone is visible. Near the mine are the famous yew trees. Advancing, Taylor's Gill forms a fine cascade after rain.	22¾	cr. Seathwaite Bridge.	8¼	
		Keppel Crag and Hind Crag on the left.		
		Seathwaite vill.		
	21½	cr. Stockley Bridge.	9½	
		The road winds precipitously up Aaron End.		Bay's Brown. Taylor's Gill Band. Saddleback is seen over Borrowdale.
Sty Head Tarn, a desolate sheet of water, beyond which Great End rises abruptly. Farther on is Scawfell Pikes.—Sprinkling Tarn, which sends a stream into Sty Head Tarn, is half a mile to the east. These tarns serve as guides in the ascent of the Pikes from Borrowdale.	19	Sty Head.	12	A magnificent pass elevated 1250 feet above the valley. The road descends very steeply between Great Gable on the right, and Great End and Scawfell on the left, to Wastdale Head, a level and secluded valley, of a few hundred acres, at the head of Wast Water, shut in by lofty mountains that rise like walls from it. Here is a chapel, but no inn. Garnets are found embedded in the slate of Gable and Lingmell.
A mountain road of six miles conducts from Wastdale Head, between Lingmell and the Screes, into Eskdale. The pedestrian and horseman may reach Ennerdale by the pass of Black Sail, or, by traversing another pass called Scarf Gap, may enter Buttermere dale at Gatescarth. This path is six miles in length.	17	Wastdale Head	14	
	15½	Head of Wast Water.	15½	This lake is 3½ miles in length, and about half a mile broad; its extreme depth is 270 feet. The grand mountains and bare rocks around this lake, invest it with a peculiar air of desolation. The Screes, whose sides "shiver in all the subdued colours of the rainbow," extend along the whole length of the opposite shore, whilst the road passes under Yewbarrow and Buckbarrow Pike.
Overbeck makes a pleasing cascade some distance above the bridge. The finest view of the valley is observed from the north-west extremity of the Screes.	14½	cr. Overbeck Bridge.	16½	
		Turn to see the panorama of mountains at the head of the valley, Yewbarrow, Kirkfell, Great Gable, Lingmell, Scawfell Pikes, and Scawfell.		Crook End, C. Rawson, Esq.
Strands is a pretty little village with two inns. The tourist making it his head quarters for a few days, will find many pleasant excursions in the vicinity. The view of Wast Water commanded from Latterbarrow, a rocky hill in the neighbourhood, is extremely fine. A curious ravine called Hawl Gill, in the south-east extremity of the Screes, is worth a visit; and those who are fond of mountain rambles, may pass along the summit of the Screes and descend to Wastdale Head. The views from this elevated situation are magnificent.	11	Strands vill.	20	From a field fronting Crook, there is one of the best views, not only of the head, but of the whole body, of the lake. From no other point of view are the colours of the Screes more beautiful, more majestic the outline, more magnificent the frowning cliffs. WILSON.
	7½	cr. Bleng Bridge.	23½	
	7	Gosforth vill.	24	The road from Gosforth to Egremont has been described in No. V.
	4	cr. Calder Bridge.	27	
		EGREMONT.	31	

ON RIGHT FROM KESWICK.	From Penrith.		From Keswick.	ON LEFT FROM KESWICK.
		KESWICK.		
One mile and three-quarters from Keswick, on an eminence to the right of the old road to Penrith, is a Druidical Circle.	17½		½	**Greta Bank Bridge.** Greta Bank, Thos. Spedding, Esq. **Latrigg, "Skiddaw's Cub."**
	15¾	cr. Naddle Bridge.	2¼	
Road into St. John's Vale, also through Matterdale to Ulleswater and Patterdale, fourteen and a half miles from Keswick.	15½		2½	
	14¾	cr. New Bridge.	3¼	The Riddings, Joseph Crosier, Esq.
Road into St. John's Vale. The road lies under Saddleback, a mountain of somewhat inferior elevation to Skiddaw. Its summit is difficult of access, but the views are extensive. On the south and east, it commands finer prospects than Skiddaw, but on other sides they are much intercepted. Its geological structure is similar to that of Skiddaw.	14	THRELKELD VILL. The stream watering this vale, is called the Glenderamakin, until its confluence with St. John's Beck, after which it is termed the Greta.	4	"And see beyond that hamlet small, The ruin'd towers of Threlkeld Hall." This hall was once the residence of Sir Lancelot Threlkeld, a powerful knight in the reign of Henry VII. It is now occupied as a farm-house. The Earl of Lonsdale is proprietor.
	12¾	Scales. Over moorish uninteresting ground.	5¾	Road to Hesketh-new-Market. From the hill near the eighth mile-stone from Keswick, there is a fine view over the vale of Threlkeld to the Newland's Mountains.
Mell Fell, a conical hill, formed of a curious conglomerate.	11	Moor End.	7	
	10	Sun Inn.	8	
Road through Matterdale to Ulleswater.	8½	Spring Field.	9½	Road to Hesketh-new-Market.
Slate has now disappeared, and new red sandstone taken its place.	6¾	Penruddock Vill. Observe the peculiar shape of Blencathara, from which the other name of that mountain is taken.	11¼	Greystock Castle, two miles on the left. The park is very extensive. The mansion is a fine building, containing some good pictures. Greystock Church, built in the reign of Edward II., contains some ancient monuments. Many relics of antiquity abound in the neighbourhood.
Road through Dacre to Pooley Bridge, at the foot of Ulleswater, four miles. Dacre Castle, formerly the residence of the famous border family of Dacre, has been converted into a farm-house. The name is derived from the exploits of one of their ancestors, at the siege of Acre—the St. Jean d'Acre of modern times—in the Holy Land under Richard Cœur de Lion. Another branch of this clan was settled at Gilsland in Cumberland. There are many ballads and traditions which still —"proclaim Douglas or Dacre's conquering name."	5		13	
	2½	Stainton Vill.	15½	One mile and a half to the right, Dalemain, E. W. Hasell, Esq.
	1¾	Red Hills.	16¼	Half a mile beyond Stainton, the road from Penrith to Ulleswater deviates to the right. Hence there is a charming view of the Vale of Penrith, and the mountains circling Ulleswater, which lake is hidden by Dunmallet, a wooded hill at its foot. Yanwath Hall, is seen on the banks of the Eamont, one mile and a half from Penrith on the right.
Bede says, that a monastery once stood at Dacre, and about 930, a congress was held here, at which King Athelstan, accompanied by the King of Cumberland, received homage from Constantine, King of Scotland.		PENRITH. Inns, The Crown; George.	18	Skirsgill, L. Dent, Esq.

CXVIII. PENRITH—ULLES WATER—PATTERDALE—KIRKSTONE—AMBLESIDE, 24½ Miles.

*** **Instead of the first five miles and three quarters of the road given below, the Tourist may cross Eamont Bridge on the road to Kendal, turning to the right a little beyond, to Yanwath vill. (two miles,) leaving King Arthur's Round Table on the left. Here is Yanwath Hall, an ancient castellated building, a good specimen of the old Westmorland Hall. Sockbridge vill. is a mile further. The hall at this place is a ruin deserving the attention of the artist. Barton church is seen on the right a mile beyond. Pooley Bridge is reached five miles and three quarters from Penrith.**

It has been recommended, that, in order to see the lower part of Ulles Water to advantage, the Westmorland margin should be traversed for three or four miles; a boat might be in readiness to convey the stranger across the lake to the road usually taken.

ON RIGHT FROM PENRITH.	From Ambles.		From Penrith.	ON LEFT FROM PENRITH.
		PENRITH.		
	23¼	Pursue the Keswick road	1¼	Skirsgill, Mrs Parkin.
Road to Keswick.	22½	for two miles.	2	
		Dalemain Park.		Dalemain, E.W. Hasell, Esq.
Waterfoot, Col. Salmond.		cr. the Dacre.		Dunmallet, upon which stood a Roman fort.
To reach Pooley Bridge a quarter of a mile distant at the foot of the lake, a turn must be made to the left. The Sun is an excellent hotel, at Pooley Bridge, where post-horses and boats can be obtained. There is a good view of the lake from Dunmallet, a hill near the village.	18¾	**ULLES WATER.** Rampsbeck Lodge on the left.	5¾	This lake is of a serpentine shape, nine miles long, a mile wide, and about 200 feet in extreme depth. It is divided by promontories into three sections, called reaches, of unequal size, the smallest being the highest, and the largest the middle reach. Four small islands adorn the uppermost, the scenery around which is of the grandest description.
Road to New Church, so called, in distinction from Old Church, which stood on the margin of the lake. The former was consecrated by Bishop Oglethorpe in 1558, while on his way to crown Queen Elizabeth; an office he had soon to regret having undertaken, when all the other prelates had refused, for he as well as the other Roman Catholic Bishops were shortly afterwards deprived.	17	Watermillock.	7½	Halsteads, William Marshall, Esq. on a promontory, called Skelley Neb. Hallin Fell projects from the opposite shore, and terminates the first reach. Swarth Fell is below Hallin Fell; between the two, Fusedale Beck enters the lake in the bay termed How Town Wyke.
This fine park, belonging to Henry Howard, Esq. of Corby, contains upwards of 1000 acres. It is well stocked with deer. At Sandwyke, on the opposite margin, a considerable stream called How Grain enters the lake.	15	Enter Gowbarrow Park.	9½	In Gowbarrow Park, says Wordsworth, the lover of Nature might linger for hours. Here is a powerful brook, which dashes among rocks through a deep glen hung on every side with a rich and happy intermixture of native wood; here are beds of luxuriant fern, aged hawthorns, and hollies decked with honeysuckles; and fallow deer glancing and bounding over the lawns and through the thickets.
Lyulph's Tower, a hunting seat, the property of Mr Howard. There is a splendid view of the lake from the front.	13½		11	
List, ye who pass by Lyulph's Tower At eve; how softly then Doth Aira Force, that torrent hoarse, Speak from the woody glen! Fit music for a solemn vale! And holier seems the ground To him who catches on the gale The spirit of a mournful tale Embodied in the sound. WORDSWORTH's *Somnambulist*.		cr. Airey Bridge. Road to Keswick through Matterdale 10½ miles.		A mile above the bridge the stream is precipitated down a fall of eighty feet. Two wooden bridges are thrown across the brook, one above the other, below the fall. The banks are beautifully wooded, and the scenery around of inconceivable magnificence. Birk Fell rises rapidly from the opposite margin.

ON RIGHT FROM PENRITH.	From Ambles.		From Penrith.	ON LEFT FROM PENRITH.
Glencoyn House, an old picturesque farm house belonging to Mr Howard.	11¾	cr. Glencoyn Beck. Enter Westmorland.	12¾	A promontory from Birk Fell terminates the second reach. The first island, House Holm.
Stybarrow Crag. This rock merely allows room for the road between it and the lake. The dale landers, headed by a Mounsey, once made a successful stand against a troop of Scottish mosstroopers at this place. The leader was thereafter styled King of Patterdale, a title borne for many years by his descendants. Bilberry Crag. Patterdale Hall	10½	cr. Glenridding Beck.	14	Glenridding House, Rev. H. Askew. This stream takes its rise in Keppel Cove and Red Tarns, which lie near the summit of Helvellyn. That mountain may be ascended through this glen. Place Fell, with a patch of cultivated ground on which are two farm houses lying at its base, has a striking effect on the opposite shore.
Patterdale Chapel. In the churchyard is one of the many large yews which grow in this country.		cr. Grisedale Beck.		A mountain road, practicable only for horsemen and pedestrians, conducts through Grisedale into Grasmere.
	9½	Patterdale vill.	15	There is a good inn at this place, which, if the Tourist have time, should be made his head quarters for some days, as there is much to see in the neighbourhood. Road into Martindale across Deepdale Beck.
The streams from Grisedale and Deepdale join their waters shortly before entering the lake. St Sundays Crag.	8¼	cr. Deepdale Beck.	16¼	The road is now through flat meadows on the banks of the stream, to another branch, which flows from Brother's Water.
Brother's Water, backed by Dove Crags and other acclivities, clothed with native wood. This small sheet of water is said to take its name from the circumstance of two brothers having been once drowned in it whilst skating.	6½	High Hartsope.	18	Hartsope Village. Hayes Water, a tarn well known to the angler, lies between High Street and Grey Crag, two miles above Hartsope. Angle Tarn in the same neighbourhood is noted for the superior flavour of its trout.
The summit of the pass is fenced in by the Red Screes on the right, and Woundale Head on the left. The large block of stone —— whose Church-like frame Gives to the savage Pass its name— stands on the right of the road. The Romans are supposed to have marched through this depression on their way northwards from the station at Ambleside. Near the summit, a road diverges on the left into the valley of Troutbeck. At the point of deviation, a small inn has lately been erected. In the descent, which is excessively steep, the views of Windermere and the vale of Ambleside are very fine. Wansfell Pike is on the left, Loughrigg Fell on the right of the vale.	3½	Enter the common and climb the pass of Kirkstone.	21	Within the mind strong fancies work, A deep delight the bosom thrills, Oft as I pass along the fork Of these fraternal hills. Aspiring road! that lov'st to hide Thy daring in a vapoury bourn; Not seldom may the hour return When thou shalt be my guide. * * * * Who comes not hither ne'er shall know, How beautiful the vale below;
		AMBLESIDE. Inns—Salutation, Commercial, and White Lion.	24½	Nor can he guess how lightly leaps The brook adown the rocky steeps. WORDSWORTH.

ON RIGHT FROM PENRITH.	From Kendal.		From Penrith.	ON LEFT FROM PENRITH.
		PENRITH.		
The Vicarage. At the corner of the field, at the first lane on the right, beyond Eamont Bridge, is King Arthur's Round Table. A short distance down the lane, on the right, is Mayborough, another relic of the dark ages. The road proceeds through Tirrel and Barton to Pooley Bridge.	25	cr. Eamont Bridge.	1	Carleton Hall, John Cowper, Esq. The Eamont and Lowther are tributaries of the Eden, before entering which they form a junction.
		Enter Westmorland.		
	24½	cr. Lowther Bridge.	1½	Brougham Hall, the Windsor of the North. In the vicinity is Brougham Castle, a fine ruin, the property of descendants from "The stout Lord Cliffords that did fight in France."
Clifton Hall, a farm-house, an ancient turretted mansion.	23¾	Clifton Vill.	2¼	
Here are the gates leading to the Earl of Lonsdale's magnificent Park of 600 acres, and to the Castle.				Upon Clifton Moor, a skirmish took place in 1745, between the retreating troops of the Pretender and the army under the Duke of Cumberland, in which fifteen were killed on both sides. Mention is made of this incident in Waverley.
Hackthorpe Hall, also a farm-house. The birth-place of John first Viscount Lonsdale. The Lowther family have immense possessions in the neighbourhood.	21	Hackthorpe Vill.	5	
	19	Thrimby Vill.	7	
Shap, anciently Heppe, a long straggling village. The remains of an abbey, founded in 1150, are a mile to the west on the banks of the Lowther. Only a tower of the Church is standing, but it appears to have been at one time an extensive structure. A road turns off at Shap to Hawes Water, six miles.	16	Shap Vill. Inns, Greyhound, King's Arms.	10	On the south-east of Shap, by the road side, are two lines of unhewn granite, called Carl Lofts. A mile to the north-east of the same village, there is an ancient circle of large stones, both these remains are supposed to be of Druidic origin.
	14	Shap Toll Bar.	12	
Wastdale Head, a granitic mountain, from which blocks, of immense size, have been carried, by some extraordinary means, into Lancashire and Staffordshire, in one direction, and to the coast of Yorkshire in another, upwards of 100 miles from the parent rock. In order to enter Yorkshire, they must have been drifted over Stainmoor, 1400 feet in elevation.	12	Over the elevated moorish tract called Shap Fells.	14	Shap Spa, a medicinal spring which annually draws a crowd of visitors, is a mile to the east in the midst of the moor. The water is of nearly similar quality to that at Leamington. There is an excellent hotel in the vicinity of the spring.
		Steep descent under Bretherdale Bank to		
	9	High Borrow Bridge, over the Lune.	17	This is the last stage to Kendal.
Low-Bridge House, Richard Fothergill, Esq.	7	Forest Hall.	19	Whinfell Beacon, 1500 feet.
	5		21	Hollow through which the Sprint from Longsleddale flows. This narrow and picturesque vale commences near Garnett Bridge, and runs six miles northwards, between steep and rocky declivities. A path at its head crosses Gatescarth Pass, having Harter Fell on the left, and Branstree on the right, into Mardale, at the head of Hawes Water.
Three miles north of Kendal from Otter Bank, a beautiful view of that town, with the Castle Hill on the left, is obtained.				
Mint House, Mrs. Elderton.	1	cr. Mint Bridge.	25	Benson Knott, 1098 feet.
		KENDAL. Inns, King's Arms, Commercial.	26	St. George's Church.

SYNOPTICAL VIEW OF THE MOUNTAINS OF THE LAKE DISTRICT.

NAME OF MOUNTAINS.	Height in Feet.	COUNTY.
Scawfell Pike	3166	Cumberland.
Scawfell	3100	Cumberland.
Helvellyn	3055	Cumb. and Westmd.
Skiddaw	3022	Cumberland.
Fairfield	2950	Westmorland.
Great Gable	2925	Cumberland.
Bowfell	2914	Westmorland.
Rydal Head	2910	Westmorland.
Pillar	2893	Cumberland.
Saddleback	2787	Cumberland.
Grasmoor	2756	Cumberland.
Red Pike	2750	Cumberland.
High Street	2700	Westmorland.
Grisedale Pike	2680	Cumberland.
Coniston Old Man	2577	Lancashire.
Hill Bell	2500	Westmorland.
Harrison Stickle } Langdale Pikes	2400	} Westmorland.
Pike o' Stickle } Langdale Pikes	2300	
Carrock Fell	2110	Cumberland.
High Pike, Caldbeck Fells . .	2101	Cumberland.
Causey Pike	2030	Cumberland.
Black Combe	1919	Cumberland.
Lord's Seat	1728	Cumberland.
Honister Crag	1700	Cumberland.
Wansfell	1590	Westmorland.
Whinfell Beacon, near Kendal .	1500	Westmorland.
Cat Bell	1448	Cumberland.
Latrigg	1160	Cumberland.
Dent Hill	1110	Cumberland.
Benson Knot, near Kendal . .	1098	Westmorland.
Loughrigg Fell	1108	Westmorland.
Penrith Beacon	1020	Cumberland.
Mell Fell	1000	Cumberland.
Kendal Fell	648	Westmorland.
Scilly Bank, near Whitehaven .	500	Cumberland.
PASSES:—		
Sty Head	1250	Cumberland.
Haws, between Buttermere Dale and Newlands . .	1160	Cumberland.
Kirkstone	1200	Westmorland.
Haws, between Buttermere and Borrowdale . .	1100	Cumberland.
Dunmail Raise	720	Cumb. and Westmd.

Highest English Mountain, Scawfell Pike, Cumberland .	3,166 feet.
Highest Welsh Mountain, Snowdon, Caernarvonshire . .	3,571 „
Highest Irish Mountain, Gurrane Tual, Kerry	3,404 „
Highest Scottish Mountain, Ben Nevis, Inverness-shire .	4,406 „
Highest European Mountain, Mont Blanc . . .	15,781 „
Highest Mountain in the World, Dhawalaghiri, Asia .	26,862 „

NAME.	COUNTY.	Extreme length in miles.	Extreme breadth in miles.	Extreme depth in feet.	Height in feet above the sea.
Windermere . .	West. & Lanc.	10	1	240	116
Ulleswater . . .	Cum. & West.	9	1	210	380
Coniston Water .	Lancashire	6	½	160	105
Bassenthwaite Water	Cumberland	4	1	68	210
Derwentwater . .	Cumberland	3	1½	72	222
Crummock Water	Cumberland	3	¾	132	240
Wast Water . .	Cumberland	3	½	270	160
Hawes Water . .	Westmorland	3	½		443
Thirlemere . . .	Cumberland	2¾	½	108	473
Ennerdale Water .	Cumberland	2½	½	80	
Esthwaite Water .	Lancashire	2	⅓	80	198
Buttermere . . .	Cumberland	1¼	½		247
Grasmere . . .	Westmorland	1¼	⅓	180	180
Lowes Water . .	Cumberland	1	½		
Brother's Water .	Westmorland	¾	½		
Rydalmere . . .	Westmorland	½	⅓		156
Red Tarn, Helvellyn	Westmorland				2400
Sprinkling Tarn, Borrowdale	Cumberland				1900

SYNOPTICAL VIEW OF WATERFALLS.

NAME.	Height in feet.	SITUATION.	COUNTY.
Scale Force . .	156	South-west side of Crummock Lake . . .	Cumberland.
Barrow Cascade .	124	East side of Derwentwater	Cumberland.
Lowdore Cascade	100	East side of Derwentwater	Cumberland.
Colwith Force .	90	Little Langdale . .	Westmorland.
Airey Force . .	80	West side of Ulleswater	Cumberland.
Dungeon Gill Force	80	South-east side of Langdale Pikes . . .	Westmorland.
Stock Gill Force .	70	Ambleside . . .	Westmorland.
Birker Force .	60	South side of Eskdale .	Cumberland.
Stanley Gill Force	60	South side of Eskdale .	Cumberland.
Sour Milk Force .	60	South side of Buttermere	Cumberland.
Upper Fall, Rydal	50	Rydal Park . . .	Westmorland.
Skelwith Force .	20	On the stream flowing from Elter Water .	Westmorland.

BY RAILWAY (EAST LANCASHIRE), 27½ Miles.

ON RIGHT FROM MANC.	From Blackb.		From Manch.	ON LEFT FROM MANC.
River Irwell, and beyond, Broughton Hall, & Sedgely Park; and farther off, Heaton Park & Hall, Earl of Wilton.	23	From Manchester, by Manchester and Bolton Railway, to Clifton Junction (p. 258).	4½	Trafford Park, Sir H. De Trafford, Bart. Pendleton. Pendlebury. Clifton; and beyond, Worsley Hall, Earl of Ellesmere. Railway to Bolton.
Irwell House. Prestwich. Outwood Lodge; 1½ m. beyond, Polefield.		cr. Manchester, Bolton, and Bury Canal, and riv. Irwell.		
Stand Hall, 1¼ mile.	21¼	Ringley Road St. cr. riv. Irwell.	6¼	Ringley, 1 mile.
	20¼	Radcliffe Bridge St.	7¼	To Bolton, 5 miles. Ainsworth, 3 miles.
Radcliffe. Unsworth Lodge.		cr. riv. Irwell.		
To Rochdale, 6½ miles. Near Bury, Chamber Hall. Here the great Sir Robt. Peel was born, and a monument to his memory has been erected near Bury.	17½	BURY ST. Follow course of river Irwell, which the line frequently crosses.	10	To Bolton, 5¼ miles. Elton. Tottington.
	15¼	Summerseat St.	12¼	
Nuttall Hall. 2 miles beyond Ramsbottom Station is a branch line to Rawtenstall and Bacup, which follows the valley of the Irwell.	13¾	Ramsbottom St. Leave valley of Irwell 1 m. before reaching	13¾	Holcome.
	10¼	Helmshore St.	17¼	
Carter Place.	9	HASLINGDEN (p. 339).	18½	To Blackburn, by road, 8 miles.
	7	Baxenden St.	20½	
Accrington House, Col. J. Peel. Railway to Burnley, and thence, by Colne and Skipton, to Leeds.	5½	ACCRINGTON St. The inhabitants of Accrington are chiefly engaged in cotton-spinning and calico-printing. Pop. 1851, 7481.	22	
	4	Church St.	23½	Oswaldtwistle.
Dunken Halgh, H. Petre, Esq. Clayton Hall. Rishton.		cr. Leeds and Liverpool Canal. BLACKBURN (see p. 339).	27½	

BURY is a considerable manufacturing town, situated on an eminence between the rivers Irwell and Roch. Although its present importance is of modern origin, it is a place of considerable antiquity, and was a Saxon town, as its name implies. The woollen manufacture, which is of ancient date, having been carried on here by the emigrant Flemings, is still prosecuted, though not on so extensive a scale, of late years, as the cotton manufacture. There are also in and near the town several extensive establishments for bleaching, calico-printing, iron founding, and machine making. The canal from Bury to Manchester and Bolton, as well as railway communication, conduces materially to its trading prosperity. Bury possesses a small model barrack, a free school, public subscription library, a news-room, a botanical institution, a medical library, a dispensary, and a mechanic's institution, several churches and chapels, besides meeting-houses, and charitable institutions. One M.P. Pop. 37,563.

On the heath near Bury, Lord Strange, afterwards Earl of Derby, mustered 20,000 men in favour of the Royal cause in 1642.

HASLINGDEN is a flourishing manufacturing town. The chapel contains a font of the time of Henry VII., as well as several monuments. The Haslingden canal communicates with Bury, Manchester, Liverpool, and Leeds. Pop. 6929.

On an eminence near the town is a tower erected by Messrs William and Charles Grant (" the Cheeryble Brothers" of Dickens), and one of whom (1852) still survives, who were the first manufacturers of the district, as a kind of public thanksgiving for the public prosperity they have reaped. From a lofty height, on the opposite side of the valley of the Irwell, where stands the Bury monument to Sir R. Peel, a fine and most extensive view of Lancashire may be obtained.

BLACKBURN, eight miles distant from Haslingden by the turnpike road, is famous for its manufacture of calicoes. It has many churches and chapels, an academy for the education of dissenting ministers, several meeting houses and a grammar school. James Hargreaves, inventor of the spinning jenny, was a native of this place Two M.P. Pop. 63,126.

About ten miles from Blackburn is the Jesuits' College of Stonyhurst.* The road leads through Ribblesdale, one of the finest and most extensive vales in England. To the left is Ribchester, a celebrated Roman station, and to the north-east, the Castle of Clitheroe, on a bold and abrupt eminence. Stonyhurst stands on a fine situation, and has a noble and commanding aspect. It was built in the reign of Elizabeth, by Sir Richard Sherburne, whose daughter carried the estate by marriage into the family of the Welds of Lulworth Castle, Dorsetshire, by whom it was disposed of to the founders of the college. This institution was established in 1794, and is conducted in a very efficient manner. About 180 boys, principally sons of the Roman Catholic nobility and gentry, receive their education in it. Charles Waterton and the Right Hon. Richard Lalor Sheil were educated here. Besides the class rooms and other accommodations necessary for the purpose of tuition, it contains a museum, in which, among other interesting objects, are the private seals of James II. and of Fenelon, and the cap, beads, seal, and reliquary of Sir Thomas More; a number of transatlantic curiosities presented by C. Waterton, Esq. of Walton Hall; a good collection of minerals and shells, bronze casts of the Cæsars, and plaster casts of the apostles, and a quaint old jewel chest which belonged to Queen Christina of Sweden. The library contains some highly illuminated MSS. In the philosophical apparatus-room there is a

* The distance is only about seven miles by the footpath in a direct line, out the carriage road is very circuitous.

fine painting, by Annibal Caracci, of the descent from the Cross. The recreation hall, a magnificent gallery, 90 feet by 20, is embellished with a great number of paintings, and hung with tapestry. The refectory was the baronial hall of the Sherburnes. The gardens are laid out in the old style, and contain some lofty well-trimmed walls of yew. Here is to be seen the identical Roman altar which Camden saw at Ribchester in 1603, one of the finest remains of classical antiquity in the country. A handsome church has lately been erected at Stonyhurst, at an expense of above L.10,000. At Mitton church, in the vicinity, there are some fine monuments of the Sherburnes. Stonyhurst is equidistant from Clitheroe, Whalley, and Ribchester.

A road leads from Blackburn to Clitheroe, 10¼ miles, passing by WHALLEY, which is seven miles from Blackburn in a N. N. E. direction, and 4½ miles from Accrington. Whalley is a parish, township, and village in the hundred of Blackburn and the honour of Clitheroe. It is the largest parish in the county, and one of the largest in the kingdom, containing 47 townships, and has an area of 180 square miles. The church is a venerable pile, containing some curiously carved stalls, &c. It was originally founded A. D. 628, and rebuilt 1100. Whalley Abbey, founded for monks of the Cistercian order, was an establishment of remarkable magnificence. The last abbot was executed in the reign of Henry VIII., for his share in the insurrection, designated "the Pilgrimage of Grace." The remains of the abbey are still sufficient to show the splendour of its architecture. The abbot house has been renovated and turned into a modern residence. Near Whalley are Read Hall, and Clerk Hill; and four miles beyond, at Great Mitton, Bashall; near which, on the river Ribble, is Waddow Hall, a fine mansion, romantically situated near the banks of the river.

CLITHEROE is situated on an eminence on the east bank of the Ribble. Here are the ruins of an ancient castle, erected by the Lacys, who came over with the Conqueror. The male line of this family became extinct in 1193, and the honour of Clitheroe passed afterwards into the possession of the famous John of Gaunt, and when his son became Henry IV. it was vested in the crown, remaining so till the time of Charles II. It is now the property of the Buccleuch family. During the commonwealth, Clitheroe castle was dismantled by order of the Parliament, and is now greatly dilapidated. Its stones contributed to build a modern mansion, which stands within its precincts. Clitheroe has an excellent grammar school, and several churches and chapels. In the vicinity of the town are extensive cotton printing works. Two miles distant is Pendle hill, 1803 feet above the level of the sea. One M.P. Pop. 10,864.

One mile before Clitheroe is Standen Hall, J. Aspinall, Esq.; and beyond, near Chatburn, Downham Hall, (W. Assheton, Esq.) and Greenbank. At Clitheroe is Clitheroe Castle, and 3½ miles distant, in a north-west direction, is Browsholme (E. Parker, Esq.), a curious building, erected in the time of Henry VII. containing, among other interesting antiquities, the original silver seal of the commonwealth.

59¼ Miles.

ON RIGHT FROM MANC.	From Leeds.		From Manch.	ON LEFT FROM MANC.
Line to Ashton and Huddersfield (see p.344.) Rochdale Canal. Branch to Oldham, 2 m.	58½	From Victoria Station, Manchester, to Miles Platting Junction St.	¾	Harpurhey. Blackley. Alkrington Hall, and beyond, Heaton Park, (Earl of Wilton.)
Chadderton Park.	53¾	Middleton Junction St.	5½	Middleton, 1 mile.
Rochdale is situated in a beautiful valley on the river Roch. It has extensive woollen manufactories, and cotton spinning and weaving are also carried on to a large extent. One M.P. Pop. 38,184.		The town of Middleton has within the last half century risen from a small village to a place of considerable extent, owing to the cotton manufacture, which is here carried on in all its branches. The printing and bleaching works are on a large scale. Pop. 9876.		Hopwood Hall, R. G. Hopwood, Esq.
The manor of Rochdale was long in the possession of the Byron family, and was sold by the poet, Lord Byron, to James Dearden, Esq., whose son now holds these princely domains.		☞ cr. Rochdale canal twice.		
	51	Blue Pits Junction St.	8¼	Branch to Heywood, 1½ miles; near it Heywood Hall.
				Castleton Hall; 1 mile beyond, Roch Bank.
Belfield.	49¼	ROCHDALE ST.	10	Castle Mere.
Clegg Hall.		☞ cr. river Beal.		Wardleworth.
	46	Littleborough St.	13¼	Smallbridge.
Langfield Moor. Walsden Moor.		Through tunnel, 1½ mile long.		
	40½	Todmorden Junction St.	18¾	Branch line to Burnley.
		Enter Yorkshire, and proceed along valley of river Calder, through three short tunnels, to		Stansfield Hall.
River Calder and Rochdale Canal.	38¾	Eastwood St.	20½	
		☞ cr. river Calder and Rochdale Canal.		Hepstonstall.
On the high moorlands through which this part of the line passes are nume-	36¼	Hebden Bridge St.	23	River Calder and Canal.

ON RIGHT FROM MANC.	From Leeds.		From Manch.	ON LEFT FROM MANC.
rous remains of antiquity, mostly of British origin.	35	Mytholmroyd St.	24¼	Wadsworth. Midgley. Luddenden.
	33¼	Luddenden Foot St.	26	
Sowerby. Tillotson was a native of this place.	31½	Through tunnel. Sowerby Bridge Junction Station.	27¾	Warley House. Branch to Halifax, 2¾ miles (see p. 343); near Halifax, Craven Lodge.
Norland.	29¾	NORTH DEAN Junction St.	29½	
		cr. river Calder, and through short tunnel to		
Elland. Stainland. Rastrick.	28¼	Elland St.	31	
		cr. river Calder.		
Upper and Lower Woodhouse.	25¼	BRIGHOUSE St.	34	Brighouse.
Bradley.		cr. Calder again.		Clifton. Kirklees Hall, Sir G. Armytage, Bart.
Junction of line from Huddersfield (see p. 345).	23¼	COOPER BRIDGE Junction St.	36	
Heaton Lodge.		cr. Calder.		Blake Hall.
	20¾	Mirfield Junction St.	38½	Branch to Bradford, 11½ miles.
		cr. Calder.		
	19	Dewsbury St.	40¼	Line to Leeds, by Dewsbury, Batley, &c. (see p. 345), 9½ miles.
Thornhill.		Cross Calder Navigation, through short tunnel.		Earls Heaton.
Horbury Bridge.		cr. river Calder.		Ossett.
Bretton Hall, W. B. Beaumont, Esq., 2 miles.	16	Horbury St.	43¼	Horbury Lodge. Lupset Hall, D. Gaskell, Esq.
Sandal Castle, an ancient ruin.		Through tunnel ½ mile long.		Thornes House, J. M. Gaskell, Esq.
	12¼	WAKEFIELD Junction St.—(see p. 356.)	47	
Kirkthorpe Hall.		cr. river Calder.		
	9¾	Normanton St. on the Midland Railway.	49½	Newland Park, Sir M. Dodsworth, Bart.
		Thence to LEEDS, as in p. 354.	59¼	

Oldham is situated on an eminence on the western bank of the Medlock and near the source of another stream called the Irk. It is only about seven miles distant from Manchester, and this circumstance, together with the advantages of railways and water carriage, and especially its mineral resources, have constituted this one of the most extensive seats of the staple manufacture of the county. The goods chiefly made here are fustian, velveteens, calicoes, and cotton and woollen cords. The silk manufacture is making progress. The original staple trade is the manufacture of hats, which still prevails to a very large extent. Mr. Thomas Henshaw, an opulent hatter and a native, founded a blind asylum at Manchester, and a blue coat school at Oldham. Hugh Oldham, Bishop of Exeter, who founded and endowed the free school of Manchester, derived his name, if not his origin, from this town. Oldham has numerous churches, chapels, and schools. It was first constituted a borough by the Reform Act, and now returns two members. No town in this vicinity has grown in size and numbers more rapidly than Oldham. In 1760, it is said to have consisted of only sixty dwellings. The population is 94,344.

Halifax is a well built and opulent town, deriving its importance from the manufacture of cloth, which was commenced here about the middle of the sixteenth century. It has numerous cotton mills and factories, and is the principal mart for stuffs, such as shalloons, serges, &c., for the sale of which an immense building, called the Piece Hall, has been erected, having 315 rooms for the lodgment of goods, which are open for sales once a week. The vicinity of Halifax abounds with coal, and it is connected by railways with all parts of the kingdom. The Calder navigation also affords a ready communication with Hull, and the Rochdale Canal with Manchester, Chester, Liverpool, and Lancaster. Halifax has numerous churches and chapels. The old church is a venerable Gothic structure. There are also several meeting houses and charitable institutions, free schools, &c. Halifax once had criminal jurisdiction, even in capital cases. Any person found guilty of theft was beheaded by means of a machine resembling the guillotine, called the "Maid of Halifax." Two M. P. Pop. 37,014.

Bradford, seven miles distant from Halifax, is a well-built and populous town, beautifully situated at the union of three extensive valleys, and forms nearly a central point with Halifax, Keighley, Leeds, Wakefield, Dewsbury, and Huddersfield. The inhabitants are chiefly employed in the manufacture of woollen cloths and cotton. There is abundance of coal and iron ore in the vicinity. The trade of the town is greatly promoted by railway traffic as well as by a canal which leads from the centre of the town to the Leeds and Liverpool canal. Bradford possesses numerous churches, chapels, meeting houses, and schools, a cloth hall, &c. The environs of the town are extremely pleasant, and the surrounding country abounds with picturesque scenery. During the great civil war the inhabitants of Bradford were distinguished for their adherence to the parliamentary cause, and twice repulsed a large body of royalists from the garrison of Leeds. Two M.P. Pop. 106,218.

At Undercliffe, near Bradford, is the Airedale College for the education of Dissenting ministers. About five miles from the town is the Moravian settlement of Fulneck, distinguished by the neatness and industry of its inhabitants.

CXXIII. MANCHESTER TO HUDDERSFIELD AND LEEDS (BY MIRFIELD AND DEWSBURY), BY RAILWAY, 42½ Miles.

ON RIGHT FROM MANC.	From Leeds.		From Manch.	ON LEFT FROM MANC.
Ashton, or Ashton-under-Lyne, is a considerable town, situated on the river Tame. It has largely increased of late years, owing to the cotton manufacture, which is here carried on in all its branches. There are also extensive collieries in the immediate neighbourhood. One M.P. Pop. 33,917.		From Victoria Station, Manchester. cr. Rochdale Canal and river Medlock, by a viaduct of 10 arches. Over Ashton Moss.		Ashton is the New Jerusalem of the followers of Joanna Southcote, who have a handsome chapel here, but their numbers have of late decreased. Ashton has a small model barrack.
	36	Ashton St.	6½	To Oldham, 3½ miles.
Staley Bridge is situated partly in Lancashire and partly in Cheshire, lying on both banks of the river Tame, which divides the counties. The cotton manufacture is largely carried on here. Pop. 24,921.	34½	STALEY BRIDGE.	8	
		Follow the course of the river Tame, and the Huddersfield Canal.		
Bucton Castle, an ancient ruin, probably of early British origin.	32	Mossley St.	10½	
		Enter Yorkshire.		
	29¾	Greenfield St.	12¾	
		cr. river Tame and Huddersfield Canal.		
Saddleworth, ¾ mile, is situated in a wild and mountainous country, near the borders of Cheshire, Lancashire, and Yorkshire. The inhabitants are employed in the manufacture of woollen cloths, kerseymeres, and shawls.	28¾	SADDLEWORTH St.	13¾	
	27½	Diggle St.	15	Dobcross.
		Through tunnel, 2¾ m. cr. Huddersfield Canal.		
	23¾	Marsden St.	18¾	
		Along valley of river Colne.		
Huddersfield Canal and river Colne.	21¼	Slaithwaite St.	21¼	
Linthwaite.	19¾	Golcar St.	22¾	
	18½	Longwood St.	24	

ON RIGHT FROM MANC.	From Leeds.		From Manch.	ON LEFT FROM MANC.
	16¾	HUDDERSFIELD (see p. 363.)	25¾	
	14	Bradley St.	28½	
Heaton Lodge.		Join Manchester and Leeds (now Yorkshire and Lancashire) Railway.		Cooper Bridge.
	13	Heaton Lodge St.	29½	
		Along Manchester and Leeds line to		Blake Hall.
	12	MIRFIELD St.	30½	Branch to Bradford, by Cleckheaton, 11½ miles.
One mile before Dewsbury, leave Manchester and Leeds line.		cr. river Calder.		
	9	DEWSBURY St.	33½	
Hanging Heaton.		Dewsbury is a market town of great antiquity. Blankets and carpeting are manufactured here to a considerable extent. Pop. 1851, 5033.		Batley Carr.
West Ardsley.	8	Batley St.	34½	
		Howley Park.		Bruntcliffe Thorne.
	5	Morley St.	37½	
Middleton Lodge, 1 m.	3	Churwell St.	39½	
Beeston.				
	1½	Wortley St.	41	Farnley Park, 1½ mile.
		cr. river Aire.		
		LEEDS. (see p. 356.)	42½	

CXXIV. PRESTON TO BLACKBURN, BURNLEY, COLNE, SKIPTON, AND LEEDS, BY RAILWAY, 66¼ Miles.

ON RIGHT FROM PREST.	From Leeds.		From Preston.	ON LEFT FROM PREST.
Leave railway to Ormskirk and Liverpool.		From Preston, by North Union Railway, to		
Leave North Union line, to Wigan, &c.		Lostock Hall Junction.		
Beyond Bamber Bridge, Cuerdon Hall, R. Townley Parker, Esq.	62½	Bamber Bridge St.	3¾	Walton-le-Dale, 1½ m. Brindle Lodge.
Hoghton Tower, Sir H. B. Hoghton, Bart. (see p. 259.)	59½	Hoghton St.	6¾	
		cr. river Darwen.		

ON RIGHT FROM PREST.	From Leeds.		From Preston.	ON LEFT FROM PREST.
	57¾	Pleasington St.	8½	Woodfold Park.
Fenniscowles, Sir W. H. Feilden, Bart.		cr. riv. Darwen again.		
	56½	Cherry Tree St.	9¾	Witton House. J. Ffeilden, Esq.
		cr. riv. Darwen.		
Railway to Bolton.	54¾	Blackburn (see p. 339.)	11½	Dunken Halgh. H. Petre, Esq.
		cr. Leeds and Liverpool Canal.		
Railway to Haslingden and Manchester (see p. 338).	50¾	Church St.	15½	Clayton Hall.
	49¼	Accrington St. (see p. 338).	17	
Hapton.		Huncoat St.		Altham; beyond, Read Hall.
		Rose Grove St.		Padiham, and beyond, Huntroyd Hall, L. N. Starkie, Esq.
Near Burnley is Towneley Hall, the seat of Chas. Towneley, Esq., a venerable mansion forming three sides of a quadrangle, the fourth side of which was removed about a hundred years ago. Here is a fine collection of family portraits. This seat was once the residence of the celebrated antiquary, C. Towneley, Esq., who formed that exquisite collection of antique marbles and statues now in the British Museum. The mansion is surrounded by noble woods, principally of ancient oak, finely dispersed and scattered over the park and demesnes to a great extent. Near Towneley is Ormerod House.		cr. Leeds and Liverpool Canal.		Palace House. Hood House. Gawthorpe Hall, Sir J. P. K. Shuttleworth, Bart.
	43¾	BURNLEY.	22½	Burnley stands on a tongue of land formed by the confluence of the Burn with the Calder. The inhabitants are chiefly engaged in the cotton manufacture. The church is an ancient building, and contains several monuments, Towneley Chapel, &c. There is a grammar school founded about the time of Edward VI. Pop. 28,700.
		cr. West Calder river, and Leeds and Liverpool Canal.		
Reedley Hollows.		Marsden St.		
Little Marsden. Marsden Hall.		Nelson St.		
In the distance, Boulsworth Hill, 1689 ft.	37¾	Colne St.	28½	Colne is a small town with numerous cotton and woollen manufactories. It has a neat church, several meeting-houses, two grammar schools, and a cloth hall. The Leeds canal passes within a mile of it. Pop. 6315
	35½	Foulridge St. Enter Yorkshire.	30¾	
	32¾	Earby St.	33½	7½ m. distant is Bolton Hall, H. Littledale, Esq., and 5 m., Gisburne Park, Lord Ribblesdale.
	31½	Thornton St.	34¾	Ingthorp Grange, 2 m.

ON RIGHT FROM PREST.	From Leeds.		From Preston.	ON LEFT FROM PREST.
				West Marton Hall, T. H. Cholmondeley, Esq., 1¼ mile.
	30¼	Elslack St.	36	Broughton Hall, Sir C. R. Tempest, Bart.
		cr. river Aire.		
Carlton. Pop. of Skipton 1851, 4962.	26¼	SKIPTON. The line hence follows almost throughout the course of the river Aire, which (as well as the Leeds and Liverpool Canal, and the turnpike road) it several times crosses.	40	Skipton Castle, Sir R. Tufton Bart.
				Bradley.
Glusburn.	23½	Cononley St.	42¾	Farnhill.
Eastburn.	21¾	Kildwick St.	44½	
Steeton Hall.	20¼	Steeton St.	46	Silsden.
Keighley is situated near the Aire, over which there is a handsome stone bridge. The inhabitants carry on a considerable trade in cotton, linen, and worsted goods. The church contains two ancient gravestones, one of which bears the date of 1023. Pop. 15,005.	17¼	KEIGHLEY St. (See also p. 363.)	49	West Morton; beyond, Rumbald's Moor.
				Riddlesden Hall.
Harden Grange, W. B. Ferrand, Esq.		cr. river Aire.		
St. Ives.	14¼	BINGLEY St.	52	
Heaton Hall. Cottingley Hall.		Bingley is beautifully situated on an eminence near the Aire. The surrounding country is pleasing and well wooded. The worsted manufactory is carried on to a considerable extent. Pop. 5238.		
		cr. river Aire.		
Branch to Bradford, 2¾ miles. Wrose. Idle.	11	Shipley St.	55¼	Baildon. Esholt. Esholt Hall, W. R. C. Stansfield, Esq.
		cr. river Aire.		
Park Hill.	7¾	Apperley St.	58½	
		cr. river Aire.		
	5¾	Calverley St.	60½	Horsforth Hall.
	4¾	Newlay St.	61½	
Bramley.				

ON RIGHT FROM PREST.	From Leeds.		From Preston.	ON LEFT FROM PREST.
	$3\frac{1}{4}$	Kirkstall St.	63	Kirkstall Abbey (see p. 356.)
Armley Park.	$1\frac{3}{4}$	Armley St.	$64\frac{1}{2}$	
		LEEDS. (See p. 356.)	$66\frac{1}{4}$	

CXXV. MANCHESTER TO YORK (THROUGH HUDDERSFIELD AND NORMANTON), BY RAILWAY, 68 Miles.

ON RIGHT FROM MANC.	From York.		From Manch.	ON LEFT FROM MANC.
	$37\frac{1}{2}$	From Manchester, by Huddersfield, to Mirfield St. (as in pp. 344, 345.)	$30\frac{1}{2}$	
	$24\frac{1}{2}$	Thence, by Wakefield, to Normanton (p. 342).	$43\frac{1}{2}$	
		Thence to YORK (as in pp. 437, 438.)	68	

CXXVI. MANCHESTER TO SHEFFIELD, GAINSBOROUGH, HULL, AND GRIMSBY, BY RAILWAY, $110\frac{1}{4}$ Miles.

ON RIGHT FROM MANC.	From Grimsby.		From Manch.	ON LEFT FROM MANC.
Line of Manchester and Birmingham railway, to Crewe.		From London road Station, Manchester, to Ardwick St.	$\frac{3}{4}$	Openshaw.
	$107\frac{3}{4}$	Through short tunnel. Gorton St.	$2\frac{1}{2}$	
		cr. Manchester and Stockport Canal.		Manchester and Ashton Canal.
Gorton House.	$106\frac{3}{4}$	Fairfield St.	$3\frac{1}{2}$	
Denton, $1\frac{1}{4}$ mile, and near it, Haughton Hall.	$105\frac{1}{4}$	Guide Bridge Junction St.	5	Branch to Ashton, $\frac{3}{4}$ mile, and Staley Bridge, $1\frac{1}{2}$ mile.
Dukinfield Hall.		cr. river Tame and Peak Forest Canal.		Dukinfield, a populous

ON RIGHT FROM MANC.	From Grimsby.	Enter Cheshire.	From Manch.	ON LEFT FROM MANC.
Hyde, ½ mile, a considerable place, devoted almost entirely to the cotton manufacture. Pop. 13,722.	102¾	Newton St.	7½	suburb of Ashton, the people of which are engaged in various branches of the cotton manufacture. (See Ashton, p. 344.)
Hyde Hall, E. H. Clarke, Esq.	100¼	Mottram St.	10	Mottram in Longdendale, 1 mile; ¾ mile beyond, Thorncliffe Hall.
Glossop, Duke of Norfolk, 1½ mile.		cr. river Etherow and enter Derbyshire.		
Branch railway to Glossop, 1 mile.	98¼	Dinting Junction St.	12	Melandra Castle, the site of a Roman camp.
	97½	Hadfield St.	12¾	
Mouslow Castle, an ancient site.		Through Longdendale, the valley in which the river Etherow runs.		The elevated valley through which the line here runs is enclosed on either hand by the mountains of the Pennine range.
This tunnel is near the point of junction of the counties of Chester, York, and Derby, one end being in Cheshire, and the other in Yorkshire: it passes under a bleak hilly moor, covered with dark heath and bog. It was six years in progress of formation, and 3485 barrels of gunpowder were consumed in blasting the rocks through which it passes.		cr. river Etherow, and re-enter Cheshire.		
	90¾	Woodhead St.	19½	Woodhead, 1¼ mile. 2½ miles distant is Holme Moss, over which the Huddersfield turnpike road passes, at an elevation of 1859 feet.
		Through tunnel, 5192 yards (nearly 3 miles) long.		
	87¾	Dunford Bridge St.	22½	
		Along valley of river Don, Yorkshire, which the line follows the whole way to Sheffield.		
	85¼	Hazlehead Bridge St.	25	
Penistone is a small market town on the banks of the Don; it is situated in a wild and dreary district, and the moors to the westward have a bleak and barren aspect. Pop. of parish, 7149.	82¼	Penistone Junction and Thurlston St.	28	Silkstone, 2½ m. and beyond Cannon Hall, G. Spencer Stanhope, Esq. Thurgoland.
		cr. river Don.		
	77¾	Wortley St.	32	Wortley Hall, Lord Wharncliffe:—2½ miles beyond, Wentworth Castle, F. W. T. V. Wentworth, Esq.
Bolsterstone.	76¾	Deep Car St.	33½	Wharncliffe Wood. Wharncliffe Park, Lord Wharncliffe.
	73¾	Oughty Bridge St.	36½	Ecclesfield, 3 miles, and beyond, the Grange (Earl of Effingham.)
Hillsborough Hall.	71¾	Wadsley Bridge St.	38½	6½ miles, Wentworth House and Park, Earl Fitzwilliam. Wards End.
	69	SHEFFIELD (see p. 376.)	41¼	Railway to Rotherham 5 miles.
		cr. river Don and Sheffield and Tinsley Canal.		Attercliffe.
	66½	Darnal St.	43¾	

ON RIGHT FROM MANC.	From Grimsby.		From Manch.	ON LEFT FROM MANC.
Handsworth.				Treeton.
		cr. river Rother and line of Midland Railway, near the		Aston and Aston Hall.
Woodhouse.	63¼	Woodhouse Junction Station on do.	47	
Beighton. Wales.	58¼	Kiveton Park St.	52	Todwick. Kiveton Park. South Anston.
Harthill, 1½ mile. Thorpe Salvin.		Enter Nottinghamshire.		Walling Wells, Sir T. W. White, Bart.
Shireoaks Park.	55¼	Shireoaks St.	55	
Chesterfield Canal.				Gateford Hall.
Worksop Manor and Park, Duke of Newcastle, and beyond, Welbeck Abbey, Duke of Portland.	53¼	WORKSOP St. (see p. 368.)	57	
		cr. river Ryton and Macclesfield Canal.		Osberton Hall, G. S. Foljambe, Esq. Ranby Hall, Duke of Newcastle.
Clumber, Duke of Newcastle, and beyond, Thoresby, Earl Manvers.		cr. river Idle.		Babworth Hall, H. B. Simpson, Esq.
Ordsall.	45¼	EAST RETFORD St.	65	West Retford. Great Northern Railway to Doncaster and York.
The Elms.				Chesterfield Canal. Clareborough.
Grove Hall, G. E. Harcourt Vernon, Esq. 1½ m. West Burton.	39½	Sturton St.	70¾	N. and S. Wheatley. Bole.
		cr. river Trent, and enter Lincolnshire.		
Somerby Park, Sir Thos. Beckett, Bart., 2 miles.	35¾	GAINSBOROUGH (p. 419.)	74½	
Thonock Hall, H. Bacon Hickman, Esq.	31	Blyton St.	79¼	Laughton, 2 miles.
Pilham.	28	Northorpe St.	82¼	Scotton, 2 miles.
Kirton in Lindsey is a small town 17 miles north of Lincoln, beautifully situated on the summit of a hill. It has a fine church, of early English architecture. Pop. of par., 2058.	25½	KIRTON LINDSEY St.	84¾	
		Cross line of ancient Ermine Street.		
Redbourne Hall, Duke of St. Albans, 1½ m.	22	Scawby and Hibaldstow St.	88¼	Scawby, 1½ mile. Scawby Hall, Sir J. Nelthorpe, Bart.
		cr. river Ancholme.		Manby Hall, (Earl of Yarborough) 4 m.
Caistor, 10 miles.	19¼	BRIGG St. (see p. 419.)	91	Barton on Humber (by road) 11 miles.
				Elsham Hall, T. G Corbett, Esq.
Line from Lincoln and	15½	Barnetby Junction.	94¾	Melton Ross.

ON RIGHT FROM MANC.	From Grimsby.		From Manch.	ON LEFT FROM MANC.
Market Raisen joins (see chap. clix). Brocklesby Park, Earl of Yarborough.	11	Brocklesby St.	99¼	Croxton. Wootton Hall, L. Upleby, Esq., 2¾ miles.
Yarborough Camp.	9¾	Ulceby Junction St.	100½	Ulceby. Branch to New Holland, on the Humber, opposite Hull, 6½ miles.
Keelby.	8	Habrough St.	102¼	
Riby, G. Tomline, Esq. 2½ miles.	4¼	Stallingborough St.	106	Estuary of the Humber.
Laceby Hall, 2½ miles.	2	Great Coates St.	108¼	
Line from Louth and Boston joins.		GREAT GRIMSBY (p. 430.)	110¼	

CXXVII. LONDON TO LEEDS, BY LEICESTER, DERBY, AND CHESTERFIELD (MIDLAND RAILWAY), 205¼ Miles.

ON RIGHT FROM LOND.	From Leeds.		From London.	ON LEFT FROM LOND.
		From London, by North Western Railway, to		
	122¼	Rugby (pp. 199, 203.)	83	Leave main line of North Western Railway.
Rugby Lodge, T. Caldecott, Esq. Cotton House.		Leaving Rugby, pass through Gilcorner tunnel, 300 feet long.		Holbrook Grange. Newbold, Sir T. G. Skipwith, Bart., and beyond Combe Abbey (Earl Craven.)
Ashby Parva.	114½	ULLESTHORPE St. (*Leicestershire.*) (From London, 91 miles; from Nottingham, 39½ m.)	90¾	Newnham-Paddox, Earl of Denbigh. Claybrooke Hall.
Dunton Bassett.				Frowlesworth.
	111¼	Broughton-Astley St.	94	
	107¾	Countesthorpe St.	97½	Cosby.
Countesthorpe.	105¾	Wigston St.	99½	
		Knighton Tunnel, 100 yards in length.		
To Uppingham, 21 m.; to Melton Mowbray, 14 m.	102½	LEICESTER (p. 354.)	102¾	Braunston Hall, C. Winstanley, Esq. To Hinkley, 12 m.; to Ashby-de-la-Zouch, 17 m.
Barkby Hall, W. Pochin, Esq.	97⅜	SYSTON St.	107⅜	Belgrave. Birstall House, and beyond, Bradgate Park.

ON RIGHT FROM LOND.	From Leeds.		From London.	ON LEFT FROM LOND.
				Wanlip Hall, Sir G. J. Palmer, Bart.
At a distance, Brookesby Hall.	94½	**Sileby St.**	110¾	Mount Sorrel, famous for its castle, which was besieged in the reign of Henry III., and totally demolished.
	92¼	**Barrow St.**	113	Quorndon Hall, E. B. Farnham, Esq.
Prestwould Hall, C. W. Packe, Esq. Burton Hall, C. J. H. Mundy, Esq.	89¾	LOUGHBOROUGH. (From London, 116 miles; from Nottingham, 14 m.) This town carries on an extensive hosiery and lace trade, and has derived great benefit from its canal, which communicates with the Trent and Soar. Pop. 10,830.	115½	To Ashby-de-la-Zouch, 12 miles. The Elms. Garendon Park, C. M. Phillipps, Esq.
Stanford Hall.				Sutton Bonnington. Kegworth village.
Here a branch turns off to Nottingham (p. 443).	85	**Kegworth St.**	120½	Lockington; and, at a distance, Donnington, Marquis of Hastings.
Thrumpton Hall.	80	Sawley St.	125¼	
	79¼	Draycott St.	126	
	77	Borrowash St.	128¼	Elvaston Castle, Earl of Harrington.
Spondon Hall.	75½	Spondon St. About 3 miles from the station are some remains of Dale Abbey.	129¾	A church existed at Spondon before the Conquest. The present edifice is an interesting specimen of the style of the fourteenth century.
Chaddesden Hall, Sir H. S. Wilmot, Bart.	73	DERBY (p. 355.)	132¼	
At a distance, Locko Park. Breadsall Priory, where Dr. Darwin lived, and where he died in 1802. In the church of Breadsall there is a monument to his memory.	67½	Duffield St. Milford Tunnel, 830 yards in length.	137¾	Markeaton, W. Mundy, Esq. Darley, R. Holden, Esq. Allestree Hall, W. Evans, Esq.; and beyond, Kedleston, Lord Scarsdale. Duffield, C. R. Colvile, Esq.
Holbrook Hall.	65½	BELPER (p. 355).	135¾	Farnagh Hall.
	62½	Ambergate St. Visitors to the Derbyshire Peak will here quit the railway for Wirksworth, 6 miles distant. Lodge Hill Tunnel, 260 yards long. The railway is now carried along the beautiful valley of the Ansa, which stream it several times crosses.	142¾	Railway to Matlock and Rowsley, branches off at Ambergate station. At a distance Alderwasley Hall, F. E. Hurt, Esq. Ruins of Wingfield manor house, occupying a commanding situation. It was dismantled by order of the Parliament in 1646.
Alfreton Hall.	59	Wingfield St.	146¼	
	55¼	Stretton St.	150	Ogston Hall, G. Turbutt, Esq.

ON RIGHT FROM LOND.	From Leeds.		From London.	ON LEFT FROM LOND.
At a distance Hardwicke Hall, (Duke of Devonshire), an interesting old mansion, erected by the celebrated Countess of Shrewsbury (see page 375).	52¾	Clay Cross St. Tunnel, one mile long. North Wingfield.	152½	
Sutton, G. Arkwright, Esq., 4 m. To Mansfield, 12 miles; Worksop, 16 miles. 6 miles to the east is Bolsover Castle (the property of the Duke of Portland), an unfinished mansion, erected in the early part of the 17th century on the site of an ancient castle built soon after the Conquest by the Peveril family. The present mansion, which stands on the brow of an eminence, was begun by Sir C. Cavendish. The Hill. Tapton Grove, G. Meynell, Esq. Tapton House.	48¾	CHESTERFIELD, a town of considerable antiquity on the west bank of the Rother. Its principal manufactures are cotton and worsted stockings; and in the vicinity are iron works and potteries. The old church, was erected during the 13th century. The spire has a singular appearance, and is much bent towards the west. There is a canal which communicates with the Trent and the Humber. Chesterfield possesses several charities. Pop. 9836. During the civil wars the Parliamentary forces were defeated at Chesterfield by the Earl of Newcastle.	156½	Wingerworth Hall. The old hall was garrisoned for the Parliament in 1643. To Buxton, 24 miles; Chapel-en-le-Firth, 24 m.; Bakewell, 12 m.; Chatsworth, 10 m.; Sheffield, 12 miles. 2½ m. distant, at Whitington, is the Revolution House, where the Revolution of 1688 was planned.
Staveley village. Barlborough Hall, the Rev. C. H. R. Rodes.	45¼	Staveley St.	160	Staveley iron-works.
	42½	Eckington St. cr. the river Rother, and enter Yorkshire.	162¾	Reinshaw, Sir S. Sitwell, Bart.
Wales — Todwick, Aston.				
	37½	Woodhouse Mill St.	167¾	To Sheffield, 6 m.
To Doncaster, 12 m. Clifton House. Eastwood House. Aldwarke Hall, G. S. Foljambe, Esq. Thrybergh Hall, J. Fullerton, Esq.	33	MASBOROUGH or ROTHERHAM St. From this station a railroad turns off to Sheffield.	172¼	To Penistone, 14 m. In the distance, the Grange (Earl of Effingham), and beyond Wentworth House (Earl Fitzwilliam).
To Doncaster, 9 miles. Fly-boats take the passengers upon the river Don to Doncaster for one shilling.	28	Swinton St. Cat-hill Tunnel, 140 yards long.	177¼	
	26	Wath St.	179¼	At a distance, Wentworth Castle, F. W. T. V. Wentworth, Esq.
	24	Darfield St.	181¼	

ON RIGHT FROM LOND.	From Leeds.		From London.	ON LEFT FROM LOND.
	19¾	BARNSLEY contains numerous forges for making wire, nails, hardware, &c., and extensive manufactories of linen, cloth, and bottles. Pop. 17,890.	185½	
Cudworth. Shafton.				Monk Bretton.
	16½	Royston and Notton St.	188¾	Notton.
Felkirk. Walton Hall (Charles Waterton, Esq., the distinguished naturalist), containing a museum open to public inspection. Crofton Hall, 1 m.		Cross Barnsley Canal.		Woolley Hall, G. Wentworth, Esq., 2 miles. Chevet Hall, Sir L. M Pilkington, Bart. Sandal Magna.
	13	OAKENSHAW ST.	192¼	Wakefield, 1¾ mile (p. 356).
Warmfield.		Junction of Manchester and Leeds line.		Newland Park, Sir C. Dodsworth, Bart.
	9¾	NORMANTON ST.	195½	Altofts Hall.
Line to York, 24½ m. (see p. 437.) Dunford House.		cr. river Calder.		
	6¾	Methley St.	198½	Methley Park, Earl of Mexborough. Oulton House.
Swillington Hall, Sir J. H. Lowther, Bart., 3 m. distant, Kippax Park, T. D. Bland, Esq., and beyond, Ledstone Park.	5	Woodlesford St.	200¼	
				Rothwell.
Leventhorpe Hall. Newsam Green. Temple Newsam, Marquis of Hertford.		River Aire runs parallel to railway, on right.		
		LEEDS. (see p. 356.)	205¼	

Leicester, on the banks of the Soar, is a place of very great antiquity, having been a city during the Saxon heptarchy. It appears, by Domesday Book, that, at the Norman conquest, it was a populous city. In the reign of Henry V., a Parliament was held here. Richard III., after his defeat and death, was buried here in a Franciscan convent, which then stood near St. Martin's Church. Cardinal Wolsey died here in the Abbey of St. Mary de Pratis. The town was formerly fortified, and the remains of the wall may be in many parts distinctly traced. The castle was a most extensive building. Its hall is still entire, and the courts of justice are held in it at the assizes. Leicester contains numerous churches and dissenting chapels. In St. Mary's Church is the monument of the Rev. T. Robinson, author of "Scripture Characters," who was Vicar for many years. There are few towns in which are to be seen so many charitable institutions. The chief manufacture of Leicester is that of hosiery goods. The lace trade is also carried on to a very considerable extent. Leicester returns two M.P. Pop. 1861, 68,056. Five miles distant is Bradgate Park, the birth-place of Lady Jane Grey; and four miles beyond it is Bardon Hill, the highest part of the county.

DERBY is situated on the banks of the Derwent, which is navigable hence to the Trent. The town is very ancient, and took its name from the river on which it is situated. On the east bank of the river, opposite to Derby, was the Roman station Derventio. Derby contains numerous churches, several dissenting meeting-houses and chapels, a Mechanics' Institute, and a Philosophical Society founded by Dr Darwin, who here composed the greater portion of his works. Here are extensive manufactories of silk, cotton, and fine worsted stockings. The silk-mill is the first and largest of its kind erected in England. Here also are large porcelain works and manufactories, where all kinds of ornaments are made of the marbles, spars, petrifactions, &c., found in the neighbourhood. All-Saints' Church contains numerous monuments of the Cavendish family. Richardson the novelist was a native of this town. A castle once existed at Derby; but the last remains of the building are said to have disappeared during the reign of Elizabeth. Several religious establishments were founded here at a very early period; but no vestiges of them now remain. Prince Charles Stuart advanced as far as Derby on his march into England, and the house in which he lodged is still pointed out. Through the noble munificence of Joseph Strutt, Esq., the working classes of Derby possess peculiar opportunities of enjoyment and gratification. This public-spirited individual appropriated nearly eleven acres of land, containing an extensive collection of trees and shrubs, for the recreation of the inhabitants and their families. This piece of land, called the Arboretum, was laid out, at the donor's expense, by the late J. C. Loudon, Esq., with great taste and judgment. The value of the Arboretum, including the ground and buildings, is estimated at £10,000. The Derby Grammar School is supposed to be one of the most ancient foundations of the sort in the kingdom. Flamsteed the astronomer (a native), received his early education in this school. Derby returns two Members to Parliament. Pop. 43,091.

BELPER, on the Derwent, is noted for its cotton mills belonging to Messrs Strutt. Their construction is worthy of notice. About 1200 or 1300 persons are constantly employed in them. About a mile and a half distant are two other cotton mills, a bleaching-mill, and an iron-forge, all belonging to the same proprietors, who have provided for the comfort and instruction of their workmen in a very praiseworthy manner. It affords his title to Lord Belper. Pop. 9509.

ROTHERHAM is pleasantly situated near the confluence of the Rother and the Don. It carries on a considerable trade in coals and lime. On the opposite bank of the river, in the village of Masborough, are the extensive iron-works established by Messrs Walker in 1746. The iron-bridge of Sunderland, and that of Southwark, in the metropolis, were cast in these foundries. Rotherham has a college for the instruction of independent ministers, a spacious church, erected in the reign of Edward IV., several chapels and meeting-houses, free grammar and charity schools, &c. Pop. 1861, 7598. About four miles distant is Wentworth House, the magnificent seat of Earl Fitzwilliam, adorned with numerous antiquities and paintings by the best masters. Near the entrance to the mansion, is the mausoleum erected by the 4th Earl Fitzwilliam in honour of his uncle, the Marquis of Rockingham.

Two miles from the Wakefield station near the river Calder is the town of WAKEFIELD, considered one of the handsomest towns in the West Riding of Yorkshire. The most remarkable of its churches is All-Saints, a spacious Gothic structure with the loftiest spire in the county. There is a very beautiful and richly adorned Gothic chapel (but not used as such), which was built by Edward IV. in memory of his father and followers who fell in a battle near this town. Wakefield has long been noted for its manufacture of woollen cloths and stuffs. It has also a considerable trade in corn and coals. Archbishop Potter and Dr. Radcliffe were natives of this town. Pop., 23,150. One M.P.

LEEDS, the largest and most flourishing town of Yorkshire, on the Aire, is the metropolis of the woollen manufacture, and the fifth town in England in point of population and commercial activity. It is an ancient town, and was probably a Roman station, but has been the scene of few historical events. Its situation is highly advantageous for manufacturing and commercial purposes. The chief articles of manufacture here are superfine cloths, kerseymeres, swansdowns, shalloons, carpets, blankets, &c.; plate-glass, earthenware, and the spinning of flax to a great extent. Its merchants also buy extensively the woollen and stuff goods made in the neighbouring towns and villages, and get them finished and dyed; so that Leeds is a general mart for all these fabrics. The Leeds cloth-halls form an interesting spectacle on the market days. Machine-making is a flourishing business in Leeds. The Leeds and Liverpool Canal connects Leeds with the Western sea, and by means of the river Aire it has a communication with the Humber. By means of railways, this town now enjoys every advantage which can be given, by the most rapid communication with all parts of Great Britain. The town-hall is a new and magnificent building; it contains a very fine organ built by Gray and Davison, upon which there are performances Tuesdays and Saturdays. The organist is Dr. Spark. Leeds contains also numerous churches and chapels, a free grammar school, a national school, commercial buildings, and a corn exchange, a philosophical and literary society, a mechanics' institute, a theatre, and various charitable institutions. Leeds was the native place of Dr. Hartley, author of "Observations on Man;" Wilson, the painter; and Smeaton, the celebrated engineer. Dr. Priestley, the distinguished philosopher, officiated for several years as the minister of the Unitarian chapel here. Leeds gives the title of Duke to the family of Osborne. Two M.P. Pop. 207,165.

About three miles from Leeds are the ruins of Kirkstall Abbey, picturesquely situated in a vale watered by the Aire. This abbey was founded in 1152 by Henry de Lacy for monks of the Cistercian order.

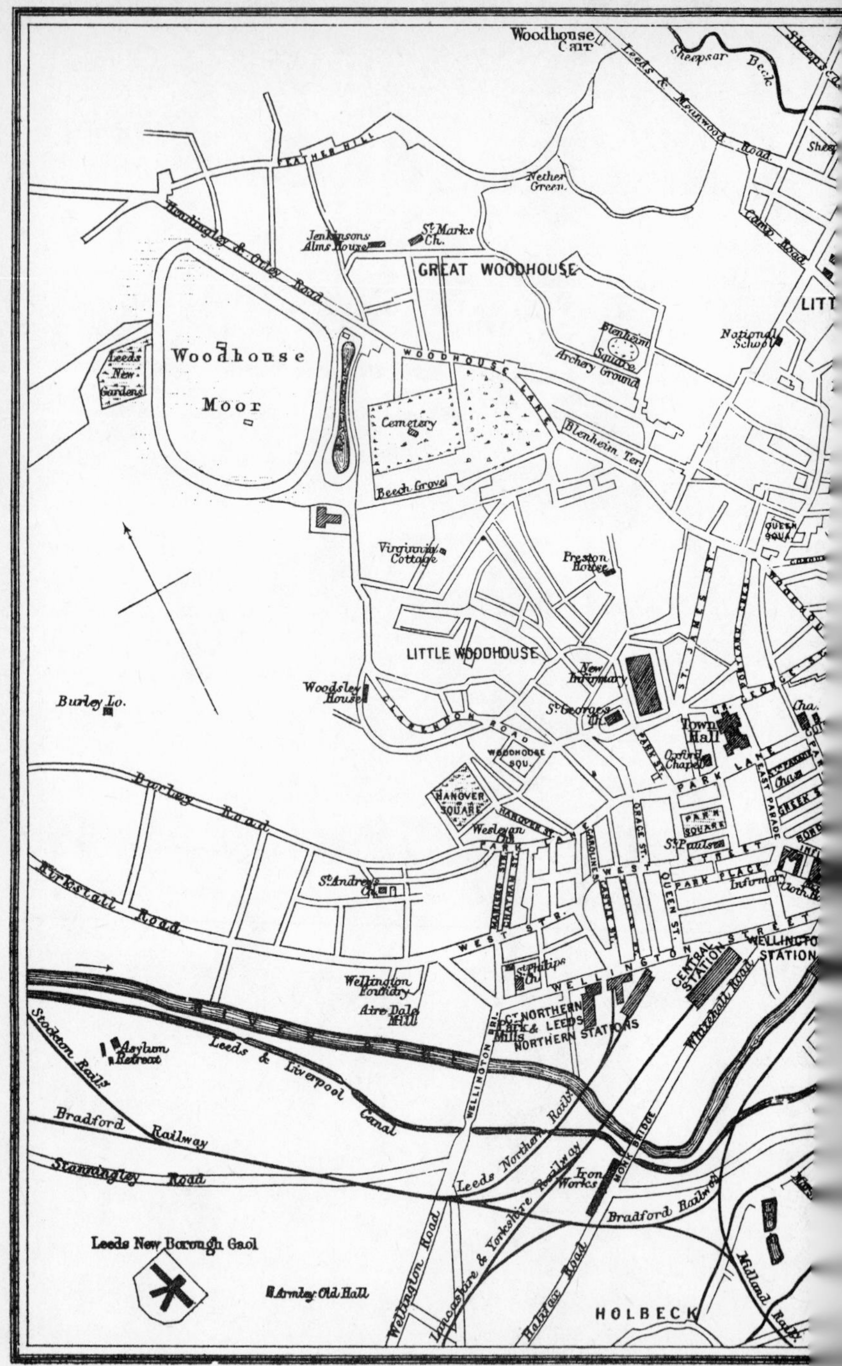
Woodhouse Carr
Leeds & Meanwood Road
Sheepsar Beck
Nether Green
Headingley & Otley Road
Jenkinsons Alms House
St. Marks Ch.
GREAT WOODHOUSE
Leeds New Gardens
Woodhouse Moor
Woodhouse Lane
Blenheim Square
Archery Ground
National School
Cemetery
Blenheim Ter.
Beech Grove
Virginia Cottage
Preston House
LITTLE WOODHOUSE
New Infirmary
Woodsley House
Clarendon Road
St. Georges Ch.
Town Hall
Burley Lo.
Woodhouse Squ.
Oxford Chapel
Park Lane
Hanover Square
Wesleyan Ch.
Burley Road
Park Square
St. Pauls
Park Place
Infirmary
Kirkstall Road
St. Andrews Ch.
West St.
Queen St.
Wellington Street
Central Station
Wellington Station
Whitehall Road
St. Philips Ch.
Wellington Foundry
Aire Dale Mill
Gt. Northern & Leeds Northern Stations
Park Mills
Stockton Rails
Asylum Retreat
Leeds & Liverpool Canal
Wellington Bri.
Bradford Railway
Stanningley Road
Leeds Northern Rail.
Iron Works
Monk Bridge
Bradford Railway
Leeds New Borough Gaol
Armley Old Hall
Wellington Road
Lancashire & Yorkshire Railway
Halifax Road
HOLBECK
Midland Railway

A. & C. B

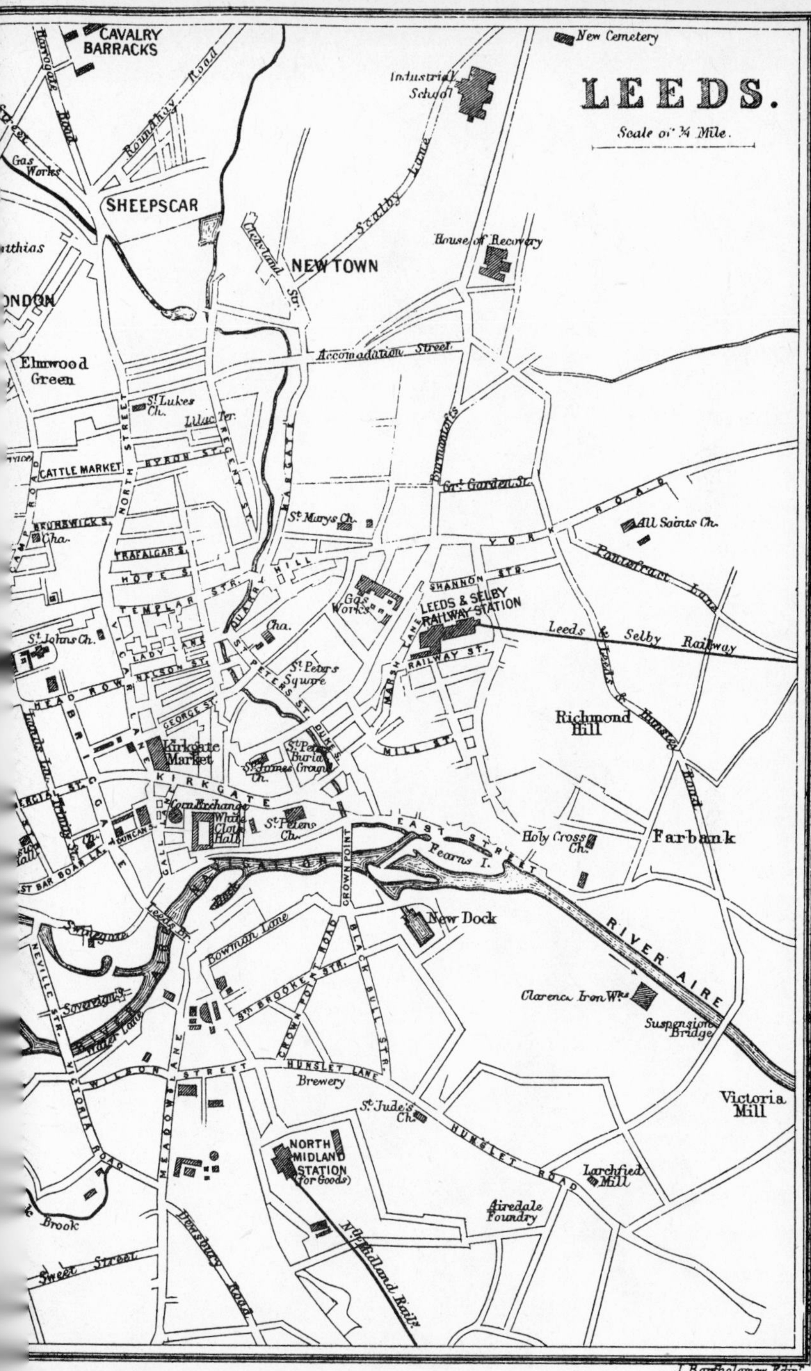

LEEDS.
Scale of ¾ Mile.
CAVALRY BARRACKS
Roundhay Road
Gas Works
SHEEPSCAR
NEW TOWN
Cleveland St.
Scalby Lane
Industrial School
New Cemetery
House of Recovery
Elmwood Green
Accomadation Street
St. Lukes Ch.
Lilac Ter.
NORTH STREET
REGENT ST.
BYRON ST.
CATTLE MARKET
MARGATE
Burmantofts
Gt. Garden St.
St. Marys Ch.
YORK ROAD
All Saints Ch.
Pontefract Lane
TRAFALGAR S.
HOPE S.
TEMPLAR ST.
QUARRY HILL
SHANNON STR.
Gas Works
LEEDS & SELBY RAILWAY STATION
Leeds & Selby Railway
RAILWAY ST.
MARSH LANE
St. Johns Ch.
LADY LANE
NELSON ST.
Cha.
St. Peters Square
ST. PETERS ST.
HEAD ROW
GEORGE ST.
DUKE S.
MILL ST.
Richmond Hill
Leeds & Hunslet Road
Kirkgate Market
St. Peters Burial Ground
St. James Ch.
KIRKGATE
Corn Exchange
White Cloth Hall
St. Peters Ch.
EAST STREET
Pearns I.
Holy Cross Ch.
Farbank
CROWN POINT
BRIGGATE
DUNCANS
Trinity Ch.
Bowman Lane
CROWN POINT ROAD
BLACK BULL STR.
New Dock
RIVER AIRE
Clarence Iron Wks.
Suspension Bridge
NEVILLE STR.
Water Lane
Sth. BROOKE STR.
MEADOW LANE
WILSON STREET
HUNSLET LANE
Brewery
St. Jude's Ch.
HUNSLET ROAD
Victoria Mill
VICTORIA ROAD
NORTH MIDLAND STATION (For Goods)
Larchfield Mill
Airedale Foundry
Brook
Sweet Street
Dewsbury Road
N. Midland Rail.
J. Bartholomew, Edin.

rgh

CXXVIII. BIRMINGHAM AND DERBY JUNCTION RAILWAY (MIDLAND RAILWAY, West Branch), $38\frac{1}{2}$ Miles in length, commences at the Hampton Station of the London and North Western Railway

ON RIGHT FROM HAMPTON STATION.	From Derby.		From H. Stat.	ON LEFT FROM HAMPTON STATION.
Packington Hall, Earl of Aylesford. Maxstoke Castle (T. Dilke, Esq.) and the ruins of Maxstoke Priory, both of which were erected in the reign of Edward III. A considerable part of the castle remains in its original state.	$33\frac{3}{4}$	**Coleshill St.** Coleshill on the Cole. The church, a fine specimen of Gothic architecture, contains a sculptured font, and numerous monuments of the Digby family. It affords the title of Viscount to the Earls Digby.	$4\frac{3}{4}$	Coleshill Park, Lord Digby, and Coleshill House.
Blyth Hall, W. S. Dugdale, Esq., formerly the property and residence of Sir Wm. Dugdale, author of the Monasticon, and historian of this county, who died here about 1685. Shustoke.	$30\frac{1}{4}$	**Whitacre Junction St.**	$8\frac{1}{4}$	Branch to Castle Bromwich and Birmingham. Hams Hall, C. B. Adderley, Esq.
At a distance is Atherstone, which carries on a considerable trade in hats.	$28\frac{3}{4}$	KINGSBURY ST.	$9\frac{3}{4}$	Middleton Hall.
	$24\frac{3}{4}$	**Wilnecote & Fazeley St.**	$13\frac{3}{4}$	Fazeley.
Tamworth Castle (the property of the Marquis of Townshend), is an ancient baronial mansion, erected by Robert Marmion, a celebrated Norman chief.	24	TAMWORTH, on the Tame, is situated partly in Staffordshire and partly in Warwick; has manufactories of woollen cloth and calicoes, as well as tanneries and ale breweries. Two M.P. Pop. 10,192.	$14\frac{1}{2}$	Branch to Lichfield; $1\frac{1}{2}$ m. Drayton Manor, Sir R. Peel, Bart. Camberford Hall.
Amington Hall, C. H. W. A. Court, Esq.	$20\frac{1}{2}$	**Haselour St.**	$18\frac{1}{4}$	Elford Hall.
	$17\frac{3}{4}$	**Oakley and Alrewas St.**	$20\frac{3}{4}$	Orgreave Hall, Earl of Lichfield.
Catton Hall, Sir R. E. Wilmot, Bart. Walton Hall. At a distance Drakelow, Sir Thos. Gresley, Bart. To Ashby-de-la-Zouch, $8\frac{3}{4}$ miles. Line from Leicester joins.	15	**Barton and Walton St.**	$23\frac{1}{2}$	Wichnor Park, J. Levett, Esq. Wichnor Manor was held by Sir P. de Somerville under the Earl of Lancaster, by the curious tenure of being bound to present a flitch of bacon to every married couple, who, after being married a year and a day, should make oath that they had never quarrelled.
At a distance Bradby Park (Earl of Chesterfield), 4 m. from which is Calke Abbey, Sir J. H. Crewe, Bart., and two m. farther, Melbourne Castle, late Viscount Melbourne. One mile distant is the village of Repton, one of the most ancient places in the county, and supposed to have been a Roman station.	11	BURTON-UPON-TRENT, an ancient town noted for its ale. Near the town hall is a curious ancient house. The bridge over the Trent appears to have been first erected about the time of the Norman conquest. Here are the ruins of an extensive abbey founded about 1002. Burton is now environed by a network of railways. Pop. 13,671.	$27\frac{1}{2}$	To Lichfield, $12\frac{1}{2}$ m. Dovecliff House, and beyond, Rolleston Hall, Sir O. Mosley, Bart. Egginton Hall, Sir H. Every, Bart.
At a distance, Foremark, Sir R. Burdett, Bart.	$6\frac{1}{2}$	**Willington St.**	32	On Egginton Heath, the Royalists and Parliamentary armies fought in 1644
Osmaston Hall, Sir R. E. Wilmot, Bart., and beyond, Elvaston Castle, Earl of Harrington.		DERBY (see p. 355).	$38\frac{1}{2}$	The Pastures.

ON RIGHT FROM LEEDS.	From Hull.		From Leeds.	ON LEFT FROM LEEDS.
Temple Newsam (Marquis of Hertford).		From Leeds. Through tunnel, 800 yards long.		Killingbeck Hall, and in the distance Bramham Park, G. Lane Fox, Esq.
Swillington, Sir J. H. Lowther, Bart.		Halton St.		
Kippax Park, T. D. Bland, Esq.		Cross Gates St.		
Ledstone Park, Rev. C. Wheler.	44½	Garforth St.	6½	Sturton; 1½ mile beyond, Parlington House late R. O. Gascoigne, Esq.
	42	Micklefield St.	9	Aberford, 3 miles, and beyond Hazlewood, Sir E. Vavasour, Bart. Huddlestone Hall. Newthorpe.
	39	Milford Junction St.	12	Sherburn, 1 m., and beyond Scarthingwell Hall, Lord Hawke. Lenerton.
Monk Frystone, R. M. Milnes, Esq., and beyond Byram Hall, Sir J. W. Ramsden, Bart.		Cross York and North Midland line.		
	35	Hambleton St.	16	
Gateforth House, and Hambleton Haugh, 1¼ mile.	33½	Thorpe Willoughby St.	17½	
Brayton.	31	SELBY ST. Selby is a flourishing town near the banks of the Ouse, by means of which, and of canals, it carries on a considerable trade. In this town there are the remains of an abbey, founded by William I., whose son Henry I. was born here. There is a curiously constructed timber bridge over the Ouse. The old church is remarkable. Pop. 5271.	20	In the distance, Escrick Park, Lord Wenlock. Branch to Market Weighton, 16 miles.
		☞ cr. river Ouse.		Barlby. Osgodby.
Hemingbrough.	28	Cliff St.	23	S. Duffield. Woodhall.
Brackenholme, 1 mile. Newsholme.		☞ cr. river Derwent.		Bowthorpe Hall. Wressell. Brind.
Howden, 1¼ mile. Belby.	22¼	HOWDEN ST. Howden is a small town of considerable antiquity, with an elegant church, and the remains of a palace which belonged to the Bishop of Durham. Pop. 2376.	28¾	Cavil. Portingten.
	19¼	Eastrington St.	31¾	

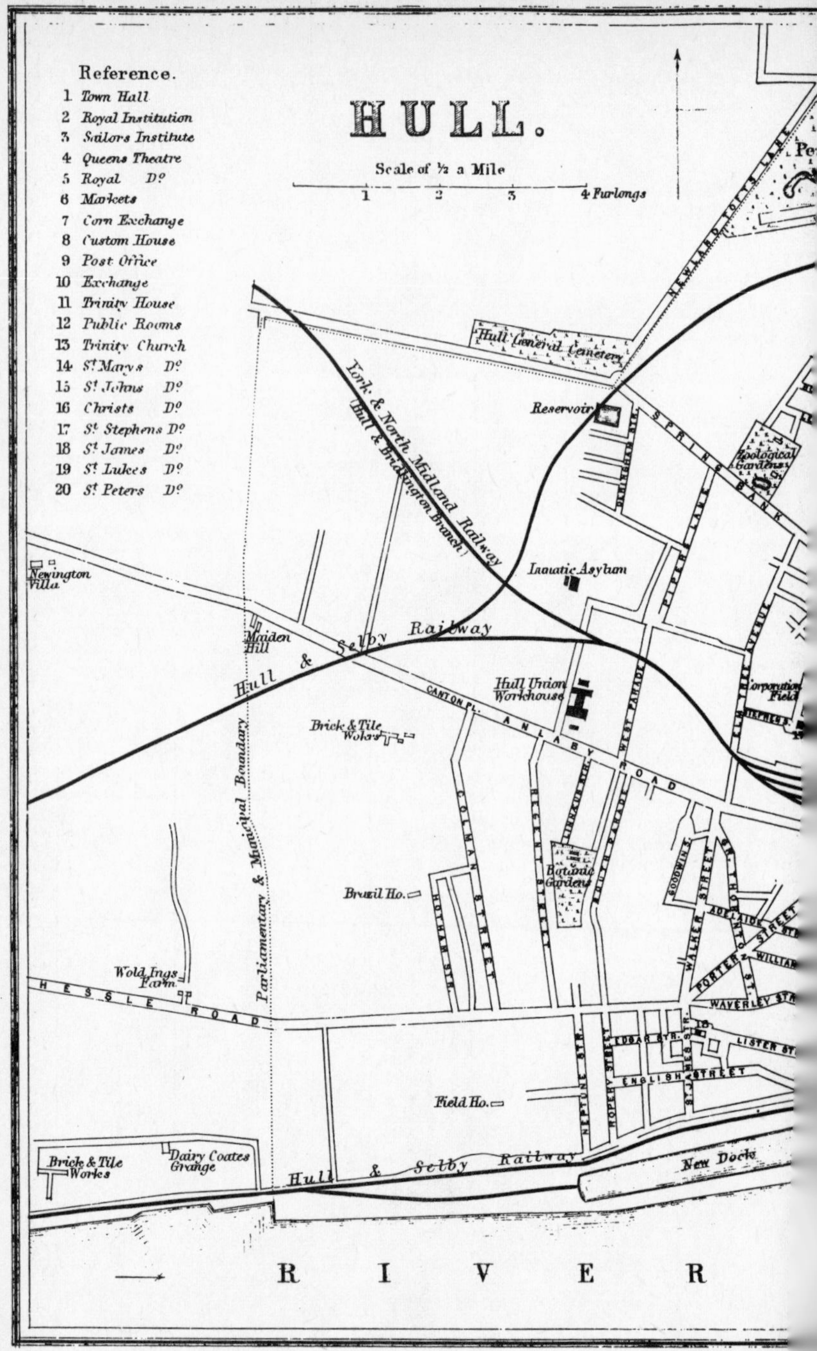
HULL.
Scale of ½ a Mile
1
2
3
4 Furlongs
Reference.
1 Town Hall
2 Royal Institution
3 Sailors Institute
4 Queens Theatre
5 Royal Dº
6 Markets
7 Corn Exchange
8 Custom House
9 Post Office
10 Exchange
11 Trinity House
12 Public Rooms
13 Trinity Church
14 St Marys Dº
15 St Johns Dº
16 Christs Dº
17 St Stephens Dº
18 St James Dº
19 St Lukes Dº
20 St Peters Dº
Hull General Cemetery
Reservoir
York & North Midland Railway
(Hull & Bridlington Branch)
Newland Tofts Lane
Spring Bank
Zoological Gardens
Lunatic Asylum
Newington Villa
Maiden Hill
Hull & Selby Railway
Hull Union Workhouse
Canton Pl.
Anlaby Road
West Parade
Corporation Field
Brick & Tile Works
Parliamentary & Municipal Boundary
Colman Street
Regent Street
Linnaeus Str.
South Parade
Botanic Gardens
Brazil Ho.
Hotham Str.
Goodwin Str.
Walker Street
Adelaide Str.
Porter Street
Waverley Str.
Wold Ings Farm
Hessle Road
Edgar Str.
English Street
Lister Str.
Neptune Str.
Ropery Street
Field Ho.
Brick & Tile Works
Dairy Coates Grange
Hull & Selby Railway
New Dock
RIVER

A. & C.

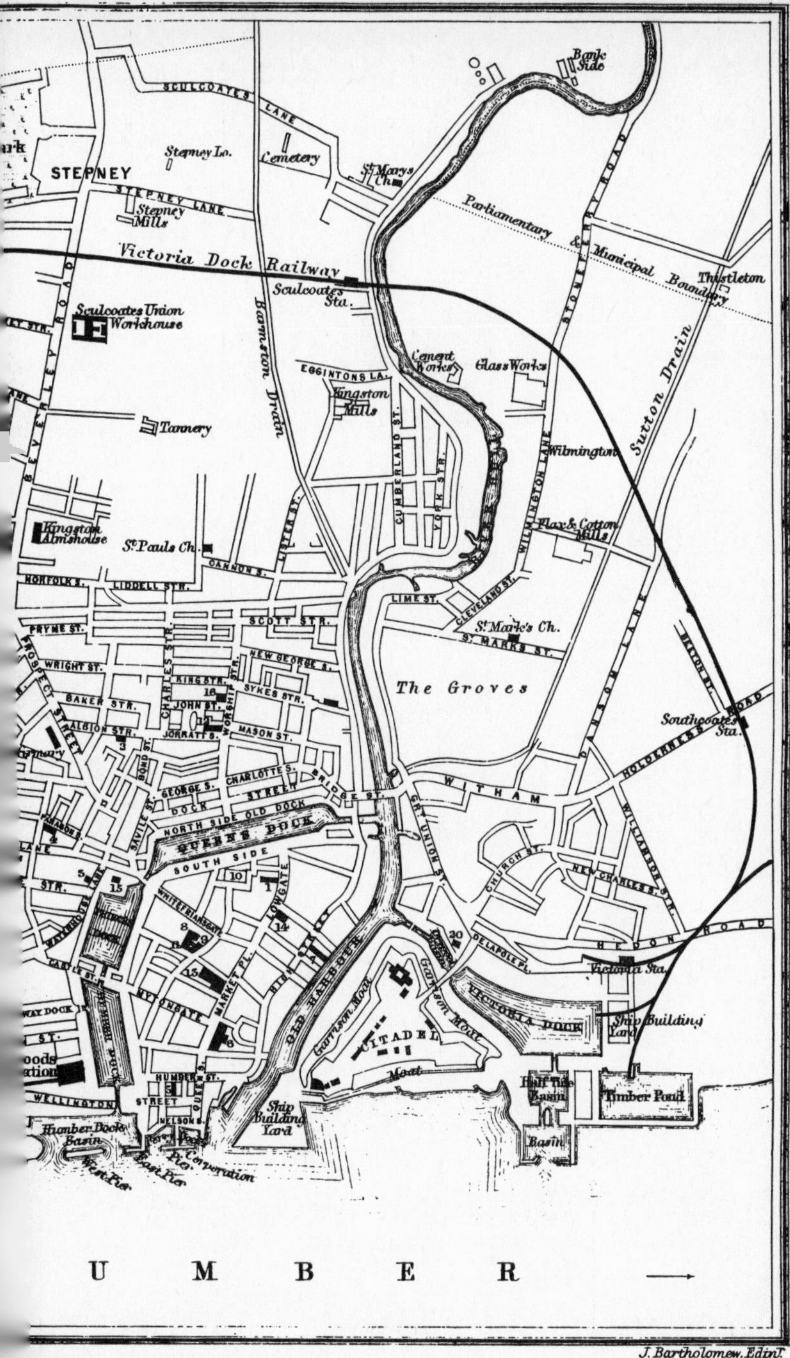

STEPNEY
Stepney Lo.
Sculcoates Lane
Cemetery
St. Marys Ch.
Stepney Lane
Stepney Mills
Bank Side
Parliamentary & Municipal Boundary
Thistleton
Victoria Dock Railway
Sculcoates Sta.
Sculcoates Union Workhouse
Beverley Road
Barnston Drain
Stoneferry Road
Sutton Drain
Cement Works
Glass Works
Eggintons La.
Kingston Mills
Tannery
Cumberland St.
York Str.
Wilmington
Wilmington Lane
Flax & Cotton Mills
Kingston Almshouse
St. Pauls Ch.
Lister St.
Cannon S.
Norfolk S.
Liddell Str.
Lime St.
Cleveland St.
St. Mark's Ch.
St. Marks St.
Pryme St.
Scott Str.
New George S.
Prospect Street
Wright St.
King Str.
Sykes Str.
The Groves
Baker Str.
Charles Str.
John St.
Worship Str.
Albion Str.
Jorratt S.
Mason St.
Dansom Lane
Southcoates Sta.
Holderness Road
George S.
Charlotte S.
Bridge St.
Dock Street
Witham
Williamson St.
North Side Old Dock
Queen's Dock
South Side
Savile St.
Bond St.
Lowgate
Gt. Union St.
Church St.
New Charles Str.
Whitefriarsgate
Market Pl.
Old Harbour
High St.
Delapole Pl.
Hedon Road
Victoria Sta.
Garrison Moat
Citadel
Moat
Victoria Dock
Ship Building Yard
Mytongate
Humber St.
Queen S.
Wellington
Street
Nelson S.
Humber Dock Basin
West Pier
East Pier
Pier
Conveyance
Ship Building Yard
Half Tide Basin
Basin
Timber Pond
U M B E R
J. Bartholomew, Edinr.

rgh.

ON RIGHT FROM LEEDS.	From Hull.		From Leeds.	ON LEFT FROM LEEDS.
				Gilberdike.
	17	Staddlethorpe St.	34	
Bromfleet.		☞ cr. Market Weighton Canal, and follow north bank of the Humber.		Scalby.
Brough probably occupies the site of a Roman station.	10½	Brough St.	40½	Welton and Welton House, T. Raikes, Esq. East Dale House. Melton Hill.
The Humber, here 1½ mile wide.				
	7½	Ferriby St.	43½	
				Hesslewood House, J. R. Pease, Esq., Tranby Lodge and Tranby House. Hessle Mount; 2 m. distant, South Ella, J. B. Broadley, Esq.
Ferry to Barton, on opposite bank of Humber.	4¾	Hessle St.	46¼	
				Railway to Bridlington and Scarborough. See p. 452.
		HULL.	51	

HULL, or Kingston-upon-Hull, situated at the mouth of the river Hull, where it enters the Humber, is one of the principal sea-ports in the united kingdom. Its distance from London is 174 miles by way of Lincoln, or by Great Northern Railway, and 236 miles by way of York. It was anciently called Wyke or Wyke-upon-Hull, but its name was changed to Kingston-upon-Hull by Edward I., who prevailed on the Abbot of Meaux, who was lord of the manor, to sell him the lordship of Myton, with the town of Wyke. He afterwards made it a royal borough. The town was regularly fortified in the reign of Edward II. During the civil war it was held for the parliament, and was twice besieged by the Royalists but without success. The old part of the town, with the exception of the fine market-place, in which there is Scheemaker's equestrian statue of William III., is ill built, with narrow streets, but that portion near the Docks consists of handsome streets and houses. Hull is admirably situated for trade, being at the mouth of the great rivers Humber, Hull, Ouse, and Trent. It has three considerable, besides graving docks, and the old harbour is to be converted into a fourth. Hull has, within these few years, become a principal steam-packet station, and has various steamers, which sail at regular intervals for Hamburgh, Rotterdam, London, Leith, Aberdeen, Berwick, Newcastle, and Yarmouth. In 1850, 258 vessels of 50 tons and upwards, and 195 of smaller dimensions belonged to Hull. It employs a few vessels in the whale-fishery, and carries on an extensive traffic in coals, oil, corn, and timber. It has also a considerable foreign trade to the Baltic, the southern parts of Europe, the West Indies, and America. The value of the exports from Hull in 1850 was £10,366,610. The building and equipment of ships is an important branch of industry. The custom-house dues amounted in 1857 to £312,629, so that of English ports Hull ranks next after London, Liverpool, and Bristol. Of places of worship, including those of every sect, there are upwards of thirty in Hull. The most important is the church of the Holy Trinity, which is said to be one of the largest edifices of the kind in the kingdom. The principal educational establishments of Hull are, Hull College, Kingston College, and a free grammar school founded by Bishop Alcock in 1486. In the latter, Andrew Marvell (who was long the representative of this town in parliament), Bishop Watson, and William Wilberforce, received a part of their education. It has also a Trinity House, and a number of charitable institutions, a large and well-selected subscription library, a good museum, a theatre, &c. The ancient gates of the town still remain, and the approaches to it are defended by batteries. The late Mr. Wilberforce was a native of, and for many years member for Hull. A column to his memory was erected Aug. 1, 1834. Two M.P. Pop. 1861, 97,661. Hornsea is the bathing-place of Hull.

CXXX. LONDON TO KENDAL THROUGH BEDFORD, NOTTINGHAM, HUDDERSFIELD, HALIFAX, AND KIRKBY LONSDALE.

ON RIGHT FROM LOND.	From Kendal.		From London.	ON LEFT FROM LOND.
Danesbury, W. Blake, Esq. Knebworth, Sir E. L. Bulwer Lytton, Bart.	239½	From London to Welwyn, *Herts*, (p. 370.)	25	Ayott St Lawrence, C. C. W. Dering, Esq. and Lamer Ho. Codicote Lo., and beyond, the Hoo, Lord Dacre.
	234¾	Langley.	29½	Paulswolden (Earl of Strathmore). Stagenhoe. King's Walden Park, W. Hale, Esq. Temple Dinsley. Hunsdon House.
2 miles east is Wymondley House, formerly an Academy for the education of Dissenting ministers. To Baldock, 5 miles. Ickleford. Arlesey Bury, S. B. Edwards, Esq. Henlow Grange.	230½	HITCHIN, a large and ancient town, pleasantly situated in a valley. The church is supposed to have been built in the time of Henry VI., and contains numerous monuments, several curious brasses of the 15th and 16th centuries, and a fine altar-piece by Rubens. Pop. 6330.	34	Hitchin Priory, F. P. D. Radcliffe, Esq. High Down, F. P. D. Radcliffe, Esq. In the distance, Wrest Park (Earl de Grey).
1 m. dist. Southill Ho., W. H. Whitbread, Esq.; beyond Old Warden, Lord Ongley. Ickwell Bury.	223½	SHEFFORD, *Bedfordsh.* Bloomfield the poet died here in 1723.	41	Chicksand Priory, Sir G. R. Osborn, Bart. Hawnes Place (Lady Carteret), and beyond Ampthill (Lord Wensleydale).

ON RIGHT FROM LOND.	From Kendal.		From London.	ON LEFT FROM LOND.
Cardington, S. C. Whitbread, Esq.	$218\frac{1}{4}$	**Cardington.**	46	
Cople House.		In the church is a monument by Bacon, in memory of S. Whitbread, Esq., and a tablet in honour of Howard, who resided several years in a house near the churchyard.		Kempston.
To Huntingdon, $23\frac{1}{2}$ m., St. Neots, 12 miles. 3 m. distant Howbury Park, F. Polhill, Esq.	$214\frac{1}{4}$	BEDFORD, (p. 364.)	50	To St. Albans, 30 m. Ampthill, 8 miles. Bromham Hall. Oakley Park, Duke of Bedford.
	$209\frac{1}{4}$	**Milton Ernest.**	55	Milton House, and, 4 m. distant, Odell Castle.
	$207\frac{3}{4}$	**Bletsoe.**	$56\frac{1}{2}$	2 m. distant Colworth House. Sharnbrook House.
Melchbourne Park, Lord St. John.	$204\frac{1}{4}$	**Knotting,** ***Fox Alehouse.***	60	Here a road leads over Ditchford Bridge through Finedon, and Burton-Latimer, to Kettering, 2 m. nearer than the other.
	$200\frac{3}{4}$	**Rushden,** ***Northamptonshire.***	$63\frac{1}{2}$	Knuston Hall. Rushden Hall, J. Williams, Esq.
To Kimbolton, 8 m.	$199\frac{1}{2}$	HIGHAM FERRERS. (p. 365.)	$64\frac{3}{4}$	
		cr. river Nen.		
	$195\frac{1}{2}$	Finedon.	$68\frac{3}{4}$	Finedon Hall.
	$193\frac{1}{4}$	Burton Latimer.	71	
Barton Seagrave Hall,	$191\frac{1}{2}$	Barton Seagrave.	$72\frac{3}{4}$	
2 miles distant Cranford Hall, Rev. Sir G. S. Robinson, Bart.	$189\frac{3}{4}$	KETTERING, (p. 365.)	$74\frac{1}{2}$	To Market Harborough, 11 miles.
Boughton, Duke of Buccleuch and Queensberry.				3 m. distant Cransley. Thorpe Malsor, T. P. Maunsell, Esq.
Geddington House.				Glendon Hall, J. Booth, Esq.
Oakley Hall, Sir Wm. De Capell Brooke, Bart.				Rushton Hall. Carlton, Sir J. H. Palmer, Bart.
In the distance Kirby, Earl of Winchilsea and Nottingham, and Deene Park, Earl of Cardigan; and beyond, Laxton Hall, Lord Carbery.	181	ROCKINGHAM (p. 365.)	$83\frac{1}{4}$	Rockingham Castle, Lord Sondes.
		cr. river Welland, and enter Rutlandshire.		
Lyndon.	$175\frac{1}{2}$	UPPINGHAM (p. 365.)	$88\frac{3}{4}$	2 m. distant Stockerston House. Ayston Hall, G. Fludyer, Esq.

ON RIGHT FROM LOND.	From Kendal.		From London.	ON LEFT FROM LOND.
At a distance, Normanton Park, Lord Aveland. Burley Park, Mr. Finch, and beyond, Exton, Earl of Gainsborough.				**Braunston.**
To Stamford, 11 miles. Grantham, 21 miles.	169¼	**OAKHAM, p. 365.**	95	2½ m dist. Cold Overton Hall, C. H. Frewen, Esq. Somerby Hall.
Stapleford Hall, Earl of Harborough, adorned with several specimens of sculpture.	164½	**Enter Leicestershire.**	100	Leesthorpe Hall. Lit. Dalby Hall, E. B. Hartopp, Esq. Thorpe Satchville.
		cr. river Eye.		
To Grantham, 16 miles.	159	MELTON MOWBRAY, the great resort of those who love the chase. Pop., 1861, 4047. The surrounding country is celebrated for sporting.	105¼	To Leicester, 15 miles. Sysonby Lodge (Earl of Bessborough). Asfordby, and beyond, Ragdale House.
3 m. distant, Goadby Ha., and beyond, Croxton Park (Duke of Rutland).	156	**Kettleby.**	108¼	Wartnaby Hall. Dalby Old Hall.
2 m. beyond, Owthorpe Hall (Sir Henry Bromley, Bart.), formerly the seat of the celebrated Col. Hutchinson, temp. Charles I.	152½	**Broughton,** ***Notts.***	111¾	
Tollerton Hall. Colwick Hall, and on the right bank of the Trent, Holme Pierrepont, Earl Manvers.	146¼	**Plumtree.**	118	Clifton Hall, Sir R. J. Clifton, Bart. Lenton Grove; Lenton Hall, F. Wright, Esq.; Lenton Priory.
		cr. river Trent.		Wollaton Hall, Lord Middleton. Strelley Hall, and beyond, Nuttall Temple, W. Holden, Esq.
Mapperley, I. Wright, Esq.	140½	NOTTINGHAM (p. 443.)	123¾	To Alfreton, 16 miles, Derby, 16 m., Ashby-de-la-Zouche, 19½ miles.
To Newark, 19½ miles. Worksop and Worksop Manor (Duke of Newcastle), 12 miles. 1 mile dist. Berry Hill, Sir E. S. Walker; 4 m. Clipstone Park.		**Enter Sherwood Forest.**		To Alfreton, 9 miles, Matlock, 16 miles. Papplewick Hall. Newstead Abbey (Col. Wildman), once the property of the Byron family, and beyond, Annesley Ha.
	126¼	MANSFIELD (p. 366).	138	
Pleasley Park.	123¼	Pleasley (*Derbyshire*). About half-a-mile from this place, is a romantic dell of great beauty, leading to the cotton-works, called Pleasley Works.	141	**3 miles distant is Hardwicke Hall, one of the seats of the Duke of Devonshire.**

ON RIGHT FROM LOND.	From Kendal.		From London.	ON LEFT FROM LOND.
Scareliff. Langwith, and beyond Langwith Lodge, Earl Bathurst.	122½	Stoney Houghton.	141¾	To Chesterfield, 9 m. Glapwell Hall, at a distance, Sutton Park. Bolsover Castle, Duke of Portland.
To Worksop and Worksop Manor, Duke of Newcastle, 6 m., and beyond Welbeck Abbey, Duke of Portland.	116½	Clown.	147¾	To Sheffield, 12½ m.
	115	Knitacre.	149¼	Barlborough Hall, Rev. C. H. R. Rodes, and beyond, Reinshaw, Sir S. Sitwell, Bart.
	111½	Enter Yorkshire.	152¾	
Aston Hall.	110½	Aughton.	153¾	To Sheffield, 7 miles. Aughton Hall.
	106½	Whiston.	157¾	
To Doncaster, 12 m. Clifton House, H. Walker, Esq., and Eastwood House. Aldwarke Hall, G. S. Foljambe, Esq. Thrybergh Hall, J. Fullerton, Esq.	104½	ROTHERHAM (p. 355.)	159¾	To Sheffield, 6 miles. The Grange, Earl of Effingham. Wentworth House, Earl Fitzwilliam. Wentworth Castle, F. W. T. V. Wentworth, Esq. Worsborough Hall, W. B. Martin, Esq.
		cr. river Don.		
To Doncaster, 15 m. Wakefield, 10½ miles.	92	BARNSLEY (p. 354.)	172¼	To Stockport, 33 m.
Birthwaite Hall.	89	Darton.	175¼	2 m. distant, Cannon Hall, J. S. Stanhope, Esq.
	85½	Bretton.	178¾	Bretton Hall, W. B. Beaumont, Esq.
To Wakefield, 6½ m. Denby Grange, Sir J. Lister Kaye, Bart.	82	Flockton.	182¼	
Whitley Hall, R. H. Beaumont, Esq.	79½	Lepton.	184¾	
		cr. river Coln.		
On the road to Manchester, 7 m. from Huddersfield, may be seen the stupendous tunnel, 3¼ miles long, through which the canal is led, made at the expense of £300,000. To Wakefield, 13 m.	75¼	HUDDERSFIELD is a large and populous town, carrying on a very extensive manufacture of serges, kerseymeres, and broad and narrow cloths. It has churches and chapels. 2 miles south of the town, on Castle Hill, are the remains of the ancient city of Cambodunum. Pop. 1861, 34,877. One M.P. See also p. 345.	189	Springwood. Spring Grove. To Chapel-en-le-Frith, 28 miles. To Stockport, 28 m.; Manchester, 25½ miles.
Fixby Hall, and beyond Kirklees Hall, Sir G. Armytage, Bart.		cr. river Calder.		
To Leeds, by Birstal, 15 miles; Bradford, 9 m.	67¼	HALIFAX (see p. 343.)	197	To Rochdale, 16½ m.; Burnley, 21½ miles.
Harden Grange, W. B. Ferrand, Esq. To Bradford, 10 m.	55¼	KEIGHLEY on the Aire carries on a considerable trade in cotton, linen, and worsted goods. Pop. 1861, 15,005. See also p. 347.	209	Knowle Ho., F. Greenwood, Esq.

ON RIGHT FROM LOND.	From Kendal.		From London.	ON LEFT FROM LOND.
		cross river Aire.		Cononley Hall, Rev. J. Swire. To Colne, 10½ miles. To Clitheroe, 19 miles.
To Otley, 15 m.,—Harrowgate, 19½ m.,—Ripley, 20 m. Skipton Castle, Sir R. Tufton, Bart., and in the distance, Bolton Abbey, Duke of Devonshire.	45¼	SKIPTON, (pp. 347 and 369.)	219	
Gargrave House. 2 miles distant, Eshton Hall, M. Wilson, Esq., and Flasby Hall, C. Preston, Esq.	40½	Gargrave.	223¾	Broughton Hall (Sir C. R. Tempest, Bart.) Bank Newton, and beyond, Ingthorpe Grange.
	38½	Cold Coniston.	225¾	
	35½	Hellifield.	228¾	Hellifield Peel, and, 1½ m. distant, Halton Place.
	33½	Long Preston.	230¾	
	29¼	SETTLE, (p. 369.)	235	
Austwick.		cross river Ribble.		Lawkland Hall. Crow Nest.
	22¼	Clapham.	242	
To Askrigg, 20 miles.	19¼	INGLETON, (p. 370.)	245	To Lancaster, 18¼ m.
	18¼	Thornton.	246	Halstead.
Hipping Ha. E. Tatham, Esq. Leck Ho.		Enter Lancashire. cross river Lune.		At a distance, Thurland Castle.
To Sedbergh, 11 miles.	12	KIRKBY LONSDALE, (p. 370) *(Westmorland).*	252	To Lancaster, 15 miles. 2 m. distant, Whittington Hall, T. Greene, Esq. Summerfield Hall, E. Tatham, Esq.
Underley Hall, W. Thompson, Esq.	9¾	Keastwick.	254½	
	4¼	Old Hutton.	260	
		cr. Lancaster Canal.		
		cross river Kent.		
		KENDAL, (p. 269).	264¼	

Bedford is situated on both sides of the river Ouse, which is navigable to the German Ocean. It is a place of great antiquity, and is supposed to be the Bedicanford of the Saxon Chronicle. It possessed an ancient castle, of which, however, no part at present remains. Bedford carries on an extensive trade in corn, malt, timber, coals, and iron. Lace and straw-plait making afford employment to a great number of poor females and children. There are in Bedford numerous churches and chapels. The church of St. Peter has a curious old Norman door, a fine antique font, and some old stained glass in the windows. There are several meeting-houses; and it is calculated that about half of the inhabitants of the town are Dissenters. There is probably no English town of similar extent, equal to Bedford in the variety and magnitude of its charitable and educational establishments. For these it is chiefly indebted to Sir W. Harpur, Alderman of London in the reign of Edward VI. The income arising from his charity now amounts to upwards of £17,000 a year. John Bunyan was pastor of a Baptist congregation in this town, and his Pilgrim's Progress was composed in the county gaol. About a mile from the town is Elstow, his birth-place. The cottage in which he was born is still standing, but it has lately received a new front. Bedford returns two members to Parliament. Pop. 1851, 11,693

HIGHAM FERRERS.—The church is a fine building, and rich in brasses and other monuments. Here is also a free school, which once formed part of a college founded by Archbishop Chichele. Pop. of par. 1861, 1152. The borough formerly returned one M.P., but is now disfranchised.

KETTERING, an ancient town, standing on a rising ground. The church contains a few interesting monuments. Dr. John Gill, the commentator, was a native of this place; and Andrew Fuller, another well-known Baptist minister, was pastor of a congregation here. The trade of Kettering consists chiefly of wool-combing and shoemaking. Pop. 5498.

In the church at Warkton, two miles from Kettering, are the monuments of the Montagu family by Roubilliac and Vangelder.

About 2 miles from Kettering is Boughton House, a seat of the Duke of Buccleuch, containing a fine collection of paintings. It was formerly the seat of the Dukes of Montagu, now extinct.

ROCKINGHAM is situated in the midst of Rockingham Forest, which was at an early period noted for its extensive iron-works; and in the reign of Edward I. is described as being 30 miles long by 8 miles broad. The church, which was partially destroyed by Oliver Cromwell, contains some fine monuments. Here are the remains of a strong fortress, erected by William the Conqueror. Within the court is the spacious mansion of Lord Sondes.

UPPINGHAM.—The church is a fine Gothic structure, containing some handsome monuments. Here are also several chapels, a free grammar-school, and an hospital. These institutions, which are well endowed, were, as well as the grammar-school at Oakham, founded by R. Johnson, Archdeacon of Leicester, A. D. 1584. Pop. 2176.

OAKHAM, the county-town of Rutland, is situated in the rich vale of Catmos. It had an ancient castle, supposed to have been erected by Walcheline de Ferrers, a younger scion of the family De Ferrers, to whom Henry II. had granted the manor. Among the possessors of the manor and castle were, Richard King of the Romans, brother of Henry III.; Edmund Earl of Kent, brother of Edward II.; De Vere, Earl of Oxford and Duke of Ireland, favourite of Richard II.; Thomas of Woodstock, uncle to the same King; Humphrey Duke of Buckingham, the supporter and victim of Richard III.; Thomas Cromwell, Earl of Essex; and George Villiers, second Duke of Buckingham, the favourite of Charles II. The remains of the castle consist principally of the hall used for the business of the county. Oakham is remarkable for an ancient custom,—the first time any peer of the realm passes through the lordship, he forfeits, to the lord of the manor, a shoe from the horse on which he rides, unless he commutes for it. A number of these shoes are nailed to the gate of the castleyard and the interior of the county hall. Some of them are gilt and stamped with the donor's name. Among them are shoes given by Queen Elizabeth, by the late Duke of York, and by George IV. when Prince Regent. Pop. 2948.

About two miles from Oakham is Burley-on-the-Hill, the magnificent seat of Mr. Finch, one of the finest mansions in England. In the reign of James I. this estate was the property of George Villiers first Duke of Buckingham, who had the honour of entertaining his royal master within its walls, when Ben Johnson's masque of the Gipsies was first performed. During the civil wars, this mansion was destroyed by the Parliamentary forces, and lay in ruins many years, till it was rebuilt by Daniel Finch, Earl of Nottingham, ancestor of the present proprietor. The architecture is of the Doric order, combining great splendour and elegance with simplicity. On the south side there is a terrace 900 feet long by 36 feet broad, commanding views of remarkable beauty. The interior is adorned with numerous portraits, pictures of the Italian school, a valuable library, &c. The park is about 6 miles in circumference. A short way beyond Burley is Exton Park, the fine mansion of the Earl of Gainsborough. 5 m. distant is Cottesmore Park, belonging to the Earl of Lonsdale.

Mansfield is seated in a valley near the little river Man, from which it probably takes its name, and is surrounded by the ancient forest of Sherwood, the scene of Robin Hood's chief exploits. It is an ancient town, with a Gothic church containing numerous monuments. The principal manufactures are those of stockings and gloves. Here are also several cotton-mills, factories of double point-net, and an iron-foundry. A railway, seven miles in length, connecting Mansfield with the Cromford Canal, has been constructed at an expense of £30,000. It has proved very advantageous to the trading interests of the place There is a free-grammar school, which was founded by royal charter in the reign of Queen Elizabeth. A handsome cross has lately been erected in the market-place to the memory of Lord George Bentinck. Pop. 1861, 8316. About 1½ mile from the town, in the neighbourhood of a village called Mansfield Woodhouse, two Roman villas were discovered in 1786, and in the vicinity of Mansfield numerous Roman coins have been found.

Sherwood Forest, (so intimately associated with the name and exploits of Robin Hood) in which Mansfield is situated, anciently extended from the town of Nottingham to Whitby in Yorkshire. Even so late as the reign of Queen Elizabeth, it contained a space equal to the present dimensions of the New Forest. It was a favourite resort of the kings of the Norman race, who had a summer palace at Clipstone built by Henry II. The mark of King John upon the forest trees here has been repeatedly found of late years in cutting them up for timber. The extensive demesnes which this forest contained have all been bestowed in grants by different monarchs, and repeated enclosures have reduced the open forest to that part which formerly went by the name of the Hye Forest, a tract of land about ten miles long by three or four wide, extending from the Nottingham road near Mansfield on the west, to Clipstone Park on the east. This tract is for the most part bare of trees. " Near Mansfield, there remains a considerable wood, Harlowe Wood, and a fine scattering of old oaks near Berry-hill, in the same neighbourhood, but the greater part is now an open waste, stretching in a succession of low hills and long-winding valleys, dark with heather. A few solitary and battered oaks standing here and there, the last melancholy remnants of these vast and ancient woods, the beautiful springs, swift and crystalline brooks, and broad sheets of water lying abroad amid the dark heath, and haunted by numbers of wild ducks and the heron, still remain. But at the Clipstone extremity of the forest, a remnant of its ancient woodlands remains, unrifled, except of its deer,—a specimen of what the whole once was, and a specimen of consummate beauty and interest. Birkland and Bilhaghe taken together form a tract of land extending from Ollerton along the side of Thoresby Park, the seat of Earl Manvers, to Clipstone Park, of about five miles in length, and one or two in width. Bilhaghe is a forest of oaks, and is clothed with the most impressive aspect of age that can perhaps be presented to the eye in these kingdoms. * * * A thousand years, ten thousand tempests, lightnings, winds, and wintry violence have all flung their utmost force on these trees, and there they stand, trunk after trunk, scathed, hollow, gray, and gnarled, stretching out their bare sturdy arms on their mingled foliage and ruin—a life in death. All is grey and old. The ground is grey,—beneath the trees are grey with clinging lichens,—the very heather and fern that spring beneath them have a character of the past.

" But Bilhaghe is only half of the forest-remains here ; in a continuous line with it lies Birkland—a tract which bears its character in its name—the land of birches. It is a forest perfectly unique. It is equally ancient with Bilhaghe, but it has a less dilapidated air. It is a region of grace and poetry. I have seen many a wood, and many a wood of birches, and some of them amazingly beautiful, too, in one quarter or another of this fair island, but in England nothing that can compare with this. * * On all sides, standing in their solemn steadfastness, you see huge, gnarled, strangely-coloured, and mossed oaks, some riven and laid bare from summit to root with the thunderbolts of past tempests. An immense tree is called the Shamble-Oak, being said to be the one in which Robin Hood hung his slaughtered deer, but which was more probably used by the keepers for that purpose. By whomsoever it was so used, however, there still remain the hooks within its vast hollow."*

Between Mansfield and Nottingham is Newstead Abbey, the seat of Mr.

* Howitt's Rural Life in England, p. 380-86.

Webb, formerly the mansion of the Byron family. Here was a priory of Black Canons, founded by Henry II., about A. D. 1170. At the Dissolution it was granted to Sir John Byron, who fitted up part of the edifice as a residence, but allowed the chapel to go to decay. Its front is an exceedingly beautiful specimen of early English achitecture, scarcely equalled by any other specimen in elegance of composition and delicacy of execution. An apartment is shewn in which Edward III. slept. The place has undergone great alterations and additions since it came into the possession of its previous owner. The grounds before the new front have been much improved, but the old gardens have been suffered to retain their ancient character. An oak planted by Lord Byron is shewn. In the Lake below the Abbey there is an artificial rock, formed at a great expense by the poet's grandfather. It is fortunate that a place so interesting from its connection with Lord Byron, should have been so carefully preserved who affords the utmost facility for the inspection of it by strangers. In the vicinity is a curious hollow rock, called Robin Hood's Stable. Beyond Newstead, and about nine miles from Nottingham, is Annesley Hall, famous as the birthplace and patrimony of Mary Chaworth, the object of Lord Byron's early attachment. And at a short distance is Hucknall church, where he rests among his ancestors. Hucknall is seven miles from Nottingham.

About 12 miles from Mansfield, and 26 from Nottingham, is the town of Worksop, delightfully situated near the northern extremity of Sherwood Forest, in what is generally called the Dukery, from there having been at one time no less than four ducal seats within a few miles. A priory was founded here in the time of Henry I., but little now remains of it except the abbey gate. The principal object of curiosity is the Abbey Church, which once belonged to the priory, and affords fine specimens of the Norman, pointed, and early English styles. The western door is a beautiful Norman composition; at the east end is the tower which was central, while the whole of the church was standing. The interior is highly ornamented, and contains a number of curious effigies. Pop. 1861, 7112. Near Worksop stood Worksop Manor, a magnificent mansion, surrounded by an extensive and finely wooded park. The ancient manor-house was erected by the celebrated Bess of Hardwick, and was accidentally destroyed by fire in 1761. The modern mansion was formerly a seat of the Dukes of Norfolk, but was purchased by the late Duke of Newcastle. In the neighbourhood are the following interesting mansions: Clumber Park, the splendid residence of the Dukes of Newcastle, containing a fine collection of paintings. The park is about 11 miles in circumference, and includes two ancient woods, from the largest of which Clumber Park derives its name,—Welbeck Abbey, the seat of the Duke of Portland, comprising some remains of the original building, which was founded for the Premonstratensian canons, A. D. 1153. The park is celebrated for the age and the size of its trees, —Thoresby, the seat of Earl Manvers, the representative of the Dukes of Kingston. The old mansion was consumed by fire in the year 1745. The park, which includes an area of about thirteen miles, contains several sheets of water, and abounds with sylvan scenery. Thoresby was the birth-place of Lady Mary Wortley Montagu. Rufford Abbey, a seat of the Earl of Scarborough, formerly the mansion of the patriotic Sir George Savile, an ancestor of the present proprietor. In the year 1148, an abbey was founded here for Cistercian monks, and some remains of it are included in the present immense structure.

Seven and a-half miles from Mansfield is Bolsover, the church of which contains a costly tomb, in honour of Henry, second Duke of Newcastle, as well as several monuments of the Cavendish family. Bolsover Castle is a noble building, belonging to the Duke of Portland.

Skipton, in the district called Craven, on the banks of the Aire, is noted for the sale of corn, cattle, and sheep. The trade of the town is greatly benefited by its proximity to the Leeds and Liverpool canal. The church contains several monuments of the Clifford family. There is also a good grammar school. The vale of Skipton is much admired for its picturesque beauty and fertility. Pop. 4533.

Skipton Castle was erected shortly after the conquest by Robert de Romeli, Lord of the honour of Skipton, and was long the property of the celebrated family of the Cliffords. It was garrisoned for the king in the time of the civil wars, and withstood a siege in the year 1645, but was ultimately obliged to surrender to the Parliament. It was the birth-place of the celebrated Anne Clifford, Countess of Dorset, Pembroke, and Montgomery, who repaired it and made it one of her principal residences. It contains ancient tapestries, and is now the property of Sir R. Tufton, Bart., the representative of her descendant, the last Earl of Thanet.

About six miles from Skipton are the ruins of Bolton priory, situated in one of the most delightful spots in England. The nave of the priory church is now used for a parochial chapel. Opposite to the western entrance the Duke of Devonshire has a small hunting seat formed out of the original gateway of the priory. The walks through the woods, and the views of the river, ruins, and surrounding scenery, are remarkably beautiful. About a mile from the priory is the celebrated Strid, a narrow passage torn by the Wharfe through its bed of solid rock, where it rushes with tremendous fury. This was the scene of the catastrophe of the boy Egrement, who, in attempting to overleap the chasm, fell in and was drowned. (See Wordsworth's poem entitled the "Force of Prayer.") In this vicinity is Barden tower, a ruined fortress of the Cliffords. Here the famous Shepherd Lord pursued his studies, under the tuition of some of the monks of Bolton.

Settle, on the Ribble, is remarkable for its situation at the foot of a lofty limestone rock, the summit of which commands a fine view. Great numbers of cattle are sold at its fairs. The parish church is about three quarters of a mile distant, at the village of Giggleswick, which has a richly-endowed grammar school, founded in the reign of Edward VI. Paley was educated here. In the neighbourhood are several slate and stone quarries. Pop. 1586.

In the vicinity of INGLETON are the Ingleborough mountains, 2360 feet high; Wharnside, 2384 feet; Pennigant, 2270 feet, all commanding extensive prospects; Thornton Scar, 300 feet in height; Thornton Force, a beautiful cascade, falling about 90 feet; and two romantic caves, called Yordas and Weathercote.

KIRKBY LONSDALE is a neat town on the west side of the Lune, over which there is an elegant bridge. It has an ancient church, and the churchyard commands a remarkably fine prospect The mills belonging to this place are worked by a small brook, the waters of which set in motion seven wheels, one above the other. Pop. of township, 1727; and of parish, 4365.

CXXXI. LONDON TO CARLISLE THROUGH HATFIELD, STAMFORD, NEWARK, DONCASTER, BOROUGHBRIDGE, AND APPLEBY, 300¾ Miles.

ON RIGHT FROM LOND.	From Carlisle.		From London.	ON LEFT FROM LOND.
Camfield (Baron Dimsdale). Bedwell Park, Sir C. E. Eardley, Bart.	289¾	London to Barnet, *Herts.* Re-enter Middlesex. Re-enter Herts.	11	Wrotham Park, Earl of Strafford. Gobions. Brookman's Park.
Hatfield Ho., Marquis of Salisbury. To Hertford, 7½ miles. Bush Hall. Digswell House, and near it, Tewin Water.	281¼	HATFIELD, (p. 372.) cross river Lea. cross river Maran.	19½	To St. Alban's, 6 miles Brocket Hall, late Viscount Melbourne.
Lockley. Panshanger (Earl Cowper). Shephall Bury.	275¾	WELWYN. (Dr. Young, author of the Night Thoughts, was rector of this place, and is buried in the church.)	25	Danesbury, W. Blake, Esq.; and, 3 miles distant, Ayott St Laurence, C. C. W. Dering, Esq.
Chivesfield Lodge.	269¼	STEVENAGE. To the south of this place, but on the east side of the road, are six barrows, said to be of Danish origin.	31½	Knebworth House, Sir E. L. Bulwer Lytton, Bart.; and, beyond, the Hoo (Lord Dacre), and Paulswolden (Earl of Strathmore). Elm Wood.
	263½	BALDOCK carries on a considerable trade in corn and malt. The church contains some curious monuments.	37¼	Rocksley House.
	259¾	Enter Bedfordshire.	41	Radwell. In the neighbourhood are several Roman remains, called Cæsar's Camp, from the outworks of which Roman relics have been from time to time dug up.
Stratton Pa., C. Barnett, Esq., and, at a distance, Sutton Park, Sir J. M. Burgoyne, Bart. Shortmead House.	255¾	BIGGLESWADE, a neat town on the Ivel, by means of which it carries on a considerable trade in timber, coals, and oats. Its chief manufactures are of straw-plait and lace. Pop. 4027. cross river Ivel.	45	2 miles distant, Old Warden, Lord Ongley; Southill, W. Whitbread. Esq.; and Ickwellbury, J. Harvey, Esq.
	254¼	Lower Caldecote.	46½	
3 m. dist. Everton Ho.	252¾	Beeston Cross.	48	To Hitchin, 13 miles. To Bedford 8 miles.

ON RIGHT FROM LOND.	From Carlisle.		From London.	ON LEFT FROM LOND.
		cr. river Ivel.		
Sandy Place; and, at a distance, the Hasells, F. Pym, Esq.	251¾	Girtford.	49	At a distance Moggerhanger House.
Tempsford Hall, and Tempsford House.	249¾	Tempsford.	51	Roxton House, C. J. Metcalfe, Esq.
		cross river Ouse.		
	247	Wiboston.	53¾	Bushmead Priory, W. H. W. Gery, Esq.
To St Neot's, 1¼ mile.	245¾	Eaton Socon.	55	
	244¼	Cross Hall.	56½	
		Enter Huntingdonshire.		
Paxton Place, and Paxton Hall.	243	Little Paxton.	57¾	Southoe Rectory.
Diddington House, late G. Thornhill, Esq.	241	Diddington.	59¾	
Stirtloe House.				
Buckden Palace, one of the Episcopal residences of the Bishop of Lincoln.	239¾	Buckden. The parish church is a very handsome structure, and contains numerous monuments.	61	
To Huntingdon, 4 m.				
Brampton Park, Duke of Manchester, and beyond it, Hinchinbrooke. Earl of Sandwich.	237¼	Brampton Hut.	63½	Alconbury Lodge.
Great Stukeley.	234¾	Alconbury.	66	
	233	Alconbury Hill.	67¾	
To York, 17 m.; to Aldborough, 1 mile.	94¾	For the route from this place to BOROUGH-BRIDGE * (see p. 382-5.)	206	Newby Hall, Earl de Grey, and 3 miles distant, Copgrove House, T. Duncombe, Esq.
Borough Bridge Hall, A. Lawson, Esq.		cr. river Ure.		To Ripon, 5 miles.
Aldborough Lodge, and Aldborough Hall.				
Newby Park.	93¾	Kirkby Hill.	207	
	87¾	York Gate Inn.	213	2 m. dis. Norton Conyers, Sir B. R. Graham, Bart.
	82¾	Leeming Lane.	218	Camp Hill.
				Firby Hall.
	80¾	Londonderry.	220	Thorp Perrow, M. Milbanke, Esq.
	79¼	Leeming.	221½	Theakstone.
				Holtby.
Kiplin Park, late Earl of Tyrconnel.	72¾	Catterick, A place of great antiquity.	228	Hornby Castle, Duke of Leeds.
				Brough Hall, Sir Wm. Lawson, Bart.
To Darlington, 8 m.		cr. river Swale.		To Richmond, 3¾ m.
Middleton Lodge, and beyond Halnaby Hall, Sir J. R. Milbanke, Bart.	68¼	Scotch Corner.	232½	Aske Hall, Earl of Zetland.
Stanwick Park, Duke of Northumberland.				

* This route is four miles longer than the route described at pages 380-385.

ON RIGHT FROM LOND.	From Carlisle.		From London.	ON LEFT FROM LOND.
Forcett Park.				
	60¼	Smallways.	240½	Barningham, M. Milbanke, Esq.
	58¼	Greta Bridge.	242½	
Rokeby Park, late J. B. S. Morritt, Esq., the friend of Sir Walter Scott.		[bridge] cr. branch of the Tees.		
Beyond Greta Bridge is a fine view of the town of Barnard Castle; 3 m. beyond is Streatlam Castle, J. Bowes, Esq.; and in the distance, Raby Castle, Duke of Cleveland.	52¼	Bowes was a Roman station, and has vestiges of a castle.	248½	
	47	Spittal House.	253¾	
	46¼	Rear Cross.	254½	
		Enter Westmorland.		
	39¼	BROUGH.	261½	
	29	Crackenthorpe.	271¾	
	26½	Kirkby Thore.	274¼	
Newbiggin Hall, W. Crackenthorpe, Esq.	24¾	Temple Sowerby.	276	
		[bridge] cr. the river Eden.		
	18¾	Brougham Castle.	282	Brougham Hall, Lord Brougham, and beyond, Lowther Castle, Earl of Lonsdale.
Skirsgill.		[bridge] cr. river Emont, and enter Cumberland.		
3 m. distant Eden Hall, Sir G. Musgrave, Bart.	18¼	PENRITH.	282½	In the distance, Greystoke Park, H. Howard, Esq.
Corby Castle, P. H. Howard, Esq.		CARLISLE.	300¾	

Hatfield, remarkable for the adjacent mansion, called Hatfield House (Marquis of Salisbury), erected at the commencement of the seventeenth century. The old house was the residence of Prince Edward, afterwards Edward VI., immediately before his accession. Queen Elizabeth lived here as a sort of prisoner during the latter part of the reign of her sister Mary. Hatfield was, soon after the accession of James I., made over, in exchange for Theobalds, to Sir R. Cecil, afterwards Earl of Salisbury, youngest son of the Lord-Treasurer Burghley, in whose family it has ever since continued. The gateway and end of the old palace are still standing. The present building was erected by Sir R. Cecil. In November 1835, the left wing was destroyed by fire, on which occasion the Dowager Marchioness of Salisbury perished in the flames. The grounds are beautifully laid out. Charles I. was a prisoner at Hatfield. Pop. of par. 3871.

Brough, situated in the wild district of Stainmoor. It is supposed to occupy the site of the Verteræ of the Romans. Here are the ruins of a castle which was erected before the Conquest. The church is a spacious ancient fabric, and the pulpit is formed out of a single stone. To the east of the town is a pillar which denotes the boundary of Yorkshire and Cumberland. Pop. of par. 1728

About eight miles farther on is APPLEBY, the county town of Westmorland, situated on the Eden. It was a place of some importance before the Conquest, but in the reign of Henry II. it was utterly destroyed by the Scots. In the time of Richard II. it met with a similar fate, and the greater part of it still lay in ruins in the time of Queen Mary. The castle stands on a lofty height rising from the river. It was founded previous to the Norman Conquest, but was almost rebuilt in 1686 by the then Earl of Thanet. It is now the property of Sir R. Tufton, Bart. It contains a large collection of curious and valuable family portraits, some valuable MSS., and among other relics, the magnificent suit of armour worn in the tiltyard by George Clifford, Earl of Cumberland, as champion to Queen Elizabeth. This castle anciently belonged to the Clifford family, and was fortified for King Charles by Lady Anne Clifford, Countess of Dorset, Pembroke, and Montgomery, but it was forced to surrender after the battle of Marston Moor. The church contains the monuments of Margaret, Countess of Cumberland, and of the celebrated Lady Anne, Countess of Dorset, Pembroke, &c., her daughter. Appleby formerly sent two M.P., but was disfranchised by the Reform Bill. Pop. of township, 960.

CXXXII. LONDON TO THIRSK, THROUGH LOUGHBOROUGH, NOTTINGHAM, CHESTERFIELD, SHEFFIELD, BARNSLEY, LEEDS, WAKEFIELD, AND RIPON, 235½ Miles.

ON RIGHT FROM LOND.	From Thirsk.		From London.	ON LEFT FROM LOND.
	94½	From Hicks's Hall to Pleasley, Derbyshire, (p. 362.)	141	
Glapwell Hall, and, at a distance, Bolsover Castle (Duke of Portland).	92½	Glapwell.	143	
Midland Railway.	90½	Heath.	145	
Sutton Hall.	86½	Hasland.	149	Hasland House, and, two miles distant, Wingerworth Hall.
To Worksop, 15 miles.	85¼	CHESTERFIELD. (See p. 353.)	150¼	To Tideswell, 16 miles—Blakewell, 13—Winster, 12—Matlock, 9½—to the Baths, 10½.
On Whittington Moor was a public-house called the Revolution House, from its having been the place where the Earl of Danby, the Earl of Devonshire, and others assembled to concert measures for effecting the Revolution of 1688.	83¾	Whittington Common.	151¾	
	79¾	Dronfield. The church has a fine tower and spire. The chancel contains three rich stone stalls, the foliage of which is very beautiful.	155¾	
Norton Hall.	77¾	Little Norton.	157¾	Beauchieff Abbey, founded in 1163 for White Canons, by Robert Fitz-Ranulph, said to have been one of the murder-
	75	⚞ cr. the river Sheaf, and enter Yorkshire.	160½	

ON RIGHT FROM LOND.	From Thirsk.		From London.	ON LEFT FROM LOND.
				ers of Thomas à Becket, in expiation of whose murder the abbey was built.
To Worksop, 19½ miles.	73¼	SHEFFIELD, (p. 376.)	162¼	To Huddersfield, 26¼ m.
		cross the river Don.		
	72¼	Pitsmoor.	163¼	
The Grange, Earl of Effingham; and Wentworth House, Earl Fitzwilliam.	67¼	Chapel Town.	168¼	3 miles distant, Wortley Hall, Lord Wharncliffe.
	65¾	Hood Hill.	169¾	Tankersley.
	62¼	Worsborough.	173¼	Worsborough Hall, W. B. Martin, Esq. Ouslethwaite House, W. Elmhirst, Esq.; and Wentworth Castle, F. W. T. V. Wentworth, Esq.
To Doncaster, 15 miles.	59¾	BARNSLEY (see p. 354.)	175¾	
	59	Old Mill Inn.	176½	To Stockport, 23 miles.
		cr. Dearne and Dove Canal and river Dearne.		
	56¼	Staincross.	179¼	Woolley Park, G. Wentworth, Esq. 3 miles distant, Bretton Hall, W. B. Beaumont, Esq.
Chevet, Sir L. M. Pilkington, Bart.	52¾	New Miller Dam.	182¾	
Woodthorpe.	51¼	Sandal Magna.	184¼	Pledwick — Kettlethorpe. Lupset Hall, D. Gaskell, Esq. Thornes House, J. M. Gaskell, Esq.
		cross river Calder.		
To Selby, 23 miles. Newland Park, Sir C. Dodsworth, Bart.	49¼	WAKEFIELD, (p. 356.)	186¼	To Huddersfield, 13 m.; to Halifax, 16 miles.
Hatfield Ha. Methley Hall, Earl of Mexborough.	48¼	Newton.	187¼	
	45½	Lofthouse.	190	Lofthouse Hall. Middleton Lodge.
	41½	Hunslet.	194	
		cross river Aire.		To Halifax by Bradford, 18 m.; to Otley, 10 m.
To Selby, 20¼ miles; to Tadcaster, 14¼ miles. 3 miles distant, Temple Newsam, containing an excellent collection of paintings.	40¼	LEEDS, (p. 356.)	195¼	2½ miles distant, Armley House. Potter Newton Hall.
	37½	Chapel Allerton.	198	
	36¼	Moor Allerton.	199¼	
	35	Alwoodley Gates.	200½	To Otley, 8 miles.
To Tadcaster, 11 miles.	32	Harewood. The church is a venerable structure, and containing, amongst other tombs, that of Judge Gascoigne, who committed Henry V. when Prince of Wales, to prison, for insulting him whilst ad-	203½	Harewood House, Earl of Harewood, a noble mansion, with gardens and pleasure grounds laid out by the celebrated Capability Brown.

ON RIGHT FROM LOND.	From Thirsk.		From London.	ON LEFT FROM LOND.
		ministering justice. Here are also the remains of Harewood Castle.		
		cross river Wharf.		
	30¼	Dunkeswick.	205¼	Rigton.
Rudding Park, Sir J. Radcliffe, Bart.	27¼	Spacey House.	208¼	
	24½	HARROWGATE (p. 377.)	211	
Bilton Park, and beyond, Scriven Park, Sir C. Slingsby, Bart.	21¾	Killinghall.	213¾	Pannal.
		cr. river Nidd.		
Nidd Hall, J. Rawson, Esq.	20½	RIPLEY, a small town, which was neatly rebuilt in the Tudor style by Sir W. Ingilby in 1829-30. The church contains several monuments of the Ingilby family, and in the church-yard is the pedestal of an ancient cross.	215	To Pateley Bridge, 9¼ miles. Ripley Castle. The gardens, which are very fine, are open to the public on Fridays.
Newby Hall, Earl De Grey.	18	South Stainley.	217½	Studley Royal, Earl De Grey, and beyond, Grantley Hall, Lord Grantley.
	12¾	RIPON (p. 378.)	222¾	
		cr. the river Ure.		
	8½	The Leeming Road.	227	Norton Conyers, Sir B. R. Graham, Bart.
Newby Park.	7	Baldersby.	228½	
	5½	Skipton Bridge.	230	
		cr. river Swale.		
	4	Bushby Stoop.	231½	
	2½	Carlton Miniott.	233	
Thirkleby Hill, 3 m.		THIRSK (p. 380.)		

At a short distance from Glapwell (p. 373) on the left, is Hardwick Hall (Duke of Devonshire,) a most interesting specimen of the Elizabethan style of domestic architecture. It stands on the brow of a bold and commanding eminence, overlooking a vale of great beauty. This fine old mansion was erected by the celebrated Countess of Shrewsbury, daughter of John Hardwick of Hardwick, and heiress of this estate. She married four times, always contriving to get the power over her husband's estates by direct devise, or by intermarrying the children of their former marriages, so that she brought together immense estates, and laid the foundation of four dukedoms. Her first husband was Sir William Cavendish, the secretary and biographer of Wolsey, her last the Earl of Shrewsbury, to whose custody Mary Queen of Scots was consigned.* The most remarkable apartments in this interesting edifice are the state-room and the gallery. At one end of the former is a canopy of state, and in another part a bed, the hangings of which are very ancient. The gallery, which is about 170 feet long, and 26 wide, extends the whole length of the eastern side of the house, and is hung with tapestry, on a part of which is the date of 1478. In the chapel there is a very rich and curious altar cloth, 30 feet long, hung round the rails of the altar, with figures of saints under canopies wrought in needle-work. The house has, with very few exceptions, been kept exactly in the

* HOWITT's Rural Life in England, 2d edit. p. 257-267.

state in which its builder left it as to furniture and arrangement. The late Duke of Devonshire brought hither his family pictures from Chatsworth. There are nearly 200 portraits in this gallery, the most interesting being those of "Bess of Hardwick," Queen Elizabeth, Mary Queen of Scots, Lady Jane Grey, Cardinal Pole, Bishop Gardiner, Sir Thomas More, Sir William Cavendish, William, first Duke of Devonshire, Hobbes the philosopher, &c. The furniture is in many instances older than the house, and was removed from the old hall. Some of the needle-work was wrought by Mary Queen of Scots, and in the entrance hall there is a statue of her by Westmacott.

At about 100 yards from the hall stand the remains of the old baronial residence where Queen Mary and Arabella Stuart were confined. In the reign of Henry VII. it was the residence of the Hardwick family, but the whole pile is now but a splendid ruin luxuriantly mantled with ivy.

Hardwick is in the parish of Ault Hucknall, and Hobbes the philosopher is buried in the church. About four miles to the west is the Tupton station of the North Midland Railway.

SHEFFIELD is situated near the confluence of the Don and the Sheaf, at the eastern foot of that extensive range of hills which runs along the centre of the island from Staffordshire to Westmorland. With the exception of a single outlet towards Doncaster, it is encompassed and overlooked by an amphitheatre of hills, and the neighbourhood presents a remarkable variety and beauty of prospect. Hallamshire, which includes the parish of Sheffield, and the adjoining parishes of Handsworth and Ecclesfield, forms a district, the origin of which may be traced back to Saxon, Roman, and even British times, but the town of Sheffield has more recently risen into importance. In the reign of Henry I. the manor of Sheffield belonged to the family of De Lovetot, who founded an hospital called St Leonards, established a corn-mill, and erected a bridge over the river Don; and the manor afterwards successively descended by marriage to the Furnivals, Talbots, and ultimately to the Howards, in whose possession it still remains. Mary Queen of Scots spent nearly fourteen years of her imprisonment in Sheffield manor-house, which stood on an eminence, a little distance from the town, and was dismantled in 1706 by the order of Thomas, Duke of Norfolk. A castle was erected at Sheffield at a very early period. During the civil wars, Sir John Gell took possession of the castle and town for the parliament; but on the approach of the Marquis of Newcastle, he retreated into Derbyshire. Sheffield Castle continued in the possession of the Royalists till after the battle of Marston Moor, when it was obliged to capitulate after a siege of some days. It was then demolished by order of the parliament, and no vestiges of it now remain.

So early as the thirteenth century, Sheffield had acquired a reputation for iron manufactures, especially for a kind of knives called "whittles." The great abundance of iron-ore, stone, and coal which are found in the vicinity might naturally have been expected to give rise to such manufactures, and the several mountain streams which unite near the town furnish an extent of water-power

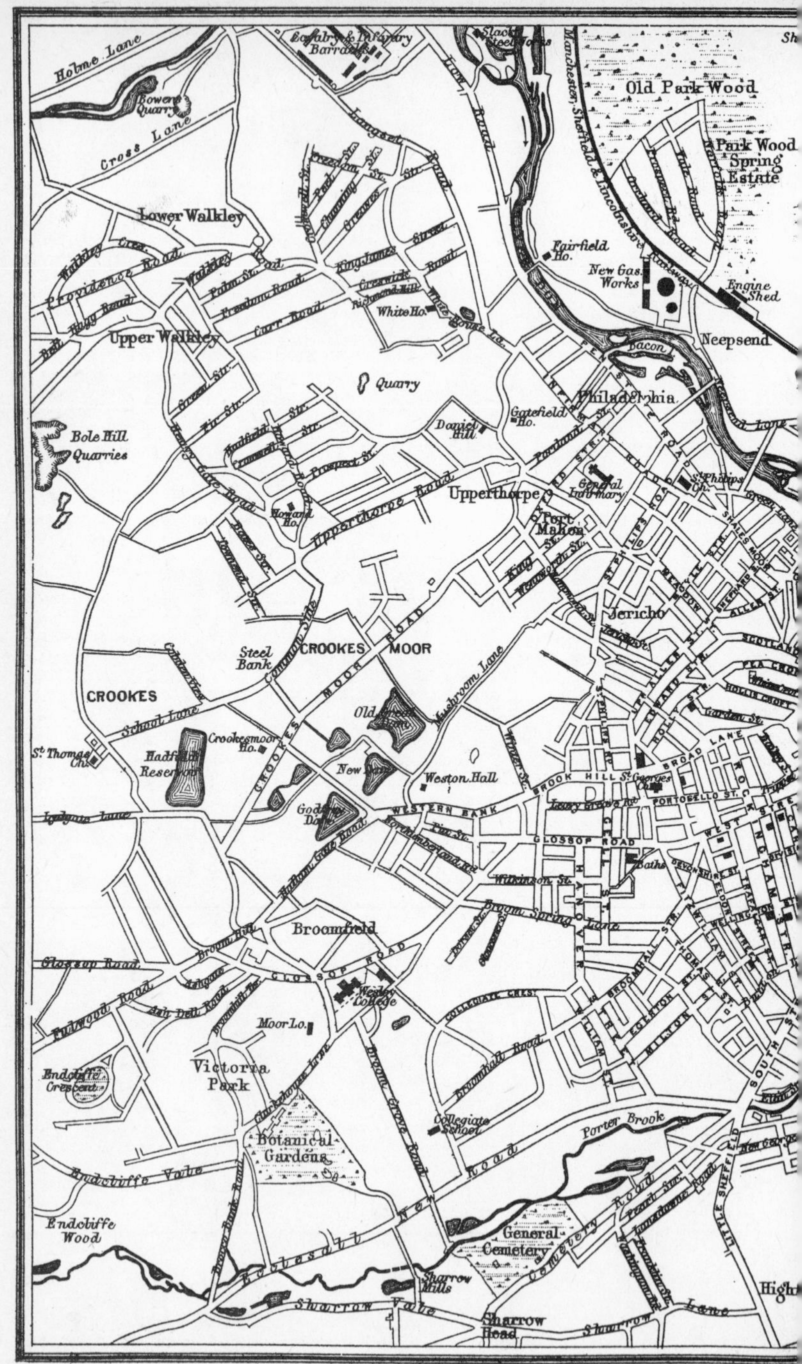

Holme Lane
Bowers Quarry
Cross Lane
Cavalry & Infantry Barracks
Langsett Road
Lower Walkley
Upper Walkley
Providence Road
Freedom Road
Carr Road
King James St.
White Ho.
Quarry
Bole Hill Quarries
Daniel Hill
Gatefield Ho.
Upperthorpe
Upperthorpe Road
Howard Ho.
Port Mahon
General Infirmary
Philadelphia
Old Park Wood
Park Wood Spring Estate
Fairfield Ho.
New Gas Works
Engine Shed
Neepsend
Manchester, Sheffield & Lincolnshire Railway
St. Philips Ch.
Jericho
Steel Bank
CROOKES MOOR
CROOKES
School Lane
Crookes Moor Road
Mushroom Lane
Crookesmoor Ho.
St. Thomas Ch.
New Dam
Weston Hall
Godfrey Dam
Broad Lane
Brook Hill
St. Georges Ch.
Portobello St.
Western Bank
Glossop Road
Wilkinson St.
Broom Spring Lane
Baths
Broomfield
Glossop Road
Fulwood Road
Wesley College
Moor Lo.
Victoria Park
Endcliffe Crescent
Broomhall Road
Collegiate Crest.
Collegiate School
Botanical Gardens
Endcliffe Vale
Porter Brook
Endcliffe Wood
Ecclesall New Road
General Cemetery
Cemetery Road
Sharrow Mills
Sharrow Vale
Sharrow Head
Sharrow Lane
Little Sheffield
A.& C.

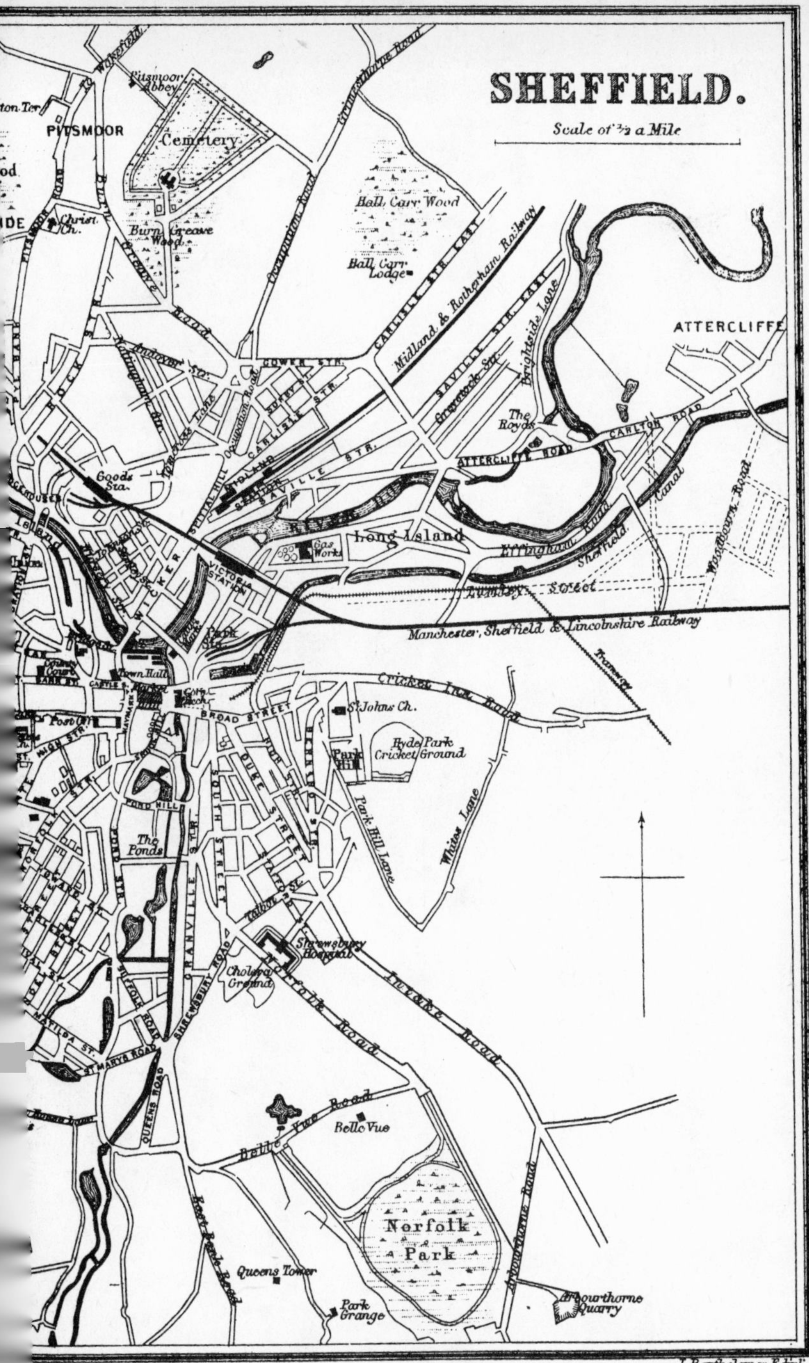

J. Bartholomew, Edinr.

urgh.

which probably few other localities could command. In the reign of Queen Elizabeth many artisans emigrated from the Netherlands into England, in consequence of the cruelties of the Duke of Alva; and the workers in iron having been settled in a body at Sheffield, the neighbourhood from this time became known for the manufacture of shears, sickles, knives, and scissars. The principal manufacture of Sheffield is cutlery in all its branches. The vast buildings used for grinding by steam form one of the curiosities of the town. Silver-plate and plated goods form also one of its staple manufactures. Brass-foundries are also numerous, and the manufacture of Britannia metal and German silver occupies many hands. Optical instruments, brushes, buttons, and combs are also made here to a considerable extent, and there are various other manufactures which arise out of, or are connected with, the staple commodities of the town.

The public buildings consist of the Town Hall, the Cutler's Hall, the Corn Exchange, erected by one of the Dukes of Norfolk, whose family own the ground upon which no inconsiderable part of the town is built, the Assembly Rooms, and Theatre, the Music Hall, two News-rooms, and the Public Baths, the Cemetery, Botanical Gardens, General Infirmary, the Dispensary, and the Shrewsbury Hospital, established and munificently endowed by an Earl of Shrewsbury. Sheffield has numerous churches and meeting-houses, and establishments for education, several Banks, a Literary and Philosophical Society, a Mechanics' Institution. Two M.P. Population, 185,172.

HARROWGATE is celebrated for its mineral springs, which are annually visited by about 2000 persons. It consists of two scattered villages, known by the names of High and Low Harrowgate, situated about a mile from each other, and possessing ample accommodation for visitors. Harrowgate possesses both chalybeate and sulphurous springs. Of the former the oldest is the Tewit Well, which was discovered about the year 1576. The Old Spa, situated on the Stray, was discovered, by Dr. Stanhope, previous to 1631. The Starbeck chalybeate is about midway between Harrowgate and Knaresborough. The saline chalybeate is situated at Low Harrowgate, and was discovered in 1819. The sulphurous springs are, the Old Sulphur Wells, situated at Low Harrowgate, close by the Leeds and Ripon road; the Crown Sulphur Well, situated in the pleasure-grounds belonging to the Crown Hotel; and the Knaresborough or Starbeck Spa, situated nearly midway between Harrowgate and Knaresborough. Harrowgate possesses a considerable number of hotels, several boarding-houses, public baths, promenade-rooms, ball and billiard-rooms, circulating libraries and reading-rooms, four places of worship, &c. Population of High and Low Harrowgate, 4737.

About three miles from Harrowgate is the town of KNARESBOROUGH, delightfully situated on the banks of the Nidd, which flows through a most romantic valley below precipitous rocks. The church of St. John the Baptist is old, and contains monuments to the Slingsbys, &c. Here are the remains of a castle which was erected soon after the conquest. It belonged at one time to Piers Gavaston the favourite of Edward II. In the year 1331 this castle was granted by Edward

III. to his son, the celebrated John of Gaunt, and was afterwards one of the places in which Richard II. was imprisoned. During the civil wars it sustained a siege from the parliamentary forces under Lord Fairfax, and at last surrendered upon honourable terms. It was afterwards dismantled by order of the parliament. Part of the principal tower is still remaining. In the walk along the bank of the Nidd, opposite the ruins of the castle, is a celebrated petrifying or dropping well, springing in a declivity at the foot of a limestone rock. Near it is a curious excavation called St Robert's Chapel, hollowed out of the solid rock; its roof is groined, and the altar adorned with Gothic ornaments. About half a mile lower down the river are the remains of a priory founded by Richard Plantagenet. A mile to the east is St Robert's Cave, remarkable on account of the discovery of a skeleton here in 1759, which led to the conviction and execution of the celebrated Eugene Aram.* Knaresborough has manufactories of linen and cotton, and its corn-market is one of the largest in the county. Two M.P. Pop. 1851, 5536. Knaresborough was the birth-place of the famous blind guide John Metcalf. He had lost his sight in infancy, and yet frequently acted as a guide over the forest during the night, or when the paths were covered with snow,—contracted for making roads, building bridges, &c. He died 1810, aged ninety-three years.

Ripon is a town of considerable antiquity, situated between the rivers Ure and Skell, over the former of which there is a handsome stone bridge of seventeen arches. At an early period it was pillaged and burnt by the Danes, and here they defeated an army of the Saxons. A conical tumulus called Ellshaw or Ailcey Hill, near the cathedral, is supposed to cover the remains of those who fell in the battle. In 1695, several Saxon coins were found on digging into this hill. Ripon suffered severely from the plague in 1534, and again in 1625. Here in 1640, commissioners were deputed by Charles I. to meet with the Scots to treat with them, and endeavour to obtain a peace. In 1643, Sir Thomas Mauleverer, with a detachment of the parliamentary army, took possession of the town, and committed many outrages on the inhabitants, but was put to flight by a detachment of Royalists under Sir John Mallory of Studley, then governor of Skipton Castle.

The most interesting building in Ripon is the cathedral, the first stone of which was laid in 1331, but the choir was probably not finished till 1494. The chapter house, however, with the crypts beneath, are supposed to be much more ancient. It is said to be one of the best proportioned churches in the kingdom. It has two uniform towers at the west end, each 110 feet high, besides the great tower called St Wilfred's tower; each of these towers originally supported a spire of wood covered with lead. Under the chapter house is a vaulted charnel house, which contains an immense collection of human remains in good preservation, piled in regular order round the walls.

Trinity church was built and endowed in 1826, at a cost of £13,000, by its first incumbent, the Rev. Edward Kilvington. Ripon contains several Dissenting

* See Sir E. Bulwer Lytton's Eugene Aram.

chapels, and hospitals, a free grammar school, founded in 1547, by Edward VI. a mechanics' institute, &c. The bishopric of Ripon was created in 1836, out of the large dioceses of York and Chester. The bishop's palace is situated on a slight eminence, about a mile north-west of the city. The foundation stone was laid on the 1st of October 1838. The market-place is a spacious square, in the centre of which stands an obelisk, 90 feet high, which is surmounted by the arms of Ripon. This obelisk was erected by William Aislaby, Esq. of Studley, who represented the borough for sixty years in Parliament. On the south side of the market-place is the town-hall, built in 1801 by Mrs Allanson of Studley. Ripon was once noted for the excellence of its spurs; it was also celebrated for its woollen manufactures. The present manufacture is chiefly saddle-trees,—it also produces linens and malt. The Ure navigation was brought up to the town by means of a short canal in 1767. Ripon sends two members to Parliament. Bishop Porteus was a native of this town. Pop. 6172.

Ripon is 208 miles north north-west of London, 27 north of Leeds, and 24 north-west by west of York. It affords the title of Earl to the Robinson family.

About three miles from Ripon is Studley Royal, the seat of Earl de Grey, adorned with a good collection of paintings. The principal object of attraction however, is the celebrated pleasure grounds, which include the venerable remains of Fountains Abbey, said to be the most perfect monastic building in England. The site of this monastery was granted in 1132, by Thurstan, Archbishop of York, to certain monks who resolved to adopt the Cistercian order. Eight years after it was burnt down, but was speedily rebuilt. The foundation of the church was laid in 1204. This abbey became, in the course of time, one of the wealthiest monasteries in the kingdom, and its possessions extended over a tract of thirty miles. At the dissolution the abbey and part of the estates were sold to Sir Richard Gresham, father of Sir Thomas. It originally covered about ten acres of ground, but scarcely more than two are now covered with the ruins. "No depredation has been committed on the sacred pile; time alone has brought it to its present state; it has fallen by a gentle decay without any violent convulsion. Built in the most elegant style of Gothic architecture, the tower and all the walls are yet standing, the roof alone being gone to ruins." The late Miss Lawrence, who was owner of the abbey, evinced a most praiseworthy regard for these interesting remains of antiquity, and from time to time expended considerable sums in their preservation. A short distance west of the abbey stands the fine old mansion of Fountains Hall, built by Sir Stephen Proctor in 1611, with materials taken from the ruins of the monastery. On an eminence opposite the hall stand some large old yew trees, under which the monks are said to have obtained shelter while engaged in building the abbey. They were originally seven in number, but three of them have been blown down.

The domain of Studley is open to the public every day except Sunday, until five o'clock in the evening. Harrowgate is fourteen miles distant.

About four miles from Ripon, and thirteen from Harrowgate, is Newby Hall.

the mansion of Earl de Grey, situated on the northern bank of the river Ure and commanding beautiful and extensive views of the surrounding country. It is supposed to contain the best private collection of statuary in the kingdom. The drawing-room is hung with tapestry of the celebrated Gobelin manufactory. The pleasure grounds are beautiful and well laid out.

Seven miles from Ripon and eighteen from Harrowgate is Hackfall, a romantic valley of great beauty, laid out in a tasteful manner. It also was the property of the late Miss Lawrence.

Three miles south-west of Ripon is Markenfield Hall, once the seat of a renowned family of that name.

Nine miles from Ripon and ten from Harrowgate, on an elevated ridge of moorland, are some vast perpendicular masses of grit, called the Brimham rocks, which are well deserving the inspection of tourists. There are several tumuli dispersed among the rocks. In the centre of this wild scene, the late Lord Grantley some years ago erected a substantial house and out-offices for the accommodation of strangers.

Grantley Hall, the seat of Lord Grantley, is four miles distant from Ripon.

In West Tanfield Church, six miles and a half from Ripon, are several tombs of the Marmion family.

THIRSK is a pleasant well-built town on the banks of the little river Codbeck, which divides the old town from the new. St Mary's church is a handsome Gothic structure, and is said to have been built with the ruins of the ancient castle which was destroyed in the reign of Henry II. It contains several monuments, and three *sedilia* or stone seats which were used by the clergy before the Reformation. There are several meeting-houses and charitable institutions, banks, &c. It is connected by railway with all parts of the kingdom. One M.P. Pop. 5350.

CXXXIII. LONDON TO NEWCASTLE-UPON-TYNE THROUGH WARE, HUNTINGDON, STAMFORD, GRANTHAM, NEWARK, DONCASTER, BOROUGHBRIDGE, DARLINGTON, AND DURHAM, 269¾ Miles.

ON RIGHT FROM LOND.	From Newcas.		From London.	ON LEFT FROM LOND.
Victoria Park.	267¼	From Shore Ditch Church to Stoke, Newington.	2½	
	266½	Stamford Hill.	3¼	
		Tottenham High Cross, so called from a cross which has stood here from time immemorial.	4½	Bruce Castle (now a school). Tottenham Park.
Enfield was formerly celebrated for its Chase, now enclosed. Here are the remains of a palace in which Edward VI. is supposed to have held his court, an ancient church, &c. Pop. of par. 12,424.	262¾	Edmonton. The Bell Inn here is immortalized by Cowper in his ballad of John Gilpin. Pop. of parish, 10,930	7	At Southgate, in the vicinity, is Arno's Grove, a fine seat, containing numerous Etruscan vases, minerals, &c. Enfield Park, and beyond, Trent Park, D. Bevan, Esq.
	260½	Enfield Highway.	9¼	

ON RIGHT FROM LOND.	From Newcas.		From London.	ON LEFT FROM LOND.
1 m. dist. in Essex are the remains of Waltham Abbey, where Harold and his brothers were buried. Here also are some powder mills.	258½	Waltham Cross, *Herts*, takes its name from a beautiful cross erected here by Edward I. in honour of his Queen Eleanor. Her remains rested here on their way to Westminster. The cross has been repaired and restored on various occasions during the last and present centuries.	11¼	Theobalds' Park, Sir H. Meux, Bart. Here is the site of the palace of Theobalds, built by Lord Burghley, and where James I. (who gave Hatfield for it) died in 1625.
Nunsbury.	256¼	Cheshunt. The manor house was the residence of Cardinal Wolsey, and Richard Cromwell died in a house near the church. Cheshunt college was removed to this place from Talgarth in 1792.	13½	Cheshunt Park.
	255	Wormley.	14¾	Wormley Bury.
		cr. New river.		
	254	Broxbourne.	15¾	Broxbourne Bury, J. Bosanquet, Esq.
2¼ miles dist., at Stanstead Abbots, are the remains of the Rye House, famous for the Rye House plot. 3 m. dist. is Hunsdon House, once the residence of Mary, Elizabeth, and Edward VI.	252¾	HODDESDON, on the Lea, has an ancient market-house, a tower of Old St. Catherine's chapel, a grammar school, &c. To the right is a curious old manor-house. Pop. 1898.	17	Between Hoddesdon and Hertford is Haileybury College, for the education of young men for the civil service in India, and beyond, Balls Park, Marq. Townshend, and Brickendon Bury. To Hertford, 4 miles.
To Bishop Stortford, 14½ miles. Dunmow, 20¼.	250½	AMWELL, (p. 387.) Pop. of parish 1851, 1652.	19¼	Amwell Bury. Source of New River. To Hertford, 2½ miles.
		cr. New river.		
	248¾	WARE, (p. 387.)	21	To Stevenage, 11¼ miles. Ware Park.
		cross the river.		Poles.
Youngsbury and Thundridgebury.	247	Wade's Mill.	22¾	1½ mile distant Sacomb Park.
To Cambridge, 24½ m.	243¼	Puckeridge.	26½	Hamells Park.
3 miles distant Albury Hall. Wyddiall Hall. Newsells Bury, and Cocken Hatch.	238¾	BUNTINGFORD carries on a trade in leather and malt.	31	Aspeden Hall. Broadfield Hall.
To Cambridge, 12¾ m. To Newmarket, 24 m.	232¼	ROYSTON, partly in Herts, partly in Cambridgeshire, carries on a trade in malt and corn. The church formerly belonged to a priory, and contains a few ancient monuments. Pop. of parish 1882.	37½	To Baldock, 8½ miles.
Kneesworth Hall, and, to the right, Melbourne Bury.		cross river Cam.		
Wimpole Hall, the	225¾	Arrington, (*Camb.*)	44	

ON RIGHT FROM LOND.	From Newcas.		From London.	ON LEFT FROM LOND.
noble mansion of the Earl of Hardwicke. Wimple church contains a splendid monument to Lord Chancellor Hardwicke.		Golden Lion.		
	223	Caxton. The birthplace of the first English printer, and of Matthew Paris the historian.	46¾	Gransden Park 2 m. distant, and Waresley Park, 5 miles.
Bourne House, Earl Delawarr. To Cambridge, 10 m.	220½		49¼	3 miles distant Croxton Park.
Papworth Hall.	217½	Papworth, St Everard.	52¼	
	216½	Papworth, St Agnes.	53¼	
		Enter Huntingdonshire.		
To Cambridge, 14¾ m.; to St Ives, 5½ miles.	212	Godmanchester.	57¾	To St Neots, 8 miles.
		cross river Ouse.		
10 m. distant Ramsey, and Ramsey Abbey, E. Fellowes, Esq.	211	HUNTINGDON, (p. 387.)	58¾	Hinchinbrooke House, (Earl of Sandwich,) and beyond Brampton Park, (Duke of Manchester.) To St Neots by Buckden Palace, (Bishop of Lincoln,) 10 miles. To Thrapston, 16½ m. Castle Hill House.
Great Stukeley Hall, L. J. Torkington, Esq.	205¾	Alconbury Hill.	64	Alconbury Lodge.
Connington Castle, J. M. Heathcote, Esq. Holme Wood.	198¾	Stilton. The cheese which bears this name was, though of Leicestershire manufacture, originally sold here.	71	Washingley Hall.
To Peterborough, 5 m. Overton Longueville and Orton Hall (Mar. of Huntly); and, on the opposite bank of the Nen, Milton Park, Earl Fitzwilliam.	197¾	Norman Cross, the place where a great number of French prisoners were confined during the war.	72	To Oundle, 8 miles; on the road to which is Elton Hall, Earl of Carysfort.
	190¼	Wansford.	79½	
		cr. river Nen, and enter Northamptonsh.		Wothorpe, in ruins, (Marquis of Exeter.)
Burghley Park, (Marquis of Exeter.) See p. 388.		cr. river Welland.		
To Market Deeping, 7½ miles; to Bourne, 10 miles.	184¼	STAMFORD, (*Lincolnsh.*) (p. 388.)	85½	To Normanton Park, Lord Aveland, 4 miles. To Uppingham, 12 m.; to Oakham, 11 miles.
1½ m. distant Tolethorpe House. Here are the remains of a Roman encampment, and an ancient Gothic Church.	182¼	Bridge Casterton. (*Rutlandshire.*)	87½	Tickencote Hall, J. M. Wingfield, Esq. Exton Hall, (Earl of Gainsborough)—a fine specimen of the architecture of the 16th century, containing a valu-
		cross river Gwash.		

ON RIGHT FROM LOND.	From Newcas.		From London.	ON LEFT FROM LOND.
At a little distance from Ram Jam House is Stretton village.	178¼	Horn Lane Toll-Gate. Before Stretton a road leads off on the left to Oakham, 7 miles distant.	97½	able collection of paintings. The park is of great extent, and contains abundance of very fine timber. Exton church is a beautiful specimen of Gothic architecture, and contains some remarkable monuments of the Harrington and Noel families, who have possessed this lordship for several ages.
Stocken Hall, Lord Aveland.	176¼	**Ram Jam House.**	93½	At a dist. Cottesmore Hall, Earl of Lonsdale.
		Enter Lincolnshire.		
At a dist. Grimsthorpe Castle, Lord Willoughby D'Eresby.	174½	South Witham.	95¼	
	173¼	North Witham.	96½	
To Corby, 4½ miles.	171½	Colsterworth.	98¼	Near this place Sir Isaac Newton was born, Dec. 1642. Buckminster Park, Earl of Dysart.
Easton Hall, Sir M. J. Cholmeley, Bart., and beyond Irnham Hall, Lord Clifford.	169¼	Stoke Rochford.	100½	Stoke House, C. Turnor, Esq.
3 miles distant Boothby Pagnell.	167	Great Ponton.	102¾	3 miles distant, Harlaxton and Hungerton Hall, G. De Ligne Gregory, Esq., and beyond, Denton House, Sir G. E. Welby, Bart., and Belvoir Castle, Duke of Rutland.
Belton House, Earl Brownlow.	163¼	GRANTHAM, (p. 388.)	106½	
Syston Park, Sir J. C. Thorold, Bart.	161½	Great Gonerby.	108¼	
	157	Foston.	112	Allington House.
2 miles distant Stubton Hall.		Enter Nottinghamshire.		Staunton Hall (Rev. J. Staunton), and Shelton Hall.
To Sleaford, 20 miles. To Lincoln, 16 miles.	149	NEWARK, (p. 388.)	120¾	To Nottingham, 19½ m. Kelham Hall, J. H. M. Sutton, Esq.
Winthorpe Hall.		cr. river Dean.		
Langford Hall.		cross river Trent.		To Southwell, 8½ miles.
Muskham House.	146½	South Muskham.	123¼	
	143¾	Cromwell.	126	
Carlton Hall.	143	Carlton.	126¾	**2 m. dist. Ossington Ha., Right Hon. J. E. Denison.**
Marnham Hall.	142	Sutton-upon-Trent.	127¾	
	140¼	Weston.	129½	
	138¼	Scarthing Moor Inn.	131½	
	136	TUXFORD, proverbial for its miry situation. The church contains several monuments.	133¾	
	134¼	West Markham.	135½	To Thoresby Park (Earl Manvers), 4 miles; beyond, Clumber Park (Duke of Newcastle).
	132¼	Gamston.	137½	
		cr. Chesterfield Canal.		
Grove Hall, G. E. Harcourt Vernon, Esq.	129	EAST RETFORD, (p. 388.)	140¾	Babworth Hall, H. Bridgeman Simpson, Esq.
To Gainsborough, 9¼ m.		cr. river Idle.		West Retford House.

ON RIGHT FROM LOND.	From Newcas.		From London.	ON LEFT FROM LOND.
	126	**Barnby Moor Inn.**	143¾	Ranby Hall.
	124½	Torworth.	145¼	
	123	Ranskill.	146¾	Blythe Hall, H. Walker, Esq.
Bawtry Hall, R. M. Milnes, Esq.	122	Scrooby.	147¾	Serlby Hall, Viscount Galway.
To Gainsborough, 12 m. To Thorne, 14 miles.	120½	BAWTRY, situated partly in Notts, partly in Yorkshire.	149¼	To Tickhill, 4 m. and beyond, Sandbeck Park, Earl of Scarborough. Hesley Hall.
At a distance Finningley Park, J. Harvey, Esq.	116	Rossington Bridge.	153¾	Rossington.
		cr. river Torne.		
Cantley Hall, J. W. Childers, Esq.	115	Tophall.	154¾	
1 m. distant Wheatley Hall, Sir W. R. C. Cooke, Bart. Booth Ferry, 22½ m.; Howden, 24¼ miles. 10 miles dist. is Thorne, a small but flourishing town on the Don, by means of which, and of the canal from this river to the Trent, it carries on a considerable trade. Pop. 2591. (See p. 428.)	111¾	DONCASTER, (p. 389.) Five m. from Doncaster is Billham Hall, in the grounds of which is the Belvidere, commanding an extensive prospect. A few miles east is Epworth, the birth-place of John Wesley.	158	Beyond, Sprotborough Hall, Sir J. W. Copley, Bart., and Melton Hall. To Worksop, 16 m.; to Rotherham, 12 m.; thence to Sheffield, 6 m. To Barnsley, 15 m.; Penistone, 23; Mottram, 40; Manchester, 51.
		cr. river Don.		
Skellow Grange.	110	York Bar.	159¾	Cusworth Park, W. Wrightson, Esq., and beyond, Hickleton Hall, Rt. Hon. Sir C. Wood, Bart.
Burghwallis, and Owston Hall, P. D. Cooke, Esq.	106¾	Red House.	163	Brodsworth Hall, Lord Rendlesham.
2 m. distant Campsall Hall, Sir J. Radcliffe, Bart., and Camp's Mount.	104¾	Robin Hood's Well.	165	Shelbrooke Park. To Pontefract, 6½ m.
Stapleton Park, J. H. Barton, Esq., and to the right Womersley, Lord Hawke.		cr. river Went.		Two miles distant Ackworth Park and Ackworth Grange.
Grove Hall.	99½	Darrington.	170¼	2 miles from Darrington a road leads off to the town of Pontefract or Pomfret, 1½ m. distant, pleasantly situated on an eminence. It is celebrated for its gardens, nurseries, liquorice, &c. Here are the ruins of a castle in which, it is alleged, Richard II. was murdered. Two M.P. Pop. 11,736. Frystone Hall, R. Monckton Milnes, Esq.
13½ miles distant is Tadcaster, a neat well built town on the Wharfe. It is supposed to have been the Calcaria of the Romans. Pop. 1851, 2527. About 3 miles from Tadcaster, between Towton and Saxton is a ridge of high land, where a famous battle was fought between the Yorkists and Lancastrians in 1461.	96½	Ferry Bridge. 13 miles distant is the town of Snaith, pleasantly situated on the Aire. In the church is a statue and tomb of a Viscount Downe. Great quantities of flax are grown in the vicinity. Close to the town is Cowick Hall, the seat of Viscount Downe.	173¼	
		cr. river Aire.		
Byrom Hall, Sir J W. Ramsden, Bart.	95¼	Brotherton.	174¼	

ON RIGHT FROM LOND.	From Newcas.		From London.	ON LEFT FROM LOND.
York Railway.	94	Fairburn.	175¾	
To Selby, 9½ miles. Leeds, Selby, and Hull Railway.	92½	Peckfield Turnpike.	177¼	Ledstone Hall, and Kippax Park, T. D. Bland, Esq. **To Leeds, 9½ miles.**
Huddleston Hall.	90	**Micklefield.**	179¾	
Lotherton Hall. To Tadcaster, 4¼ miles. Haslewood Hall, Sir Edwd. Vavasour, Bart. This seat has belonged to the ancestors of the present proprietor since the time of William the Conqueror, with the exception of a short period during the reign of Henry III., when it was pledged to a Jew for £350. It is famous for the extent and richness of its prospects. The chapel contains a number of monuments in memory of different individuals of the family.	87¼	ABERFORD, a small town, with the ruins of an ancient castle, said to have been built soon after the Conquest. The town stands on a limestone rock of inconsiderable elevation, and consists chiefly of one long straggling street. Pop. 1009.	182½	To Leeds, 10 miles. Near Aberford, Parlington Ho., late R. O. Gascoigne, Esq. A little farther, Becca Hall, W. Markham, Esq.; and near it Potterton Lodge.
	83	**Bramham.** 2½ miles farther, to Tadcaster, 4¾ miles. cr. river Wharfe.	186	Bramham Biggin, Lord Headley; Bramham Ho. and Lodge; Bramham Park (G. L. Fox, Esq.) erected in the early part of last century by Lord Bingley. About 6 miles distant is Harewood House, the splendid seat of the Earl of Harewood.
Wetherby Grange. The country surrounding Wetherby is pleasingly diversified. To York, 13 miles. Ingmanthorpe Hall.	79¾	WETHERBY, a small town on the Wharfe, over which there is a handsome bridge. Above the bridge is a cascade.	190	To Harrowgate, 7 m.; Knaresborough by Spofforth, 8 m. A little below Wetherby is St. Helen's ford, where the Roman military way crossed the Wharfe. 1 mile from Wetherby, Linton Spring, Stockeld Park, P. Middleton, Esq.
Thornville Royal and Allerton Park, Lord Stourton.	76¾	Walshford Bridge. cr. river Nidd. 3 miles beyond Walshford Bridge a road leads off to York, distant 12 miles.	193	Ribston Hall, (Sir F. L. H. Goodricke, Bart.) in the gardens of which the famous apple was first cultivated. Here may be seen a monument to the standard bearer of the ninth Roman legion, which was discovered at York in the 17th century.
From Boroughbridge to York, 17 m., Thirsk, 10½ miles. 1 mile distant is Aldborough, formerly a Roman station. In the wall of the church vestry is a basso relievo of Mercury, and in the churchyard is a gravestone with the figure of a woman in a Saxon dress. Boroughbridge Hall, A. Lawson, Esq.	67¾	BOROUGH BRIDGE carries on an extensive trade in hardware. In the market-place is a handsome fluted Doric column. It was at Boroughbridge that Edward II. defeated the Earl of Lancaster.	202	To Knaresborough, 4 m. About half a mile dist. are three immense stones called the *Arrows*, generally supposed to have been erected by the Romans.

ON RIGHT FROM LOND.	From Newcas.		From London.	ON LEFT FROM LOND.
Aldborough Lodge, A. Lawson, Esq. Aldborough Hall, and, 3 miles distant across the Swale, Myton Hall, S. Stapylton, Esq.				2 m. dist. Newby Hall, Earl de Grey, and 3 m. dist. Copgrove House, T. Duncombe, Esq.
		cr. river Ure.		
To Easingwold, 10 m.	63¾	Dishforth.	206	To Carlisle, 95½ miles.
		cr. river Swale.		
To Thirsk, 4 miles.	61¼	Topcliffe.	208½	Newby Park, G. Hudson, Esq., and beyond, at a distance, Norton Conyers, Sir B. R. Graham, Bart. To Ripon, 8 miles.
To Thirsk, 3 miles.	57¼	Sand Hutton.	212½	
Wood End, Lady Crompton.	55¼	Newsham.	214½	
	53¾	South Otterington.	216	Newby Wiske.
	52½	North Otterington.	217¼	
	49¾	NORTHALLERTON has a Gothic church, a spacious market-place, and a prison on Howard's plan. Near this town was fought in 1138, the celebrated battle of the Standard, in which David King of Scotland was defeated. The spot still bears the name of Standard Hill. One M.P. Pop. 4755.	220	To Scorton, 9½ miles; Richmond, 14½; Bedale, 7½; Leyburn, 20 miles. Hutton Bonville Hall.
Hornby Grange.	42¾	Great Smeaton, remarkable for the beauty of the surrounding scenery, and for the extensive prospects which it commands.	227	
Croft Hall, Sir W. R. C. Chaytor, Bart. And 2 m. dist. Neasham Hall.	37¾	Croft has a much frequented mineral spring.	232	To Richmond, 9 m. Barnard Castle, 18 m.
		cr. river Tees and enter Durham.		
		cr. river Skerne.		
To Yarm, 10 m., Stockton, 14 miles. Coatham Hall.	33	DARLINGTON, (p. 389.) Five miles from Darlington is Dinsdale or Middleton Spa, with a good hotel. One mile distant is Grange Hall.	236¾	Blackwell Grange, (W. Allan, Esq.) containing a very extensive museum of natural history. To Barnard Castle, 16 m. Bishop Aukland, 12 m. Catterick Bridge, 12½.
Ketton House, Rev. Sir C. Hardinge, Bart.	27¾	Aycliffe.	242	
Great Chilton.	24	Rushy Ford.	245¾	Windlestone Hall, Sir W. Eden, Bart., and beyond, Auckland Castle (Bishop of Durham).

ON RIGHT FROM LOND.	From Newcas.		From London	ON LEFT FROM LOND.
Croxdale Hall, G. Salvin, Esq.	19¼	Butcher Race.	250½	
	18½	Sunderland Bridge.	251¼	2 m. dist. Whitworth Pa., R. D. Shafto, Esq., and near it, Brancepeth Castle, Hon. G. J. J. Hamilton Russell.
3 m. distant, Sherburn Hall, and 1 mile beyond, Durham, Aycliffe Heads, Ruins of Finchale Abbey.		cr. river Wear.		
	14½	DURHAM (p. 389.)	255¼	Burn Hall. Oswald House.
		cr. river Wear.		
Lumley Castle, Earl of Scarborough, and Lambton Castle, Earl of Durham.	8½	CHESTER-LE-STREET. (See p. 391.)	261¼	
	7½	Pelton.	262¼	
	5½	Birtley.	264¼	
Usworth House.	4	Ayton Bank.	265¾	2 m. distant Ravensworth Castle, Lord Ravensworth.
To Sunderland over the Iron Bridge 10½ m.	¼	GATESHEAD. Pop. 1851, 25,568. See p. 394.	269½	1 m. distant Red Heugh, and 5 m. distant Axwell Pa., Sir T. Clavering, Bart.
		cr. river Tyne and enter Northumberland.		
Heaton House and Benton House.		NEWCASTLE-UPON-TYNE (p. 391.)	269¾	Elswick Hall, J. H. Hinde, Esq.

Amwell, on a branch of the river Lea, is said to have derived its name from Emma's Well, a spring near the church. In a small island formed by the stream is a monument to the memory of Sir Hugh Myddleton, who achieved the task of conveying the New River water to London. Izaak Walton lived at Amwell.

Ware, a market-town on the Lea, with a considerable trade in malt and corn. The church of St Mary contains many curious monuments, and in the churchyard is the tomb of Dr Mead, who died (1652) aged (it is alleged) 148 years. At the Saracen's Head Inn may be seen the great bed of Ware, 12 feet square, which is incorrectly said to have been the state bed of Edward IV. Pop. 5002.

Huntingdon is situated on the north bank of the Ouse. It stands on the Ermin Street; and there was a Roman station, the Durolipons of Antoninus, on the site, either of the town, or its suburb, Godmanchester. In the year 917, Edward the Elder built a castle here, of the outworks of which, traces yet remain. In the civil war the royal troops entered Huntingdon after a short resistance, and plundered it. Before the Reformation, Huntingdon contained fifteen churches, of which but two remain. It contains also several chapels and meeting-houses, a town-hall, and assembly-rooms, a county gaol, a small theatre, and a race course, a free grammar school, and many other schools of various kinds. Godmanchester also contains numerous schools. The trade of the town is principally in wool, corn, and malt, and it has several breweries and manufactories. Oliver Cromwell was a native of Huntingdon. 1 m. distant is Hinchinbroke House (Earl of Sandwich) formerly the property of the Cromwell family. The great room in which Queen Elizabeth and James I. were entertained is still preserved. The mansion occupies the site of a Benedictine nunnery. Beyond it is Brampton Park, the seat of the Duke of Manchester. Huntingdon is connected by railways with all parts of the kingdom. Two M.P. Pop. 6254.

STAMFORD is a town of great antiquity, and had fourteen parish churches, only five of which now remain. That of St Martin contains several monuments of the Cecil family. The great Lord Burghley was interred here. Stamford contains also several chapels, a town-hall, assembly rooms, a theatre, free grammar, blue-coat, and national schools, several charitable institutions, &c. Its principal trade is in malt, coal, and freestone. Two M.P. Pop. 8047.

Close by Stamford is Burghley House, (Marquis of Exeter,) a magnificent mansion, erected by Lord Treasurer Burghley, on the site of a very ancient fabric, and situated in a noble park. It contains a hall supported by 12 columns of Scagliola marble, a grand staircase, painted by Stothard, two libraries, containing many curious MSS., a very valuable collection of pictures, a splendid state bed, &c. The approach from Stamford is through an avenue of oaks of remarkable size.

GRANTHAM is situated on the Roman Ermine Street and Witham. St Wulfan's church is a spacious structure, and has a spire 273 feet high. It contains a curious font and several monuments. Grantham formerly possessed several religious houses, some remains of which still exist. In the free grammar school here, Sir Isaac Newton received part of his education. Two M.P. Pop. 11,121.

Three miles distant is Belton House (Earl Brownlow), designed by Wren and adorned by Gibbons, contains many family portraits and other paintings. Beyond Belton is Syston Park, Sir J. C. Thorold, Bart. Five miles distant is Belvoir Castle, the magnificent mansion of the Duke of Rutland, occupying the summit of a hill. Belvoir was destroyed by fire in 1816, but it has since been rebuilt on a magnificent scale. It contains one of the best collections of pictures in the kingdom. The castle was originally founded by Robert de Todeni. It commands a prospect of remarkable extent and beauty. To Folkingham, 13 miles; to Donington, 19¾ miles. To Melton Mowbray, 16 miles; to Bingham, 14 miles.

NEWARK is situated on a branch of the Trent. Here are the ruins of a castle in which King John died, A D. 1216. The church of St Mary Magdalene is one of the largest and most elegant in the kingdom. It was in great part rebuilt in the time of Henry VI. The interior has some good wood screen-work and stained glass, with various brasses and other ancient monuments. It has lately undergone repairs, and will well repay a visit. Here are also a new church, a handsome town-hall, a free grammar school, several meeting-houses, and charitable institutions. The principal trade of Newark is in corn, malt, and cattle. Lightfoot and Bishop Warburton were natives of Newark. Two M.P. Pop. 1851, 11,330. It is connected by railway with all parts of the kingdom, and gives the title of viscount to Earl Manvers. In the civil wars, Newark zealously supported the King, and was incorporated by Charles II. on account of its loyalty to his father. Near Newark is the Beacon Hill, which was the scene of an action between the Royalists under Prince Rupert, and the Parliamentary forces under Sir J. Meldrum. Between Newark and Southwell, 8 m. distant, is the field where Charles I. surrendered himself to the Scotch commissioners.

NEWCASTLE UPON TYNE
& GATESHEAD.
THE T
Spital Tongues
Spital Tongues Colliery
Belle Grove Ho.
NUNS MOOR
Cavalry & Infantry Barracks
CAST
LEAZ
North Elswick Hall
ST NICHOLAS CEMETERY
New Mills
Barrack Road
Wingrove Ho.
Union Workhouse
Carlisle & Hexham Road
West House
Gloucester H.
Highfield Ho.
Spring Garden Ter.
Wellington St.
Pitt St.
Hill St.
Stanhope St.
Diana St.
Buckingham Str.
William St.
Tindal St.
Arthur Hill
Westgate Cemetery
Westgate Hill
Bentinck Road
Gloucester Road
St. Pauls Ch.
Elswick Row
Rye Hill
Summerhill Grove
Victoria Str.
Westmoreland St.
St John's Cemetery
Elswick West Villas
Elswick Hall
Dean House
Low Dean House
Elswick Glue Manufactory
Elswick Dean
Mechanics Institute
Westmoreland Road
South Parade
St. Mary's Ch.
Lawton St.
Elswick Villas
Ryehill Str.
George Str.
Blandford Street
Blenheim Str.
Dukes St.
Cambridge Street
Maple St.
Pine Street
Sycamore Street
Hinde Str.
Park R.
De Grey St.
Armstrong Street
Penn St.
Railway Street
Newcastle & Carlisle Railway
Low Elswick
Elswick Lead Wks.
Elswick Foundry
Gas Works
The Haughs
The Kings Meadows
Clarence Is.
R
Sadlers Landing
Newcastle & Carlisle Ry
Team
Dunston
(Redheugh Branch)
Tanfield Branch

A. & C

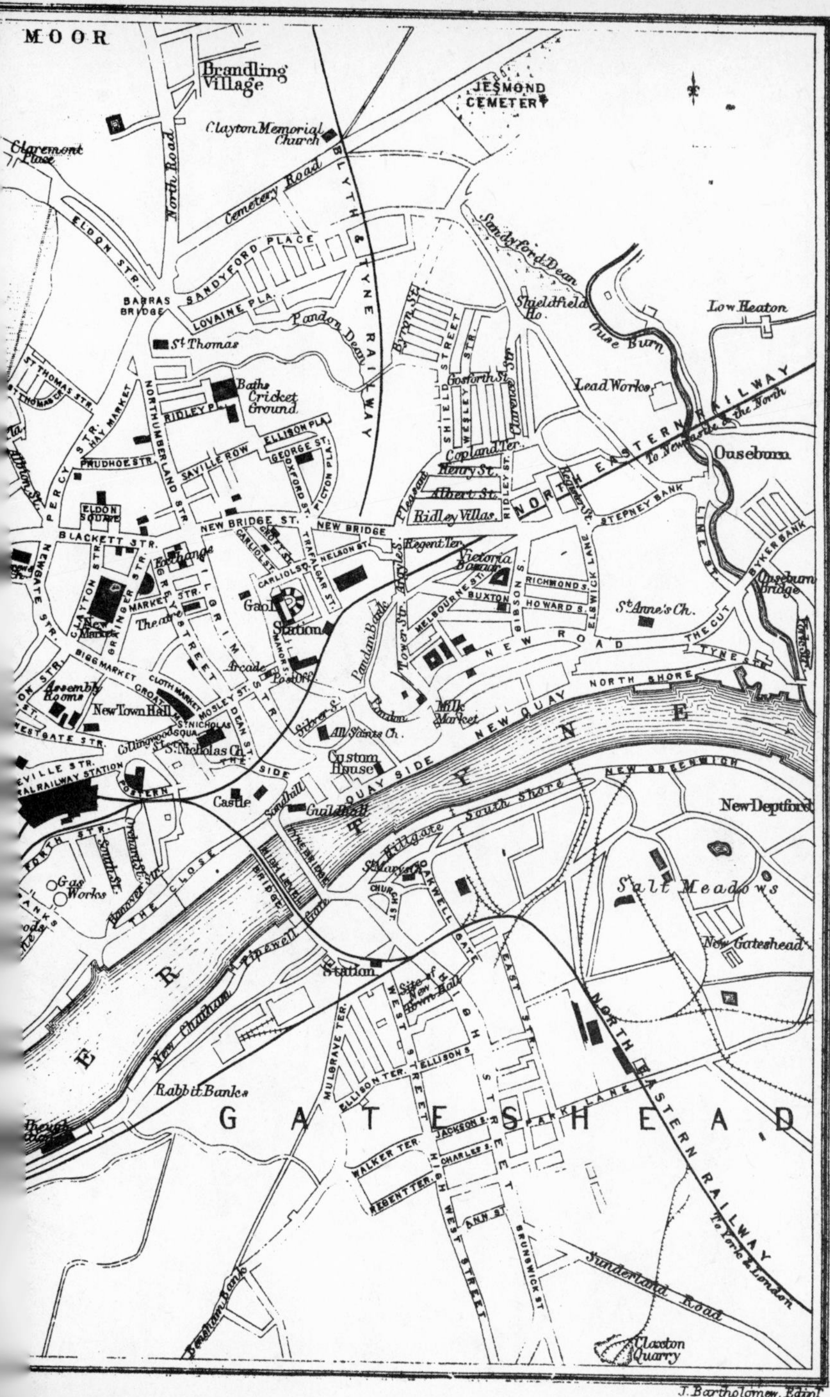

J. Bartholomew, Edinr.

urgh.

East Retford, on the Idle, carries on a considerable trade, particularly in hops, and has manufactories of paper, sailcloth, &c. It has two churches, besides chapels, a free grammar school, and an hospital. East Retford, with the Hundred of Basset Law, returns two M.P. Pop. of Parl. borough, 1861, 47,330.

Doncaster, on the Don, is one of the cleanest and most beautiful towns in the kingdom. It was the *Danum* of Antoninus, and was called *Dona Ceastre* by the Saxons, from which its present name is derived. The town stands on the Watling Street of the Romans, and coins, urns, and other Roman remains, are occasionally dug up in the neighbourhood. Doncaster has a few iron foundries, and possesses one of the largest corn markets in the kingdom. The public buildings most worthy of notice are the mansion-house, a handsome structure, which cost about £10,000;—St. George's Church, a spacious and elegant structure, with a fine tower, and painted east window; Christ Church, the town hall, gaol, theatre, race-stand, &c. Here are also several chapels and meeting houses, numerous educational establishments, and public charities. The famous races at Doncaster are held in the third week of September. Potteric Car, on the south of the town, was a morass of many miles in extent till the year 1766. It is now completely drained, and yields luxuriant crops. Pop. 16,406.

Darlington is situated on the Skerne, over which is a bridge of three arches. St. Cuthbert's church, built by the celebrated Hugh de Pudsey, is of the 12th century, and cruciform, with a lofty spire; and the town has places of worship for Methodists, and other Protestant Dissenters, and for Roman Catholics. Darlington carries on a considerable trade. The chief occupations of the inhabitants are combing wool, spinning flax, grinding optical glasses, and founding iron. Pop. 1861, 15,781. Darlington is remarkable for the extent of its Quaker population. It gives title of Earl to the Duke of Cleveland.

Durham, a city of great antiquity, stands on a remarkable eminence nearly surrounded by the river Wear. There does not appear to have been any town where Durham now stands till about the end of the tenth century, when the monks of Lindisfarne rested there with the remains of St Cuthbert. Soon after a church was built by Bishop Aldune, and dedicated to St Cuthbert, whose remains were removed and enshrined in it. Durham suffered severely from the cruelties of William the Conqueror, who repeatedly laid waste the surrounding country with fire and sword. In 1072, a strong castle was built here; and the bishop assumed the title of Count Palatine. In 1093, the old church built by Aldune was pulled down, and the present magnificent edifice begun by William de Carilepho the bishop, and Turgot the prior. Durham has figured conspicuously in all the great transactions that have agitated the north. It suffered often from the invasions of the Scots; and was frequently the head quarters of Edward III. and of other monarchs and commanders on their excursions against Scotland. Durham was deeply indebted to Bishop Hugh Pudsey (Earl of Northumberland) who was appointed to the bishopric in 1153. To him it owes the Galilee, one of the most curious and beautiful portions of the cathedral,—a sumptuous shrine for the relics of the venerable Bede, the restoration of the borough of Elvet, the building of Elvet bridge, and the completion of the city-wall along the bank of the Wear. To him the citizens of Durham were indebted for their first charter. One of his successors, Anthony Beck, rivalled him in the greatness of his wealth and the magnificence of his public works. He is said to have been the adviser of Edward I. in his dishonest policy towards Scotland. Among many other distinguished men Durham has numbered among its prelates Bishop Hatfield, founder of Durham College, Oxford, now extinct, Bishops Langley and Cosin, Lord Crewe, the testator of the magnificent charity of Bamborough Castle and lands, Bishops Talbot, Butler, the author of the Analogy of Religion, Egerton, Thurlow, Shute Barrington, and Dr. Maltby, the present holder of this see (1853). The cathedral, a magnificent edifice, stands on the highest part of the eminence which is occupied by the city. It was founded in the year 1093, and the successive additions which have been made to it are not only a perfect specimen of the Norman architecture, but a striking illustration of the gradual changes in the English style to the beginning of the fifteenth century. It was repaired and restored in the end of last century. It contains the remains of St Cuthbert, brought to light in 1827, of the venerable Bede, several of whose MSS. are in the cathedral library, of Ralph Lord Neville, who commanded the English at the battle of Neville's Cross, &c. In the churchyard is a monument to Robert Dodsley, the bookseller, author of the Economy of Human Life. The cathedral library contains a number of curious and interesting works, MSS. and relics. The castle of Durham, which stands opposite the cathedral, was erected by William the Conqueror, and, till recently, was the residence of the Bishops of the Palatinate. A university was established at Durham during the Commonwealth, but, on the restoration of monarchy, it was dissolved. Another university was opened in 1833, and is now attended by numerous students. Its funds are drawn by act of Parliament from the property of the bishopric. The Norman chapel of the castle is appropriated to the use of the college. The dining-hall is used as the college-hall, and the keep has been restored in good taste, and fitted up as college-chambers. This university is allowed to grant degrees in the several faculties, and a royal charter was granted to it in 1837. Besides the cathedral, Durham possesses numerous churches, chapels, and meeting-houses, a Roman Catholic chapel, the court-houses, a new prison, erected in 1809, at the cost of £120,000; the Guildhall, erected by Bishop Tunstall in 1555; an infirmary, a theatre, the remains of Finchale Abbey in a vale near the river, a mechanics' institute, and numerous educational and charitable institutions. The walks round the city afford the most charming promenades. About three-quarters of a mile distant is the site of the Maiden Castle, a fortress ascribed to the Romans, as also some remains of the Icknield Street. Saline, chalybeate, and sulphurous springs are found in the neighbourhood. One mile west of the city is Neville's Cross, erected by Ralph Lord Neville in memory of the defeat and capture of David II. Two M.P. Pop 1861, 14,088. Durham is connected by railways with all parts of the kingdom. It gives the title of Earl to the Lambton family.

To Sunderland, 13 miles; Sedgefield, 11; Stockton, 21½; Witton Gilbert, 3½; Lanchester, 8; Wolsingham, 15; Stanhope, 20½; St John Weardale, 27½; Bishop Auckland, 10¼; Staindrop, 19; Barnard Castle, 24¼.

Six miles from Durham is Chester le Street, built upon an old Roman road, and on or near a Roman station. It became, A. D. 882, the seat of the bishopric, which was removed hither from Lindisfarne. In 995, a Danish invasion drove away the bishop and his clergy, who afterwards settled at Durham. The church is an interesting building, with a fine tower 156 feet in height. It was formerly a collegiate church, and has been famous from the time of St Cuthbert, whose remains rested here 113 years before they were conveyed to Durham. This church contains a collection of stone effigies of the Lords of Lumley from Lyulph, the Saxon founder of the family, to the reign of Elizabeth. They are fourteen in number, each resting on its altar tomb, and the name, armorial bearings, and immediate connections of each knight or baron are displayed on a tablet on the wall above his tomb. Pop. 2550.

One mile distant is Lumley Castle, a seat of the Earl of Scarborough. This noble building stands on a fine gradual elevation above the Wear. It is a quadrangle of yellow freestone, having an open court or area in the centre, with four uniform towers. A noble gatehouse projects from the centre, with overhanging turrets. The castle is supposed to have been built in the latter part of the fourteenth century. The apartments are unfurnished, and the pictures are chiefly portraits of the ancient family of the Lumleys. The great hall is ninety feet long, and exhibits striking features of feudal customs and old English manners. About a mile distant is Lambton Castle, the seat of the Earl of Durham, which was built in 1797 on the site of the old house of Harraton, the former seat of the Hedworths. It occupies an elevated situation on the banks of the Wear, and is surrounded by extensive grounds.

Newcastle-upon-Tyne is supposed to have derived its origin from Pons Ælii, the second station from the eastern extremity of the Roman wall. Previous to the Conquest the place was called Monkchester, from the number of monastic institutions; its present name was derived from a castle erected here by Robert, eldest son of William the Conqueror, on his return from an expedition into Scotland. Newcastle was anciently the resort of numerous pilgrims, who came to visit the holy well of Jesus' Mount, now Jesmond, a mile north-east of the town. One of the principal streets in Newcastle is still called Pilgrim Street. Another ancient town, called Pampedon, appears to have been included in the limits of the modern Newcastle; its name may be traced in the modern Pandon Hall, Pandon Bank, &c. Newcastle has been the seat of many most interesting events in the history of England. David I. of Scotland made himself master of the town in the reign of Stephen, and obliged the people to swear allegiance to the Empress Maud. Here John of England and William the Lion of Scotland had a conference in the year 1209. Here again Alexander II. of Scotland and his Queen came, in 1235-36, and had a conference with Henry III. of England. Here John Balliol did homage to Edward I. for the crown of Scotland. In 1293, the famous Sir William Wallace, in one of his inroads into England, made several vehement but unsuccessful attacks upon the town. In 1318, during the reign of Edward II., an unsuccessful attempt at a permanent peace between the Scots and English was made here—two nuncios from the Pope, and two envoys from Philip of France, besides the English and Scotch commissioners, being present. In 1342, David Bruce, King of Scotland, made an unsuccessful attack upon the town shortly before the battle of Neville's Cross; and, twelve years afterwards, commissioners met here to consult on his ransom. In 1644, Newcastle was besieged by the Scottish army under General Alexander Leslie, Earl of Leven, but Sir Thomas Glenham, for the Marquis of Newcastle, who was governor for the king, successfully defended the town against him. In the same year, however, the Scots under the Earl of Leven took it by storm; but Sir John Marley, then mayor, retired to the castle, with about 500 men, which he held till terms of capitulation were obtained. In 1636, above 5000 persons died of the plague at Newcastle. In 1646, Charles I. was brought hither from Newark by the Scots, to whom he had surrendered himself. Newcastle is supposed to have been incorporated by William Rufus; but the first mayor was appointed in the reign of Henry III.

The town, which has more than doubled its size during the present century, is situated on the summit and declivities of three lofty eminences, rising from the north bank of the Tyne, and ten miles from its mouth. The town of Gateshead occupies the opposite bank, and may be regarded as a sort of suburb of Newcastle. "A strange mixture of ancient and modern objects strikes your eye in the more lofty and prominent features of Newcastle. There stands, tall, and stalwart, and square, and black as ink, the old donjon-keep of Robert Curthose, the son of the Conqueror. To the left still higher towers over the town the fine steeple of St Nicholas, and to the right the new and lofty column in honour of the 2d Earl Grey. Here, along the banks of the river, you see ranges, one above another, of dim and dingy buildings, that have stood for centuries amid the smoke of the great capital of coal; and there, on its bold eminence, a Grecian fabric, standing proudly aloft, like the temple of Minerva in Athens. Beyond it, again, you catch the tops of houses, and ranges of streets, that indicate a degree of modern magnificence which at once astonishes you in the midst of so much that is different, and stimulates you to a nearer inspection."*

Newcastle has undergone a most wonderful change during the last few years. In the centre of the town the old and narrow streets have been swept away, and some of the noblest and most magnificent streets and squares in the kingdom erected in their room. The person by whose genius and industry this marvellous

* HOWITT's Visits to Remarkable Places 2d Series, p. 287.

change has been effected is Mr Grainger, a native of the town, who raised himself to great importance from the condition of a charity boy, and the apprentice to a carpenter and builder. The total cost of his improvements on Newcastle in the five years ended August 1839, amounted to £645,690; and the total value of the whole property created by him during the same period, to £995,000.* Besides these magnificent operations, Mr Grainger's plan comprehends the erection of extensive quays, of ranges of manufactories, and also of villas and terraces on the high ground in the neighbourhood of the town.

The other objects of interest in Newcastle are St Nicholas' Church, large and cruciform, with a beautiful spire, the upper portion of the lantern assuming the form of an imperial crown, and a valuable library, containing, among other curious books, the illuminated Bible of Hexham Abbey; St Andrew's Church, a very ancient structure, part of it of Norman architecture; St John the Baptist's Church, containing an ancient font and several ancient monuments; All Saints' Church, a modern edifice of Grecian architecture, with a steeple 202 feet high; St Ann's, St Thomas's, Mary Magdalene, &c.; the Infirmary, the Keelmen's Hospital, the monument erected to the 2d Earl Grey, surmounted by a statue of that nobleman; the Royal Arcade, 250 feet long, by 20 wide and 35 feet high, the Incorporated Company's Hall, &c. The new covered market is pronounced to be the finest in the kingdom. Its area is more than two acres. One of the most remarkable features of the town is Stephenson's double bridge, nearly 120 feet high, which on its higher level conveys the railway across the Tyne, and has an ordinary roadway underneath. Newcastle also possesses several meeting-houses, hospitals, schools, and other charitable institutions, a literary and scientific institution, containing a fine library and reading room, a museum of Egyptian, and a gallery of Roman antiquities, &c. The free grammar school was founded by Thomas Horsley, who was mayor of Newcastle in 1525. Here the late Earl of Eldon, and Lords Stowell and Collingwood, the poet Akenside, and other eminent persons received the earlier part of their education.

The principal business of Newcastle is the shipment of coals, the produce of the surrounding coal-pits. About three millions of tons of coals are shipped annually from the river Tyne. The other chief articles of export are lead, cast and wrought iron, glass and pottery, copperas and other chemical productions, soap, colours, grindstones, salt, and pickled salmon. The imports are wine, spirituous liquors, and fruit, corn, timber, flax, tallow, and hides from the Baltic, and tobacco and various other articles from North America. The customs revenue of this port in 1857 was £291,782. Newcastle possesses glass-houses, potteries, and manufactories of iron, steel, engines, and woollen cloths. A number of persons are engaged in ship-building, and the branches of trade connected with it. The shipping belonging to the port in 1851 amounted to 110 sailing vessels under 50, and 803 over 50 tons, besides 130 steamers under 50, and eight over 50 tons; total tonnage, 202,376 tons. Newcastle is connected by means of railways with all parts of the kingdom.

* Penny Magazine, March, April, and May, 1840.

Newcastle returns two members to Parliament. Pop. 1861, 111,151.

GATESHEAD in Durham may be regarded as a suburb of Newcastle, to which it is united by a stone bridge. St. Mary's church is a handsome building. There are several manufactories of glass and of wrought and cast iron in the town, and in the vicinity are numerous coal-pits. One M.P. Pop. 1861, 59,411.

Total population, Newcastle and Gateshead, 170,562.

CXXXIV. FROM NEWCASTLE TO BERWICK-UPON-TWEED THROUGH MORPETH AND ALNWICK, 63½ Miles.

ON RIGHT FROM NEWC.	From Berwick.		From Newcas.	ON LEFT FROM NEWC.
				Fenham Hall.
	60½	Gosforth Turnpike.	3	At a distance, Woolsington, M. Bell, Esq.
Gosforth House, T. Smith, Esq.		cross the Ouse Burn.		
Seaton Burn.	57½	Six-Mile-House.	6	
Arcot, and 5 miles distant on the coast, the ruins of Seaton Delaval, the property of Lord Hastings.		cr. Seaton Burn.		Blagdon House, Sir M. W. Ridley, Bart.
Four miles distant from Shield Green is Widdrington Castle, and 7 m. distant on the coast, Cresswell Hall, A. J. B. Cresswell, Esq. Widdrington Castle was a noble structure, but was unfortunately destroyed by fire. The only remaining part of it is an octangular embattled tower, to which a square modern edifice has been added. The family of Widdrington was formerly of great consideration in this county. The first baron lost his life at the battle of Wiganlane, in the cause of Charles II. His grandson forfeited the estate in the Rebellion of 1715. A lady of this family is the heroine of Percy's beautiful ballad, the Hermit of Warkworth.	55½	Shotton Edge.	8	
	54	Stannington Bridge.	9½	
		cr. the river Blyth.		
	53½	Stannington.	10	
	51½	Clifton.	12	
		cr. riv. Wansbeck.		To Jedburgh, 47½ m.
	48¾	MORPETH, (p. 395.)	14¾	2 miles distant, the ruins of Mitford Castle, and near them, Mitford Castle, R.-Admiral R. Mitford.
	44½	Shield Green.	19	Causey Park. Linden Hall, C. Bigge, Esq.
		cr. the Eshot Burn.		
	39¾	West Moor.	23¾	
	38¾	West Thirston.	24¾	
		cr. the riv. Coquet.		
	38½	Felton.	25	Felton Park, T. Riddell, Esq. Swarland Hall.
	36¾	Nelson's Monument.	26¾	
	35¼	Newton.	28¼	Swansfield and Hulne Abbey, Duke of Northumberland, and beyond, Lemmington Hall.
To Alnmouth, 4¼ miles.				
Alnwick Castle, Duke of Northumberland, and 4 miles distant on the coast, Howick House, Earl Grey.	29½	ALNWICK, (see p. 395.)	34	To Rothbury, 11½ m.
		cr. the river Alne.		

ON RIGHT FROM NEWC.	From Berwick.		From Newcas.	ON LEFT FROM NEWC.
Heckley House. Rock Castle.	23½	North Charlton.	40¼	
Charlton Hall, and Falloden, Right Hon. Sir George Grey, Bart. Ellingham Hall, Sir E. Haggerston, Bart.	19¾	Warnford.	44¼	Twizell House, P. J. Selby, Esq.; and in the distance, Chillingham Park, Earl of Tankerville.
Adderstone House. Belford Hall, Rev. J. D. Clark.	15	BELFORD, (p. 398.)	48½	
Easington, and 4 miles distant, Bambrough Castle (see p. 398).	12¾	Detchant.	50¾	Middleton Hall.
	10	Fenwick, (*Durham.*)	53½	Kyloe.
Haggerston Castle, Sir E. Blount, Bart.	7	Haggerston.	56½	
Cheswick House, J. S. Donaldson-Selby, Esq.	½	Tweedmouth.	63	Longridge.
		cr. river Tweed.		
		BERWICK-UPON-TWEED, (p. 399.) *	63½	

Morpeth is pleasantly situated on the northern bank of the river Wansbeck, among woody undulating hills. It is a place of considerable antiquity; and, in 1215, was burnt by its own inhabitants out of hatred to King John. Its weekly cattle-market is one of the largest in England. The town-hall was erected in 1714 by the 3d Earl of Carlisle, from designs by Vanbrugh. The free school was founded by Edward VI. Of the ancient castle, only a few fragments and the gate, now remain. One M.P. Pop. 13,794.

About two miles from Morpeth are the ruins of Mitford Castle and of Mitford manor-house, and, at a short distance, the splendid modern mansion of Admiral Mitford. The valley from Morpeth to Mitford is one of the most lovely in England. The Wansbeck winds through it between lofty precipitous banks, flanked by fine woods.

Alnwick is situated on a declivity on the south bank of the river Alne. It is but 310 miles N. by W. from London by the old road, though farther by railway. The town is well laid out, the streets spacious and well-paved, the houses are chiefly of stone, of modern date, and some of them of considerable elegance. Bondgate, one of the streets, takes its name from a gate erected by Hotspur, and still standing. The town possesses a town-hall and clock-house, a free school, several churches, and chapels. The most interesting object is the ancient castle, the residence of the Duke of Northumberland, which has been restored, and occupies an elevated situation on the south bank of the Alne, covering about five acres. This noble baronial mansion belonged to William Tyson, a Saxon baron, who

* For the route from Berwick to Edinburgh, see Black's Picturesque Tourist of Scotland.

was slain at the battle of Hastings, and it came into the possession of the Percy family in 1310. Grose says, the original building is supposed to have been founded by the Romans. In 1093, it withstood a memorable siege against Malcolm, King of Scots, and his son, Prince Edward, both of whom were slain before it. William the Lion, King of Scotland, was taken prisoner here in 1174. King John burnt it down in 1215. It had been suffered to go very much to decay, till it was completely repaired several years since, and it is now one of the most magnificent specimens in the kingdom of an old baronial residence. The building is of freestone, and, as well as the repairs and ornaments, is in the Gothic style, and in excellent taste. It consists of three courts, enclosing about five acres, and is flanked by sixteen towers, the battlements of which are decorated with statues representing men in the act of defence. The interior is fitted up in a style becoming the residence of a nobleman of the highest rank and most ancient descent, and is in admirable keeping with its exterior. The chapel is very richly adorned, and contains a tomb of white marble in honour of Elizabeth, 1st Duchess of Northumberland, daughter and heiress of Algernon, Duke of Somerset and Earl of Northumberland. The grounds are extensive and beautiful, and contain the remains of two ancient abbeys—Alnwick and Hulne. In the woods opposite to the castle stands a picturesque cross, rebuilt in 1774 on the spot where King Malcolm of Scotland fell. The place where William the Lion was taken prisoner is also marked by a monument. In the grounds stands the tower of Brislee, erected by the late Duke in 1762. The view from its top is extensive and magnificent.

Alnwick Abbey, beautifully seated on the northern bank of the Alne, was the first house of the Premonstratensians in England. They settled here in 1147. It was for some time the seat of the Brandlings, and after them, of the Doubledays, whose heirs sold it to the Duke of Northumberland. A gateway tower of it remains, on which are armorial shields of the Percys, crosses, and a niche richly crowned with open Gothic work.

Hulne Abbey stands in a woody and delightful solitude three miles above Alnwick. It was founded in 1240. Its outer walls and gateways are still very entire. The most perfect part of it is a fine tower which was fitted up in the Gothic style by the 2d Duke of Northumberland.

At the proclaiming of the July fair in Alnwick, the old feudal custom of keeping watch and ward is kept up by the Duke's tenants, and those who owe suit and service. This is a very ancient custom, and originated in the necessity of watching the Scotch, who used to make inroads the night before the July fair.

The ceremony of making free burgesses at Alnwick is of a very peculiar kind. The candidates are compelled to pass through a miry pool about twenty feet across, and from four to five feet deep in many places. On St Mark's day, the candidates, mounted and clad in white, with white night-caps on their heads, and swords by their sides, are accompanied by the bailiff and chamberlains similarly mounted and armed, and preceded by music to the pool. This has been previously deepened, and its bottom made uneven with stones, holes, stakes, and ropes of straw. They then dismount, scramble through the pool, and after changing their befouled garments, ride round the boundaries of the town. According to tradition, the observance of this custom was enjoined by King John as a punishment to the inhabitants for their carelessness. Owing to their neglect of the roads near the town, it is said the king lost his way, and was bemired in a bog. There are three free schools in Alnwick supported by the corporation, and a national school for 200 boys, founded by the 2d Duke of Northumberland in 1810, to commemorate the completion of the fiftieth year of the reign of George III. Pop. 5670.

Six miles from Alnwick are the noble ruins of Warkworth Castle, an ancient fortress held at different periods by the descendants of Roger Fitz-Roger, and by the families of Umfraville and Percy, to the latter of which it still belongs. This castle was the favourite residence of the Percy family, but in 1672 its timber and lead were granted to one of their agents, and the principal parts of it unroofed. It is a noble pile, finely situated on an eminence above the river Coquet, commanding a very extensive and beautiful view. As was justly observed by Grose, nothing can be more magnificent and picturesque from what part soever it be viewed. The keep or principal part of the building stands on the north side, and is elevated on an artificial mound several feet higher than the other portions. The whole building is very large, and comprehends many apartments. The great baronial hall is nearly 40 feet long by 24 wide and 20 high. The castle and moat, according to an ancient survey, contained nearly six acres of ground. It includes in front of the keep an area of more than an acre, surrounded with walls and towers. These walls are in many places entire, and thirty-five feet high. The entire gateway or principal entrance was once a stately building defended by a portcullis, and containing apartments for several officers of the castle, of which a few only now remain, inhabited by the person who has charge of the ruins. Among the lower apartments the dungeon yet remains. The fabric is now preserved with great care.

About half a mile from the castle is the famous Hermitage, consisting of two apartments hewn out of the rock. The principal apartment, or chapel, is about 18 feet long, 7½ wide, by 7½ high. At the east end is an altar, with a niche behind it for a crucifix, and near the altar is a cavity containing a cenotaph, with a recumbent female figure, having the hands raised in the attitude of prayer. In the inner apartment are another altar and a niche for a couch. According to tradition this hermitage was the abode of one of the family of Bertram of Bothal, who spent here a life of penitence for the murder of his brother. The Percy family after his death maintained a chantry priest here till the dissolution of the monasteries, when the endowment reverted to the family, having never been endowed in mortmain. This tradition is the subject of a beautiful ballad, by Dr. Percy, Bishop of Dromore.

The town of Warkworth is on the south side of the river Coquet. The church of St Lawrence is elegant and spacious, has a spire 100 feet high, and is to some extent of considerable antiquity. Pop. of par. 1851, 4439.

Six and a half miles from Alnwick, on the coast, are the ruins of Dunstanburgh Castle, erected in 1315 by Thomas Plantagenet, Earl of Lancaster. It was destroyed during the wars of the Roses. Nothing at present remains of it but its outworks, which are in the form of a crescent. Its area contains about nine acres. The village of Dunston is celebrated as the supposed birth-place of Duns Scotus, "the most subtle doctor," and opponent of Aquinas, "the angelic doctor."

Between four and five miles to the right of Alnwick, and about a mile from the sea, is Howick House, the seat of Earl Grey.

Belford is a neat town, standing on a gradual slope, about two miles from the sea. It has a church and several chapels, and in the vicinity are the ruins of an ancient chapel, surrounded by oak trees. Pop. 1067.

About five miles from Belford is Bambrough Castle, standing upon a basalt rock, which rises 150 feet above the level of the sea. In natural strength there is not a situation in the whole county equal to that of Bambrough. A castle is said to have been erected here by Ida, King of Bernicia, so early as A.D. 559, and named by him Bebban-brough, in honour of his queen, Bebba. In every succeeding age, down to the reign of Edward IV., it figured conspicuously in the contests which agitated the country; but it has never altogether recovered the injury which it received in a siege after the battle of Hexham. By a grant of the Crown, in the time of James I., it came into the family of the Forsters, and was forfeited by Thomas Forster in 1715; but his maternal uncle, Nathaniel Lord Crewe, Bishop of Durham, purchased the estate, and bequeathed it to charitable purposes. The trustees under his will reside here in turn. Archdeacon Sharp, about the year 1757, expended large sums of money in repairing the castle, and rendering it habitable. The whole of the extensive accommodations of the castle, (which includes within its exterior walls no less a space than eight acres,) except the library and the residence of the trustee, are devoted to objects of active benevolence. Here is a market for flour and groceries, which are sold to the poor at prime cost, and an infirmary, where advice and medicine are given gratis. Here are also large schools, endowed for the gratuitous education of the children of the poor, and twenty poor girls are, from their ninth year till they are fit for service, lodged, clothed, and educated. Besides the good done to the neighbourhood, this admirable charity has proved of incalculable benefit to those who have suffered from shipwreck. Life-boats and all kinds of implements useful in saving crews and vessels in distress, are always in readiness. Apartments are fitted up for shipwrecked sailors, and a constant patrol is kept up every stormy night for eight miles along this tempestuous coast. The castle contains an extensive and valuable library, the bequest of Dr. Sharp, which is open to any person residing within ten miles. In the court-room there are various portraits, and among them those of the founder, Lord Crewe, and his Lady. In this room are four large pieces of tapestry, brought from Ripon Abbey. In 1770, while clearing the cellar, a draw-well was discovered, 145 feet deep, and cut through solid rock. The great tower of the castle commands an extensive sea and land prospect. Opposite to Bambrough are the Farn Isles, abounding with sea-fowl of various kinds. It was here that Grace Darling was instrumental in saving the people wrecked in the Rothesay Castle steamer.

BERWICK-UPON-TWEED is situated upon a gentle declivity close by the German Ocean, on the north side of the mouth of the river Tweed. It is a well-built town. and is surrounded by walls in a regular style of fortification. It contains several churches and chapels, schools, banks, &c. 2 M.P. Pop. 1861, 13,265. It is governed by a mayor, aldermen, &c. The trade of the port is considerable, and it has railway communication with all parts of the kingdom. Berwick occupies a prominent place in the history of the Border wars, and has been often taken and retaken both by the Scots and English. It was finally ceded to the English in 1482, and, since then, has remained subject to the laws of England, though forming, politically, a distinct territory. Its castle, so celebrated in the early history of these kingdoms, is now a shapeless ruin.

Near Berwick is Lindisfarne, or the Holy Island, once the seat of a bishopric, and containing the ruins of an ancient monastery.

CXXXV. FROM NEWCASTLE TO COLDSTREAM THROUGH WOOLER, 60½ Miles.

ON RIGHT FROM NEWC.	From Coldstr.		From Newcas.	ON LEFT FROM NEWC.
	45¾	From Newcastle to MORPETH (p. 394.)	14¾	
Causey Park. Linden Hall, C. Bigge, Esq.	39¼	Longhorsley.	21¼	Todburn Park.
Felton Hall, T. Riddell, Esq.	35¼	cr. river Coquet.	24¼	Brinkburn Abbey, which was founded for Black Canons in the time of Henry I. The shell of the church is still very entire.
		Weldon Bridge.		5¾ miles distant is Rothbury, delightfully situated in a retired spot on the banks of the Coquet. The church is a very ancient building, and contains an antiquated font and several monuments. On the opposite side of the river is Whitton Tower, now the rectory. The living is one of the richest in the kingdom.
	35½	Low Framlington.	25	
Swarland Hall.	34½	Long Framlington.	26	
Crossing Rimside Moor you have a view of Alnwick tower in the distance.				Lorbottle. Calally Castle, E. J. Clavering, Esq.
3 miles distant Broome Park, W. Burrell, Esq., and Lemmington Hall.		Bridge of Alne.		1 mile distant Eslington, Lord Ravensworth, beyond which is Collingwood House.
	26½	cr. river Alne.	34	¾ m. distant is the village of Whittingham, and north of it the small town of Glanton.
Shawdon Hall.	24¾	Glanton.	35¾	Glanton Pike House.

ON RIGHT FROM NEWC.	From Coldstr.		From Newcas.	ON LEFT FROM NEWC.
Percy's Cross was erected in memory of Sir Ralph Percy, who was slain here by Lord Montacute in a severe skirmish in 1463 before the battle of Hexham.	21½	Percy's Cross.	39	
Chillingham Castle (Earl of Tankerville) famous for the breed of wild cattle preserved here.	15¾	Woolerhaugh Head.	44¾	Roddam Hall, W. Roddam, Esq.
		cr. Wooler Water.		Earle, C. Selby, Esq.
Lilburn Tower, E. Collingwood, Esq. Fowberry Tower, Sir F. Blake, Bart. Weetwood, Rev. L. S. Orde.	14	WOOLER.	46½	The church of Wooler is neat, and the town has also several chapels. There are some entrenchments and cairns near the town, and the thick walls of an ancient tower. About 1 mile distant is a hill called Humbledon Heugh, on the top of which there is a circular entrenchment with a large cairn. Pop. of par. 1697
Ewart Park, Sir Horace St Paul, Bart.	11¼	Akeld.	49¼	
		cr. river Glen.		
Ford Castle, Marquis of Waterford. Etal Hall, Earl of Glasgow.	8¼	Millfield.	52¼	Near Milfield is Flodden Field, where the celebrated battle was fought between James IV. of Scotland and the Earl of Surry, A.D. 1513, in which the former was defeated and slain.
Pallinsburn House.	5½	Pallinsburn.	55¼	
3 m. distant Tilmouth House and Twizel Castle, Sir F. Blake, Bart.	1¼	Cornhill.	59¼	
		cr. river Tweed, and enter Scotland.		
Lennel House, Earl of Haddington, and beyond, The Hirsel, Earl of Home.		COLDSTREAM.	60½	Lees, Sir John Marjoribanks, Bart.

COLDSTREAM, occupying a level and elevated situation on the north bank of the Tweed, crossed here by a handsome bridge. The population of the town was, in 1861, 1834. In consequence of its proximity to England, Coldstream, like Gretna Green, is celebrated for its irregular marriages. General Monk resided in Coldstream during the winter of 1659-60, before he marched into England to restore Charles II., and here he raised a regiment now well known as the Coldstream Guards. On the bank of the Tweed, to the west of the town, is Lees, the beautiful seat of Sir John Marjoribanks, Bart., and on the north-west is Hirsel, the seat of the Earl of Home. About a mile and a half to the east of the town are the ruins of Lennel Church, which was the name of the parish before Coldstream existed. Near it is Lennel House (Earl of Haddington), in which the venerable Patrick Brydone, author of "Travels in Sicily and Malta," spent the latter years of his long life.* Following the course of the river, we come to Tilmouth, where the Till, a narrow, sullen, deep, dark,

* There are two roads from Coldstream to Berwick, one along the north bank and one along the south bank of the Tweed. The latter is the more interesting, and is generally preferred.

and slow stream, flows into the Tweed. On its banks stands Twizel Castle (Sir Francis Blake, Bart.) Beneath the Castle the ancient bridge is still standing by which the English crossed the Till before the battle of Flodden.* The glen is romantic and delightful, with steep banks on each side, covered with copsewood. On the opposite bank of the Tweed is Milne-Graden (David Milne, Esq.), once the seat of the Kerrs of Graden, and, at an earlier period, the residence of the chief of a border clan, known by the name of Graden. A few miles eastward is Ladykirk, nine miles from Berwick. Near this is Ladykirk, the seat of D. Robertson, Esq. The church of this parish is an ancient Gothic building, said to have been erected by James IV., in consequence of a vow made to the Virgin, when he found himself in great danger while fording the Tweed in this neighbourhood. By this ford the English and Scottish armies made most of their mutual invasions. In the adjacent field, called Holywell Haugh, Edward I. met the Scottish nobility, to settle the dispute between Bruce and Balliol, relative to the Scotch crown. On the opposite bank of the Tweed stands the celebrated castle of Norham. The description of this ancient fortress, in the poem of Marmion, is too well known to require quotation here. The extent of its ruins, as well as its historical importance, shows it to have been a place of magnificence as well as strength. In 1164, it was almost rebuilt by Hugh Pudsey, Bishop of Durham, who added a huge keep or donjon. After 1174 it seems to have been chiefly garrisoned by the King, and considered as a royal fortress. It was the residence of Edward I. when umpire on the claims of Bruce and Balliol to the Scottish throne. It was repeatedly taken and retaken during the wars between England and Scotland. The ruins of the castle are at present considerable as well as picturesque. They consist of a large shattered tower, with many vaults and fragments of other edifices enclosed within an outward wall of great circuit. Two miles from Norham are the ruins of Dudhoe Castle.

* ——————— "they crossed
The Till, by Twisel Bridge.
High sight it is, and haughty, while
They dive into the deep defile;
Beneath the cavern'd cliff they fall,
Beneath the castle's airy wall.
By rock, by oak, by hawthorn tree,
Troop after troop are disappearing;
Troop after troop their banners rearing,
Upon the eastern bank you see,
Still pouring down the rocky den,
Where flows the sullen Till,
And, rising from the dim wood glen
Standards on standards, men on men,
In slow succession still,
And sweeping o'er the Gothic arch,
And pressing on in ceaseless march,
To gain the opposing hill."

Marmion, c. vi.

ON RIGHT FROM NEWC.	From Edinb.		From Newcas.	ON LEFT FROM NEWC.
				Fenham Hall.
Woolsington, M. Bell, Esq.	98¾	Woolsington.	4½	
	95¾	Ponteland.	7½	2½ m. distant, Dissington. E. Collingwood, Esq.
		cr. the river Pont.		
Kirchley Hall, S. C. H. Ogle, Esq.	93¼	Higham Dykes.	10	Milbourne Hall.
	90	Belsay Castle.	13¼	Belsay Castle, Sir C. M. L Monck, Bart.
Bolam House, Lord Decies.	87¾	Low House.	15½	2 m. distant Capheaton, Sir J. E. Swinburne, Bart.
		cr. river Wansbeck.		
	84¾	Wallington.	18½	Wallington, Sir W. C. Trevelyan, Bart. Little Harle Tower, and Kirk Harle, Sir L. Loraine, Bart
2 miles distant is Rothley Castle, built for effect by the late Sir E. Blackett, Bart.	81	Division of the road. (To Morpeth, 12¼ miles; to Alnwick, 22¼.)	22¼	
Farther to the right is Longwitton Hall, J. M. Fenwicke, Esq.; Netherwitton, and Nunnykirk, C. W. Orde, Esq.	74½	Elsdon.	28¾	
	69¼	Ellishaw.	34	To Hexham, 23 miles.
	62¼	Byrness.	41	Corbridge, 22 miles.
	55¼	Carter Fell Turnpike.	48	
Edgerston, W. Oliver Rutherfurd, Esq.		Enter Scotland.		
	45	JEDBURGH.*	58¼	
	6¼	DALKEITH.	97	
		EDINBURGH.	103¼	

CXXXVII. LONDON TO SEDBERGH, BY BOROUGHBRIDGE, LEYBURN, AND ASKRIGG, 266½ Miles.

ON RIGHT FROM LOND.	From Sedber.		From London.	ON LEFT FROM LOND.
Newby Park.	53½	From Hicks's Hall, to York Gate Inn (p. 371.)	213	Norton Conyers, Sir B. R. Graham, Bart.
	56½	Nosterfield.	220	Sleningford Hall, J. Dalton, Esq.
		cr. the river Ure.		
	43	MASHAM.	223½	Swinton Park.
3 m. distant Thorp Perrow Park, M. Milbanke, Esq.; 2 m. distant, Clifton Castle; and beyond it, Thornton Hall, Sir C. Dodsworth, Bart.	40½	Nether Ellington.	226	
	38	Jerveaux Abbey.	228½	Jerveaux Abbey, a very fine ruin, is the property of the Marquis of Ailesbury.

* For a description of the road from Jedburgh to Edinburgh, see Black's Picturesque Tourist.

ON RIGHT FROM LOND.	From Sedber.		From London.	ON LEFT FROM LOND.
	36	East Witton.	230½	
	35½	Cover Bridge.	231½	1 mile distant is Middleham, remarkable for the ruins of its castle and the beauty of the surrounding scenery. Middleham Castle was the residence of the celebrated Earl of Warwick, the king-maker.
		cr. river Cover.		
Danby Park, S. T. Scroope, Esq.	35¼	Ulshaw Bridge.	231¼	
		cr. the river Ure.		
	33½	Spennithorne.	233	
1½ m. distant, Burton, Constable; farther to the right, Haukwell Hall; and in the distance, Hornby Castle (Duke of Leeds.)	32½	Harmby.	234	
	31½	LEYBURN. This town has been entirely rebuilt within these few years. On the west side is a delightful terrace-promenade about a mile long, and commanding a fine prospect. Thence there is an opening into a wood called Queen's Gap, through which it is said Mary Queen of Scots passed when she attempted to escape from Bolton Castle. There are several chapels in the town.	235	Leyburn Hall. At a short distance is Wensley Dale, a romantic and picturesque spot, watered by the Ure, and abounding in cascades. On the north side of the dale stands Bolton Castle, in which the Queen of Scots was confined two years. The remains of this fortress are very considerable, and the walls are of great strength. The surrounding scenery is very beautiful Here is also Bolton Hall, (Lord Bolton,) an elegant modern mansion.
To Richmond, 10 m.	30½	Wensley.	236	Swinethwaite Hall.
Elm House.	27	Redmire.	239½	
To Reeth, 6 miles, a small market town, which is situated on an eminence, and commands very beautiful views. Pop. 1343.	24½	Carperby.	242	Nappa Hall.
	20	ASKRIGG has an old church, grammar school, and alms houses. In the vicinity of this place, and of Aysgarth, Carperby, and Bishop's Dale are the celebrated falls of the Ure.	246½	The fall at Heaning, about 2 miles from Aysgarth, is remarkably beautiful.
Hardrow Force is situated about ¼ of a mile from the Hawes. The descent by a rude stair leads into a natural amphitheatre, the walls being perfectly perpendicular and of mountain limestone. The chasm is 100 feet deep, of like breadth, and in length about 400, though from its assuming a curved form towards the outer extremity, when it opens into the face of the hill, the visitor seems enclosed in a huge pit. The fall is from the upper extremity of the chasm, and not unfrequently resembles a crystal pillar 100 feet high, supporting the little wooden bridge, and groups of larches above it. This is undoubtedly one of the most wonderful waterfalls in the kingdom.	14½	Hardrow. The waterfall at this place deserves particular notice.	252	To Lancaster, 38½ m. To Hawes, ¾ mile.
	11½	Thwaite Bridge.	255	
		cr. the river Ure.		
	6½	Little Town.	260	
	5½	Smorthwaite Bridge.	261	
	3½	Morthwaite Bridge.	263	
		SEDBERGH. About 5 miles from Sedbergh is Dent, situated in the beautiful secluded vale of Dent Dale. The inhabitants are employed in knitting stockings. Sedbergh has several chapels and a free grammar school.	266½	Ingmire Hall, T. S. Upton, Esq.

ON RIGHT FROM LOND.	From Durham.		From London.	ON LEFT FROM LOND.
To Darlington, 8 miles.	26	From Hicks's Hall to Scotch Corner, (p. 371.)	232½	To Barnard Castle, 15 miles.
Middleton Lodge, and beyond, Halnaby Hall. Sir J. R. Milbanke, Bart.		cross river Tees, and enter Durham.		Aske Hall (Earl of Zetland) 1 m. Stanwick Park, D. of Northumberland, 3 m. Carlton Hall and Forcett Park.
To Darlington, 6 miles. 2 m. dist. Walworth Castle.	19½	Pierse Bridge.	239	To Barnard Castle, 10 miles. Cliffe Hall.
Redworth House, R. Surtees, Esq. Brusselton Tower, a pleasure-house, commanding delightful views.	13	West Auckland.	245½	To Wolsingham, 11 m.; to Jedburgh by Witton-le-Wear, 76½ miles.
	10	BISHOP AUCKLAND.	248½	Auckland Castle, Bishop of Durham, and, in the distance, Witton Castle, Sir W. R. C. Chaytor, Bart.
Howlish Hall, and at Westerton a circular tower, erected as an observatory.		7 miles farther join the road from Darlington to Durham, (p. 386-87.)		
Croxdale Hall, G. Salvin, Esq. Windlestone Hall, Sir William Eden, Bart.	3½	Sunderland Bridge.	255	2 miles distant, Whitworth Pa., R. D. Shafto, Esq., and near it Brancepeth Castle, Viscount Boyne.
		cr. the river Wear.		Burn Hall. Oswald House.
		DURHAM (see p. 389).	258½	
		OR From Hicks's Hall to		
	19½	Pierse Bridge as above,	239	
	14¼	Heighington.	244¼	
	10½	Eldon.	248	
		Merrington.		From Merrington church there is a very extensive and beautiful prospect.
		2½ miles farther join the road to Durham through Bishop Auckland.		
	3½	Sunderland Bridge.	255	
		cross river Wear.		
		DURHAM, (see p. 389).	258½	

Ten miles from Pierse Bridge is BARNARD CASTLE on the River Tees. The name of this town was derived from a castle which was erected here shortly after the Norman Conquest by Barnard, son of Guy Balliol, who came into England with the Conqueror. The extensive ruins of this fortress are situated on the summit of a rocky eminence, and include within their area a circumference of upwards of six acres. Balliol's Tower, at the western extremity of the building, is a round tower of great size and antiquity, and remarkable for the curious construction of its vaulted roof. The prospect from the top of the tower commands a rich and magnificent view of the wooded valley of the Tees. Upon the forfeiture of John Balliol, the first King of Scotland of that family, this fortress was seized by Edward I. It subsequently passed into the possession of the Beauchamps, Earls of Warwick, the Staffords, Dukes of Buckingham, and ultimately of the Nevills, Earls of Westmorland. During the insurrection, in which the last representative of the last-mentioned family engaged with the Earl of Northumberland, against Queen Elizabeth, for the purpose of restoring the Roman Catholic faith, Barnard Castle was seized by Sir George Bowes, and held out for ten days against all the forces of the insurgents. (See Wordsworth's White Doe of Rylstone.) On the forfeiture of the Earl of Westmoreland, Barnard Castle reverted to the Crown, and was sold or leased to Car, Earl of Somerset, the guilty favourite of James I. It was afterwards granted to Sir Harry Vane the elder, and is now the property of his descendant, the Duke of Cleveland.* Barnard Castle is the scene of part of Sir Walter Scott's poem of Rokeby. The town of Barnard Castle has one of the largest corn-markets in the north of England. The inhabitants are chiefly employed in tanning, and in the manufacture of carpets, plaids, and stockings. Pop. 1851, 4357. Two miles from the town is a chalybeate spring.

Between two and three miles from Barnard Castle is Streatlam Castle (John Bowes, Esq.), situated in a secluded but romantic vale encircled by lofty and irregular hills. The park displays some rich natural scenery.

About five miles and a quarter from Barnard Castle is Staindrop, about a mile from which is Raby Castle, the fine old baronial mansion of the Duke of Cleveland. Raby Castle was the ancient seat of the Nevills, formerly one of the most powerful families in the kingdom. Camden states, that from this house sprung six Earls of Westmorland, two Earls of Salisbury and Warwick, an Earl of Kent, a Marquis of Montagu,† a Baron Ferrers of Oversley, Barons Latimer, Barons (now Earls of) Abergavenny, one Queen, five Duchesses, besides Countesses and Baronesses, an Archbishop of York, and a great number of inferior gentlemen. The famous Earl of Warwick, the "King-maker," was of this house. The origin of the family of the Nevills is to be found in Saxon times. Canute gave Staindropshire to the church of Durham, and the prior and convent granted the same district to Dolphin, son of Uchtred, and Raby soon became the seat of the honour. The grandson of Dolphin married Isabel, sister and heiress of Henry de Nevill, and heiress of the castles and lordships of Sheriff Hutton and Brancepeth, and a whole train of estates and manors dependent on those two great fees. The family adopted thenceforth the surname of Nevill.‡ Raby is said to have been built by John Lord Nevill, son of Ralph Lord Nevill, who was one of the leaders at the

* See Appendix to Rokeby, Note A.

† Camden might have added a Duke of Bedford to the list. The son of the Marquis of Montagu was created a Duke by this title, but was deprived by Edward IV. of his dukedom *on account of his poverty and inability to maintain the dignity.*

‡ Howitt's Visit to Remarkable Places, 2d Series, p. 231-261.

battle of Nevill's Cross. His successor was created Earl of Westmorland by Richard II., and became brother-in-law to Henry IV. This mighty line was destroyed in the reign of Queen Elizabeth, in consequence of the part which the sixth and last Earl took in the disastrous "Rising of the North." Their immense estates were confiscated, and the Earl was forced to flee into Scotland, where he found a safe retreat with Kerr of Ferniherst. He afterwards escaped into Flanders, where he entered as a colonel into the Spanish service, and protracted a life of unavailing regret to extreme old age. Brancepeth was sold by the Crown in the reign of Charles I., and, after passing through several hands, is now the property of Viscount Boyne. Raby Castle and estates were sold to Sir Harry Vane, and have descended from him in a direct line to their present possessor, the Duke of Cleveland. The first view of this fine old mansion impresses the spectator with a strong feeling of the old feudal grandeur. Pennant says of it, "It is a noble massy building of its kind, uninjured by any modern strokes inconsistent with the general taste of the edifice, but simply magnificent it strikes by its magnitude and that idea of strength and command naturally annexed to the view of vast walls, lofty towers, battlements, and the surrounding outworks of an old baron's residence. The building itself, besides the courts, covers an acre of land." The interior is fitted up with all the conveniences and elegancies of modern refinement. The old baronial hall, which forms one side of the square of the inner area, is of the grandest proportions, 90 feet in length, 36 in breadth, and 34 in height. The roof is flat and made of wood; the joints ornamented with escutcheons of the family of the Nevills. Here, it is said, assembled in their time 700 knights who held of that family. The kitchen, which forms a lofty square of 30 feet, is a singular relic of the ancient baronial time. The old tower of Bertram Bulmer and Clifford tower command extensive and splendid prospects. The park is noble.

Bishop Auckland is a small but neat town on an eminence, bounded on the south-east by the river Gaunless, and on the north by the Wear. Auckland Castle, the palace of the Bishop of Durham, stands on a hill above the town, and is a splendid but irregular pile, erected at different periods. Its situation, amidst hills and green sloping lawns, rocks, woods, and water, is very beautiful, and was selected by the celebrated Bishop Anthony Beck, who built here a fine castellated manor-house, which, at the time of the Commonwealth, fell into the hands of Sir Arthur Haselrigge. He destroyed the old buildings, and erected a splendid house here, which, however, on the Restoration, was again pulled down by Bishop Cosin. The present edifice has been raised by his successors to its present condition and greatness. It contains some noble rooms, adorned with several fine paintings; and in the chapel is a monument by Nollekens, in memory of Bishop Trevor, and a picture of the resurrection by Sir Joshua Reynolds. The town has several mines in its neighbourhood, and is connected by railways with all parts of the kingdom. It has also several chapels, free schools, &c. Pop. 6480.

Brancepeth Castle, the property of Viscount Boyne in right of his wife, is situated between Bishop Auckland and Durham, at the distance of about four miles from the latter. This stately building was erected by the family of the Bulmers, most probably during the early part of Stephen's reign. It is supposed to have derived its name, The Brawn's path, from a huge brawn or boar, said to have once haunted this spot, and to have been killed by one of its lords. The castle was restored or rebuilt by the grandfather of the present possessor's wife, but still retains much of its original appearance and massive strength, and is one of the noblest mansions in the country. In the entrance-hall there is a suit of armour, richly inlaid with gold, said to be that of David Bruce, King of Scotland, taken at Nevill's Cross. The baron's hall contains a fine collection of armour and arms of all sorts. The rooms are very fine, and adorned with some good paintings. The country around is rich and pleasant. In the church are various monuments of the Nevills.

CXXXIX. LONDON TO ALSTON THROUGH WOLSINGHAM, STANHOPE, AND ST. JOHN'S WEARDALE, 282¾ Miles.

ON RIGHT FROM LOND.	From Alston.		From London.	ON LEFT FROM LOND.
To Bishop Auckland, 3 miles.	37¼	From Hicks's Hall to WEST AUCKLAND (p. 404.) cr. the river Wear.	245½	To Barnard Castle, 11¼ miles.
Witton Castle, Sir William R. C. Chaytor, Bart.	32¾	Witton le Wear.	250	3 m. distant, across the Wear, Hopeland House.
Witton Hall. Bishop Auckland Railway.	30¾	Horden Head.	252	
To Durham, 11¾ m.	29¾	Harperley Lane Head.	253	Harperley Park, G. H. Wilkinson, Esq.
Wolsingham is situated on a point of land formed by the confluence of the Wear and Weserow. At a short distance are the remains of a spacious structure, supposed to be part of a monastery founded by Henry de Pudsey. Above the town is an eminence commanding an extensive and delightful prospect. One mile from Wolsingham is Bishopoak, and, farther to the right, Fawnlees.	26¼	WOLSINGHAM.	256½	
	23¼	Frosterley.	259½	Stanhope, a small town on the Wear, chiefly inhabited by miners. Near it, to the west, on an eminence called Castle Hill, are the remains of an ancient fortress; and on the north is a cavern abounding with stalactites. In the vicinity is Stanhope Castle. The Stanhope and Tyne Railway connects this town with South Shields, &c. The living is a very rich one.
	20½	STANHOPE.	262½	
	18	East Gate.	264¾	
	14¾	West Gate.	268	
	13¼	St. John's Weardale.	269½	
		Enter Cumberland.		
	6¼	Kilhope Cross.	276½	
		ALSTON MOOR.	282¾	

Alston stands on an eminence near the Tyne, over which is an ancient bridge. The surrounding country is bleak and desolate. In the vicinity are rich and extensive lead mines, belonging to Greenwich hospital. Eleven and a quarter miles from Alston is Haltwhistle (Northumberland), on the Newcastle and Carlisle Railway (see p. 266), an ancient town containing two old border towers,—a church, adorned with old monuments, and a remarkable oval mound, called Castle Banks, in the centre of which is a fine spring. Two and a half miles from Haltwhistle is Fetherstone Castle, a noble edifice belonging to J. G. F. Wallace, Esq.; and about three miles north-west of the town are the remains of Thirlwall Castle, formerly one of the boundary fortresses between England and Scotland.

CXL. LONDON TO SUNDERLAND BY BOROUGHBRIDGE, THIRSK, YARM, AND STOCKTON, 268½ Miles.

ON RIGHT FROM LOND.	From Sunder.		From London.	ON LEFT FROM LOND.
	62½	From Hicks's Hall to BOROUGHBRIDGE, by Ware and Royston, (p. 385) is 202 miles; by Baldock and Biggleswade (p. 371.)	206	
To Easingwold, 10 m.		cr. river Ure.		To Carlisle, 95½ miles.
	58½	Dishforth.	210	
		cr. river Swale.		
	56	Topcliffe.	212½	Newby Park. To Northallerton, 12½ miles.
Thirkeley Park. To York, 23¾ miles; to Helmsley Blackmoor, 13 m.; Kirkby Moorside, 18½ m.; Pickering 26½ m.	51	THIRSK (p. 380.)	217½	To Ripon, 12¾ m.; Northallerton, 8¾ m.
	50	South Kilvington.	218½	
	49	North Kilvington.	219½	
	47	Knayton.	221½	Brawith Hall.
	46	Barrowby.	222½	
Silton.	45	Leake.	223½	2 miles distant, Crossby Cote.
Thimbleby Lodge. Arncliffe Hall. To Stokesley, 7½ miles;	39	Tontine Inn.	229½	Harlsey Hall, J. C. Maynard, Esq.

ON RIGHT FROM LOND.	From Sunder.		From London.	ON LEFT FROM LOND.
thence to Guisborough, 7½ miles.*				
	37	Trenholme.	231½	Rounton Grange.
Rudby.	34½	Crathorne.	234	
	33	Kirkleavington.	235½	
	31	YARM. (See p. 411.)	237½	To Northallerton, 17 miles; Richmond, 21 m.
The Fryerage, T. Meynell, Esq.				
		☞ cr. River Tees and enter Durham.		
Two miles dist. Acklam Hall, T. Hustler, Esq.	27	STOCKTON. (See p. 411.)	241½	
	25½	Norton Inn.	243	To Thorpe, 3¾ miles; thence to Layton, 2½ miles; thence to Sedgefield, 1¾ mile.
Billingham Grange.	24½	Billingham.	244	
	22½	Wolviston.	246	Wynyard Park, Earl Vane.
To Greatham, 2½ m.; thence to Stranton, 3 miles; thence to Hartlepool, 2 miles.	19	Red Lion Inn.	249½	To Hartlepool, by Hart, 5½ miles.
Elwick Hall.	16	Sheraton.	252½	
		Hartlepool Railway.		
Castle Eden, R. Burdon, Esq., a spacious castellated edifice, beautifully situated on the summit of a wooded precipice, forming the southern boundary of the romantic defile called Castle Eden Dean.	13	Castle Eden Inn.	255½	
	12	Shotton.	256½	
	9	Easington.	259½	Near Bishop Wearmouth are, Thornhill—High Barns — Low Barns — Ford — Low Pallion—and across the Wear, Hilton Place and Hilton Castle (J. Bowes, Esq.), formerly the baronial residence of the Hiltons, who possessed the manor from the time of Athelstan till the year 1746. It stands in a charming vale on the north side of the river Wear.
	7½	Cold Hesledon.	261	
	6½	Dalton le Dale.	262	
Seaham Hall, Earl Vane.	3½	Ryhope.	265	
The Grange—Salem House—Middle Hendon—Building Hill—Hendon—Hendon Lodge.	¾	Bishop Wearmouth.	267¾	
		SUNDERLAND. (See p. 412.)	268½	

* Guisborough was the first place in England where alum-works were erected. Here are the ruins of an abbey which was once the burial-place of the nobility of the surrounding country. One mile south-east is a mineral spring. Four miles north-west is a lofty hill, commanding a very extensive prospect; and four miles south-west is Roseberry Topping, a peaked mountain, 1022 feet high, which also commands fine views. The country around Guisborough is very beautiful. Three miles distant are Wilton Castle (Sir John H. Lowther, Bart.) and Skelton Castle, near which is Upleatham Hall. Five miles distant is Kirkleatham Hall, surrounded by tasteful grounds. Near the hall is Turner's Hospital, founded, in 1676, by Sir W. Turner for 40 poor people. In Kirkleatham church is a splendid mausoleum. Beyond, is Marsk Hall, Earl of Zetland. Seven miles from Guisborough are Redcar and Coatham, two small villages much frequented for sea-bathing. The sands extend eight miles.

ON RIGHT FROM LOND.	From Tynem.		From London.	ON LEFT FROM LOND.
	21¼	From Hicks's Hall to Durham by Ware, (p. 387), is 255¼ miles, by Baldock, (p. 370).	259¼	
	18¾	Blue House.	261¾	
Belmont, and 2 miles distant, Elemore Hall.	17¼	Rainton Pitt Houses.	263¼	
Great Eppleton, and Little Eppleton, and Hetton Hall.	16¼	East Rainton.	264¼	2 miles distant Murton House.
	14½	Houghton le Spring.	266	2 miles distant, South Biddick.
1½ mile distant Tunstall Lodge.	12	East Harrington.	268½	High Barns and Low Barns.
	9	Bishop Wearmouth.	271½	Ford and Pallion House.
Thornhill and the Grange.	8¼	SUNDERLAND (see p. 412). The Iron Bridge. cross river Wear.	272¼	
	8¼	Monk Wearmouth.	272¼	
	7¼	Fulwell Inn.	273	
Whitburn, Sir Hedworth Williamson, Bart.	5½	Cleadon.	275	
Cleadon House and West House.	3¾	Harton.	276¾	Biddick House.
	3	Westoe.	277½	
	2	SOUTH SHIELDS (see p. 413).	278½	Hebburn Hall, C. Ellison, Esq.
		Cross the river Tyne by the Ferry.		
	1½	NORTH SHIELDS (see p. 414). (*Northumberland*).	279	
		TYNEMOUTH (see p. 414).	280½	Tynemouth Lodge, and, 2 miles distant, Whitley Park.
		OR,		
	9	From Hicks's Hall to Bishop Wearmouth.	267¾	
		Thence to Tynemouth as above.	276¾	
		OR,		
	9	From Hicks's Hall to NEWCASTLE-UPON-TYNE, (p. 387).	273¾	
	8	Useborn.	274¾	
	7	Byker.	275¾	
	2½	Chirton.	280¼	Heaton Hall, beyond which is Benton House, and Little Benton.
Chirton House.	1½	NORTH SHIELDS (see p. 414).	281¼	
		TYNEMOUTH (see p. 414).	282¾	

YARM stands on a narrow neck of land, washed on three sides by the river Tees. Owing to the extreme lowness of its situation, it has suffered severely by inundations. The town carries on a small trade in corn, bacon, &c. The church has a fine stained glass window. Pop. of par. 1401

STOCKTON is situated on the left bank of the Tees. It is 242 miles from the General Post-Office, London, by the coach road through Barnet, Biggleswade, Stamford, &c., and 276 miles by railway through Rugby, Leicester, Derby, York, and Darlington. It is one of the handsomest and cleanest towns in the north of England. The bishops of Durham had, from an early period, a residence here, where Bishop Morton took refuge when the army of Charles I. was defeated by the Scots in the skirmish at Newburn, (A.D. 1640.) It was demolished by order of the Parliament in 1652. The traces of the moat and embankment still mark the site. Stockton possesses several churches, chapels, and meeting-houses, a town-hall, custom-house, a mechanics' institution, grammar, blue-coat, charity, and national schools; a news-room, assembly rooms, billiard-rooms, and a small theatre. There is a race-course on the opposite side of the Tees. The principal manufacture of the town is that of engines and of linen and sail-cloth. There are also iron and brass foundries, breweries, and some corn-mills, and some ship-building, rope and sail making, and yarn and worsted spinning are carried on. There are extensive coal-works and some brick-yards near the town, and a salmon and other fisheries in the Tees. The harbour of Stockton is formed by the river Tees. A considerable trade is carried on with the Baltic, Holland, Hamburgh, and British America; and coastwise, with London, Leith, Hull, Sunderland, &c. Customs revenue of Stockton, 1857, £86,689. Communication is maintained with London and Newcastle by steam-packets, and with Darlington, York, Manchester, Birmingham, London, &c., by railway. The Stockton, Darlington, and Wear Valley Railway has a terminus on the quay. It is the first railway on which locomotive engines were employed. A branch to Middlesbrough, a port in Yorkshire, where the Stockton steamers stop, parts from the main line to the south of the town of Stockton, and is carried over the Tees by a suspension bridge. This railway extends from the Teesmouth by Billingham, Whitton, Preston le Skerne, and West Auckland, to the coal-fields of Witton and Cockfield, a distance of 30 miles. Pop. 13,357.

Four and a half miles from Stockton is Wynyard Park, the seat of Earl Vane.

Twelve miles from Stockton is HARTLEPOOL, situated on a small peninsula jutting out into the sea, a few miles from the mouth of the Tees. This peninsula, which is one of the most marked features of the eastern coast, is partly formed by a pool called the Slake, dry at low water. The name of the town was derived from Hart-le-pol, the Pool or Slake of Hart. A monastery, which is mentioned by Bede, was founded here at a very early period. St Hilda was the abbess of it. Mention is made of Hartlepool as a harbour of some consequence so early as 1171. In the thirteenth century it belonged to the Bruces of Annandale, in Scotland, the progenitors of the royal family of that name The town was erected into a borough by John, A.D. 1200. After Bruce ascended the Scottish throne, his English possessions were forfeited, and Hartlepool was granted to the Cliffords, in whose possession it long remained. It suffered severely from the Scots in 1312, and again in 1315, a year after the battle of Bannockburn. It was seized by the insurgents in the great Northern Rebellion in the reign of Elizabeth. During the civil wars it was taken by the Scottish army in 1644, and retained by them till 1647.

Hartlepool was fortified during the course of the thirteenth century by walls, which inclosed it on every side except on the east, where the steep cliffs rendered this unnecessary. A considerable part of these walls still remains, which only fifty years ago exhibited an almost perfect specimen of the defences of former times. The old haven is now entirely disused. The present harbour, which is formed by a pier run out on the south side of the town, is very accessible in every wind to laden vessels under 100 tons, and is well lighted. The town has greatly increased of late, and the formation of the railway and of wet docks will add much to its prosperity. It is much resorted to for sea-bathing. The inhabitants are chiefly engaged in the coasting trade and fishing.

Hartlepool possesses a church, a large and curious building, chiefly in the early English style, several meeting-houses, and town-hall. There was formerly a monastery of Franciscan friars here. Out of the rocks on the shore of the peninsula the sea has excavated several caverns, which may be explored for nearly fifty yards. There are two chalybeate springs near the town.

The Rev. Wm. Romaine was a native of Hartlepool. Pop. 12,603.

HOUGHTON-LE-SPRING is situated at the head of a fine vale, sheltered on the north and east by limestone hills. The church is a spacious building in the form of a cross; some portions of it are in the early English, and some in the decorated style. It contains the monument of Bernard Gilpin, "the Apostle of the North," and one of the most pious of the English Reformers, who was for some time Rector of Houghton. On the north-east of the church-yard is the grammar school, which he founded with the aid of some friends. Pop. 1861, 3824 The mansion of Houghton Hall is supposed to have been built in the reign of Elizabeth or James.

SUNDERLAND is situated on the south side of the mouth of the Wear. The Parliamentary borough comprehends, besides the parish of Sunderland, the townships of Bishop Wearmouth and Bishop Wearmouth Pans, Monkwearmouth, and Monkwearmouth Shore, and Southwick, on the north side of the river.

Monkwearmouth was a place of some note in the Anglo-Saxon and Anglo-Norman period. A monastery was founded here in the year 674, which was destroyed by the Danes in the ninth century. It was restored after the Conquest, but was soon after reduced to be a cell of the monastery of St Cuthbert. Bishop Wearmouth received a charter from Hugh Pudsey in the twelfth century, and, in 1634, it received a new charter of incorporation from Bishop Morton. During the civil wars it was garrisoned for the Parliament. The town was chiefly indebted for its earlier prosperity to the coal trade. The river is crossed by an iron bridge of one arch, erected near the close of last century at a cost of £61,800. The span of the arch is 236 feet, and the height above low water 94 feet to the centre of the arch, so that ships of 300 tons pass under it by lowering their top gallant masts. The harbour at Sunderland is formed by two piers on the north and south sides of the river. The new docks, completed in 1850, enclosing eighteen acres, add greatly to the accommodation. Near the termination of the north pier, a light-house was built in 1802. However, in 1841, an alarming breach took place in that pier, and the light-house was, by the ingenuity of Mr. Murray, engineer, moved in an entire state nearly 150 yards, to the eastern extremity of the new pier. There is not the slightest appearance of crack in any part of the building, though the gross weight moved was 338 tons. The principal manufactures of Sunderland are of bottle and flint-glass, anchors, chain-cables, &c., and ship-building and rope-making are carried on to a very great extent. Brick-making, coal-mining, and quarrying grindstones, also afford extensive employment in the neighbourhood. This port possessed in the beginning of 1851, 77 sailing vessels, under, and 894 over, 50 tons, besides 32 small steamers. Total tonnage, 207,804 tons. Upwards of 500 vessels are engaged in the coal trade, which is very extensive. Lime, glass, and grindstones are also exported. Timber and iron are imported from the Baltic; butter, cheese, and flax, from Holland, &c. Total customs revenue, 1861, £95,734. A considerable fishery is carried on. The borough contains numerous churches, chapels, and meeting-houses; a custom-house, mechanics' institute, and an exchange, several banks, a theatre, and assembly rooms. On the town moor are extensive barracks. Near the town, on the coast, is a chalybeate spring. A quarter of a mile above the bridge is the celebrated Pemberton shaft, 273 fathoms deep. Two M.P. Pop. of parl. borough 1861, 85,797. By means of railways Sunderland is connected with all parts of the kingdom.

South Shields is situated on the south bank of the Tyne, near its mouth. It derived its name and origin from the fishermen of the Tyne, who built here along the shore sheds, locally termed "sheels," or "shields," to defend themselves from the weather. The Romans had a station at South Shields, and various Roman antiquities have been found here. The principal trade of the town is in coal, great quantities of which are shipped here. Ship-building is carried on with great activity, and there are very extensive glass-works, a pottery, and manufactures of soda and alum, breweries, and rope-walks. South Shields was once noted for the manufacture of salt, but that branch of industry is now nearly extinct. The church of St. Hilda contains several monuments, and a model of the life-boat, presented by Mr. Greathead, the inventor, an inhabitant of this town. South Shields has numerous churches and chapels, banks, and charitable institutions, a mechanics' institute, a theatre, &c. The borough is in the parish of Jarrow, famous for its Benedictine monastery, of which some remains still exist. The original building was destroyed in the invasion of William the Conqueror, but was subsequently repaired, and ultimately became a cell to Durham. Some remains of the ancient conventual church are embodied in the present church of Jarrow, and in the vestry there is preserved a chair which is said to have been the seat of the venerable Bede, who, born near it, spent the greater part of his life in the monastery of Jarrow. His well is still shown. South Shields was incorporated 1850. One M.P. Pop. of parl. bor. 35,239.

South Shields is connected by railway with all parts of the empire.

NORTH SHIELDS extends about a mile along the north bank of the Tyne, opposite South Shields. It is a town of considerable antiquity, having arisen about the time of Edward I., under the protection of the prior of Tynemouth, who established a market, and formed a harbour; but in consequence of the opposition of the burgesses of Newcastle, who regarded the formation of this town as a violation of their charter, he was compelled to destroy the buildings he had erected. During the time of the Commonwealth an act was passed by Cromwell for the formation of quays, and the establishment of a market; but it was not till the eighteenth century that the restrictions upon the trade of the place were removed. North Shields possesses a spacious new church, and numerous chapels, a scientific and mechanics' institute, a subscription library, and a theatre. It is a railway station, and a place of very considerable trade, and exports great quantities of coals, chiefly to London, and the eastern coasts of England and Scotland. Ship-building and its kindred branches of manufacture are actively carried on. At the entrance of the town from the sea are two lighthouses, and near them is Clifford's Fort. It forms a part of the parl. borough of Tynemouth. Pop. of North Shields 9595.

TYNEMOUTH is a parliamentary borough and seaport at the mouth of the Tyne, where ships receive their cargoes from Newcastle. It has been supposed that the Romans had a post on the site of Tynemouth Castle. On the same site a religious house was afterwards erected, which was enclosed and fortified in the time of William the Conqueror. Here Malcolm III., King of Scotland, and his son Prince Edward were interred. It was twice besieged and taken, during the great civil war. Considerable remains still exist both of the priory and the castle. The priory church was used as the parish church until the time of Charles II., when a new church was built at North Shields. There are a lighthouse and some other modern buildings in the castle. Tynemouth is much frequented in the bathing season, and some good baths have recently been erected. The Marsden Rocks, a few miles from Tynemouth, are frequently visited by parties of pleasure. Tynemouth sends one M.P. Pop. of par. bor. 1861, 34,021. The parliamentary borough comprehends the township of Tynemouth, North Shields, Chirton, Preston, and Cullercoates.

Cullercoates is a small bathing town two miles from Tynemouth. Eight miles from Tynemouth is Seaton Delaval, formerly the seat of the Delavals, now the property of Lord Hastings. It was erected from designs by Sir John Vanbrugh, and was one of the finest mansions in Northumberland, but was unfortunately destroyed by fire in 1822. There is a mausoleum within the grounds, and the chapel, which is as old as the time of William the Conqueror, is one of the most complete and beautiful little pieces of antiquity in England.

CXLII. FROM LONDON TO KIRKBY MOORSIDE THROUGH HELMSLEY BLACKMOOR, 227¾ Miles.

ON RIGHT FROM LOND.	From Kirkby.		From London.	ON LEFT FROM LOND.
	28½	From Hicks's Hall to YORK (see p. 438).	199¼	
	24½	Wiggington.	203¼	
Sutton Hall.	20½	Sutton on the Forest.	207¼	
Stillington Hall. Brandsby Hall, F. Cholmeley, Esq.	17½	Stillington.	210¼	To Easingwold, 2½ m.
3 miles dist. Hovingham Hall. Helmsley is a small market-town on a declivity near the Rye. The inhabitants are employed	10½	Gilling.	217¼	Gilling Castle, C. Fairfax, Esq. and Newburgh Hall, Sir G. Wombwell, Bart.
in agriculture and the	9½	Oswaldkirk.	218¼	Oswaldkirk Hall.
linen manufacture. Here are the ruins of a castle which was taken by Fairfax in the civil war. The grounds of Duncombe Park, half a mile distant, are laid out with great taste, and command fine prospects. Four miles distant are the ruins of Rivaulx	7	Sproxton.	220¾	Duncombe Park, Lord Feversham, an elegant mansion, containing a fine collection of paintings. It was formerly called Helmsley, ("once proud Buckingham's delight"), and was the seat of the Villiers, Dukes of Buckingham.
		cr. river Rye.		
Abbey, founded in 1181 for Cistercian monks. The situation is one of remarkable beauty. Five	5½	HELMSLEY BLACKMOOR.	222¼	To Bilsdale, 9½ miles, thence to Kirkby, 3½ m., —thence to Stokesley, 2½ m.
miles from Helmsley are the ruins of Ryland Abbey.	3	Nawton.	224¾	
		KIRKBY MOORSIDE.	227¾	Kirkby Moorside is remarkable as the place where the last Duke of Buckingham of the Villiers family died miserably in 1687, as described in the well known lines of Pope.

CXLIII. LONDON TO WHITBY THROUGH BALDOCK, STAMFORD, GRANTHAM, DONCASTER, YORK, AND NEW MALTON, 246 Miles.

ON RIGHT FROM LOND.	From Whitby.		From London.	ON LEFT FROM LOND.
	46¾	From Hicks's Hall to York.	199¼	
Stockton. Sand Hutton, J. Walker, Esq.	39	Lobster Inn.	207	3 m. distant, Sheriff Hutton Park, L. Thompson, Esq., and ruins of the Castle.
Howsham Hall.	36	Spittle Bridge.	210	
	34½	Whitwell.	211½	
Hutton Lodge. Welham House, R. Bower, Esq. To Scarborough, 22¼ m. To Beverley, 28½ miles.	28¾	NEW MALTON, a well built town, on the Derwent, and the York and Scarborough Railway. It has been supposed to be the Roman Camelodunum. Here are the remains of an ancient castle, two churches, several meeting-houses, a theatre, and assembly rooms. The town carries on a large trade in corn, butter, and hams. Two M. P. Pop. 8072.	217¼	Castle Howard, the magnificent seat of the Earl of Carlisle, built from a design of Sir John Vanbrugh, on the site of the old castle of Hinderskelf, which was destroyed by an accidental fire. It is enriched with a splendid collection of paintings, statues, busts, &c. The grounds are beautiful and extensive.
	27¾	Old Malton.	218¼	
	25¼	Howe Bridge.	220¾	Kirkby Hall.
		cr. river Derwent.		
To Scarborough, 20½ m. Kingthorpe Hall.	20¼	PICKERING contains a spacious and ancient church, and the ruins of a castle which sustained a siege against the parliamentary army during the civil wars. Pop. of township 2640.	225¾	To Kirkby Moorside, 8 m.
	15¾	Lockton.	230¼	
	11¾	Saltersgate.	234¼	
	6¾	Silpho Cross.	239¼	
Sleights Hall.	4¼	Sleights.	241¾	Esk Hall.
		cr. river Esk.		
	3½	Carrend.	242½	Aislaby Hall.
				Carr Hall.
Sneaton. Larpool Hall, E. Turton, Esq.	2	Ruswarp.	244	
				High Stakesby.
Stakesby.				
		WHITBY, (p. 424.)	246	Mulgrave Castle, Marquis of Normanby, 3 m.
				Field House, C. Richardson, Esq.
Whitby Abbey.				

CXLIV. LONDON TO SCARBOROUGH THROUGH YORK AND NEW MALTON, 239½ Miles.

ON RIGHT FROM LOND.	From Scarbor.		From London.	ON LEFT FROM LOND.
	22¼	From Hicks's Hall to New Malton.	217¼	Hildenley, Sir G. Strickland, Bart.; beyond, Easthorpe, and in the distance Castle Howard (Earl of Carlisle).
		cr. river Derwent.		
Sutton. Settrington Hall.	21¾	Norton.	217¾	
Newton Hall.	17¾	Rillington.	221¾	
	13¼	Yeddingham Bridge.	226¼	Scampston Hall, W. St. Quintin, Esq. Knapton. Ebberston.
		cr. river Derwent.		
	9¾	Snainton.	229¾	To Pickering by Eberstone, 7½ miles.
High Hall, Sir D. Cayley, Bart.	8	Brompton.	231½	
Wykeham Abbey, a modern mansion erected on the site of a priory, founded 1153.	6½	Wykeham.	233	
	5¾	Hutton-Bushel.	233¾	Hutton Bushel Hall.
	4¾	East Ayton.	234¾	
		cr. river Derwent.		
	1	Falsgrave.	238½	
		SCARBOROUGH, (p. 423).	239½	

CXLV. LONDON TO WHITBY THROUGH LINCOLN, HULL, AND SCARBOROUGH, 231¼ Miles.

ON RIGHT FROM LOND	From Whitby.		From London.	ON LEFT FROM LOND.
Beyond Norman Cross you have a fine view of Whittlesea-Mere, an extensive sheet of water, about 2 m. long, and 1 m. across.	159¼	From Hicks's Hall to Norman Cross, *Huntingdonshire.*	72	At a distance, Overton Longueville, and Orton Hall, Marq. of Huntly.
		Junction of the road.		To Oundle, 12½ miles.
To March through Whittlesea, 16½ miles.		cr. river Nen, and enter *Northamptonshire.*		
To Whittlesea, 5½ m.	158¾	PETERBOROUGH, (p, 420).	72½	Thorpe Hall, and beyond Milton Park (Earl Fitzwilliam).
Thorney, 7 miles; Wisbeach, 19½ m.; Downham, Market, 32½ m.; Swaffham, 45½ m.	150¼	Walton.	80	To Oundle, 13½ miles; Weldon, 22¼ m.; Market Harborough, 37 m.; Lutterworth, 50 m.
	150¾	Werrington.	80½	
To Crowland, 5½ m.	149	Glinton.	82¼	
To Spalding, 12 miles.	147¼	Northborough.	84	
		cr. river Welland, and enter Lincolnshire.		

ON RIGHT FROM LOND.	From Whitby.		From London.	ON LEFT FROM LOND.
To Spalding, $11\frac{1}{2}$ m.	$145\frac{1}{4}$	MARKET-DEEPING, so called from its situation, the ground to the east of this place being the lowest in the county. Pop. of par. 1337.	86	To Stamford, $8\frac{1}{2}$ m. On the way, Uffington House, Earl of Lindsey.
	143	Langtoft.	$88\frac{1}{4}$	Casewick Hall, Rt. Hon. Sir J. Trollope, Bt.
	$142\frac{1}{4}$	Baston.	89	
Thetford House.	$141\frac{1}{2}$	Kate's Bridge.	$89\frac{3}{4}$	Shillingthorpe.
		☞ cross river Glen.		
	$140\frac{1}{4}$	Thurlby.	91	
To Spalding, 12 m.	138	BOURNE, (p. 421.)	$93\frac{1}{4}$	To Stamford, $10\frac{1}{4}$ m. To Corby, 8 miles.
	$135\frac{1}{2}$	Morton.	$95\frac{3}{4}$	Grimsthorpe (Lord Willoughby d'Eresby), and beyond, Irnham Park (Lord Clifford).
To Donington, $12\frac{3}{4}$ m.	$131\frac{1}{4}$	Aslackby.	100	
To Donington, $9\frac{3}{4}$ m.	$129\frac{1}{4}$	FOLKINGHAM. Here was anciently a castle, but only the moats and mounds remain. The site is now occupied by a gaol. The church is large and handsome.	102	
	127	Newton-Goss.	$104\frac{1}{4}$	To Grantham, 11 m.
	$126\frac{1}{4}$	Osbournby.	105	
Aswarby Hall, Sir T. Whichcote, Bart.	125	Aswarby.	$106\frac{1}{4}$	2 miles distant, Culverthorpe Hall (J. A. Honblin, Esq.); and in the distance, Belton House (Earl Brownlow).
	$122\frac{1}{4}$	Silk-Willoughby.	109	
To Boston, 18 m.; to Tattershall, $13\frac{3}{4}$ miles. At a distance are the remains of the ancient monastic edifice of Haverholme priory, which have been incorporated into the modern mansion of the Earl of Winchilsea and Nottingham.	$119\frac{3}{4}$	SLEAFORD. The bishops of Lincoln had a castle here, which is now quite level with the ground. The church is a handsome building, containing several monuments to the Carr family. Pop. 3745.	$111\frac{1}{2}$	Rauceby (A. Peacock, Esq.)
	$118\frac{3}{4}$	Holdingham.	$112\frac{1}{2}$	To Newark upon Trent, 18 miles.
	$118\frac{1}{4}$	Leasingham.	113	
Bloxholme Hall, Rt. Hon. R. A. C. N. Hamilton. Ashby House.				
Blankney Hall, C. Chaplin, Esq.	$110\frac{1}{4}$	Green Man Inn.	121	Wellingore.
At a distance, Nocton Hall, Earl of Ripon. Branston Hall, Hon. A. L. Melville. Canwick Hall, Major G. W. T. Sibthorp.	$109\frac{1}{4}$	Dunstan Pillar, a quadrangular stone-shaft, which rises to the height of about 100 feet, and is surmounted by a statue of Geo. III. It was erected as a guide for travellers when the roads were intricate, and the heath was an extensive waste.	122	Coleby Hall (Sir C. R. Tempest, Bart.), surrounded by pleasing grounds. Harmston Hall.
		☞ cr. river Wytham.		
To Wragby, $10\frac{3}{4}$ m.; thence to Horncastle, 10 m. To New Bolingbroke, $27\frac{1}{4}$ miles.	$101\frac{3}{4}$	LINCOLN, (p. 421.)	$129\frac{1}{2}$	To Newark, 16 miles; Southwell, $24\frac{1}{4}$ miles; Mansfield $36\frac{1}{4}$ miles.

ON RIGHT FROM LOND.	From Whitby.		From London.	ON LEFT FROM LOND.
Riseholme Palace (Bishop of Lincoln.) Hackthorne Hall, R. Cracroft, Esq. Caenby Hall. To Market Rasen, 10m.	96½	Midge Inn.	134¾	Burton Hall, Lord Monson. Aisthorpe Hall. Summer Castle; Fillingham Castle, J. Dalton, Esq.
Norton Place, Sir M. J. Cholmeley, Bart.	90½	Spittal-in-the-Street.	140¾	Glentworth, Earl of Scarborough. To Gainsborough, 10 miles.*
Redbourne Hall, Duke of St Albans.	84	Redbourne.	147½	To Kirton in Lindsey, 2 miles.
	82½	Hibaldstow.	148¾	
		cr. river Ancholme.		
To Caistor, 10 miles. Elsham Hall, T. G. Corbett, Esq., and beyond, at a considerable distance, Brocklesby Hall, Earl of Yarborough.	74½	BRIGG, or GLANFORD BRIGG. This town carries on a considerable trade in corn, coals, and timber. Pop. 1851, 3097.	151¾	Scawby Hall, Sir J. Nelthorpe, Bart. 4 miles distant Manby Hall, Earl of Yarborough. Appleby Hall.
2½ m. distant, Barrow Hall, and beyond, Wootton House. 5 m. distant are Thornton College and the ruins of Thornton Abbey, founded by William le Gros, Earl of Albemarle, A.D. 1139. Various portions of the building are yet tolerably entire. The abbot's lodge is occupied as a farm house. To Hedon, 8 miles.	68¾	BARTON upon Humber, a town of great antiquity, a railway station, and noted as the principal place of passage to Hull. It carries on a considerable trade in corn and flower. The church of St. Peter is very ancient, and its tower remarkable. Waterside Inn. There is a regular steam-packet from Barton to Hull. cross Humber.	162½	
	61¾	HULL, (*Yorkshire.*) (See p. 359.)	169½	To South Cave, 12½ m. Tranby House. Cottingham Castle.
On right bank of the Hull, Hull Bank.	59½	Newland.	171¾	
	57	Dunswell.	174¼	
	54½	Woodmansey.	176¾	
To Hornsea, 13 miles.	52¾	BEVERLEY, (p. 422.)	178½	To Hessle, 9 miles.
To Bridlington by Brandsburton, 23½ miles.	51¾	Molescroft.	179½	To York, 29¼ miles. To New Malton, 27 m.
	50	Leckonfield.	181¼	Cherry Burton House. High Hall. Low Hall.

* Gainsborough is situate on the right bank of the river Trent, twenty-one miles above its junction with the estuary of the Humber. The town, consisting principally of one long street, running parallel to the river, is clean, well paved, and lighted. It possesses a well built church, erected in 1748, several dissenting places of worship, a town hall, and a small theatre. Here is an ancient building called the Old Hall, composed of oak timber framing, and forming three sides of a quadrangle. It was formerly surrounded by a moat. The town has a considerable coasting and inward trade, arising from canals, and the navigable state of the river, which admits steamers and vessels of from 150 to 200 tons. Pop. 6320.

ON RIGHT FROM LOND.	From Whitby.		From London.	ON LEFT FROM LOND.
	47½	Scorborough.	183¾	At a distance South Dalton Hall, Lord Hotham.
	46¼	Beswick.	185	
Watton Abbey.	45	Watton.	186¼	Kilnwick Hall, C. Grimston, Esq.
	43	Hutton Cranswick.	188¼	3 m. distant Neswick Hall.
2 m. dist. Pockthorpe. To Bridlington by Nafferton and Burton Agnes, 11½ miles.	39½	GREAT DRIFFIELD, a pleasant town at the foot of the Wolds, carries on a considerable trade in corn. Pop. of township 4244.	191¾	Sunderlandwick Hall. To York, 28¼ miles.
	38	Kendal House.	193¼	At a distance Sledmere Pa., Sir Tatton Sykes, Bart.
11 m. distant is Bridlington, a neat town, which derived its origin from an Augustine Priory founded in the reign of Henry I. 1 mile S. E. of the town is Bridlington Quay, much frequented for sea bathing. Pop. of township 1861, 5775. (See p. 427.)*	33½	Langtoft.	197¾	To York by Sledmere, 30 miles.
	29½	Foxholes.	201¾	Ganton Hall, Sir T. D. Legard, Bart.
	25¼	Staxton.	206	To New Malton, 14¾ miles.
	22¼	Seamer.	209	At a distance High Hall, Sir D. Cayley, Bart.
Hunmanby, 4¾ miles.	19¼	Falsegrave.	212	Wykeham Abbey, and Hutton Bushel Hall.
To Bridlington, 18 m.	18¼	SCARBOROUGH (p. 423.)	213	To New Malton, 20 m.
	14¾	Burniston.	216½	
	13¾	Cloughton.	217½	
	10¾	Staintondale.	220½	
	8¼	Peak Alum-works. An examination of the extensive alum-works at this place will amply repay the tourist's trouble.	223	The country adjacent to Whitby, throughout an extent of 30 miles along the coast, and from 8 miles to 12 miles in breadth inland, is an almost uninterrupted alum rock.
	6½	Mill-Beck.	224¾	
	5¼	Thorpe Town, Robin Hood's Bay.	226	
	3¼	Hawsker.	228	
	2½	Stainsacre Lane.	228¾	
1 mile distant, High Stakesby and Low Stakesby.		WHITBY (p. 424.)	231¼	Mulgrave Castle, Marquis of Normanby, 3 m.

Peterborough.—This city was anciently called Medeshamstede, and owes its origin to a celebrated Benedictine abbey, founded soon after the revival of Christi-

* Three and a half miles from Bridlington is the fishing village of Flamborough, formerly a town of considerable importance. Here are the remains of a Danish tower. The church contains a curious monumental inscription. Two miles distant is the celebrated promontory called Flamborough Head. (See p. 427.)

anity among the Saxons. This abbey was destroyed by the Danes about 807, and was, in 966, restored after remaining desolate for upwards of a century and a half. The ancient name of the city was then superseded by the present, derived from the saint to whom it was dedicated. At the dissolution of the religious houses, the Abbey of Peterborough was one of the most magnificent, and was selected as the seat of one of the new bishoprics erected by Henry VIII. During the great civil wars, the conventual buildings were utterly demolished, and the cathedral itself was much injured, and its monuments defaced. The cathedral is a noble structure, measuring on the outside 471 feet in length, and 180 in breadth, chiefly in the Norman style, and erected at various periods. Here were interred Queen Katherine of Arragon and Mary Queen of Scots; but the remains of the latter were afterwards removed to Westminster Abbey. At the west end of the cathedral is a large court, on the south side of which is a range of the ancient monastic buildings. The remains of the cloisters are in good preservation. In the church of St John the Baptist is a tablet with some exquisite figures by Flaxman. The city contains also a theatre, several schools, banks, and meeting-houses, jail, &c. The trade carried on is chiefly in corn, coal, timber, lime, bricks, and stone. The Nen is navigable for boats, and the city is connected by railway with all parts of the kingdom. Dr Paley was a native of Peterborough. Two M.P. Pop. 11,735.

About two miles from Peterborough is Milton Park, the seat of Earl Fitzwilliam. Several pieces of stained glass were removed hither from the windows of Fotheringhay Castle, when that building was demolished. Here is also a portrait of Mary Queen of Scots, and another of James I. when a boy, said to have been given by Mary to Sir W. Fitzwilliam on the morning of her execution.

Bourne is a small town in south Lincolnshire, where was formerly a castle, the seat of a lordship of some note in the Saxon times. Hereward, the Anglo-Saxon chieftain, who opposed the most protracted resistance to William the Conqueror, was the son of the Lord of Bourne. In the centre of the market-place is the town-hall, in the room of one built by the great Lord Burghley, a native of the town. The church is a large and handsome building. The principal business carried on is tanning and wool-stapling. Here is a medicinal spring, which is much frequented, and there are traces of the site of an Augustinian priory. Pop. 1861, 3066. Between three and four miles from Bourne, is Grimsthorpe Castle, the seat of Lord Willoughby d'Eresby, an irregular structure, erected at various periods, from the time of Henry VIII. till 1723. It has a beautiful chapel, and a fine collection of pictures. The grounds are very extensive and beautiful.

Lincoln, the capital of Lincolnshire, is a place of great antiquity, and was of considerable importance under the Romans. At the time of the Norman Conquest it was one of the most important places in the kingdom. William the Conqueror caused a strong castle to be erected here in 1086. King Stephen was defeated and taken prisoner here in 1141 by Robert Earl of Gloucester, natural brother to the Empress Maud. Lincoln was the scene of important operations during the civil wars in John's reign, and here the party of the Dauphin was completely overthrown by the Earl of Pembroke during the minority of Henry III. During the great civil war, the royalists obtained possession of the city, but it was stormed by the Parliamentary army under the Earl of Manchester, May 5, 1644. The most interesting of the public buildings is the Cathedral, which is reckoned one of the finest in the kingdom. It is situated on the summit of a hill, and is visible at a distance of many miles. It was founded under William Rufus, but re-erected by Henry II. and dedicated to the Virgin. The west front, two circular windows, the choir, and screen, and the Lady Chapel, are peculiarly beautiful and interesting. The celebrated bell, the Great Tom of Lincoln, cast in 1610, was cracked in 1827, and broken up in 1834. With six others, it was recast into the present large bell and two quarter bells, and placed in the central tower in 1835. It is 6 feet 10½ inches in diameter at the mouth, and weighs 5 tons 8 cwt., nearly a ton more than the old bell. The only bells in the kingdom which exceed it in size are the "Mighty Tom" of Oxford, (7 tons 15 cwt.), and Great Tom of Exeter, (6 tons.) On the north side of the cathedral are the cloisters, in which is preserved a Roman pavement. The library contains some curious specimens of Roman antiquities. In the cathedral are numerous monuments; among others, those of Catherine Swinford, wife of John of Gaunt; of Joan, Countess of Westmorland, their daughter; and of several bishops and deans of the cathedral; but many of the older monuments have been removed or were totally destroyed during the civil wars. The other buildings worthy of notice are the Chapter House, the ruins of the Bishops' Palace, the remains of the castle, with the county jail and Court House; the Newport Gate, one of the finest remnants of Roman architecture in England; the remains of John of Gaunt's Palace; the guildhall; city jail, &c. The city abounds in antiquities, and especially in monastic and other architectural remains. The other churches of Lincoln are fourteen in number; formerly there were upwards of fifty, and most of them standing at the time of the Reformation. There are also several dissenting places of worship, public libraries, (in one of which is an old copy of Magna Charta,) a mechanics' institute, a theatre, assembly rooms, and race-course. The chief trade is in flour, and there are some extensive breweries, noted for ale. The Witham and Trent communicate by the Foss Dyke, a work of Roman origin, twelve miles long, and the city is connected by railway with all parts of the kingdom. It returns two M.P., and affords the title of Earl to the Duke of Newcastle. Pop. 20,999.

Beverley, an extensive and pleasant town near the Hull, at the foot of the York Wolds. The houses are good, and the principal street is terminated by an ancient gateway. The market-place, which comprises an area of nearly four acres, is ornamented with an octangular market-cross. It is supposed that in ancient times, the marshes of Deira, to the north of the Humber, became lakes or meres whenever the river Hull overflowed the country. Beverley probably took its name from one of these lakes,—Beverlac, the lake of beavers, so named from the beavers with which the neighbouring river Hull abounded. In the early part

SCARBOROUGH

of the eighth century, a church was founded here by John, Archbishop of York who afterwards converted it into a monastery. Athelstan changed it from a monastery into a college. Various important privileges were conferred upon the town by the same monarch. During the great civil wars, Beverley was frequently the scene of agitation; and it was here that Sir John Hotham, who had represented the town in several successive parliaments, was arrested by his nephew, on his flight from Hull, as a traitor to the commonwealth. The present trade of Beverley is chiefly confined to tanned leather, oatmeal, malt, corn, and coal. The town communicates with the river Hull by a canal, called Beverley Beck. The finest object in Beverley is the superb collegiate church of St John, or Minster, adorned with several monuments to the Percys. This edifice has been built at different periods, and exhibits various styles of Gothic architecture. The principal window, at the east end, is said to be copied from that of York. The celebrated Percy-Shrine, which is within the choir, is of most exquisite workmanship. St Mary's Church is also exceedingly handsome and spacious. In ancient times, there was also a monastery of Blackfriars, another of Franciscans or Greyfriars, and an establishment of knights hospitallers. Beverley has a grammar-school of great antiquity, several meeting-houses, two hospitals, several schools, banks, houses of correction, &c. Bishops Alcock, Fisher, and Green, were natives of this place. Beverley returns two M.P., and gives the title of Earl to a branch of the Northumberland family. Pop. 1861, 10,868.

Scarborough is delightfully situated in the recess of a bay, whence it rises in the form of an amphitheatre to the summit of a cliff or scar. Its name, signifying a fortified rock, is of Saxon derivation; and there is reason to suppose that it was also a Roman settlement. It ranks among the most ancient boroughs which send members to Parliament. The town was in ancient times defended by strong walls, a moat, and earthen mound. The castle, which stands on a promontory, elevated more than 300 feet above the level of the sea, was built in the reign of King Stephen by William le Gros, Earl of Albemarle and Holderness, and has been the scene of many events remarkable in history. Here, Piers de Gavaston sought refuge from his enemies; but, being taken, was beheaded by them. During the civil wars, the castle underwent two sieges by the Parliamentary forces; the first of which lasted upwards of twelve months, the garrison having at length been compelled, by disease and famine, to surrender on honourable terms. It was afterwards dismantled by order of the Parliament, but underwent a temporary repair on the breaking out of the Rebellion in 1745, and is still occupied by a small garrison, who are accommodated in barracks of modern erection. Scarborough combines the advantages of sea-bathing with mineral-baths, and its neighbourhood presents a beach of the finest sand in the kingdom. The two mineral springs are on the very edge of the sea-water, and are found to contain carbonate and sulphate of lime, magnesia, and oxide of iron. There are also excellent baths, and the most complete accommodation for the enjoyment of sea-bathing. Scarborough possesses numerous churches and chapels, a theatre, assembly-rooms, banks, libraries, &c., and a remarkable bridge, erected upon piers 75 feet high, over a chasm 400 feet wide which separates the town from the spa. The scenery in the neighbourhood of the town is of a beautiful and romantic character. About four miles from Scarborough is the picturesque village of Hackness, where also is Hackness Hall (Sir J. V. B. Johnstone, Bart.), a noble mansion near the supposed site of St Hilda's Cell. Scarborough returns two M.P., and is connected by railway with all parts of the kingdom. Pop. 18,377.

WHITBY was originally the seat of an abbey, founded by Oswy, King of Northumberland, in the seventh century, which, having been destroyed by the Danes, was rebuilt after the conquest in a style of great magnificence. In 1540, Whitby was only a small fishing-town, containing about thirty or forty houses. The erection of the alum-works at Sands End, in the year 1615, contributed greatly to its prosperity. The town is built along the sloping banks of the Esk, which forms the harbour, and divides the town into two parts, connected by a draw-bridge, so constructed as to admit vessels of 500 tons burden. The principal objects worthy of notice are the venerable remains of the Abbey Church, situated on a high cliff commanding a fine view; the docks, extending along both sides of the river; the piers, the town-house, baths, library, museum, &c. St Mary's Church, near the top of a hill, is approached from the bottom of the vale by 190 stone steps. It contains several monuments of the Cholmeley family, and the tomb of General Lascells, a native of Whitby, who was killed at Prestonpans. Whitby carries on an extensive trade in alum and coals, and also in ship-building. The vicinity abounds in beautiful and romantic scenery. Three miles distant is Mulgrave Castle, the seat of the Marquis of Normanby. Whitby has railway communication with all parts of the kingdom. One M.P. Pop. 1861, 12,051.

CXLVI. LONDON TO MARKET HARBOROUGH THROUGH NEWPORT PAGNELL, OLNEY, WELLINGBOROUGH, AND KETTERING, 85½ Miles.

ON RIGHT FROM LOND.	From M. Harbor.		From London.	ON LEFT FROM LOND.
	35¼	From Hicks's Hall to NEWPORT PAGNELL, (See p. 223.)	50	At a distance Gayhurst, Lord Carington, and Tirringham.
Chicheley House, Rev. A. Chester.		cr. the river Ouse.		
	33¼	Sherrington.	52	
	31¼	Emberton.	54	
		cr. the river Ouse.		

From M. Harbor.		From London.
30¼	OLNEY.	55
28¾	Warrington.	56½
	Enter Northamptonshire.	
25¼	Bozeat.	60
22¼	Wollaston.	63
19¼	Long Bridge.	66
	cr. the river Nen.	
18¼	WELLINGBOROUGH. (To Northampton, 11 miles; Thrapston, 11 miles.)	67
16¾	Great Harrowden.	68½
14¾	Isham.	70½
11¼	KETTERING (p. 365.)	74
7¼	Rothwell.	78
5¾	Desborough.	79½
3¾	The Fox Inn.	81½
¾	Little Bowden.	84½
	cr. river Welland, and enter Leicestershire.	
	MARKET HARBOROUGH. (p. 224.)	85¼

ON RIGHT FROM LOND.

Clifton House, Turvey House, and Turvey Abbey.

Wellingborough is supposed to have derived its name from the number of medicinal springs in its neighbourhood, and one called Redwell was formerly of celebrity. Charles I. and his Queen lived here in tents a whole season to drink the water. All Saint's Church is extensive, and has carved stalls on each side of the chancel. Olney has also several chapels and a free school. It carries on a considerable trade in corn, and the manufacture of boots, shoes, and lace. Pop. 6067.

11 m. from Wellingborough is

Thrapston, on the Nen, by means of which it possesses a considerable trade. Pop. 1851, 1183. About two miles distant is Drayton House, a noble antiquated structure, supposed to have been erected about the middle of the 15th century. The church of Lowick in the vicinity is adorned with monuments, brasses, and stained glass. Beyond, about four miles distant, is Lilford Hall, a handsome mansion, belonging to Lord Lilford, and about 4 miles farther,

Oundle, a neat town, almost surrounded by the Nen, possessing, besides a handsome church with a tower, several chapels, a market-house, &c. Pop. 1861, 2450. 3½ miles from Oundle is Fotheringhay (Lord Overstone), where formerly stood the castle in which Mary Queen of Scots was confined and executed. 6 miles from Oundle is

Apthorpe, the church of which contains a monument to Sir W. Mildmay, Chancellor of the Exchequer to Queen Elizabeth, and founder of Emmanuel College, Cambridge. In the vicinity is Apthorpe Hall, the seat of the Earl of Westmoreland.

ON LEFT FROM LOND.

Weston Underwood, Sir R. G. Throckmorton, Bart.

Olney is a small but neat town on the Ouse, surrounded by delightful scenery. The church is spacious. Many of the females here are employed in making worsted stockings and in silk weaving. Cowper the poet resided here for a number of years.

2 miles from Bozeat is Castle Ashby, Marquis of Northampton, a large quadrangular structure, containing numerous portraits. The dates 1625 and 1635 are seen in the balustrades of the turrets. In the park is the church, a neat building, with a curious ancient porch, and an old altar tomb with the statue of a cross-legged knight.

2 miles from Kettering on the right is Boughton House, Duke of Buccleuch, formerly the seat of the Dukes of Montagu; and 9 miles from Kettering is Weldon, noted for its quarries of stone, which is capable of taking a high polish. In the neighbourhood are the traces of a town, and the remains of the pavement of a Roman mansion.

CXLVII. LONDON TO BEDFORD THROUGH ST ALBANS AND LUTON, 51 Miles.

ON RIGHT FROM LOND.	From Bedford.		From London.	ON LEFT FROM LOND.
	30	From Hicks's Hall to ST ALBANS, (p. 196.)	21	Gorhambury (Earl of Verulam.)
Sandridge Lodge. Harpenden Lodge, and at a distance, East Hide.	25¾	Harpenden. Enter Bedfordshire.	25¼	Stockwood 1 m.
Luton Hoo Park, the seat of J. G. Leigh, Esq. a noble mansion.	22	Gibraltar Inn.	29	
	20	LUTON. cr. the river Lea.	31	LUTON has a church with fine embattled tower and curious font, and monuments, a chapel founded in the reign of Henry VI., and a window representing St George and the Dragon. Its chief manufacture is straw plait. Pop. 1861, 15,329.
Hexton House. Silsoe has a chapel with an altar piece by Mrs Lloyd. Near Silsoe is Wrest Park, Earl de Grey, adorned with a number of paintings, chiefly portraits, and possessing fine grounds and gardens. In the church-yard of Flitton, one mile distant, is the mausoleum of the family of Grey, Earls and Dukes of Kent.	13½	Barton in the Clay.	37½	
	11¾	New Inn.	39¼	
	10½	Silsoe.	40½	Three miles from Clophill is AMPTHILL, a small town, having an ancient moat house, a new market-house, and an old church. In the vicinity is Ampthill Park, a mansion of the late Lord Holland (occupied by Lord Wensleydale) containing a valuable collection of paintings, a library, and a museum. The park is remarkable for its oaks. Henry VIII.'s queen, Katherine, resided in the old mansion while her divorce was in agitation. The Alameda a beautiful grove of linden trees, was planted by the late Lord Holland for the inhabitants of Ampthill.
2½ miles distant from Clophill is Chicksand Priory, and beyond, Southill, Duke of Bedford.	8¾	Clophill.	42¼	
One mile beyond West End is Hawnes House (Marquis of Bath).	6¾	West End.	44¼	
	4	Wilshamstead.	47	
	1¾	Elstow.	49¼	
		BEDFORD, (p. 364.)	51	

CXLVIII. LONDON TO HIGHAM FERRERS THROUGH KIMBOLTON, 71¼ Miles.

ON RIGHT FROM LOND.	From H. Ferr.		From London.	ON LEFT FROM LOND.
	16¼	From Hicks's Hall to Eaton Socon, (p. 371.)	55	Kimbolton Castle, a noble mansion of considerable antiquity, has been successively the property of the Bohuns, Staffords, and Wingfields, and is now the seat of the Duke of Manchester. Katherine of Aragon, the divorced Queen of Henry VIII. died here. St Andrew's church contains several monuments of the Montagu family
	14¾	Cross Hall.	56½	
At a dist. Paxton Place.	13¾	Hail Weston, *Hunting.*	57½	
Gaines Hall (J. Duberley, Esq.,) and on the opposite side of the road, Staughton House, D. Onslow, Esq.	11	Staughton Highway.	60¼	
	9	Stonley.	62¼	
	8	KIMBOLTON.	63¼	
	6¼	Tilbrook, *Bedford.*	64¾	
	2	Chelveston, *Northamp.*	69¼	
		HIGHAM FERRERS, (p. 365.)	71¼	

ON RIGHT FROM LOND.	From F. Head.		From London.	ON LEFT FROM LOND.
	46½	From Hicks's Hall to YORK. (See p. 438.)	199¼	Stamford Bridge was the scene of a decisive and sanguinary conflict between the English and Norwegians, in which the former, under Harold, completely defeated the latter, and slew their king Harfager.
	43¾	Grimston.	202	
	40½	Gate Helmsley.	205¼	
	39	Stamford Bridge.	206¾	Helmsley Lodge.
		cr. river Derwent.		Aldby Park, H. Darley, Esq.
	34	Garrowby Street Inn.	211¾	Garrowby Hall, Right Hon. Sir C. Wood, Bart.
	28	Fridaythorpe.	217¾	
	26½	Fimber.	219½	
Sledmere Park, (Sir Tatton Sykes, Bart.), an elegant mansion, the grounds of which are richly ornamented with temples, pavilions, &c. There is a lofty arched gateway over the road.	22½	Sledmere.	223½	
Thorpe Hall, Lord Macdonald.	10½	Rudston.	235½	
Boynton Hall, Sir G. Strickland, Bart., M.P.	8½	Boynton.	237½	
BRIDLINGTON (see also p. 420) is pleasantly situated near the coast. Some vestiges of an Augustine Priory still remain. The last prior was executed at London for treason. About a mile south-east of the town is Bridlington Quay, much resorted to for sea-bathing and its mineral springs. The harbour is formed by two piers, the northernmost of which affords an excellent promenade, and commands a fine view of Flamborough Head and the bay. The harbour is defended by two batteries. Pop. 5775.	5½	BRIDLINGTON. (See also p. 420.)	240½	Flamborough (see also p. 420) is now only a fishing village. The church is an ancient structure, and contains a curious monumental inscription to the memory of Sir Marmaduke Constable. At the west end of the town are the remains of a Danish tower. Two miles distant is the celebrated promontory called Flamborough Head, the stupendous cliffs of which rise perpendicularly from 300 to 450 feet. They are composed of a mouldering limestone rock which, at the base, is worn into numerous extensive caverns by the violence of the waves.
At Sewerby is Sewerby House, Y. Greame, Esq., and beyond it, at Marton, Marton Hall, R. Creyke, Esq.	4	Sewerby.	241¾	
	2	Flamborough.	245¾	
		Flamborough Head.		

CL. LONDON TO HULL BY YORK, MARKET WEIGHTON, AND BEVERLEY, 236½ Miles.

ON RIGHT FROM LOND.	From Hull.		From London	ON LEFT FROM LOND.
		From Hicks's Hall to		
	37¼	YORK, (see p. 438.)	199¼	
	34½	Grimston.	202	To Bridlington, 38¼ m.
	31½	Kexby Bridge.	205	Kexby Bridge House.
		cr. river Derwent.		
Bolton Hall.	29¾	Wilberfoss.	206¾	
	26½	Barmby Moor.	210	To Pocklington, 2 m.
Melbourne Hall, Sir H. M. Vavasour, Bart.	24¼	Pocklington New Inn.	212¼	To Pocklington, 1½ m.
2 miles distant, Everingham Hall, Lord Herries.	23½	Hayton.	213	
	21	Shipton.	215½	Londesborough Park, Lord Londesborough.
2 m. distant, Houghton Hall, Hon. C. Langdale, and 3 miles farther Hotham Hall.	19	MARKET WEIGHTON. (See p. 429.)	217½	
	11¾	Bishop Burton.	224¾	High Hall, South Dalton Hall, Lord Hotham, and Cherry Burton House.
To Hessle, 9 miles; South Cave, 12 m.	9	BEVERLEY, (p. 422.)	227½	
	7¼	Woodmansey.	229¼	
	4¾	Dunswell.	231¾	Hull Bank, for many years the seat of the Burton family.
	2¼	Newland.	234¾	
		HULL, (see p. 359.)	236½	

CLI. LONDON TO MARKET WEIGHTON BY BAWTRY, THORNE, AND HOWDEN, 191¾ Miles.

ON RIGHT FROM LOND.	From M. Wei.		From London.	ON LEFT FROM LOND.
		From Hicks's Hall to		
	38¾	BAWTRY, by Ware (p. 384), 149 miles, by Baldock, (p. 370.)	153	
	37½	Austerfield.	154¼	
	34¾	Finningley.	157	Finningley Park, J. Harvey, Esq.
	33¾	Blaxton.	158	Thorne, a small but flourishing town on the Don, carries on a considerable trade. The surrounding country is so low, that it has been necessary to enclose the neighbouring rivers and canal by strong high banks to prevent inundations. Pop. 2591.
		cr. Stainforth and Keadby Canal.		
	25¼	THORNE (See also p. 384).	166½	
	20¾	New Bridge.	171	Cowick Hall, Viscount Downe, and beyond, across the river Aire, Carleton Hall, Lord Beaumont.

ON RIGHT FROM LOND.	From M. Wei.		From London.	ON LEFT FROM LOND.
		cr. the Dutch river.		The Dutch river is a canal, so called because it was cut in the reign of Charles II., by Van Mulden, and his Dutch and Flemish settlers.
	18¼	Rawcliffe.	173¼	
	15¼	Armin.	176½	
	13¾	Booth Ferry.	178	Two or three miles east of Booth Ferry, and on the Ouse, is the rising port of GOOLE, which carries on a considerable trade, and has extensive docks and warehouses. Pop. 5850.
		cr. the river Ouse.		
HOWDEN is a small town of considerable antiquity, with the remains of a palace of the Bishops of Durham. The church is one of the finest specimens of Gothic architecture in the kingdom, has a good tower, and some curious monuments. Pop. 2376.	12	HOWDEN. (To South Cave, 12 m. thence to Hull, 12½ m.)	179¾	
	10¼	Benland.	181½	
Near Holme is Holme Hall, (Hon. C. Langdale.) for several centuries the property of the Constables of Flamborough, who sold it to Sir Marmaduke Langdale, the steady adherent of Charles I.	8½	Howden Grange.	183¼	Near Holme is Spalding Moor, on which is a remarkable hill. 120 feet high, commanding an extensive prospect. The village is on the plain, but the church is situated on the top of the hill.
	7	Welham Bridge.	184¾	
Market Weighton carries on a considerable trade by means of a canal, which communicates with the Humber. Here are several barrows containing human bones, and the remains of armour.	5	Holme.	186¾	Beyond Holme is Melbourne Hall (Sir H. M. Vavasour, Bart.); and, 2 miles distant from Holme, is Everingham Hall, (Lord Herries), a noble modern mansion, in which is a fine portrait of Charles I. by Vandyke. Near the entrance to the grounds is a curious Saxon font.
2 miles distant Houghton Hall, Hon. C. Langdale.		MARKET WEIGHTON.	191¾	

CLII. LONDON TO GREAT GRIMSBY THROUGH LINCOLN & MARKET RASEN.

ON RIGHT FROM LOND.	From G. Grim.		From London.	ON LEFT FROM LOND.
	34	From Hicks's Hall to Lincoln, (p. 418.)	129½	
	18½	Market Rasen, so called from the stream on which it is situated, has a church, three dissenting chapels, and a free school. Pop. of par. 2563.	145	
		GREAT GRIMSBY. (See p. 430).	163½	

There is another and better road to Great Grimsby by Market Rasen and Caistor, but it is 5½ miles longer.

CAISTOR, a place of great antiquity, is supposed to derive its name from the Roman word "Castrum." Some Roman and Saxon antiquities have been discovered here. The church is partly of Norman and partly of early English architecture. There are also several chapels, banks, &c., in this town.

GREAT GRIMSBY, anciently Gryme, is an ancient town near the Humber, by means of which it carries on a considerable trade. It was of sufficient importance to furnish Edward III. with 11 vessels and 170 mariners for his armament against Calais; but the harbour gradually fell to decay, until it was renovated about the beginning of the present century. There are large warehouses and timber-yards attached to the harbour, and the new docks and tidal basin, commenced in 1849, and to occupy 43 acres, will, combined with its railways, soon render Grimsby a formidable rival to Hull. Amount of customs' duties in 1857, £27,852. St James's church contains some ancient monuments, and a large font of early English character, and the steeple is a beautiful specimen of English pointed architecture. One M.P. Pop. of Parl. borough, 15,060.

CLIII. LONDON TO GREAT GRIMSBY THROUGH SPALDING, BOSTON, SPILSBY, AND LOUTH.

ON RIGHT FROM LOND.	From G. Grims.		From London.	ON LEFT FROM LOND.
From Spalding to Crowland is 9 miles; to Holbeach, 7½ miles.		From Hicks's Hall to Alconbury Hill* (p. 371.)	67¾	Milton Park, Earl Fitzwilliam.
		Norman Cross.	75¾	
CROWLAND is a place of great antiquity, and is noted as the site of an extensive abbey, of which the church, founded by King Ethelbald in 716, still remains. Here is also a bridge, supposed to have been originally erected about 860, and remarkable for its curious construction. Pop. 1851, 2466. 5 m. distant is Thorney, where is a church that formed part of an ancient abbey, the possessions of which were granted, at the time of Edward VI. to the Earl of Bedford, whose descendant, the present Duke, is owner of the town and of 19,000 acres of the surrounding lands.		PETERBOROUGH. (See p. 420.)	81¾	
	76¾	Northborough.	88	About 8 m. from Spalding, on the right is HOLBEACH, a town of great antiquity; has a Gothic church, and two grammar schools. Pop. 1851, 2245.
		cr. river Welland, and enter Lincolnshire.		
	75¼	St James's Deeping.	89½	
	64¾	SPALDING, a town of great antiquity, carries on a considerable trade in wool. The principal buildings are, the church, town-hall, court-house, theatre, Assembly Rooms, &c. Pop. 1851, 7627.	100	DONINGTON has an ancient church, on which are vestiges of a Roman inscription. To Donington, 4 m. SWINESHEAD has a handsome church and a free school. King John first rested here after the loss of his baggage in crossing the neighbouring marshes.
	62½	Pinchbeck.	102¼	Pinchbeck has a fine old church.
		cr. the river Glen.		
	60¾	Surfleet.	104	To Swineshead, 7½ m.
	55	Sutterton.	109¾	West Skirbeck House.
Wyberton Hall, and Frampton Hall.	52¾	Kirton.	112	To Swineshead, 6¾ m.. and thence to Sleaford, 11¼ miles.
	48¾	BOSTON (see p. 431.)	116	
		cr. river Witham.		
	47¼	Burton Corner.	117¼	Revesby Abbey, J. B. Stanhope, Esq.
	44	Sibsey.	120¾	To Tattershall,† 9½ m.
To Wainfleet, 12 miles.	40	Stickney.	124¾	To New Bolingbroke, 2¾ miles.
	38	Stickford.	126¾	

* The road is four miles shorter by the route through Ware and Royston, p. 382.

† At Tattershall are the remains of a castle erected by Sir R. Cromwell in the 15th century, and the ruins of a church, which was once a magnificent structure.

ON RIGHT FROM LOND.	From G. Grims.		From London.	ON LEFT FROM LOND.
				Hagnaby Priory.
	35	West Keal.	129¾	
	34½	East Keal.	130¼	
	32½	Spilsby.	132¼	
To Wainfleet, 8¾ miles. Candlesby House and Gunby Hall, A. Massingberd, Esq. Dalby Hall.		The church contains several monuments to the Willoughbys.		
	30¼	Partney.	134½	2 miles distant Sausthorpe Hall. Langton Hall. Harrington Hall, 3 m.
Well Hall, Rt. Hon. R. A. C. N. Hamilton. To Alford, 3 miles.	26¼	Ulceby Cross.	138½	
South Thoresby Hall, C. T. Wood, Esq.	24½	Calceby Beck Houses.	140¼	Calceby Ruins. South Ormesby House,
Burwell Park (H. Lister, Esq.) the birth-place of the celebrated Sarah Duchess of Marlborough.	21¾	Burwell.	143	C. J. H. M. Massingberd, Esq. Walmsgate.
To Saltfleet, 11½ m. Little Grimsby House.	15½	LOUTH, (p. 432.)	149¼	To Wragby, 14½ m.; to Market Rasen, 13 m. To Horncastle,* 13 m.
	12½	Fotherby.	152¼	Fanthorpe Hall.
	11½	Utterby.	153¼	
	9¾	Ludborough.	155	
	7¾	North Thoresby.	157	3 miles distant Hawerby House.
	6	Waith.	158¾	
	4¾	Holton-le-Clay.	160	
Weelsby House.	2	Scartho.	162¾	2 m. distant Waltham Hall. To Caistor, 11 miles.
		GREAT GRIMSBY, (p. 430.)	164¾	Bradley and beyond, Laceby Hall.

BOSTON is by some supposed to have derived its name (Botolph's Town) from St. Botolph's Monastery, which stood here. This monastery was built A. D. 654, and was destroyed by the Danes A.D. 870. Various other religious houses existed here, but not a vestige of them now remains. The most interesting building in Boston is St. Botolph's church, which was built in 1309. It is a spacious and noble pile, 245 feet long, and 98 feet wide within the walls. Its tower is one of the loftiest in the kingdom, being 300 feet high, lantern-shaped at the top, and visible at sea for nearly 40 miles. Boston carries on an extensive trade with the north of Europe in hemp, iron, timber, and tar. There are some few manufactures here

* Horncastle, on the Bane, is noted for its horse fairs, and has a considerable trade in tanning. It is supposed to have been the Castra Hibernia of the Romans. Pop. 1851, 4921. Near it is Scrivelsby Court (Sir H. Dymoke, Bart.), the seat of the Dymoke family, champions of England.

for sail-cloth, canvas, and sacking. There are also iron and brass foundries. By means of the Witham and the canals connected with it, Boston has a navigable communication with Lincoln, Gainsborough, Nottingham, and Derby, and is connected by railway with all parts of the kingdom. Boston has a guild-hall, assembly-rooms, several churches, chapels, and banks, free grammar, blue-coat, and national schools, a theatre, several charitable institutions, &c. Boston affords the title of baron to the Irby family. Fox, the martyrologist, was a native of Boston. Two M.P. Pop. 17,893

LOUTH is pleasantly situated at the eastern foot of the Wolds, and on the bank of the little river Ludd. The church of St. James is one of the finest in the county. It has a lofty and elegant tower, surmounted by a rich octagonal spire, the whole 288 feet high. The east window is remarkable for its beautiful tracery. The grounds of the vicarage house are curiously laid out, as if attached to a hermitage. Louth possesses a session-house, a house of correction, a guild-hall, assembly rooms, several churches, chapels, and banks, a small theatre, &c. There are some manufactories of carpets, rugs, and blankets, of soap and paper, besides breweries, &c. An export trade is carried on in corn and wool. Louth is a station on the Great Northern Railway. Pop. 10,560

CLIV. LONDON TO CAMBRIDGE THROUGH WARE, 51 Miles.

ON RIGHT FROM LOND.	From Camb.		From London.	ON LEFT FROM LOND.
	24½	From Shoreditch Ch. to Puckeridge, *Herts.*	26½	Hamells Park.
1 m. distant, Albury.	23¾	Braughin.	27¼	
Hormead Bury.	20½	Hare Street.	30½	Wyddiall Hall.
	16½	Barkway.	34½	
Cocken Hatch.				
Haydon.	14	Barley.	37	Newsells Bury.
	11	Tun Bull's House.	40	
	8	Foulmire, *Cambridgesh.*	42	1¾ mile distant, Shepreth Hall, and in the distance, Wimpole Hall, Earl of Hardwicke.
2 m. distant, Whittlesford Hall.	6¼	Newton.	44¾	
1½ mile distant, Great Shelford House, and beyond, Gog Magog Hills, Lord Godolphin.	4¾	Hauxton.	46¼	To Royston, 10½ m.
	2¼	Trumpington.	48¾	Trumpington Hall.
		CAMBRIDGE (see p. 433.)	51	3½m. distant, Madingley Park, Sir St Vincent Cotton, Bart.

ON RIGHT FROM LOND.	From Camb.		From London.	ON LEFT FROM LOND.
	13	From Shoreditch Ch. to Royston (pp. 380-381).	37½	
		Enter Cambridgeshire.		Kneesworth Hall.
	9¾	Melbourne.	40¾	Melbourne Bury.
	5¼	Haston.	45¼	Shrepreth Hall, and in the distance, Wimple Hall, Earl of Hardwicke, (see pp. 381-2).
		Hauxton.		
	4½	Junction of the road.	46¼	
In the distance, Gog Magog Hills, Lord Godolphin.	2	Trumpington.	48½	Trumpington Hall.
		CAMBRIDGE.	50½	In the distance, Madingley, Sir S. V. Cotton, Bart.

CAMBRIDGE, the county town of Cambridgeshire, stands on the river Cam, which is navigable to the Ouse, and communicates with the sea through the port of Lynn. It derives its name from the river on which it is situated. The ancient name of the river was Granta; and in Doomsday Book the town is called Grentebridge. Cambridge is a town of great antiquity. It was burned by the Danes in 871, and again in 1010. A castle was built here by William the Conqueror, but it was early suffered to go to decay, and all that now remains of it is the gate house. The chief object of attraction at Cambridge is the university, which consists of seventeen colleges and halls, situated in different parts of the town. The origin of this university is involved in obscurity, but it is supposed that Cambridge first became a seat of learning in the seventh century. According to Mr. Hallam, the date of its first incorporation is tne fifteenth of Henry III., or 1231. Others say, however, that this is a mistake, and that Henry only sent a royal letter, directing that lodgings for the students should be valued according to the custom of the university, by two masters and two townsmen. The first formal charter which is extant was granted by Edward I. in the twentieth year of his reign. Some important privileges were granted to the university by Edward III. in 1333, in consequence of which such jealousy was created among the townsmen, that they at length, in 1381, broke out into open violence, and seized on and destroyed the university charters. All the present colleges or halls have been founded since the time of Edward I. Each college is a separate corporate body, holding the buildings and libraries, and possessing large funds in money, in land, in houses, and in advowsons. The constitutions of these colleges are various, as well as the amount of their property and the mode in which the scholars, fellows, and masters are appointed and remunerated. The university is a corporation by itself, to which the public library, the senate-house, the printing-press, the observatory, and some other establishments belong, and it also possesses power to make regulations for the government of the whole body, as well as to choose several of the professors.* The Chancellor is the head of the

* Some of the professors are selected by the Crown, and hence their titles of Regius Professors.

university. The office may be tenable beyond two years by the tacit consent of the university. The Vice-Chancellor is elected annually from the heads of colleges. The members on the boards of the university amount to nearly 7200.

The following are the colleges and halls in the order of their foundation:—

St. Peter's College founded in 1257 by Hugh de Balsham, Bishop of Ely, and enlarged in 1826.

Clare Hall, founded 1326, by Dr. Richard Baden, as University hall, and refounded 1344, by Lady Elizabeth, sister of Gilbert de Burgh, Earl of Clare. It was rebuilt in 1638, and has a chapel built in the beginning of last century.

Pembroke Hall, founded 1343, by Mary de Valence, Countess of Pembroke, and improved by Henry VI. Her husband's death so affected her as to lead her into retirement, and she spent her income for charitable and useful objects. William Pitt was a student here.

Gonville and Caius College, founded 1349, by Edmund Gonville, and enlarged 1558, by Dr. John Caius, who was educated in this college, and whose monument adorns the chapel. Sir Thomas Gresham, Jeremy Taylor, and Lord Chancellor Thurlow, received their education here.

Trinity Hall, founded in 1350, by Wm. Bateman, Bishop of Norwich, is appropriated chiefly to the study of civil law, and has a law library.

Corpus Christi College was founded in 1351 by two societies or guilds of Cambridge, and rebuilt in 1823, from designs by W. Wilkins, Esq.

King's College was founded in 1441, by Henry VI., for the reception of scholars from Eton. The chapel is a magnificent pile, and the distinguishing feature of Cambridge. The roof is remarkably beautiful, arched, but unsupported by pillars, and the whole forms one of the richest and most perfect specimens of the perpendicular style. All the windows except one are of stained glass, and the floor of the choir is of black and white marble. Parallel with the chapel is a noble range of buildings containing the library and the hall. Walsingham, Waller the Poet, Sir R. Walpole, &c., were of this college.

Queen's College was founded in 1446, by Margaret of Anjou, and enlarged in 1465, by the Queen of Edward IV. It possesses an extensive library, chapel, gardens, &c.

Catherine Hall was founded in 1475, by Robert Woodlark, D.D., Chancellor of the University, and has Bishop Sherlock's library.

Jesus College was founded in 1496, by John Alcock, Bishop of Ely. The hall and gardens are fine. Flamstead, Roger North, Sterne, and Coleridge were students.

Christ's College was founded in 1466, by Henry VI., but was refounded in 1505-6, by Lady Margaret, Countess of Richmond, mother of Henry VII., who also founded the Lady Margaret Professorship of Divinity, the first professorship on the record of the university. Erasmus was made the Lady Margaret's Professor of Divinity in 1510. In the gardens is a mulberry tree planted by Milton.

St. John's College was founded in 1511 by the same Lady Margaret, mother of Henry VII., and has been much enlarged during the present century. It has been peculiarly prolific of eminent men.

Magdalene College founded in 1542, by Thomas Baron Audley. It contains the Pepysian library, with curious MSS. This collection, mentioned with such pride in his Diary,* was the gift of Samuel Pepys. He was of this College.

Trinity, the chief college of the university, was founded in 1546 by Henry VIII. and afterwards augmented by Queen Mary. The chapel was begun by Queen Mary, and finished by Queen Elizabeth. This college boasts a fine library, and is rich in portraits, busts, &c. Among the rest are a statue of Sir Isaac Newton by Roubilliac, a bust of Porson by Chantrey, and Thorwaldsen's statue of Byron which was rejected by the Dean and Chapter of Westminster. The master's lodge has always, since the time of Elizabeth, been the residence of the monarch during a royal visit. Trinity College rose at once from infancy to maturity. During the reigns of Elizabeth and James I. a greater number of bishops proceeded from this than from any other college; and at the beginning of the 17th century, it could claim at the same time the two Archbishops, and no less than seven other prelates on the English bench. When the present translation of the Bible was executed, six of the translators were resident fellows of the College. Among the eminent persons who have been educated at Trinity college may be mentioned, Sir R. Cotton, Sir H. Spelman, Bacon, Coke, Dr. Donne, John Ray, Barrow, Newton, Cowley, Dryden, Andrew Marvell, Dr. Conyers Middleton, Lord Byron, &c. And among the masters of this college have been, Archbishop Whitgift, Bishop Wilkins, Bishop Pearson, Isaac Barrow, and Richard Bentley.

Emmanuel College, founded 1584, by Sir Walter Mildmay. It possesses the Sancroft library, numerous portraits, a handsome hall, and gardens.

Sidney Sussex College, founded 1598, in accordance with the will of Lady Frances Sydney, Countess of Sussex, has a hall, chapel, and gardens. Oliver Cromwell was educated here.

Downing College, founded in 1800, in terms of the will of Sir George Downing, Bart. who died in 1749; but the appropriation of the estates, and the granting of the charter, were delayed by litigation. It has a good library.

The other public buildings belonging to the university are the Senate-House, a magnificent building of the Corinthian order, adorned with statues of George I. and II., Charles, Duke of Somerset, and William Pitt, the first and third by Rysbrach, and the last by Nollekens; the public schools and university library, to which a copy of every book published in the empire is sent. In the vestibule of the latter is a fine bust of Dr. E. D. Clarke, by Chantrey; here also is the celebrated MS. of the four Gospels and Acts of the Apostles, given by Beza, —the Botanic Garden, occupying three or four acres—the Pitt Press, a handsome building erected in 1831,—the Observatory, an edifice in the Grecian style, erected 1822-1824, at an expense of upwards of £18,000,—the Fitzwilliam Museum, a magnificent pile, commenced in 1837 and lately finished, contains a fine collection of books, paintings, drawings, &c. bequeathed in 1816 to the university, together with £100,000 South Sea annuities, by Richard Viscount Fitz-

* Pepys' Diary, vol. iii. p. 298, &c.

william, an Irish Peer. The principal churches of Cambridge are Great St Mary's, or University Church, All Saints, in which is a monument by Chantrey to the memory of H. Kirke White, Great St Andrews, containing a cerotaph for Captain Cook, St Benedict's, St Michael's, and St Sepulchre's round chapel, an interesting relic of antiquity, lately restored by the Camden Society. There are also several other churches and chapels, besides many charitable institutions, a free grammar-school, a county prison, built on Howard's plan; Addenbrooke's Hospital, founded by a physician of that name, but considerably increased by a bequest of Mr. Bowtell, a bookbinder of the town; the Town-Hall, and the conduit behind it, given by Hobson the carrier, celebrated by Milton in two whimsical epitaphs. Bishop Jeremy Taylor, and Cumberland the dramatist, were natives of Cambridge. Two M.P. are returned by the town, and two by the university. Cambridge usually affords the title of Duke to a branch of the Royal family. Pop. 1861, 26,361. Stourbridge Fair, annually held at Cambridge in September, is one of the most ancient, and was formerly one of the largest, in England.

CLVI. LONDON TO HARROWGATE, RIPON, AND THIRSK (THROUGH LEEDS) BY RAILWAY, 244¾ Miles.

ON RIGHT FROM LOND.	From Thirsk.		From London.	ON LEFT FROM LOND.
	39	From London to LEEDS (p. 351.)	205¼	Armley.
Burley Lodge.		cr. riv. Aire.		
Headingley. New Grange.	36	Headingley and Kirkstall St.	208¼	Kirkstall Abbey, in ruins.
Cookridge Wood.	33½	Horsforth St.	210¾	
Cookridge Hall. Bramhope Grove. Breary. Kirskill Hall.				Bramhope.
3½ miles Harewood House, Earl of Harewood (see p. 374).	29¾	Arthington and Poole St.	214½	To Otley, 4 miles. To Ilkley, 9½ miles.
		cr. riv. Wharfe.		Castley.
Arthington Hall.	27½	Weeton St.	216¾	Rigton.
Rudding Park, Sir J. Radcliffe, Bart.	24¼	Pannal St.	220	
Knaresborough, 1½ m. (p. 377).	21	HARROWGATE AND KNARESBOROUGH St.	223¼	Harrowgate, 1 mile (see p. 377).
Conyngham Hall, 1¼ m.		cr. riv. Nidd.		Bilton.
Scriven Park, Sir C. Slingsby, Bart., 1½ mile. Nidd Hall. S. Stainley. Leonard Burton.	18	Ripley St. (See p. 375.)	226¼	To Ripley, 1½ mile, and beyond, Ripley Park, Markington.
Bishop Monkton. Newby Hall, Earl de Grey, 1½ mile. Littlethorpe.	15	Wormald Green St.	229¼	Whitcliffe. 2½ m. distant, Studley Royal and Fountains Abbey (Earl de Grey.)

ON RIGHT FROM LOND.	From Thirsk.		From London.	ON LEFT FROM LOND.
Hutton Conyers.	10	RIPON (see p. 378.)	234¼	The Palace, Bishop of Ripon. Nunwick.
		cr. river Ure.		Norton Conyers, Sir B. R. Graham, Bart. Here the Leeds northern line proceeds by Melmerby, and Newby Wiske to Northallerton and Stockton.
	5¼	Baldersby St.	239	
Catton. Newby Park, 1½ mile.		cr. river Swale.		Skipton.
	3	Topcliffe St.	241¼	Carlton Miniot.
		Cross line of York, Newcastle, and Berwick Railway.		
		THIRSK (see p. 380.)	244¼	

From the Church Fenton Station, on the York and North Midland Railway, there is also a branch railway to Harrowgate, by which route the total distance from London to Harrowgate is 225¼ miles, that is, two miles longer than the above (see p. 438.)

CLVII. LONDON TO YORK THROUGH LEICESTER AND DERBY, BY RAILWAY, 219¾ Miles.

ON RIGHT FROM LOND.	From York.		From London.	ON LEFT FROM LOND.
		From London, by North Western Railway, to		
	137	RUGBY JUNCTION. (p. 203.)	82¾	Leave line of London and North Western Railway.
		Thence by Midland Railway through Leicester, Derby, and Chesterfield, to		Before reaching Normanton, Manchester and Leeds Railway joins.
Castleford, on the river Calder, occupies the site of a Roman station, the *Legeolium* of the Itinerary.	24½	NORMANTON. (pp. 351-354.)	195¼	Leave line of Midland Railway, to Leeds, 8¾ m.
		By York and North Midland Railway, through tunnel, 1½ mile long, to		Methley Park, Earl of Mexborough.
To Pontefract, 2¾ m. Fyrstone Hall, R. M. Milnes, Esq. Bryam Hall, Sir J. W. Ramsden, Bart.	20½	Castleford St.	199¼	Kippax Park, 1¾ m., T. D. Bland, Esq. Ledsham, and beyond, Ledstone Park.
		cr. river Calder.		Fairburn

ON RIGHT FROM LOND.	From York.		From London.	ON LEFT FROM LOND.
	16¾	Burton Salmon St.	203	
Monk Frystone, R. M. Milnes, Esq.				Frystone Lodge.
Selby, 8 m. (see p. 358.)	15	Milford Junction St. Cross Line of Leeds and Shelby Railway.	204¾	
Sherburn, situated on the road from Doncaster to York, had formerly a palace of the Archbishops of York, but it is now entirely demolished.	13	Sherburn St.	206¾	Scarthingwell Hall, Lord Hawke.
Cawood, 4 m. distant from the Ulleskelf Station, is a small market-town on the river Ouse. Here was formerly one of the chief residences of the Archbishops of York, a magnificent palace, where Wolsey was arrested on the charge of high treason, shortly before his death.*	10¾	Church Fenton Junction St.	209	Branch to Harrowgate, 16½ m.; – 2¼ m. dist. on this line is Towton, the scene of a sanguinary engagement during the wars of the Roses fought on Palm Sunday, the 29th March 1461.
	9	Ulleskelf St.	210½	Grimston Hall, Lord Londesborough, beyond, Tadcaster (see p. 384.)
		cr. river Wharfe.		
Bolton Lodge, Sir W. M. S. Milner, Bart. Nun Appleton, 2 m., Sir W. M. S. Milner, Bart.	7¾	Bolton Percy St. Here there is a fine church, containing several interesting monuments. It was built in 1423.	212	Oxton Hall, 2 miles. Steeton Hall. Colton Lodge.
Appleton Roebuck.	3¾	Copmanthorpe St.	216	
Bishopsthorpe, the palace of the Archbishop of York. Middlethorpe. Dring Houses.				Askham Bryan.
		YORK.	219¾	

YORK is a very ancient city, and is said to have been founded 983 years B.C. Little is known of its history till A.D. 150, when it was one of the greatest Roman stations in the province, having an imperial palace, a tribunal, and a regular government within its walls. The Emperor Severus lived in the palace three years, and died there. He was succeeded by his sons Caracalla and Geta, the former of whom murdered the latter in York, and returned to Rome. About a century after, Carausius landed in Britain, and was proclaimed emperor at York. Constantine the Great was born in this city in 272, and his father Constantius died there in 307. York has had a conspicuous share in all the national troubles, especially in the civil wars of the Roses and temp. Charles I. The walls, gates, and posterns, are to a considerable extent still perfect. The portions of walls which remain are surmounted by a delightful promenade commanding a beautiful prospect of the surrounding country. The ca-

* See Cavendish's Narrative, app. to Galt's Life of Wolsey, 3d ed. p. 222.

thedral is the finest building of the kind in the empire, displaying the most charming features of the various styles of Gothic. It is by internal measurement 524 feet long, 222 feet from north to south in transepts, and 99 feet high. It was first founded in 626, by Edwin, the Saxon King of Northumberland, and through succeeding ages has been enlarged, repaired, and improved with great taste. It suffered severely from fire in 1829, and again in 1840. From the time of Paulinus, the first archbishop, who was appointed in 625, down to the present moment, there have been no fewer than 92 archbishops of York. Besides the cathedral, there are twenty-one parish churches within the walls, and three in the suburbs. The city is thus peculiarly attractive to the ecclesiologist. The other objects of public interest are the city walls; the castle originally built by William I., since restored, and now used as a gaol (including within its walls Clifford's Tower, said to have been raised by the Romans); the ruins of St Mary's Abbey; the Yorkshire Museum and gardens; the Assembly Rooms; the public cemetery, &c. The charitable institutions of the city are very numerous. It contains upwards of twelve dissenting chapels. York carries on a considerable river trade, and has some traffic in gloves, linens, glass, and drugs, as well as in printing and bookselling, and it derives great advantage from the influx of visitors to the assizes and the races. The learned Alcuin was a native of York, as were also Flaxman and Etty the Academicians. York usually gives the title of Duke to the second son of the sovereign. Two M.P. Pop. 45,385.

The Great Northern Railway forms, however, the most direct line of communication between the Metropolis and the north of England. From the London terminus at King's Cross, this line proceeds northward by Barnet, Hatfield, Stevenage, Hitchin, Biggleswade, St Neot's, and Huntingdon, to Peterborough; thence by Grantham, Newark, East Retford, Bawtry, Doncaster, and Womersley, joining the York and North Midland at Burton-Salmon. A loop line leaves the main trunk at Peterborough, and passes to the eastward through Spalding, Boston, Lincoln, and Gainsborough to Retford.

The distance from London to Peterborough, by this route, is 76¼ miles;—the total distance from London to York, 191 miles, and from London to Hull, 173¼ miles.—(See description of Great Northern lines.)

CLVIII. YORK TO DURHAM, NEWCASTLE, AND BERWICK, BY RAILWAY, 153¾ Miles.

ON RIGHT FROM YORK.	From Berwick.		From York.	ON LEFT FROM YORK.
	153¾	From York.		
Skelton.		cr. river Ouse.		Nether Poppleton.
	148	Shipton St.	5¾	Overton.
4 miles distant, Sutton Hall, W. C. Harland, Esq.	144	Tollerton St.	9¾	Newton-on-Ouse, and Benningbrough Hall.
				Alne.

ON RIGHT FROM YORK.	From Berwick.		From York.	ON LEFT FROM YORK.
Easingwold, 2 miles.	142½	ALNE St.	11¼	
	140¼	Raskelf St.	13½	Branch to Boroughbridge, 5¾ miles.
	137½	Pill Moor Junction St.	16¼	
	135½	Sessay St.	18¼	
2 miles distant, Thirkleby Park.		Cross line from Leeds and Harrowgate (p. 437).		Dalton; beyond, Topcliffe on Swale, and Newby Park.
Woodend, Lady Crompton. Thornton-le-Moor.	131¼	THIRSK St. (See p. 380).	22½	Breckenbrough. Newsham.
	126½	Otterington St.	26¼	North Otterington.
Brompton. Lazenby. Birkby.	123½	NORTH ALLERTON JUNCTION St. (See p. 386).	30¼	Branch to Leeming Lane, 5½ miles. Yafforth. Lazenby Hall. Hutton Bonville.
	116¼	Cowton St.	37½	Pepper Hall, 1½ mile.
	114½	Dalton Junction St.	39¼	Halnaby Hall, Sir J. R. Milbanke, Bart.
The ruins of Richmond Castle are situated on the south side of the town, overlooking the Swale, which runs in a deep valley beneath. The keep is about 100 feet high, and the shell almost entire. The walls are 11 feet thick. This castle was founded by Alain Rufus, Earl of Bretagne, who came over with William the Conqueror. Near the castle, on the opposite bank of the Swale, are the ruins of the Priory of St. Martin; and north of the town are the ruins and fine tower of a Greyfriary. Here are also the ruins of St. Nicholas's Hospital.		Branch to Richmond, 9½ miles.		Richmond is delightfully situated on a lofty eminence rising from the Swale. It has two old churches, St. Mary's and Trinity, several dissenting chapels, a town-hall, free grammar and other schools. It is noted for its extensive corn market, and has a considerable traffic in lead. The surrounding country is remarkably picturesque. 2 M.P. Pop. 1861, 5134. Near the town is Aske Hall, the seat of the Earl of Zetland.
Croft Hall, Sir W. R. C. Chaytor, Bart.		cr. river Tees, and enter Durham.		Clarvaux Castle.
Neasham Hall, 2½ m.	112	Croft St.	41¾	Blackwell Grange.

ON RIGHT FROM YORK.	From Berwick.		From York.	ON LEFT FROM YORK.
	109¼	DARLINGTON (p. 389).	44½	
Ketton House, Rev. Sir C. Hardinge, Bart.		Cross Stockton and Darlington Railway.		
		cr. river Skerne twice.		Coatham.
	103¾	Aycliffe St.	50	
		cr. river Skerne and Clarence Railway.		Windlestone Hall, Sir Wm. Eden, Bart., 3½ m.
Hardwick Hall, 1½ m.	99	Bradbury St.	54¾	
Branch to Hartlepool, 15½ m. Quarrington. Cassop. Whitwell.	96¼	Ferry Hill Junction St.	57½	Great Chilton. Branch to Willington and Byers Green. Whitworth Park, R. D. Shafto, Esq., 4 m. Brancepeth Castle, Viscount Boyne, 4½ miles.
Branch to Sunderland, 13 miles.	91¾	Shincliffe St.	62	
	89¼	Sherburn St.	64½	Croxdale Hall, G. Salvin, Esq.
Ellemore Hall. Pittington.	88¼	Belmont Junction St.	65½	Sherburn Hall. Branch to Durham, 2 m.
W. Rainton. E. Rainton. Morton.	87	Leamside St.	66¾	River Wear, and beyond, the Ruins of Finchale Abbey.
	84¾	Fence Houses St.	69	Great Lumley. Lumley Castle, Earl of Scarborough. Lambton Castle, Earl of Durham.
Painshaw Hill, on the summit of which is a monument, erected in 1844, in honour of the late Earl of Durham.	82¾	Pensher or Painshaw St.	71	
		cr. river Wear.		
Barmston.	81½	Washington St.	72¼	Usworth Place.
Hylton Place. Hylton Castle, J. Bowes, Esq.	77½	Boldon St.	76¼	
Branch to South Shields, 3 miles, and to Sunderland, 5 m. Jarrow. Monkton. Hebburn Hall, C. Ellison, Esq.	76	Brockley Whins Junction St.	77¾	S. Wardley. Ayton Banks, 2 m.
Nether Heworth.	70	GATESHEAD (see p. 394.)	83¾	Ravensworth Castle, Lord Ravensworth, 3¾ m. Dunston Hall, (a lunatic asylum), 2¾ m. and beyond, Axwell Park, Sir W. A. Clavering, Bart.
		cr. river Tyne, and enter Northumberland.		

ON RIGHT FROM YORK.	From Berwick.		From York.	ON LEFT FROM YORK.
Branch to North Shields and Tynemouth, 6 miles. Benton House.	66½	NEWCASTLE (p. 391.)	87¼	Fenham Hall, 2 miles. Long Benton. Gosforth House; 2½ miles beyond, Woolsington House, M. Bell, Esq.
	61	Killingworth St.	92¾	Seaton Burn. Arcot.
4 m. distant, near the coast, Seaton Delaval, Lord Hastings.	57	Cramlington St.	96¾	
Blyth, 6 miles distant, at the mouth of a small river of the same name, has considerable trade in coals. Pop. 1953. Horton.		cr. river Blyth.		Blagdon Park, Sir M. W. Ridley, Bart. Stannington.
Bedlington.	53	Netherton St.	100¾	
	50¼	MORPETH (p. 395.)	103½	Mitford Castle ruins 2¼ miles, and Mitford House.
Bothal, Duke of Portland.		cr. river Wansbeck.		
	46¾	Longhirst St.	107	Longhirst House. Ulgham.
Creswell Hall, A. J. B. Creswell, Esq., 2 m.		cr. Line Water.		Causey Park.
Widdrington Castle. (See p. 394.)	43½	Widdrington St.	110¼	Eshot Hall; 3 miles beyond, Linden Hall. Felton Park, T. Riddell, Esq.
	38¼	Acklington St.	115½	Acton House.
		cr. river Coquet.		Swarland Hall. Newton Hall.
	35	Warkworth St.	118¾	Shilbottle.
Warkworth Castle and Hermitage, 1 mile (see p. 397.)		cr. river Alne.		
Alnmouth, on the coast, 2 miles.	32	Bilton Junction St.	121¼	Branch to Alnwick, 3 miles. Alnwick Castle and Abbey, Duke of Northumberland (p. 396.)
Howick House, Earl Grey. Dunston Hill.	29¼	Long Houghton St.	124½	Hulne Abbey. Swansfield. Rennington.
On the coast, Dunstanborough Castle, 3 m. Ebleton.	24	Christon Bank St.	129¾	Rock Castle. Charlton Hall. Falloden House, Rt. Hon. Sir G. Grey, Bart.
Beadnell House, 3½ m.	21	Chat Hill St.	132¾	Ellingham Hall, Sir G. Huggerston, Bart.
	19¼	Newham St.	134½	Twizell House, P. J. Selby, Esq.
On the coast, 3 miles distant, the ruins of Bamborough Castle (see p. 398); beyond, Farn Islands.	17¾	Lucker St.	136	Alderstone House. Bells Hill.
Budle House.	14½	BELFORD (p. 398.)	139½	Belford Hall. Easington House.
Holy Island (see p. 399.)		The line hence runs near the sea-shore.		Middleton Hall. Kyloe.

ON RIGHT FROM YORK.	From Berwick.		From York.	ON LEFT FROM YORK.
The Sea.	8	Beal St.	145¾	Haggerston Castle, Sir E. Blount, Bart. Ancroft, 2 miles.
Spittal.	3	Scremerston St.	150¾	Cheswick House, J. S. Donaldson Selby, Esq.
	1¼	Tweedmouth Junction St. cr. river Tweed.	152½	Line to Kelso, &c., branches off.
		BERWICK, (see p. 399).	153¾	
		Thence to Edinburgh, by railway, 58 miles.		

CLIX. LONDON TO HULL, THROUGH RUGBY, LEICESTER, NOTTINGHAM, AND LINCOLN, BY RAILWAY, 208 Miles.

ON RIGHT FROM LOND.	From Hull.		From London.	ON LEFT FROM LOND.
	208	From London, by North Western Railway, to		
	125¼	Rugby (p. 203).	82¾	
		Thence, by Midland Railway, to		
Kingston-upon-Soar.	87¾	Kegworth St. (p. 352).	120¼	Ratcliffe-upon-Soar.
Thrumpton Hall.		cr. river Trent. and enter Derbyshire.		
	83½	Long Eaton Junction.	124½	Line to Derby, 9 miles.
Barton. Attenborough. Clifton Hall, Sir R. J. Clifton, Bart.		Enter Nottinghamshire.		Chilwell Hall. Bramcote and Bramcote Park, 1½ mile.
	80½	Beeston St.	127½	
Wilford.				Lenton Hall. Lenton Firs; beyond, Wollaton Hall, Lord Middleton.
Colwick Hall; and beyond, Holme Pierrepoint (Earl Manvers).	77¾	NOTTINGHAM.	130¼	Branch to Mansfield, 17½ miles.

NOTTINGHAM is situated on the north bank of the river Lene, about a mile north of the Trent. Its early history is involved in obscurity. It at one time belonged to the Danes, and was one of their Mercian burghs which connected their Northumbrian and East Anglian dominions. William the Conqueror built a castle here, the government of which he conferred upon his natural son,

William Peveril. This strong fortress was the object of contest during the reigns of Stephen, Richard I., John, Henry III., &c. In 1330, Roger Mortimer, the paramour of Queen Isabella, was seized here by her son, Edward III. In the civil wars of his time, Charles I. set up his standard at Nottingham, but the place was taken next year by the Parliament, who garrisoned the castle, of which the famous Colonel Hutchinson was governor. It was dismantled during the Commonwealth, and upon the Restoration the ancient fortress was replaced by the present edifice, which belongs to the Duke of Newcastle. It was burnt during the Reform Bill riots, and remains in ruins. The castle stands on a rock perpendicular on three sides, at the south-west corner of the town.

The principal public buildings of this town are, the exchange, the county hall and gaol, the town hall, the mechanics' hall, the new corn exchange, the house of correction, the infirmary, the lunatic asylum, St. Mary's Church, on a striking elevation (recently restored at great expense, and containing some fine monuments), St. Peter's, and several other churches belonging to the Establishment. Nottingham has also several handsome meeting-houses, a large Roman Catholic Chapel, and numerous alms houses; a spacious market place, containing 5½ acres, considered the largest in the kingdom; a small theatre, a race-course, extensive cavalry barracks, free schools, and several banks. About a mile south of the town is the Trent Bridge, of nineteen arches, an ancient structure, and exhibiting, from frequent repairs, great architectural variety.

The principal manufactures of Nottingham are, bobbin-net and lace, and cotton and silk hosiery, shoes, and gloves. There are several mills for spinning cotton and woollen yarn, and for throwing silk; also dye-houses and iron-foundries. Nottingham ale has a high reputation. The Nottingham Canal joins the Trent a mile from the town. The Midland Railway Company have a commodious first-class station in the meadows adjacent to the town. The environs of Nottingham are very pleasant, and abound with gardens belonging to the inhabitants. Nottingham returns two members to Parliament. The population of the Parliamentary Borough in 1861 was 74,693. The outlying suburbs, viz., the villages of Sneinton, Lenton, and Radford, have a population of more than 20,000. A considerable part of the land round the town was, until recently, commonable to the burgesses during a third of every year, and, consequently could not be used for building purposes. But an act has been obtained for its enclosure—numerous new streets, public walks, and places of recreation have been laid out; public baths and wash-houses, and numerous private edifices have been built and are in course of erection on the land which has thus been brought into the market. Gilbert Wakefield, Dr. Kippis, and Henry Kirke White were natives of Nottingham. Seven miles distant is Hucknall Church where Lord Byron was interred in 1824.

ON RIGHT FROM LOND.	From Hull.		From London.	ON LEFT FROM LOND.
Colwick Hall.	74¼	Carleton St.	133¾	Gedling, and Gedling House, Rev. P. Williams.
	72¼	Burton Joyce St.	135¾	1 mile beyond Fiskerton Station is a branch to Southwell, pleasantly situated in a well wooded country, on the banks of the little river Greet. Southwell is a place of great antiquity, and was formerly more extensive than at present. It possesses a collegiate church, supposed to be the oldest ecclesiastical structure in England, except St Augustine's Monastery at Canterbury.* The Archbishops of York formerly had a palace here, now in ruins. Pop. 3095.
	70	Lowdham St.	138	
Bleasby Hall, R. K. Kelham, Esq.	66¾	Thurgarton St. A fine old church here.	141¼	
Morton.	63¾	Fiskerton St.	144¼	
		cr. riv. Greet (a noted trout stream) and branch of river Trent.		
Winthorpe Hall. Langford.	60¼	NEWARK (see p. 388.)	147¾	Kelham Hall, J. H. Manners Sutton, Esq.
		Cross line of Great Northern Railway.		On opposite side of Trent, Muskham Grange and Muskham House, J. Handley, Esq.
	55	Collingham St.	153	South Scarle.
		Cross boundary, and enter Lincolnshire.		
Thurlby Hall, Sir E. G. Bromhead, Bt., 3 m.	52¼	Swinderby St.	155¾	Eagle.
S. Hyckham.	50	Thorpe St.	158	
N. Hyckham.	47¾	Hykeham St.	160¼	
Bracebridge. Boultham.		cr. river Witham.		
Line to Boston branches off.	44¾	LINCOLN (p. 421).	163¼	Line from Gainsborough joins.
Canwick Hall, Major G. W. T. Sibthorp, 1 mile. Greetwell.		cr. river Witham again.		
Cherry Willingham. Fiskerton.	39¼	Reepham St.	168¾	
Wragby, 5 m. distant, is a small market-town, with a church of considerable architectural beauty. Pop. 610.	37¾	Langworth St.	170¼	Sudbrooke Holme, R. Ellison, Esq.
		cr. Langworth riv.		
Stainton.	34¾	Snelland St.	173¼	
Holton Hall, 2 miles. Lissington. Linwood.	33¼	Wickenby St.	174¾	Friesthorpe. Faldingworth. Buslingthorpe.
Willingham House 2½ m.; and beyond Bayon's Manor, Right Hon. C. T. D'Eyncourt. Walesby.	23¼	MARKET RASEN, a small market-town, 13½ miles N.E. of Lincoln.	178¾	Middle Rasen. Kirkby cum Osgodby.

* It is 264 feet long, and has three towers. The stone carving of the chapter house is most elaborate.

ON RIGHT FROM LOND.	From Hull.		From London.	ON LEFT FROM LOND.
	26½	Usselby St.	181½	
Normanby. Claxby.		The line here runs along the base of the Wolds.		N. Owersby.
	23¾	Holton St.	184¼	
To Caistor, 3 miles (p. 429.)	22	Moortown St.	186	S. Kelsey, 2½ miles; near it, Kelsey Hall.
Grasby.	20½	N. Kelsey St.	187½	
Searby cum Owmsby. Somerby.	18¾	Howsham St.	189¼	Cadney, 2 miles.
Bigby.	14¾	BARNETBY ST.	193¼	Junction of line from Glanford Brigg and Gainsborough (p. 350.)
Barnetby. Brocklesby Park (Earl of Yarborough.)	10¼	Brocklesby St.	197¾	
Branch to Grimsby, 9¾ miles (see p. 351.)	9	ULCEBY JUNCTION ST.	199	
N. Killingholme.				Wootton, and Wootton Hall, L. Uppleby, Esq.
	6½	Thornton Abbey St.	201½	Thornton Curtis.
Thornton College, &c.; beyond, East Halton, and Mouth of Humber.	4¾	Goxhill St.	203¼	Barrow.
	2½	NEW HOLLAND, And on the opposite bank of the Humber, which is crossed by steam-boats so formed as to receive the carriages on their decks.	205½	Railway to Barton, 3½ miles
		HULL, (see p. 359.)	208	

CLX. LONDON TO NORTHAMPTON AND PETERBOROUGH, BY RAILWAY, 110¼ Miles.

ON RIGHT FROM LOND.	From Peterbr.		From London.	ON LEFT FROM LOND.
Courteen Hall, Sir C. Wake, Bart. Milton Mazor.	47¼	From London by North Western Railway to BLISWORTH JUNCTION St. (p. 202.)	63	Leave main line of N. Western Railway.
		Nearly along line of Northampton Canal to		
Delapré Abbey, Major-General E. Bouverie.	42½	NORTHAMPTON, (p. 226.) The line hence follows throughout the course of the Nen, which it crosses in several places.	67¾	Abington Abbey (a lunatic asylum), 1 m.
Hardingstone. Great Houghton. Little Houghton.				Weston Favell. Overstone House (Lord Overstone.)

ON RIGHT FROM LOND.	From Peterbr.		From London.	ON LEFT FROM LOND.
Brafield, 1½ mile. Cogenhoe.	38½	Billing Road St.	71¾	Little Billing. Great Billing.
Whiston. Castle Ashby, Marquis of Northampton (see p. 425).	35½	Castle Ashby St.	74¾	Ecton Lodge. Earls Barton, 1½ mile. Great Doddington.
Woollaston Hall. To Olney, 11 miles.	31½	WELLINGBOROUGH St. (See pp. 424-5.) cr. river Nen.	78¾	Wellingborough, 1½ m.
Irchester, 1 mile, the site of a Roman encampment.	29½	Ditchford St.	80¾	Finedon Hall, 2¾ m.
Knuston Hall, 1¾ mile.		cr. river Nen.		
Higham Ferrers, 1 m. Stanwick.	27¼	HIGHAM FERRERS St. (See p. 365.)	83	Irthlingborough, 1 m. Kettering, 9 miles.
Raunds, 1½ mile. Ringstead. Denford.	24½	Ringstead St. cr. river Nen several times.	85¾	Little Addington. Great Addington. Woodford.
To Huntingdon, 17 m. Titchmarsh.	21¼	THRAPSTON (p. 425).	89	Drayton House, 2 m. Islip.
Wigsthorpe.	18¾	Thorpe St.	91½	Lowick, 2 miles. Aldwinkle.
		Cross coach-road from Thrapston to Oundle.		Woodford House, 4 m. Cranford, Rev. Sir G. T. Robinson, Bart., 5 m.
Barnewell Castle.	15½	Barnewell St. cr. river Nen twice.	94¾	Lilford Hall (Lord Lilford.) Pilton.
Polebrooke, 1¾ mile. Ashton.	13	OUNDLE (see p. 425). Pop. 1851, 2689.	97¼	Stoke Doyle. Glapthorn. Fotheringhay, (see p. 425).
Elton Hall (Earl of Carysfort).	8	cr. river Nen. Elton St. cr. riv. Nen, and enter Huntingdonshire.	102¼	Kingscliffe, 5 miles, is a small town, which formerly had a market, now discontinued.
	6½	WANSFORD St.	103¾	Stamford, 7½ miles (see p. 388); 1 mile before Stamford is Burghley House, Marquis of Exeter.
Chesterton, 1¾ mile.		cr. riv. Nen, and re-enter Northamptonshire. Cross line of ancient Ermine Street, a Roman Road.		Walcot Hall, 5 miles.
To Huntingdon, 19¼ miles; Stilton, 6½ m.	5¼	Castor St.	105	Near Castor, at Water Newton, on the opposite side of the Nen, is the site of a Roman station, the *Durobrivæ* of the Itinerary.
		cr. riv. Nen again, and re-enter Huntingdonshire.		
Alwalton Castle. Overton Longueville, and near it, Orton Hall Marq. of Huntly.	2¾	Overton St.	107½	Milton Park, Earl Fitzwilliam. Thorpe Hall.
		PETERBOROUGH (p. 420).	110¼	

ON RIGHT FROM LOND.	From Hull.		From London.	ON LEFT FROM LOND.
		From London by North Western Railway, as on preceding page, to		
Paston. Werrington.	98¼	PETERBOROUGH. (See p. 420.)	110¼	5 miles beyond, Peterborough, leave line of railway to Stamford and Melton Mowbray. Glinton.
		Thence by Great Northern line, to		
Crowland, 2½ miles (see p. 430.)	89¼	Peakirk, Crowland, &c. St.	119¼	Market Deeping, 2 m. distant, a small town of great antiquity. The land to the eastward of it is said to be the lowest in the county, whence its appellation is derived. Pop. 1337.
		cr. river Welland, and enter Lincolnshire.		
	87½	St James Deeping St.	121	
	83½	Littleworth and Deeping Fen St.	125	
		Proceed through the district of the Fens, an immense level tract which occupies parts of the counties of Lincoln, Cambridge, Norfolk, Suffolk, Huntingdon, and Northampton, extending about 50 miles from north to south, and 30 from east to west, and comprehending nearly 400,000 acres. This district is intersected by numerous artificial channels, by means of which it has been effectually drained, and converted, from a vast swamp, into a highly fertile and productive region.		
Holbeach (see p. 430), 8 miles.	77½	SPALDING St. (see p. 430.)	131	Pinchbeck. Surfleet.
The church of St. Peter and St. Paul in Algarkirk is an ancient structure, with a tower and five bells.	73¾	Surfleet St.	134¾	Gosberton; near it, Cressy Hall.
		cr. river Glen.		
	70½	Sutterton and Algarkirk St.	138	Swineshead, 5 miles (see p. 430.) Kirton. Frampton Hill.
Frampton Hall.	68½	Kirton St.	140	W. Skirbeck House.
Wyberton.	64½	BOSTON (p. 431.)	144	Railway to Lincoln, 25 m., by Tattershall.
		cr. river Witham.		
	59½	Sibsey St.	149	
	57¾	Old Leeke St.	150¾	
	54½	East Ville St.	154	To New Bolingbroke, 7½ miles.
	51	Little Steeping St.	157½	
Wainfleet, 5 miles, a small market-town situated on a navigable creek of the sea, on the north side of the estuary of the Wash. It has a grammar school, founded in 1459. Pop. 1392. Irby. Bratoft.	49¾	FIRSBY St.	158¾	Spilsby, 4 m. distant, a small market-town, 26 miles east of Lincoln, is the chief place in the southern part of Lindsey division. Pop. 1467. Gunby Hall, A. Massingberd, Esq. Candlesby House; beyond, Gillingham House.
Burgh, 2 miles. Orby.	46¾	BURGH St.	161¾	Welton. Claxby.
Willoughby.	43½	Willoughby St.	165	Well Hall, Rt. Hon R. A. C. N. Hamilton.

ON RIGHT FROM LOND.	From Hull.		From London.	ON LEFT FROM LOND.
Farlsthorpe.	41	ALFORD ST. a small market-town. Pop. 1945.	167½	Rigsby. Haugh. S. Thoresby. Bellean Hall.
Saleby. Authorpe.	38	Claythorpe St.	170½	Claythorpe Hall.
Tothill. S. Reston.	36	Authorpe St.	172½	Burwell Park, H. Leister, Esq.
N. Reston.	33½	Legbourne St.	175	Muckton.
Stewton.	30¼	LOUTH (p. 432).	178¼	Little Cawthorpe. Kenwick Hall.
Keddington. Little Grimsby. Yarborough.		cross Louth Navigation.		Fanthorpe Hall. Fotherby. Utterby.
Covenham St Mary. Fulstow.	24¼	Ludborough St.	184¼	
Tetney.	23¼	N. THORESBY St.	185¼	Grainsby. Waith.
	21¼	Holton-le-Clay St.	187¼	
Humberstone. Clee.	19¼	Waltham St.	189¼	Waltham Hall. Scartho.
	16¼	GREAT GRIMSBY, (see p. 430). Thence to	192¼	
	6½	Ulceby, as in p. 446.	202	
		From Ulceby to New Holland, and HULL, as in p. 446.	208½	

CLXII. LONDON TO HULL, THROUGH CAMBRIDGE, ELY, PETERBOROUGH, AND BOSTON, BY RAILWAY, 200¾ Miles.

ON RIGHT FROM LOND.	From Hull.		From London.	ON LEFT FROM LOND.
		From Bishopsgate St., London, to		
Stepney. Bow Common.	199¾	Mile End St. cr. Regent's Canal.	1	
Branch to Blackwall Railway.	198¼	Victoria Park and Bow St.	2½	Victoria Park, an extensive space, recently purchased by government, and enclosed for the recreation of the inhabitants of the eastern parts of the metropolis.
Bow is said to have derived its name from its old bridge, of one arch or bow. Between Bow and Stratford was an ancient bridge over the Lea, said to have been built by order of Matilda, queen of Henry I. Bromley		Cross line of E. and W. India Docks and North Western Railway Junction. cr. river Lea, and enter Essex.		

ON RIGHT FROM LOND.	From Hull.		From London.	ON LEFT FROM LOND.
Leave line to Colchester, and branch to N. Woolwich. Leytonstone and Leytonstone House, and beyond, Wanstead.	197	Stratford St. The line here turns northward, and proceeds along the course of the river Lea.	3¾	Hackney. Defoe lived here. Clapton. Low Leyton.
Wanstead House, a noble building, was demolished by the 4th Earl of Mornington.	195	Lea Bridge St. cr. river Lea, and re-enter Middlesex.	5¾	Stamford Hill.
West Ham. Walthamstow.	193	TOTTENHAM St. Pop. of parish 1851, 9120.	7¾	Tottenham High Cross. Bruce Castle, now a school.
River Lea; and beyond, Chingford.	192	PARK St.	8¾	Tottenham Place. Tottenham. Branch to Enfield, 3 m.
	191½	Water Lane St.	9½	Edmonton, rendered classic by Cowper's "John Gilpin."
Waltham Abbey, 1 m. distant, derives its name from an Abbey of very ancient origin, which was enlarged by Harold, who was buried within its precincts. All that now remains of the building is a part of the west end of the Ladye Chapel, now used as the parochial church. An ancient gate at some distance, partly built with Roman bricks, marks one of the entrances of the Abbey garden. Pop. of town 1861, 2873, and of parish, 5044.	189	PONDERS END St. Enter Hertfordshire.	11¾	Forty Hall. Theobald's Park, Sir H. Meux, Bart.
	186	WALTHAM St.	14¾	Waltham Cross, an exquisite relic (see p. 381.)
	184½	Cheshunt St.	16¼	Cheshunt (see p. 381.) Cheshunt Park. Wormley.
	181¾	Broxbourne Junction St. cr. river Lea, and enter Essex.	19	Hoddesdon, 2½ m. Branch to Ware and Hertford, 7 miles. 1 mile distant on this branch is the Rye House, celebrated as the scene of the plot to which its name has become attached.
Nazeing.	178¾	Roydon St. Along valley of river Stort.	22	Stanstead Abbots. Hunsdon House, 1 m. Eastwick.
Parndon House. Little Parndon.	176½	Burnt Mill St.	24½	New Place; beyond, Gilston, once the property of Ward, the author of "Tremaine."
Latton Priory. Harlow, 1 mile (see p. 162.) At High Laver, 4½ m. distant, John Locke was buried.	174½	HARLOW St.	26¼	
Hyde Hall, Earl of Roden. At Hatfield Broad Oak, 6 miles distant, are the remains of a Benedictine priory. Little Hallingbury. Walbury. Great Hallingbury.	172¼	Sawbridgeworth St. Cross river Stort, and re-enter Hertfordshire.	28½	Thorley.

ON RIGHT FROM LOND.	From Hull.		From London.	ON LEFT FROM LOND.
	168½	BISHOP STORTFORD (see p. 463). Pop. 4673.	32¼	Hadham.
Birchanger. Stanstead Mountfichet, which has an old church, and the slight remains of an ancient castle, built in the time of William I.	165¼	Re-enter Essex. Stanstead St.	35½	Farnham. Manewden, 2 miles.
Standstead Hall, and beyond Easton Park, Viscount Maynard.	163½	Elsenham St.	37½	
Henham on the Hill. Widdington. Debden Hall. Shortgrove Hall.	159	Newport St.	41¾	Ugley, 1 m. Quendon Hall. Wendens Ambo.
Audley End, the noble seat of Lord Braybrooke, contains some good pictures, and has an extensive aviary. Littlebury.	157¼	AUDLEY END St. Enter Cambridgeshire.	43½	Great Chesterford is the site of a Roman station:—at the adjacent village of Ickleton, extensive Roman remains have been found.
Little Chesterford. To Linton, 5 miles, a small market town. Branch Railway to Newmarket, 18 miles.	153¼	CHESTERFORD St. Enter valley of river Cam or Granta, one of the feeders of which the line crosses several times.	47½	Ickleton. Hinxton. Duxford.
	149¾	Whittlesford St.	51	Whittlesford Hall.
Pampisford. Sawston.	146½	Shelford St.	54¼	Great Shelford House. Little Shelford.
Stapleford. Gog Magog Hills, Lord Godolphin. Cherry Hinton, 1½ m. Branch to Newmarket. Fen Ditton. Horningsea.	143¼	Cambridge Junction St. (see p. 433.) ☞ cr. river Cam, and continue along its valley.	57½	Trumpington; and beyond, Grantchester. In the distance, Madingley Hall, Sir St. Vincent Cotton, Bart. Branch to St Ives and Huntingdon, 19½ miles. Chesterton. Milton. Milton Hall.
	137¾	Waterbeach St. Proceed through the district of the Fens. ☞ cr. river Ouse.	63	Cottenham, 3½ miles, gave the title of Earl to the late Lord Chancellor Cottenham. Stretham. Thetford.
Barraway. Stuntney. Leave main line to Norwich (see p. 485.) Wood House.	128½	Ely, Peterborough, and Lynn Junction St. (See p. 456.)	72¼	That part of Cambridgeshire which lies to the north of the Ouse is called the Isle of Ely, and has a separate jurisdiction. It forms a part of the great Fen district.
	125¾	Chittisham St. ☞ cr. Old and New Bedford rivers, two artificial channels, cut in order to give a better outfall to the waters of the Ouse, by avoiding its circutous course.	75	

ON RIGHT FROM LOND.	From Hull.		From London.	ON LEFT FROM LOND.
	$118\frac{3}{4}$	MANEA St.	82	
		cr. old riv. Nen.		
Branch to Wisbeach, 9 miles.	$113\frac{1}{2}$	MARCH JUNCTION St. March is a small market-town, with some trade in coals, timber, and corn. Pop. 3600. See also p. 459.	$87\frac{1}{2}$	Branch from St Ives joins here, $18\frac{3}{4}$ miles.
The great level of the Fens, through which this part of the line runs, is commonly called the Bedford Level, from the circumstance of the 4th Earl of Bedford having formed a company for its drainage in the time of Charles I. The attempt was renewed during the reign of Charles II., by whom a charter was granted (in 1664) to an incorporated company, under the control and management of which the draining of	$105\frac{3}{4}$	Eastrea St.	95	this district has been maintained to the present day. Notwithstanding, however, the vast expense which has been incurred, the work is still imperfect. But great improvement has taken place within the last few years, and steam engines are now used for the purpose of raising the water into the numerous artificial cuts by which it is carried off to the sea.
		cr. Whittlesea Dyke.		
	$104\frac{1}{2}$	Whittlesea St. (see p. 458).	$96\frac{1}{2}$	
		cr. King's Dyke.		
	$98\frac{1}{4}$	PETERBOROUGH.	$102\frac{1}{2}$	
		Thence to New Holland (HULL), as in p. 448.	$200\frac{3}{4}$	

CLXIII. HULL TO BRIDLINGTON AND SCARBOROUGH, BY RAILWAY, $53\frac{1}{2}$ Miles.

ON RIGHT FROM HULL.	From Scarbor.		From Hull.	ON LEFT FROM HULL.
Newland. Hull Bank, $1\frac{1}{2}$ mile.	$49\frac{1}{2}$	From Hull to Cottingham St.	4	Leave Hull and Selby line. Cottingham Castle. Risby Hall, $2\frac{1}{2}$ miles.
Cottingham Parks. Beverley Parks. Woodmansey.	$45\frac{1}{4}$	BEVERLEY (p. 422).	$8\frac{1}{4}$	Molescroft. Leckonfield. Scorbrough.
Hornsea, $12\frac{1}{2}$ miles distant, a small town on the coast, on the west side of which is a lake called Hornsea Mere, nearly 440 acres in extent.	$40\frac{1}{2}$	Lockington St.	13	Dalton Hall, Lord Hotham, 5 m.
Watton Abbey.	$37\frac{1}{4}$	Hutton Cranswick St.	$16\frac{1}{4}$	Beswick. Watton; near it, Kilnwick Hall.
Skerne.		cr. small feeder of River Hull.		Neswick Hall, 3 miles. Sunderlandwick Hall.
4 miles north of Driffield are some tumuli called the Danes' Graves.	34	GREAT DRIFFIELD (p. 420). The line runs along the base of the York Wolds, on the high grounds of which are numerous remains of antiquity, both of Roman and Saxon times.	$19\frac{1}{2}$	Sledmere Castle, Sir Tatton Sykes, Bart., $7\frac{1}{2}$ m.
Foston.	32	Nafferton St.	$21\frac{1}{2}$	Pockthorpe Hall, 3 m. Lowthorpe Hall.
Great Kelk.	$29\frac{3}{4}$	Lowthorpe St.	$23\frac{3}{4}$	Ruston Parva. Harpham.

ON RIGHT FROM HULL.	From Scarbor.		From Hull.	ON LEFT FROM HULL.
Fraisthorpe.	28	Burton Agnes St.	$25\frac{1}{2}$	Burton Agnes Hall, Sir H. Boynton, Bart.
	25	Carnaby St.	$28\frac{1}{2}$	Thornholm. Haisthorpe. Bessingby.
The Sea. Sewerby House.	$22\frac{3}{4}$	BRIDLINGTON (pp. 420 and 427).	$30\frac{3}{4}$	Boynton Hall, Sir G. Strickland, Bart. $3\frac{1}{2}$ m.
Marton Hall, R. Creyke, Esq. Flamborough, 2 miles (see pp. 420 and 427).	$20\frac{1}{4}$	Marton St.	$33\frac{1}{4}$	Rudstone, 6 miles; and near it, Thorpe Hall, Lord Macdonald.
Across the peninsula which terminates in Flamboro' Head is an ancient work called the Danes' Dyke.	19	Bempton St. The line here runs parallel to the coast, at a distance of about a mile.	$34\frac{1}{2}$	
Buckton.	$16\frac{1}{4}$	Speeton St.	$37\frac{1}{4}$	
Reighton. Filey Bay.	12	Hunmanby St.	$41\frac{1}{2}$	Burton Fleming, 3 m. Muston.
	$9\frac{1}{4}$	FILEY St.	$44\frac{1}{4}$	
	$7\frac{1}{4}$	Gristhorpe St.	$46\frac{1}{4}$	Flotmanby, 1 mile. Folkton, $1\frac{1}{2}$ mile.
Lebberston.	$5\frac{1}{2}$	Cayton St.	48	
	3	Seamer Junction St.	$50\frac{1}{2}$	Junction of line from York and Malton.
Osgodby, $1\frac{1}{2}$ mile. Oliver's Mount, with tumuli.		SCARBOROUGH (p. 423).	$53\frac{1}{2}$	Falsgrave, and in the distance, Hackness Hall Sir J. V. B. Johnstone, Bart.

CLXIV. YORK TO SCARBOROUGH, BY RAILWAY, $42\frac{3}{4}$ Miles.

ON RIGHT FROM YORK.	From Scarbor.		From York.	ON LEFT FROM YORK.
Line to Market-Weighton, by Pocklington, 23 miles. West and East Huntington. Earswick.		From York to		Clifton.
Towthorpe.	$37\frac{3}{4}$	Haxby St. cr. river Foss.	5	
	$35\frac{1}{2}$	Strensall St.	$7\frac{1}{4}$	Lillings-Ambo.
	$32\frac{3}{4}$	Flaxton St.	10	Thornton-le-Clay. Foston.
Bossall, $1\frac{1}{2}$ m., and beyond, Aldby Park, H. Darley, Esq. Howsham Hall, (G. Cholmley, Esq.) on the Derwent. Westow.	$30\frac{3}{4}$	Barton St. cr. Spittle Beck, and follow course of river Derwent, along which the railway winds for some miles.	12	Crambe.
Kirkham Abbey.	27	Kirkham St.	$15\frac{3}{4}$	Whitwell.

ON RIGHT FROM YORK.	From Scarbor.		From York.	ON LEFT FROM YORK.
Firby.	26¼	Castle Howard St.	16½	Castle Howard, 2½ m., Earl of Carlisle (p. 416.)
	23¾	Hutton St.	19	Hilderley, Sir G. Strickland, Bart., and Easthorpe Hall.
Welham House.		cr. river Derwent.		Mosley Bank.
Scagglethorpe, 1 mile.	21	NEW MALTON, (p. 416.)	21¾	Old Malton.
	16½	Rillington Junction St.	26¼	Line to Pickering and Whitby, 30½ miles.
Scampston Hall. Knapton Hall.	14½	Knapton St.	28¼	Yeddingham.
West and East Heslerton; beyond, the elevated tract of the York Wolds.	12¾	Heslerton St.	30	
	9¼	Sherburn St.	33½	Valley of river Derwent.
Potter Brompton. Binnington; and beyond, Ganton Hall, Sir T. D. Legard, Bart.	7¾	Ganton St.	35	2 miles distant, Wykeham Abbey.
Willerby. Staxton.	3	Seamer Junction St. Here the line from Hull and Bridlington joins (see p. 453).	39¾	
		SCARBOROUGH, (p. 423).	42¾	Hackness Hall, Sir J. V. B. Johnstone, Bart., 5 miles.

CLXV. YORK TO PICKERING AND WHITBY, BY RAILWAY, 56¾ Miles.

ON RIGHT FROM YORK.	From Whitby.		From York.	ON LEFT FROM YORK.
Leave line to Scarborough, 16½ miles. Scampston Hall.	30½	From York to Rillington Junction St. (as above).	26¼	
		cr. river Derwent.		
Thornton-le-Dale, 2 m.	27½	Marishes Road St.	29¼	
About 5 miles distant are some remarkable ancient entrenchments, called Scamridge Dykes, probably either of Danish or Saxon origin. Kingthorpe. Lockton.	24	PICKERING (see p. 416.) The line hence runs through Newton Dale, one of the narrow valleys which extend in a longitudinal direction through the high region of the North York Moorlands.	32¾	Kirkby Misterton, 1½ mile.
Blackhow Topping, a lofty eminence, 2½ miles. On the adjacent moorlands are numerous tumuli, and other ancient works.	18	Levisham St.	38¾	Newton. Near Cawthorn, 2 m. distant, are the remains of two Roman camps, and beyond, at Cropton, one of British origin.
	9¼	Goathland St.	47½	Goathland Moor.

ON RIGHT FROM YORK.	From Whitby.		From York.	ON LEFT FROM YORK.
	6¼	Grosmont St.	50½	Egton, 1¼ mile, a small market town, on the north side of the river Esk. Pop. 1128.
Sleights Moor.		The line hence follows the course of the river Esk, which it crosses several times.		Aislaby Moor.
	3	Sleights St.	53¾	
Ugglebarnby. Sneaton.	1½	Ruswarp St.	55¼	Aislaby. Stakesby.
Larpool Hall, E. Turton, Esq.		WHITBY (see p. 424).	56¾	Mulgrave Castle, Marquis of Normanby, 3 m.

CLXVI. LONDON TO WELLS (NORFOLK), THROUGH CAMBRIDGE, ELY, AND LYNN, 123 miles.

ON RIGHT FROM LOND.	From Wells.		From London.	ON LEFT FROM LOND.
Gog Magog Hills, Lord Godolphin.	72	From London to CAMBRIDGE (page 433.)	51	In the distance Madingley, Sir St. V. Cotton, Bart.
		cr. river Cam.		
Milton Hall.	68¾	Milton.	54¼	
	67	Waterbeach.	56	
	61¾	Stretham Bridge.	61¼	
		cr. the West Water.		
	60¼	Stretham.	62¾	
To Newmarket, 13½ m. Mildenhall, 16½ m.	56	ELY (page 456.)	67	To St. Ives by Earith, 17½ m.; Huntingdon by Chatteris, 27 m.; Wisbeach, 28½ miles.
New Barns Hall.	54	Chettisham.	69	
	53	Woodhouse.	70	Wood House.
	51	Littleport.	72	
	50	Littleport Bridge.	73	
		cr. the river Ouse.		
	47	Brandon Creek Bridge, and enter *Norfolk.*	76	
		cr. riv. Brandon.		
	45¾	Southery Ferry.	77¼	
	45	Southery.	78	
Wood Hall.	43¼	Modney Bridge.	79¾	
	42	Hilgay.	81	
		cr. the river Stoke.		
	41	Fordham.	82	
Ryston Hall, E. R. Pratt, Esq., and 1½ mile to the right, Dereham Abbey.	39¾	Denver.	83¼	

ON RIGHT FROM LOND.	From Wells.		From London.	ON LEFT FROM LOND.
Crow Hall. To Swaffham, 14½ m.	38½	DOWNHAM MARKET.	84½	To Wisbeach, 13 m.
Stow Hall, Sir T. Hare, Bart.	36	Stow Bardolph.	87	Wallington Hall.
	34¼	South Runcton.	88¾	Watlington Hall.
	32¾	Tottenhill.	90¼	To Wisbeach, 12 m.
To Stoke Ferry, 9½ m.		cr. the Setchey.		
	31	SETCHEY.	92	
	29¾	West Winch.	93¼	
To Swaffham, 14½ m.	28½	Hardwick.	94½	To Wisbeach, 12½ m.; Holbeach, 18½ m.
To Norwich by Gayton and East Dereham, 40½ miles.	27¼	LYNN (p. 457).	95¾	
	26¼	Gaywood.	96¾	To Castle Rising, 2½ m.
	25¼	South Wootton.	97¾	
	19¾	Hillington.	103¼	Hillington Hall, Sir W. J. H. B. Ffolkes, Bart.
To Fakenham, 13¼ m.; to Wells by West and East Rudham, 19 miles.	19¼	Junction of the Road.	103¾	
Houghton, Marquis of Cholmondeley, a magnificent seat, built by Sir Robert Walpole.	18¾	Flitcham.	104¼	Anmer Hall, H. Coldham, Esq., and beyond Sandringham Hall, seat of the Prince of Wales, 2 m. from Wolverton station.
	14	Great Bircham.	109	
Bagthorpe Hall.	13¼	Bircham Newton.	109¾	
Docking Hall, Stanhoe Hall, and Barwick House, D. Hoste, Esq.	11¼	Docking.	111¾	
Burnham Hall.				
To Fakenham, 10 m.; New Walsingham, 7½ m.	5¾	Burnham Westgate.	117¼	Hunstanton Cliff, 10¼ miles.
Near Burnham is Burnham Thorpe, the birth-place of Lord Nelson. His father was rector of the parish.	5	Burnham Overy.	118	
Holkham Hall, Earl of Leicester, a magnificent mansion, commenced in 1734 by Lord Lovel, afterwards Earl of Leicester of a former creation, from designs by Palladio and Inigo Jones, and finished in 1760. Both as regards its natural and artificial beauties it is one of the finest residences in England.	1½	Holkham Staith.	121½	
		WELLS.	123	WELLS is a small seaport town with a tolerable harbour, but difficult of access. Corn and malt are shipped, and coals, timber, deals, bark, oil cake, tar, and wine are imported. Here is an oyster fishery.

ELY stands on a considerable eminence in the Isle of Ely, a large tract of high land encompassed with fens that were formerly covered with water. A monastery was founded here about 670. In 870, it was pillaged and destroyed by the Danes, and was not rebuilt till about a century later, when a charter was granted by Edgar, which was confirmed by Canute and Edward the Confessor, and subsequently by the Pope. The isle was gallantly defended against William the Conqueror; but, after repeated attacks, the inhabitants were obliged to surrender. In 1107, Ely was erected into a bishopric by Henry I. After the dissolution of the monasteries, Henry VIII. converted the conventual church into a cathedral. This building displays a singular mixture of various styles of architecture, and has an unfinished appearance, but, as a whole, it is a noble structure. The interior is exceedingly beautiful, and much has been done during the present century to restore and beautify the various chapels it contains. The stalls are fine specimens of wood carving. The whole length of the edifice is upwards of 520 feet. The Church of the Holy Trinity, formerly the Lady Chapel, is attached to the cathedral. It was commenced in the reign of Edward II., and is one of the most perfect buildings of that age. The Church of St Mary is also handsome. Here are also several meeting-houses, a grammar-school, founded by Henry VIII., a national school, charity school, &c. Ely has a considerable manufactory for earthenware and tobacco pipes, and there are several mills in the isle for the preparation of oil from flax, hemp, and cole seed. Pop. 7428.

The Bishop of Ely has considerable patronage at Cambridge.

Lynn or Lynn Regis, a place of great antiquity, is situated on the right bank of the Ouse, about eight or nine miles from the sea. It is divided into several parts by four small rivers, called fleets, and was formerly encompassed on the land side by a foss, defended by a wall and bastions. The harbour is difficult of entrance, but capable of receiving 300 sail of vessels. There is a large quantity of wine imported from Portugal and Spain, and of hemp, wood, and flax, and other articles from the Baltic. Customs' revenue, 1861, £16,174. The market-place is very extensive and handsome, and the quays for landing wine are convenient. The principal church, St Margaret's, is one of the largest parochial churches in England, and is especially rich in monumental brasses. It was erected in 1160, and repaired and enlarged in 1741. There are several other churches or chapels, various meeting-houses, a guild-hall, custom-house, theatre, hospital, a free grammar-school, St Ann's Fort, the promenade called the Mall, the ruins of the Grey Friars' Church, a mechanics' institute, &c. There is communication by railway between Lynn and all the principal towns of the empire. Two M.P.

Castle Rising, five miles north-west of Lynn, and two miles from the Wash on the Rising river, is a place of great antiquity. Some have supposed that Alfred the Great built a castle here. At any rate, a castle enclosing a fragment of a more ancient building, erected here by William de Albini, existed before 1176. Of this fortress there are considerable remains. Here Isabella, Queen of Edward II., was kept in confinement by her son Edward III. from 1330 till her death in 1368. The church is an ancient structure, and contains a highly ornamented font. There is a national school and an hospital, with a chapel, built by the Earl of Northampton in 1613. Disfranchised by Reform Bill. Pop. 377.

Sandringham Hall, the seat of H. R. H. the Prince of Wales, is two miles east of Wolverton Station, immediately to the north of Castle Rising. The estate is described as one of great beauty, affording a rich variety of scenery, and abounding with game. H. R. H. acquired the property in 1862, and its cost is said to have been £150,000.

Flitcham was formerly called Felixham and St. Mary de Fontibus, from the numerous springs in the vicinity. Four miles distant is Houghton Hall (Marquis of Cholmondeley), a stately fabric erected by Sir Robert Walpole.

CLXVII. LONDON TO LYNN THROUGH ROYSTON, CAMBRIDGE, ST. IVES, CHATTERIS, MARCH, AND WISBEACH, 107¼ Miles.

ON RIGHT FROM LOND.	From Lynn.		From London.	ON LEFT FROM LOND.
	56¾	From Shoreditch Ch. to Cambridge, (p. 433.)	50½	Madingley, Sir St. V. Cotten, Bart. St Neots, 17 m.
To Ely, 16 m.		cr. the river Cam.		St Ives, a small town, pleasantly situated on the Ouse, over which is a curious and ancient stone
Somersham was formerly annexed to the monastery of Ely, and	50½	Lolworth.	56¾	bridge, & a modern arched causeway. This town
contained a palace belonging to that see, the site of which is now occupied by other build-	46½	Fen Stanton. *Huntingdonshire.*	60¾	was nearly destroyed by fire in 1689. It carries on a considerable trade in malt
ings. The church is a spacious and noble edi-	44½	ST. IVES.	62¾	and coal, and its market is noted for the sale of
fice, containing several ancient brasses and monuments. The chancel	38¾	Somersham.	68½	cattle, sheep, pigs, poultry, &c. The church, a light, neat structure, with
is supposed to be of the time of Henry III.	33¾	Chatteris Ferry.	73½	a handsome tower, contains numerous sepulchral monuments. Here
Chatteris has a church, a national school, and the remains of a chapel at Hunney Farm.		cr. the river Nen, and enter the Isle of Ely, *Camb.*		are several meeting-houses, and some remains of an ancient priory. Slepe Hall, at St Ives,
Wisbeach derives its name from its situation on the banks of the river Ouse or Wis, which flows through it. It is about eight miles from	31¾	Chatteris.	75½	was the residence of Oliver Cromwell when he rented Wood Farm in the
the German Ocean. The old castle was rebuilt by Thurloe,	30	Carter's Bridge.*	77¼	vicinity. Pop. 3321.

* About 7 miles distant is Ramsey, with an elegant church. Pop. 2354. In the vicinity is Ramsey Mere, a beautiful lake abounding with pike, perch, and eels. Near the town is Ramsey Abbey, the beautiful seat of E. Fellowes, Esq. Eight miles from Ramsey is Whittlesey. Pop. 4496. Whittlesey Mere produces excellent fish, and is much frequented by pleasure-parties.

ON RIGHT FROM LOND.	From Lynn.		From London.	ON LEFT FROM LOND.
Secretary of State to Cromwell, from the designs of Inigo Jones, but has disappeared. The church of St Mary is a spacious and handsome fabric, but of singular construction, being furnished with two naves. It has a very beautiful tower and contains numerous monuments. Wisbeach has also another church, a chapel of ease, several meeting-houses, a custom-house and town hall, a theatre, free and national school, a literary society, assembly rooms, &c. The Rose and Crown Inn has been occupied as a tavern since 1475. There is a circus erected on the site of the castle. The chief articles of traffic are corn, coals, timber, and wine Here are large cattle fairs, and the surrounding country produces wool, hemp, and flax. Wisbeach is a railway station, and there is a canal from it to the river Nen at Outwell, and thence to the Ouse at Salter's Lodge Sluice. Pop. 1861, 9276. King John lost all his baggage and treasures in attempting to cross the Wash. Leverington church, 2 m. distant, contains a curious font, and some painted glass.		cr. Vermuden's Drain.		
	27¾	Doddington, the richest living in England (£7300 per annum).	79½	
	26¼	Wimblington.	81	MARCH, a village in the parish of Doddington, has a spacious and elegant church. Sir H. Peyton, Bart. has a seat at Doddington. Pop. 3600 (see also p. 452).
	23¾	MARCH.	83½	
		cr. the river Nen, (To Peterborough by Whittlesey, 16½ miles.)		
	18½	Guyhern Ferry.	88¾	WALPOLE with the neighbouring villages of Walton and Walsoken, derives its name from its situation, adjacent to an old Roman wall, for securing the country against the inundation of the sea. Numerous Roman bricks, and an aqueduct formed of earthen pipes, were found here in 1727. Walpole St Peter possesses one of the most beautiful parish churches in England, erected about 1423. At a place called Cross Keys, in Walpole St Andrew parish, an embankment, more than 1½ m. long, has been thrown across the Wash, and the river is carried to the sea by a canal, crossed by a drawbridge. A direct communication has thus been opened between Norfolk and Lincolnshire, and the distance between this part of the country and the north of England lessened by 20 miles.
	12¾	WISBEACH.	94½	
		cr. the river Nen, and enter Norfolk.		
	11¾	Walsoken.	95½	
	9¾	Walton Highway.	97½	
	7¾	Walpole Highway.	99½	
	6¼	Rose and Crown.	101	
	4¼	Tun Green.	103	
		cr. the Eau Brink Cut.		
		LYNN, (p. 457).	107¾	

CLXVIII. LONDON TO LYNN BY EPPING, NEWMARKET, AND BRANDON, 102¼ Miles.

ON RIGHT FROM LOND.	From Lynn.		From London.	ON LEFT FROM LOND.
	33	From Whitechapel Church to Barton Mills, (pp. 462-463.)	69¼	
		cr. the river Lark.		1 mile distant is Mildenhall on the Lark, which is here navigable for barges. The church has a richly carved roof, and a steeple 109 feet high.
Lakenheath Hall.				
Brandon, a small well built town on the Little Ouse, had once a great manufactory for gun flints. It gives the	27	Wangford.	75¼	North Court Lodge.
	24	BRANDON.	78¼	Brandon Park (H. Bliss, Esq.)

ON RIGHT FROM LOND.	From Lynn.		From London.	ON LEFT FROM LOND.
title of Duke of Brandon to the Duke of Hamilton and Brandon. In the vicinity are extensive rabbit warrens. Pop. 1851, 2022.		cr. the Little Ouse river, and enter Norfolk.		To Swaffham, 14¾ m.
2 miles distant, Santon Downham, Earl Cadogan.				
Weeting Hall. In the distance, Wretham Park, W. Birch, Esq.	22¾	Weeting All Saints.	79½	3 miles distant, Hockwold Hall. Feltwell Lodge.
3 miles distant, Diddlington Hall, Lord Berners.	18¼	Methwold.	84	
		cr. the river Stoke.		
3 miles distant, Oxburgh Hall, Sir H. R. P. Bedingfield, Bart., a venerable seat, exhibiting a peculiarly interesting specimen of ancient domestic architecture.	14	STOKE FERRY.	88¼	
	12¼	Wereham.	90	1 mile distant, Dereham Abbey.
Stradsett Hall, W. Bagge, Esq., and, 3 miles distant, Barton Bendish Hall, Sir H. Berney, Bart.	9	Stradsett.	93¼	To Downham Market, 3¾ miles.
4 miles distant, Marham Hall.	7½	Shouldham Thorpe.	94¾	2 miles distant, Wallington Hall, and near it Stow Hall, Sir T. Hare, Bart.
	4¾	Junction of the road.	97½	
		cr. the riv. Setchey.		
	3¾	SETCHEY.	98½	1 mile distant, Watlington Hall.
		LYNN (see p. 457).	102¼	

CLXIX. LONDON TO WELLS BY NEWMARKET, BRANDON, SWAFFHAM, AND FAKENHAM, 118½ Miles.

ON RIGHT FROM LOND.	From Wells.		From London.	ON LEFT FROM LOND.
	40¼	From Whitechapel Ch. to Brandon (p. 459).	78¼	
		cr. the Little Ouse river.		To Lynn, 24 miles.
	35½	Mundford, *Norfolk*.	83	
Lyndford Hall, Sir J Sutton, Bart., and West Tofts Hall, and Buckenham House.	34½	Ickborough.	84	2½ miles distant Diddlington Hall, Lord Berners.
Hilborough Hall, and, 2 miles distant, Pickenham Hall.	31¼	Hilborough.	87¼	Cley Hall.
4 miles distant, Necton Hall, W. Mason, Esq. Dunham Lodge.	25½	SWAFFHAM (p. 461).	93	
	22¾	Castle Acre, *Guide Post*.	95¾	To Castle Acre, 1½ m.

ON RIGHT FROM LOND.	From Wells.		From London.	ON LEFT FROM LOND.
Lexham Hall.	21¼	Newton.	97¼	Narford Hall, A. Fountaine, Esq. Near the above is Narburgh Hall, and, at West Acre, the remains of the Abbey, and beyond West Acre, High House, A. Hamond, Esq.
	16½	Weasanham, St Peter's.	102	
	13½	Rainham Hall.	105	Rainham Ha. (Marquis of Townshend,) erected in 1636, contains among other paintings the famous one of Belisarius, by Salvator Rosa.
	11¾	Toft Trees.	106¾	
FAKENHAM is situated near the river Wensom, on a pleasant declivity. It has a handsome church, and one of the largest corn-markets in the county.	9¾	FAKENHAM.	108¾	
	6¾	East Barsham.	111¾	
To Foulsham, 8¼ m.; to Holt, 12 miles.	5¾	Houghton-in-the-Hole.	112¾	To Lynn, 21¾ miles.
To Norwich, 27 miles. Walsingham Abbey, H. Lee Warner, Esq.	5	NEW OR LITTLE WALSINGHAM.	113½	
	3	Wighton.	115½	To Docking, 11 miles; Burnham Thorpe, 6¼ m.; thence to Burnham Westgate, 1½ miles.
	2	Warham Hall.	116½	
	1	Lime Kiln.	117½	Holkham House, Earl of Leicester (see p. 456.)
		WELLS (see p. 456).	118½	

SWAFFHAM is situated on an eminence, and consists of four principal streets. It is a railway station, and noted for its butter-market. The church, which is the finest parish church in the neighbourhood, is large and cruciform, and consists of a nave with two aisles, a chancel, and two transept chapels. It contains several monuments, a roof of finely carved oak, and a library. Here are also several meeting-houses, assembly rooms, theatre, house of correction, &c. Races are held annually on an extensive heath to the south of the town, and coursing-matches are also frequent on the same ground. Pop. 2974.

CASTLE ACRE is supposed to have been a Roman station, as several coins and a tesselated pavement have been dug up here. A castle was erected at this place by William, Earl of Warren and Surrey, to whom the lordship had been granted by his father-in-law, William the Conqueror. Some fragments of the building still remain, and the principal street of the present village passes through one of the main entrances of the castle. There are also considerable remains of a priory of Cluniac monks, founded by Earl Warren, near the castle. The parish church is ancient.

NEW OR LITTLE WALSINGHAM is situated near the river Stiffkey. A monastery for Black Canons was founded here in the reign of William the Conqueror; and pilgrimages, by foreigners of all nations, were made to the chapel or shrine of an idol called "Our Lady of Walsingham." belonging to this foundation.

Several kings and queens of England (among them Henry VIII., in the commencement of his reign), paid their devotions here. Erasmus, who visited it, has described the riches of the chapel. There are some fine remains of the convent, the principal part of which are included in the pleasure-grounds of Walsingham Abbey, the seat of H. Lee Warner, Esq. New Walsingham has a spacious church, containing an ancient font, richly sculptured. The bridewell was formerly a lazar-house for lepers. Pop. 1069.

CLXX. LONDON TO NORWICH BY EPPING, NEWMARKET, THETFORD, AND WYMONDHAM, 108½ Miles.

ON RIGHT FROM LOND.	From Norwich		From London.	ON LEFT FROM LOND.
7 m. from Stratford is Chigwell, where there is a free school, in which W. Penn was educated.	107½	From Whitechapel Church to Mile-End.	1	
The vicinity abounds with noble mansions. Chipping Ongar, 10½ miles farther, has an ancient church, partly built with Roman bricks.	106	Bow.	2½	
		cr. river Lea, and enter Essex.		
	105	Stratford.	3½	
To Romford, 8½ miles.	103	Leytonstone.	5½	
Stratford House, Wanstead Grove.	101¾	Snaresbrook.	6¾	Walthamstow House.
Woodford contains numerous country residences of the London citizens. In the churchyard is a yew tree of extraordinary size, and an elegant monument erected in memory of the descendants of Sir Edmundbury Godfrey, who formerly lived here. Cromwell and Milton are said to have resided in this village.	101	Woodford.	7½	Higham House.
	99½	Woodford Wells.	9	Woodford Wells were formerly much celebrated for their medicinal properties, but have now fallen into disuse.
	98½	The Bald-faced Stag.	10	
Loughton Hall, a fine old mansion with beautiful grounds.	97	Loughton.	11½	Gilwell House.
To Chipping Ongar, 7¼ miles. 1 m. distant Coppersale Hall, and 3 miles distant Hill Hall, Sir W. Bowyer Smijth, Bart.	91¾	EPPING (see p. 464).	16¾	Copped Hall, one of the finest seats in the county (late H. J. Conyers, Esq.) Warleys. A new road has lately been made to Epping to the left of the old one.
	87½	Potter's Street.	21	To Ware, 9½ m., thence to Hertford, 2 miles.
Hubert Hall.	85½	Bromley.	23	
Durrington House.	85¼	Harlow, noted for its fair called Harlow Bush Fair, held on the 9th of September.	23¼	Mark Hall, Parndon House, and beyond, Gilston Park and Hunsdon House.
Hyde Hall, Earl of Roden.	83	Sawbridgeworth, *Herts*.	25½	
Walbury Hall.	81	Spelbrook.	27½	Thorley Hall.

ON RIGHT FROM LOND.	From Norwich.		From London	ON LEFT FROM LOND.
		cross river Stort.		
Twyford House. To Dunmow, 8½ miles.	78½	Hockerill.	30	¾ of a mile distant is Bishop's Stortford, a populous and extensive town on the Stort. It carries on a considerable trade by means of canal and railway. The church contains several monuments. On the east side of the town are the ruins of the castle. Pop. 4673.
In the distance Easton Park, (Viscount Maynard).	75¾	Stanstead Mountfitchet, *Essex*.	32¾	
Orford House.	73½	Ugley.	35	
	72½	Quendon.	36	
1 mile distant, Debden Hall, Shortgrove, and Audley End, the noble seat of Lord Braybrooke.	70	Newport. Has a fine church.	38½	Quendon Flats.
SAFFRON WALDON, 2¾ miles distant, has one of the most beautiful parish churches in England. Here are alms houses, founded by Edward VI., a free school, meeting-houses, &c. Audley End is a portion of the magnificent structure erected about 1610, on the site of the ancient abbey. Pop. 5474.	66¼	Littlebury.	42¼	
	64¾	Little Chesterford.	43¾	
		cross river Cam.		To Cambridge, 10½ m.
	63¾	Great Chesterford. Was an ancient Roman Station.	44¾	Babraham Hall, R. J. Adeane, Esq., and 2 m. dist. Gog Magog Hills, Lord Godolphin. On the top of these hills is a triple entrenchment, with two ditches, supposed to be of British origin.
To Linton, 4¼ miles. Abington Park, T. Mortlock, Esq.	59¼	Bourn Bridge, *Cambridgeshire*.	49¼	
Abington Hall, Abington Lodge, Hildersham Hall, and Hildersham Rookery.	58	Worsted Lodge. Junction of the Roman road.	50½	2 miles distant Fulbourn House. Here Ely Cathedral is seen at a distance of 18 m. in a direct line.
Valley House, and, 4 miles to the right of it, West Wratting Park, Sir C. Watson, Bart. 2 miles distant Dullingham House.	54¼	Green Man.	54¼	2 m. Wilbraham Temple, E. Hicks, Esq., and beyond, Bottisham Hall, S. Jenyns, Esq.
2 miles distant Stetchworth Park, R. J. Eaton, Esq.	49½	DEVIL'S DITCH. (p. 464.)	59	Just before the 56th milestone you have a view of Cambridge. 4 miles distant Swaffham House, J. P. Allix, Esq.
2 m. distant Cheveley Park, Duke of Rutland. To Bury St. Edmunds, 12 miles. At a distance Dalham Hall, Sir R. Affleck, Bart.	47¾	NEWMARKET, (p. 464.)	60¾	To Cambridge, 13 m. 2 miles distant Exning Lodge. 4 miles distant Fordham Abbey. 1½ mile beyond Newmarket, and, 2 miles distant, Chippenham Park, surrounded by fine grounds.
		Enter Suffolk.		
Herringswell House, G. Mure, Esq.; and beyond, Cavenham Hall, H. S. Waddington, Esq.	42¼	The Red Lodge.	66¼	
	39½	Barton Mills.	69¼	To Mildenhall, 1 m., and Barton Hall, Lt. Gen. Sir H. E. Bunbury, Bart. K C.B.
		cross river Larke.		

ON RIGHT FROM LOND.	From Norwich.		From London.	ON LEFT FROM LOND.
Elvedon Hall, Earl of Albemarle.	32¼	Elvedon.	76¼	
		cr. the Little Ouse river.		
Euston Hall, Duke of Grafton, beyond which is Schadewell Lodge, Sir R. J. Buxton, Bart. Russhford Lodge, Riddlesworth Hall, and Kilverstone Hall.	28½	THETFORD (p. 465.) (To Bury St Edmunds, 12¼ m.; to East Harling, 9¼ m.)	80	King's House. In the distance, Santon Downham Hall, Earl Cadogan.
1½ mile distant West Harling Hall.	21¼	Larling Heath.	87¼	Wretham Hall, W. Birch, Esq. Hockham Hall, H. Partridge, Esq.
2 miles distant Eccles Hall, and farther to the right, Quidenham Hall, Earl of Albemarle. Hargham Hall, Sir T. B. Beevor, Bart.	20¼	Larlingford.	88¼	Shropham Hall, H. Hemsworth, Esq. Attleborough Hall, Sir W. B Smijth, Bart.
	14½	Attleborough.	94	To Watton, 10 miles; to Hingham, 5¼ miles. Burfield Hall; Cavick House.
Stanfield Hall (late J. Jermy, Esq., the victim of Rush), and near it, Ketteringham Hall, Sir J. P. Boileau, Bart.	8½	WYMONDHAM (p. 465.)	100	2 m. distant Kimberley Hall, Lord Wodehouse, containing a fine portrait of Vandyke by himself, and surrounded by beautiful grounds.
	5	Hethersett.	103½	Melton Hall, and Colney Hall.
Intwood Hall, J. S. Muskett, Esq. Cringleford Hall, Keswick Hall, H. Gurney, Esq., and Keswick Ho., R. H. Gurney, Esq.	2½	Cringleford.	106	
		cross river Yare.		
	2	Eaton.	106½	Earlham Hall, J. J. Gurney, Esq., and Eaton Hall.
		NORWICH (p. 465.)	108½	

Epping is situated in a district formerly very woody, and preserved by our ancient monarchs for the enjoyment of the sports of the field. It was then called Waltham Forest, and extended almost to the capital. In the same neighbourhood also was Hainault Forest, lately disafforested, where a fair was held for many centuries, under a remarkable tree, well known by the name of Fairlop Oak, which existed till recently, and was of prodigious size. A stag was annually turned out in the forest for the amusement of the public on Easter Monday. The town of Epping is singularly irregular in its appearance. It preserves the fame it has long enjoyed for its cream, butter, sausages, and pork. About a mile from Epping in the forest, is Queen Elizabeth's hunting lodge.

DEVIL'S DITCH is an ancient Roman entrenchment, which runs in a straight line for several miles across Newmarket heath.

NEWMARKET, situated partly in Cambridge and partly in Suffolk, derives its celebrity from horse-racing, for which it is the most famous place in the kingdom. The races are held seven times a-year. The first, called the Craven meeting, commences on Easter Monday, then follow two spring meetings, one in July, and three in October. Most of the houses in Newmarket are of modern construction, and many of them are very handsome. Charles II. built a seat here, afterwards burnt, but which frequently became the residence of royalty subsequent to his time. The town possesses two churches and several meeting-houses. Pop. 4069.

At Swaffham St Cyriac, five miles from Newmarket, is a curiously constructed church, the lower part of which is square, the second storey has eight sides, and the upper storey sixteen.

THETFORD was formerly a town of considerable size and importance, having had a Cluniac priory, a nunnery, a Dominican friary, and several smaller religious houses, all of which are now destroyed. Of the twenty churches which it once possessed, only three now remain,—St Peter's, commonly called the "black church," because built chiefly of flint—St Cuthbert's on the Norfolk side, and St Mary's on the Suffolk side of the river. Here are also several dissenting chapels and meeting-houses. Considerable remains of the Cluniac priory and of the nunnery still exist, and some relics of the other ancient religious structures. There is an ancient grammar-school; and, near the town, a chalybeate spring, with a handsome pump-room, reading-room, and baths, erected in 1819. Thetford was the occasional residence of Henry I., Henry II., Elizabeth, and James I. Tom Paine was a native of this place. It carries on a small trade in corn and coals. Two M.P. Pop. 4208.

WYMONDHAM or WYNDHAM is a town of considerable extent, and has been much improved of late years. A priory of black monks was established here before 1107 by William de Albini, chief butler to Henry I. The only part of the conventual buildings now remaining is a portion of the church, which is at present used as the parish church.

NORWICH, the capital of Norfolk, is situated on the Wensum, and Eastern Counties Railway. It is a place of great antiquity, and was a flourishing town in the time of Edward the Confessor. The most interesting buildings in Norwich are the castle and the cathedral. The former is supposed to have been rebuilt by Roger Bigod, in the reign of William the conqueror, and comprehended an area of not less than twenty-three acres. The keep maintains its ancient form externally, but the inner part has been much altered, in order to adapt it to the purpose of a gaol, to which it has been long applied. The entrance tower, known as Bigod's tower, has lately been restored. The foundation of the cathedral was laid in 1094 by Herbert Losinga, the Bishop, in whose time the see was removed from Thetford to Norwich. The work was carried on by succeeding bishops, and the spire was not erected till 1361. The architecture is chiefly Norman. The spire is 315 feet high, and the interior, 411 feet by 191 feet, is adorned with a fine font and numerous interesting monuments. On the north side of the cathedral is the bishop's palace, a large irregular edifice, built by different prelates. It, as well as the cathedral, suffered much from the mistaken zeal of the Puritans. Losigna laid the foundations of a Benedictine priory at the same time as those of the cathedral, but only a few traces of the former remain. Norwich contains thirty-six churches and numerous meeting-houses. Some of the churches are valuable specimens of ancient architecture. The most conspicuous is that of St Peter's, Mancroft, a large and handsome edifice, in which is a tablet to the memory of Sir Thomas Browne, the author of the "Religio Medici." The other objects most worthy of notice are, St Julian's Church, exhibiting some fine specimens of Saxon architecture; St Lawrence, with a square tower 112 feet high; St Andrew's Hall, formerly the nave of the church belonging to the Black Friars, now the common hall of the city, adorned with paintings and other ornaments, and used for the musical festivals held here; Erpingham's gate, an elegant specimen of ancient architecture, facing the west end of the cathedral; the free and numerous other schools, the shire hall in the castle ditch, the new city gaol, the infirmary, numerous banks, theatres, barracks, a public library, the museum of natural history and antiquities, &c. The charitable institutions and charities, such as hospitals and alms-houses, are very numerous.

The most important trade of the town consists of the manufacture of silk, worsted, and cotton into shawls, crapes, bombazines, damasks, camlets, and imitations of the Irish and French stuffs. There is also a considerable manufacture of shoes.

Dr Caius, one of the founders of Gonville and Caius College, Cambridge, Dr Samuel Clarke, Harmer the biblical critic, Beloe the translator, and Archbishop Parker, were natives of Norwich. Two M.P. Pop. 74,891.

About 4 miles from Norwich is Costessy Hall, the fine seat of Jerningham, Lord Stafford. The house is partly ancient, partly modern. Contiguous to the house is a handsome Gothic chapel.

Twelve miles from Norwich is WORSTEAD, formerly the seat of a considerable manufacture, introduced by the Flemings, of woollen twists and stuffs, called from it "worsted goods," but this manufacture was, in the reigns of Richard II. and Henry IV., removed to Norwich. The church is a fine building, with a beautiful tower, and contains a font of peculiar richness, and a curious wooden screen.

CLXXI. LONDON TO NORWICH, BY CHELMSFORD, BRAINTREE, SUDBURY, BURY ST EDMUNDS, AND THETFORD, 111¾ Miles.

ON RIGHT FROM LOND.	From Norwich.		From London.	ON LEFT FROM LOND.
	111¾	From Whitechapel Ch.		
	82¾	to CHELMSFORD. (pp. 470, 471.)	29	
Boreham House, Sir J. Tyssen Tyrell, Bart.	80¼	Broomfield.	31½	Dunmow, 8½ miles from Little Waltham, is pleasantly situated on an eminence. The church is old, and in the centre of the town is a cross, erected in 1578, and repaired in 1761. 2 miles to the east, at Little Dunmow, was a priory of Augustine canons, founded in 1104. The site of the buildings is now partly occupied by the manor-house. The well-known tenure of the "flitch of bacon" is that by which the manor of Little Dunmow is held. In the vicinity is Easton Lo., (Viscount Maynard) which suffered severely from fire a few years ago.
Waltham Lodge.	78½	Little Waltham.	33¼	
Terling Place, Lord Rayleigh.		cr. river Chelmer.		
	75½	Blackwater, St. Anne's.	36¼	
Braintree is a large straggling town, containing a spacious church, standing on an eminence, several meeting-houses and charitable institutions. The silk manufacture employs many of the inhabitants. Pop. 4305.	73¾	Young's End.	38	To Dunmow, 8¼ miles.
	71¼	BRAINTREE. To Colchester through Coggeshall, 15½ m.; to Witham, 7 miles; Maldon, 13¼ miles.	40½	
	70½	Bocking Street.	41¼	
Stisted Hall.		cross river Blackwater.		
Halstead has a good grammar school and several churches and chapels, banks, &c. The principal manufacture is fine velvet. Pop. 1851, 5658.	68¾	High Garret.	43	About 2 miles from Halstead is Gosfield Hall, a seat of the late E. G. Barnard, Esq., presenting an interesting specimen of the old baronial hall. Here is a gallery called Queen Elizabeth's, in commemoration of her having twice visited this place. There is also a curious sculptured stone chimney-piece, representing the Battle of Bosworth Field. Its park is extensive, and contains many fine old trees.
		cross river Colne.		
To Colchester, 13½ m.	65¼	HALSTEAD.	46½	
Colne Park.				
Twinstead, Sir G. W. Denys, Bart.	62¼	Parmer's Street.	49½	
Twinstead Hall, (Earl of Pomfret).	59½	Bulmer Tye.	52¼	
Ryes Lodge.				
Sudbury was one of the first places at which Edward III. settled the Flemings, whom he invited over to instruct his subjects in the woollen manufacture. Here are some remains of a priory of the order of St Augustine. Archbishop Simon of Sudbury, Gainsborough the painter, and Dr. Enfield, were born at Sudbury.		cr. river Stour, and enter Suffolk.		To Castle Hedingham, 5¼ miles.
	57¼	SUDBURY was once a place of much greater importance than at present. It has three handsome churches and a small silk manufactory. The Stour is navigable to this town. Sudbury returned one M.P. till 1844, when it was disfranchised. Pop. 6879.	54½	Auberries. 1 mile distant, Brandon Hall. Borley.

ON RIGHT FROM LOND.	From Norwich.		From London.	ON LEFT FROM LOND.
To Lavenham, 7 miles.				
Acton Place.	55¼	Rodbridge.	56½	Liston Hall.
Melford Hall, Sir Wm. Parker, Bt. The church of Long Melford is handsome, containing several brasses and monuments, and a font with some curious carving on the top of it.	53¼	Long Melford. Wolsey was a native of this place.	58½	Melford Place. Kentwell Hall. Chadacre Hall.
	49¾	Alpheton.	62	
Bradfield Hall, an ancient edifice, once the residence of Arthur Young, the writer on Agriculture.	45¾	Bradfield.	66	
Rushbrooke Park (R. F. B. Rushbrooke, Esq.) a fine specimen of the Elizabethan style.	43¼	Welnetham.	68½	Hawstead House, and at Bury, Hardwick House, Lady Cullum.
To Ixworth, 6½ miles. St Edmund's Hill.	40¾	BURY ST EDMUNDS, (p. 469.)	71	To Newmarket, 14 m. Ickworth Park, Marquis of Bristol, (see p. 469) and Great Saxham Hall, W. Mills, Esq.
	38¾	Fornham, St Martin.	73	Fornham St Genevieve, Duke of Norfolk; and Hengrave Hall, Sir T. R. Gage, Bart.
Ampton Hall, Lord Calthorpe, and Livermere Hall.	36¼	Ingham.	75½	Culford Hall, R. Benyon de Beauvoir, Esq.
	32½	Rymer House.	79¼	
Euston Hall, Duke of Grafton. In the park is an elegant banquetting-house, built by Kent.	30½	Barnham.	81¼	3 miles distant, Elvedon Hall (Earl of Albemarle.)
		cr. Little Ouse river, and enter Norfolk.		
Kilverstone Hall, J. Wright, Esq. 3 miles dist., Schadewell Lodge, Sir Robt. J. Buxton, Bart.	28½	THETFORD, (p. 465.)	83¼	In the distance, Santon Downham Hall (Earl Cadogan.)
Ketteringham Hall, Sir J. P. Boileau, Bart.	8½	Wymondham.	103½	Kimberley Hall (Lord Wodehouse), 2 m.
		NORWICH, (see p. 465.)	111¾	Costessey Park (Lord Stafford), 4 m.

CLXXII. LONDON TO NORWICH, BY CHELMSFORD, BRAINTREE, SUDBURY, BURY ST EDMUNDS, IXWORTH, AND SCOLE INN, 112¼ Miles.

ON RIGHT FROM LOND.	From Norwich.		From London.	ON LEFT FROM LOND.
St Edmund's Hill, and beyond it Rougham Old Hall, P. Bennet, Esq., and Rougham New Hall. Bury St Edmunds is an ancient town on the East Union Railway and the Larke, which, with the Ouse, is navigable to Lynn. Its splendid Abbey of St Edmund was the second in the kingdom, but is now only a magnificent pile of ruins. The principal buildings are the town hall, originally a church; St Mary's church, an ancient structure, adorned with an elegant roof and a beautiful porch, and containing the tomb of Mary Queen of France, and afterwards Duchess of Suffolk, daughter of Henry VII.; St James's church is early English. The church gate, as it is called, is considered a noble specimen of Saxon architecture; the abbey gate, distinguished by a beautiful arch and numerous sculptural embellishments; a theatre, Assembly Rooms, Mechanics' Institute, new jail, &c. Here are also a botanical garden, a free grammar school, and several meeting houses and charitable institutions. Sir Nicholas Bacon, Bishop Gardiner, Bishop Blomfield of London, and many other eminent men, were natives of this town. 2 M.P. Pop. 13,318.	112¼	**From Whitechapel Church to**		About a mile from the entrance to Bury is Ickworth Park (Marquis of Bristol), a splendid building, erected by the celebrated Earl of Bristol, Bishop of Derry, and containing a fine collection of modern sculpture. The park is 11 miles in circumference.
	41¼	BURY ST EDMUNDS.	71	
	38½	**Barton.**	73¾	Barton Hall, Lieut. Gen. Sir H. E. Bunbury, Bart. 3 m. N.W. is Hengrave Hall (Sir T. R. Gage, Bart.), a noble specimen of ancient architecture.
	34¾	IXWORTH. 3 miles distant, Langham Hall, Sir H. C. Blake, Bart., and near it Stowlangtoft Hall, H. Wilson, Esq.	77½	Troston Hall, the seat of R. E. Loft, Esq.
	31¾	Stanton.	80½	
	26½	BOTESDALE derives its name from a chapel here dedicated to St Botolph. It has a free school founded by Sir Nicholas Bacon, Lord Keeper to Queen Elizabeth.	85¾	Redgrave Hall, G. Wilson, Esq. once the seat of Chief Justice Holt. The village church, which is situated in the park, contains some interesting monuments. To Palgrave, 2 miles; thence to Diss, 1 mile.
	21	**Stuston.** Half a mile farther join the road to Scole Inn from Ipswich, (p. 475.)	91¼	Diss on the Waveney is a neat and prosperous town, the inhabitants of which are for the most part employed in the manufacture of hose and hempen cloth. The windows of the church are arranged in a peculiar manner, being disposed in pairs, five on each side of the nave, and a plain pilaster between every pair. Pop. 1861, 3164 (see also p. 473.)
	19½	cr. the Waveney, and enter Norfolk.	92¾	
	19¼	Scole Inn or Osmondiston.	93	Scole Inn was built about 190 years ago, by a Mr Peck, a merchant of Norwich. It was profusely decorated with carved work, and formerly possessed a curious sign representing the arms of the chief towns and families of the county (see also p. 473.)
	10½	Stratton, St Mary.	101¾	
	9½	Stratton, St Michael.	102¾	
		cr. the river Yare.		Costessey Park (Lord Stafford), 4 m.
		NORWICH, (p. 465.)	112¼	

ON RIGHT FROM LOND.	From Norwich.		From London.	ON LEFT FROM LOND.
	110	From Whitechapel Ch. to Mile End.	1	
Stepney.	$108\frac{1}{2}$	Bow.	$2\frac{1}{2}$	
		cr. the river Lea, and enter Essex.		
Upton House. To Barking, by West and East Ham, $3\frac{1}{2}$ miles. Plashet.	$107\frac{1}{2}$	Stratford.	$3\frac{1}{2}$	To Low Leyton, 2 m., thence to Walthamstow, 2 miles.
	$104\frac{1}{4}$	Ilford Bridge.	$6\frac{3}{4}$	Ilford Place, Cranbrook House, and Valentines, containing some fine carving by Gibbons, and in the hot-house a very remarkable vine.
		cr. the riv. Roothing.		
	102	Chadwell.	9	
	100	The Whalebone.	10	The whalebone is said to have belonged to a whale taken in the same year in which Oliver Cromwell died.
Romford is a populous town and railway station, with a good road trade, and is noted for its corn and cattle markets, and its ale. A new church has supplanted the old one (erected in 1407), and contains several ancient monuments, which were removed thither. Pop. 4361. To Gray's Thurrock, $12\frac{1}{2}$ miles.	$99\frac{1}{4}$	ROMFORD. (See p. 487.)	$11\frac{3}{4}$	To Epping Forest, Marshalls, and Gidea Hall.
Hare Hall, an elegant mansion.	$98\frac{1}{4}$	Hare Street.	$12\frac{3}{4}$	Dagnam Park, Sir R. D. Neave, Bart.
Warley Pl., and Warley Lodge.	$94\frac{1}{2}$	Brook Street.	$16\frac{1}{2}$	Rocketts, How Hatch, and Weald Hall, C. T. Tower, Esq.
Thorndon Hall, (Lord Petre,) a magnificent mansion, erected under the direction of Payne. The chapel is adorned with a fine painting of the Nativity. To Tilbury Fort, $16\frac{1}{2}$ m.	93	BRENTWOOD. Here is a free school and a new church, and in the High Street are the remains of a town-hall and prison. Pop. 2811.	18	Brentwood is a railway station, and carries on a considerable road trade.
To Billericay, $4\frac{1}{2}$ miles; 2 m. dist. Hutton Hall.	92	Shenfield.	19	Shenfield Place. Fitzwalter Park.
Ingatestone Hall, formerly the mansion of the Petre family.	90	Mountnessing Street.	21	Thoby Priory.
	88	Ingatestone.	23	The Hyde, J. Disney, Esq. Mill Green House.
To Maldon, $12\frac{1}{2}$ miles.	86	Margaretting Street.	25	Coptfold Hall. Writtle Lodge, and in the distance, Skreens, T. W. Bramston, Esq.
	$84\frac{1}{2}$	Stisted.	$26\frac{1}{2}$	
	$83\frac{1}{2}$	Widford.	$27\frac{1}{2}$	Highlands.

ON RIGHT FROM LOND.	From Norwich.		From London.	ON LEFT FROM LOND.
Chelmsford, the county town of Essex, and a railway station on the Chelmer. It has a new and spacious church, several meeting-houses, two gaols, a shire hall and corn exchange, assize court, and assembly-rooms, a house of correction, a free grammar-school, theatre, race-course, &c. Pop. 5513.	82¾	Moulsham, and Moulsham Hall, Sir H. B. P. St John Mildmay, Bart.	28¼	MALDON, 8 miles from Chelmsford, is an ancient populous town, and a railway station. It has several churches, chapels, banks, &c., is a bonding port, and carries on a considerable trade in coals, iron, deals, &c. Two M.P. Pop. 6261. See also p. 488.
		cr. the riv. Chelmer.		
Great Baddow, 4 m., and 5½ m. distant is Danbury, the church of which stands on a Danish camp, and contains the tombs of three cross-legged knights, curiously carved. Danbury Palace, Bishop of Rochester.	82	CHELMSFORD.	29	2⅓ m. distant Broomfield. To Chipping Ongar, 10½ miles; Epping, 17½; Dunmow, 12¾; Braintree, 11½ miles.
Springfield Lyons.	80¾	Springfield.	30¼	Springfield Place.
Boreham House, Sir J. T. Tyrell, Bart. Crix.	77¾	Boreham Street.	33¼	
Hatfield Priory.	76	Hatfield Peverell.	35	2 m. distant, Terling Place, Lord Rayleigh. To Braintree, 7 miles.
		cr. the river Brain.		
In the vicinity of Witham, are the remains of a camp. To Maldon, 5½ miles.	73¼	WITHAM, a place of great antiquity, near the confluence of the Brain and Blackwater. The church contains several interesting monuments.	37¾	The Grove—Witham Place—Witham Lodge—Faulkbourn Hall, J. Bullock, Esq.
1 m. distant Braxted Park, C. Du Cane, Esq., a handsome mansion, finely situated in an extensive park. The interior is elegantly fitted up. At Coggeshall are some vestiges of an abbey built by King Stephen.	71¾	Riven Hall End.	39¼	1½ mile distant, Riven Hall Place.
	70	Kelvedon. (To Coggeshall, 3 miles.)	41	Felix Hall, T. S. Western, Esq. Colchester is supposed to have been the Roman colony of Camelodunum. Here are the remains of a castle formerly of great strength, and of the town wall, the ruins of St John's Abbey, and St Botolph's priory, an ancient chapel, an arched vault used as a prison, the moat hall, a neat theatre, numerous churches and chapels, schools, &c. Some of the churches are interesting on account of their architectural ornaments, and the monuments they contain. 10 miles from Colchester, on the right, is St Osyth, where are the remains of an Au-
		cr. the river Blackwater.		
Layer Marney Tower, Quintin Dick, Esq.	69	Gore Pits.	42	
Copford Hall. Birch Hall, C. G. Round, Esq.	63¾	Stanway.	47¼	
Stanway Hall.	62	Lexden.	49	
9 miles distant is West Mersea, a small bathing place. Donyland Hall, and Berechurch Hall, late Sir G. H. Smyth, Bart. Wivenhoe Park, J. G. Rebow, Esq.	60¼	COLCHESTER, situated on the south bank of the river Colne. The town is famous for its oysters 2 M.P. Pop. 1861, 23,809. Colchester is connected with all parts of the kingdom by railways.	50¾	

ON RIGHT FROM LOND.	From Norwich.		From London.	ON LEFT FROM LOND.
	60	The Obelisk. cr. the river Colne.	51	gustine Priory, founded in the twelfth century. The quadrangle is almost entire, and is entered by a beautiful gateway. The church of St Osyth contains several monuments.
Dedham, and beyond, Lawford Hall; in the distance Mistley Park, near Manningtree.	52¾	Stratford Bridge. cr. the river Stour, and enter Suffolk.	58¼	Langham Hall; and beyond, Boxted, G. Poley, Esq.
	51¾	Stratford St Mary.	59¼	3 miles distant, Tendring Hall, Sir R. C. Rowley, Bart., and Horksley Park.
Wherstead Lodge, W. Scrope, Esq., and five miles distant, Wolverstone Hall, J. Berners, Esq. delightfully situated on the west bank of the Orwell. The park is extensive and well stocked with deer.	48¾	Cross Green.	62¼	
	45¾	Copdock.	65¼	Hintlesham Hall, J. H. L. Anstruther, Esq., & 3 miles distant Bramford Hall. To Bramford, 3 miles, thence to Great Blackenham 3 miles, thence to Needham Market, 3½ m., thence to Stow Market, 3½ miles.
Christchurch Park, W. C. Fonnereau, Esq., and Red House.	42½	Hadleigh Guide Post. cr. the river Orwell.	68½	
4 miles distant, Nacton Broke Hall, Sir G. N. Broke, Bart.,* built by Lord Chief Baron Broke in 1526, and Orwell Park, G. Tomline, Esq.	42	IPSWICH, (p. 477.) To Saxmundham, 20½ m.	69	The Chauntry, Sir Fitzroy Kelly.
1 m. dist. Shrubland Hall, Sir W. Fowle Middleton, Bart.	38½	Claydon.	72½	To Needham Market, 5 miles, thence to Stow Market, 3½ miles.
Crowfield Hall, now a farm house.	35¾	Coddenham Bridge.	75¼	
4 miles distant is Helmingham Hall, a seat of the Earl of Dysart, a quadrangular structure erected about the time of Henry VIII. It is completely surrounded by a moat, and is approached by two drawbridges. It contains some fine paintings, a good library, and a large collection of ancient armour.	31½	Little Stonham. 3½ miles from Stonham is Debenham, the church of which contains several ancient monuments, and 4 m. beyond is Worlingworth Hall, now a farm house.	79½	The park attached to Helmingham Hall, contains some of the finest oaks in this part of the kingdom, many of them of great age. The church, which adjoins the park, contains many splendid memorials of the Tollemache family.
	27½	Brockford Street.	83½	
	26¾	Thwaite.	84¼	Thornham Hall, Lord Henniker.
	25	Stoke Ash.	86	
At the fourth milestone from Brockford,—to Eye 2 miles.	24¼	Old Black Bull.	86¾	

* The father of the present baronet was the gallant Sir Philip B. Vere Broke, who obtained a baronetcy in consideration of the victory he achieved in 1813, as Captain of the Shannon over the United States Frigate, the Chesapeake.

ON RIGHT FROM LOND.	From Norwich.		From London.	ON LEFT FROM LOND.
Yaxley Hall. Brome Hall, and beyond, Oakley Park, Sir E. C. Kerrison, Bart.	23	Yaxley. (1¼ mile farther; to Eye, 1½ mile.)	88	To the left is the town of EYE. The church is spacious and handsome. Eye formerly possessed a castle, and to the east of the town may still be seen the ruins of a Benedictine monastery. 1 M.P. Pop. 1861, 7038. (See also p. 489.)
	19½	cr. river Waveney, and enter Norfolk.	91½	
Scole Inn was formerly noted for a singularly carved sign, representing the arms of the chief towns and families in the county, and for a large circular bed of immense size. (See also p. 469.)	19¼	Scole Inn, or Osmondistone.	91¾	To Diss, 2½ miles. Diss (see also p. 469) is a neat flourishing town on the Waveney. The inhabitants are principally employed in the manufacture of hempen cloth, hose, and stays. The church is remarkable for the disposition of its windows. Here are also Presbyterian and Quakers' meeting-houses, and a charity school. Pop. 3164.
	16¾	Dickleburgh.	94¼	
	14½	Tivetshall Green.	96½	
	10½	Stratton, St Mary.	100½	
1 mile distant Boyland Hall, F. W. Irby, Esq.	9½	Stratton, St Michael.	101½	7½ m. from Diss is NEW BUCKENHAM, where are the ruins of an ancient castle, and a spacious church, containing a richly carved screen, and some interesting monuments.
	8¼	Bird-in-Hand.	102¾	
Shottesham Park. Dunston Hall.	6½	Newton Flotman.	104½	Mangreen Hall.
	2¼	Harford Bridge. cr. the river Yare.	108¾	To New Buckenham, 13¼ miles.
		NORWICH, (p. 465.)	111	To Wymondham, 8½ m.

CLXXIV. LONDON TO CROMER BY NEWMARKET, BRANDON, WALTON, AND EAST DEREHAM, 128¾ Miles.

ON RIGHT FROM LOND.	From Cromer.	From Whitechapel Church to	From London.	ON LEFT FROM LOND.
	50½	BRANDON, (p. 459.)	78¼	
		cr. the Little Ouse and enter Norfolk.		
1½ mile from Watton is Merton Hall (Lord Walsingham), a fine antiquated mansion in the Gothic style, standing in an extensive park, diversified with rich plantations.	46½	Lyndford Lodges.	82¼	West Tofts Hall and Lyndford Hall, Sir J. Sutton, Bart.
	45½	West Tofts Hall.	83½	
	43¾	Stanford.	85	At Stanford Buckenham House, Lord Petre
	40¾	Clermont Lodge.	88	WATTON, a small town, noted for its butter. The church has a round tower, and is supposed to be of the time of Henry I.
1 mile from Shipdham is Letton Hall, B. Gurdon, Esq.	38	WATTON.	90¾	
	33¼	Shipdham.	95½	

ON RIGHT FROM LOND.	From Cromer.		From London.	ON LEFT FROM LOND.
	32½	Market Street.	96¼	near the old manor-house. In the vicinity is Wayland Wood, where, according to tradition two infants were murdered by their uncle, which gave rise to the ballad of the Children of the Wood. Pop. 1365.
East Dereham is a town of considerable antiquity. Here was anciently a nunnery, founded in the 8th century. The church is a large cruciform building of considerable antiquity, containing a rich font of the 15th century, a curious old chest, in which are deposited the records of the church, and a marble monument to the poet Cowper, who was buried here A. D. 1800. Pop. 3070	28¾	EAST DEREHAM.	103½	
	24¾	Swanton Morley.	104	2 miles from East Dereham, Bylaugh Hall, E. Lombe, Esq., built by the Court of Chancery.
		cr. river Wensum.		
Near Swanton Morley, Elsing Hall.	21½	Bawdeswell.	107½	Near Swanton Morley is Billingford Hall, W. Pearce, Esq.
		(To Foulsham, 3 miles.)		
At Bawdeswell, Bawdeswell Hall. FOULSHAM was nearly destroyed by fire in 1770. The church is a handsome building of flint and stone. Pop. 1048. 5 m. north of Foulsham is Melton Constable, Lord Hastings.	17½	REEPHAM. It was formerly remarkable for three churches in one churchyard.	111¼	
	16¼	Sall Hall. Sall Hall, Sir R. P. Jodrell, Bart. 2 m. distant, Heydon Hall, W. E. Lytton Bulwer, Esq.	112½	
At Cawston, Haverland Hall, E. Fellowes, Esq.	14¾	Cawston.	114	
		(To Holt, 10¾ miles.)		
AYLSHAM, on the Bure, has a church said to have been erected by John of Gaunt, containing numerous brasses, a curious font, and a painted glass window. Here are also several chapels, banks, free school, &c. Pop. 2388.	10½	AYLSHAM,*	118¼	About 1 mile beyond Aylsham is Blickling Hall, containing a good library, and surrounded by fine grounds. Blickling was at one time the property of Sir T. Boleyne, Earl of Wiltshire and Ormonde, the father of Anne Boleyne, who was married here to Henry VIII.
	8¾	Ingworth Mill.	120	
At Hanworth Green, Gunton Hall, Lord Suffield.	5¼	Hanworth Green. At Hanworth Green is Hanworth Park.	133½	Beyond Blickling is Wolterton Park, the seat of the Earl of Orford.
CROMER is situated on one of the highest cliffs on the Norfolk coast, and carries on some trade in coals, timber, tiles, oil-cake, and other goods. There is a lighthouse on the cliff, and a life-boat. The church is an ancient building of great beauty. Cromer is much frequented in the bathing season, There was anciently a town or village on this part of the coast called Shipden, which was destroyed by the sea about the beginning of the 15th century. The sea still continues to gain on the land.	3¾	Powder Hill.	125	Felbrigg Park. W. H. Wyndham, Esq., and near it the church, a handsome edifice, containing monuments of the Felbrigg and Windham families. Felbrigg is an ancient mansion, occupying one of the finest situations in Norfolk, and surrounded by extensive and venerable woods. It contains a large collection of valuable paintings by some of the most eminent masters. It was the seat of the Right Hon. W. Windham, the celebrated statesman.
		CROMER.	128¾	

* About 11¾ miles from Aylsham is HOLT, the birth-place of Sir Thomas Gresham, where there is a free school founded by that celebrated merchant. Pop. 1635. 4½ miles farther is Cley, a small sea port, into which (it has been erroneously asserted) the Earl of Carrick, afterwards James I. of Scotland, was driven by a storm in 1405. He was in reality captured off Flamborough Head, and carried to London. (See Tytler's History, vol. ii. p. 451.) 5 m. from Holt is Melton Constable, the seat of Lord Hastings.

CLXXV. LONDON TO CROMER, BY NORWICH AND NORTH WALSHAM.

131¾ Miles.

ON RIGHT FROM LOND.	From Cromer.		From London.	ON LEFT FROM LOND.
	23¼	From Whitechapel Ch. to NORWICH, (p. 465).	108½	Catton Hall.
Sprowston Hall and Rackheath Hall, Sir H. J. Stracey, Bart., and Beeston St. Andrew Hall.	21	Sprowston.	110¾	Horsham Hall. Spixworth Park, J Longe, Esq.
	18½	Crostwick.	113¼	Near Horstead, Horstead Hall.
At Crostwick, Wroxham Hall.		cr. the Stone Beck.		Stratton, Strawless Hall, R. Marsham, Esq.
	16½	Horstead.	115¼	
		cr. the river Bure.		
Coltishall Hall, Rev. R. Ward.	16	Coltishall.	115¾	At Scottowe Common, Scottowe Hall, Sir H. T. E. Durrant, Bart.
	13¾	Scottowe Common.	118	
Westwick Hall, and, 1¾ mile distant, Worstead Hall, and, 2 m. farther on the right, Honing Hall, E. G. Cubitt, Esq.	12¼	Westwick Hall Park.	119½	NORTH WALSHAM stands on a gentle eminence above the river Ant. The town was almost entirely burnt in 1600. A market cross, erected in the time of Edward III., was rebuilt after the fire. The church is spacious; and there are several chapels, banks, a free school, a theatre, &c. A canal affords communication with Yarmouth.
	9	NORTH WALSHAM.	122¾	
3 miles from North Walsham, Witton Park, Lord Wodehouse.	6½	Antingham.	125¼	
	4	Thorpe Market.	127¾	
		Cromer (see p. 474).	131¾	At Antingham, Gunton Hall, Lord Suffield.

CLXXVI. LONDON TO YARMOUTH THROUGH CHELMSFORD, IPSWICH, SCOLE INN, BUNGAY, AND BECCLES, 126½ Miles.

ON RIGHT FROM LOND.	From Yarm.		From London.	ON LEFT FROM LOND.
Hoxne Hall, and beyond Broome Hall, Sir E. C. Kerrison, Bart.	34¾	From Whitechapel Ch. to Scole Inn, *Norfolk* (p. 469.)	91¾	
	33¾	Billingford Common.	92¾	
	32½	Thorpe Abbotts.	94	
	30¾	Brockdish Street.	95¾	
	29	Needham.	97½	To Norwich, 19¼ miles.
	27¾	HARLESTON.	98¾	Redenhall (church of the 14th century). Gawdy Hall.
	26¼	Redenhall.	100¼	
Flixton Hall, Sir R. S. Adair, Bart.	25½	Wortwell.	101	Denton House, 1 m.
BUNGAY is a railway station, and is situated on the Waveney, navigable for barges up to the town. It was almost destroyed by fire in 1688, but has since been neatly rebuilt. It has two parish churches, one of which has a fine tower. Here also are remains of a Benedictine nunnery, and of a very strong castle, fortified in the reign of Stephen, but demolished in that of Henry III. Bungay has a handsome market place and cross, a theatre, assembly rooms, free grammar school, &c. Here also are several mineral	21¼	Earsham.	105¼	Earsham House, Sir W. W. Dalling, Bart.
		cr. river Waveney.		
	20¼	BUNGAY, (*Suffolk.*) To Norwick, 14 miles; to (Loddon, 6¼ miles.)	106¼	2 m. from Bungay, Ditchingham Park, J. J. Bedingfield, Esq.; Hedenham Park, Broome Hall.
	18½	Mettingham. Ruins of Mettingham Castle.	108	
	17¼	Shipmeadow.	109¼	1½ m. Ellingham Hall, and, 3 m. distant, Kirby Cane Hall (Lord Berners).

ON RIGHT FROM LOND.	From Yarm		From London.	ON LEFT FROM LOND.
springs. By means of the railway and the Waveney the town carries on some trade in corn, malt, flour, coal, lime, &c., and has lime-kilns, malting-houses, &c. Pop. 3805.	16¼	Barsham.	110¼	Ashendens.
	14¾	BECCLES.	111¾	Beccles is a well built town on the Waveney. It has an elegant Gothic church, the porch of which is a good specimen of later English. In the south part of the town is the ruins of another church. Here are also a handsome town hall, several chapels, banks, free school, and grammar school. A common of about 1400 acres belongs to the town. Pop. 4266.
		cr. river Waveney.		
1½ m. from Beccles, Worlingham Hall, Earl of Gosford, and N. Cove Hall.	13¼	Gillingham All Saints. (*Norfolk.*)	113¼	
	11	Toft Monks.	115½	
At Gillingham, All Saints, Gillingham Hall.	9½	Haddiscoe.	117	
Near St Olave's Bridge are the ruins of Herringfleet Abbey and Herringfleet Hall, J. Leathes, Esq.	7¼	St Olave's Bridge.	119½	At Gillingham, All Saints, Geldeston Hall, J. Kerrich, Esq.
		cr. river Waveney.		
	6½	Fritton, (*Suffolk.*)	120	At Toft Monks, Raveningham Hall, Sir E. Bacon, Bart.
At Fritton, Fritton Hall; and 1¾ m. distant, Somerleyton Hall, Sir S. M. Peto, Esq. See p. 479.	1¼	South Town.	125¼	
	¼	Yarmouth Bridge.	126¼	
		cr. the river Yare.		
		YARMOUTH, (p. 479.)		Breydon Water.

CLXXVII. LONDON TO YARMOUTH, THROUGH IPSWICH, WOODBRIDGE, SAXMUNDHAM, AND LOWESTOFT, 124 Miles.

ON RIGHT FROM LOND.	From Yarm.		From London.	ON LEFT FROM LOND.
Kesgrave Lodge, R. Newton Shawe, Esq.	55	From Whitechapel Ch. to Ipswich, (p. 477.)	69	Christ Church Park. W. C. Fonnereau, Esq.
	51½	Kesgrave.	72½	Bealings Hall. 2 m. Playford Hall. Beacon Hill House, Sir E. S. Gooch, Bart.
Martlesham Place.	49	Martlesham Street.	75	Seckford Almshouses.
River Deben. Ufford Place, Captain C. Brook.	47¼	WOODBRIDGE, (p. 478.)	76¾	The Priory, and 3 m. distant, Grundisbrugh Hall, Sir J. Blois, Bart.
To Orford, 11 m., and 1 m. thence, Sudbourne Hall (Marquis of Hertford); Melton Lodge.	45¾	Melton.	78¼	Bredfield Hall.
	44½	Ufford Street.	79½	
Loudham Hall E. Whitbread, Esq., and near it the remains of Campsey Abbey. 2 m. Rendlesham Hall, Lord Rendlesham.	43¼	Pettistree.	80¾	Thorpe Hall, C. Baldry, Esq.
	42½	Wickham Market.	81½	Glevering Hall, A. Arcdeckne, Esq. Easton Park, Duke of Hamilton and Brandon.
2 m. Campsey Ash High House, John Shepherd, Esq.		cross river Deben. (To Hatcheston, 2½ m.; thence to Framlingham, 3¼ miles.)		Great Glemham Hall, J. Moseley, Esq.; Marlesford Hall, and 2 miles distant, Parham Hall, S. F. Corrance, Esq., and Parham Lodge.
Little Glemham Hall, Hon. Mrs. North.	39½	Glemham.	84½	
	37¾	Stratford, St Andrew.	86¼	
		cross river Alde.		

ON RIGHT FROM LOND.	From Yarm.		From London.	ON LEFT FROM LOND.
7¼ m. ALDBOROUGH, a fashionable watering-place, and the birthplace of the poet Crabbe.	37¼	Farnham.	86¾	Benhall Lodge, Rev. E. Holland, and Benhall House.
Hurts Hall, W. Long, Esq.	34½	SAXMUNDHAM.*	89½	Carlton Hall, E. Fuller, Esq.
	33¼	Kelsale.	90¾	
To Darsham Hall, 1 m.; to Darsham, 2 m.; thence to Dunwich, 4 m.	30¼	Yoxford.	93¾	Cockfield Hall, Sir J. Blois, Bart.; Thorington Hall, Col. H. Bence Bence, 2 m.; and 2 m. farther, Heveningham Hall (Lord Huntingfield)
	25¾	Blythburgh.	98¼	
		cross river Blythe.		
	25	Bulchamp.	99	Henham Park, Earl of Stradbroke.
To Southwold, 3½ m., (p. 407.)	21¾	Wangford.	102¼	
Benacre Hall, Sir E. S. Gooch, Bart.	18	Wrentham.	106	
	16½	Benacre Turnpike.	107½	2 m. dist. Sotterley Ha.
	14¾	Kessingland.	109¼	1 m. distant Henstead House, Rev. T. Sheriffe.
	11¾	Pakefield.	112¼	2 m. Carlton Colville.
	11¼	Kirkley.	112¾	½ m. Mutford Bridge, Lake Lothing.
Gunton Old Hall, and Gunton New Hall.	10	LOWESTOFT, (p. 478.)	114	1½ m. Flixton High Ho.
Battery Hill.	5½	Hopton.	118½	2¼ miles Blundeston Hall; and farther to the left, Somerleyton Hall, Sir S. M. Peto, Bart.; and Hobland Hall.
	2¼	Gorleston.	121¾	
		2 m. Burgh Castle, a fine ruin.		
Across the river, Nelson's monument.	1¼	South Town.	122¾	
	¼	Yarmouth Bridge.	123¾	
		☞ cr. river Yare, and enter Norfolk.		
North Sea.		YARMOUTH, (p. 479.)	124	Breyden Water.

IPSWICH, the capital of Suffolk, and a place of great antiquity, stands on the side of a gentle elevation rising from the river Orwell, the banks of which present very pleasing prospects. Ipswich formerly contained nineteen parish churches, and still retains twelve, besides three in the Liberty, and several places of worship for Dissenters. In St. Peter's is an ancient font, and in St. Lawrence's a painting by Sir Robert Ker Porter. Ipswich has town and shire halls, an extensive county jail, a commodious market-place, corn-exchange, banks, barracks, baths, theatre, assembly-rooms, public library, free schools, mechanics' institute, custom-house, &c. A college was established here by Cardinal Wolsey, who was said to have been born in a house, still standing, in St. Nicholas parish; but the

* 10¾ miles from Saxmundham is Halesworth on the Blythe, by means of which, and of a canal to Southwold, it carries on a considerable trade. A great quantity of hemp is grown in the vicinity, and many of the inhabitants are employed in spinning yarn. Pop. 2382.

institution fell with the founder. Ipswich was formerly, though no longer, celebrated for its woollen manufactures. It chiefly depends at present on the manufacture of agricultural implements and on ship-building, and the exportation of ship-timber, corn, malt, &c.; but it has a considerable import trade for wines, spirits, timber, ship stores, and other commodities. Customs Rev., 1850, £29,126 1s. 2d. Vessels sail every tide from Ipswich to Harwich and back again—an excursion rendered peculiarly delightful by the beauty of the scenery. Ipswich is connected by railway with all parts of the kingdom. About a mile from the town is the race-course, and a beautiful promenade, called Christ Church Park, is open to the public. Two M.P. Pop. 37,950.

WOODBRIDGE stands on the river Deben, and is a place of great antiquity. It has a spacious market place, in the centre of which is the old shire hall. St. Mary's, the old church, contains several monuments, is spacious, and is supposed to have been erected in the time of Edward III. It has a square buttressed tower 180 feet high. Here are also meeting-houses, richly endowed almshouses, a custom-house, a small theatre, and barracks, dock-yards, &c. Woodbridge is a place of considerable trade, exporting corn, malt, and flour, and importing coal, timber, and general merchandize. Pop. 4513.

About nine or ten miles from Woodbridge is FRAMLINGHAM, a town of great antiquity, on the Alde. The church is large, with a tower 90 feet high, in which is a peal of eight bells. The roof of the nave is of curiously carved oak. The church contains several monuments of the Howard family; among others, that of the accomplished poet, Earl of Surrey, beheaded by Henry VIII. Here are the ruins of a magnificent castle, which, with the manor, were bequeathed by Sir Robert Hitcham to Pembroke Hall, Cambridge. It was to this castle that Queen Mary repaired when Lady Jane Grey was placed upon the throne. Pop. of parish, 2252.

ORFORD, twelve miles from Woodbridge, has an ancient castle, of which only the keep now remains. The church contains an ancient font and several monuments. One mile distant is Sudbourne Hall, a seat of the Marquis of Hertford. Orford gives the title of Earl to the Walpole family. Pop. 948.

SOUTHWOLD, almost surrounded by the Blythe, is pleasantly situated on an eminence overlooking the sea, and much frequented in the bathing season. It was nearly destroyed by fire in 1659. Pop. 1861, 2032. In Southwold Bay or Sole Bay, the famous naval engagement took place in 1672, between the Dutch under De Ruyter, and the English under the Duke of York, afterwards James II.

LOWESTOFT, a place of great antiquity, stands on a cliff facing the sea, viewed from which it is a remarkably picturesque object. The parish church, about half a mile west of the town, is large, handsome, and contains several ancient monuments. In the churchyard is the tomb of Potter, the translator of Æschylus, Sophocles, &c. There are also meeting-houses, a town-hall, two light-houses, a theatre, lunatic asylum, &c. &c. One of the principal branches of industry are the fisheries and fishcuring, for the London and Norwich markets. There are rope and twine manufactories. Lowestoft has lately been much frequented as a bathing place, for which its sands are well adapted. The town is greatly indebted to Sir S· M. Peto, Bart., of Somerleyton Hall, who purchased the harbour in 1844, and originated a company for the improvement of the port and town, the deepening of Lake Lothing, &c. He carried also the branch railway from Reedham to Lowestoft, thus placing the latter in a very advantageous commercial position. Pop. 10,663.

Great Yarmouth, a considerable seaport town and a place of great antiquity. The old town is situated on the eastern bank of the Yare, and is connected with the new town, called Little Yarmouth, by means of a bridge. The old town had walls, and consists of four parallel steeets, and of about 150 narrow cross lanes, called rows. The best dwelling-houses are situated along the quay, which is considered the finest in the kingdom, having in the centre a noble promenade, planted on each side with trees. The principal buildings are the old church, erected in 1123, and recently restored, several chapels, banks, a town-hall, theatre, assembly-room, bathing-house, &c. There are several charitable institutions, the principal of which is the Seamen's Hospital, and extensive barracks, containing a large armoury. There is an extensive manufactory for crapes and other silk goods. Ship-building, and the various trades connected with it, are carried on to some extent. The rivers Yare, Waveney, and Bure, which unite in Breydon Water, contiguous to the town, secure to Yarmouth an extensive inland trade. The exportation of grain and malt is considerable; but the principal business of this port consists of the herring and mackerel fisheries. An extensive timber trade with the Baltic is also carried on, and Yarmouth Roads have long been the principal rendezvous for the collier trade. Customs Revenue, 1850, £38,372 : 11 : 11. It is one of the termini of the Eastern Counties Railway, and thus holds communication with all important parts of the kingdom. Two M.P. Pop. 1861, 34,810. Near Yarmouth is a beautiful fluted column, 140 feet high, in memory of Lord Nelson.

Southend (Essex) is situated on an acclivity at the mouth of the Thames opposite to Sheerness. It has of late years risen into some importance as a bathing-place. Here is an assembly-room, a theatre, library, meeting-house, baths, bathing machines, &c. Near this place a stone marks the termination of the jurisdiction of the corporation of London over the Thames. Steam vessels sail thither regularly during summer.

On the Naze, a projecting piece of land, on the east coast of Essex, 18 miles from Colchester, is the village of Walton, of late in some repute as a bathing place.

CLXXVIII. LONDON TO HARWICH. THROUGH CHELMSFORD AND COLCHESTER, 71½ Miles.

ON RIGHT FROM LOND.	From Harwich		From London.	ON LEFT FROM LOND.
	20½	From Whitechapel Ch. to COLCHESTER. (See p. 471.)	51	
Ardleigh Park; and to Great Bromley Hall and Bromley Lodge, 4 miles.	15¾	Ardleigh.	55¾	
Manningtree was anciently called Sciddinchon. It is a railway station, and carries on a considerable trade in malt, corn, coals, deals, iron, and fish.	13¼	Wignell Street.	58¼	
	11½	MANNINGTREE.	60	HARWICH, a railway station, situated on a tongue of land opposite the mouth of the Stour and the Orwell, has a spacious harbour, capable of containing more than 100 sail of the line. It was a place of importance during the war, as almost the only means of communication with the north of Europe. The chief employments are ship-building and other kindred trades. Here is a dockyard, well furnished with storehouses, &c., a church, town hall and gaol, custom house, &c. In summer it is much frequented as a bathing-place. Landguard fort, defending the harbour, was erected by James I. 2 M.P. Pop. 5070.
Mistley Hall.	10¾	Mistley Thorn.	60¾	
Wix Abbey.	8½	Bradfield.	63	
Ramsey Hall.	3¾	Ramsey Street.	67¾	
	3¼	Ramsey.	68¼	
	2	Dover Court.	69½	4 miles across the Orwell, Felixstowe, Sir. S. Fludyer, Bart.
		HARWICH.	71½	

CLXXIX. LONDON TO SOUTHEND, THROUGH BARKING, RAINHAM, STANFORD LE HOPE, AND HADLEIGH, 39¾ Miles.

ON RIGHT FROM LOND.	From South'd.		From London.	ON LEFT FROM LOND.
The West India Docks, erected at the expense of £1,200,000.	38	From Whitechapel Ch. to Limehouse.	1¾	
		cr. the river Lea, and enter Essex.		BARKING was formerly celebrated for its nunnery, said to have been the first convent for women in England. The church contains several brasses and other monuments. Barking and its neighbourhood supply London with vast quantities of vegetables. 1 m. dist. is Eastbury House, a curious antique building, traditionally associated with the gunpowder plot, as the place where the conspirators held their meetings. Pop. of Barking, 5076.
	33¾	East Ham.	6	
		cr. river Roding.		
Between Barking and Rainham, Belvidere, the seat of Sir C. E. Eardley, Bart. is seen across the Thames.	32¾	BARKING.	7	
	27¼	Rainham.	12½	
	26	Winnington.	13¾	
Tilbury Fort, the principal defence of the Thames above Sheerness, is mounted with a great number of cannon, and strongly garrisoned during war. Near this place Queen Elizabeth reviewed her army when the country was threatened by the Spanish Armada.	25½	Junction of the Road. (To Purfleet, 1½ miles.)	14¼	At Purfleet are large government powder magazines.
	23¾	Avely.	16	Near Winnington is Bell House, Sir T. B. Lennard, Bt.
	21¼	Stifford.	18½	1½ mile from Stifford is Belmont Castle.
	19	Baker Street.	20¾	
	18½	Division of the Road. (To Tilbury Fort, 4 miles.)	21¼	
	15½	Stanford le Hope.	24½	

ON RIGHT FROM LOND.	From South'd.		From London.	ON LEFT FROM LOND.
At Hadleigh are the remains of a castle situated on the brow of a steep hill, commanding a fine view of the Thames. The church is an ancient building. Near Hadleigh is Hadleigh Hall, now a school.	11½	Vange.	28¼	
	9¾	Pitsea.	30	
	5	Hadleigh.	34¾	Thundersley.
	3	Leigh.	36¾	
		SOUTHEND (p. 479.)	39¾	

CLXXX. LONDON TO SOUTHEND THROUGH ROMFORD, BRENTWOOD, BILLERICAY, AND RAYLEIGH, 41¾ Miles.

ON RIGHT FROM LOND.	From South'd.		From London.	ON LEFT FROM LOND.
BILLERICAY is situated on an eminence commanding fine views of the Thames and the coast of Kent. Here is a church said to have been founded in the time of Edward III. The tower may be of that age, but the body of the chapel is comparatively modern. Pop. 1390.	41¾	From Whitechapel Ch.		
	23¾	to BRENTWOOD (p. 470.)	18	Rayleigh was formerly a town of some importance. It has an old church, and some traces of an old castle. 5 m. distant is Rochford, near which is Rochford Hall, where Anne Boleyne was born in 1507.
	22¾	Shenfield.	19	
	18½	BILLERICAY.	23¼	
	8	Rayleigh.	33¾	
	5½	Hadleigh Common.	36¼	
		SOUTHEND (p. 479.)	41¾	

CLXXXI. LONDON TO BEDFORD, BY RAILWAY, 63 Miles.

ON RIGHT FROM LOND.	From Bedford.		From London.	ON LEFT FROM LOND.
	63	From London by North Western Railway, to		
	16¼	Bletchley Junction St. (p. 202.)	46¾	Leave main line of London and North Western Railway.
	15	Fenny Stratford St.	48	
Little Brickhill, and beyond, Great Brickhill, P. D. Duncombe, Esq.		Fenny Stratford stands on the line of the Roman Watling Street, and is probably the site of the ancient Magiovintum. Dr Willis, the antiquarian, died here in 1760, and was buried in the chapel. Pop. 1199.		Bow Brickhill.
		cr. river Ouzel. Enter Bedfordshire.		Wavendon Hall, Sir H. A. Hoare, Bart.
Woburn Abbey, Duke of Bedford.	12	Woburn Sands St.	51	Husborn Crawley. Holcot, 2 miles, and
Segenhoe Park.	9¼	Ridgmount St.	53	Holcot House.

ON RIGHT FROM LOND.	From Bedford.		From London.	ON LEFT FROM LOND.
	7½	Lidlington St.	55½	
Ampthill and Ampthill Park (Lord Wensleydale), 2¼ m. (see p. 426).	6	Ampthill (Marston) St.	57	
Houghton Conquest; and 1½ m. beyond, Hawnes Park (Marquis of Bath.)				Wootton.
Wilshamstead.				Kempston, and Kempston Hall.
Elstow.	63	BEDFORD (p. 364.)	63	

CLXXXII. PETERBOROUGH TO STAMFORD, MELTON-MOWBRAY, AND LEICESTER, BY RAILWAY, 53 Miles.

ON RIGHT FROM PETERB.	From Leicest.		From Peterb.	ON LEFT FROM PETERB.
	53	From PETERBOROUGH (see p. 420), to		Thorpe Hall.
Paston.	50	Walton St.	3	Milton Park, Earl Fitzwilliam.
Werrington. Glinton, 1½ miles.				Marholm.
Etton.	46¾	Helpstone St.	6¼	
				Bainton. Walcot Hall, 1½ m.
Stamford is situated on the line of the Roman Ermine Street. Two miles to the north-west, at the village of Great Casterton, Roman antiquities have been found.	43	Uffington St.	10	Uffington House (Earl of Lindsey).
		Along banks of river Welland.		
	40¼	STAMFORD St. (see p. 388.)	12¾	Burghley House, Marquis of Exeter (see p. 388).
Tinwell.		cr. river Welland, and enter Rutlandshire.		
Normanton Pa., 2 m., Lord Aveland; 3 m. farther, Exton Hall (Earl of Gainsborough).	36¾	Ketton St.	16¼	
	34¼	Luffenham St.	18¾	S. Luffenham. Pilton.
Lyndon.	30¼	Manton and Uppingham St.	22¾	Wing. Manton Lodge. Uppingham, 3½ miles (see p. 365).
Egleton.		cr. river Gwash.		
1 mile distant Burley Park, Mr. Finch.	26¾	OAKHAM St. (see p. 365.)	26¼	
		Through Vale of Catmoss.		Barleythorpe. Langham.
Melton-Mowbray and Oakham canal.	23¾	Ashwell St.	29¼	
Teigh.	21¼	Whissendine St.	31¾	
Edmondthorpe Hall, 1¾ miles.		cr. canal.		

ON RIGHT FROM PETERB.	From Leicest.		From Peterb.	ON LEFT FROM PETERB.
	$18\frac{3}{4}$	Saxby St.	$34\frac{1}{4}$	Stapleford Hall, Earl of Harborough.
Freeby. Brentingby. Thorpe Arnold; 5 m. distant, Goadby Hall.		Along valley of river Wreak, which the line crosses several times.		Burton Lazars; beyond, Little Dalby Hall, 3 miles.
Sysonby Lodge, Earl of Bessborough, 2 miles.	15	MELTON-MOWBRAY St. (see p. 362).	38	
Sysonby.	$12\frac{1}{4}$	Kirby St.	$40\frac{3}{4}$	
	$11\frac{1}{4}$	Frisby St.	$41\frac{3}{4}$	Frisby.
Ashfordby. Hoby.				Rotherby. Brookesby Hall.
	$9\frac{1}{4}$	Brookesby St.	$43\frac{3}{4}$	
Thrussington.	8	Rearsby St.	45	
Ratcliffeon Wreak.				Queniborough, 1 mile.
	$4\frac{3}{4}$	Syston Junction St.	$48\frac{1}{4}$	Barkby Hall, W. Pochin, Esq., 1 mile.
Wanlip Hall, Sir G. J. Palmer, Bart.		Join Midland Railway.		
Thurmaston. Birstall House. Belgrave.		LEICESTER (p. 354).	53	Humberstone.

CLXXXIII. LONDON TO WARE AND HERTFORD, BY RAILWAY, 26 Miles.

ON RIGHT FROM LOND.	From Hertford		From London.	ON LEFT FROM LOND.
Leave main line of Northern and Eastern Railway.	7	From Bishopsgate St. to Broxbourne Junction St. (as in p. 450).	19	Hoddesdon, a small market town, 17 miles from London, and 4 miles to the south-east of Hertford. Pop. 1851, 1854. (See p. 381).
The Rye House, the scene of the pretended conspiracy of 1683, is in the present day the frequent resort of the London angler, who finds good sport in the Lea and the New River, both in its immediate vicinity.		cr. New River. and follow its course.		
	$5\frac{1}{4}$	Rye House St.	$20\frac{3}{4}$	Haileybury College, 2 miles, belonging to the East India Company.
Faseney Park.	4	St. Margaret's St.	22	Amwell, a pretty village (see p. 387). A votive urn, surrounded by a thicket of evergreens, was erected here in 1800, to the memory of Sir Hugh Myddleton, by whose patriotic exertions the waters of New River were originally conveyed to the metropolis.
The Priory and Poles. Ware Park.	$1\frac{3}{4}$	WARE St. (see p. 387).	$24\frac{1}{4}$	
Hertford, the county town of Herts, is situated on the south bank of the river Lea. A castle was erected here in the tenth century, of which a few remains still exist. But the present castle was		HERTFORD.	26	Balls Park, Marquis of Townshend; Brickendonbury, and beyond, Panshanger (Earl Cowper).

built in the time of Charles I., and is now a school. At the east end of the town is an establishment belonging to Christ's Hospital (popularly known as the Blue Coat School), London, and used as a preparatory school for younger children, who are received here prior to their admission to the metropolitan establishment. It is a large building, capable of accomodating 600 children. Hertford is a pleasant, busy, and respectable town. Its principal trade is in mealing and malting. Two M.P. Pop. 6769.

CLXXXIV. LONDON TO HUNTINGDON, BY RAILWAY, 77 Miles.

ON RIGHT FROM LOND.	From Huntin.		From London.	ON LEFT FROM LOND.
		From London by Northern and Eastern Railway, to		
Leave main line to Ely and Norwich.	19½	CAMBRIDGE (p. 433).	57½	
		cr. river Cam.		
		Cross line of Roman road.		
Impington Park.	14¾	Histon St.	62¼	Girton:—2 miles beyond, Madingley Park, Sir St. V. Cotton, Bart.
Cottenham, 2½ miles.	12½	Oakington St.	64½	
Rampton, 1¼ mile.	10	Long Stanton St.	67	Long Stanton Hall.
	7¾	Swavesey St.	69¼	
		Enter Huntingdonshire.		
Branch to March and Wisbeach, 28¼ miles. Houghton. Witton. Hartford.	5	ST. IVES JUNCTION ST. (See p. 458.)	71¾	Hemingford Grey. Hemingford Abbots.
		Follow course of river Ouse, which the line crosses twice, to		
		HUNTINGDON (see p. 387).	77	Godmanchester, the site of the ancient *Durolipons*, a Roman station.

CLXXXV. LONDON TO MARCH AND WISBEACH, BY RAILWAY, 100 Miles.

ON RIGHT FROM LOND.	From Wisb.		From London.	ON LEFT FROM LOND
		From London to		
	28¼	ST. IVES JUNCTION ST. (as above).	71	Leave line to Huntingdon 5¼ miles.
Needingworth.		cr. riv. Ouse.		Woodhurst.
Bluntisham. Colne.	22¼	Somersham St. (see p. 458.)	77	
Numerous drains, or *droves*, crossing the Fens.		Proceed through the district of the Fens.		6 miles distant is Ramsey (p. 458), and Ramsey Abbey, E. Fellowes, Esq.
		Enter Cambridgeshire.		
	17	Chatteris St.	83	Doddington, 1½ mile (the richest living in England), Sir H. Peyton. Bart.
	13¼	Wimblington and Doddington St.	86¾	
		cr. Old riv. Nen.		
Line from Ely joins (see p. 452).	9	MARCH JUNCTION ST. (p. 452.)	91	Line to Peterborough, 15 miles.
		Continue through the Fens, to		
		WISBEACH (p. 458).	100	

EASTERN COUNTIES RAILWAY
(LONDON TO CAMBRIDGE, ELY, NORWICH & YARMOUTH.)

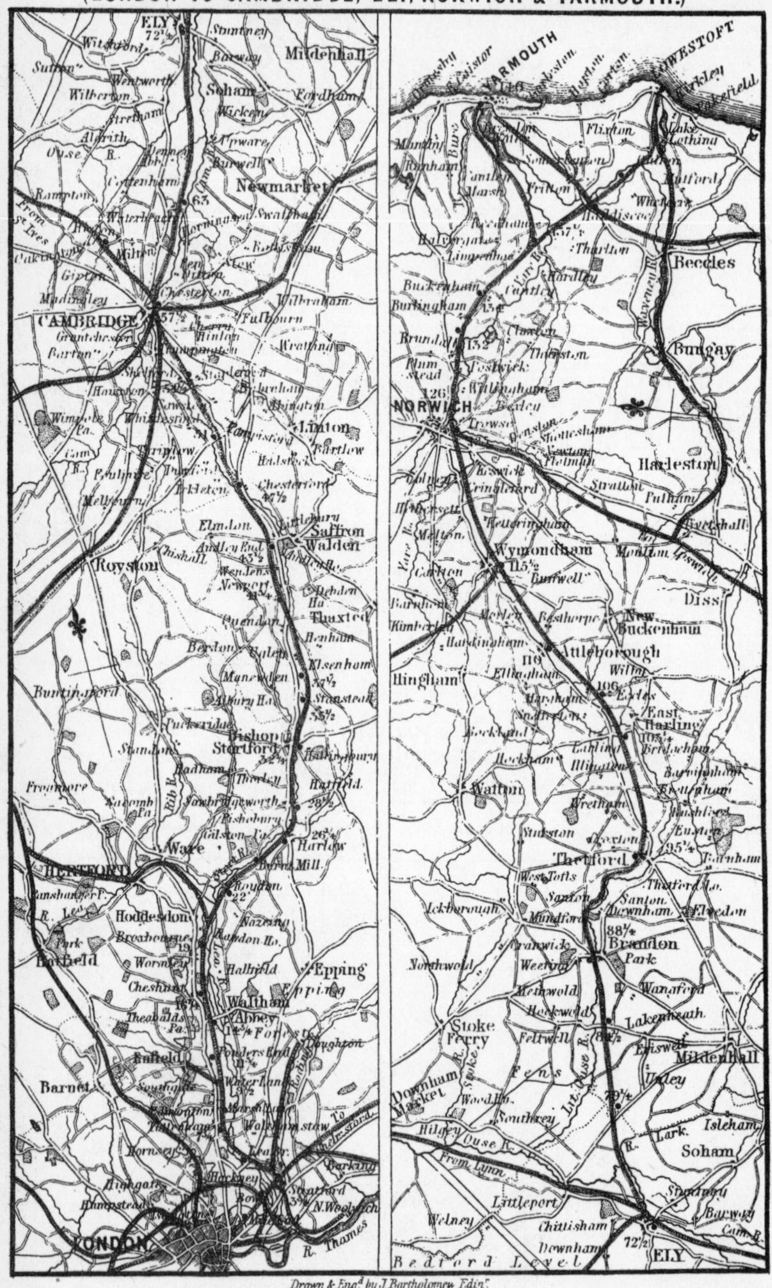

Drawn & Engd. by J. Bartholomew Edinr.

Published by A. & C. Black, Edinburgh.

ON RIGHT FROM LOND.	From Lynn.		From London.	ON LEFT FROM LOND.
		From London to		
Line to Norwich and Yarmouth.	26¾	ELY ST. (p. 451). The line hence runs throughout along the valley of the Ouse, the course of which it nearly follows.	72¼	Line to March and Peterborough. New Barns. Wood House.
	21	Littleport St.	78	
Southery.		Enter Norfolk.		
	15½	Hilgay Fen St.	83½	
	14	Ouse Bridge St.	85	
Hilgay. Wood Hall.		cr. river Ouse.		
Fordham.	12½	Denver St.	86½	
Ryston Hall, E. R. Pratt, Esq.; 1½ miles beyond, Dereham Abbey. Crow Hall.	11	DOWNHAM MARKET.	88	Downham Market is situated on the side of a hill on the east bank of the Ouse, over which is a good bridge. Near the church there were formerly some monastic buildings, particularly a priory of Benedictine monks. Downham is celebrated for its butter market. Pop. 2458.
Bexwell. Wimbotsham. Stow Hall, Sir Thos. Hare, Bart.	8½	Stow St.	90½	
Wallington Hall. South Runcton.	7¼	Holme St.	91¾	Branch to Wisbeach, 10 miles.
Watlington Hall.	6	Watlington St.	93	Wiggenhall St. Mary Magdalene. Wiggenhall St. Peter's. Wiggenhall St. Mary's
West Winch; beyond, N. Runcton, D. Gurney, Esq.		cr. Nar or Setchey River.		Wiggenhall St. German's, 1 mile.
		LYNN (see p. 457).	99	

CLXXXVII. LONDON TO NORWICH AND YARMOUTH, THROUGH CAMBRIDGE, BY RAILWAY, 146 Miles.

ON RIGHT FROM LOND.	From Yarm.		From London.	ON LEFT FROM LOND.
		From London to		
	73¾	ELY ST. (p. 451.)	72¼	Lines to Peterborough and Lynn.
		cr. river Ouse, near the junction of river Lark.		
To Mildenhall, 8 miles (see p. 459).	66¾	Mildenhall Road St. Enter Suffolk, near the junction of the three	79¼	

ON RIGHT FROM LOND.	From Yarm.		From London.	ON LEFT FROM LOND.
		counties of Norfolk, Suffolk, and Cambridge. Along valley of Little Ouse to		
Lakenheath, 2 miles. Mildenhall, 7 miles.	61½	Lakenheath St.	84½	Hockwold; beyond, Feltwell St Nicholas, and Feltwell St. Mary.
Brandon Hall. Brandon Park, H. Blipp, Esq. N. Court Lodge.		Leave the Fen country, and enter a wooded and picturesque district. cr. river Ouse, and enter Norfolk.		Weeting All Saints.
	57¾	BRANDON St. (see p. 459.)	88¼	
Santon Downham, and Downham Hall (Earl Cadogan.)		Along north bank of Little Ouse river to		
3 miles distant, Elvedon Hall (Earl of Albemarle); and, 3½ miles, Euston Hall, Duke of Grafton, standing in a magnificent park.	50¾	THETFORD (p. 465.) Over Croxton and Roundham Heaths.	95¼	3½ miles distant, Wretham Hall, W. Birch, Esq.
Snare Hill. Kilverstone Hall. Schadwell Lodge, 2 m. Bridgeham; and beyond, W. Harling Hall.				Illington; beyond, Hockham Magna Hall, H. Partridge, Esq. Larling.
East Harling, 1 mile distant, is a small and decayed market town. Population, 1062.	42¾	Harling Road St.	106¼	Snetterton.
Eccles Hall; and, 1 m. beyond, Quiddenham Hall, Earl of Albemarle.	39¾	Eccles Road St.	106¼	Hargham Hall, Sir T. B. Beevor, Bart.
Wilby Hall. Old Buckenham, 2 m.; and beyond, New Buckenham, a small market town. Population (of the two), 1971. Besthorpe.	36	ATTLEBOROUGH St.	110	Attleborough is a small and unimportant market town, 14 miles south-west of Norwich. Pop. 1959. Morley St Peters, and Morley Botolph.
Stanfield Hall, the seat of the late J. Jermy, Esq. has been rendered memorable in the annals of crime, by the untimely fate of its late occupant and his son, whose murder (in 1848), under circumstances of great atrocity, is still fresh in public recollection. Ketteringham Hall, Sir J. P. Boileau, Bart. Intwood Hall. Keswick. Junction of Eastern Union Railway.	30½	WYMONDHAM JUNCTION ST. (see p. 465).	115½	Line from Lynn and Dereham joins here. Kimberley Hall, 2 m. Lord Wodehouse. Hethersett Hall. New Hall. Cringleford Hall. Eaton Hall; and beyond, Earlham Hall, J. J. Gurney, Esq., and Colney Hall. 4 miles distant, Costessey Hall, Lord Stafford.

EASTERN COUNTIES & EASTERN UNION RAILWAYS.

(LONDON TO IPSWICH, BURY & NORWICH.)

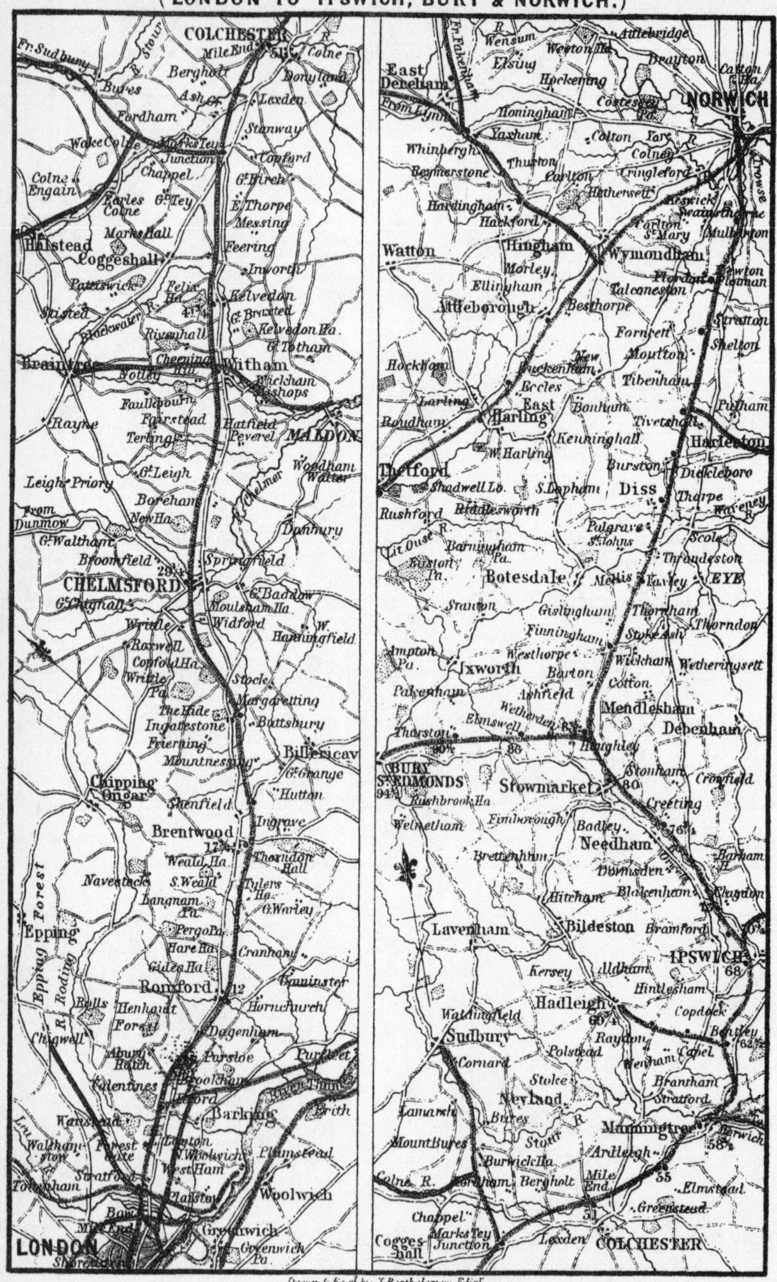

Drawn & Engd. by J. Bartholomew, Edinr.

Published by A. & C. Black Edinburgh.

ON RIGHT FROM LOND.	From Yarm.		From London.	ON LEFT FROM LOND.
	21	Trowse St.	125	
To Bungay, 14 miles (see p. 475).	20	NORWICH (see p. 465.)	126	Thorpe.
Whitlingham. Postwick. Surlingham.				Plumstead; and near, Plumstead House and Plumstead Hall. Witton.
River Yare.		Follow north bank of river Yare.		
	14	Brundall St.	132	Brundall House. Strumpshaw Hall.
To Carleton, and beyond, Langley Park, Sir W. B. Proctor, Bart.	12	Buckenham St.	134	Hassingham. Cantley.
Branch to Lowestoft, through Somerleyton and Mutford, 11½ m. (see p. 479). Marshes of the Yare and Waveney.	8	Reedham Junction St.	138	Limpenhoe. Wickhampton.
		Pass along north side of Breydon Water, a lake of considerable size, to		Berney Arms.
Breydon Water.		YARMOUTH (see p. 479).	146	

CLXXXVIII. LONDON TO NORWICH, THROUGH IPSWICH, HAUGHLEY, AND DISS, BY RAILWAY, 113½ Miles.

ON RIGHT FROM LOND.	From Norwich.	From Bishopsgate St., London, to	From London.	ON LEFT FROM LOND.
Line to North Woolwich, 5 m. Westham.	119¾	Stratford St. (p. 450).	3¾	Leave line to Cambridge and Ely.
	108½	Forest Gate St.	5	Epping Forrest.
Little Ilford.		cr. river Roding.		Wanstead. Valentines.
Barking, 1½ miles (see p. 480).	106½	Ilford St.	7	Hainault Forest, lately disafforested, 1 m.
	101½	ROMFORD St. (see p. 470).	12	Gidea Hall. Hare Hall.
Hornchurch, 1½ m.		cr. small river Ingerbourne.		Dagnam Park, Sir R. S. Neave, Bart. S. Weald; and beyond, Weald Hall.
Thorndon Hall, Lord Petre (see p. 470). Hutton, and Hutton Hall. Mountnessing. Ingatestone Hall.	95¾	BRENTWOOD St. (see p. 470).	17¾	Shenfield. Fitzwalter.
Buttsbury.	90¼	Ingatestone St.	23¼	The Hyde. Margaretting.

ON RIGHT FROM LOND.	From Norwich.		From London.	ON LEFT FROM LOND.
		cr. river Wid, a feeder of the Chelmer.		Coptfold Hall, and Highlands.
Moulsham Hall, Sir H. B. P. St John Mildmay, Bart. Springfield Lyons. Boreham House, Sir John T. Tyrell, Bart. Crix. Hatfieldbury. Hartfield Priory.	84¼	CHELMSFORD St. (see p. 471.) Viaduct across river Chelmer.	29¼	Widford, at or near which was probably a Roman station, the *Cæsaromagus* of the Itinerary. Springfield Place. New Hall, 1 mile. Terling Place, Lord Rayleigh, 2 m.
Hatfield Peverell, 1 m. Maldon, 5¾ m. distant by railway, is situated on the south side of the river Blackwater, which below the town expands into a wide estuary. It has several churches, and an old town-hall, and imports coal, iron, corn, &c. It returns two M.P. Pop. 1861, 6261. (See also p. 471.)	75¼	Witham Junction St. Here the Maldon and Baintree line crosses. 1 mile beyond Witham, on the right, at the distance of one mile, is Braxted Park, C. du Cane, Esq.	38¼	Witham Place; and beyond, Faulkbourn Hall. Braintree, 6¼ miles by railway. Rivenhall Place, 1½ m.
	71¾	Kelvedon St. cr. river Blackwater.	41¾	Felix Hall, J. S. Western, Esq. COGGESHALL, 2 m. distant, a small market-town, on the river Blackwater. Pop. 3166. Little Tey.
Inworth. East Thorpe. Copford Place; and beyond, Copford Hall. Stanway. Lexden House, and Lexden Park, J. Mills, Esq.	67¼	Marks Tey Junction St. cr. river Colne.	46¼	Branch to Sudbury, 11¾ miles (see p. 467.) Fordham, 2 miles. West Bergholt, 1½ m.
Town of Colchester, 1 mile (see p. 471.) Ardleigh Park, 1½ m.	62¼	COLCHESTER St. (See p. 471.)	51¼	
Great Bromley, 2½ m.	58	Ardleigh St.	55½	Ardleigh Hall; 1½ m. distant, Hill House. Dedham Grove, 1½ m. East Bergholt Hall, Sir R. Hughes, Bart.
Lawford Hall. Mistley Hall. Brantham. To Harwich, 11½ m. Estuary of river Stour.	54½	MANNINGTREE St. (See p. 480.) cr. river Stour, and enter Suffolk.	59	West Lodge.
Tattingstone Place, T. S. Western, Esq. Tattingstone Hall, now a farm-house. Wherstead Lodge, W. Scrope, Esq. Freston, 1½ mile; beyond, Wolverstone Hall, and Chelmondiston, and, on the opposite bank of Orwell, Orwell Park, G. Tomline, Esq.; and Nactonbroke Hall, Sir G. N. Broke, Bart.	51	Bentley Junction St.	62½	Branch to HADLEIGH, 7¼ m., a small market-town on the river Bret, formerly of more importance than at present. Pop. 2779. Copdock.

ON RIGHT FROM LOND.	From Norwich.		From London.	ON LEFT FROM LOND.
Stoke Park.		cr. river Gipping.		
To Woodbridge, 8 m. (see p. 478).	45½	IPSWICH St. (p. 477).	68	Chauntry, Sir Fitzroy Kelly. Sproughton.
Christ Church Park, W. C. Fonnereau, Esq.		Through short tunnel, and along course of river Gipping.		
Whitton.	42¾	Brandford St. Follow river Gipping, which below the town of Ipswich bears the name of the Orwell, and at its mouth joins the Stour off Harwich.	70¾	Bramford Hall; 3 m. distant, Hintlesham Hall, J. H. L. Anstruther, Esq. Somersham. Little Blakenham.
Claydon Hill.	40½	Claydon St.	73	Great Blakenham. Bayleham. Darmsden.
Barham. Shrubland Park, Sir W. F. Fowle Middleton, Bt. Bosmere Hall;—3 m. beyond, Crowfield Hall; and 2 miles further Helmingham Hall, Earl of Dysart.	36¾	NEEDHAM MARKET St. Needham Market is a small market-town on the Gipping. Pop. 1353.	76¾	Barking Hall, Earl of Ashburnham; 2 miles distant, Battisford Hall.
Creeting. Debenham, 8½ m. distant from Needham Market, is a small market town on the river Deben. The church is old. Pop. 1667. One mile north of Debenham is Aspall Hall, C. Chevallier, Esq.; and 5 miles to the north-east, Worlingworth Hall, now a farm house.	33¼	STOW MARKET St. Stow Market is a well built town near the Gipping, which has been rendered navigable from Ipswich to this place. The manufacture of sacking, ropes, twine, and hempen cloth, is carried on here, and it has a good market for barley. There are some hop plantations in the neighbourhood. Pop. 3531.	80¼	Badley. Combs. Finborough Hall. Tott Hill. Harleston, 2 miles.
Old Newton. Gipping Chapel. Cotton.	31	Haughley Junction St.	82½	Line to Bury St Edmonds, 12 miles. Bacton.
Wickham Skeith. Thornham Hall, Lord Henniker.	27½	Finningham St.	86	Gislingham.
2 m. distant is Yaxley Hall; and 1 m. further, the small town of Eye, which returns 1 M.P. (see p. 473); beyond, Broome Hall, Sir E. C. Kerrison, Bart.	22½	Mellis (Eye) St.	91	Burgate; 2 miles beyond, Botesdale, a small and decayed market town. Pop. 359. (See p. 469). Near Bottesdale is Redgrave Hall, G. St V. Wilson, Esq.
		cr. river Waveney, and enter Norfolk.		
Thrandeston. Palgrave. Scole Inn or Osmondiston.	19	DISS St. (see pp. 469 & 473).	94½	Wortham. Roydon.
Frenze. Gissing. Tivetshall.	16½	Burston St.	97	Winfarthing. Tibbenham; and 3½ m. distant, New Buckenham (see p. 473.)

ON RIGHT FROM LOND.	From Norwich.		From London.	ON LEFT FROM LOND.
	13½	Tivetshall St.	100	
Moulton. Wacton. Tharston Hall.	10	Forncett St.	103½	Aslacton. Forncett.
Long Stratton; and beyond, Boyland Hall, F. W. Irby, Esq.	7½	Flordon St.	106	Hapton. Flordon.
Tasburg, probably the site of *Ad Taum*, a Roman station.	4½	Swainsthorpe St.	109½	Newton Flotman. Swainsthorpe.
Shottesham Park. Dunston Hall. Caistor St Edmunds. Bixley Hall, 1¾ miles; and beyond, Kirby Hall.		cr. river Yare. NORWICH (see p. 465.)	113½	Mangreen Hall. Keswick. Costessey Park, Lord Stafford.

CLXXXIX. NORWICH TO EAST DEREHAM, SWAFFHAM, AND LYNN, BY RAILWAY, 48¾ Miles.

ON RIGHT FROM NORW.	From Lynn.		From Norwich.	ON LEFT FROM NORW.
	48¾ 38¼	From Norwich to Wymondham St. (pp. 486-7.)	10½	Leave railway to Thetford, &c.
Crownthorpe. Kimberley Hall, Lord Wodehouse. Coston.	32¾	Hardingham St.	16	Wicklewood. Hardingham Hall, 1½ mile.
Runhall. Thuxton Hall.		cr. river Blackwater.		Thuxton. Garveston Hall.
	28¾	Yaxham St.	20	Letton Hall, B. Gruden, Esq.
Branch to Fakenham, 12½ miles (see p. 461); 4½ miles distant, on this branch, is Elmham Hall and Park, Lord Sondes.	26¾	EAST DEREHAM St. (see p. 474.)	22	Whinbergh.
Quebec Castle, near E. Dereham, and in the distance, Bylaugh Hall, E. Lombe, Esq.	22¾	Wendling St.	26	
Beeston.	19¾	Fransham St.	29	
Great Dunham. 3 m. distant is Castle Acre, at which was formerly a strong fortress, said to have covered 18 acres (see p. 461.)	18½	Little Dunham St.	30¼	Dunham Lodge.
At Narborough, Roman remains have been found.	14½	SWAFFHAM St. Swaffham, a market-town, standing on high ground, and considered very salubrious. It has a large ancient church having some curious	34¼	Wolverton Place. Necton Hall, 2 miles. Cockley Cley, 4 m. and near it, Cley Hall. E. A. Applethwait, Esq. To Brandon, by road, 16 miles.

ON RIGHT FROM NORW.	From Lynn.		From Norwich.	ON LEFT FROM NORW.
		monuments and a carved roof. Races are annually held on the adjacent heath. Pop. 2974. (See also p. 461).		Beechamwell, 3 miles.
Narburgh Hall, A. Fountaine, Esq; beyond, Narford Hall.	8½	Narburgh St.	40¼	
		cr. river Nar.		
	7	Bilney St.	41¾	Pentney.
Gayton Hall, 2 miles.				Bilney Lodge, 1 mile.
	5	East Winch St.	43¾	Winch Hall.
	3	Middleton St.	45¾	Middleton, 1 mile.
Mintlyn.		LYNN St. (p. 457).	48¾	N. Runcton, 2 miles, D. Gurney, Esq.; and beyond, West Winch.

CXC. NORWICH TO ELY, PETERBOROUGH, AND LEICESTER, BY RAILWAY, 137 Miles.

ON RIGHT FROM NORW.	From Leicest.		From Norwich	ON LEFT FROM NORW.
	137	From NORWICH by Brandon and Thetford, to		
Line to Downham and Lynn.	83¼	ELY (as in pp. 485, 486, and 487.)	53¾	Line to Cambridge and London.
	53	Thence, by March, to PETERBOROUGH. (as in pp. 451-2).	84	Line to Blisworth, on London and North Western Railway.
		From Peterborough to LEICESTER (pp. 482-3).	137	

CXCI. LONDON TO NEWMARKET, BY RAILWAY, 69 Miles.

ON RIGHT FROM LOND.	From Newm.		From London.	ON LEFT FROM LOND.
	11½	From Bishopsgate St. London, to Cambridge St. (see p. 451).	57½	Leave line of Northern and Eastern Railway.
Gog Magog Hills, Lord Godolphin.	9½	Cherry Hinton St.	59½	

ON RIGHT FROM LOND.	From Newm.		From London.	ON LEFT FROM LOND.
At West Wratting 4½ miles distant, Wratting Park, Sir C. Watson, Bart.	7½	Fulbourn St.	61½	Fulbourn. Great Wilbraham, and Wilbraham Temple, E. Hicks, Esq.
	5½	Six Mile Bottom St.	63½	Bottisham Hall, 3½ m. Upper Hare Park. Lower Hare Park.
Dullingham Hall. Stetchworth House. Cheveley Park, 2 m., Duke of Rutland.	3½	Dullingham St.	65½	The Race Course.
		NEWMARKET (see p. 464.)	69	

CXCII. LONDON TO BURY ST EDMUNDS, BY RAILWAY, 94½ Miles.

ON RIGHT FROM LOND.	From Bury.		From London.	ON LEFT FROM LOND.
Leave line to Norwich, by Diss, 30 miles.		From London, by Eastern Counties Railway, to		
	12	Haughley Junction St. (p. 489.)	82½	Haughley, and ruins of Haughley Castle. Plashwood.
Wetherden Hall.				Haughley Park. Wetherden. Haughley Place.
Ashfield Lodge, 2½ m., Lord Thurlow. Langham Hall, 3 m., Sir H. C. Blake, Bart. Norton.	8½	Elmswell St.	86	Woolpit; and 2½ m. beyond, Drinkstone Park. Tostock Hall. Tostock Place. Beyton. Rougham Hall, P. Bennet, Jun., Esq.
Pakenham, 1½ miles; and Nether Hall, W. C. Basset, Esq. Pakenham Lodge. Barton Mere House. Pakenham New House. Little Haugh House. Great Barton; and beyond, Barton Hall, Lieutenant-General Sir E. H. Bunbury, Bart.	4	Thurston St.	90½	Rushbrooke Park, 2 miles, R. F. B. Rushbrooke. St Edmunds Hill.
		BURY ST EDMUNDS (p. 469.)	94½	Ickworth Park, Marquis of Bristol.

CXCIII. LONDON TO YORK, BY GREAT NORTHERN RAILWAY, *via* GRANTHAM AND NEWARK, 191 Miles.

ON RIGHT FROM LOND.	From York.		From London.	ON LEFT FROM LOND.
Hackney.	191	From London Terminus at King's Cross.		
To Enfield, Tottenham, and Edmonton.	187	Hornsey St.	4	Highgate. South Lodge, in the neighbourhood, was the seat of Earl Chatham, when only a member of the House of Commons.
	184¾	Colney Hatch and Southgate St.	6¼	
Trent Park.	181¾	BARNET ST. (See pp. 196 and 370).	9¼	Barnet, and beyond, Wrotham Park, Earl of Strafford.
	178¼	Potters Bar and South Mims St. (See p. 196).	12¾	The tower of the church at South Mims is a picturesque object, being entirely mantled with ivy.
Hatfield House (Marquis of Salisbury), see pp. 196, 370, and 372; and beyond, Bedwell Park, Sir C. E. Eardley, Bart.	171¼	HATFIELD St. per St Albans and Luton.	17¾	Brocket Hall. In the distance, Hoo Park, Lord Dacre.
Tewin House (Viscount Uxbridge).	169	Welwyn St. (See pp. 360 and 370).	22	Knebsworth Park, Sir E. Bulwer Lytton, Bart.
Panshanger Park. The property of Earl Cowper, who permits free access to the parks and grounds, and also to his picture-gallery.	162	Stevenage St. (See p. 370).	28½	
	159	HITCHIN St. (see p. 360).	32	At the village of Hexton, 4½ miles west of Hitchin, a battle was fought in 914 between the Danes and Saxons, in which the latter were victorious; and a little to the east of the village there is an ancient entrenchment, called Ravensburg Castle, which occupies seven acres. There are also numerous barrows in the vicinity, supposed to contains the bones of those slain in battle.
	154	Arlsey and Shefford Road St.	37	
Sutton Park, Sir J. M. Burgoyne, Bart.	151	BIGGLESWADE St. (See p. 370).	41	
Sandy was an important Roman station.	147	Sandy St.	44	
St Neots. Pop. 1851, 2951.	139¼	St Neots St.	51¾	
	135¼	Offord St.	55¾	
	132	HUNTINGDON St. (See p. 387).	59	Brompton Park.
Whittlesey Mere.	121¾	Holme St.	69¼	Orton Hall, Marquis of Huntly.
Branch to Boston, Lincoln, and Retford.	114¾	PETERBOROUGH St. (See pp. 417, 420, &c.)	76¼	Milton Park, Earl Fitzwilliam.
	106¼	Tallington St.	84¾	
	102½	Essendine St.	88½	
Grimsthorpe Park, Lord Willoughby d'Eresby.	99	Little Bytham St.	92	
	94	CORBY St.	97	Easton Hall, Sir M. J. Cholmley, Bart.

ON RIGHT FROM LOND.	From York.		From London.	ON LEFT FROM LOND.
	89	Great Ponton St. (See p. 383.)	102	
Belton House, Earl of Brownlow.	85¾	GRANTHAM St. (See pp. 383, 388.)	105¼	Branch to Nottingham. In the distance, Belvoir Castle, Duke of Rutland.
Marston Moor.	79½	Haigham and Marston St.	111½	
	75¾	Claypole St.	115¼	
Branch to Lincoln.	71	NEWARK St. (See pp. 383 and 388.)	120	Branch to Nottingham. Kelham Hall, J. Manners Sutton, Esq.
	64¾	Carlton St. (See p. 383.)	126¼	Ossington Hall, Rt. Hon. J. E. Denison.
	59¼	TUXFORD St. (See p. 383.)	131¾	
The Boston and Lincoln branch rejoins main line here.	52½	RETFORD St. (See pp. 383 and 388.)	138½	
		Manchester and Lincolnshire line crosses here.		
	49	Sutton St.	142	
Near Ranskill are the remains of a priory of Gilbertine monks.	46¾	Ranskill St.	144¼	Serlby Hall, Viscount Galway.
	45	Scrooby St.	146	
Bawtry Hall, R. M. Milnes, Esq.	43	BAWTRY St. (See p. 384.)	148	
	39½	Rossington St.	151½	
Cantley Hall, J. W. Childers, Esq.	34¾	DONCASTER St. (See pp. 384, 389.)	156¼	Cusworth Park.
	32¾	Arksey and Stockbridge St.	158¼	
Askerne is noted for its mineral waters, and has risen, in the course of a few years, from a straggling village to a well built town.	28½	Askerne St.	162½	
	26½	Norton St.	164½	
	24½	Womersley St.	166½	
Line to Goole.	20	Knottingley Junction St.	171	
	14¾	Milford Junction St.	176¼	
		Leeds and Selby line crosses		
	12¾	Sherborne St.	178¼	
		(and thence to York, as on p. 438).	191	

ON RIGHT FROM LOND.	From York.		From London.	ON LEFT FROM LOND.
	134¼	From King's Cross St. London, to Peterborough St. (as on preceding page.)	76¼	
	103½	Thence to Boston St. (as on p. 448.)	107	
To Thornton le Fen.	98½	Langrick St.	112	
	92¼	Dogdyke St.	118¼	
	91½	TATTERSHALL St. (See p. 430, note).	119	Tattershall was a Roman station, and traces of encampments are still visible at a short distance, where several coins and relics have been found.
At Kirkstead is a very curious chapel, with a groined roof, and in the interior a rude figure in stone, representing a knight templar, with the form of a cross on his bassinet.	87¾	KIRKSTEAD St.	122¾	
	86	Stixwould St. St. for Woodhall Spa and Horncastle.	124¼	
	84	Southrey St.	126½	
Tupholme Hall, and beyond Gautby Hall.	81½	BARDNEY St. for Wragby.	129	
The church of St. John is a handsome Gothic structure, surmounted by a lofty tower at the west end.	75	Washingborough St.	135½	Washingborough Hall.
	72¼	Lincoln St. (See pp. 421-22).	138¼	
Line to Gainsborough 10¾ m.	66¼	Saxilby Junction St.	144¼	Kettlethorpe Hall.
Babworth Hall, H. J. B. Simpson, Esq.	52½	Retford St. (See p. 388).	158	Grove Park, and beyond Headon Park.
		and thence to York, (as on preceding page).	210½	

ON RIGHT FROM BRIST.	From Glouces.		From Bristol.	ON LEFT FROM BRIST.
	37½	Bristol St. of Bristol and Gloucester Railway.		Stoke House, Duke of Beaufort.
	31⅓	Mangotsfield Station.	6	Hill House.
Chipping Sodbury, and beyond Dodington Park, (C. W. Codrington, Esq.). and Badminton, (Duke of Beaufort).	27½	Yate Station.	10½	
	22½	Wickwar Station.	15	
	20½	Charfield Station.	17	Cromhall Park, Earl of Ducie. Tortworth Lodge, Earl of Ducie.
In the distance, Kingscote Park, T. H. Kingscote, Esq.	15¼	Berkeley Road Station.	22¼	Berkeley Castle, Admiral Sir M. Berkeley.
Spring Park, Earl of Ducie.	10¾	Frocester Station.	26¾	
Standish Park.	9	Stonehouse Station.	28½	Hardwick Court and Quedgley House.
		Gloucester. (See p. 156).	37½	

CXCVI. LONDON TO GLOUCESTER, CHEPSTOW, CARDIFF, AND SWANSEA (SOUTH WALES), BY RAILWAY, 216 Miles.

ON RIGHT FROM LOND.	From Swansea.		From London.	ON LEFT FROM LOND.
	216	London to		
	102	Gloucester. (as on p. 114).	114	
	96¾	Oakle Station.	119¼	
	91¼	Newnham Station.	124¾	
	85½	Gatcombe Station.	130½	
	82½	Lydney Station.	133½	
	74½	Chepstow Station. (See p. 144).	141½	
	69½	Portskewet Station.	146½	
	65	Magor Station.	151	Llanwern, Rev. Sir C. J. Salusbury, Bart.
Tredegar House, Sir C. M. R. G. Morgan, Bart.	57½	Newport Station. (See p. 128)	158½	

ON RIGHT FROM LOND.	From Swansea.		From London.	ON LEFT FROM LOND.
	52¼	Marshfield Station.	163¾	
Branch Lines to Merthyr Tydvil, Aberdare, &c.	45¾	Cardiff Station. (See p. 128).	170¼	
Llandaff. (See p. 129.)	43½	Ely and Llandaff St.	172½	
	41¾	St. Fagans Station.	147¼	In the distance Weuvoe Castle, R. F. Jenner, Esq.
Llantrissant.	34¾	Llantrissant Station.	181¼	
	29½	Pencoed Station	186½	
Bridgend.	25¾	Bridgend Station.	190¼	Ewenny and Ewenny Abbey.
Margam Park, C. R. M. Talbot, Esq.	20	Pyle Station.	196	
	13½	Port-Talbot Station.	202½	
	10¼	Briton Ferry Station.	205¾	
Gnoll Castle, H. J. Grant, Esq.	8	Neath Station. (See p. 130-1).	208	
	4¾	Llansamlet Station.	211¼	
		Swansea Station. (See p. 131).	216	

CXCVII. LONDON TO BANBURY, THROUGH BUCKINGHAM, BY RAILWAY, 78 Miles.

ON RIGHT FROM LOND.	From Banbury.		From London.	ON LEFT FROM LOND.
Branch to Bedford (*via* Woburn and Ampthill.)	31¼	London to Bletchley Junction St. (See p. 202).	46¾	
Little Horwood Rectory, Philip Dauncey, Esq.		Swanbourne Station.		Swanbourne House, Right Hon. Sir T. F. Fremantle, Bart.
	23¾	Winslow Station.	54¼	Branch to Oxford.
Addington House, formerly General Poulett, late Lord Nugent.				
Stowe, Duke of Buckingham and Chandos. (See pp. 176, 192). Shalstone House, Thomas Fitzgerald, Esq.	17	Buckingham Station. (Buckingham, see pp. 176, 192).	61	Evenley Hall, Hon. P. S. Pierrepoint.

ON RIGHT FROM LOND.	From Banbury.		From London.	ON LEFT FROM LOND.
Biddlesdon Park, late George Morgan, Esq.	9¾	**Brackley Station.**	68¼	Stean Park, Earl Spencer.
		Farthingoe Station.		**Farthingoe House.**
Thenford House. Marston House.				
		Banbury Station. (See pp. 176, 192). A line of rail runs from this place to Oxford, through Doddington and Woodstock, (part of the Great Western Railway).	78	

CXCVIII. LONDON TO OXFORD, THROUGH WINSLOW, BICESTER, AND ISLIP, 78 Miles.

ON RIGHT FROM LOND.	From Oxford.		From London.	ON LEFT FROM LOND.
	78	**London to**		
	24	**Winslow Junction St.** (See p. 191).	54	
	20	**Claydon Station.**	58	Claydon House, Sir Harry Verney, Bart. Doddershall House, Grenville Pigott, Esq. Wootton House, Marquis of Chandos.
	14	**Launton Station.**	64	
Bicester House.	11¾	**Bicester Station.**	66¼	
Middleton Park, Earl of Jersey. Bucknell House (and Kennel), T. T. Drake, Esq.				
Kirtlington Park, Sir G. Dashwood, Bart.	5	**Islip Station.**	73	
Bletchington House, Viscount Valentia.				
Blenheim, Duke of Marlborough. (See p. 172, 189).		**Oxford Station.** (See pp. 162, 166, 186, 187, 189).	78	

THE
CALEDONIAN RAILWAY
AND
THE NORTH BRITISH RAILWAY,
THE TRUNK LINES FROM THE BORDERS OF ENGLAND INTO SCOTLAND.

THE two great lines of communication between England and Scotland consist of the *Caledonian Railway* (from Carlisle to Glasgow and Edinburgh), on the west,—and the *North British Railway* (between Berwick and Edinburgh), on the east side of the island. The general direction of the former of these is given in page 256. On account, however, of the importance of these trunk lines between the two countries, it is believed that a sketch of them will form an acceptable addition to the present work, and they are accordingly given in detail in the following pages—Edinburgh and Glasgow being the starting-points of the former line, and Edinburgh the starting-point of the latter,—the journeys are exhibited from these cities southward to the English border.

EDINBURGH—LANARK.

ON RIGHT FROM EDINBURGH.	From Carlisle	From Edinburgh	ON LEFT FROM EDINBURGH.
Granton.			North British Railway.
Edinburgh station. Edinburgh and Glasgow Railway.	100		**Edinburgh station.** Dalry village. Merchiston.
Slateford station. Corstorphine Hill. Riccarton—Sir Willm. Gibson Craig, Bart.	97	3	**Slateford station.** Viaduct over Water of Leith. Hailes House. Baberton House — Captain Christie.
Currie station. Dalmahoy House—Earl of Morton. Dalmahoy Crags, 680 feet high.	95	5	**Currie station.** Currie village. Ruins of Lennox Castle. Ravelrig Hill. Balerno. Meadowbank — Lord Meadowbank.
Kirknewton station. East Calder village. Bellfield House. Mid-Calder village, on an eminence. Contentibus. Beautiful view of Firth of Forth and Fife hills from the viaduct.	90	10	**Kirknewton station.** Kirknewton village. Ormiston village. Viaduct over the Lin water, in 6 arches of 60 feet span, and 103 feet above the stream.
West Calder station. West Calder village. Harwood. Cobinshaw Reservoir. Mosshat.	85	15	**West Calder station.** Harburn—Mr. Cochrane. The surrounding country at this part is bleak and uninteresting. Woolfords.
Auchengray station. Branch to Wilsontown Iron-Works. Cleugh House.	79½	20½	**Auchengray station.** Ampherlaw—Dr Somerville. Carnwath village.
Carnwath station.	74	26	**Carnwath station.**
Carstairs station. Where the trains unite.			**Carstairs station,** Where the trains unite.
Lanark station. Cleghorn—Mr. A. E. Lockhart. Jerviswood—Earl of Haddington. Cartland Crags on the Mouse Water, are about a mile west of Lanark. They rise on both sides about 400 feet high, and form a deep chasm, where a cave in the face of the rock, termed Wallace's Cave, is pointed out by tradition as the hiding-place of that hero after he had slain Haselrig the English sheriff.	72	28	**Lanark station.** In the vicinity of Lanark are the Falls of the Clyde. At Bonnington Linn (the uppermost fall) the water is thrown over a perdendicular rock about 30 feet in height into a deep hollow or basin. Corra Linn, the largest of the falls, is half a mile below the former. The river here makes three distinct leaps, in height altogether of about 84 feet. Pop. of Lanark, 5384.

I. GLASGOW–ABINGTON.

ON RIGHT FROM GLASGOW.	From Carlisle	From Glasgow	ON LEFT FROM GLASGOW.
Glasgow station.	101		**Glasgow station.**
Rutherglen.			
Cambuslang.			
Garnkirk station.			**Garnkirk station.**
The Priory—Lord Blantyre. Ruins of Bothwell Castle.			
Coatbridge station.		9½	**Coatbridge station.** Cross the Monkland Canal by a wooden viaduct. Woodhall in the distance.
Bothwell village. Hamilton.			
Holytown station.			**Holytown station.**
Motherwell station. Dalziel House—Mr. J. G. C. Hamilton.	89	12	**Motherwell station.** Cleland House—Earl of Stair.
Wishaw station.	86	15	**Wishaw station.** Wishaw Castle—Lord Belhaven.
Overtown station. Dalserf village. Mauldslie Castle. Milton—Mr. Wm. Lockhart.	84½	16½	**Overtown station.**
Carluke station.	82	19	**Carluke station.** Carluke village.
	80½	20½	
Lee House—Sir N. M. Lockhart, Bart. Jerviswood—Earl of Haddington. Town of Lanark.			Kilcadzow village.
Lanark station. Falls of the Clyde.	76	25	**Lanark station.** Viaduct over Mouse Water. Carstairs village.
Carstairs junction st. Carstairs House—Mr. Henry Monteith.	73½	27½	**Carstairs junction st.** Branch to Edinburgh.
Carstairs junction st. Viaduct over the Clyde.	73½	27½	**Carstairs junction st.** Carnwath village.
Pittenain House. Cairngrife House. Carmichael House—Sir W. Anstruther, Bart.			Liberton village. Covington Castle—ruins.
Thankerton station. Tinto Hill, 2300 feet high. Fatlips Castle.	68½	32½	**Thankerton station.** Symington village.
Symington station. Wiston village. Dungavel Hill.	66½	34½	**Symington station—for Biggar.**
Hardington—Mr. R. MacQueen. Roberton village.	64	37	Lamington village. Woodend. Clyde's Bridge. Duneaton.
Abington station.	57½	43½	**Abington station.** Castle in ruins.
Crawford village.	56	45	

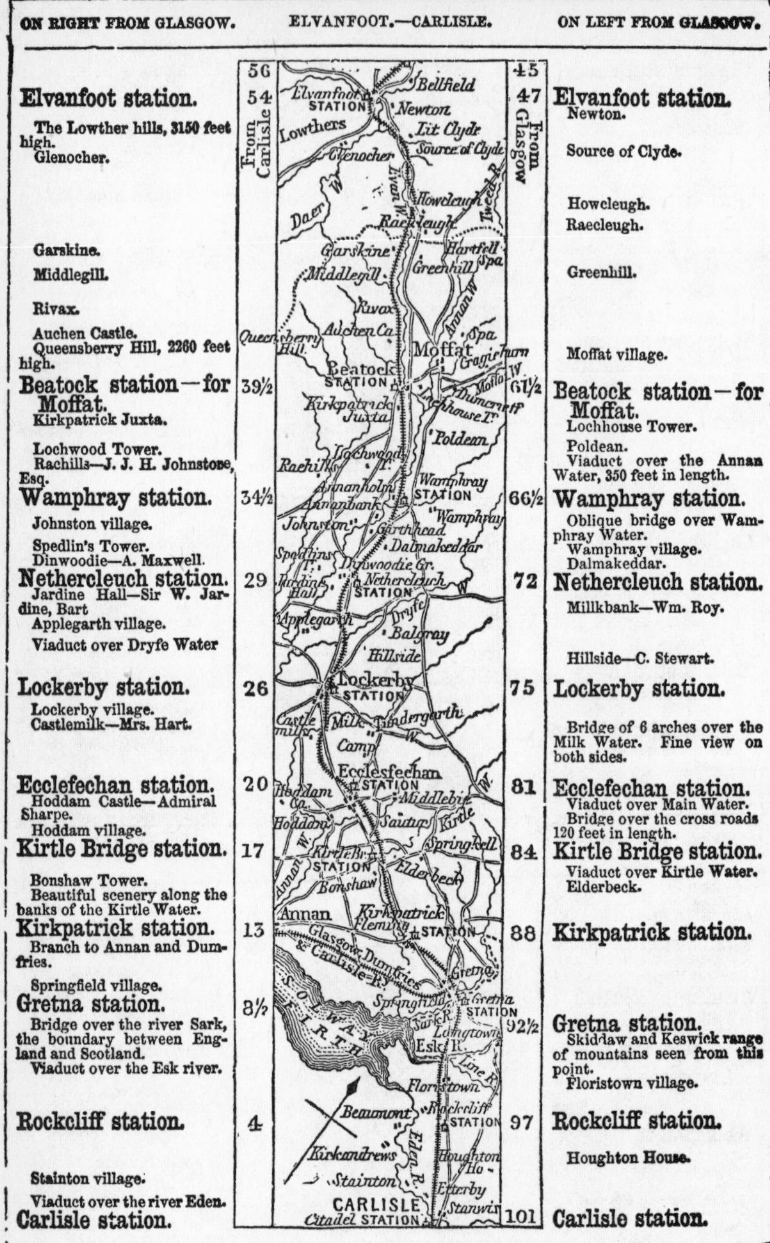

ON RIGHT FROM GLASGOW.	From Carlisle	ELVANFOOT.—CARLISLE.	From Glasgow	ON LEFT FROM GLASGOW.
Elvanfoot station. The Lowther hills, 3150 feet high. Glenocher.	54		47	**Elvanfoot station.** Newton. Source of Clyde.
Garskine. Middlegill. Rivax. Auchen Castle. Queensberry Hill, 2260 feet high.				Howcleugh. Raecleugh. Greenhill. Moffat village.
Beatock station—for Moffat. Kirkpatrick Juxta. Lochwood Tower. Rachills—J. J. H. Johnstone, Esq.	39½		61½	**Beatock station—for Moffat.** Lochhouse Tower. Poldean. Viaduct over the Annan Water, 350 feet in length.
Wamphray station. Johnston village. Spedlin's Tower. Dinwoodie—A. Maxwell.	34½		66½	**Wamphray station.** Oblique bridge over Wamphray Water. Wamphray village. Dalmakeddar.
Nethercleuch station. Jardine Hall—Sir W. Jardine, Bart. Applegarth village. Viaduct over Dryfe Water	29		72	**Nethercleuch station.** Millkbank—Wm. Roy. Hillside—C. Stewart.
Lockerby station. Lockerby village. Castlemilk—Mrs. Hart.	26		75	**Lockerby station.** Bridge of 6 arches over the Milk Water. Fine view on both sides.
Ecclefechan station. Hoddam Castle—Admiral Sharpe. Hoddam village.	20		81	**Ecclefechan station.** Viaduct over Main Water. Bridge over the cross roads 120 feet in length.
Kirtle Bridge station. Bonshaw Tower. Beautiful scenery along the banks of the Kirtle Water.	17		84	**Kirtle Bridge station.** Viaduct over Kirtle Water. Elderbeck.
Kirkpatrick station. Branch to Annan and Dumfries. Springfield village.	13		88	**Kirkpatrick station.**
Gretna station. Bridge over the river Sark, the boundary between England and Scotland. Viaduct over the Esk river.	8½		92½	**Gretna station.** Skiddaw and Keswick range of mountains seen from this point. Floristown village.
Rockcliff station. Stainton village. Viaduct over the river Eden.	4		97	**Rockcliff station.** Houghton House.
Carlisle station.			101	**Carlisle station.**

EDINBURGH.—DUNBAR.—BERWICK-ON-TWEED.—58 MILES.
WITH BRANCH LINE TO HADDINGTON.—17 MILES.

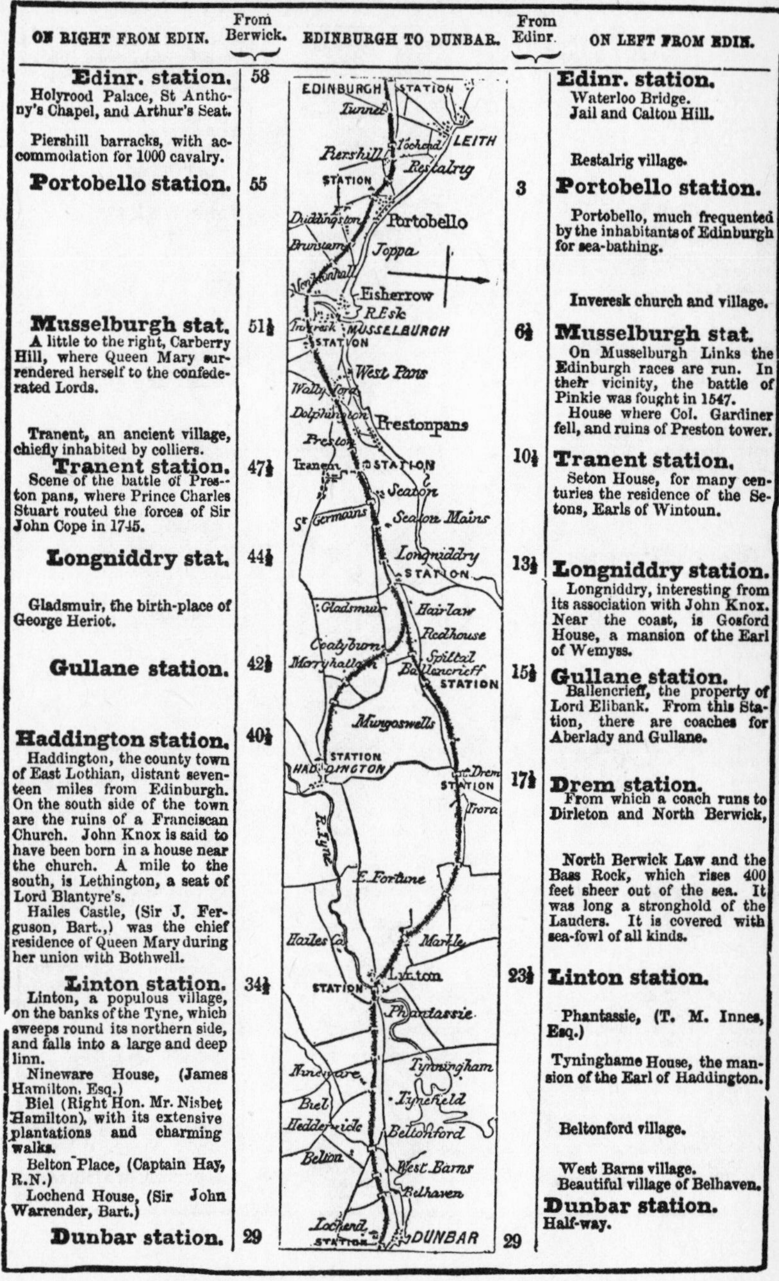

ON RIGHT FROM EDIN.	From Berwick.	EDINBURGH TO DUNBAR.	From Edinr.	ON LEFT FROM EDIN.
Edinr. station. Holyrood Palace, St Anthony's Chapel, and Arthur's Seat.	58			**Edinr. station.** Waterloo Bridge. Jail and Calton Hill.
Piershill barracks, with accommodation for 1000 cavalry.				Restalrig village.
Portobello station.	55		3	**Portobello station.** Portobello, much frequented by the inhabitants of Edinburgh for sea-bathing.
				Inveresk church and village.
Musselburgh stat. A little to the right, Carberry Hill, where Queen Mary surrendered herself to the confederated Lords.	51½		6½	**Musselburgh stat.** On Musselburgh Links the Edinburgh races are run. In their vicinity, the battle of Pinkie was fought in 1547. House where Col. Gardiner fell, and ruins of Preston tower.
Tranent, an ancient village, chiefly inhabited by colliers. **Tranent station.** Scene of the battle of Preston pans, where Prince Charles Stuart routed the forces of Sir John Cope in 1745.	47½		10½	**Tranent station.** Seton House, for many centuries the residence of the Setons, Earls of Wintoun.
Longniddry stat. Gladsmuir, the birth-place of George Heriot.	44½		13½	**Longniddry station.** Longniddry, interesting from its association with John Knox. Near the coast, is Gosford House, a mansion of the Earl of Wemyss.
Gullane station.	42½		15½	**Gullane station.** Ballencrieff, the property of Lord Elibank. From this Station, there are coaches for Aberlady and Gullane.
Haddington station. Haddington, the county town of East Lothian, distant seventeen miles from Edinburgh. On the south side of the town are the ruins of a Franciscan Church. John Knox is said to have been born in a house near the church. A mile to the south, is Lethington, a seat of Lord Blantyre's. Hailes Castle, (Sir J. Ferguson, Bart.,) was the chief residence of Queen Mary during her union with Bothwell.	40½		17½	**Drem station.** From which a coach runs to Dirleton and North Berwick, North Berwick Law and the Bass Rock, which rises 400 feet sheer out of the sea. It was long a stronghold of the Lauders. It is covered with sea-fowl of all kinds.
Linton station. Linton, a populous village, on the banks of the Tyne, which sweeps round its northern side, and falls into a large and deep linn. Nineware House, (James Hamilton, Esq.) Biel (Right Hon. Mr. Nisbet Hamilton), with its extensive plantations and charming walks. Belton Place, (Captain Hay, R.N.) Lochend House, (Sir John Warrender, Bart.)	34½		23½	**Linton station.** Phantassie, (T. M. Innes, Esq.) Tyninghame House, the mansion of the Earl of Haddington. Beltonford village. West Barns village. Beautiful village of Belhaven.
Dunbar station.	29		29	**Dunbar station.** Half-way.

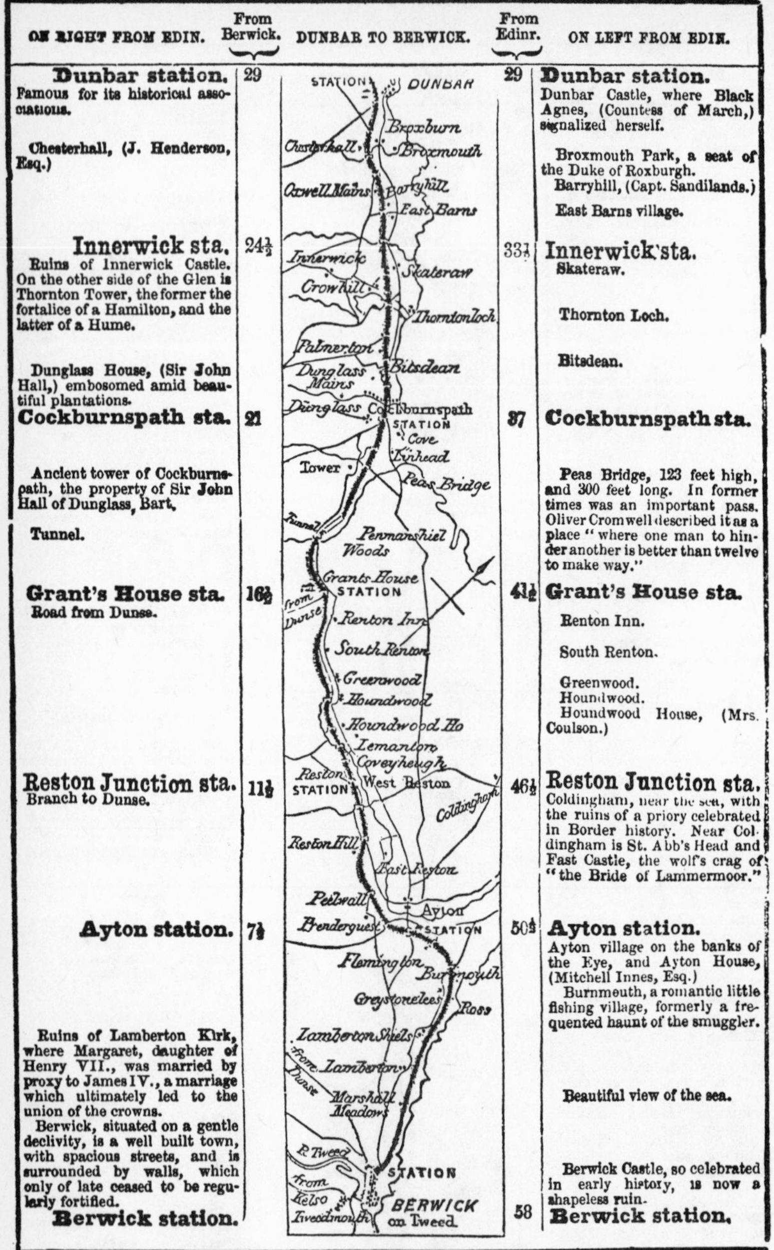

ON RIGHT FROM EDIN.	From Berwick.	DUNBAR TO BERWICK.	From Edinr.	ON LEFT FROM EDIN.
Dunbar station. Famous for its historical associations. Chesterhall, (J. Henderson, Esq.)	29		29	**Dunbar station.** Dunbar Castle, where Black Agnes, (Countess of March,) signalized herself. Broxmouth Park, a seat of the Duke of Roxburgh. Barryhill, (Capt. Sandilands.) East Barns village.
Innerwick sta. Ruins of Innerwick Castle. On the other side of the Glen is Thornton Tower, the former the fortalice of a Hamilton, and the latter of a Hume. Dunglass House, (Sir John Hall,) embosomed amid beautiful plantations.	24½		33½	**Innerwick sta.** Skateraw. Thornton Loch. Bitsdean.
Cockburnspath sta. Ancient tower of Cockburnspath, the property of Sir John Hall of Dunglass, Bart. Tunnel.	21		37	**Cockburnspath sta.** Peas Bridge, 123 feet high, and 300 feet long. In former times was an important pass. Oliver Cromwell described it as a place "where one man to hinder another is better than twelve to make way."
Grant's House sta. Road from Dunse.	16½		41½	**Grant's House sta.** Renton Inn. South Renton. Greenwood. Houndwood. Houndwood House, (Mrs. Coulson.)
Reston Junction sta. Branch to Dunse.	11½		46½	**Reston Junction sta.** Coldingham, near the sea, with the ruins of a priory celebrated in Border history. Near Coldingham is St. Abb's Head and Fast Castle, the wolf's crag of "the Bride of Lammermoor."
Ayton station. Ruins of Lamberton Kirk, where Margaret, daughter of Henry VII., was married by proxy to James IV., a marriage which ultimately led to the union of the crowns. Berwick, situated on a gentle declivity, is a well built town, with spacious streets, and is surrounded by walls, which only of late ceased to be regularly fortified.	7½		50½	**Ayton station.** Ayton village on the banks of the Eye, and Ayton House, (Mitchell Innes, Esq.) Burnmouth, a romantic little fishing village, formerly a frequented haunt of the smuggler. Beautiful view of the sea. Berwick Castle, so celebrated in early history, is now a shapeless ruin.
Berwick station.			58	**Berwick station.**

INDEX.

The Hotels are placed in Italics after the Names of the Towns.